D1597039

Applied Quantitative Methods
for Trading and Investment

Wiley Finance Series

Applied Quantitative Methods for Trading and Investment

Edited by

Christian L. Dunis
Jason Laws

and

Patrick Naïm

WILEY

Copyright © 2003   John Wiley & Sons Ltd, The Atrium, Southern Gate, Chichester,
West Sussex PO19 8SQ, England

Telephone (+44) 1243 779777

Email (for orders and customer service enquiries): cs-books@wiley.co.uk
Visit our Home Page on www.wileyeurope.com or www.wiley.com

All Rights Reserved. No part of this publication may be reproduced, stored in a retrieval system or
transmitted in any form or by any means, electronic, mechanical, photocopying, recording, scanning or
otherwise, except under the terms of the Copyright, Designs and Patents Act 1988 or under the terms of a
licence issued by the Copyright Licensing Agency Ltd, 90 Tottenham Court Road, London W1T 4LP, UK,
without the permission in writing of the Publisher. Requests to the Publisher should be addressed to the
Permissions Department, John Wiley & Sons Ltd, The Atrium, Southern Gate, Chichester, West Sussex PO19
8SQ, England, or emailed to permreq@wiley.co.uk, or faxed to (+44) 1243 770620.

This publication is designed to provide accurate and authoritative information in regard to the subject matter
covered. It is sold on the understanding that the Publisher is not engaged in rendering professional services. If
professional advice or other expert assistance is required, the services of a competent professional should be
sought.

Other Wiley Editorial Offices

John Wiley & Sons Inc., 111 River Street, Hoboken, NJ 07030, USA

Jossey-Bass, 989 Market Street, San Francisco, CA 94103-1741, USA

Wiley-VCH Verlag GmbH, Boschstr. 12, D-69469 Weinheim, Germany

John Wiley & Sons Australia Ltd, 33 Park Road, Milton, Queensland 4064, Australia

John Wiley & Sons (Asia) Pte Ltd, 2 Clementi Loop #02-01, Jin Xing Distripark, Singapore 129809

John Wiley & Sons Canada Ltd, 22 Worcester Road, Etobicoke, Ontario, Canada M9W 1L1

Wiley also publishes its books in a variety of electronic formats. Some content that appears
in print may not be available in electronic books.

Library of Congress Cataloging-in-Publication Data

Applied quantitative methods for trading and investment / edited by Christian Dunis, Jason
    Laws, and Patrick Naïm
       p. cm. — (Wiley finance series)
     Includes bibliographical references and index.
     ISBN 0-470-84885-5 (cased : alk. paper)
      1. Finance—Mathematical models. 2. Investments—Mathematical models. 3.
    Speculation—Mathematical models. I. Dunis, Christian. II. Laws, Jason. III. Naïm,
    Patrick. IV. Series

    HG106.A67 2003
    332.6′01′5195—dc21

                                                   2003049721

British Library Cataloguing in Publication Data

A catalogue record for this book is available from the British Library

ISBN 0-470-84885-5

Typeset in 10/12pt Times by Laserwords Private Limited, Chennai, India
Printed and bound in Great Britain by TJ International, Padstow, Cornwall
This book is printed on acid-free paper responsibly manufactured from sustainable forestry
in which at least two trees are planted for each one used for paper production.

Contents

About the Contributors

George T. Albanis is currently working at Hypovereinsbank – HVB Group. He obtained his PhD from City University Business School, London and holds a BSc in Economics from the University of Piraeus, Greece and Master's degrees in Business Finance and in Decision Modelling and Information Systems from Brunel University, London. An experienced programmer, his interests are applications of advanced nonlinear techniques for financial prediction in fixed income and credit derivatives markets, and quantification of risk in financial modelling.

Yves Bentz is Vice President with Crédit Suisse First Boston, specialising in high frequency equity trading strategies and statistical arbitrage. He was previously a quantitative trader with Morgan Stanley and with Beaghton Capital Management in London where he developed automated equity and derivatives trading strategies. Yves holds a PhD from the University of London (London Business School). He has published several research papers on factor modelling and nonlinear modelling, in particular stochastic parameter models and nonparametric statistics and their applications to investment management.

Monica Billio is Associate Professor of Econometrics at Università Ca' Foscari of Venice. She graduated in Economics at Università Ca' Foscari di Venezia and holds a PhD degree in Applied Mathematics from the Université Paris IX Dauphine. Her fields of interest are simulation-based methods and the econometrics of finance.

Frédérick Bourgoin is an Associate Portfolio Manager in the Active Fixed Income Portfolio Management Team at Barclays Global Investors in London where he is involved in the development of the active bond and currency strategies, as well as the risk management systems. Prior to joining BGI, he was a risk manager and quantitative analyst at Portman Asset Management. Frédérick holds a Post-Graduate Degree in Finance from ESSEC Business School and an MSc in Econometrics and Mathematical Economics from Panthéon-Sorbonne University in Paris.

Neil Burgess is a Vice President in the Institutional Equity Division at Morgan Stanley where he works in the area of quantitative programme trading, leading and coordinating new developments in trading systems and strategies for equities and equity derivatives between Europe and the USA. He obtained his PhD from London University. He has published widely in the field of emerging computational techniques and has acted as a programme committee member for international conferences: Forecasting Financial Markets, Computational Finance and Intelligent Data Engineering and Learning.

Nuno Cassola holds a PhD in Economics from the University of Kent at Canterbury. He worked as an Associate Professor at the Technical University of Lisbon from 1992 until 1994. He then joined the Research Department of the Banco de Portugal in 1994 where he became Head of the Monetary and Financial Division in 1996. In 1999 he joined the European Central Bank in Frankfurt where he is currently Principal Economist in the Monetary Policy Stance Division of the Monetary Policy Directorate.

Christian L. Dunis is Girobank Professor of Banking and Finance at Liverpool Business School, and Director of its Centre for International Banking, Economics and Finance (CIBEF). He is also a consultant to asset management firms, a Visiting Professor of International Finance at Venice International University and an Official Reviewer attached to the European Commission for the Evaluation of Applications to Finance of Emerging Software Technologies. He is an Editor of the *European Journal of Finance* and has published widely in the field of financial markets analysis and forecasting. He has organised the Forecasting Financial Markets Conference since 1994.

Xuehuan Huang graduated from Liverpool Business School with an MSc in International Banking and Finance and from China's Shenzen University with a BA in Business Management. After working as an auditor with Ernst & Young, she is currently a financial analyst at Bayer DS European headquarters.

Vassilios Karalis is an Associate Researcher at the Centre for International Banking, Economics and Finance of Liverpool Business School (CIBEF). Vassilios holds an MSc in International Banking and Finance from Liverpool Business School and a BSc in Mathematics with specialisation in probabilities, statistics and operational research from the University of Ioannina, Hellas.

Jason Laws is a Lecturer in International Banking and Finance at Liverpool John Moores University. He is also the Course Director for the MSc in International Banking, Economics and Finance at Liverpool Business School. He has taught extensively in the area of investment theory and derivative securities at all levels, both in the UK and in Asia. Jason is also an active member of CIBEF and has published in a number of academic journals. His research interests are focused on volatility modelling and the implementation of trading strategies.

Pierre Lequeux joined the Global Fixed Income division of ABN AMRO Asset Management London in 1999. As Head of Currency Management, he has responsibility for the quantitative and fundamental currency investment process. He was previously Head of the Quantitative Research and Trading desk at Banque Nationale de Paris, London branch, which he joined in 1987. Pierre is also an Associate Researcher at the Centre for International Banking, Economics and Finance of Liverpool Business School (CIBEF) and a member of the editorial board of *Derivatives Use, Trading & Regulation*.

Jorge Barros Luís is Head of Credit Risk Modelling with Banco Português de Investimento. Previous positions include Economist at the European Central Bank and Banco de Portugal, Chief-Economist at Banif Investimento and Adviser to the Minister of Finance and to the Secretary of State for the Treasury of the Portuguese Government. Jorge holds a PhD in Economics from the University of York and has published several papers on yield curve modelling and information extraction from option prices.

Patrick Naïm is an engineer of the Ecole Centrale de Paris. He is the founder and chairman of Elseware, a company specialised in the application of nonlinear methods to financial management problems. He is currently working for some of the largest French institutions and coordinating research projects in the field at a European level.

Bruno B. Roche is Head of Research in the Global Management Research group of a major multinational company where he leads a specialist team whose role is to provide world class expertise, methodologies, technologies and knowledge management in multiple areas which have a global critical impact (e.g. financial markets, risk management and advertising effectiveness). He is also a Researcher at the Solvay Business School at the University of Brussels.

Michael Rockinger is Professor of Finance at the HEC School of Business of the University of Lausanne. He has been scientific consultant at the French Central Bank for many years. He is also affiliated with CEPR and FAME. Previously, Michael taught Finance at all levels at HEC-Paris. His research interests are various, one of them is the modelling of asset prices. Michael earned his PhD in Economics at Harvard University. He is also a graduate in Mathematics from the Swiss Federal Institute of Technology (EPFL) and holder of a Master's degree from the University of Lausanne.

Domenico Sartore is Full Professor of Econometrics at Università Ca' Foscari di Venezia. Previously he taught at the University of Milan and the University of Padua. At present, he is President of the economics and finance consultancy GRETA (Gruppi di Ricerca Economica Teorica ed Applicata) in Venice. His field of interest is the econometrics of finance, where he has published many papers.

Mark Williams is an Associate Researcher at the Centre for International Banking, Economics and Finance of Liverpool Business School (CIBEF). Mark holds an MSc in International Banking and Finance from Liverpool Business School and a BSc in Economics from Manchester Metropolitan University.

Preface

Applied Quantitative Methods for Trading and Investment is intended as a quantitative finance textbook very much geared towards *applied* quantitative financial analysis, with detailed empirical examples, software applications, screen dumps, etc. Examples on the accompanying CD-Rom detail the data, software and techniques used, so that contrary to what frequently happens with most textbook examples, they clarify the analysis by being reasonably easily reproducible by the reader.

We expect this book to have a wide spectrum of uses and be adopted by financial market practitioners and in universities. For the former readership, it will be of interest to quantitative researchers involved in investment and/or risk management, to fund managers and quantitative proprietary traders, and also to sophisticated private investors who will learn how to use techniques generally employed by market professionals in large institutions to manage their own money. For the latter, it will be relevant for students on MSc, MBA and PhD programmes in Finance where a quantitative techniques unit is part of the course, and to students in scientific disciplines wishing to work in the field of quantitative finance.

Despite the large number of publications in the field of computational finance in recent years, most of these have been geared towards derivatives pricing and/or risk management.[1] In the field of financial econometrics, most books have been subject specific,[2] with very few truly comprehensive publications.[3] Even then, these books on financial econometrics have been in reality mostly *theoretical*, with empirical applications essentially focused on validating or invalidating economic and financial theories through econometric and statistical methods.

What distinguishes this book from others is that it focuses on a wide spectrum of methods for modelling financial markets in the context of *practical financial applications*. On top of "traditional" financial econometrics, the methods used also include *technical analysis* systems and many *nonparametric tools* from the fields of data mining and artificial intelligence. Although we do not pretend to have covered all possible methodologies,

---

[1] See, for instance, Wilmott, P. (1998), *Derivatives: The Theory and Practice of Financial Engineering*, John Wiley, Chichester and Alexander, C. (2001), *Market Models*, John Wiley, Chichester.

[2] See, for instance, Dunis, C., A. Timmermann and J. Moody (2001), *Developments in Forecast Combination and Portfolio Choice*, John Wiley, Chichester.

[3] See Campbell, J. Y., A. W. Lo and A. C. MacKinlay (1997), *The Econometrics of Financial Markets*, Princeton University Press, Princeton and Gouriéroux, C. and J. Jasiak (2002), *Financial Econometrics*, Princeton University Press, Princeton.

we believe that the wide breadth of potential methods retained in this manual is highly desirable and one of its strengths. At the same time, we have been careful to present even the most advanced techniques in a way that is accessible to most potential readers, making sure that those interested in the practical utilisation of such methods could skip the more theoretical developments without hindering comprehension, and concentrate on the relevant practical application: in this respect, the accompanying CD-Rom should prove an invaluable asset.

An applied book of this nature, with its extensive range of methodologies and applications covered, could only benefit from being a collaborative effort of several people with the appropriate experience in their field. In order to retain the practitioner's perspective while ensuring the methodological soundness and, should we say, academic respectability of the selected applications at the same time, we have assembled a small team of quantitative market professionals, fund managers and proprietary traders, and academics who have taught applied quantitative methods in finance at the postgraduate level in their respective institutions and also worked as scientific consultants to asset management firms.

As mentioned above, the range of applications and techniques applied is quite large. The different applications cover foreign exchange trading models with three chapters, one using technical analysis, one advanced regression methods including nonparametric Neural Network Regression (NNR) models and one a volatility filter-based system relying on Markov switching regimes; one chapter on equity statistical arbitrage and portfolio immunisation based on cointegration; two chapters on stock portfolio optimisation, one using Kalman filtering techniques in the presence of time-varying betas and the other using matrix algebra and Excel Solver to derive an optimal emerging stock market portfolio; one chapter on yield curve modelling through the use of affine models; one chapter on credit classification with decision trees, rule induction and neural network classification models; two chapters on volatility modelling and trading, one using Excel to compute both univariate and multivariate GARCH volatility and correlation in the stock market, the other using straddle strategies based on GARCH and Recurrent Network Regression (RNR) to build a forex volatility trading model; one chapter on Value at Risk (VaR) and option pricing in the presence of stochastic volatility; one chapter on the information contained in derivatives prices through the use of risk-neutral density functions and, finally, one chapter on weather risk management when confronted with missing temperature data.

The first part of the book is concerned with applications relying upon advanced modelling techniques. The applications include currencies, equities, volatility, the term structure of interest rates and credit classification. The second part of the book includes three chapters where the applications on equities, VaR, option pricing and currency trading employ similar methodologies, namely Kalman filter and regime switching. In the final part of the book there are five chapters where a variety of financial applications ranging from technical trading to missing data analysis are predominantly implemented using Excel.

In the following we provide further details on each chapter included in the book.

1. "Applications of Advanced Regression Analysis for Trading and Investment" by C. L. Dunis and M. Williams: this chapter examines the use of regression models in trading and investment with an application to EUR/USD exchange rate forecasting and trading models. In particular, NNR models are benchmarked against some other traditional regression-based and alternative forecasting techniques to ascertain

their potential added value as a forecasting and quantitative trading tool. In addition to evaluating the various models out-of-sample from May 2000 to July 2001 using traditional forecasting accuracy measures, such as root-mean-squared errors, models are also assessed using financial criteria, such as risk-adjusted measures of return. Transaction costs are also taken into account. Overall, it is concluded that regression models, and in particular NNR models, do have the ability to forecast EUR/USD returns for the period investigated, and add value as a forecasting and quantitative trading tool.

2. "Using Cointegration to Hedge and Trade International Equities" by A. N. Burgess: this chapter analyses how to hedge and trade a portfolio of international equities, applying the econometric concept of cointegration. The concepts are illustrated with respect to a particular set of data, namely the 50 equities which constituted the STOXX 50 index as of 4 July 2002. The daily closing prices of these equities are investigated over a period from 14 September 1998 to 3 July 2002 – the longest period over which continuous data is available across the whole set of stocks in this particular universe. Despite some spurious effects due to the non-synchronous closing times of the markets on which these equities trade, the data are deemed suitable for illustration purposes. Overall, depending on the particular task in hand, it is shown that the techniques applied can be successfully used to identify potential hedges for a given equity position and/or to identify potential trades which might be taken from a statistical arbitrage perspective.

3. "Modelling the Term Structure of Interest Rates: An Application of Gaussian Affine Models to the German Yield Curve" by N. Cassola and J. B. Luís: this chapter shows that a two-factor constant volatility model describes quite well the dynamics and the shape of the German yield curve between 1986 and 1998. The analysis supports the expectations theory with constant term premiums and thus the term premium structure can be calculated and short-term interest rate expectations derived from the adjusted forward rate curve. The analysis is carried out in Matlab and the authors include all of the files with which to reproduce the analysis. Their findings will be of interest to risk managers analysing the shape of the yield curve under different scenarios and also to policy makers in assessing the impact of fiscal and monetary policy.

4. "Forecasting and Trading Currency Volatility: An Application of Recurrent Neural Regression and Model Combination" by C. L. Dunis and X. Huang: this chapter examines the use of nonparametric Neural Network Regression (NNR) and Recurrent Neural Network (RNN) regression models for forecasting and trading currency volatility, with an application to the GBP/USD and USD/JPY exchange rates. The results of the NNR and RNN models are benchmarked against the simpler GARCH alternative and implied volatility. Two simple model combinations are also analysed. Alternative FX volatility forecasting models are tested out-of-sample over the period April 1999–May 2000, not only in terms of forecasting accuracy, but also in terms of trading efficiency: in order to do so, a realistic volatility trading strategy is implemented, using FX option straddles once mispriced options have been identified. Allowing for transaction costs, most trading strategies retained produce positive returns. RNN models appear as the best single modelling approach, yet model combination which has the best overall performance in terms of forecasting accuracy fails to improve the RNN-based volatility trading results.

5. "Implementing Neural Networks, Classification Trees, and Rule Induction Classification Techniques: An Application to Credit Risk" by G. T. Albanis: this chapter
   shows how to implement several classification tools for data mining applications in
   finance. Two freely available softwares on classification neural networks and decision trees, respectively, and one commercial software for constructing decision trees
   and rule induction classifiers are demonstrated, using two datasets that are available
   in the public domain. The first dataset is known as the Australian credit approval
   dataset. The application consists of constructing a classification rule for assessing the
   quality of credit card applicants. The second dataset is known as the German credit
   dataset. The aim in this application is to construct a classification rule for assessing the credit quality of German borrowers. Beyond these examples, the methods
   demonstrated in this chapter can be applied to many other quantitative trading and
   investment problems, such as the determination of outperforming/underperforming
   stocks, bond rating, etc.
6. "Switching Regime Volatility: An Empirical Evaluation" by B. B. Roche and M.
   Rockinger: this chapter describes in a pedagogical fashion, using daily observations
   of the USD/DEM exchange rate from October 1995 to October 1998, how to estimate
   a univariate switching model for daily foreign exchange returns which are assumed to
   be drawn in a Markovian way from alternative Gaussian distributions with different
   means and variances. The application shows that the USD/DEM exchange rate can
   be modelled as a mixture of normal distributions with changes in volatility, but not
   in mean, where regimes with high and low volatility alternate. The usefulness of
   this methodology is demonstrated in a real life application, i.e. through the profit
   performance comparison of simple hedging strategies.
7. "Quantitative Equity Investment Management with Time-Varying Factor Sensitivities"
   by Y. Bentz: this chapter describes three methods used in modern equity investment
   management for estimating time-varying factor sensitivities. Factor models enable
   investment managers, quantitative traders and risk managers to model co-movements
   among assets in an efficient way by concentrating the correlation structure into a small
   number of factors. Unfortunately, the correlation structure is not constant but evolves
   in time and so do the factor sensitivities. As a result, the sensitivity estimates have to
   be constantly updated in order to keep up with the changes. The first method, based
   on rolling regressions, is the most popular but also the least accurate. The second
   method is based on a weighted regression approach which overcomes some of the
   limitations of the first method by giving more importance to recent observations.
   Finally, a Kalman filter-based stochastic parameter regression model is shown to
   optimally estimate nonstationary factor exposures.
8. "Stochastic Volatility Models: A Survey with Applications to Option Pricing and
   Value at Risk" by M. Billio and D. Sartore: this chapter analyses the impact on Value
   at Risk and option pricing of the presence of stochastic volatility, using data for the
   FTSE100 stock index. Given the time-varying volatility exhibited by most financial
   data, there has been a growing interest in time series models of changing variance in
   recent years and the literature on stochastic volatility models has expanded greatly:
   for these models, volatility depends on some unobserved components or a latent
   structure. This chapter discusses some of the most important ideas, focusing on the
   simplest forms of the techniques and models available. It considers some motivations
   for stochastic volatility models: empirical stylised facts, pricing of contingent assets

and risk evaluation, and distinguishes between models with continuous and discrete volatility, the latter depending on a hidden Markov chain. A stochastic volatility estimation program is presented and several applications to option pricing and risk evaluation are discussed.

9. "Portfolio Analysis Using Excel" by J. Laws analyses the familiar Markovitz model using Excel. This topic is taught on Finance degrees and Master's programmes all over the world, increasingly through the use of Excel. The author takes time out to explain how the spreadsheet is set up and how simple short-cuts can make analysis of this type of problem quick and straightforward. In the first section of the chapter the author uses a two-variable example to show how portfolio risk and return vary with the input weights, then he goes on to show how to determine the optimal weights, in a risk minimisation sense, using both linear expressions and matrix algebra. In the second part of the chapter the author extends the number of assets to seven and illustrates that using matrix algebra within Excel, the Markovitz analysis of an n-asset portfolio is as straightforward as the analysis of a two-asset portfolio. The author takes special care in showing how the correlation matrix can be generated most efficiently and how within the same framework the optimisation objective can be modified without fuss.

10. "Applied Volatility and Correlation Modelling Using Excel" by F. Bourgoin. The originality of this chapter lies in the fact that the author manages to implement a range of univariate and multivariate models within the software package, Excel. This is extremely useful as a large proportion of finance practitioners, students and researchers are familiar with this package. Using S&P500 return data the author generates one-step-ahead forecasts of volatility using the J.P. Morgan RiskMetrics model, the J.P. Morgan RiskMetrics model with optimal decay, a GARCH(1,1) model with and without a variance reduction technique and finally using the GJR model to account for asymmetric reaction to news. A comparison of forecasts is made and some useful insights into the efficacy of the models highlighted. In the second part of the chapter the author uses return data on the DAX30 and CAC40 to model the correlation structure using a number of models. As with the univariate approach this includes the J.P. Morgan RiskMetrics model with and without optimal decay, a GARCH model with and without variance reduction and finally the so-called "Fast GARCH" model of which the author has previously made significant contributions to the literature.

11. "Optimal Allocation of Trend-Following Rules: An Application Case of Theoretical Results" by P. Lequeux uses sophisticated Excel modelling tools to determine what should be the optimal weighting of trading rules to maximise the information ratio. The trading rules utilised in the chapter are moving average trading rules ranging in order from 2 to 117 days and they are applied to a sample of five currency pairs (USD–JPY, EUR–USD, GBP–USD, USD–CAD and AUD–USD) over the period 15/02/1996 to 12/03/2002. The analysis could however be applied to any financial asset and any linear trading rule. In the applied example the author attempts to determine ex-ante what would be the optimal weighting between moving averages of order 2, 3, 5, 9, 32, 61 and 117 to maximise the delivered information ratio. To assist in understanding, the model has been programmed into a spreadsheet to give the reader the possibility to experiment. The results show that in four currency

pairs out of five the optimal weighting procedure is superior, when measured by the information ratio, to an equally weighted basket of trading rules.

12. "Portfolio Management and Information from Over-the-Counter Currency Options" by J. B. Luís: this chapter looks at the informational content of risk-reversals and strangles derived from OTC at-the-money forward volatilities. Three empirical applications of the literature are presented: one on the EUR/USD, followed by the analysis of implied correlations and the credibility of the Portuguese exchange rate policy during the transition to the EMU, and of the Danish exchange rate policy around the euro referendum in September 2000. This chapter is supported by the necessary Excel files to allow the reader to validate the author's results and/or apply the analysis to a different dataset.

13. "Filling Analysis for Missing Data: An Application to Weather Risk Management" by C. L. Dunis and V. Karalis: this chapter analyses the use of alternative methods when confronted with missing data, a common problem when not enough historical data or clean historical data exist, which will typically be the case when trying to develop a decision tool either for a new asset in a given asset class (say a recently issued stock in a given company sector) or for a new asset class as such (for instance weather derivatives). The application to weather data derives from the fact that most weather derivatives pricing methodologies rely heavily on clean data. The statistical imputation accuracy of different filling methods for missing historical records of temperature data is compared: the Expectation Maximisation (EM) algorithm, the Data Augmentation (DA) algorithm, the Kalman Filter (KF), Neural Networks Regression (NNR) models and, finally, Principal Component Analysis (PCA). Overall, it is found that, for the periods and the data series concerned, the results of PCA outperformed the other methodologies in all cases of missing observations analysed.

Overall, the objective of *Applied Quantitative Methods for Trading and Investment* is not to make new contributions to finance theory and/or financial econometrics: more simply, but also more practically, it is to enable its readers to make competent use of advanced methods for modelling financial markets.

We hope that, with the numerous files and software programs made available on the accompanying CD-Rom, it will constitute a valuable reference textbook for quantitative market professionals, academics and finance graduate students.

Many of the authors of chapters contained in this book have an affiliation to the Forecasting Financial Markets (FFM) conference which has been held each May since 1993. The editors of the text and several of the authors are members or associates of the Centre for International Banking, Economics and Finance (CIBEF) at Liverpool John Moores University. Details of both the conference and CIBEF may be found at www.cibef.com.

February 2003

Applications of Advanced Regression Analysis for Trading and Investment*

CHRISTIAN L. DUNIS AND MARK WILLIAMS

ABSTRACT

This chapter examines and analyses the use of regression models in trading and investment with an application to foreign exchange (FX) forecasting and trading models. It is not intended as a general survey of all potential applications of regression methods to the field of quantitative trading and investment, as this would be well beyond the scope of a single chapter. For instance, time-varying parameter models are not covered here as they are the focus of another chapter in this book and Neural Network Regression (NNR) models are also covered in yet another chapter.

In this chapter, NNR models are benchmarked against some other traditional regression-based and alternative forecasting techniques to ascertain their potential added value as a forecasting and quantitative trading tool.

In addition to evaluating the various models using traditional forecasting accuracy measures, such as root-mean-squared errors, they are also assessed using financial criteria, such as risk-adjusted measures of return.

Having constructed a synthetic EUR/USD series for the period up to 4 January 1999, the models were developed using the same in-sample data, leaving the remainder for out-of-sample forecasting, October 1994 to May 2000, and May 2000 to July 2001, respectively. The out-of-sample period results were tested in terms of forecasting accuracy, and in terms of trading performance via a simulated trading strategy. Transaction costs are also taken into account.

It is concluded that regression models, and in particular NNR models do have the ability to forecast EUR/USD returns for the period investigated, and add value as a forecasting and quantitative trading tool.

1.1 INTRODUCTION

Since the breakdown of the Bretton Woods system of fixed exchange rates in 1971–1973 and the implementation of the floating exchange rate system, researchers have been motivated to explain the movements of exchange rates. The global FX market is massive with

---

* The views expressed herein are those of the authors, and not necessarily those of Girobank.

Applied Quantitative Methods for Trading and Investment. Edited by C.L. Dunis, J. Laws and P. Naïm
© 2003 John Wiley & Sons, Ltd ISBN: 0-470-84885-5

an estimated current daily trading volume of USD 1.5 trillion, the largest part concerning spot deals, and is considered deep and very liquid. By currency pairs, the EUR/USD is the most actively traded.

The primary factors affecting exchange rates include economic indicators, such as growth, interest rates and inflation, and political factors. Psychological factors also play a part given the large amount of speculative dealing in the market. In addition, the movement of several large FX dealers in the same direction can move the market. The interaction of these factors is complex, making FX prediction generally difficult.

There is justifiable scepticism in the ability to make money by predicting price changes in any given market. This scepticism reflects the efficient market hypothesis according to which markets fully integrate all of the available information, and prices fully adjust immediately once new information becomes available. In essence, the markets are fully efficient, making prediction useless. However, in actual markets the reaction to new information is not necessarily so immediate. It is the existence of market inefficiencies that allows forecasting. However, the FX spot market is generally considered the most efficient, again making prediction difficult.

Forecasting exchange rates is vital for fund managers, borrowers, corporate treasurers, and specialised traders. However, the difficulties involved are demonstrated by the fact that only three out of every 10 spot foreign exchange dealers make a profit in any given year (Carney and Cunningham, 1996).

It is often difficult to identify a forecasting model because the underlying laws may not be clearly understood. In addition, FX time series may display signs of nonlinearity which traditional linear forecasting techniques are ill equipped to handle, often producing unsatisfactory results. Researchers confronted with problems of this nature increasingly resort to techniques that are heuristic and nonlinear. Such techniques include the use of NNR models.

The prediction of FX time series is one of the most challenging problems in forecasting. Our main motivation in this chapter is to determine whether regression models and, among these, NNR models can extract any more from the data than traditional techniques. Over the past few years, NNR models have provided an attractive alternative tool for researchers and analysts, claiming improved performance over traditional techniques. However, they have received less attention within financial areas than in other fields.

Typically, NNR models are optimised using a mathematical criterion, and subsequently analysed using similar measures. However, statistical measures are often inappropriate for financial applications. Evaluation using financial measures may be more appropriate, such as risk-adjusted measures of return. In essence, trading driven by a model with a small forecast error may not be as profitable as a model selected using financial criteria.

The motivation for this chapter is to determine the added value, or otherwise, of NNR models by benchmarking their results against traditional regression-based and other forecasting techniques. Accordingly, financial trading models are developed for the EUR/USD exchange rate, using daily data from 17 October 1994 to 18 May 2000 for in-sample estimation, leaving the period from 19 May 2000 to 3 July 2001 for out-of-sample forecasting.[1] The trading models are evaluated in terms of forecasting accuracy *and* in terms of trading performance via a simulated trading strategy.

---

[1] The EUR/USD exchange rate only exists from 4 January 1999: it was retropolated from 17 October 1994 to 31 December 1998 and a synthetic EUR/USD series was created for that period using the fixed EUR/DEM conversion rate agreed in 1998, combined with the USD/DEM daily market rate.

Our results clearly show that NNR models do indeed add value to the forecasting process.

The chapter is organised as follows. Section 1.2 presents a brief review of some of the research in FX markets. Section 1.3 describes the data used, addressing issues such as stationarity. Section 1.4 presents the benchmark models selected and our methodology. Section 1.5 briefly discusses NNR model theory and methodology, raising some issues surrounding the technique. Section 1.6 describes the out-of-sample forecasting accuracy and trading simulation results. Finally, Section 1.7 provides some concluding remarks.

1.2 LITERATURE REVIEW

It is outside the scope of this chapter to provide an exhaustive survey of all FX applications. However, we present a brief review of some of the material concerning financial applications of NNR models that began to emerge in the late 1980s.

Bellgard and Goldschmidt (1999) examined the forecasting accuracy and trading performance of several traditional techniques, including random walk, exponential smoothing, and ARMA models with Recurrent Neural Network (RNN) models.[2] The research was based on the Australian dollar to US dollar (AUD/USD) exchange rate using half hourly data during 1996. They conclude that statistical forecasting accuracy measures do not have a direct bearing on profitability, and FX time series exhibit nonlinear patterns that are better exploited by neural network models.

Tyree and Long (1995) disagree, finding the random walk model more effective than the NNR models examined. They argue that although price changes are not strictly random, in their case the US dollar to Deutsche Mark (USD/DEM) daily price changes from 1990 to 1994, from a forecasting perspective what little structure is actually present may well be too negligible to be of any use. They acknowledge that the random walk is unlikely to be the optimal forecasting technique. However, they do not assess the performance of the models financially.

The USD/DEM daily price changes were also the focus for Refenes and Zaidi (1993). However they use the period 1984 to 1992, and take a different approach. They developed a hybrid system for managing exchange rate strategies. The idea was to use a neural network model to predict which of a portfolio of strategies is likely to perform best in the current context. The evaluation was based upon returns, and concludes that the hybrid system is superior to the traditional techniques of moving averages and mean-reverting processes.

El-Shazly and El-Shazly (1997) examined the one-month forecasting performance of an NNR model compared with the forward rate of the British pound (GBP), German Mark (DEM), and Japanese yen (JPY) against a common currency, although they do not state which, using weekly data from 1988 to 1994. Evaluation was based on forecasting accuracy and in terms of correctly forecasting the direction of the exchange rate. Essentially, they conclude that neural networks outperformed the forward rate both in terms of accuracy and correctness.

Similar FX rates are the focus for Gençay (1999). He examined the predictability of daily spot exchange rates using four models applied to five currencies, namely the French franc (FRF), DEM, JPY, Swiss franc (CHF), and GBP against a common currency from

---

[2] A brief discussion of RNN models is presented in Section 1.5.

1973 to 1992. The models include random walk, GARCH(1,1), NNR models and nearest neighbours. The models are evaluated in terms of forecasting accuracy and correctness of sign. Essentially, he concludes that non-parametric models dominate parametric ones. Of the non-parametric models, nearest neighbours dominate NNR models.

Yao *et al.* (1996) also analysed the predictability of the GBP, DEM, JPY, CHF, and AUD against the USD, from 1984 to 1995, but using weekly data. However, they take an ARMA model as a benchmark. Correctness of sign and trading performance were used to evaluate the models. They conclude that NNR models produce a higher correctness of sign, and consequently produce higher returns, than ARMA models. In addition, they state that without the use of extensive market data or knowledge, useful predictions can be made and significant paper profit can be achieved.

Yao *et al.* (1997) examine the ability to forecast the daily USD/CHF exchange rate using data from 1983 to 1995. To evaluate the performance of the NNR model, "buy and hold" and "trend following" strategies were used as benchmarks. Again, the performance was evaluated through correctness of sign and via a trading simulation. Essentially, compared with the two benchmarks, the NNR model performed better and produced greater paper profit.

Carney and Cunningham (1996) used four data sets over the period 1979 to 1995 to examine the single-step and multi-step prediction of the weekly GBP/USD, daily GBP/USD, weekly DEM/SEK (Swedish krona) and daily GBP/DEM exchange rates. The neural network models were benchmarked by a naïve forecast and the evaluation was based on forecasting accuracy. The results were mixed, but concluded that neural network models are useful techniques that can make sense of complex data that defies traditional analysis.

A number of the successful forecasting claims using NNR models have been published. Unfortunately, some of the work suffers from inadequate documentation regarding methodology, for example El-Shazly and El-Shazly (1997), and Gençay (1999). This makes it difficult to both replicate previous work and obtain an accurate assessment of just how well NNR modelling techniques perform in comparison to other forecasting techniques, whether regression-based or not.

Notwithstanding, it seems pertinent to evaluate the use of NNR models as an alternative to traditional forecasting techniques, with the intention to ascertain their potential added value to this specific application, namely forecasting the EUR/USD exchange rate.

1.3 THE EXCHANGE RATE AND RELATED FINANCIAL DATA

The FX market is perhaps the only market that is open 24 hours a day, seven days a week. The market opens in Australasia, followed by the Far East, the Middle East and Europe, and finally America. Upon the close of America, Australasia returns to the market and begins the next 24-hour cycle. The implication for forecasting applications is that in certain circumstances, because of time-zone differences, researchers should be mindful when considering which data and which subsequent time lags to include.

In any time series analysis it is critical that the data used is clean and error free since the learning of patterns is totally data-dependent. Also significant in the study of FX time series forecasting is the rate at which data from the market is sampled. The sampling frequency depends on the objectives of the researcher and the availability of data. For example, intraday time series can be extremely noisy and "a typical off-floor trader...

would most likely use daily data if designing a neural network as a component of an overall trading system" (Kaastra and Boyd, 1996: 220). For these reasons the time series used in this chapter are all daily closing data obtained from a historical database provided by Datastream.

The investigation is based on the London daily closing prices for the EUR/USD exchange rate.[3] In the absence of an indisputable theory of exchange rate determination, we assumed that the EUR/USD exchange rate could be explained by that rate's recent evolution, volatility spillovers from other financial markets, and macro-economic and monetary policy expectations. With this in mind it seemed reasonable to include, as potential inputs, other leading traded exchange rates, the evolution of important stock and commodity prices, and, as a measure of macro-economic and monetary policy expectations, the evolution of the yield curve. The data retained is presented in Table 1.1 along with the relevant Datastream mnemonics, and can be reviewed in Sheet 1 of the DataAppendix.xls Excel spreadsheet.

Table 1.1   Data and Datastream mnemonics

Number	Variable	Mnemonics
1	*FTSE 100 – PRICE INDEX*	FTSE100
2	*DAX 30 PERFORMANCE – PRICE INDEX*	DAXINDX
3	*S&P 500 COMPOSITE – PRICE INDEX*	S&PCOMP
4	*NIKKEI 225 STOCK AVERAGE – PRICE INDEX*	JAPDOWA
5	*FRANCE CAC 40 – PRICE INDEX*	FRCAC40
6	*MILAN MIB 30 – PRICE INDEX*	ITMIB30
7	*DJ EURO STOXX 50 – PRICE INDEX*	DJES50I
8	*US EURO-$ 3 MONTH (LDN:FT) – MIDDLE RATE*	ECUS$3M
9	*JAPAN EURO-$ 3 MONTH (LDN:FT) – MIDDLE RATE*	ECJAP3M
10	*EURO EURO-CURRENCY 3 MTH (LDN:FT) – MIDDLE RATE*	ECEUR3M
11	*GERMANY EURO-MARK 3 MTH (LDN:FT) – MIDDLE RATE*	ECWGM3M
12	*FRANCE EURO-FRANC 3 MTH (LDN:FT) – MIDDLE RATE*	ECFFR3M
13	*UK EURO-£ 3 MONTH (LDN:FT) – MIDDLE RATE*	ECUK£3M
14	*ITALY EURO-LIRE 3 MTH (LDN:FT) – MIDDLE RATE*	ECITL3M
15	*JAPAN BENCHMARK BOND-RYLD.10 YR (DS) – RED. YIELD*	JPBRYLD
16	*ECU BENCHMARK BOND 10 YR (DS) 'DEAD' – RED. YIELD*	ECBRYLD
17	*GERMANY BENCHMARK BOND 10 YR (DS) – RED. YIELD*	BDBRYLD
18	*FRANCE BENCHMARK BOND 10 YR (DS) – RED. YIELD*	FRBRYLD
19	*UK BENCHMARK BOND 10 YR (DS) – RED. YIELD*	UKMBRYD
20	*US TREAS. BENCHMARK BOND 10 YR (DS) – RED. YIELD*	USBD10Y
21	*ITALY BENCHMARK BOND 10 YR (DS) – RED. YIELD*	ITBRYLD
22	*JAPANESE YEN TO US $ (WMR) – EXCHANGE RATE*	JAPAYE$
23	*US $ TO UK £ (WMR) – EXCHANGE RATE*	USDOLLR
24	*US $ TO EURO (WMR) – EXCHANGE RATE*	USEURSP
25	*Brent Crude-Current Month, fob US $/BBL*	OILBREN
26	*GOLD BULLION $/TROY OUNCE*	GOLDBLN
27	*Bridge/CRB Commodity Futures Index – PRICE INDEX*	NYFECRB

---

[3] EUR/USD is quoted as the number of USD per euro: for example, a value of 1.2657 is USD1.2657 per euro. The EUR/USD series for the period 1994–1998 was constructed as indicated in footnote 1.

All the series span the period from 17 October 1994 to 3 July 2001, totalling 1749 trading days. The data is divided into two periods: the first period runs from 17 October 1994 to 18 May 2000 (1459 observations) used for model estimation and is classified in-sample, while the second period from 19 May 2000 to 3 July 2001 (290 observations) is reserved for out-of-sample forecasting and evaluation. The division amounts to approximately 17% being retained for out-of-sample purposes.

Over the review period there has been an overall appreciation of the USD against the euro, as presented in Figure 1.1. The summary statistics of the EUR/USD for the examined period are presented in Figure 1.2, highlighting a slight skewness and low kurtosis. The Jarque–Bera statistic confirms that the EUR/USD series is non-normal at the 99% confidence interval. Therefore, the indication is that the series requires some type of transformation. The use of data in levels in the FX market has many problems, "FX price movements are generally non-stationary and quite random in nature, and therefore not very suitable for learning purposes... Therefore for most neural network studies and analysis concerned with the FX market, price inputs are not a desirable set" (Mehta, 1995: 191).

To overcome these problems, the EUR/USD series is transformed into rates of return. Given the price level $P_1, P_2, \ldots, P_t$, the rate of return at time t is formed by:

$$R_t = \left(\frac{P_t}{P_{t-1}}\right) - 1 \tag{1.1}$$

An example of this transformation can be reviewed in Sheet 1 column C of the oos_Naïve.xls Excel spreadsheet, and is also presented in Figure 1.5. See also the comment in cell C4 for an explanation of the calculations within this column.

An advantage of using a returns series is that it helps in making the time series stationary, a useful statistical property.

Formal confirmation that the EUR/USD returns series is stationary is confirmed at the 1% significance level by both the Augmented Dickey–Fuller (ADF) and Phillips–Perron (PP) test statistics, the results of which are presented in Tables 1.2 and 1.3.

The EUR/USD returns series is presented in Figure 1.3. Transformation into returns often creates a noisy time series. Formal confirmation through testing the significance of

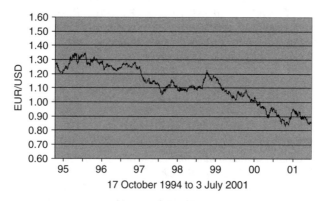

Figure 1.1   EUR/USD London daily closing prices (17 October 1994 to 3 July 2001)[4]

---

[4] Retropolated series for 17 October 1994 to 31 December 1998.

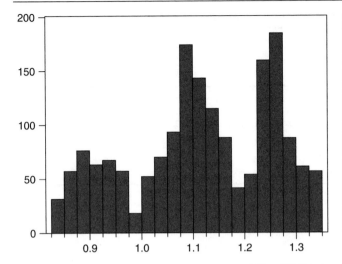

Figure 1.2 EUR/USD summary statistics (17 October 1994 to 3 July 2001)

Table 1.2 EUR/USD returns ADF test

ADF test statistic	**−18.37959**			
		1%	critical value[a]	**−3.4371**
		5%	critical value	−2.8637
		10%	critical value	−2.5679

[a]MacKinnon critical values for rejection of hypothesis of a unit root.

Augmented Dickey–Fuller Test Equation
Dependent Variable: D(DR_USEURSP)
Method: Least Squares
Sample(adjusted): 7 1749
Included observations: 1743 after adjusting endpoints

Variable	Coefficient	Std. error	t-Statistic	Prob.
DR_USEURSP(−1)	−0.979008	0.053266	−18.37959	0.0000
D(DR_USEURSP(−1))	−0.002841	0.047641	−0.059636	0.9525
D(DR_USEURSP(−2))	−0.015731	0.041288	−0.381009	0.7032
D(DR_USEURSP(−3))	−0.011964	0.033684	−0.355179	0.7225
D(DR_USEURSP(−4))	−0.014248	0.024022	−0.593095	0.5532
C	−0.000212	0.000138	−1.536692	0.1246

R-squared	0.491277	Mean dependent var.		1.04E-06
Adjusted R-squared	0.489812	S.D. dependent var.		0.008048
S.E. of regression	0.005748	Akaike info. criterion		−7.476417
Sum squared resid.	0.057394	Schwarz criterion		−7.457610
Log likelihood	6521.697	F-statistic		335.4858
Durbin–Watson stat.	1.999488	Prob(F-statistic)		0.000000

Table 1.3   EUR/USD returns PP test

PP test statistic	**−41.04039**		1%	critical value[a]	**−3.4370**
			5%	critical value	−2.8637
			10%	critical value	−2.5679

[a]MacKinnon critical values for rejection of hypothesis of a unit root.

Lag truncation for Bartlett kernel: 7	(Newey−West suggests: 7)	
Residual variance with no correction		3.29E-05
Residual variance with correction		3.26E-05

Phillips−Perron Test Equation
Dependent Variable: D(DR_USEURSP)
Method: Least Squares
Sample(adjusted): 3 1749
Included observations: 1747 after adjusting endpoints

Variable	Coefficient	Std. error	t-Statistic	Prob.
DR_USEURSP(−1)	−0.982298	0.023933	−41.04333	0.0000
C	−0.000212	0.000137	−1.539927	0.1238
R-squared	0.491188	Mean dependent var.		−1.36E-06
Adjusted R-squared	0.490896	S.D. dependent var.		0.008041
S.E. of regression	0.005737	Akaike info. criterion		−7.482575
Sum squared resid.	0.057436	Schwarz criterion		−7.476318
Log likelihood	6538.030	F-statistic		1684.555
Durbin−Watson stat.	1.999532	Prob(F-statistic)		0.000000

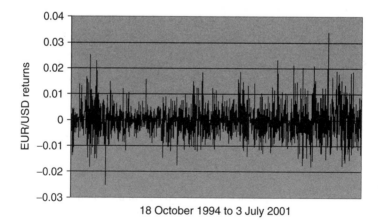

18 October 1994 to 3 July 2001

Figure 1.3   The EUR/USD returns series (18 October 1994 to 3 July 2001)

the autocorrelation coefficients reveals that the EUR/USD returns series is white noise at the 99% confidence interval, the results of which are presented in Table 1.4. For such series the best predictor of a future value is zero. In addition, very noisy data often makes forecasting difficult.

The EUR/USD returns summary statistics for the examined period are presented in Figure 1.4. They reveal a slight skewness and high kurtosis and, again, the Jarque–Bera statistic confirms that the EUR/USD series is non-normal at the 99% confidence interval. However, such features are "common in high frequency financial time series data" (Gençay, 1999: 94).

Table 1.4 EUR/USD returns correlogram

Sample: 1 1749
Included observations: 1748

	Autocorrelation	Partial correlation	Q-Stat.	Prob.
1	0.018	0.018	0.5487	**0.459**
2	−0.012	−0.013	0.8200	**0.664**
3	0.003	0.004	0.8394	**0.840**
4	−0.002	−0.002	0.8451	**0.932**
5	0.014	0.014	1.1911	**0.946**
6	−0.009	−0.010	1.3364	**0.970**
7	0.007	0.008	1.4197	**0.985**
8	−0.019	−0.019	2.0371	**0.980**
9	0.001	0.002	2.0405	**0.991**
10	0.012	0.012	2.3133	**0.993**
11	0.012	0.012	2.5787	**0.995**
12	−0.028	−0.029	3.9879	**0.984**

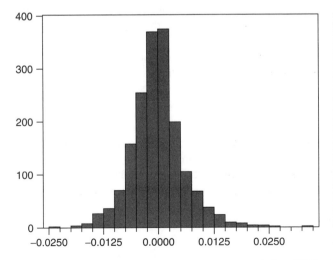

Series:DR_USEURSP	
Sample 2 1749	
Observations 1748	
Mean	−0.000214
Median	−0.000377
Maximum	0.033767
Minimum	−0.024898
Std. Dev.	0.005735
Skewness	0.434503
Kurtosis	5.009624
Jarque–Bera	349.1455
Probability	0.000000

Figure 1.4 EUR/USD returns summary statistics (17 October 1994 to 3 July 2001)

A further transformation includes the creation of interest rate yield curve series, generated by:

$$yc = 10 \text{ year benchmark bond yields} - 3 \text{ month interest rates} \tag{1.2}$$

In addition, all of the time series are transformed into returns series in the manner described above to account for their non-stationarity.

1.4 BENCHMARK MODELS: THEORY AND METHODOLOGY

The premise of this chapter is to examine the use of regression models in EUR/USD forecasting and trading models. In particular, the performance of NNR models is compared with other traditional forecasting techniques to ascertain their potential added value as a forecasting tool. Such methods include ARMA modelling, logit estimation, Moving Average Convergence/Divergence (MACD) technical models, and a naïve strategy. Except for the straightforward naïve strategy, all benchmark models were estimated on our in-sample period. As all of these methods are well documented in the literature, they are simply outlined below.

1.4.1 Naïve strategy

The naïve strategy simply assumes that the most recent period change is the best predictor of the future. The simplest model is defined by:

$$\hat{Y}_{t+1} = Y_t \tag{1.3}$$

where Y_t is the actual rate of return at period t and $\hat{Y}_{t+1}$ is the forecast rate of return for the next period.

The naïve forecast can be reviewed in Sheet 1 column E of the oos_Naïve.xls Excel spreadsheet, and is also presented in Figure 1.5. Also, please note the comments within the spreadsheet that document the calculations used within the naïve, ARMA, logit, and NNR strategies.

The performance of the strategy is evaluated in terms of forecasting accuracy and in terms of trading performance via a simulated trading strategy.

1.4.2 MACD strategy

Moving average methods are considered quick and inexpensive and as a result are routinely used in financial markets. The techniques use an average of past observations to smooth short-term fluctuations. In essence, "a moving average is obtained by finding the mean for a specified set of values and then using it to forecast the next period" (Hanke and Reitsch, 1998: 143).

The moving average is defined as:

$$M_t = \hat{Y}_{t+1} = \frac{(Y_t + Y_{t-1} + Y_{t-2} + \cdots + Y_{t-n+1})}{n} \tag{1.4}$$

Microsoft Excel - oos_Naive

File Edit View Insert Format Tools Data Window Help

Arial 10 B I U € % ‚

U30

Trading Days	USD to 1 Euro	Daily returns	Daily returns Rise or Fall	Naïve Forecast	Trading Signal	# Transactions Calculation	Positions	Last Entry	Transaction Profit/Loss	Winning Trades
19/05/2000	0.8928	-0.10%	0	0.30%				0.8928	0	0
22/05/2000	0.904	1.25%	1	-0.10%				-0.904	0.0112	1
23/05/2000	0.9088	0.53%	1	1.25%				0.9088	-0.0048	0
24/05/2000	0.9074	-0.15%	0	0.53%				0.9088	0	
25/05/2000	0.9069	-0.06%	0	-0.15%				-0.9069	-0.0019	0
26/05/2000	0.9259	2.10%	1	-0.06%	-1		0	-0.9069	0	
29/05/2000	0.9277	0.19%	1	2.10%	1	1	0.9277	0.9277	-0.0208	0
30/05/2000	0.9325	0.52%	1	0.19%	1		0	0.9277	0	
31/05/2000	0.9274	-0.55%	0	0.52%	1		0	0.9277	0	
01/06/2000	0.9311	0.40%	1	-0.55%	-1	1	-0.9311	-0.9311	0.0034	1
02/06/2000	0.9442	1.41%	1	0.40%	1	1	0.9442	0.9442	-0.0131	0
05/06/2000	0.9445	0.03%	1	1.41%	1		0	0.9442	0	
06/06/2000	0.9589	1.52%	1	0.03%	1		0	0.9442	0	
07/06/2000	0.9571	-0.19%	0	1.52%	1		0	0.9442	0	
08/06/2000	0.9535	-0.38%	0	-0.19%	-1	1	-0.9535	-0.9535	0.0093	1
09/06/2000	0.951	-0.26%	0	-0.38%	-1		0	-0.9535	0	
12/06/2000	0.9539	0.30%	1	-0.26%	-1		0	-0.9535	0	
13/06/2000	0.9607	0.71%	1	0.30%	1	1	0.9607	0.9607	-0.0072	0
14/06/2000	0.959	-0.18%	0	0.71%	1		0	0.9607	0	
15/06/2000	0.9526	-0.67%	0	-0.18%	-1	1	-0.9526	-0.9526	-0.0081	0
16/06/2000	0.9608	0.86%	1	-0.67%	-1		0	-0.9526	0	
19/06/2000	0.9603	-0.05%	0	0.86%	1	1	0.9603	0.9603	-0.0077	0
20/06/2000	0.9554	-0.51%	0	-0.05%	-1	1	-0.9554	-0.9554	-0.0049	0
21/06/2000	0.9462	-0.96%	0	-0.51%	-1		0	-0.9554	0	
22/06/2000	0.9395	-0.71%	0	-0.96%	-1		0	-0.9554	0	
23/06/2000	0.9365	-0.32%	0	-0.71%	-1		0	-0.9554	0	
26/06/2000	0.9371	0.06%	1	-0.32%	-1		0	-0.9554	0	
27/06/2000	0.9433	0.66%	1	0.06%	1	1	0.9433	0.9433	0.0121	1
28/06/2000	0.9459	0.28%	1	0.66%	1		0	0.9433	0	
29/06/2000	0.9525	0.70%	1	0.28%	1		0	0.9433	0	

Comment box: The forecast in this period (cell E6) is equal to the daily returns of the previous period (cell C5). In general, the forecast at time *t+1* is simply the value of the daily return at time *t*.

Sheet 1 / Sheet 2

Figure 1.5 Naïve forecast Excel spreadsheet (out-of-sample)

where M_t is the moving average at time t, n is the number of terms in the moving average, Y_t is the actual level at period t[5] and $\hat{Y}_{t+1}$ is the level forecast for the next period.

The MACD strategy used is quite simple. Two moving average series $M_{1,t}$ and $M_{2,t}$ are created with different moving average lengths n and m. The decision rule for taking positions in the market is straightforward. If the short-term moving average (SMA) intersects the long-term moving average (LMA) from below a "long" position is taken. Conversely, if the LMA is intersected from above a "short" position is taken.[6] This strategy can be reviewed in Sheet 1 column E of the is_35&1MA.xls Excel spreadsheet, and is also presented in Figure 1.6. Again, please note the comments within the spreadsheet that document the calculations used within the MACD strategy.

The forecaster must use judgement when determining the number of periods n and m on which to base the moving averages. The combination that performed best over the in-sample period was retained for out-of-sample evaluation. The model selected was a combination of the EUR/USD series and its 35-day moving average, namely $n = 1$ and $m = 35$ respectively, or a $(1,35)$ combination. A graphical representation of the combination is presented in Figure 1.7. The performance of this strategy is evaluated in terms of forecasting accuracy via the correct directional change measure, and in terms of trading performance.

Several other "adequate" models were produced and their performance evaluated. The trading performance of some of these combinations, such as the $(1,40)$ combination, and

---

[5] In this strategy the EUR/USD levels series is used as opposed to the returns series.
[6] A "long" EUR/USD position means buying euros at the current price, while a "short" position means selling euros at the current price.

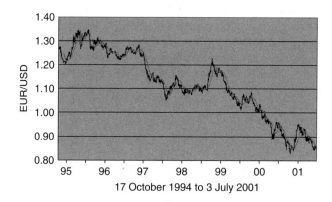

	A	B	C	D	E	F	G	H	I	J	K	
1				Daily returns	Trading	# Transactions			Transaction	Winning		Daily
2	Trading Days	USD to 1 Euro	Daily returns	Rise or Fall	Signal	Calculation	Positions	Last Entry	Profit/Loss	Trades	Daily Change	Pr
37	02/12/1994	1.2093	-0.44%	0	-1	1	-1.2093	-1.2093	0	0	-0.0053	
38	05/12/1994	1.212	0.22%	1	-1		0	-1.2093	0		0.0027	-0.0
39	06/12/1994	1.2141	0.17%	1	-1		0	-1.2093	0		0.0021	-0.0
40	07/12/1994	1.2143	0.02%	1	-1		0	-1.2093	0		0.0002	-0.0
41	08/12/1994	1.2105	-0.31%	0	-1		0	-1.2093	0		-0.0038	0.0
42	09/12/1994	1.2113	0.07%	1	-1		0	-1.2093	0		0.0008	-0.0
43	12/12/1994	1.213	0.14%	1	-1		0	-1.2093	0		0.0017	-0.0
44	13/12/1994	1.2115	-0.12%	0	-1		0	-1.2093	0		-0.0015	0.0
45	14/12/1994	1.2142	0.22%	1	-1		0	-1.2093	0		0.0027	-0.0
46	15/12/1994	1.2127	-0.12%	0	-1		0	-1.2093	0		-0.0015	0.0
47	16/12/1994	1.2132	0.04%	1	-1		0	-1.2093	0		0.0005	-0.0
48	19/12/1994	1.211	-0.18%	0	-1		0	-1.2093	0		-0.0022	0.0
49	20/12/1994	1.2119	0.07%	1	-1		0	-1.2093	0		0.0009	-0.0
50	21/12/1994	1.2127	0.07%	1	-1		0	-1.2093	0		0.0008	0.0
51	22/12/1994	1.2045	-0.68%	0	-1		0	-1.2093	0		-0.0082	-0.0
52	23/12/1994	1.2058	0.11%	1	-1		0	-1.2093	0		0.0013	-0.0
53	26/12/1994	1.2058	0.00%	0	-1		0	-1.2093	0		0	
54	27/12/1994	1.2062	0.03%	1	-1		0	-1.2093	0		0.0004	-0.0
55	28/12/1994	1.2083	0.17%	1	-1						0.0021	-0.0
56	29/12/1994	1.225	1.38%	1	1				57	0	0.0167	-0.0
57	30/12/1994	1.2264	0.11%	1	1						0.0014	0.0
58	02/01/1995	1.2264	0.00%	0	1						0	
59	03/01/1995	1.2244	-0.16%	0	1						-0.002	-0.
60	04/01/1995	1.221	-0.28%	0	1		0	1.225	0		-0.0034	-0.0
61	05/01/1995	1.2256	0.38%	1	1		0	1.225	0		0.0046	-0.0
62	06/01/1995	1.2202	-0.44%	0	1		0	1.225	0		-0.0054	-0.0
63	09/01/1995	1.2229	0.22%	1	1		0	1.225	0		0.0027	-0.0
64	10/01/1995	1.2328	0.81%	1	1		0	1.225	0		0.0099	0.0
65	11/01/1995	1.2326	-0.02%	0	1		0	1.225	0		-0.0002	-0.0
66	12/01/1995	1.2361	0.28%	1	1		0	1.225	0		0.0035	0.0

Callout (near rows 55–56): SMA intersects LMA from below, therefore a long position is taken in this period (cell E56), this is the first point at which the blue line intersects the red line in Figure 7. Prior to this period a short position was held.

Figure 1.6   EUR/USD and 35-day moving average combination Excel spreadsheet

Figure 1.7   EUR/USD and 35-day moving average combination

the (1,35) combination results were only marginally different. For example, the Sharpe ratio differs only by 0.01, and the average gain/loss ratio by 0.02. However, the (1,35) combination has the lowest maximum drawdown at −12.43% and lowest probability of a 10% loss at 0.02%.[7] The evaluation can be reviewed in Sheet 2 of the is_35&1MA.xls and is_40&1MA.xls Excel spreadsheets, and is also presented in Figures 1.8 and 1.9,

---

[7] A discussion of the statistical and trading performance measures used to evaluate the strategies is presented below in Section 1.6.

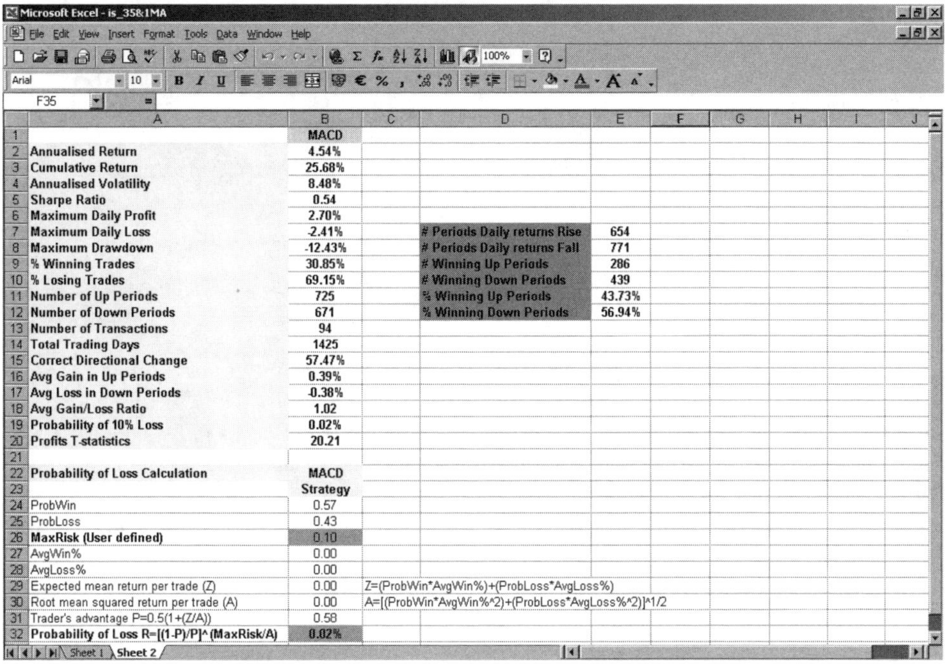

Figure 1.8 (1,35) combination moving average Excel spreadsheet (in-sample)

respectively. On balance, the (1,35) combination was considered "best" and therefore retained for further analysis.

1.4.3 ARMA methodology

ARMA models are particularly useful when information is limited to a single stationary series,[8] or when economic theory is not useful. They are a "highly refined curve-fitting device that uses current and past values of the dependent variable to produce accurate short-term forecasts" (Hanke and Reitsch, 1998: 407).

The ARMA methodology does not assume any particular pattern in a time series, but uses an iterative approach to identify a possible model from a general class of models. Once a tentative model has been selected, it is subjected to tests of adequacy. If the specified model is not satisfactory, the process is repeated using other models until a satisfactory model is found. Sometimes, it is possible that two or more models may approximate the series equally well, in this case the most parsimonious model should prevail. For a full discussion on the procedure refer to Box *et al.* (1994), Gouriéroux and Monfort (1995), or Pindyck and Rubinfeld (1998).

The ARMA model takes the form:

$$Y_t = \phi_0 + \phi_1 Y_{t-1} + \phi_2 Y_{t-2} + \cdots + \phi_p Y_{t-p} + \varepsilon_t - w_1 \varepsilon_{t-1} - w_2 \varepsilon_{t-2} - \cdots - w_q \varepsilon_{t-q}$$

$$(1.5)$$

---

[8] The general class of ARMA models is for stationary time series. If the series is not stationary an appropriate transformation is required.

	A	B	C	D	E	F	G	H	I	J
1		MACD								
2	Annualised Return	4.49%								
3	Cumulative Return	25.28%								
4	Annualised Volatility	8.50%								
5	Sharpe Ratio	0.53								
6	Maximum Daily Profit	2.69%								
7	Maximum Daily Loss	-2.41%		# Periods Daily returns Rise	651					
8	Maximum Drawdown	-14.54%		# Periods Daily returns Fall	769					
9	% Winning Trades	30.49%		# Winning Up Periods	290					
10	% Losing Trades	69.51%		# Winning Down Periods	439					
11	Number of Up Periods	729		% Winning Up Periods	44.55%					
12	Number of Down Periods	662		% Winning Down Periods	57.09%					
13	Number of Transactions	82								
14	Total Trading Days	1420								
15	Correct Directional Change	57.04%								
16	Avg Gain in Up Periods	0.38%								
17	Avg Loss in Down Periods	-0.38%								
18	Avg Gain/Loss Ratio	1.00								
19	Probability of 10% Loss	0.06%								
20	Profits T-statistics	19.89								
21										
22	Probability of Loss Calculation	MACD								
23		Strategy								
24	ProbWin	0.57								
25	ProbLoss	0.43								
26	MaxRisk (User defined)	0.10								
27	AvgWin%	0.00								
28	AvgLoss%	0.00								
29	Expected mean return per trade (Z)	0.00		Z=(ProbWin*AvgWin%)+(ProbLoss*AvgLoss%)						
30	Root mean squared return per trade (A)	0.00		A=[(ProbWin*AvgWin%^2)+(ProbLoss*AvgLoss%^2)]^1/2						
31	Trader's advantage P=0.5(1+(Z/A))	0.57								
32	Probability of Loss R=[(1-P)/P]^ (MaxRisk/A)	0.06%								

Figure 1.9 (1,40) combination moving average Excel spreadsheet (in-sample)

where Y_t is the dependent variable at time t; $Y_{t-1}, Y_{t-2}, \ldots, Y_{t-p}$ are the lagged dependent variables; $\phi_0, \phi_1, \ldots, \phi_p$ are regression coefficients; ε_t is the residual term; $\varepsilon_{t-1}, \varepsilon_{t-2}, \ldots, \varepsilon_{t-p}$ are previous values of the residual; $w_1, w_2, \ldots, w_q$ are weights.

Several ARMA specifications were tried out, for example ARMA(5,5) and ARMA(10,10) models were produced to test for any "weekly" effects, which can be reviewed in the arma.wf1 EViews workfile. The ARMA(10,10) model was estimated but was unsatisfactory as several coefficients were not even significant at the 90% confidence interval (equation arma1010). The results of this are presented in Table 1.5. The model was primarily modified through testing the significance of variables via the likelihood ratio (LR) test for redundant or omitted variables and Ramsey's RESET test for model misspecification.

Once the non-significant terms are removed all of the coefficients of the restricted ARMA(10,10) model become significant at the 99% confidence interval (equation arma13610). The overall significance of the model is tested using the F-test. The null hypothesis that all coefficients except the constant are not significantly different from zero is rejected at the 99% confidence interval. The results of this are presented in Table 1.6. Examination of the autocorrelation function of the error terms reveals that the residuals are random at the 99% confidence interval and a further confirmation is given by the serial correlation LM test. The results of this are presented in Tables 1.7 and 1.8. The model is also tested for general misspecification via Ramsey's RESET test. The null hypothesis of correct specification is accepted at the 99% confidence interval. The results of this are presented in Table 1.9.

Table 1.5 ARMA(10,10) EUR/USD returns estimation

Dependent Variable: DR_USEURSP
Method: Least Squares
Sample(adjusted): 12 1459
Included observations: 1448 after adjusting endpoints
Convergence achieved after 20 iterations
White Heteroskedasticity–Consistent Standard Errors & Covariance
Backcast: 2 11

Variable	Coefficient	Std. error	t-Statistic	Prob.
C	−0.000220	0.000140	−1.565764	0.1176
AR(1)	−0.042510	0.049798	−0.853645	**0.3934**
AR(2)	−0.210934	0.095356	−2.212073	0.0271
AR(3)	−0.359378	0.061740	−5.820806	0.0000
AR(4)	−0.041003	0.079423	−0.516264	**0.6058**
AR(5)	0.001376	0.067652	0.020338	**0.9838**
AR(6)	0.132413	0.054071	2.448866	0.0145
AR(7)	−0.238913	0.052594	−4.542616	0.0000
AR(8)	0.182816	0.046878	3.899801	0.0001
AR(9)	0.026431	0.060321	0.438169	**0.6613**
AR(10)	−0.615601	0.076171	−8.081867	0.0000
MA(1)	0.037787	0.040142	0.941343	**0.3467**
MA(2)	0.227952	0.095346	2.390785	0.0169
MA(3)	0.341293	0.058345	5.849551	0.0000
MA(4)	0.036997	0.074796	0.494633	**0.6209**
MA(5)	−0.004544	0.059140	−0.076834	**0.9388**
MA(6)	−0.140714	0.046739	−3.010598	0.0027
MA(7)	0.253016	0.042340	5.975838	0.0000
MA(8)	−0.206445	0.040077	−5.151153	0.0000
MA(9)	−0.014011	0.048037	−0.291661	**0.7706**
MA(10)	0.643684	0.074271	8.666665	0.0000

R-squared	0.016351	Mean dependent var.		−0.000225
Adjusted R-squared	0.002565	S.D. dependent var.		0.005363
S.E. of regression	0.005356	Akaike info. criterion		−7.606665
Sum squared resid.	0.040942	Schwarz criterion		−7.530121
Log likelihood	5528.226	F-statistic		1.186064
Durbin–Watson stat.	1.974747	Prob(F-statistic)		0.256910

Inverted AR roots	0.84 + 0.31i	0.84 − 0.31i	0.55 − 0.82i	0.55 + 0.82i
	0.07 + 0.98i	0.07 − 0.98i	−0.59 − 0.78i	−0.59 + 0.78i
	−0.90 + 0.21i	−0.90 − 0.21i		
Inverted MA roots	0.85 + 0.31i	0.85 − 0.31i	0.55 − 0.82i	0.55 + 0.82i
	0.07 − 0.99i	0.07 + 0.99i	−0.59 − 0.79i	−0.59 + 0.79i
	−0.90 + 0.20i	−0.90 − 0.20i		

Table 1.6   Restricted ARMA(10,10) EUR/USD returns estimation

Dependent Variable: DR_USEURSP
Method: Least Squares
Sample(adjusted): 12 1459
Included observations: 1448 after adjusting endpoints
Convergence achieved after 50 iterations
White Heteroskedasticity–Consistent Standard Errors & Covariance
Backcast: 2 11

Variable	Coefficient	Std. error	t-Statistic	Prob.
C	−0.000221	0.000144	−1.531755	0.1258
AR(1)	0.263934	0.049312	5.352331	**0.0000**
AR(3)	−0.444082	0.040711	−10.90827	**0.0000**
AR(6)	−0.334221	0.035517	−9.410267	**0.0000**
AR(10)	−0.636137	0.043255	−14.70664	**0.0000**
MA(1)	−0.247033	0.046078	−5.361213	**0.0000**
MA(3)	0.428264	0.030768	13.91921	**0.0000**
MA(6)	0.353457	0.028224	12.52307	**0.0000**
MA(10)	0.675965	0.041063	16.46159	**0.0000**
R-squared	0.015268	Mean dependent var.		−0.000225
Adjusted R-squared	0.009793	S.D. dependent var.		0.005363
S.E. of regression	0.005337	Akaike info. criterion		−7.622139
Sum squared resid.	0.040987	Schwarz criterion		−7.589334
Log likelihood	5527.429	F-statistic		2.788872
Durbin–Watson stat.	2.019754	Prob(F-statistic)		**0.004583**
Inverted AR roots	0.89 + 0.37i	0.89 − 0.37i	0.61 + 0.78i	0.61 − 0.78i
	0.08 − 0.98i	0.08 + 0.98i	−0.53 − 0.70i	−0.53 + 0.70i
	−0.92 + 0.31i	−0.92 − 0.31i		
Inverted MA roots	0.90 − 0.37i	0.90 + 0.37i	0.61 + 0.78i	0.61 − 0.78i
	0.07 + 0.99i	0.07 − 0.99i	−0.54 − 0.70i	−0.54 + 0.70i
	−0.93 + 0.31i	−0.93 − 0.31i		

The selected ARMA model, namely the restricted ARMA(10,10) model, takes the form:

$$Y_t = -0.0002 + 0.2639Y_{t-1} - 0.4440Y_{t-3} - 0.3342Y_{t-6} - 0.6361Y_{t-10}$$
$$- 0.2470\varepsilon_{t-1} + 0.4283\varepsilon_{t-3} + 0.3535\varepsilon_{t-6} + 0.6760\varepsilon_{t-10}$$

The restricted ARMA(10,10) model was retained for out-of-sample estimation. The performance of the strategy is evaluated in terms of traditional forecasting accuracy and in terms of trading performance. Several other models were produced and their performance evaluated, for example an alternative restricted ARMA(10,10) model was produced (equation arma16710). The decision to retain the original restricted ARMA(10,10) model is because it has significantly better in-sample trading results than the alternative ARMA(10,10) model. The annualised return, Sharpe ratio and correct directional change of the original model were 12.65%, 1.49 and 53.80%, respectively. The corresponding

Table 1.7   Restricted ARMA(10,10) correlogram of residuals

Sample: 12 1459
Included observations: 1448
Q-statistic probabilities adjusted for 8 ARMA term(s)

	Autocorrelation	Partial correlation	Q-Stat.	Prob.
1	−0.010	−0.010	0.1509	
2	−0.004	−0.004	0.1777	
3	0.004	0.004	0.1973	
4	−0.001	−0.001	0.1990	
5	0.000	0.000	0.1991	
6	−0.019	−0.019	0.7099	
7	−0.004	−0.004	0.7284	
8	−0.015	−0.015	1.0573	
9	0.000	0.000	1.0573	**0.304**
10	0.009	0.009	1.1824	**0.554**
11	0.031	0.032	2.6122	**0.455**
12	−0.024	−0.024	3.4600	**0.484**
13	0.019	0.018	3.9761	**0.553**
14	−0.028	−0.028	5.0897	**0.532**
15	0.008	0.008	5.1808	**0.638**

values for the alternative model were 9.47%, 1.11 and 52.35%. The evaluation can be reviewed in Sheet 2 of the is_arma13610.xls and is_arma16710.xls Excel spreadsheets, and is also presented in Figures 1.10 and 1.11, respectively. Ultimately, we chose the model that satisfied the usual statistical tests and that also recorded the best in-sample trading performance.

1.4.4   Logit estimation

The logit model belongs to a group of models termed "classification models". They are a multivariate statistical technique used to estimate the probability of an upward or downward movement in a variable. As a result they are well suited to rates of return applications where a recommendation for trading is required. For a full discussion of the procedure refer to Maddala (2001), Pesaran and Pesaran (1997), or Thomas (1997).

The approach assumes the following regression model:

$$Y_t^* = \beta_0 + \beta_1 X_{1,t} + \beta_2 X_{2,t} + \cdots + \beta_p X_{p,t} + \varepsilon_t \tag{1.6}$$

where Y_t^* is the dependent variable at time t; $X_{1,t}, X_{2,t}, \ldots, X_{p,t}$ are the explanatory variables at time t; $\beta_0, \beta_1, \ldots, \beta_p$ are the regression coefficients; ε_t is the residual term.

However, Y_t^* is not directly observed; what is observed is a dummy variable Y_t defined by:

$$Y_t = \begin{cases} 1 & \text{if } Y_t^* > 0 \\ 0 & \text{otherwise} \end{cases} \tag{1.7}$$

Therefore, the model requires a transformation of the explained variable, namely the EUR/USD returns series into a binary series. The procedure is quite simple: a binary

Table 1.8   Restricted ARMA(10,10) serial correlation LM test

Breusch–Godfrey Serial Correlation LM Test

F-statistic	0.582234	Probability	**0.558781**
Obs*R-squared	1.172430	Probability	**0.556429**

Dependent Variable: RESID
Method: Least Squares
Presample missing value lagged residuals set to zero

Variable	Coefficient	Std. error	t-Statistic	Prob.
C	8.33E-07	0.000144	0.005776	0.9954
AR(1)	0.000600	0.040612	0.014773	0.9882
AR(3)	0.019545	0.035886	0.544639	0.5861
AR(6)	0.018085	0.031876	0.567366	0.5706
AR(10)	−0.028997	0.037436	−0.774561	0.4387
MA(1)	−0.000884	0.038411	−0.023012	0.9816
MA(3)	−0.015096	0.026538	−0.568839	0.5696
MA(6)	−0.014584	0.026053	−0.559792	0.5757
MA(10)	0.029482	0.035369	0.833563	0.4047
RESID(−1)	−0.010425	0.031188	−0.334276	0.7382
RESID(−2)	−0.004640	0.026803	−0.173111	0.8626

R-squared	0.000810	Mean dependent var.	1.42E-07
Adjusted R-squared	−0.006144	S.D. dependent var.	0.005322
S.E. of regression	0.005338	Akaike info. criterion	−7.620186
Sum squared resid.	0.040953	Schwarz criterion	−7.580092
Log likelihood	5528.015	F-statistic	0.116447
Durbin–Watson stat.	1.998650	Prob(F-statistic)	0.999652

Table 1.9   Restricted ARMA(10,10) RESET test for model misspecification

Ramsey RESET Test

F-statistic	0.785468	Probability	0.375622
Log likelihood ratio	0.790715	Probability	**0.373884**

variable equal to one is produced if the return is positive, and zero otherwise. The same transformation for the explanatory variables, although not necessary, was performed for homogeneity reasons.

A basic regression technique is used to produce the logit model. The idea is to start with a model containing several variables, including lagged dependent terms, then through a series of tests the model is modified.

The selected logit model, which we shall name logit1 (equation logit1 of the logit.wf1 EViews workfile), takes the form:

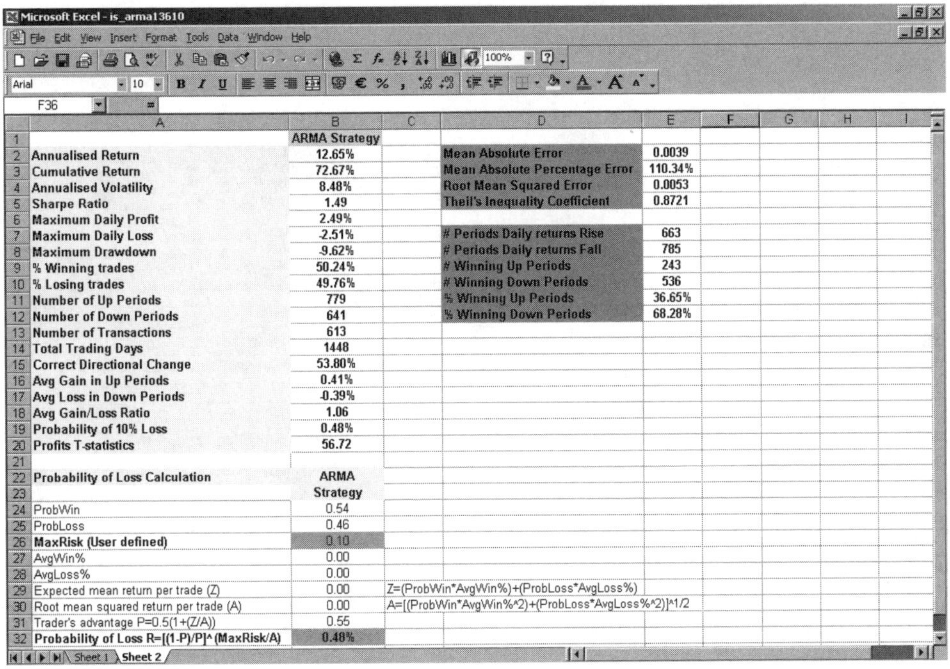

Figure 1.10   Restricted ARMA(10,10) model Excel spreadsheet (in-sample)

$$Y_t^* = 0.2492 - 0.3613X_{1,t} - 0.2872X_{2,t} + 0.2862X_{3,t} + 0.2525X_{4,t}$$
$$- 0.3692X_{5,t} - 0.3937X_{6,t} + \varepsilon_t$$

where $X_{1,t}, \ldots, X_{6,t}$ are the JP_yc(-2), UK_yc(-9), JAPDOWA(-1), ITMIB30(-19), JAPAYE\$(-10), and OILBREN(-1) binary explanatory variables, respectively.[9]

All of the coefficients in the model are significant at the 98% confidence interval. The overall significance of the model is tested using the LR test. The null hypothesis that all coefficients except the constant are not significantly different from zero is rejected at the 99% confidence interval. The results of this are presented in Table 1.10.

To justify the use of Japanese variables, which seems difficult from an economic perspective, the joint overall significance of this subset of variables is tested using the LR test for redundant variables. The null hypothesis that these coefficients, except the constant, are not jointly significantly different from zero is rejected at the 99% confidence interval. The results of this are presented in Table 1.11. In addition, a model that did not include the Japanese variables, but was otherwise identical to logit1, was produced and the trading performance evaluated, which we shall name nojap (equation nojap of the logit.wf1 EViews workfile). The Sharpe ratio, average gain/loss ratio and correct directional change of the nojap model were 1.34, 1.01 and 54.38%, respectively. The corresponding values for the logit1 model were 2.26, 1.01 and 58.13%. The evaluation can be reviewed in Sheet 2 of the is_logit1.xls and is_nojap.xls Excel spreadsheets, and is also presented in Figures 1.12 and 1.13, respectively.

---

[9] Datastream mnemonics as mentioned in Table 1.1, yield curves and lags in brackets are used to save space.

	A	B	C	D	E	F	G	H	I
1		ARMA Strategy							
2	Annualised Return	9.47%		Mean Absolute Error	0.0039				
3	Cumulative Return	54.42%		Mean Absolute Percentage Error	105.57%				
4	Annualised Volatility	8.50%		Root Mean Squared Error	0.0053				
5	Sharpe Ratio	1.11		Theil's Inequality Coefficient	0.9040				
6	Maximum Daily Profit	2.49%							
7	Maximum Daily Loss	-2.51%		# Periods Daily returns Rise	663				
8	Maximum Drawdown	-8.57%		# Periods Daily returns Fall	785				
9	% Winning trades	52.60%		# Winning Up Periods	196				
10	% Losing trades	47.40%		# Winning Down Periods	562				
11	Number of Up Periods	758		% Winning Up Periods	29.56%				
12	Number of Down Periods	662		% Winning Down Periods	71.59%				
13	Number of Transactions	346							
14	Total Trading Days	1448							
15	Correct Directional Change	52.35%							
16	Avg Gain in Up Periods	0.41%							
17	Avg Loss in Down Periods	-0.39%							
18	Avg Gain/Loss Ratio	1.06							
19	Probability of 10% Loss	2.35%							
20	Profits T-statistics	42.40							
21									
22	Probability of Loss Calculation	ARMA							
23		Strategy							
24	ProbWin	0.52							
25	ProbLoss	0.48							
26	MaxRisk (User defined)	0.10							
27	AvgWin%	0.00							
28	AvgLoss%	0.00							
29	Expected mean return per trade (Z)	0.00		Z=(ProbWin*AvgWin%)+(ProbLoss*AvgLoss%)					
30	Root mean squared return per trade (A)	0.00		A=[(ProbWin*AvgWin%^2)+(ProbLoss*AvgLoss%^2)]^1/2					
31	Trader's advantage P=0.5(1+(Z/A))	0.54							
32	Probability of Loss R=[(1-P)/P]^(MaxRisk/A)	2.35%							

Figure 1.11   Alternative restricted ARMA(10,10) model Excel spreadsheet (in-sample)

The logit1 model was retained for out-of-sample estimation. As, in practice, the estimation of the model is based upon the cumulative distribution of the logistic function for the error term, the forecasts produced range between zero and one, requiring transformation into a binary series. Again, the procedure is quite simple: a binary variable equal to one is produced if the forecast is greater than 0.5 and zero otherwise.

The performance of the strategy is evaluated in terms of forecast accuracy via the correct directional change measure and in terms of trading performance. Several other adequate models were produced and their performance evaluated. None performed better in-sample, therefore the logit1 model was retained.

1.5   NEURAL NETWORK MODELS: THEORY AND METHODOLOGY

Neural networks are "data-driven self-adaptive methods in that there are few *a priori* assumptions about the models under study" (Zhang *et al.*, 1998: 35). As a result, they are well suited to problems where economic theory is of little use. In addition, neural networks are universal approximators capable of approximating any continuous function (Hornik *et al.*, 1989).

Many researchers are confronted with problems where important nonlinearities exist between the independent variables and the dependent variable. Often, in such circumstances, traditional forecasting methods lack explanatory power. Recently, nonlinear models have attempted to cover this shortfall. In particular, NNR models have been applied with increasing success to financial markets, which often contain nonlinearities (Dunis and Jalilov, 2002).

Table 1.10   Logit1 EUR/USD returns estimation

Dependent Variable: BDR_USEURSP
Method: ML – Binary Logit
Sample(adjusted): 20 1459
Included observations: 1440 after adjusting endpoints
Convergence achieved after 3 iterations
Covariance matrix computed using second derivatives

Variable	Coefficient	Std. error	z-Statistic	Prob.
C	0.249231	0.140579	1.772894	0.0762
BDR_JP_YC(−2)	−0.361289	0.108911	−3.317273	**0.0009**
BDR_UK_YC(−9)	−0.287220	0.108397	−2.649696	**0.0081**
BDR_JAPDOWA(−1)	0.286214	0.108687	2.633369	**0.0085**
BDR_ITMIB31(−19)	0.252454	0.108056	2.336325	**0.0195**
BDR_JAPAYE$(−10)	−0.369227	0.108341	−3.408025	**0.0007**
BDR_OILBREN(−1)	−0.393689	0.108476	−3.629261	**0.0003**
Mean dependent var.	0.457639	S.D. dependent var.		0.498375
S.E. of regression	0.490514	Akaike info. criterion		1.353305
Sum squared resid.	344.7857	Schwarz criterion		1.378935
Log likelihood	−967.3795	Hannan–Quinn criterion		1.362872
Restr. log likelihood	−992.9577	Avg. log likelihood		−0.671791
LR statistic (6 df)	51.15635	McFadden R-squared		0.025760
Prob(LR statistic)	**2.76E-09**			
Obs. with dep = 0	781	Total obs.		1440
Obs. with dep = 1	659			

Theoretically, the advantage of NNR models over traditional forecasting methods is because, as is often the case, the model best adapted to a particular problem cannot be identified. It is then better to resort to a method that is a generalisation of many models, than to rely on an *a priori* model (Dunis and Huang, 2002).

However, NNR models have been criticised and their widespread success has been hindered because of their "black-box" nature, excessive training times, danger of overfitting, and the large number of "parameters" required for training. As a result, deciding on the appropriate network involves much trial and error.

For a full discussion on neural networks, please refer to Haykin (1999), Kaastra and Boyd (1996), Kingdon (1997), or Zhang *et al.* (1998). Notwithstanding, we provide below a brief description of NNR models and procedures.

1.5.1   Neural network models

The will to understand the functioning of the brain is the basis for the study of neural networks. Mathematical modelling started in the 1940s with the work of McCulloch and Pitts, whose research was based on the study of networks composed of a number of simple interconnected processing elements called neurons or nodes. If the description is correct,

Table 1.11 Logit1 estimation redundant variables LR test

Redundant Variables: BDR_JP_YC(−2), BDR_JAPDOWA(−1), BDR_JAPAYE$(−10)

F-statistic	9.722023	Probability	0.000002
Log likelihood ratio	28.52168	Probability	**0.000003**

Test Equation:
Dependent Variable: BDR_USEURSP
Method: ML – Binary Logit
Sample: 20 1459
Included observations: 1440
Convergence achieved after 3 iterations
Covariance matrix computed using second derivatives

Variable	Coefficient	Std. error	z-Statistic	Prob.
C	−0.013577	0.105280	−0.128959	0.8974
BDR_UK_YC(−9)	−0.247254	0.106979	−2.311245	0.0208
BDR_ITMIB31(−19)	0.254096	0.106725	2.380861	0.0173
BDR_OILBREN(−1)	−0.345654	0.106781	−3.237047	0.0012

Mean dependent var.	0.457639	S.D. dependent var.	0.498375
S.E. of regression	0.494963	Akaike info. criterion	1.368945
Sum squared resid.	351.8032	Schwarz criterion	1.383590
Log likelihood	−981.6403	Hannan–Quinn criterion	1.374412
Restr. log likelihood	−992.9577	Avg. log likelihood	−0.681695
LR statistic (3 df)	22.63467	McFadden R-squared	0.011398
Prob(LR statistic)	4.81E-05		
Obs. with dep = 0	781	Total obs.	1440
Obs. with dep = 1	659		

they can be turned into models mimicking some of the brain's functions, possibly with the ability to learn from examples and then to generalise on unseen examples.

A neural network is typically organised into several layers of elementary processing units or nodes. The first layer is the input layer, the number of nodes corresponding to the number of variables, and the last layer is the output layer, the number of nodes corresponding to the forecasting horizon for a forecasting problem.[10] The input and output layer can be separated by one or more hidden layers, with each layer containing one or more hidden nodes.[11] The nodes in adjacent layers are fully connected. Each neuron receives information from the preceding layer and transmits to the following layer only.[12] The neuron performs a weighted summation of its inputs; if the sum passes a threshold the neuron transmits, otherwise it remains inactive. In addition, a bias neuron may be connected to each neuron in the hidden and output layers. The bias has a value of positive

[10] Linear regression models may be viewed analogously to neural networks with no hidden layers (Kaastra and Boyd, 1996).
[11] Networks with hidden layers are multilayer networks; a multilayer perceptron network is used for this chapter.
[12] If the flow of information through the network is from the input to the output, it is known as "feedforward".

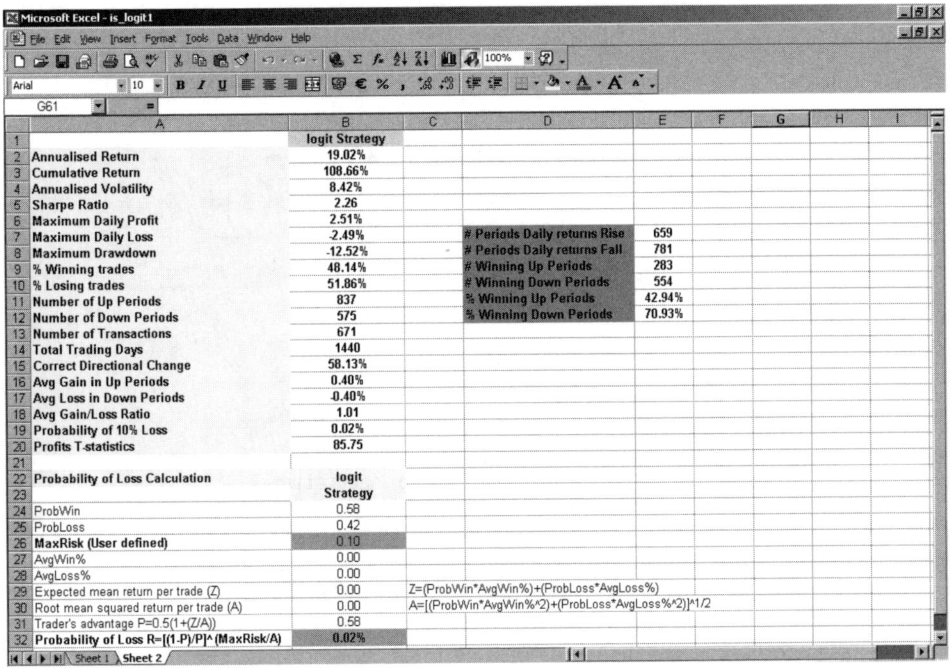

Microsoft Excel - is_logit1

G61

	A	B	C	D	E
1		logit Strategy			
2	Annualised Return	19.02%			
3	Cumulative Return	108.66%			
4	Annualised Volatility	8.42%			
5	Sharpe Ratio	2.26			
6	Maximum Daily Profit	2.51%			
7	Maximum Daily Loss	-2.49%		# Periods Daily returns Rise	659
8	Maximum Drawdown	-12.52%		# Periods Daily returns Fall	781
9	% Winning trades	48.14%		# Winning Up Periods	283
10	% Losing trades	51.86%		# Winning Down Periods	554
11	Number of Up Periods	837		% Winning Up Periods	42.94%
12	Number of Down Periods	575		% Winning Down Periods	70.93%
13	Number of Transactions	671			
14	Total Trading Days	1440			
15	Correct Directional Change	58.13%			
16	Avg Gain in Up Periods	0.40%			
17	Avg Loss in Down Periods	-0.40%			
18	Avg Gain/Loss Ratio	1.01			
19	Probability of 10% Loss	0.02%			
20	Profits T-statistics	85.75			
21					
22	Probability of Loss Calculation	logit			
23		Strategy			
24	ProbWin	0.58			
25	ProbLoss	0.42			
26	MaxRisk (User defined)	0.10			
27	AvgWin%	0.00			
28	AvgLoss%	0.00			
29	Expected mean return per trade (Z)	0.00	Z=(ProbWin*AvgWin%)+(ProbLoss*AvgLoss%)		
30	Root mean squared return per trade (A)	0.00	A=[(ProbWin*AvgWin%^2)+(ProbLoss*AvgLoss%^2)]^1/2		
31	Trader's advantage P=0.5(1+(Z/A))	0.58			
32	Probability of Loss R=[(1-P)/P]^(MaxRisk/A)	0.02%			

Sheet 1 Sheet 2

Figure 1.12 Logit1 estimation Excel spreadsheet (in-sample)

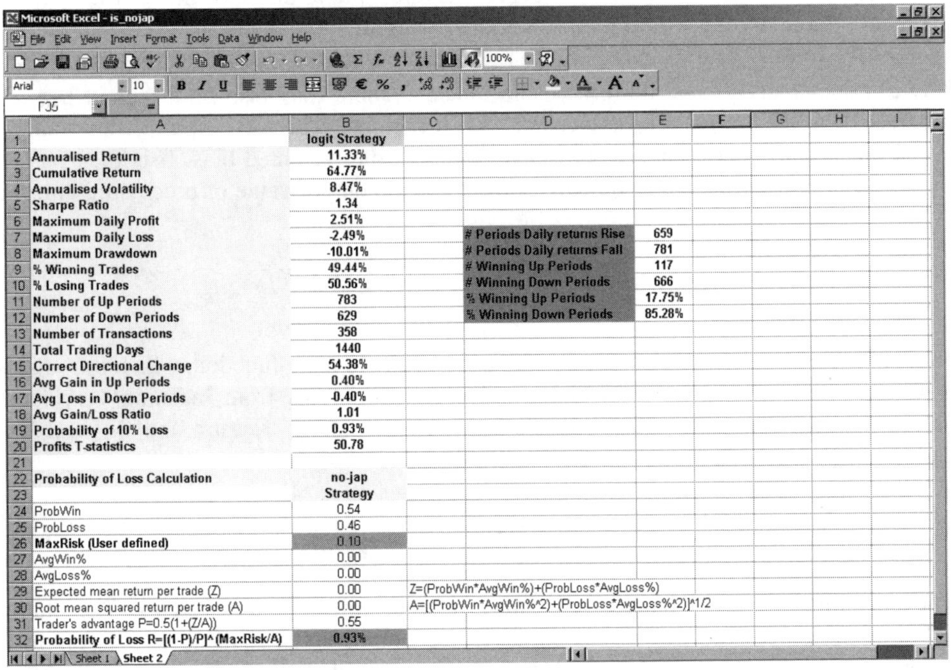

Microsoft Excel - is_nojap

F35

	A	B	C	D	E
1		logit Strategy			
2	Annualised Return	11.33%			
3	Cumulative Return	64.77%			
4	Annualised Volatility	8.47%			
5	Sharpe Ratio	1.34			
6	Maximum Daily Profit	2.51%			
7	Maximum Daily Loss	-2.49%		# Periods Daily returns Rise	659
8	Maximum Drawdown	-10.01%		# Periods Daily returns Fall	781
9	% Winning Trades	49.44%		# Winning Up Periods	117
10	% Losing Trades	50.56%		# Winning Down Periods	666
11	Number of Up Periods	783		% Winning Up Periods	17.75%
12	Number of Down Periods	629		% Winning Down Periods	85.28%
13	Number of Transactions	358			
14	Total Trading Days	1440			
15	Correct Directional Change	54.38%			
16	Avg Gain in Up Periods	0.40%			
17	Avg Loss in Down Periods	-0.40%			
18	Avg Gain/Loss Ratio	1.01			
19	Probability of 10% Loss	0.93%			
20	Profits T-statistics	50.78			
21					
22	Probability of Loss Calculation	no-jap			
23		Strategy			
24	ProbWin	0.54			
25	ProbLoss	0.46			
26	MaxRisk (User defined)	0.10			
27	AvgWin%	0.00			
28	AvgLoss%	0.00			
29	Expected mean return per trade (Z)	0.00	Z=(ProbWin*AvgWin%)+(ProbLoss*AvgLoss%)		
30	Root mean squared return per trade (A)	0.00	A=[(ProbWin*AvgWin%^2)+(ProbLoss*AvgLoss%^2)]^1/2		
31	Trader's advantage P=0.5(1+(Z/A))	0.55			
32	Probability of Loss R=[(1-P)/P]^(MaxRisk/A)	0.93%			

Sheet 1 Sheet 2

Figure 1.13 Nojap estimation Excel spreadsheet (in-sample)

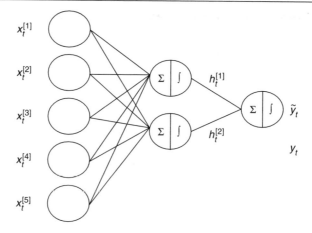

where $x_t^{[i]}$ (i = 1, 2, ..., 5) are the NNR model inputs at time t
$h_t^{[j]}$ (j = 1, 2) are the hidden nodes outputs
y_t and $\tilde{y}_t$ are the actual value and NNR model output, respectively

Figure 1.14   A single output fully connected NNR model

one and is analogous to the intercept in traditional regression models. An example of a fully connected NNR model with one hidden layer and two nodes is presented in Figure 1.14.

The vector $A = (x^{[1]}, x^{[2]}, \ldots, x^{[n]})$ represents the input to the NNR model where $x_t^{[i]}$ is the level of activity of the ith input. Associated with the input vector is a series of weight vectors $W_j = (w_{1j}, w_{2j}, \ldots, w_{nj})$ so that w_{ij} represents the strength of the connection between the input $x_t^{[i]}$ and the processing unit b_j. There may also be the input bias φ_j modulated by the weight w_{0j} associated with the inputs. The total input of the node b_j is the dot product between vectors A and W_j, less the weighted bias. It is then passed through a nonlinear activation function to produce the output value of processing unit b_j:

$$b_j = f\left(\sum_{i=1}^{n} x^{[i]} w_{ij} - w_{0j} \varphi_j\right) = f(X_j) \tag{1.8}$$

Typically, the activation function takes the form of the logistic function, which introduces a degree of nonlinearity to the model and prevents outputs from reaching very large values that can "paralyse" NNR models and inhibit training (Kaastra and Boyd, 1996; Zhang *et al.*, 1998). Here we use the logistic function:

$$f(X_j) = \frac{1}{1 + e^{-X_j}} \tag{1.9}$$

The modelling process begins by assigning random values to the weights. The output value of the processing unit is passed on to the output layer. If the output is optimal, the process is halted, if not, the weights are adjusted and the process continues until an optimal solution is found. The output error, namely the difference between the actual value and the NNR model output, is the optimisation criterion. Commonly, the criterion is the root-mean-squared error (RMSE). The RMSE is systematically minimised through the adjustment of the weights. Basically, training is the process of determining the optimal solutions network weights, as they represent the knowledge learned by the network. Since inadequacies in the output are fed back through the network to adjust the network weights, the NNR model is trained by backpropagation[13] (Shapiro, 2000).

A common practice is to divide the time series into three sets called the training, test and validation (out-of-sample) sets, and to partition them as roughly $\frac{2}{3}$, $\frac{1}{6}$ and $\frac{1}{6}$, respectively. The testing set is used to evaluate the generalisation ability of the network. The technique consists of tracking the error on the training and test sets. Typically, the error on the training set continually decreases, however the test set error starts by decreasing and then begins to increase. From this point the network has stopped learning the similarities between the training and test sets, and has started to learn meaningless differences, namely the noise within the training data. For good generalisation ability, training should stop when the test set error reaches its lowest point. The stopping rule reduces the likelihood of overfitting, i.e. that the network will become overtrained (Dunis and Huang, 2002; Mehta, 1995).

An evaluation of the performance of the trained network is made on new examples not used in network selection, namely the validation set. Crucially, the validation set should never be used to discriminate between networks, as any set that is used to choose the best network is, by definition, a test set. In addition, good generalisation ability requires that the training and test sets are representative of the population, inappropriate selection will affect the network generalisation ability and forecast performance (Kaastra and Boyd, 1996; Zhang et al., 1998).

1.5.2 Issues in neural network modelling

Despite the satisfactory features of NNR models, the process of building them should not be taken lightly. There are many issues that can affect the network's performance and should be considered carefully.

The issue of finding the most parsimonious model is always a problem for statistical methods and particularly important for NNR models because of the problem of overfitting. Parsimonious models not only have the recognition ability but also the more important generalisation ability. Overfitting and generalisation are always going to be a problem for real-world situations, and this is particularly true for financial applications where time series may well be quasi-random, or at least contain noise.

One of the most commonly used heuristics to ensure good generalisation is the application of some form of Occam's Razor. The principle states, "unnecessary complex models *should not* be preferred to simpler ones. However ... more complex models always fit the data better" (Kingdon, 1997: 49). The two objectives are, of course, contradictory. The solution is to find a model with the smallest possible complexity, and yet which can still describe the data set (Haykin, 1999; Kingdon, 1997).

A reasonable strategy in designing NNR models is to start with one layer containing a few hidden nodes, and increase the complexity while monitoring the generalisation ability. The issue of determining the optimal number of layers and hidden nodes is a crucial factor

---

[13] Backpropagation networks are the most common multilayer network and are the most used type in financial time series forecasting (Kaastra and Boyd, 1996). We use them exclusively here.

for good network design, as the hidden nodes provide the ability to generalise. However, in most situations there is no way to determine the best number of hidden nodes without training several networks. Several rules of thumb have been proposed to aid the process, however none work well for all applications. Notwithstanding, simplicity must be the aim (Mehta, 1995).

Since NNR models are pattern matchers, the representation of data is critical for a successful network design. The raw data for the input and output variables are rarely fed into the network, they are generally scaled between the upper and lower bounds of the activation function. For the logistic function the range is [0,1], avoiding the function's saturation zones. Practically, as here, a normalisation [0.2,0.8] is often used with the logistic function, as its limits are only reached for infinite input values (Zhang et al., 1998).

Crucial for backpropagation learning is the learning rate of the network as it determines the size of the weight changes. Smaller learning rates slow the learning process, while larger rates cause the error function to change wildly without continuously improving. To improve the process a momentum parameter is used which allows for larger learning rates. The parameter determines how past weight changes affect current weight changes, by making the next weight change in approximately the same direction as the previous one[14] (Kaastra and Boyd, 1996; Zhang et al., 1998).

1.5.3 Neural network modelling procedure

Conforming to standard heuristics, the training, test and validation sets were partitioned as approximately $\frac{2}{3}$, $\frac{1}{6}$ and $\frac{1}{6}$, respectively. The training set runs from 17 October 1994 to 8 April 1999 (1169 observations), the test set runs from 9 April 1999 to 18 May 2000 (290 observations), and the validation set runs from 19 May 2000 to 3 July 2001 (290 observations), reserved for out-of-sample forecasting and evaluation, identical to the out-of-sample period for the benchmark models.

To start, traditional linear cross-correlation analysis helped establish the existence of a relationship between EUR/USD returns and potential explanatory variables. Although NNR models attempt to map nonlinearities, linear cross-correlation analysis can give some indication of which variables to include in a model, or at least a starting point to the analysis (Diekmann and Gutjahr, 1998; Dunis and Huang, 2002).

The analysis was performed for all potential explanatory variables. Lagged terms that were most significant as determined via the cross-correlation analysis are presented in Table 1.12.

The lagged terms SPCOMP(-1) and US_yc(-1) could not be used because of time-zone differences between London and the USA, as discussed at the beginning of Section 1.3. As an initial substitute SPCOMP(-2) and US_yc(-2) were used. In addition, various lagged terms of the EUR/USD returns were included as explanatory variables.

Variable selection was achieved via a forward stepwise NNR procedure, namely potential explanatory variables were progressively added to the network. If adding a new variable improved the level of explained variance (EV) over the previous "best" network, the pool of explanatory variables was updated.[15] Since the aim of the model-building

---

[14] The problem of convergence did not occur within this research; as a result, a learning rate of 0.1 and momentum of zero were used exclusively.
[15] EV is an approximation of the coefficient of determination, R^2, in traditional regression techniques.

Table 1.12 Most significant lag of each potential explanatory variable (in returns)

Variable	Best lag
DAXINDX	10
DJES50I	10
FRCAC40	10
FTSE100	5
GOLDBLN	19
ITMIB	9
JAPAYE$	10
OILBREN	1
JAPDOWA	15
SPCOMP	1
USDOLLR	12
BD_yc	19
EC_yc	2
FR_yc	9
IT_yc	2
JP_yc	6
UK_yc	19
US_yc	1
NYFECRB	20

procedure is to build a model with good generalisation ability, a model that has a higher EV level has a better ability. In addition, a good measure of this ability is to compare the EV level of the test and validation sets: if the test set and validation set levels are similar, the model has been built to generalise well.

The decision to use explained variance is because the EUR/USD returns series is a stationary series and stationarity remains important if NNR models are assessed on the level of explained variance (Dunis and Huang, 2002). The EV levels for the training, test and validation sets of the selected NNR model, which we shall name nnr1 (nnr1.prv Previa file), are presented in Table 1.13.

An EV level equal to, or greater than, 80% was used as the NNR learning termination criterion. In addition, if the NNR model did not reach this level within 1500 learning sweeps, again the learning terminates. The criteria selected are reasonable for daily data and were used exclusively here.

If after several attempts there was failure to improve on the previous "best" model, variables in the model were alternated in an attempt to find a better combination. This

Table 1.13 nnr1 model EV for the training, test and validation sets

Training set	Test set	Validation set
3.4%	2.3%	2.2%

procedure recognises the likelihood that some variables may only be relevant predictors when in combination with certain other variables.

Once a tentative model is selected, post-training weights analysis helps establish the importance of the explanatory variables, as there are no standard statistical tests for NNR models. The idea is to find a measure of the contribution a given weight has to the overall output of the network, in essence allowing detection of insignificant variables. Such analysis includes an examination of a Hinton graph, which represents graphically the weight matrix within the network. The principle is to include in the network variables that are strongly significant. In addition, a small bias weight is preferred (Diekmann and Gutjahr, 1998; Kingdon, 1997; Previa, 2001). The input to a hidden layer Hinton graph of the nnr1 model produced by Previa is presented in Figure 1.15. The graph suggests that the explanatory variables of the selected model are strongly significant, both positive (green) and negative (black), and that there is a small bias weight. In addition, the input to hidden layer weight matrix of the nnr1 model produced by Previa is presented in Table 1.14.

The nnr1 model contained the returns of the explanatory variables presented in Table 1.15, having one hidden layer containing five hidden nodes.

Again, to justify the use of the Japanese variables a further model that did not include these variables, but was otherwise identical to nnr1, was produced and the performance evaluated, which we shall name nojap (nojap.prv Previa file). The EV levels of the training

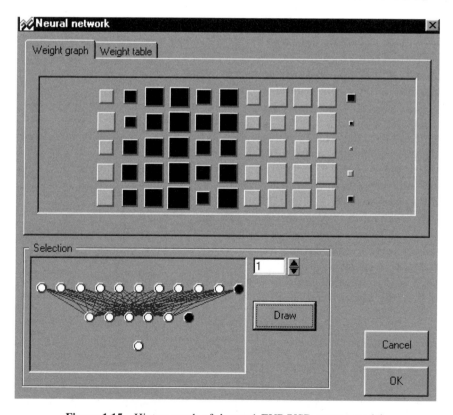

Figure 1.15   Hinton graph of the nnr1 EUR/USD returns model

Table 1.14   Input to hidden layer weight matrix of the nnr1 EUR/USD returns model

	GOLD BLN (−19)	JAPAY E$ (−10)	JAP DOWA (−15)	OIL BREN (−1)	US DOLLR (−12)	FR_yc (−2)	IT_yc (−6)	JP_yc (−9)	JAPAY E$ (−1)	JAP DOWA (−1)	Bias
C[1,0]	0.2316	−0.2120	−0.4336	−0.4579	−0.2621	−0.3911	0.2408	0.4295	0.4067	0.4403	−0.0824
C[1,1]	0.4016	−0.1752	−0.3589	−0.5474	−0.3663	−0.4623	0.2438	0.2786	0.2757	0.4831	−0.0225
C[1,2]	0.2490	−0.3037	−0.4462	−0.5139	−0.2506	−0.3491	0.2900	0.3634	0.2737	0.4132	−0.0088
C[1,3]	0.3382	−0.3588	−0.4089	−0.5446	−0.2730	−0.4531	0.2555	0.4661	0.4153	0.5245	0.0373
C[1,4]	0.3338	−0.3283	−0.4086	−0.6108	−0.2362	−0.4828	0.3088	0.4192	0.4254	0.4779	−0.0447

Table 1.15   nnr1 model explanatory variables (in returns)

Variable	Lag
GOLDBLN	19
JAPAYE$	10
JAPDOWA	15
OILBREN	1
USDOLLR	12
FR_yc	2
IT_yc	6
JP_yc	9
JAPAYE$	1
JAPDOWA	1

and test sets of the nojap model were 1.4 and 0.6 respectively, which are much lower than the nnr1 model.

The nnr1 model was retained for out-of-sample estimation. The performance of the strategy is evaluated in terms of traditional forecasting accuracy and in terms of trading performance.

Several other adequate models were produced and their performance evaluated, including RNN models.[16] In essence, the only difference from NNR models is the addition of a loop back from a hidden or the output layer to the input layer. The loop back is then used as an input in the next period. There is no theoretical or empirical answer to whether the hidden layer or the output should be looped back. However, the looping back of either allows RNN models to keep the memory of the past,[17] a useful property in forecasting applications. This feature comes at a cost, as RNN models require more connections, raising the issue of complexity. Since simplicity is the aim, a less complex model that can still describe the data set is preferred.

The statistical forecasting accuracy results of the nnr1 model and the RNN model, which we shall name rnn1 (rnn1.prv Previa file), were only marginally different, namely the mean absolute percentage error (MAPE) differs by 0.09%. However, in terms of

---

[16] For a discussion on recurrent neural network models refer to Dunis and Huang (2002).

[17] The looping back of the output layer is an error feedback mechanism, implying the use of a nonlinear error-correction model (Dunis and Huang, 2002).

	A	B	C	D	E
1		nnr Strategy			
2	Annualised Return	18.18%		Mean Absolute Error	0.0038
3	Cumulative Return	103.90%		Mean Absolute Percentage Error	137.82%
4	Annualised Volatility	8.42%		Root Mean Squared Error	0.0053
5	Sharpe Ratio	2.16		Theil's Inequality Coefficient	0.8405
6	Maximum Daily Profit	2.51%			
7	Maximum Daily Loss	-2.49%		# Periods Daily returns Rise	675
8	Maximum Drawdown	-9.11%		# Periods Daily returns Fall	765
9	% Winning trades	48.12%		# Winning Up Periods	245
10	% Losing trades	51.88%		# Winning Down Periods	569
11	Number of Up Periods	814		% Winning Up Periods	36.30%
12	Number of Down Periods	626		% Winning Down Periods	74.38%
13	Number of Transactions	611			
14	Total Trading Days	1440			
15	Correct Directional Change	56.53%			
16	Avg Gain in Up Periods	0.41%			
17	Avg Loss in Down Periods	-0.37%			
18	Avg Gain/Loss Ratio	1.12			
19	Probability of 10% Loss	0.01%			
20	Profits T-statistics	81.91			
21					
22	Probability of Loss Calculation	nnr1			
23		Strategy			
24	ProbWin	0.57			
25	ProbLoss	0.43			
26	MaxRisk (User defined)	0.10			
27	AvgWin%	0.00			
28	AvgLoss%	0.00			
29	Expected mean return per trade (Z)	0.00	Z=(ProbWin*AvgWin%)+(ProbLoss*AvgLoss%)		
30	Root mean squared return per trade (A)	0.00	A=[(ProbWin*AvgWin%^2)+(ProbLoss*AvgLoss%^2)]^1/2		
31	Trader's advantage P=0.5(1+(Z/A))	0.59			
32	Probability of Loss R=[(1-P)/P]^(MaxRisk/A)	0.01%			

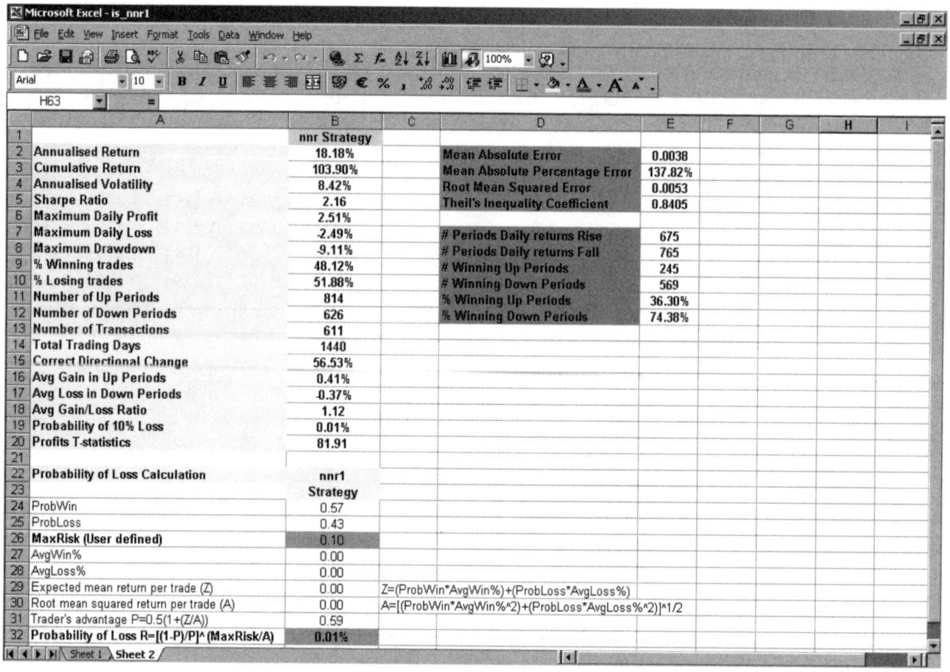

Figure 1.16 nnr1 model Excel spreadsheet (in-sample)

	A	B	C	D	E
1		rnn Strategy			
2	Annualised Return	18.38%		Mean Absolute Error	0.0038
3	Cumulative Return	105.04%		Mean Absolute Percentage Error	137.91%
4	Annualised Volatility	8.42%		Root Mean Squared Error	0.0053
5	Sharpe Ratio	2.18		Theil's Inequality Coefficient	0.8405
6	Maximum Daily Profit	2.51%			
7	Maximum Daily Loss	-2.49%		# Periods Daily returns Rise	675
8	Maximum Drawdown	-9.11%		# Periods Daily returns Fall	765
9	% Winning trades	48.04%		# Winning Up Periods	247
10	% Losing trades	51.96%		# Winning Down Periods	569
11	Number of Up Periods	816		% Winning Up Periods	36.59%
12	Number of Down Periods	624		% Winning Down Periods	74.38%
13	Number of Transactions	612			
14	Total Trading Days	1440			
15	Correct Directional Change	56.67%			
16	Avg Gain in Up Periods	0.41%			
17	Avg Loss in Down Periods	-0.37%			
18	Avg Gain/Loss Ratio	1.11			
19	Probability of 10% Loss	0.01%			
20	Profits T-statistics	82.83			
21					
22	Probability of Loss Calculation	rnn1			
23		Strategy			
24	ProbWin	0.57			
25	ProbLoss	0.43			
26	MaxRisk (User defined)	0.10			
27	AvgWin%	0.00			
28	AvgLoss%	0.00			
29	Expected mean return per trade (Z)	0.00	Z=(ProbWin*AvgWin%)+(ProbLoss*AvgLoss%)		
30	Root mean squared return per trade (A)	0.00	A=[(ProbWin*AvgWin%^2)+(ProbLoss*AvgLoss%^2)]^1/2		
31	Trader's advantage P=0.5(1+(Z/A))	0.59			
32	Probability of Loss R=[(1-P)/P]^(MaxRisk/A)	0.01%			

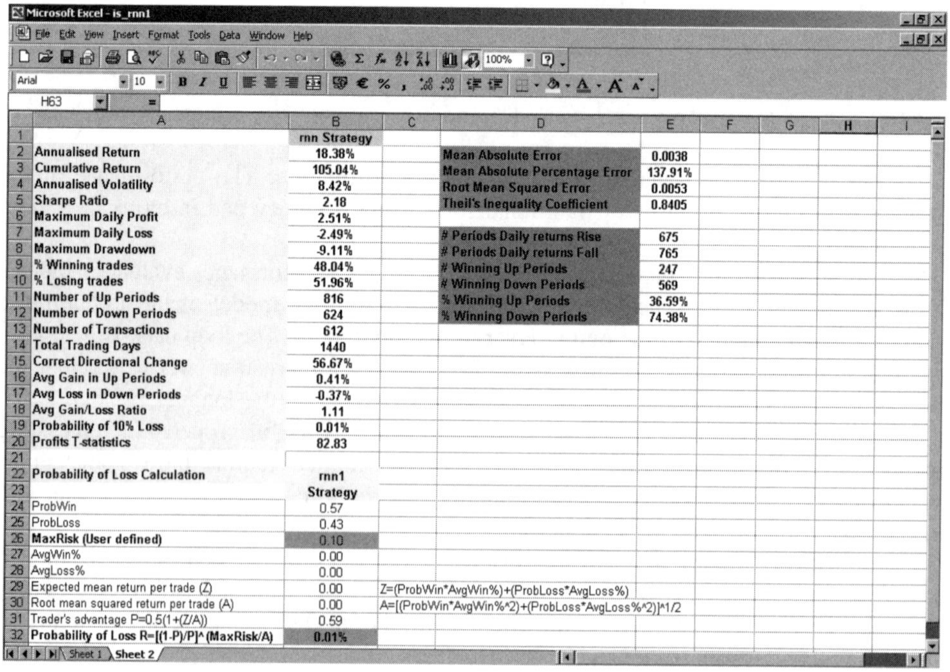

Figure 1.17 rnn1 model Excel spreadsheet (in-sample)

trading performance there is little to separate the nnr1 and rnn1 models. The evaluation can be reviewed in Sheet 2 of the is_nnr1.xls and is_rnn1.xls Excel spreadsheets, and is also presented in Figures 1.16 and 1.17, respectively.

The decision to retain the nnr1 model over the rnn1 model is because the rnn1 model is more complex and yet does not possess any decisive added value over the simpler model.

1.6 FORECASTING ACCURACY AND TRADING SIMULATION

To compare the performance of the strategies, it is necessary to evaluate them on previously unseen data. This situation is likely to be the closest to a true forecasting or trading situation. To achieve this, all models retained an identical out-of-sample period allowing a direct comparison of their forecasting accuracy and trading performance.

1.6.1 Out-of-sample forecasting accuracy measures

Several criteria are used to make comparisons between the forecasting ability of the benchmark and NNR models, including mean absolute error (MAE), RMSE,[18] MAPE, and Theil's inequality coefficient (Theil-U).[19] For a full discussion on these measures, refer to Hanke and Reitsch (1998) and Pindyck and Rubinfeld (1998). We also include correct directional change (CDC), which measures the capacity of a model to correctly predict the subsequent actual change of a forecast variable, an important issue in a trading strategy that relies on the direction of a forecast rather than its level. The statistical performance measures used to analyse the forecasting techniques are presented in Table 1.16.

1.6.2 Out-of-sample trading performance measures

Statistical performance measures are often inappropriate for financial applications. Typically, modelling techniques are optimised using a mathematical criterion, but ultimately the results are analysed on a financial criterion upon which it is not optimised. In other words, the forecast error may have been minimised during model estimation, but the evaluation of the true merit should be based on the performance of a trading strategy. Without actual trading, the best means of evaluating performance is via a simulated trading strategy. The procedure to create the buy and sell signals is quite simple: a EUR/USD buy signal is produced if the forecast is positive, and a sell otherwise.[20]

For many traders and analysts market direction is more important than the value of the forecast itself, as in financial markets money can be made simply by knowing the direction the series will move. In essence, "low forecast errors and trading profits are not synonymous since a single large trade forecasted incorrectly ... could have accounted for most of the trading system's profits" (Kaastra and Boyd, 1996: 229).

The trading performance measures used to analyse the forecasting techniques are presented in Tables 1.17 and 1.18. Most measures are self-explanatory and are commonly used in the fund management industry. Some of the more important measures include the Sharpe ratio, maximum drawdown and average gain/loss ratio. The Sharpe ratio is a

---

[18] The MAE and RMSE statistics are scale-dependent measures but allow a comparison between the actual and forecast values, the lower the values the better the forecasting accuracy.

[19] When it is more important to evaluate the forecast errors independently of the scale of the variables, the MAPE and Theil-U are used. They are constructed to lie within [0,1], zero indicating a perfect fit.

[20] A buy signal is to buy euros at the current price or continue holding euros, while a sell signal is to sell euros at the current price or continue holding US dollars.

Table 1.16   Statistical performance measures

Performance measure	Description

Mean absolute error

$$\text{MAE} = \frac{1}{T} \sum_{t=1}^{T} |\tilde{y}_t - y_t| \tag{1.10}$$

Mean absolute percentage error

$$\text{MAPE} = \frac{100}{T} \sum_{t=1}^{T} \left| \frac{\tilde{y}_t - y_t}{y_t} \right| \tag{1.11}$$

Root-mean-squared error

$$\text{RMSE} = \sqrt{\frac{1}{T} \sum_{t=1}^{T} (\tilde{y}_t - y_t)^2} \tag{1.12}$$

Theil's inequality coefficient

$$U = \frac{\sqrt{\frac{1}{T} \sum_{t=1}^{T} (\tilde{y}_t - y_t)^2}}{\sqrt{\frac{1}{T} \sum_{t=1}^{T} (\tilde{y}_t)^2} + \sqrt{\frac{1}{T} \sum_{t=1}^{T} (y_t)^2}} \tag{1.13}$$

Correct directional change

$$\text{CDC} = \frac{100}{N} \sum_{t=1}^{N} D_t \tag{1.14}$$

where $D_t = 1$ if $y_t \cdot \tilde{y}_t > 0$ else $D_t = 0$

y_t is the actual change at time t.
$\tilde{y}_t$ is the forecast change.
$t = 1$ to $t = T$ for the forecast period.

risk-adjusted measure of return, with higher ratios preferred to those that are lower, the maximum drawdown is a measure of downside risk and the average gain/loss ratio is a measure of overall gain, a value above one being preferred (Dunis and Jalilov, 2002; Fernandez-Rodriguez *et al.*, 2000).

The application of these measures may be a better standard for determining the quality of the forecasts. After all, the financial gain from a given strategy depends on trading performance, not on forecast accuracy.

1.6.3   Out-of-sample forecasting accuracy results

The forecasting accuracy statistics do not provide very conclusive results. Each of the models evaluated, except the logit model, are nominated "best" at least once. Interestingly, the naïve model has the lowest Theil-U statistic at 0.6901; if this model is believed to be the "best" model there is likely to be no added value using more complicated forecasting techniques. The ARMA model has the lowest MAPE statistic at 101.51%, and equals the MAE of the NNR model at 0.0056. The NNR model has the lowest RMSE statistic, however the value is only marginally less than the ARMA model. The MACD model has the highest CDC measure, predicting daily changes accurately 60.00% of the time. It is difficult to select a "best" performer from these results, however a majority decision rule

Table 1.17 Trading simulation performance measures

Performance measure	Description	
Annualised return	$$R^A = 252 \times \frac{1}{N} \sum_{t=1}^{N} R_t$$	(1.15)
Cumulative return	$$R^C = \sum_{t=1}^{N} R_T$$	(1.16)
Annualised volatility	$$\sigma^A = \sqrt{252} \times \sqrt{\frac{1}{N-1} \sum_{t=1}^{N} (R_t - \overline{R})^2}$$	(1.17)
Sharpe ratio	$$SR = \frac{R^A}{\sigma^A}$$	(1.18)
Maximum daily profit	Maximum value of R_t over the period	(1.19)
Maximum daily loss	Minimum value of R_t over the period	(1.20)
Maximum drawdown	Maximum negative value of $\sum (R_T)$ over the period $$MD = \min_{t=1,\dots,N} \left(R_t^c - \max_{i=1,\dots,t} \left(R_i^c \right) \right)$$	(1.21)
% Winning trades	$$WT = 100 \times \frac{\sum_{t=1}^{N} F_t}{NT}$$ where $F_t = 1$ if transaction profit$_t > 0$	(1.22)
% Losing trades	$$LT = 100 \times \frac{\sum_{t=1}^{N} G_t}{NT}$$ where $G_t = 1$ if transaction profit$_t < 0$	(1.23)
Number of up periods	Nup = number of $R_t > 0$	(1.24)
Number of down periods	Ndown = number of $R_t < 0$	(1.25)
Number of transactions	$$NT = \sum_{t=1}^{N} L_t$$ where $L_t = 1$ if trading signal$_t \neq$ trading signal$_{t-1}$	(1.26)
Total trading days	Number of all R_t's	(1.27)
Avg. gain in up periods	$AG = $ (Sum of all $R_t > 0$)/Nup	(1.28)
Avg. loss in down periods	$AL = $ (Sum of all $R_t < 0$)/Ndown	(1.29)
Avg. gain/loss ratio	$GL = AG/AL$	(1.30)
Probability of 10% loss	$$PoL = \left[\frac{(1-P)}{P} \right]^{\left(\frac{MaxRisk}{\Lambda} \right)}$$ where $P = 0.5 \times \left(1 + \left(\frac{\langle (WT \times AG) + (LT \times AL) \rangle}{\sqrt{[(WT \times AG^2) + (LT \times AL^2)]}} \right) \right)$ and $\Lambda = \sqrt{[(WT \times AG^2) + (LT \times AL^2)]}$ MaxRisk is the risk level defined by the user; this research, 10%	(1.31)
Profits T-statistics	$$T\text{-statistics} = \sqrt{N} \times \frac{R^A}{\sigma^A}$$	(1.32)

Source: Dunis and Jalilov (2002).

Table 1.18 Trading simulation performance measures

Performance measure	Description	
Number of periods daily returns rise	$$NPR = \sum_{t=1}^{N} Q_t$$ where $Q_t = 1$ if $y_t > 0$ else $Q_t = 0$	(1.33)
Number of periods daily returns fall	$$NPF = \sum_{t=1}^{N} S_t$$ where $S_t = 1$ if $y_t < 0$ else $S_t = 0$	(1.34)
Number of winning up periods	$$NWU = \sum_{t=1}^{N} B_t$$ where $B_t = 1$ if $R_t > 0$ and $y_t > 0$ else $B_t = 0$	(1.35)
Number of winning down periods	$$NWD = \sum_{t=1}^{N} E_t$$ where $E_t = 1$ if $R_t > 0$ and $y_t < 0$ else $E_t = 0$	(1.36)
Winning up periods (%)	$WUP = 100 \times (NWU/NPR)$	(1.37)
Winning down periods (%)	$WDP = 100 \times (NWD/NPF)$	(1.38)

Table 1.19 Forecasting accuracy results[21]

	Naïve	MACD	ARMA	Logit	NNR
Mean absolute error	0.0080	–	**0.0056**	–	**0.0056**
Mean absolute percentage error	317.31%	–	**101.51%**	–	107.38%
Root-mean-squared error	0.0102	–	0.0074	–	**0.0073**
Theil's inequality coefficient	**0.6901**	–	0.9045	–	0.8788
Correct directional change	55.86%	**60.00%**	56.55%	53.79%	57.24%

might select the NNR model as the overall "best" model because it is nominated "best" twice and also "second best" by the other three statistics. A comparison of the forecasting accuracy results is presented in Table 1.19.

1.6.4 Out-of-sample trading performance results

A comparison of the trading performance results is presented in Table 1.20 and Figure 1.18. The results of the NNR model are quite impressive. It generally outperforms the benchmark strategies, both in terms of overall profitability with an annualised return of 29.68% and a cumulative return of 34.16%, and in terms of risk-adjusted performance with a Sharpe ratio of 2.57. The logit model has the lowest downside risk as measured by maximum drawdown at −5.79%, and the MACD model has the lowest downside risk

---

[21] As the MACD model is not based on forecasting the next period and binary variables are used in the logit model, statistical accuracy comparisons with these models were not always possible.

Table 1.20   Trading performance results

	Naïve	MACD	ARMA	Logit	NNR
Annualised return	21.34%	11.34%	12.91%	21.05%	**29.68%**
Cumulative return	24.56%	13.05%	14.85%	24.22%	**34.16%**
Annualised volatility	11.64%	11.69%	11.69%	11.64%	**11.56%**
Sharpe ratio	1.83	0.97	1.10	1.81	**2.57**
Maximum daily profit	**3.38%**	1.84%	**3.38%**	1.88%	**3.38%**
Maximum daily loss	−2.10%	−3.23%	−2.10%	−3.38%	**−1.82%**
Maximum drawdown	−9.06%	−7.75%	−10.10%	**−5.79%**	−9.12%
% Winning trades	37.01%	24.00%	52.71%	49.65%	**52.94%**
% Losing trades	62.99%	76.00%	47.29%	50.35%	**47.06%**
Number of up periods	162	149	164	156	**166**
Number of down periods	126	138	124	132	**122**
Number of transactions	127	**25**	129	141	136
Total trading days	290	290	290	290	290
Avg. gain in up periods	0.58%	0.60%	0.55%	**0.61%**	0.60%
Avg. loss in down periods	−0.56%	−0.55%	−0.61%	**−0.53%**	−0.54%
Avg. gain/loss ratio	1.05	1.08	0.91	**1.14**	1.12
Probability of 10% loss	0.70%	**0.02%**	5.70%	0.76%	0.09%
Profits T-statistics	31.23	16.51	18.81	30.79	**43.71**
Number of periods daily returns rise	128	128	128	128	128
Number of periods daily returns fall	162	162	162	162	162
Number of winning up periods	**65**	45	56	49	52
Number of winning down periods	97	104	108	106	**114**
% Winning up periods	**50.78%**	35.16%	43.75%	38.28%	40.63%
% Winning down periods	59.88%	64.20%	66.67%	66.05%	**70.37%**

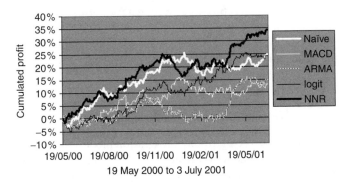

Figure 1.18   Cumulated profit graph

as measured by the probability of a 10% loss at 0.02%, however this is only marginally less than the NNR model at 0.09%.

The NNR model predicted the highest number of winning down periods at 114, while the naïve model forecast the highest number of winning up periods at 65. Interestingly, all models were more successful at forecasting a fall in the EUR/USD returns series, as indicated by a greater percentage of winning down periods to winning up periods.

The logit model has the highest number of transactions at 141, while the NNR model has the second highest at 136. The MACD strategy has the lowest number of transactions at 25. In essence, the MACD strategy has longer "holding" periods compared to the other models, suggesting that the MACD strategy is not compared "like with like" to the other models.

More than with statistical performance measures, financial criteria clearly single out the NNR model as the one with the most consistent performance. Therefore it is considered the "best" model for this particular application.

1.6.5 Transaction costs

So far, our results have been presented without accounting for transaction costs during the trading simulation. However, it is not realistic to account for the success or otherwise of a trading system unless transaction costs are taken into account. Between market makers, a cost of 3 pips (0.0003 EUR/USD) per trade (one way) for a tradable amount, typically USD 5–10 million, would be normal. The procedure to approximate the transaction costs for the NNR model is quite simple.

A cost of 3 pips per trade and an average out-of-sample EUR/USD of 0.8971 produce an average cost of 0.033% per trade:

$$\frac{0.0003}{0.8971} = 0.033\%$$

The NNR model made 136 transactions. Since the EUR/USD time series is a series of bid rates and because, apart from the first trade, each signal implies two transactions, one to close the existing position and a second one to enter the new position indicated by the model signal, the approximate out-of-sample transaction costs for the NNR model trading strategy are about 4.55%:

$$136 \times 0.033\% = 4.55\%$$

Therefore, even accounting for transaction costs, the extra returns achieved with the NNR model still make this strategy the most attractive one despite its relatively high trading frequency.

1.7 CONCLUDING REMARKS

This chapter has evaluated the use of different regression models in forecasting and trading the EUR/USD exchange rate. The performance was measured statistically and financially via a trading simulation taking into account the impact of transaction costs on models with higher trading frequencies. The logic behind the trading simulation is, if profit from a trading simulation is compared solely on the basis of statistical measures, the optimum model from a financial perspective would rarely be chosen.

The NNR model was benchmarked against more traditional regression-based and other benchmark forecasting techniques to determine any added value to the forecasting process. Having constructed a synthetic EUR/USD series for the period up to 4 January 1999, the models were developed using the same in-sample data, 17 October 1994 to 18 May 2000, leaving the remaining period, 19 May 2000 to 3 July 2001, for out-of-sample forecasting.

Forecasting techniques rely on the weaknesses of the efficient market hypothesis, acknowledging the existence of market inefficiencies, with markets displaying even weak signs of predictability. However, FX markets are relatively efficient, reducing the scope of a profitable strategy. Consequently, the FX managed futures industry average Sharpe ratio is only 0.8, although a percentage of winning trades greater than 60% is often required to run a profitable FX trading desk (Grabbe, 1996 as cited in Bellgard and Goldschmidt, 1999: 10). In this respect, it is worth noting that only one of our models reached a 60% winning trades accuracy, namely the MACD model at 60.00%. Nevertheless, all of the models examined in this chapter achieved an out-of-sample Sharpe ratio higher than 0.8, the highest of which was again the NNR model at 2.57. This seems to confirm that the use of quantitative trading is more appropriate in a fund management than in a treasury type of context.

Forecasting techniques are dependent on the quality and nature of the data used. If the solution to a problem is not within the data, then no technique can extract it. In addition, sufficient information should be contained within the in-sample period to be representative of all cases within the out-of-sample period. For example, a downward trending series typically has more falls represented in the data than rises. The EUR/USD is such a series within the in-sample period. Consequently, the forecasting techniques used are estimated using more negative values than positive values. The probable implication is that the models are more likely to successfully forecast a fall in the EUR/USD, as indicated by our results, with all models forecasting a higher percentage of winning down periods than winning up periods. However, the naïve model does not learn to generalise *per se*, and as a result has the smallest difference between the number of winning up to winning down periods.

Overall our results confirm the credibility and potential of regression models and particularly NNR models as a forecasting technique. However, while NNR models offer a promising alternative to more traditional techniques, they suffer from a number of limitations. They are not the panacea. One of the major disadvantages is the inability to explain their reasoning, which has led some to consider that "neural nets are truly black boxes. Once you have trained a neural net and are generating predictions, you still do not know why the decisions are being made and can't find out by just looking at the net. It is not unlike attempting to capture the structure of knowledge by dissecting the human brain" (Fishman *et al.*, 1991 as cited in El-Shazly and El-Shazly, 1997: 355). In essence, the neural network learning procedure is not very transparent, requiring a lot of understanding. In addition, statistical inference techniques such as significance testing cannot always be applied, resulting in a reliance on a heuristic approach. The complexity of NNR models suggests that they are capable of superior forecasts, as shown in this chapter, however this is not always the case. They are essentially nonlinear techniques and may be less capable in linear applications than traditional forecasting techniques (Balkin and Ord, 2000; Campbell *et al.*, 1997; Lisboa and Vellido, 2000; Refenes and Zaidi, 1993).

Although the results support the success of neural network models in financial applications, there is room for increased success. Such a possibility lies with optimising the neural network model on a financial criterion, and not a mathematical criterion. As the profitability of a trading strategy relies on correctly forecasting the direction of change, namely CDC, to optimise the neural network model on such a measure could improve trading performance. However, backpropagation networks optimise by minimising a differentiable function such as squared error, they cannot minimise a function based on loss, or conversely, maximise a function based on profit. Notwithstanding, there is possibility to explore this idea further, provided the neural network software has the ability to select such an optimisation criterion.

Future work might also include the addition of hourly data as a possible explanatory variable. Alternatively, the use of first differences instead of rates of return series may be investigated, as first differences are perhaps the most effective way to generate data sets for neural network learning (Mehta, 1995).

Further investigation into RNN models is possible, or into combining forecasts. Many researchers agree that individual forecasting methods are misspecified in some manner, suggesting that combining multiple forecasts leads to increased forecast accuracy (Dunis and Huang, 2002). However, initial investigations proved unsuccessful, with the NNR model remaining the "best" model. Two simple model combinations were examined, a simple averaging of the naïve, ARMA and NNR model forecasts, and a regression-type combined forecast using the naïve, ARMA and NNR models.[22] The regression-type combined forecast follows the Granger and Ramanathan procedure (gr.wf1 EViews workfile). The evaluation can be reviewed in Sheet 2 of the oos_gr.xls Excel spreadsheet, and is also presented in Figure 1.19. The lack of success using the combination models was undoubtedly because the performance of the benchmark models was so much weaker than that of the NNR model. It is unlikely that combining relatively "poor" models with an otherwise "good" one will outperform the "good" model alone.

The main conclusion that can be drawn from this chapter is that there are indeed nonlinearities present within financial markets and that a neural network model can be

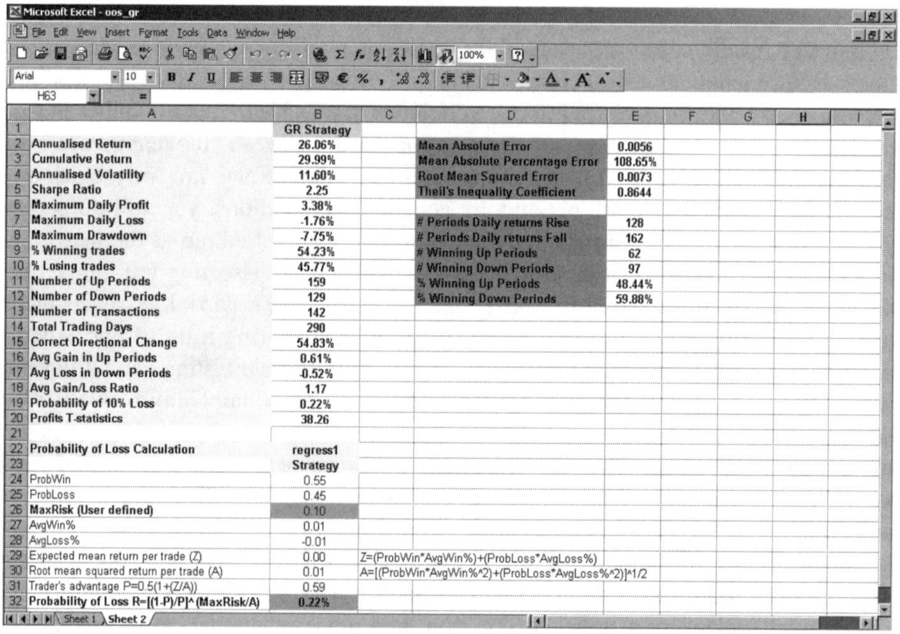

	A	B	C	D	E
1		GR Strategy			
2	Annualised Return	26.06%		Mean Absolute Error	0.0056
3	Cumulative Return	29.99%		Mean Absolute Percentage Error	108.65%
4	Annualised Volatility	11.60%		Root Mean Squared Error	0.0073
5	Sharpe Ratio	2.25		Theil's Inequality Coefficient	0.8644
6	Maximum Daily Profit	3.38%			
7	Maximum Daily Loss	-1.76%		# Periods Daily returns Rise	128
8	Maximum Drawdown	-7.75%		# Periods Daily returns Fall	162
9	% Winning trades	54.23%		# Winning Up Periods	62
10	% Losing trades	45.77%		# Winning Down Periods	97
11	Number of Up Periods	159		% Winning Up Periods	48.44%
12	Number of Down Periods	129		% Winning Down Periods	59.88%
13	Number of Transactions	142			
14	Total Trading Days	290			
15	Correct Directional Change	54.83%			
16	Avg Gain in Up Periods	0.61%			
17	Avg Loss in Down Periods	-0.52%			
18	Avg Gain/Loss Ratio	1.17			
19	Probability of 10% Loss	0.22%			
20	Profits T-statistics	38.26			
21					
22	Probability of Loss Calculation	regress1			
23		Strategy			
24	ProbWin	0.55			
25	ProbLoss	0.45			
26	MaxRisk (User defined)	0.10			
27	AvgWin%	0.01			
28	AvgLoss%	-0.01			
29	Expected mean return per trade (Z)	0.00	Z=(ProbWin*AvgWin%)+(ProbLoss*AvgLoss%)		
30	Root mean squared return per trade (A)	0.01	A=[(ProbWin*AvgWin%^2)+(ProbLoss*AvgLoss%^2)]^1/2		
31	Trader's advantage P=0.5(1+(Z/A))	0.59			
32	Probability of Loss R=[(1-P)/P]^(MaxRisk/A)	0.22%			

Figure 1.19 Regression-type combined forecast Excel spreadsheet (out-of-sample)

[22] For a full discussion on the procedures, refer to Clemen (1989), Granger and Ramanathan (1984), and Hashem (1997).

trained to recognise them. However, despite the limitations and potential improvements mentioned above, our results strongly suggest that regression models and particularly NNR models can add value to the forecasting process. For the EUR/USD exchange rate and the period considered, NNR models clearly outperform the more traditional modelling techniques analysed in this chapter.

REFERENCES

Balkin, S. D. and J. K. Ord (2000), "Automatic Neural Network Modelling for Univariate Time Series", *International Journal of Forecasting*, **16**, 509–515.

Bellgard, C. and P. Goldschmidt (1999), "Forecasting Across Frequencies: Linearity and Non-Linearity", *University of Western Australia Research Paper, Proceedings of the International Conference on Advanced Technology*, Australia, (www.imm.ecel.uwa.edu.au/~cbellgar/).

Box, G. E. P., G. M. Jenkins and G. C. Reinsel (1994), *Time Series Analysis: Forecasting and Control*, Prentice Hall, Englewood Cliffs, NJ.

Campbell, I. Y., A. W. Lo and A. C. MacKinley (1997), "Nonlinearities in Financial Data", in *The Econometrics of Financial Markets*, Princeton University Press, Princeton, NJ, pp. 512–524.

Carney, J. C. and P. Cunningham (1996), "Neural Networks and Currency Exchange Rate Prediction", *Trinity College Working Paper, Foresight Business Journal web page*, (www.maths.tcd.ie/pub/fbj/forex4.html).

Clemen, R. T. (1989), "Combining Forecasts: A Review and Annotated Bibliography", *International Journal of Forecasting*, **5**, 559–583.

Diekmann, A. and S. Gutjahr (1998), "Prediction of the Euro–Dollar Future Using Neural Networks – A Case Study for Financial Time Series Prediction", *University of Karlsruhe Working Paper, Proceedings of the International Symposium on Intelligent Data Engineering and Learning (IDEAL'98)*, Hong Kong, (http://citeseer.nj.nec.com/diekmann98prediction.html).

Dunis, C. and X. Huang (2002), "Forecasting and Trading Currency Volatility: An Application of Recurrent Neural Regression and Model Combination", *The Journal of Forecasting*, **21**, 317–354.

Dunis, C. and J. Jalilov (2002), "Neural Network Regression and Alternative Forecasting Techniques for Predicting Financial Variables", *Neural Network World*, **2**, 113–139.

El-Shazly, M. R. and H. E. El-Shazly (1997), "Comparing the Forecasting Performance of Neural Networks and Forward Exchange Rates", *Journal of Multinational Financial Management*, **7**, 345–356.

Fernandez-Rodriguez, F., C. Gonzalez-Martel and S. Sosvilla-Rivero (2000), "On the Profitability of Technical Trading Rules Based on Artificial Neural Networks: Evidence from the Madrid Stock Market", *Economics Letters*, **69**, 89–94.

Fishman, M. B., D. S. Barr and W. J. Loick (1991), "Using Neural Nets in Market Analysis", *Technical Analysis of Stocks and Commodities*, **9**, 4, 135–138.

Gençay, R. (1999), "Linear, Non-linear and Essential Foreign Exchange Rate Prediction with Simple Technical Trading Rules", *Journal of International Economics*, **47**, 91–107.

Gouriéroux, C. and A. Monfort (1995), *Time Series and Dynamic Models*, translated and edited by G. Gallo, Cambridge University Press, Cambridge.

Grabbe, J. O. (1996), *International Financial Markets*, 3rd edition, Prentice Hall, Englewood Cliffs, NJ.

Granger, C. W. J. and R. Ramanathan (1984), "Improved Methods of Combining Forecasts", *Journal of Forecasting*, **3**, 197–204.

Hanke, J. E. and A. G. Reitsch (1998), *Business Forecasting*, 6th edition, Prentice Hall, Englewood Cliffs, NJ.

Hashem, S. (1997), "Optimal Linear Combinations of Neural Networks", *Neural Networks*, **10**, 4, 599–614 (www.emsl.pnl.gov:2080/people/bionames/hashem_s.html).

Haykin, S. (1999), *Neural Networks: A Comprehensive Foundation*, 2nd edition, Prentice Hall, Englewood Cliffs, NJ.

Hornik, K., M. Stinchcombe and H. White (1989), "Multilayer Feedforward Networks Are Universal Approximators", *Neural Networks*, **2**, 359–366.

Kaastra, I. and M. Boyd (1996), "Designing a Neural Network for Forecasting Financial and Economic Time Series", *Neurocomputing*, **10**, 215–236.

Kingdon, J. (1997), *Intelligent Systems and Financial Forecasting*, Springer, London.

Lisboa, P. J. G. and A. Vellido (2000), "Business Applications of Neural Networks", in P. J. G. Lisboa, B. Edisbury and A. Vellido (eds), *Business Applications of Neural Networks: The State-of-the-Art of Real-World Applications*, World Scientific, Singapore, pp. vii–xxii.

Maddala, G. S. (2001), *Introduction to Econometrics*, 3rd edition, Prentice Hall, Englewood Cliffs, NJ.

Mehta, M. (1995), "Foreign Exchange Markets", in A. N. Refenes (ed.), *Neural Networks in the Capital Markets*, John Wiley, Chichester, pp. 176–198.

Pesaran, M. H. and B. Pesaran (1997), "Lessons in Logit and Probit Estimation", in *Interactive Econometric Analysis Working with Microfit 4*, Oxford University Press, Oxford, pp. 263–275.

Pindyck, R. S. and D. L. Rubinfeld (1998), *Econometric Models and Economic Forecasts*, 4th edition, McGraw-Hill, New York.

Previa (2001), *Previa Version 1.5 User's Guide*, (www.elseware.fr/previa).

Refenes, A. N. and A. Zaidi (1993), "Managing Exchange Rate Prediction Strategies with Neural Networks", in P. J. G. Lisboa and M. J. Taylor (eds), *Techniques and Applications of Neural Networks*, Ellis Horwood, Hemel Hempstead, pp. 109–116.

Shapiro, A. F. (2000), "A Hitchhiker's Guide to the Techniques of Adaptive Nonlinear Models", *Insurance, Mathematics and Economics*, **26**, 119–132.

Thomas, R. L. (1997), *Modern Econometrics. An Introduction*, Addison-Wesley, Harlow.

Tyree, E. W. and J. A. Long (1995), "Forecasting Currency Exchange Rates: Neural Networks and the Random Walk Model", *City University Working Paper, Proceedings of the Third International Conference on Artificial Intelligence Applications*, New York, (http://citeseer.nj.nec.com/131893.html).

Yao, J., H. Poh and T. Jasic (1996), "Foreign Exchange Rates Forecasting with Neural Networks", *National University of Singapore Working Paper, Proceedings of the International Conference on Neural Information Processing*, Hong Kong, (http://citeseer.nj.com/yao96foreign.html).

Yao, J., Y. Li and C. L. Tan (1997), "Forecasting the Exchange Rates of CHF vs USD Using Neural Networks", *Journal of Computational Intelligence in Finance*, **15**, 2, 7–13.

Zhang, G., B. E. Patuwo and M. Y. Hu (1998), "Forecasting with Artificial Neural Networks: The State of The Art", *International Journal of Forecasting*, **14**, 35–62.

2

Using Cointegration to Hedge and Trade International Equities

A. NEIL BURGESS

ABSTRACT

In this chapter, we examine the application of the econometric concept of cointegration as a tool for hedging and trading international equities. The concepts are illustrated with respect to a particular set of data, namely the 50 equities which constituted the STOXX 50 index as of 4 July 2002. The daily closing prices of these equities are investigated over a period from 14 September 1998 to 3 July 2002 – the longest period over which continuous data is available across the whole set of stocks in this particular universe. The use of daily closing prices will introduce some spurious effects due to the non-synchronous closing times of the markets on which these equities trade. In spite of this, however, the data are deemed suitable for the purposes of illustrating the tools in question and also of indicating the potential benefits to be gained from intelligent application of these tools. We consider cointegration as a framework for modelling the inter-relationships between equities prices, in a manner which can be seen as a sophisticated form of "relative value" analysis. Depending on the particular task in hand, cointegration techniques can be used to identify potential hedges for a given equity position and/or to identify potential trades which might be taken from a statistical arbitrage perspective.

2.1 INTRODUCTION

In this section we describe the econometric concept of "cointegration", and explain our motivation for developing trading tools based upon a cointegration perspective.

Cointegration is essentially an econometric tool for identifying situations where stable relationships exist between a set of time series. In econometrics, cointegration testing is typically seen as an end in itself, with the objective of testing an economic hypothesis regarding the presence of an equilibrium relationship between a set of economic variables. A possible second stage of cointegration modelling is to estimate the dynamics of the mechanism by which short-term deviations from the equilibrium are corrected, i.e. to construct an error-correction model (ECM).

The first aspect of cointegration modelling is interesting from the perspective of "hedging" assets against each other. The estimated equilibrium relationship will be one in which the effect of common risk factors is neutralised or at least minimised, allowing low-risk

Applied Quantitative Methods for Trading and Investment. Edited by C.L. Dunis, J. Laws and P. Naïm
© 2003 John Wiley & Sons, Ltd ISBN: 0-470-84885-5

combinations of assets to be created. The second aspect is interesting as a potential source of statistical arbitrage strategies. Deviations from the long-term "fair price" relationship can be considered as statistical "mispricings" and error-correction models can be used to capture any predictable component in the tendency of these mispricings to revert towards the longer term equilibrium.

Whilst the econometric methods used in cointegration modelling form the basis of our approach, they involve a number of restrictive assumptions which limit the extent to which they can be applied in practice. From our somewhat contrasting perspective, the use of tools from cointegration modelling is seen as a "means to an end", with the "end" being the creation of successful trading strategies. In this chapter we explore the application of cointegration-inspired tools to the task of trading and hedging international equities.

For both trading and hedging, the cointegration perspective can be viewed as an extension and generalisation of more established methods. In the case of statistical arbitrage, cointegration can be thought of as a principled extension of the relative value strategies, such as "pairs trading", which are in common use by market practitioners. In the case of hedging, the use of a cointegration approach can be viewed as extending factor-model hedging to include situations where the underlying risk factors are not measurable directly, but are instead manifested implicitly through their effect on asset prices.

The structure of the rest of the chapter is as follows. In Section 2.2 we provide a more detailed description of the econometric basis of our approach and illustrate the way in which cointegration models are constructed and how variance ratio tests can be used as a means of identifying potentially predictable components in asset price dynamics. In Section 2.3 we explain how cointegration can be used to perform implicit factor hedging. In Section 2.4 we explain how cointegration can be used to construct sophisticated relative-value models as a potential basis for statistical arbitrage trading strategies. In Section 2.5 we present a controlled simulation in which we show how cointegration methods can be used to "reverse engineer" certain aspects of the underlying dynamics of a set of time series. In Section 2.6 we describe the application of cointegration techniques to a particular set of asset prices, namely the daily closing prices of the 50 equities which constituted the STOXX 50 index as of 4 July 2002; a detailed description of the methodology is provided along with a discussion of the accompanying spreadsheet which contains the analysis itself. Finally, Section 2.7 contains a brief discussion of further practical issues together with a concluding summary of the chapter.

2.2 TIME SERIES MODELLING AND COINTEGRATION

In this section we review alternative methods for representing and modelling time series. Whilst often overlooked, the choice of problem representation can play a decisive role in determining the success or failure of any subsequent modelling or forecasting procedure. In particular, the representation will determine the extent to which the statistical properties of the data are stable over time, or "stationary".

Stable statistical properties are important because most types of model are more suited to tasks of *interpolation* (queries within the range of past data) rather than *extrapolation* (queries outside the range of known data). Where the statistical properties of a system are "nonstationary", i.e. changing over time, future queries may lie in regions outside the known data range, resulting in a degradation in the performance of any associated model.

The most common solution to the problems posed by nonstationarity is to attempt to identify a representation of the data which minimises these effects. Figure 2.1 illustrates

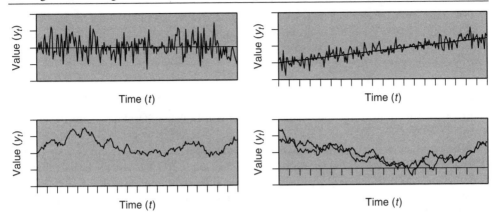

Figure 2.1 Time series with different characteristics, particularly with regard to stationarity: (top left) stationary time series; (top right) trend-stationary time series; (bottom left) integrated time series; (bottom right) cointegrated time series

different classes of time series from the viewpoint of the transformations that are required to achieve stationarity.

A naturally stationary series, such as that shown in the top-left chart, is one which has a stable range of values over time. Such a series can be directly included in a model, either as a dependent or independent variable, without creating any undue risk of extrapolation.

The top-right chart shows an example of a "trend-stationary" variable; it is stationary around a known trend which is a deterministic function of time. A stationary representation of such a variable can be obtained by "de-trending" the variable relative to the underlying trend. Some economic time series fall into this category.

Series such as that in the bottom-left chart are known as "difference stationary" because the period-to-period *differences* in the series are stationary although the series itself is not. Turning this around, such series can also be viewed as "integrated series", which represent the integration (sum) of a stationary time series. Artificial random-walk series and most asset prices fall into this category, i.e. prices are nonstationary but price differences, returns, are stationary.

The two series in the bottom-right chart represent a so-called *cointegrated* set of variables. Whilst the individual series are nonstationary we can construct a combined series (in this case the difference between the two) which is stationary. As we shall demonstrate below, some sets of asset prices exhibit cointegration to a greater or lesser degree, leading to interesting and valuable opportunities for both trading and hedging the assets within the set. Another way of looking at cointegration is that we are "de-trending" the series against each other, rather than against time.

The class into which a time series or set of time series fall, whether stationary, integrated, or cointegrated, has important implications both for the modelling approach which should be adopted and the nature of any potentially predictable components that the time series may contain. Details of a wide range of statistical tests, for identifying both the type of time series (stationary, nonstationary, cointegrated) and the presence of any potentially predictable component in the time series dynamics, are provided in Burgess (1999). In this chapter we will concentrate on two main tests: regression-based tests for the presence of cointegration, and variance ratio tests for the presence of potential predictability.

The most popular method of testing for cointegration is that introduced by Granger (1983) and is based upon the concept of a "cointegrating regression". In this approach a particular time series (the "target series") $y_{0,t}$ is regressed upon the remainder of the set of time series (the "cointegrating series") $y_{1,t}, \ldots, y_{n,t}$:

$$y_{0,t} = \alpha + \beta_1 y_{1,t} + \beta_2 y_{2,t} + \cdots + \beta_n y_{n,t} + d_t \tag{2.1}$$

If the series are cointegrated then statistical tests will indicate that d_t is stationary and the parameter vector $\alpha = (1, -\alpha, -\beta_1, -\beta_2, \ldots, -\beta_n)$ is referred to as the *cointegrating vector*. Two standard tests recommended by Engle and Granger (1987) are the Dickey–Fuller (DF) and the Cointegrating Regression Durbin–Watson (CRDW). The Dickey–Fuller test is described later in this chapter, as part of the controlled simulation in Section 2.5. An extensive review of approaches to constructing and testing for cointegrating relationships is contained in Burgess (1999).

Variance ratio tests are a powerful way of testing for potential predictability in time series dynamics. They are derived from a property of *unpredictable* series where the variance of the differences in the series grows linearly with the length of the period over which they are measured. A simple intuition for this property is presented in Figure 2.2.

In the limiting case where all steps are in the same direction the variance of the series will grow as a function of time squared, at the other extreme of pure reversion the variance of the series will be independent of time (and close to zero). A random diffusion will be a weighted combination of both behaviours and will exhibit variance which grows linearly with time.

This effect has been used as the basis of statistical tests for deviations from random-walk behaviour by a number of authors starting with Lo and MacKinlay (1988) and Cochrane (1988). The motivation for testing for deviations from random-walk behaviour is that they suggest the presence of a potentially predictable component in the dynamics of a time series. The τ-period variance ratio is simply the normalised ratio of the variance of τ-period differences to the variance of single-period differences:

$$\text{VR}(\tau) = \frac{\sum_t (\Delta^\tau y_t - \overline{\Delta^\tau y})^2}{\tau \sum_t (\Delta y_t - \overline{\Delta y})^2} \tag{2.2}$$

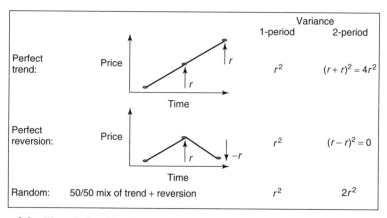

Figure 2.2 The relationship between variance and time for a simple diffusion process

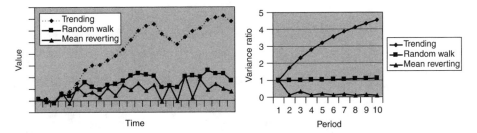

Figure 2.3   Example time series with different characteristics (left) and their variance ratio functions (right)

By viewing the variance ratio statistics for different periods collectively, we form the variance ratio function (VRF) of the time series (Burgess, 1999). A positive gradient to the VRF indicates positive autocorrelation in the time series dynamics and hence trending behaviour; conversely a negative gradient to the VRF indicates negative autocorrelation and mean-reverting or cyclical behaviour. Figure 2.3 shows examples of time series with different characteristics, together with their associated VRFs. Further examples are contained in Burgess (1999).

For the random walk series, the variance grows linearly with the period τ and hence the VRF remains close to one. For a trending series the variance grows at a greater than linear rate and so the VRF rises as the period over which the differences are calculated increases. Finally, for the mean-reverting series the converse is true: the variance grows sublinearly and hence the VRF falls below one.

2.3   IMPLICIT HEDGING OF UNKNOWN COMMON RISK FACTORS

The relevance of cointegration to hedging is based upon the recognition that much of the "risk" or stochastic component in asset returns is caused by variations in factors which have a common effect on many assets. This viewpoint forms the basis of traditional asset pricing models such as the CAPM (Capital Asset Pricing Model) of Sharpe (1964) and the APT (Arbitrage Pricing Theory) of Ross (1976). Essentially these pricing models take the form:

$$\Delta y_{i,t} = \alpha_i + \beta_{i,Mkt}\Delta Mkt_t + \beta_{i,1}\Delta f_{1,t} + \cdots + \beta_{i,n}\Delta f_{n,t} + \varepsilon_{i,t} \tag{2.3}$$

This general formulation relates changes in asset prices Δy_t to sources of systematic risk (changes in the market, ΔMkt_t, and in other economic "risk factors", $\Delta f_{j,t}$) together with an idiosyncratic asset-specific component $\varepsilon_{i,t}$.

The presence of market-wide risk factors creates the possibility of hedging or reducing risk through the construction of appropriate combinations of assets. Consider a portfolio consisting of a long (bought) position in an asset y_1 and a short (sold) position in an asset y_2. If the asset price dynamics in each case follow a data-generating process of the form shown in equation (2.3), then the *combined* returns $\Delta y_{1,t} - \Delta y_{2,t}$ are given by:

$$\Delta y_{1,t} - \Delta y_{2,t} = (\alpha_1 - \alpha_2)$$
$$+ (\beta_{1,Mkt} - \beta_{2,Mkt})\Delta Mkt_t + (\beta_{1,1} - \beta_{2,1})\Delta f_{1,t} + \cdots + (\beta_{1,n} - \beta_{2,n})\Delta f_{n,t}$$
$$+ (\varepsilon_{1,t} - \varepsilon_{2,t})$$
$$\tag{2.4}$$

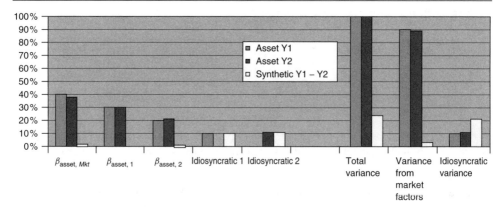

Figure 2.4 Attribution of price variance across risk factors: whilst the individual assets Y1 and Y2 are primarily influenced by changes in market-wide risk factors, the price changes of the "synthetic asset" Y1 − Y2 are largely immunised from such effects

If the factor exposures are similar, i.e. $\beta_{1,j} \approx \beta_{2,j}$, then the proportion of variance which is caused by market-wide factors will be correspondingly reduced. This effect is illustrated in Figure 2.4.

A common approach to hedging is to assume that we can explicitly identify at least reasonable approximations to the underlying risk factors $\Delta f_{j,t}$ and factor sensitivities $\beta_{i,j}$ and then to create portfolios in which the combined exposure to the different risk factors lies within a desired tolerance. However, in cases where this may not be the optimal approach, cointegration provides an alternative method of *implicitly* hedging the common underlying sources of risk.

More specifically, given an asset universe U_A and a particular "target asset", $T \in U_A$, a cointegrating regression can be used to create a "synthetic asset" $SA(T)$ which is a linear combination of assets which exhibits the maximum possible long-term correlation with the target asset T. The coefficients of the linear combination are estimated by regressing the historical price of T on the historical prices of a set of "constituent" assets $C \subset U_A - T$:

$$SA(T)_t = \sum_{C_i \in C} \beta_i C_{i,t} \quad \text{s.t.} \quad \{\beta_i\} = \arg\min \sum_{t=1,\dots,n} \left(T_t - \sum_{C_i \in C} \beta_i C_{i,t} \right)^2 \quad (2.5)$$

As the aim of the regression is to minimise the squared differences, this is a standard ordinary least squares (OLS) regression, and the optimal "cointegrating vector" $\beta = (\beta_1, \dots, \beta_{n_c})^T$ of constituent weights can be calculated directly by:

$$\beta_{OLS} = (\mathbf{C}^T\mathbf{C})^{-1}\mathbf{C}\mathbf{t} \quad (2.6)$$

where $\mathbf{C}$ is the $n_c(= |C|) \times n$ matrix of historical prices of the constituents and $\mathbf{t} = (T_1, \dots, T_n)^T$ is the vector of historical prices of the target asset.

The standard properties of the OLS procedure used in regression ensure both that the synthetic asset will be an unbiased estimator for the target asset, i.e. $E[T_t] = SA(T)_t$, and also that the deviation between the two price series will be minimal in a mean-squared-error sense. The synthetic asset can be considered an optimal statistical hedge for the target series, given a particular set of constituent assets C.

From an economic perspective the set of constituent assets C act as proxies for the unobserved common risk factors. In maximising the correlation between the target asset and the synthetic asset the construction procedure cannot (by definition) account for the "asset-specific" components of price dynamics, but must instead indirectly optimise the sensitivities to common sources of economic risk. The synthetic asset represents a combination which as closely as possible matches the underlying factor exposures of the target asset without requiring either the risk factors or the exposures to be identified explicitly. In Section 2.5, this procedure is illustrated in detail by a controlled experiment in which the cointegration approach is applied to simulated data with known properties.

2.4 RELATIVE VALUE AND STATISTICAL ARBITRAGE

In the previous section we saw that appropriately constructed combinations of prices can be largely immunised against market-wide sources of risk. Such combinations of assets are potentially amenable to statistical arbitrage because they represent opportunities to exploit predictable components in asset-specific price dynamics in a manner which is (statistically) independent of changes in the level of the market as a whole, or other market-wide sources of risk. Furthermore, as the asset-specific component of the dynamics is not directly observable by market participants it is plausible that regularities in the dynamics may exist from this perspective which have not yet been "arbitraged away" by market participants.

To motivate the use of statistical arbitrage strategies, we briefly relate the opportunities they offer to those of more traditional "riskless" arbitrage strategies. The basic concept of riskless arbitrage is that where the future cash-flows of an asset can be replicated by a combination of other assets, the price of forming the replicating portfolio should be approximately the same as the price of the original asset. Thus the no-arbitrage condition can be represented in a general form as:

$$|\text{payoff}(X_t - \text{SA}(X_t))| < \text{Transaction cost} \qquad (2.7)$$

where X_t is an arbitrary asset (or combination of assets), $\text{SA}(X_t)$ is a "synthetic asset" which is constructed to replicate the payoff of X_t and "transaction cost" represents the net costs involved in constructing (buying) the synthetic asset and selling the "underlying" X_t (or vice versa). This general relationship forms the basis of the "no-arbitrage" pricing approach used in the pricing of financial "derivatives" such as options, forwards and futures.[1] From this perspective, the price difference $X_t - \text{SA}(X_t)$ can be thought of as the *mispricing* between the two (sets of) assets.

A specific example of riskless arbitrage is index arbitrage in the UK equities market. Index arbitrage (see for example Hull (1993)) occurs between the equities constituting a particular market index, and the associated futures contract on the index itself. Typically the futures contract F_t will be defined so as to pay a value equal to the level of the index

---

[1] See Hull (1993) for a good introduction to derivative securities and no-arbitrage relationships.

at some future "expiration date" T. Denoting the current (spot) stock prices as S_t^i, the no-arbitrage relationship, specialising the general case in equation (2.7), is given by:

$$\left| F_t - \sum_i w_i S_t^i e^{(r-q_i)(T-t)} \right| < \text{cost} \qquad (2.8)$$

where w_i is the weight of stock i in determining the market index, r is the risk-free interest rate, and q_i is the dividend rate for stock i. In the context of equation (2.7) the weighted combination of constituent equities can be considered as the synthetic asset which replicates the index futures contract.

When the "basis" $F_t - \sum_i w_i S_t^i e^{(r-q_i)(T-t)}$ exceeds the transaction costs of a particular trader, the arbitrageur can "lock in" a riskless profit by selling the (overpriced) futures contract F_t and buying the (underpriced) combination of constituent equities. When the magnitude of the mispricing between the spot and future grows, there are frequently large corrections in the basis which are caused by index arbitrage activity, as illustrated in Figure 2.5 for the UK FTSE 100 index.

Many complex arbitrage relationships exist and "riskless" arbitrage is an important subject in its own right. However such strategies are inherently self-limiting – as competition amongst arbitrageurs grows, the magnitude and duration of mispricings decreases. Furthermore, in practice, even arbitrage which is technically "riskless" will still involve a certain level of risk due to uncertain future dividend rates q_i, trading risks, and so on. From this perspective the true attraction of index arbitrage strategies lies less in the theoretical price relationship than in a favourable property of the mispricing dynamics – namely a tendency for the basis risk to "mean revert" or fluctuate around a stable level.

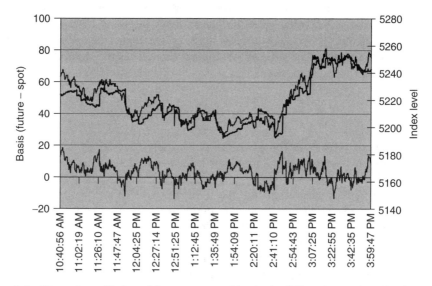

Figure 2.5 Illustration of index arbitrage opportunities in the UK equity market; the data consists of 3200 prices for the FTSE 100 index (in bold) and the derivative futures contract expiring Sept. 98; the lower curve shows the so-called "basis", the deviation from the theoretical fair price relationship between the two series; the data sample covers the period from 10.40am to 4pm on 15 September 1998; some of the abrupt price shifts will be due to arbitrage activity

Building upon this insight, the premise of "statistical arbitrage" is that regularities in combinations of asset prices can be exploited as the basis of profitable trading strategies, irrespective of the presence or absence of a theoretical fair price relationship between the set of assets involved.

Whilst clearly subject to a higher degree of risk than "true" arbitrage strategies, statistical arbitrage opportunities offer the hope of being both more persistent and more prevalent in the markets. More persistent because risk-free arbitrage opportunities are rapidly eliminated by market activity. More prevalent because in principle they may occur between any set of assets rather than solely in cases where a suitable "risk-free" hedging strategy can be implemented.

A simple form of statistical arbitrage is "pairs trading", which is in common use by a number of market participants, such as hedge funds, proprietary trading desks and other "risk arbitrageurs". Pairs trading is based on a relative value analysis of two asset prices. The two assets might be selected either on the basis of intuition, economic fundamentals, long-term correlations or simply past experience. A promising candidate for a pairs strategy might look like the example in Figure 2.6, between HSBC and Standard Chartered.

The pairs in Figure 2.6 show a clear similarity to the riskless arbitrage opportunities shown in Figure 2.5. In both cases the two prices "move together" in the long term, with temporary deviations from the long-term correlation which exhibit a strong mean-reversion pattern. Note however that in the "statistical arbitrage" case the magnitude of the deviations is greater (around ±10% as opposed to <0.5%) and so is the time period over which the price corrections occur (days or weeks as opposed to seconds or minutes).

Opportunities for pairs trading in this simple form, however, are dependent upon the existence of similar pairs of assets and thus are naturally limited. By constructing synthetic "pairs" in the form of appropriate combinations of two or more assets, cointegration techniques provide a sophisticated and powerful method to generalise the relative value approach and create a wider range of potential trading opportunities. Once a cointegrating

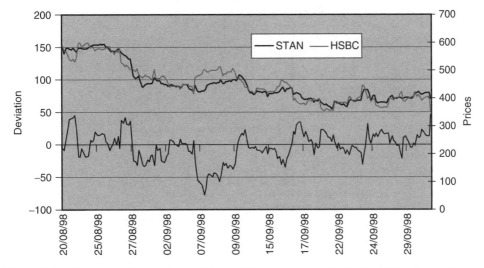

Figure 2.6 Illustration of potential statistical arbitrage opportunities in the UK equity market; the chart shows equity prices for Standard Chartered and HSBC, sampled on an hourly basis from 20 August to 30 September 1998. Note the mean-reverting nature of the deviation

regression has been performed to estimate the "fair price" relationship between a set of assets, tools such as variance ratio analysis can be used to detect deterministic components in the mispricing dynamics that could be used as the basis of a "statarb" strategy.

In this and the previous section we have provided a motivation for the use of cointegration-based techniques for both hedging and trading. In the following section we supplement this qualitative motivation with some quantitative results obtained from applying the techniques in a controlled simulation with known time series dynamics.

2.5 ILLUSTRATION OF COINTEGRATION IN A CONTROLLED SIMULATION

Now that we have described the rationale for applying cointegration-based techniques in trading, the next sections provide examples of how these techniques can be used in practice. In Section 2.6 we will explore the application of cointegration techniques to real asset prices. But before we do that, this section highlights the way in which the techniques work by means of an artificial example in which the underlying dynamics of the time series are controlled. Consider the example of a set of three assets, each following a two-factor version of the data-generating process shown in equation (2.3). In this controlled example we *specify* the factor exposures of three assets X, Y and Z as shown in Table 2.1, i.e. price changes within the set of three assets X, Y and Z are driven by a total of five factors, two common risk factors f_1 and f_2 and three asset-specific components $\varepsilon_1, \varepsilon_2, \varepsilon_3$. Furthermore let us specify that f_1 and f_2 follow random-walk processes whilst the dynamics of the asset-specific factors contain a mean-reverting component. As discussed in Section 2.4, these dynamics might also be plausibly the case in reality because predictable effects in market-wide factors would be easily observed and thus "arbitraged away", whilst small predictable components in asset-specific dynamics might be less obvious and hence also more persistent.

Based on the assumptions described above, let us specify the full dynamics of the resulting time series by the following equations:

$$
\begin{aligned}
&\Delta f_{i,t} = \eta_{i,t} && i = 1, 2 && \eta_{i,t} \sim N(0,1) \\
&\Delta \varepsilon_{j,t} = -0.1\varepsilon_{j,t} + e_{j,t} && j = 1, 2, 3 && e_{j,t} \sim N(0,0.25) \\
&\Delta X_t = \Delta f_{1,t} + \Delta f_{2,t} + \Delta \varepsilon_{1,t} && && \qquad (2.9) \\
&\Delta Y_t = \Delta f_{1,t} + 0.5\Delta f_{2,t} + \Delta \varepsilon_{2,t} \\
&\Delta Z_t = 0.5\Delta f_{1,t} + \Delta f_{2,t} + \Delta \varepsilon_{3,t}
\end{aligned}
$$

Table 2.1 Price sensitivity of three assets X, Y and Z to changes in common risk factors f_1 and f_2 and asset-specific effects $\varepsilon_1, \varepsilon_2, \varepsilon_3$

Asset	f_1	f_2	ε_1	ε_2	ε_3
X	1	1	1	0	0
Y	1	0.5	0	1	0
Z	0.5	1	0	0	1

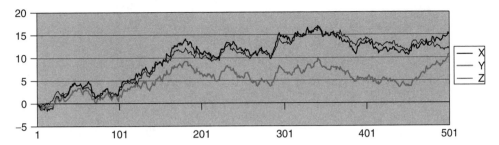

Figure 2.7 Realisation of three simulated asset price series which are driven by two underlying common factors in addition to asset-specific components

i.e. the unobserved "factor" dynamics of f_1 and f_2 are driven by the pure noise terms $\eta_{i,t}$; the also-unobserved asset-specific dynamics $\varepsilon_{j,t}$ are a combination of noise terms $e_{j,t}$ with "error correction" mean-reversion terms with parameter -0.1; the observed asset dynamics X_t, Y_t and Z_t are determined by their different exposures to the five underlying factors.

The precise "shapes" of the time series will depend on the sampled innovations $\eta_{i,t}$ and $e_{i,t}$. A particular realisation of the asset prices generated by the system is shown in Figure 2.7 and this is used as the basis of the analysis below. Note that the common factor exposures create a broad similarity between the observed price movements of the three assets.

As described in Section 2.3, we estimate the underlying fair price relationship from the observed data by performing a cointegrating regression. In this case, we arbitrarily select X as the "target series" and regress on the other two "cointegrating series" Y and Z. The resulting relationship estimated by the regression is given by:

$$X_t = 0.632Y_t + 0.703Z_t + m_t \tag{2.10}$$

Due to sampling error, the estimated relationship differs slightly from the true underlying relationship $X_t = 2/3Y_t + 2/3Z_t + m_t^*$, which would precisely cancel the factor exposures and leave a pure combination (m_t^*) of the asset-specific terms. However, it is clear that the cointegrating regression has been able to construct a combination which largely neutralises the common risk factors, and that it has done this without any explicit knowledge of (or even estimation of) the factor exposures shown in Table 2.1. It is because they bypass the need to estimate explicit factor exposures that we refer to cointegration techniques as performing "implicit" hedging of market-wide risk factors.

In this example, the asset-specific dynamics have been constructed so as to be mean reverting, so the error term of the regression can be considered as a statistical "mispricing" which represents the temporary deviation from the estimated "fair price" relationship between the three assets. Unlike the nonstationary asset prices X, Y and Z, the estimated mispricing m_t, which is illustrated in Figure 2.8, can clearly be seen to be mean reverting.

The mean-reverting nature of the mispricing time series, compared to the close to random-walk behaviour of the original time series X, Y and Z, is highlighted by the variance ratio profiles shown in Figure 2.9. Whilst the variance ratio for all three original assets remains close to unity in each case, the variance ratio of the mispricing falls substantially below one as the period over which the differences are calculated increases. This indicates that the volatility which is present in the short-term dynamics is not reflected in

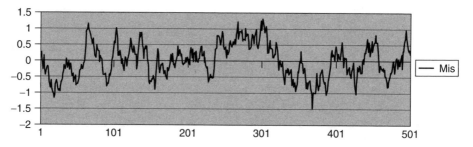

Figure 2.8 The estimated "mispricing" time series, $m_t = X_t - (0.632Y_t + 0.703Z_t)$

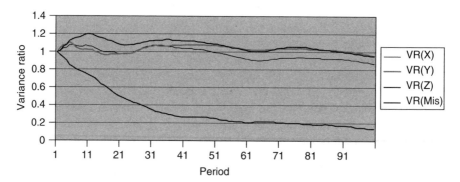

Figure 2.9 Variance ratio profiles for the time series X, Y and Z and $m_t = X_t - (0.632Y_t + 0.703Z_t)$

the long-term volatility, thus providing evidence for a substantial mean-reverting component in the mispricing dynamics.

Let us now evaluate the effectiveness of the cointegration procedure at "reverse engineering" the underlying factor dynamics. In attempting to replicate the "target" time series X the cointegrating regression procedure creates the "synthetic asset" $0.632Y + 0.703Z$ which has similar exposures to the common factors f_1 and f_2. Thus in the mispricing time series $X_t - (0.632Y_t + 0.703Z_t)$ the *net* exposure to the common factors is close to zero, allowing the mean-reverting asset-specific effects ε_1, ε_2, ε_3 to dominate the mispricing dynamics. This "statistical hedging" of the common risk factors is quantified in Table 2.2, which reports the proportion of the variance of each observed time series which is associated with each of the underlying factors.

This demonstrates that the use of cointegrating regression can immunise against common underlying factors which are not observed *directly* but instead proxied by the observed asset prices. Whilst the variance of changes in the original time series X, Y and Z is primarily (70–90%) associated with the common risk factors f_1 and f_2, the effect of these factors on the mispricing m is minimal (0.2%). Conversely, the relative effect of the asset-specific factors is greatly magnified, growing from 10–30% in the original time series to 99.8% in the relative mispricing m.

By magnifying the component of the dynamics which is associated with asset-specific effects, we would expect to magnify the predictable component which (by construction) is present in the asset-specific effects but not in the common factors. This effect can be

Table 2.2 Sensitivity of price changes of the original time series X, Y and Z and the "mispricing" time series $X_t - (0.632Y_t + 0.703Z_t)$. The table entries show the proportion of the variance of each time series which is associated with changes in common risk factors f_1 and f_2 and asset-specific effects $\varepsilon_1, \varepsilon_2, \varepsilon_3$

	X	Y	Z	m
f_1	46.1%	64.2%	16.8%	0.2%
f_2	41.5%	10.1%	67.8%	0.0%
ε_1	11.5%	0.2%	0.0%	54.5%
ε_2	0.5%	25.1%	0.1%	23.7%
ε_3	0.4%	0.4%	15.3%	21.6%
Total	100.0%	100.0%	100.0%	100.0%

quantified by considering the Dickey–Fuller statistics obtained from simple ECMs of the time series dynamics:

$$DF(s_t) = \hat{\beta}/\sigma_{\hat{\beta}} \text{ from regression } \Delta s_t = \alpha - \hat{\beta} s_t + \eta_t \quad \text{where} \quad \eta_t \text{ is a noise term}$$
(2.11)

i.e. we regress *changes* in the time series (Δs_t) against the *level* of the series (s_t) and test for a statistically significant error-correcting coefficient β. The details of the estimated ECMs for our experiment are presented in Table 2.3.

The DF statistic approximately follows a t-distribution so, roughly speaking, DF values greater than two indicate significant evidence for a mean-reverting/error-correction effect. For the underlying (but unobserved) factors, the low DF statistics for f_1 and f_2 confirm the lack of predictable components in these common factors, whilst the high DF values for $\varepsilon_1, \varepsilon_2$ and ε_3 (4.908, 5.644 and 4.454 respectively) confirm the highly significant degree of mean reversion in the asset-specific effects.

In the observed series, X, Y and Z, the mean-reverting effect is "watered down" by the unpredictable factor effects, with the result that the corresponding DF statistics are small (actually slightly negative) and present no evidence of a predictable component.

Table 2.3 Details of simple error-correction models estimated to quantify the mean-reverting component in both the unobserved factors and the observed time series. Values in bold correspond to cases where the estimated mean-reversion coefficient $\hat{\beta}$ is significant at the 0.1% level. The rows in the table are: estimated reversion parameter $\hat{\beta}$; standard error of estimate; associated DF statistic (approximately equivalent to the t-statistic in a standard regression); proportion of variance explained by model (R^2)

Factor/asset	f_1	f_2	ε_1	ε_2	ε_3	X	Y	Z	m
Estimated $\hat{\beta}$	*0.014*	*−0.001*	**0.096**	**0.124**	**0.079**	−0.001	−0.000	−0.001	**0.077**
Std. error $\sigma_{\hat{\beta}}$	*0.008*	*0.001*	0.020	0.022	0.018	0.002	0.003	0.001	0.018
DF(s_t)	*1.631*	*−0.580*	4.908	5.644	4.454	−0.452	−0.004	−0.591	4.398
R^2	*0.5%*	*0%*	*4.8%*	*6.2%*	*4.0%*	0%	0%	0%	3.9%

This picture changes dramatically when we look at the constructed "mispricing" m which has a high DF statistic of 4.398 – almost as high as for the true asset-specific effects.

The actual magnitude (as opposed to statistical significance) of the detected mean-reversion effect is given by the R^2 values in the table. The results confirm that the predictable component of the dynamics is almost as strongly present in the mispricing time series as in the underlying, but unobserved, asset-specific dynamics themselves. The magnitude of the deterministic component in the mispricing is 3.9%, which is comparable to the 4.8%, 6.2% and 4.0% in the true asset-specific dynamics, and a negligible amount in the case of the original time series X, Y and Z.

These results from our controlled experiment serve to illustrate the power of the co-integration approach to remove market-wide risk factors and highlight the asset-specific components of price dynamics, which in this case were constructed to contain a mean-reverting effect. However the qualitative reasoning presented in Sections 2.3 and 2.4, together with quantitative evidence from other sources, suggests that similar results may be obtained for real asset prices. In the following section we apply essentially the same techniques as those used in this controlled experiment to analyse price relationships between real assets, namely the equities which constitute the European-wide STOXX 50 index.

2.6   APPLICATION TO INTERNATIONAL EQUITIES

In this section we describe an application of the cointegration tools and techniques described above to data from those international equities which comprised the STOXX 50 index as of 4 July 2002. We describe this analysis with reference to the accompanying Excel workbook named "equity coint.xls" on the CD-Rom.

The set of equities which constitute our universe are listed in the first sheet of the workbook (named "Constituents"). The full set of equities included in the analysis are listed in Table 2.4.

The second sheet in the workbook is named "Prices" and contains the raw data for the analysis. This consists of daily closing prices which have been adjusted to remove the effects of stock splits, dividends and other corporate actions. The time frame for the analysis is from 14 September 1998 to 3 July 2002, which is the longest period over which continuous data is available across the whole set of stocks. This comprises almost 4 years of data, giving 993 daily observations.

Note that this data does not provide a true "snapshot" of the European equity markets due to the complication that the closing times differ across the different national exchanges. For a practical trading system this would induce serious distortions to our models, but for our purposes here the close prices serve adequately to illustrate the use of the tools we have described above.

The third sheet ("Pairs") contains a simple relative value analysis of a pair of assets at a time. The sheet also serves to illustrate the data itself and the use of variance ratio functions to identify the underlying time series dynamics. A screen shot of this worksheet is shown in Figure 2.10.

Cells D37 and D38 are used to select two equities whose prices we wish to compare. The equities are selected by entering numbers from 1 to 50 corresponding to the reference numbers shown in Table 2.4. The example given shows the case of selecting the British oil-stock BP (BP.L, number 6 in the set) and the French oil-stock Total-Fina (TOTF.PA, number 27 in the set). The lower chart plots BP against Total and also shows the synthetic

Table 2.4 The list of companies included in the analysis. The 50 stocks correspond to the constituents of the pan-European STOXX 50 index as of 4 July 2002

Ref.	Name	Symbol	Ref.	Name	Symbol
1	British Telecom	BT.L	26	Zurich Financial	ZURZn.VX
2	Glaxo Smithkline	GSK.L	27	Total-Fina	TOTF.PA
3	Alcatel	CGEP.PA	28	Suez	LYOE.PA
4	UBS	UBSZn.VX	29	Oreal	OREP.PA
5	Daimler Chrysler	DCXGn.DE	30	Telecom Italia	TIT.MI
6	BP	BP.L	31	ENI	ENI.MI
7	Astro-Zeneca	AZN.L	32	Eon	EONG.DE
8	Nokia	NOK1V.HE	33	Siemens	SIEGn.DE
9	Novartis	NOVZn.VX	34	Deutsche Bank	DBKGn.DE
10	Ericsson	ERICb.ST	35	Generali	GASI.MI
11	Philips	PHG.AS	36	Deutsche Telecom	DTEGn.DE
12	ING	ING.AS	37	BBVA	BBVA.MC
13	ABN Amro	AAH.AS	38	Allianz	ALVG.DE
14	Aegon	AEGN.AS	39	Bayer	BAYG.DE
15	Unilever	UNc.AS	40	Barclays	BARC.L
16	Royal Dutch	RD.AS	41	HSBC	HSBA.L
17	Swiss Re	RUKZn.VX	42	Diageo	DGE.L
18	Roche	ROCZg.VX	43	Lloyds Bank	LLOY.L
19	Vivendi	EAUG.PA	44	Prudential	PRU.L
20	BSCH	SAN.MC	45	Royal Bank of Scotland	RBOS.L
21	Nestle	NESZn.VX	46	Shell	SHEL.L
22	Carrefour	CARR.PA	47	Vodafone	VOD.L
23	BNP-Paribas	BNPP.PA	48	Telefonica	TEF.MC
24	Aviva	AV.L	49	Munich Re	MUVGn.DE
25	AXA	AXAF.PA	50	Credit Swiss	CSGZn.VX

asset which represents the relative return on the two stocks. All three series have been normalised to represent log price changes since the beginning of the analysis period. A close-up of the chart is shown in Figure 2.11.

In this case we see that there appears to be a semi-stable equilibrium which exists between the two asset prices. For long periods of time the relative price tends to fluctuate around an equilibrium or "fair price" level, however significant shifts in the relationship also occur, such as the 30% shift in the relative value which occurred during the early part of 2000. The apparent existence of a relationship between the two price series, together with the instability in this relationship, serve to respectively illustrate the opportunities and the risks which arise from a relative value approach to trading.

The top half of the sheet contains a variance ratio analysis of the price dynamics of the selected equities and the synthetic asset corresponding to their relative prices. The cells in the range C5:E34 contain array formulae to calculate the n-period variances for each of the three time series, with n varying between 1 and 30. To the right of these variances, cells H5:J34 contain the variance ratios, with each n-period variance normalised by n times the one-period variance. These three functions are plotted in the chart to the right of the numbers, with the example for BP and Total-Fina shown in Figure 2.12.

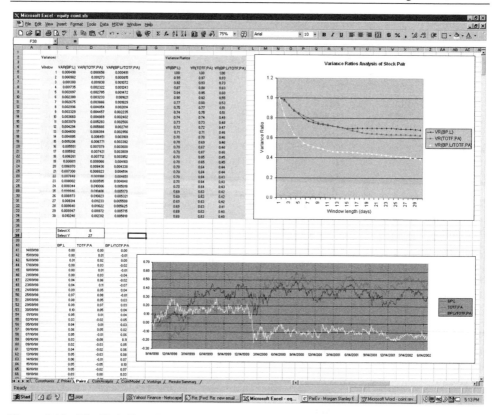

Figure 2.10 The "Pairs" worksheet containing a pairwise relative value analysis, the selected stocks are BP (number 6) and Total-Fina (number 27)

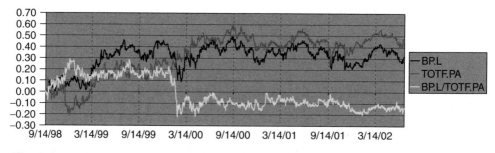

Figure 2.11 Relative prices for BP, Total, and the synthetic asset which is the ratio of the two

In this case we see that the variance ratio functions for the two securities show declining profiles, indicating the presence of reverting components in their time series dynamics. The mean-reversion tendency is significantly more prominent in the synthetic asset (BP/Total) than for either of the individual assets, providing further evidence to support the presence of a potentially predictable component in the relative price dynamics.

Given such evidence of mean-reverting dynamics we could move on to implement a statistical arbitrage strategy based on the types of trading rules described by Burgess

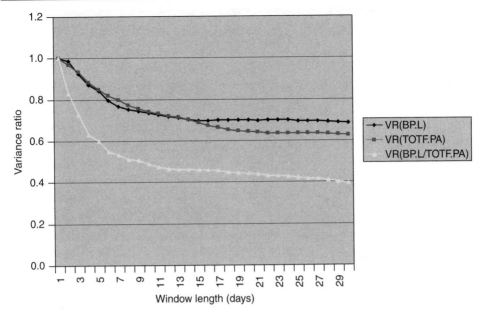

Figure 2.12   Variance ratio functions for BP, Total, and the synthetic asset which is the ratio of the two

(1999) and Towers (2000). Note however that in this particular case at least some of this effect will be due to the non-synchronous sampling of the close price in the French and UK markets. Because of this non-synchronicity a more sophisticated analysis (and probably additional data) would be needed to evaluate the true magnitude of the mean-reverting effect in the relative price of these equities and its viability as the basis for a profitable trading strategy.

Whilst pairs analysis works well for some equities, it is highly sensitive to the properties of each asset price and works better for some stocks than for others. Essentially it requires that for a given equity, there is one (and only one) equity which has similar exposures to each and every underlying factor. For a given equity there may be zero, one or more than one closely matching pairs and only in the case of a single matching pair is the simple approach likely to be close to optimal. These complications mean that pairs analysis is essentially opportunistic in nature rather than representing a general strategy which can be applied across a broad asset universe.

Cointegration modelling is essentially an extension of pairs analysis which is designed to overcome these limitations. Rather than requiring the existence of a single perfect match we instead *create* an optimally matching "synthetic asset" in the form of a weighted combination of one or more assets. The remaining sheets in the workbook demonstrate the workings and results of this more sophisticated form of relative value modelling.

Firstly, the sheet "CointAnalysis" illustrates the construction of a synthetic asset to match a chosen "target" asset. A screen shot of this worksheet is shown in Figure 2.13. The top-left of the worksheet contains various control parameters and diagnostic information. The chart in the top-centre of the worksheet presents a variance ratio analysis of the statistical mispricing. The bottom-left chart is a visualisation of the synthetic asset and the chart in the bottom-right shows the evolution of the various price series over time.

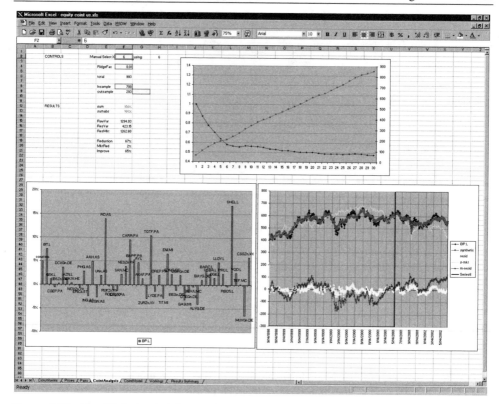

Figure 2.13 The "CointAnalysis" worksheet showing the construction of a synthetic asset to match asset number 6: British Petroleum (BP.L)

CONTROLS	Manual Select X	6	using:	6
	RidgeFac	0.01		
	total	993		
	Insample	700		
	outsample	293		

Figure 2.14 The controls for the cointegration analysis

The controls for the cointegration analysis are contained in the top-left of the worksheet. As elsewhere in the workbook, the convention is that user-specified controls are contained in cells with a black border and yellow background. In this case there are four such cells, as shown in Figure 2.14.

Firstly, the target series is specified in cell F2, using the reference numbers listed in Table 2.4. In this case we remain with the same example as before: asset number 6, British Petroleum, or BP.L for short. Note that in order to allow the generation of automatic tables, the actual control cell is H2, and cell F2 acts as a kind of manual override.

The second control cell is F4, labelled "RidgeFac". This represents an important modification of the basic methodology, which is necessary to avoid the problems caused by regressing on large numbers of variables. Rather than using a standard regression, this more practical methodology uses a "ridge regression" in which the resulting parameters are in some sense "smoothed" or "regularised" and this cell controls the amount of smoothing (Hoerl and Kennard, 1970a,b).

The final control parameters consist of the number of observations which should be used to construct the model (the "in-sample" set) and the subsequent number of observations which should be used to evaluate the model performance (the "out-of-sample" set). Cell F6 indicates the number of observations available in total, which for this analysis is 993. Cell F8 is used to specify the number of "in-sample" observations. In this case we use 700 observations, representing approximately two-thirds of the available data. By default, all of the remaining observations are used to perform the "out-sample" evaluation. This number can be overridden using cell G9, but in this case is left as the default, giving 293 observations for the out-of-sample results analysis.

The data for the regression is collected on the "CointModel" worksheet. The target asset is stored in column H of this worksheet; a constant column of ones is placed in column J; and the 49 cointegrating assets are remapped to the adjacent columns K through to BG. It is useful to have the 50 independent variables in contiguous columns in order to simplify the matrix algebra used to compute the solution to the cointegrating regression.

The calculations for the cointegrating regression are performed on the "Workings" sheet. The worksheet performs a "ridge regression" (Hoerl and Kennard, 1970a,b) in which the solution is given by $\boldsymbol{\beta} = (\mathbf{C}^T\mathbf{C} + \lambda\sigma\mathbf{I})^{-1}\mathbf{C}t$. The target vector $\mathbf{t}$ and data matrix $\mathbf{C}$ (the 49 other asset price series supplemented by a column of ones) are referenced from the "CointModel" worksheet. The regularisation parameter lambda (λ) is referenced from cell F4 of the "CointAnalysis" worksheet. The covariance matrix $\mathbf{C}^T\mathbf{C}$ is calculated in cells G4:BD53. The vector $\mathbf{C}t$ is calculated in BI4:BI53. The enhanced covariance matrix, $\mathbf{C}^T\mathbf{C} + \lambda\sigma\mathbf{I}$, is constructed in cells BM4:DJ53 by re-scaling the diagonal elements of $\mathbf{C}^T\mathbf{C}$. The inverse of this enhanced matrix is calculated in cells G56:BD105. Finally the beta parameters are calculated in cells BI56:BI105 by multiplying this inverse by the vector $\mathbf{C}t$.

With the regularisation parameter set to $\lambda = 0$, the solution reduces to the standard OLS regression: $\boldsymbol{\beta} = (\mathbf{C}^T\mathbf{C})^{-1}\mathbf{C}t$. Lambda acts as a scaling coefficient for the diagonal component of the covariance matrix $\mathbf{C}^T\mathbf{C}$, proportionally downweighting the off-diagonal covariance terms and reducing the apparent correlation between the different series. As we will see below this has an important effect in stabilising the regression and enabling us to use 50 regressor variables, more than would normally be practically feasible.

The resulting beta vector is copied across to cells J25:BG25 of the "CointModel" worksheet and used to construct the synthetic asset. This is calculated as the beta-weighted average of the 50 constituent assets (including constant term) and is stored in cells G40:G1032. Note that once the betas have been estimated from the first 700 observations (in this case), the same weights can be applied to subsequent data to calculate the values of the synthetic asset during the out-of-sample period. For purposes of visualising the composition of the synthetic asset, we take the beta vector and multiply through by the scale of the individual time series. The resulting "effective weights" are illustrated in the lower left-hand chart on the "CointAnalysis" worksheet which is also reproduced in Figure 2.15.

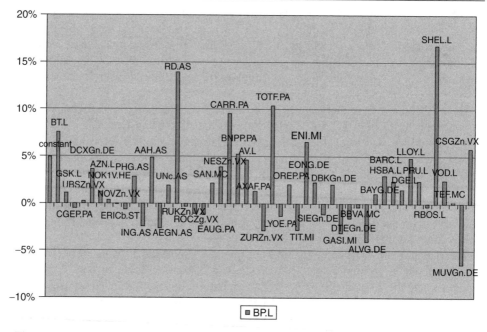

Figure 2.15   Effective weights for the synthetic asset for British Petroleum (BP.L) $\lambda = 0.01$

In the case of BP, the synthetic asset weights are dominated by other oil stocks, particularly Royal Dutch/Shell (RD.AS and SHEL.L) and Total-Fina (TOTF.PA), however most of the other stocks also have non-zero, though small, weightings indicating that the best historical fit to BP price movements is obtained by taking into account a wide range of other stocks.

Given the target asset and the constructed synthetic asset we can calculate the difference in price which is equivalent to the residual of the regression. The evolution of this time series represents the performance of a hedged portfolio with a long position in the target asset and an offsetting short position in the synthetic asset. If the synthetic asset is a good hedge for the target, this residual price should have low volatility and remain close to zero. In order to evaluate the effectiveness of the cointegration procedure we compare this price residual to that obtained by a simpler procedure, namely hedging with an equally weighted "market" portfolio. These time series are visualised in the bottom right-hand chart of the "CointAnalysis" worksheet, which is reproduced in Figure 2.16.

The vertical line divides the time axis into the in-sample and out-of-sample periods. During the in-sample period we expect the synthetic asset to closely match the target (BP.L) simply by construction; similarly the corresponding "residual" is stable around the zero level. Note that the synthetic asset is an average across a number of stocks and in this case, as would be typical, has a smoother price trajectory than the target asset itself but on the whole does tend to track the longer term price movements observed in the target series. The synthetic market price obtained as an unweighted average across the set of stocks appears to be less successful in following the price of the target asset and this is also observed in the higher volatility of the corresponding (market) residual.

During the out-of-sample period, the synthetic asset price will only track the target asset to the extent to which it has a similar exposure to the underlying risk factors which drive

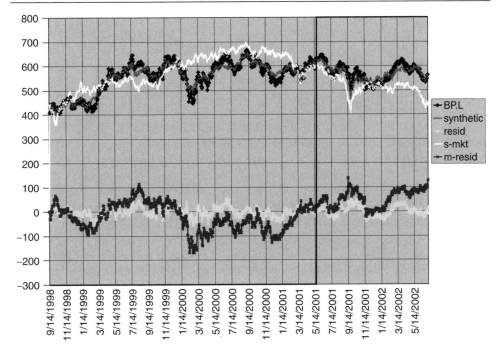

Figure 2.16 Hedged and unhedged time series for the cointegration model for BP

asset prices. In this case the model for BP appears quite successful, the residual remains in a similar price range as during the in-sample period and seems also to be relatively stable around the zero level.

The "CointAnalysis" worksheet also displays some basic measures which quantify some properties of the synthetic asset and the out-of-sample performance. The values corresponding to this example are shown in Figure 2.17.

The first two values characterise the makeup of the synthetic asset. The "sum" figure corresponds to the normalised sum of the asset weights, typically we would expect this to be close to 100%. The "sumabs" figure corresponds to the normalised sum of the absolute asset weights; if there are some negative weights, these will typically be offset

RESULTS	sum	100%
	sumabs	166%
	RawVar	1294.93
	ResVar	423.15
	ResMkt	1262.60
	Reduction	67%
	MktRed	2%
	Improve	65%

Figure 2.17 Characteristics of the cointegration model for BP.L

by positive weights over and above 100% and the sum of the absolute weights will reflect this. The figure indicates that the sum of the absolute weights is 166% in this case, reflecting negative weights totalling about 33% and offset by approximately 133% of positive weights, to give a total of 166%. Cross-checking against the visualisation of the weights in Figure 2.15, these numbers seem to be reasonable.

The sum of the absolute weights can be quite an important issue, as it provides an estimate of the quantity of assets we need to buy and sell in order to use the synthetic asset as a hedge. This measure also highlights the importance of using regularisation. For instance, with regularisation set to zero, the sum of the absolute weights for the BP.L synthetic asset becomes 404%, indicating that each unit of BP needs to be hedged against a long–short combination of equities totalling four times the value invested in BP!

The remaining figures serve to quantify the effectiveness of the synthetic asset at hedging the volatility in the target asset. These measures are calculated during the out-of-sample period in order to produce unbiased results. The "RawVar" figure corresponds to the volatility of the asset, measured in terms of price variance, the "ResVar" is the residual variance when hedged by the synthetic asset, and "ResMkt" is the residual variance when hedged against an equally-weighted "market" portfolio. The final three figures represent the proportional effectiveness of the hedging procedure. Thus in this case, the "Reduction" of 67% indicates that the synthetic asset hedge removes 67% of the out-of-sample volatility. The "market" portfolio is not a good hedge in this case, only removing 2% of the volatility in BP, and thus the cointegration approach improves on the market hedge by 65% of the original volatility. This particular example serves to highlight the potentially large improvement which can be obtained by replacing market-based hedging with the cointegration approach, but it is only fair to note that in other cases the market hedge performs equally well or even better than the cointegration approach. A fairer comparison, across the whole set of 50 stocks, will be presented towards the end of this section.

The final part of the "CointAnalysis" worksheet presents a variance ratio analysis of the time series dynamics of the hedged portfolio, with the result being shown in the chart at the top of the worksheet. The calculations underlying this chart are contained in the top-left corner of the "CointModel" worksheet. The results for the BP.L model are shown in Figure 2.18.

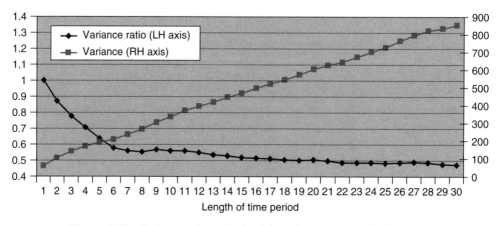

Figure 2.18   Variance ratio analysis of the cointegration model for BP.L

The variance ratio chart clearly indicates the decaying pattern which corresponds to mean-reverting dynamics. The 30-period variance ratio is just below 0.5, indicating that the variance computed over 30-day intervals is less than half as high as would be expected, given the observed 1-day variance. This suggests that, from a relative value perspective, over 50% of the short-term volatility in BP is essentially spurious price fluctuation which has a strong tendency to cancel itself out over a longer time-scale. This pattern can also be observed, though less clearly, from the concave shape of the variance curve itself. As these figures are out-of-sample results they would suggest the possibility of finding a suitable statistical arbitrage strategy to exploit this mean-reverting component in the relative price dynamics of BP against the synthetic asset portfolio. In this case, however, the same caveat as before applies in that the non-synchronous nature of our close-price data may overstate the size of the true reversion effect.

Before moving on to consider the performance across our broader universe, let us first consider the importance of the regularisation parameter. Remember that the results we have been describing above correspond to a model constructed with $\lambda = 0.01$. Let us now compare this model to the model we obtain by leaving all other parameters the same but replacing the "RidgeFac" value in cell F4 with 0.1. The composition of the new synthetic asset is shown in Figure 2.19.

With this higher degree of regularisation, the weights become more uniform. Very few are now negative and the highest weight (for Shell, SHEL.L) is reduced from approximately 18% to only 6%. The "sum" of the weights falls to 98% and the "sumabs" to 103%. In this case, however, the new synthetic asset is a less effective hedge for price movements in BP. The residual variance of the hedged portfolio rises to 702.56 (from the 423 shown in Figure 2.17), and the reduction in variance due to the hedge is now only 46% (from 67% previously). Thus, in this particular case, increasing the degree of

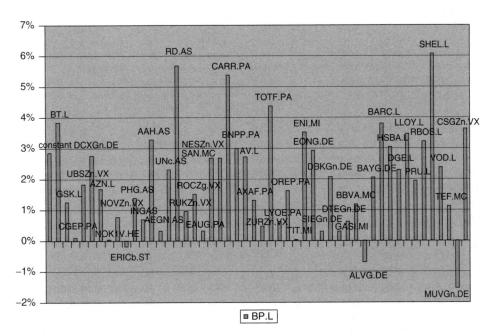

Figure 2.19 Effective weights for the synthetic asset for British Petroleum (BP.L) $\lambda = 0.1$

regularisation has decreased the effectiveness of the synthetic asset as a hedging portfolio. This should not be surprising, as in the limit we would expect a heavily regularised synthetic asset to closely match the equally-weighted portfolio, which we know is not a very good hedge in this case.

It is easy to confirm that moving to the opposite extreme also leads to a performance degradation: with the ridge factor set to zero, not only does the sum of absolute weights rise to the unattractive 404% mentioned above, but the residual variance of 611.01 (53% reduction) is also worse than the 423 (67%) for the intermediate case of $\lambda = 0.01$. These results indicate a pattern which is typical of much statistical modelling: a certain degree of regularisation tends to be beneficial, but beyond a certain point the smoothing becomes excessive and begins to degrade the model performance.

Whilst the case of this one model, for BP, is both interesting and illustrative, it is important to know whether these results are merely a lucky "one off" or whether they represent an approach which can be applied more generally. For this reason the final worksheet in the analysis, called "Results Summary", contains a table of results generated by taking each of the 50 assets in turn as the "target" asset. A particular sample of these results is shown in Table 2.5.

Table 2.5 Performance of cointegration model across the universe of equities

Stock	VarRed	MktRed	RelImp	HdgeFac	In-sample	Out-sample	SumWts	AbsSumWts
BP.L	67%	2%	65%	0.01	700	293	100%	166%
BT.L	47%	31%	16%	0.01	700	293	103%	373%
GSK.L	56%	38%	18%	0.01	700	293	100%	188%
CGEP.PA	82%	58%	24%	0.01	700	293	114%	506%
UBSZn.VX	46%	49%	−3%	0.01	700	293	100%	143%
DCXGn.DE	−1%	46%	−47%	0.01	700	293	101%	289%
BP.L	67%	2%	65%	0.01	700	293	100%	166%
AZN.L	54%	37%	17%	0.01	700	293	98%	172%
NOK1V.HE	62%	36%	27%	0.01	700	293	101%	377%
NOVZn.VX	−37%	−50%	13%	0.01	700	293	101%	170%
ERICb.ST	67%	42%	25%	0.01	700	293	93%	396%
PHG.AS	31%	31%	0%	0.01	700	293	96%	193%
ING.AS	39%	60%	−21%	0.01	700	293	104%	165%
AAH.AS	39%	40%	−1%	0.01	700	293	100%	141%
AEGN.AS	86%	64%	22%	0.01	700	293	101%	230%
UNc.AS	21%	−68%	88%	0.01	700	293	98%	179%
RD.AS	68%	67%	1%	0.01	700	293	102%	160%
RUKZn.VX	69%	62%	8%	0.01	700	293	98%	154%
ROCZg.VX	−60%	46%	−105%	0.01	700	293	99%	158%
EAUG.PA	49%	41%	8%	0.01	700	293	105%	231%
SAN.MC	86%	79%	7%	0.01	700	293	101%	117%
NESZn.VX	32%	−43%	75%	0.01	700	293	98%	148%
CARR.PA	39%	50%	−11%	0.01	700	293	100%	277%
BNPP.PA	3%	−42%	45%	0.01	700	293	93%	151%
AV.L	26%	40%	−15%	0.01	700	293	103%	163%
AXAF.PA	60%	56%	4%	0.01	700	293	103%	154%
ZURZn.VX	75%	64%	11%	0.01	700	293	107%	289%

Table 2.5   (*continued*)

Stock	VarRed	MktRed	RelImp	HdgeFac	In-sample	Out-sample	SumWts	AbsSumWts
TOTF.PA	57%	−6%	64%	0.01	700	293	98%	161%
LYOE.PA	53%	29%	24%	0.01	700	293	98%	152%
OREP.PA	−140%	−161%	21%	0.01	700	293	97%	130%
TIT.MI	76%	83%	−6%	0.01	700	293	100%	224%
ENI.MI	44%	−48%	91%	0.01	700	293	99%	152%
EONG.DE	−28%	−104%	75%	0.01	700	293	98%	157%
SIEGn.DE	63%	37%	26%	0.01	700	293	99%	211%
DBKGn.DE	70%	64%	6%	0.01	700	293	101%	196%
GASI.MI	37%	56%	−19%	0.01	700	293	103%	169%
DTEGn.DE	46%	60%	−13%	0.01	700	293	98%	379%
BBVA.MC	81%	86%	−5%	0.01	700	293	102%	154%
ALVG.DE	88%	73%	15%	0.01	700	293	100%	174%
BAYG.DE	63%	69%	−6%	0.01	700	293	106%	185%
BARC.L	71%	−26%	97%	0.01	700	293	100%	190%
HSBA.L	71%	44%	27%	0.01	700	293	99%	211%
DGE.L	23%	−48%	71%	0.01	700	293	97%	155%
LLOY.L	−61%	−97%	36%	0.01	700	293	99%	196%
PRU.L	67%	62%	5%	0.01	700	293	98%	202%
RBOS.L	66%	−48%	115%	0.01	700	293	96%	219%
SHEL.L	33%	53%	−20%	0.01	700	293	102%	157%
VOD.L	33%	23%	10%	0.01	700	293	104%	207%
TEF.MC	77%	57%	20%	0.01	700	293	101%	237%
MUVGn.DE	70%	61%	9%	0.01	700	293	99%	228%
CSGZn.VX	47%	69%	−22%	0.01	700	293	102%	147%
Mean	42%	24%	18%	0.01	700	293	100%	206%
Median	53%	43%	12%	0.01	700	293	100%	176%

The metrics in the table are precisely the same as those which are presented for individual models on the "CointAnalysis" worksheet (and in fact are directly derived from those values). Whilst the performance varies substantially from one equity to another, the figures for both mean and median performance confirm the general applicability of the approach. During what has been a very turbulent time for the equity markets, the synthetic hedge portfolios manage to reduce the out-of-sample volatility by a factor of 42% (mean) or 53% (median) – note that the mean performance is more heavily affected by one or two particularly unsuccessful "outliers". This performance represents a significant improvement over that obtained by hedging using an equally weighted combination of assets representing the market portfolio. These results suggest that the cointegration approach to hedging asset-specific risk deserves to be taken seriously.

Our study also provides some evidence to support the possibility of creating statistical arbitrage strategies based on cointegration effects within this set of equities. Evidence for the presence of mean-reverting components in the asset price dynamics is reflected in the downward-sloping variance ratio profiles shown in Figure 2.20.

Both the mean and median profiles show a significant decline in normalised variance, with the 30-day variance just under 70% of that which would be expected from

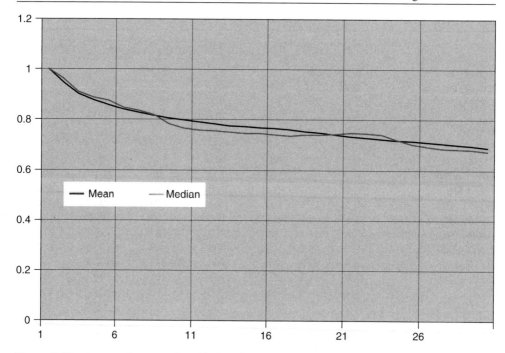

Figure 2.20   Average (mean and median) variance ratio profiles for the residual dynamics, calculated across the full set of 50 equities

extrapolating the 1-day variance. This evidence in itself is clearly not conclusive, especially considering the non-synchronous nature of our data sampling due to the different closing times in the various markets. However, this result, together with previous studies (e.g. Burgess, 1999) seems to strongly suggest that reverting components exist in the asset-specific components of price volatility which may in principle be open to exploitation using suitable statistical arbitrage strategies.

2.7   DISCUSSION AND CONCLUSIONS

The major objective of our methodology is to construct combinations of time series which are either decorrelated with major sources of economic risk and/or contain a deterministic (and hence potentially predictable) component in the dynamics.

Given a particular asset there are two main methods for constructing combinations of one or more assets with similar net exposures to market-wide risk factors. The cointegration tools described in this chapter represent an "implicit" approach to factor modelling in which neither the factors nor the sensitivities are estimated explicitly, but are instead addressed from the perspective of the impact which they cause on sets of related asset prices.

The standard approach to estimating explicit factor models is to postulate a set of financial and economic variables as the risk factors and to use regression-based techniques to estimate the sensitivity coefficients $\beta_{i,j}$ (e.g. the sensitivity of a particular stock to, say, long-term interest rates). Evidence for mean-reverting dynamics in the residuals of factor models was reported by Jacobs and Levy (1988). However, the task of constructing such models is a difficult problem in itself, and the interested reader is directed to a recent extensive study by Bentz (1999).

A second approach which is sometimes referred to as "statistical" factor modelling is to perform multivariate analysis of asset price returns and reconstruct the unobserved risk factors as linear combinations of observed asset returns. The technique of "principal components analysis" (PCA) is a natural tool in this case as it generates sequences of linear combinations (factors) which account for the greatest possible amount of the total variance, subject to the constraint of being orthogonal to the previous factors in the sequence. Some examples of applications of PCA to statistical arbitrage modelling are described in Burgess (1996), Schreiner (1998), Towers (1998), Tjangdjaja *et al.* (1998) and Towers and Burgess (1998).

Still within the area of statistical factor modelling, a generalisation of PCA which has recently attracted much attention in engineering disciplines is so-called "independent components analysis" (ICA), which is based upon algorithms developed for the blind separation of signals (Bell and Sejnowski, 1995; Amari *et al.*, 1996). In ICA the orthogonality condition of PCA is strengthened to one of complete statistical *independence*, thus taking into account higher moments. Whilst ICA techniques offer exciting potential in computational finance, particularly in that they account not only for expectations ("returns") but also for variances ("risk"), applications in this domain are still rare (see Moody and Wu (1997), Back and Weigend (1998)).

The explicit and statistical factor modelling approaches are those which are currently most used in practice, with explicit factor models typically used for hedging and risk control and statistical factor models typically used from a statistical arbitrage perspective. However we believe that the implicit factor modelling offered by the cointegration approach presents a viable alternative to these more established techniques, both for hedging and for trading. By dealing with asset prices directly, cointegration modelling presents both technical and conceptual advantages over the other methods. The technical motivation for the cointegration approach is that it avoids the need for explicit estimation of risk factors and factor sensitivities, thus eliminating a potential source of estimation error from the modelling process as a whole. The conceptual benefit of the cointegration approach is that it can be viewed as a sophisticated version of "relative value" analysis. The synthetic assets constructed by the cointegration procedure can be viewed from a hedging perspective as "tracking baskets" and from a statistical arbitrage perspective as "synthetic pairs" and thus are consistent with the way in which many traders naturally consider relationships between sets of assets. The cointegration approach also has its weaknesses, for instance there are many different methods for constructing cointegration relationships and it is not clear which works best in practice. Furthermore, in some cases it is a positive benefit to explicitly model market-wide risk factors, particularly if they are felt to contain predictable components. Thus, whilst there are both pros and cons to the cointegration approach, we feel that in a practical discipline such as investment finance it is important to take a "broad church" view and apply whichever set of tools works best in a given situation. The aim of this chapter has been to provide a demonstration of and a motivation for the relatively unused cointegration approach, in order to add another set of tools to the financial toolbox.

In conclusion, this chapter has examined the application of the econometric concept of cointegration as a tool for hedging and trading international equities. Section 2.2 introduced cointegration within the perspective of different frameworks for analysing and modelling financial time series. Sections 2.3 and 2.4 described two complementary perspectives in which cointegration is viewed as a basis for implicitly hedging unknown risk factors and also as a basis for suggesting possible opportunities for statistical arbitrage. Section 2.5 provided a controlled simulation in which the cointegration approach was demonstrated upon artificial time series with known properties. Finally, the spreadsheet analysis in Section 2.6 demonstrates an application of these tools to a real-world problem. The data used for this demonstration consisted of the daily closing prices of the 50 equities which constituted the STOXX 50 index as of 4 July 2002, analysed over a period from 14 September 1998 to 3 July 2002. We have noted that the use of daily closing prices will introduce some spurious effects due to the non-synchronous closing times of the markets on which these equities trade, so the specific results themselves can only be taken as indicative of a more realistic study. This caveat admitted, the results nevertheless serve both to illustrate the use of the tools and also to suggest the potential benefits which may be gained from their intelligent application to the tasks of hedging and trading international equities.

REFERENCES

Amari, S., A. Cichocki and H. H. Yang (1996), "A New Learning Algorithm for Blind Signal Separation", in D. S. Touretzky *et al.* (eds), *Advances in Neural Information Processing Systems 8*, MIT Press, Cambridge, MA, pp. 757–763.

Back, A. D. and A. S. Weigend (1998), "Discovering Structure in Finance using Independent Component Analysis", in A-P. N. Refenes *et al.* (eds), *Decision Technologies for Computational Finance*, Kluwer Academic Publishers, Dordrecht, pp. 309–322.

Bell, A. and T. Sejnowski (1995), "An Information-maximisation Approach to Blind Separation and Blind Deconvolution", *Neural Computation*, 7(6), 1129–1159.

Bentz, Y. (1999), *Identifying and Modelling Conditional Factor Sensitivities: An Application to Equity Investment Management*, unpublished PhD thesis, London Business School.

Burgess, A. N. (1996), "Statistical Yield Curve Arbitrage in Eurodollar Futures using Neural Networks", in A-P. N. Refenes *et al.* (eds), *Neural Networks in Financial Engineering*, World Scientific, Singapore, pp. 98–110.

Burgess, A. N. (1999), *A Computational Methodology for Modelling the Dynamics of Statistical Arbitrage*, unpublished PhD thesis, London Business School. (http://cocreativity.net/papers.html).

Cochrane, J. H. (1988), "How Big is the Random Walk in GNP?", *Journal of Political Economy*, **96**, 5, 893–920.

Engle, R. F. and C. W. J. Granger (1987), "Cointegration and Error-correction: Representation, Estimation and Testing", *Econometrica*, **55**, 251–276.

Granger, C. W. J. (1983), "Cointegrated Variables and Error-correcting Models", *UCSD Discussion Paper*.

Hoerl, A. E. and R. W. Kennard (1970a), "Ridge Regression: Biased Estimation for Nonorthogonal Problems", *Technometrics*, **12**, 55–67.

Hoerl, A. E. and R. W. Kennard (1970b), "Ridge Regression: Application to Nonorthogonal Problems", *Technometrics*, **12**, 69–82.

Hull, J. C. (1993), *Options, Futures and Other Derivative Securities*, Prentice Hall, Englewood Cliffs, NJ.

Jacobs, B. I. and K. N. Levy (1988), "Disentangling Equity Return Regularities: New Insights and Investment Opportunities", *Financial Analysts Journal*, May–June 1988, 18–43.

Lo, A. W. and A. C. MacKinlay (1988), "Stock Market Prices Do Not Follow Random Walks: Evidence from a Simple Specification Test", *The Review of Financial Studies*, 1988, **1**, 1, 41–66.

Moody, J. E. and L. Wu (1997), "What is the 'True Price'? – State Space Models for High-frequency FX Data", in A. S. Weigend *et al.* (eds), *Decision Technologies for Financial Engineering*, World Scientific, Singapore, pp. 346–358.

Ross, S. A. (1976), "The Arbitrage Pricing Theory of Capital Asset Pricing", *Journal of Economic Theory*, **13**, 341–360.

Schreiner, P. (1998), *Statistical Arbitrage in Euromark Futures using Intraday Data*, unpublished MSc thesis, Department of Mathematics, King's College, London.

Sharpe, W. F. (1964), "Capital Asset Prices: A Theory of Market Equilibrium", *Journal of Finance*, **19**, 425–442.

Tjangdjaja, J., P. Lajbcygier and N. Burgess (1998), "Statistical Arbitrage Using Principal Component Analysis For Term Structure of Interest Rates", in L. Xu *et al.* (eds), *Intelligent Data Engineering and Learning*, Springer-Verlag, Singapore, pp. 43–53.

Towers, N. (1998), *Statistical Fixed Income Arbitrage*, Deliverable Report D4.6, ESPRIT project "High performance Arbitrage detection and Trading" (HAT), Decision Technology Centre, London Business School.

Towers, N. (2000), *Decision Technologies for Trading Predictability in Financial Markets*, unpublished PhD thesis, London Business School.

Towers, N. and A. N. Burgess (1998), "Optimisation of Trading Strategies using Parametrised Decision Rules", in L. Xu *et al.* (eds), *Intelligent Data Engineering and Learning*, Springer-Verlag, Singapore, pp. 163–170.

3

Modelling the Term Structure of Interest Rates: An Application of Gaussian Affine Models to the German Yield Curve[*]

NUNO CASSOLA AND JORGE BARROS LUÍS

ABSTRACT

This chapter shows that a two-factor constant volatility model describes quite well the time series and the cross sectional behaviour of the German yield curve between 1972 and 1998. The empirical analysis supports the expectations theory with constant term premiums. Thus, an average term premium structure can be calculated and short-term interest rate expectations can be derived from the adjusted forward rate curve. The non-observable factors that explain the German yield curve are extracted using a Kalman filter technique. Following the conjecture that these factors capture, respectively, the expected short-term real interest rate and the expected inflation rate, alternative methods of identifying one of the factors with the inflation process are discussed. The first factor (real interest rate) is more important for explaining interest rate movements at the short-end of the yield curve. The second factor (inflation) carries greater weight in explaining the longer end of the yield curve. These findings are of interest to risk managers for analysing the shape of the yield curve under different scenarios and to policy makers for assessing the impact of fiscal and monetary policies. The Matlab codes necessary to reproduce the results are presented in great detail.

3.1 INTRODUCTION

The identification of the factors that determine the time-series and cross-section behaviour of the term structure of interest rates is a recurrent topic in the finance literature. Even though the interest rates for different maturities typically exhibit high correlations, these are far from being perfectly correlated. The main conclusion from the literature is that the yield curve is determined by different factors, usually described by its level, slope and curvature. Nevertheless, the identification of the yield curve factors is a controversial subject that has several empirical and practical implications, namely for the management of portfolios of fixed income securities, influencing the investment and hedging strategies within the context of portfolios of fixed income securities.

---

[*] This chapter is based on Cassola and Luís (2003) and on the PhD thesis of the second author (Luís, 2001).

Applied Quantitative Methods for Trading and Investment. Edited by C.L. Dunis, J. Laws and P. Naïm
© 2003 John Wiley & Sons, Ltd ISBN: 0-470-84885-5

Moreover, a better knowledge of these factors would facilitate the task of risk managers, in particular for Value-at-Risk (VaR) purposes. In fact by simulating different paths for the factors the behaviour of the yield curve under different scenarios could be traced and alternative empirical distributions for interest rates could be retrieved (see e.g. Bolder (2001)). The analysis of the determining factors of the yield curve is also relevant for policy makers, namely in assessing the impact of monetary and fiscal policies (see, for instance, Fleming and Remolona (1998) and Bliss (1997)).

In this chapter, the German yield curve is analysed, given its relevance in the international bond markets and its informational content about future macroeconomic developments in one of the major European Union economies. Two databases are used in this chapter, the files "datgerse.txt" and "datgersb.txt", which are both included on the CD-Rom. The first database comprises monthly averages of nine daily spot rates for maturities of 1 and 3 months and 1, 2, 3, 4, 5, 7 and 10 years, between January 1986 and December 1998. The spot rates were estimated using the Nelson and Siegel (1987) and Svensson (1994) smoothing techniques from raw market data on euro–Deutschemark short-term interest rates and par yields of German government bonds.[1] The smoothed estimates were used to construct one-period forward rates and perform forward rate regressions.[2]

As illustrated in Figure 3.1, the German end-month interest rates fluctuated markedly in the period from January 1986 to December 1998 (between 3% and 10%). These interest rate moves corresponded to significant shifts in the shape of the yield curve (Figure 3.2). In fact, during this period the yield curve moved from a flat pattern to a positively sloped curve. The sharp deceleration of the German economic growth between 1992 and 1993 was accompanied by a negatively sloped yield curve. Finally, at the end of the sample period, the yield curve returned to an almost null slope, achieving the lowest levels in the sample.

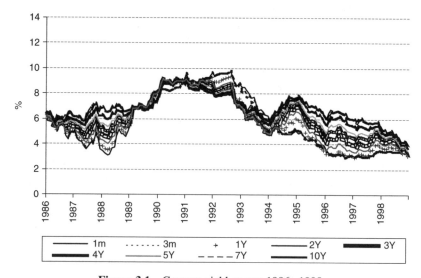

Figure 3.1   German yield curve: 1986–1998

[1] A TSP 4.3 routine was written for the estimation of spot rates. A likelihood ratio test was adopted for choosing between the Nelson and Siegel (1987) and the Svensson (1994) methods, in each sample day, as described in Cassola and Luís (1996).

[2] On this issue the research assistance of Fátima Silva, then affiliated with the Research Department of the Banco de Portugal, is acknowledged.

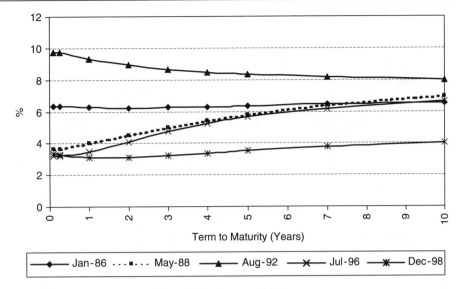

Figure 3.2   German yield curves

The second database for Germany covers a longer period, between September 1972 and December 1998.[3] However this sample includes only spot rates for annual maturities between 1 and 10 years, excluding the 9-year maturity (Figure 3.3). For the overlapping period, interest rates in the two data sets are very similar for equivalent maturities, which suggests robustness of market data and smoothing techniques.

The analysis assumes that bond yields are functions of several macroeconomic and financial variables, observable or latent. In affine models, parameters are linear in both the maturity of the assets and the factors, which makes these models easier to implement.[4] Additionally, compared to principal component analysis, affine models have the advantage of allowing for correlation among the factors, providing several outputs that are relevant for financial market participants and policy makers, such as forward rates and the structure of term premia.

Affine models are the result of four decades of evolution in asset pricing theory. In the context of yield curve modelling these can be seen as developments of the one-factor models by Vasicek (1977) and Cox *et al.* (1985a), where the short-term interest rate was the single factor.[5] Multifactor models were developed because of the discrepancy between the yield curve implied by the theory and the observed time-series properties of bond yields, namely the fact that the observed curves are substantially more concave than implied by the theory (see, for instance, Backus *et al.* (1998)).[6]

---

[3] We are grateful to Manfred Kremer, then affiliated with the Research Department of the Bundesbank, for providing the data.

[4] See Campbell *et al.* (1997, chap. 11) or Backus *et al.* (1998) for graduate textbook presentations of affine models.

[5] These models differ basically due to the fact that the latter allowed for the volatility of the short-term interest rate to be stochastic. In order to incorporate the supply side of financial assets, Cox *et al.* (1985b) derived a general equilibrium model that yields a closed-form expression for asset prices.

[6] One of the first multifactor models was developed by Ross (1976), with the Arbitrage Pricing Theory (APT). Contrary to the consumption CAPM (CCAPM) developed by Breeden (1979), the APT does not try to identify the factors with the consumption marginal rate of substitution.

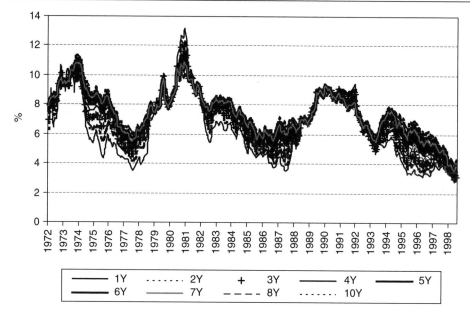

Figure 3.3   German yield curve: 1986–1998

Most papers on affine models have focused on the US term structure. The pronounced hump-shape of the US yield curve and the empirical work pioneered by Litterman and Scheinkman (1991) have led to the conclusion that three factors are required to explain the movements of the whole term structure of interest rates. These factors are usually identified as the level, the slope and the curvature of the term structure. Most studies have concluded that the level is the most important factor in explaining interest rate variations over time.

Moreover, given the apparent stochastic properties of the volatility of interest rates, Gaussian or constant volatility models are often rejected. Therefore, several papers have used three-factor models with stochastic volatility in order to fit the term structure of interest rates (see, for instance, Balduzzi *et al.* (1996) and Gong and Remolona (1997a)).

However, stochastic volatility models pose admissibility problems, as the factors determining the volatility of interest rates enter "square rooted" and thus must be positive. In addition, the parameters of a three-factor model with stochastic volatility are often very difficult to estimate. In fact, frequently small deviations of the parameters from the estimated values generate widely different and implausible term structures.

Alternatively a constant volatility or Gaussian model can be fitted. In the German case, Figure 3.1 suggests that this may be a reasonable choice, though in this chart end-month data is presented. These models overcome the empirical problems posed by stochastic volatility models and are also capable of reproducing a wide variety of shapes of the yield curve, though they face some shortcomings regarding the limiting properties of the instantaneous forward rate.[7]

Furthermore, some term structures may have properties identifiable with a smaller number of factors. For instance, according to Buhler *et al.* (1999), principal component

---

[7] See, e.g., Campbell *et al.* (1997), p. 433, on the limitations of a one-factor homoskedastic model.

analysis reveals that two factors explain more than 95% of the variation in the German term structure of interest rates consistently from 1970 up to 1999. Consequently, a decision on the number of factors is also required.

The flexibility of affine models allows for considering observable as well as non-observable factors, such as macroeconomic variables. The advantage of estimating these models using only latent or non-observable factors is that it avoids making *ex-ante* restrictions on the behaviour of the factors determining the yield curve. In this chapter, we will start by incorporating only latent factors.

In order to fit affine models to a cross-section/time-series of interest rates three practical questions have to be answered: (i) how many factors should be considered; (ii) what are the properties of the factors; and (iii) how can they be identified. A sensible way to proceed about the first question is by performing forward rate regressions in line with Backus *et al.* (1997), to assess the adequacy of Gaussian models.

Regarding the second question, two- and three-factor models were estimated.[8] Given that the two-factor Gaussian model can be specified in such a way that the short-term interest rate is equal to the sum of a constant with the two latent factors, the usual conjecture is that these factors reflect the real interest rate and the expected inflation rate.[9] A third factor may be included reflecting potential international influences on the domestic yield curve. Considering the fact that the two- and three-factor models are nested, a chi-square test can be used to select the best model.

Regarding the third issue, the link between the two factors and observable variables is assessed in three different ways: the first two are based on the explicit identification of one of the factors with the inflation rate and relating the other factor to the *ex-ante* real interest rate, in line with Zin (1997). Within this framework, a first exercise consisted in identifying one factor with the inflation rate process, modelled as an AR(1) process, following Fung *et al.* (1999). The second factor was left unconstrained and assumed to reflect the "real" determinants of the term structure of interest rates, such as the output gap or the real interest rate.

A second exercise was performed based on the assumption that the inflation is given by two factors, one of them being a common factor with the term structure. The joint factor can be taken as a proxy for core inflation. It can be shown that this assumption provides the general case of a joint model developed in Fung *et al.* (1999), where the factor loadings are not restricted to the values of the parameters of the interest rate loadings. Consequently, the second factor of the term structure is left unconstrained and should reflect the "real" determinants of the term structure of interest rates, such as the output gap or the real interest rate, while the second factor of inflation should reflect non-core inflation movements.[10] The third way chosen to analyse the identification issue

---

[8] The three-factor model was run only for the shorter database, given that the longer database does not include information on the money market rates. Therefore, it is reasonable to assume that two factors are enough to explain the behaviour of the yield curve in the range of maturities included in that database.

[9] This corresponds to the Fisher hypothesis. The two-factor model is also consistent with the idea that the Bundesbank followed a type of Taylor rule in setting official interest rates as recently documented by Clarida *et al.* (1998) and Clarida and Gertler (1997). In accordance with such a rule the short-term interest rate was adjusted in response to the deviation of inflation and output from their targets.

[10] In Remolona *et al.* (1998), inflation-indexed bonds issued by the UK government are used for this purpose. However, these securities do not exist in Germany. Consequently, the analysis in this chapter is conducted on a nominal basis, following Campbell *et al.* (1997). The best-known examples of inflation-linked securities are the inflation-indexed government bonds that exist only in a few countries, namely in the UK, the USA and France (see, for instance, Deacon and Derry (1994) and Gong and Remolona (1997b)).

is based on econometric evidence about the leading indicator properties of one factor for inflation developments in Germany.

The latent factors are estimated by a Kalman filter, while a maximum likelihood procedure is used to estimate the time-constant parameters of the yield curve, following the pioneering work by Chen and Scott (1993a,b).[11] This econometric technique allows a wide range of model specifications (including observable and non-observable factors), which compute the optimal estimate for the state variables at a given moment using all the past information available. In Figure 3.4 the reader finds a brief summary of the exercise performed in this chapter.

Two Matlab routines, supplied on the accompanying CD-Rom, were used for each of the three model specifications, one for the Kalman filter and the other for the maximum likelihood estimation. The leading properties of the factor were assessed using a RATS 4.0 standard program.[12] The results obtained in this chapter illustrate that both two- and three-factor models fit quite well the yield and the volatility curves, also providing reasonable estimates for the one-period forward and term premium curves.[13]

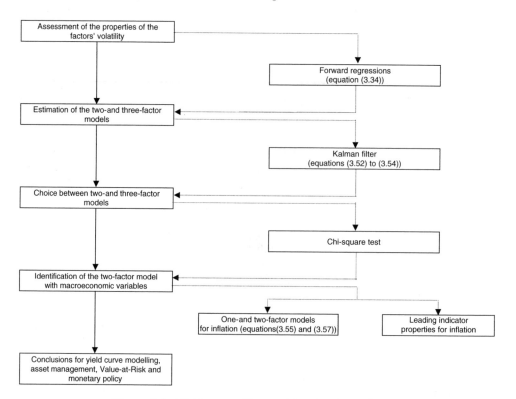

Figure 3.4   Yield curve affine models using latent factors

---

[11] The model is derived in discrete time, as in this way it matches the frequency of the data, allows the identification of the factors with observable macroeconomic variables and avoids the problem of estimating a continuous-time model with discrete-time data (see, for example, Aït-Sahalia (1996)).

[12] The chapter does not present the routine to assess the leading indicator properties, given that a routine adapted from Doan (1995) was used.

[13] The Matlab codes were written based upon codes made available by Mike Wickens and Eli Remolona. Initially, the two-factor model was run only with the equations for the yields, disregarding the volatilities. The

However, two periods of poorer model performance are identified, both related to world-wide gyrations in bond markets – Spring 1994 and 1998 – which were characterised by sharp changes in long-term interest rates while short-term rates remained stable. Thus, it seems that the third factor fails to capture the potential external influences on German interest rates. In addition, the two-factor model fits quite well the yield and the volatility curve, providing a good fit of the time series of bond yields and more reasonable estimates for the one-period forward and term premium curves than the three-factor model.

The remainder of the chapter is structured as follows. In Section 3.2 some background on asset pricing is presented. In Section 3.3 the theoretical framework of Duffie and Kan (1996) (DK hereafter) affine models is explained. In Section 3.4 a test of the expectations theory is developed that will be used to empirically motivate the Gaussian model. In Section 3.5 we discuss alternative ways of identifying the factors in the model. The econometric methodology is presented in Section 3.6. Section 3.7 includes the presentation of the data and the results of the estimation. The main conclusions are stated in Section 3.8.

3.2   BACKGROUND ISSUES ON ASSET PRICING

A fundamental result in modern asset pricing theory is that the price of any financial asset corresponds to the present value of its expected future cash-flows, this present value being obtained by applying a positive stochastic discount factor (hereafter sdf, denoted by M_t). If the future cash-flows correspond only to the financial asset price in the next period we have:

$$P_t = E_t[P_{t+1}M_{t+1}] \tag{3.1}$$

Another fundamental result in finance theory is that asset prices and returns are related to their risk, which is the ability of the asset to offer higher cash-flows when they are more needed. In fact, the more an asset helps to smooth income fluctuations, the less risky it is and the higher will be its demand for insuring against "bad times". Employing some simple algebra in equation (3.1), the following equation illustrates this link between asset prices and their risk:

$$P_t = E_t[P_{t+1}]\frac{1}{1 + i_{t+1}^f} + \text{Cov}_t[P_{t+1}, M_{t+1}] \tag{3.2}$$

This result shows that the asset price is the discounted expected value of its future payoff, adjusted by the covariance of its payoff with the sdf and where the discount factor is the inverse of the return on a risk-free asset. The covariance term consists of a risk factor and it is positive for assets that pay higher returns when they are more needed. The same result may be obtained for interest rates, instead of prices:

$$E_t[i_{t+1}] = i_{t+1}^f - \frac{\text{Cov}_t[M_{t+1}, i_{t+1}]}{E_t[M_{t+1}]} \tag{3.3}$$

---

estimates obtained for the volatilities proved unreasonable. Consequently, we opted for including the volatility equations in the Kalman filter. This procedure can be considered as corresponding to estimating the model imposing restrictions on the parameters in order to get well-behaved volatility curves.

According to equation (3.3), the excess return of any asset over the risk-free asset depends on the covariance of its rate of return with the stochastic discount factor. Thus, an asset whose payoff has a negative correlation with the stochastic discount factor pays a risk premium. With some additional self-explanatory algebra, the following result is obtained:

$$E_t[i_{t+1}] = i_{t+1}^f + \frac{\text{Cov}_t[M_{t+1}, i_{t+1}]}{\text{Var}_t[M_{t+1}]} \left(-\frac{\text{Var}_t[M_{t+1}]}{E_t[M_{t+1}]} \right) = i_{t+1}^f + \beta_{i_{t+1}, M_{t+1}} \lambda_t \qquad (3.4)$$

In equation (3.4), $\beta_{i_{t+1}, M_{t+1}}$ is the coefficient of a regression of i_{t+1} on M_{t+1}, i.e., it measures the correlation between the asset's return and the sdf or the quantity of risk, while $\lambda_t = -\text{Var}_t[M_{t+1}]/E_t[M_{t+1}]$ is the market price of risk. Therefore, as in the static CAPM, the excess return over the risk-free interest rate of any financial asset depends on the quantity of risk and its market price.

3.3 DUFFIE–KAN AFFINE MODELS OF THE TERM STRUCTURE

Affine models are built upon a log-linear relationship between asset prices and the sdf, on the one side, and the factors or state variables, on the other side. These models were originally developed by Duffie and Kan (1996), for the term structure of interest rates. As referred to in Balduzzi et al. (1996), "Duffie and Kan (1996) show that a wide range of choices of stochastic processes for interest rate factors yield bond pricing solutions of a form now widely called exponential-affine models".

Let us start by writing equation (3.1) in logs:

$$p_t = \log(E_t[P_{t+1} M_{t+1}]) \qquad (3.5)$$

where lowercase letters denote the logs of the corresponding uppercase letters. With the assumption of joint log-normality of bond prices and the nominal pricing kernel and using the statistical result that if $\log X \sim N(\mu, \sigma^2)$ then $\log E(X) = \mu + \sigma^2/2$ it is obtained from equation (3.5) that:

$$p_t = E_t[m_{t+1} + p_{t+1}] + \tfrac{1}{2}\text{Var}_t[m_{t+1} + p_{t+1}] \qquad (3.6)$$

Duffie and Kan (1996) define a general class of multifactor affine models of the term structure, where the log of the pricing kernel is a linear function of several factors $s_t^{\text{T}} = (s_{1,t}, \ldots, s_{k,t})$. DK models offer the advantage of nesting the most important term structure models, from Vasicek (1977) and Cox et al. (1985a) one-factor models to three-factor models like the one presented in Gong and Remolona (1997a). An additional feature of these models is that they allow the estimation of the term structure simultaneously on a cross-section and a time-series basis. Furthermore they provide a way of computing and estimating simple closed-form expressions for the spot, forward, volatility and term premium curves.

Expressed in discrete time, the discount factors in DK models are specified as:

$$-m_{t+1} = \xi + \gamma^{\text{T}} s_t + \lambda^{\text{T}} V(s_t)^{1/2} \varepsilon_{t+1} \qquad (3.7)$$

where $V(s_t)$ is the variance–covariance matrix of the random shocks to the sdf and is defined as a diagonal matrix with elements $v_i(z_t) = \alpha_i + \beta_i^T s_t$. Under certain conditions, the volatility functions $v_i(s_t)$ are positive;[14] β_i has non-negative elements and ε_t are the independent shocks normally distributed as $\varepsilon_t \sim N(0, I)$. Following equation (3.4), the parameters in λ^T are the market prices of risk, as they govern the covariance between the stochastic discount factor and the latent factors of the yield curve. Thus, the higher these parameters are the higher is the covariance between the discount factor and the asset return and the lower is its expected rate of return or the less risky the asset is (when the covariance is negative).

The k-dimensional vector of factors s_t is defined as follows:

$$s_{t+1} = (I - \Phi)\theta + \Phi s_t + V(s_t)^{1/2}\varepsilon_{t+1} \tag{3.8}$$

where Φ has positive diagonal elements which ensure that the factors are stationary and θ is the long-run mean of the factors. Asset prices are also log-linear functions of the factors. Adding a second subscript in order to identify the term to maturity (denoted by n), bond prices are given as follows:

$$-p_{n,t} = A_n + B_n^T s_t \tag{3.9}$$

where A_n is a parameter and B_n a vector of parameters to be estimated. The parameters in B_n are commonly known as the factor loadings, given that their values measure the impact of a one-standard deviation shock to the factors on the log of asset prices.

In term structure models, the identification of the parameters is easier, considering the restrictions imposed by the maturing bond price. In fact, when the term structure is modelled using zero-coupon bonds paying one monetary unit, the log of the price of a maturing bond must be zero. Consequently, from equation (3.6), the common normalisation $A_0 = B_0 = 0$ results. The following recursive restrictions between the parameters are obtained by computing the moments in equation (3.6), using equations (3.7) and (3.9), equating the independent terms and the terms in s_t in equation (3.8) respectively to A_n and B_n in equation (3.9) and assuming $p_{0,t} = 0$ and independent shocks:

$$A_n = A_{n-1} + \xi + B_{n-1}^T(I - \Phi)\theta - \frac{1}{2}\sum_{i=1}^{k}(\lambda_i + B_{i,n-1})^2\alpha_i \tag{3.10}$$

$$B_n^T = (\gamma^T + B_{n-1}^T\Phi) - \frac{1}{2}\sum_{i=1}^{k}(\lambda_i + B_{i,n-1})^2\beta_i^T \tag{3.11}$$

Our empirical analysis is based on interest rates of nominal zero-coupon bonds or spot rates, which can easily be computed from bond prices as:

$$y_{n,t} = -\frac{p_{n,t}}{n} \tag{3.12}$$

Consequently, from equations (3.9) and (3.12), the yield curve is defined as:

$$y_{n,t} = \frac{1}{n}(A_n + B_n^T s_t) \tag{3.13}$$

---

[14] See Backus *et al.* (1998).

Using equations (3.10), (3.11) and (3.13), the short-term or one-period interest rate is:

$$y_{1,t} = \xi - \frac{1}{2}\sum_{i=1}^{k}\lambda_i^2\alpha_i + \left[\gamma^{\mathrm{T}} - \frac{1}{2}\sum_{i=1}^{k}\lambda_i^2\beta_i^{\mathrm{T}}\right]s_t \tag{3.14}$$

Correspondingly, the expected value of the short rate is:

$$
\begin{aligned}
E_t(y_{1,t+n}) &= E_t\left(\xi - \frac{1}{2}\sum_{i=1}^{k}\lambda_i^2\alpha_i + \left[\gamma^{\mathrm{T}} - \frac{1}{2}\sum_{i=1}^{k}\lambda_i^2\beta_i^{\mathrm{T}}\right]s_{t+n}\right) \\
&= \xi - \frac{1}{2}\sum_{i=1}^{k}\lambda_i^2\alpha_i + \left[\gamma^{\mathrm{T}} - \frac{1}{2}\sum_{i=1}^{k}\lambda_i^2\beta_i^{\mathrm{T}}\right]E_t(s_{t+n}) \\
&= \xi - \frac{1}{2}\sum_{i=1}^{k}\lambda_i^2\alpha_i + \left(\gamma^{\mathrm{T}} - \frac{1}{2}\sum_{i=1}^{k}\lambda_i^2\beta_i^{\mathrm{T}}\right)[(I - \Phi^n)\theta + \Phi^n s_t] \tag{3.15}
\end{aligned}
$$

The volatility curve of the yields is derived from the variance–covariance matrix in the specification of the factors. From equations (3.8) and (3.13), the volatility curve is given by:

$$\mathrm{Var}_t(y_{n,t+1}) = \frac{1}{n^2}B_n^{\mathrm{T}}V(s_t)B_n \tag{3.16}$$

The instantaneous or one-period forward rate is the log of the inverse of the gross return:

$$f_{n,t} = p_{n,t} - p_{n+1,t} \tag{3.17}$$

According to the definition in equation (3.17), the price equation in (3.9) and the recursive restrictions in (3.13) and (3.14), the one-period forward curve is:

$$
\begin{aligned}
f_{n,t} &= (A_{n+1} + B_{n+1}^{\mathrm{T}}s_t) - (A_n + B_n^{\mathrm{T}}s_t) \\
&= \xi + B_n^{\mathrm{T}}(I - \Phi)\theta - \frac{1}{2}\sum_{i=1}^{k}(\lambda_i + B_{i,n})^2\alpha_i \\
&\quad + \left[\gamma^{\mathrm{T}} + B_n^{\mathrm{T}}(\Phi - I) - \frac{1}{2}\sum_{i=1}^{k}(\lambda_i + B_{i,n})^2\beta_i^{\mathrm{T}}\right]s_t \tag{3.18}
\end{aligned}
$$

The term premium is usually computed as the one-period log excess return of the n-period bond over the short rate. Using equations (3.9)–(3.11) and (3.14), it is equal to:

$$
\begin{aligned}
\Lambda_{n,t} &= E_t p_{n,t+1} - p_{n+1,t} - y_{1,t} \\
&= -\sum_{i=1}^{k}\left[\lambda_i B_{i,n}\alpha_i + \frac{B_{i,n}^2\alpha_i}{2}\right] - \sum_{i=1}^{k}(\lambda_i B_{i,n} + B_{i,n}^2)\beta_i^{\mathrm{T}}s_t \tag{3.19}
\end{aligned}
$$

From equations (3.15), (3.18) and (3.19), one can conclude that the forward rate is equal to the expected future short-term interest rate plus the term premium and a constant term that is related to the mean of the factors. Computing the term premium from the basic pricing equation, the following result is obtained:[15]

$$\Lambda_{n,t} = -\lambda^{\mathrm{T}} V(s_t) B_n - \frac{B_n^{\mathrm{T}} V(s_t) B_n}{2} \tag{3.20}$$

The first component in equation (3.20) is a pure risk premium, where λ is the price associated with the quantity of risk $V(s_t)B_n$. The parameters in λ determine the signal of the term premium. The second component is a Jensen inequality term. From equation (3.20) one can conclude that at least one of the market prices of risk must be negative in order to have a positive term premium.

The model estimated belongs to the class of Gaussian or constant volatility models. It is a generalisation of the Vasicek (1977) one-factor model and a particular case of the DK model, implying that some form of the expectations theory holds. As will be seen, this model seems to be adequate to fit the German term structure, given that the expectations theory is valid to a close approximation in this case. Following equation (3.7), the sdf in a two- or a three-factor Gaussian model is written as:[16]

$$-m_{t+1} = \delta + \sum_{i=1}^{k} \left(\frac{\lambda_i^2}{2} \sigma_i^2 + s_{i,t} + \lambda_i \sigma_i \varepsilon_{i,t+1} \right) \tag{3.21}$$

with $k = 2$ or 3. The factors are assumed to follow a first-order autoregressive order, with zero mean:[17]

$$s_{i,t+1} = \varphi_i s_{i,t} + \sigma_i \varepsilon_{i,t+1} \tag{3.22}$$

Within the DK framework, these models are characterised by:

$$\theta_i = 0$$

$$\Phi = \mathrm{diag}(\varphi_1, \varphi_2)$$

$$\alpha_i = \sigma_i^2$$

$$\beta_i = 0 \tag{3.23}$$

$$\xi = \delta + \sum_{i=1}^{k} \frac{\lambda_i^2}{2} \sigma_i^2$$

$$\gamma_i = 1$$

The recursive restrictions are:

$$A_n = A_{n-1} + \delta + \frac{1}{2} \sum_{i=1}^{k} [\lambda_i^2 \sigma_i^2 - (\lambda_i \sigma_i + B_{i,n-1} \sigma_i)^2] \tag{3.24}$$

$$B_{i,n} = (1 + B_{i,n-1} \varphi_i) \tag{3.25}$$

---

[15] Given that $V(s_t)$ was previously defined as a diagonal matrix with elements $v_i(s_t) = \alpha_i + \beta_i^{\mathrm{T}} s_t$, equation (3.20) corresponds to equation (3.19).

[16] As will be seen later, this specification was chosen in order to write the short-term interest rate as the sum of a constant (δ) with the factors.

[17] This corresponds to considering the differences between the "true" factors and their means.

As can be seen from equation (3.24), in a homoskedastic model, the element on the right-hand side of equation (3.10) related to the risk is zero. Thus, there are no interactions between the risk and the factors influencing the term structure, i.e., the term premium is constant. Given equations (3.14), (3.24) and (3.25), the short-term interest rate is:[18]

$$y_{1,t} = \delta + \sum_{i=1}^{k} s_{i,t} \qquad (3.26)$$

These models have the appealing feature that the short term is the sum of the factors. Our conjecture is that the yield curve may be determined by two factors, one of them being related to inflation and the other to a real factor, possibly the *ex-ante real* interest rate. Following equations (3.24) and (3.25), the one-period forward rate is given by:

$$f_{n,t} = \delta + \frac{1}{2} \sum_{i=1}^{k} \left[\lambda_i^2 \sigma_i^2 - \left(\lambda_i \sigma_i + \frac{1 - \varphi_i^n}{1 - \varphi_i} \sigma_i \right)^2 \right] + \sum_{i=1}^{k} [\varphi_i^n s_{i,t}] \qquad (3.27)$$

This specification of the forward-rate curve accommodates very different shapes. However, the limiting forward rate cannot be simultaneously finite and time-varying. In fact, if $\varphi_i < 1$, the limiting value will not depend on the factors, corresponding to the following expression:[19]

$$\lim_{n \to \infty} f_{n,t} = \delta + \sum_{i=1}^{k} \left[-\frac{\lambda_i \sigma_i^2}{(1 - \varphi_i)} - \frac{\sigma_i^2}{2(1 - \varphi_i)^2} \right] \qquad (3.28)$$

From equations (3.16) and (3.25), the volatility curve is:

$$\text{Var}_t(y_{n,t+1}) = \frac{1}{n^2} \sum_{i=1}^{k} (B_{i,n}^2 \sigma_i^2) \qquad (3.29)$$

Notice that as the factors have constant volatility, given by $\text{Var}_t(s_{i,t+1}) = \sigma_i^2$, the volatility of the yields does not depend on the level of the factors. Finally, the term

---

[18] As referred to in Campbell *et al.* (1997), in a one-factor model setting, the $B_{i,n}$ coefficients in a Gaussian model measure the sensitivity of the log of bond prices to changes in short-term interest rate. This is different from duration, as it does not correspond to the impact on bond prices of changes in the respective yields, but instead in the short rate.

[19] If $\varphi_i = 1$ interest rates are non-stationary. In that case, the limiting value of the instantaneous forward $y_{n,t} = -(p_{n,t}/n)$ is time-varying but assumes infinite values. Effectively, $(1 - \varphi_i^n)/(1 - \varphi_i) = n$ in this case. Thus, the expression for the instantaneous forward will be given by:

$$f_{n,t} = \delta + \sum_{i=1}^{k} \left[-n\lambda_i \sigma_i^2 - \frac{1}{2} n^2 \sigma_i^2 \right] + \sum_{i=1}^{k} s_{i,t}.$$

Accordingly, even if $\lambda_i < 0$, the forward rate curve may start by increasing, but at the longer end it will decrease infinitely. Obviously, if $\lambda_i > 0$, the forward rate curve will decrease monotonously.

premium in these models will be:

$$\Lambda_{n,t} = E_t p_{n,t+1} - p_{n+1,t} - y_{1,t}$$

$$= \frac{1}{2} \sum_{i=1}^{k} \left[\lambda_i^2 \sigma_i^2 - \left(\lambda_i \sigma_i + \frac{1 - \varphi_i^n}{1 - \varphi_i} \sigma_i \right)^2 \right]$$

$$= \sum_{i=1}^{k} \left[-\lambda_i \sigma_i^2 B_{i,n} - \frac{B_{i,n}^2 \sigma_i^2}{2} \right] \tag{3.30}$$

According to equations (3.27) and (3.30), the one-period forward rate in these Gaussian models corresponds to the sum of the term premium with a constant and with the factors weighted by the autoregressive parameters of the factors. Once again, the limiting case is worth noting. When $\varphi_i < 1$, the limiting value of the risk premium differs from the forward only by δ. Thus, within constant volatility models, the expected short-term rate for a very distant settlement date is δ, i.e., the average short-term interest rate. From equations (3.22) and (3.26), the expected value of the short rate for any future date $t + n$ can be computed:

$$E_t(y_{1,t+n}) = \delta + \sum_{i=1}^{k} [\varphi_i^n s_{i,t}] \tag{3.31}$$

Comparing equations (3.27), (3.30) and (3.31) we conclude that the expectations theory of the term structure holds with constant term premiums:[20]

$$f_{n,t} = E_t(y_{1,t+n}) + \Lambda_n \tag{3.32}$$

Thus, assessing the adequacy of Gaussian models corresponds to testing the validity of the expectations theory of the term structure with constant term premiums.

3.4 A FORWARD RATE TEST OF THE EXPECTATIONS THEORY

Equation (3.32) implies that forward rates are martingales if the term structure of risk premium is flat. In fact, by the law of iterated expectations, it is obtained as:

$$f_{n,t} = E_t(E_{t+1}(y_{1,t+n}) + \Lambda_n) = E_t(f_{n-1,t+1}) + (\Lambda_n - \Lambda_{n-1}) \tag{3.33}$$

As in the steady state it is expected that short-term interest rates remain constant, according to equation (3.33) the one-period forward curve should be flat under the absence of risk premium ($\Lambda_n = 0$). As noted by Backus *et al.* (1998), equation (3.33) leads to a forward regression test of the expectations theory of the term structure. The regression is:[21]

$$f_{n-1,t+1} - y_{1,t} = \text{constant} + c_n(f_{n,t} - y_{1,t}) + \text{residual} \tag{3.34}$$

---

[20] Also known as the non-pure version of the expectations theory.
[21] The term related to the slope of the term structure of risk premium is included in the constant, as it is assumed to be time-constant.

with $c_n = 1$. A rejection of this hypothesis can be taken as evidence that term premiums vary with time, i.e., that the expectations theory does not hold.

It can be shown that the theoretical values of c_n implied by the two-factor model correspond to:

$$c_n = \frac{(B_1 + B_n - B_{n+1})^T \Gamma_0 (B_1 - \Phi^T(B_n - B_{n-1}))}{(B_1 + B_n - B_{n+1})^T \Gamma_0 (B_1 + B_n - B_{n+1})} \tag{3.35}$$

In the general case:

$$\lim_{n \to \infty} c_n = \frac{B_1^T \Gamma_0 B_1}{B_1^T \Gamma_0 B_1} = 1 \quad \text{as} \quad B_{n-1} = B_n = B_{n+1} \quad \text{when} \quad n \to \infty$$

3.5   IDENTIFICATION

Contrary to the pioneer interest rate models, such as Cox et al. (1985a), where the short-term interest rate influenced the whole term structure, the latent factor models do not use explicit determinants of the yield curve. Therefore, as referred to in Backus et al. (1997), the major outstanding issue in this context is the economic interpretation of the interest rate behaviour approximated with affine models, in terms of its monetary and real economic factors. Our conjecture is that two factors seem to drive the German term structure of interest rates: one factor related to the *ex-ante* real interest rate and a second factor linked to inflation expectations.

As previously stated, the identification will thus be assessed in three different ways, the first being based on the model developed in Fung et al. (1999). As it is supposed that one of the latent factors is related to inflation, one factor is identified with that variable, which is assumed to be an AR(1) process. The inflation, denoted by π_t, will thus be defined as:[22]

$$(\pi_{t+1} - \overline{\pi}) = \rho(\pi_t - \overline{\pi}) + u_{t+1} \tag{3.36}$$

where $\overline{\pi}$ is the unconditional mean of the inflation rate and ρ is a parameter that measures the rate of mean reversion. Considering that the short-term interest rate is a risk-free rate, as there are no expectation revisions in a one-period investment, the hypothesis is that it is the sum of the short-term real interest rate $(r_{1,t})$ with the one-period inflation rate expectation:

$$y_{1,t} - \delta = (r_{1,t} - \overline{r}) + E_t(\pi_{t+1} - \overline{\pi}) \tag{3.37}$$

where the long-run mean of the short-term interest rate is equal to the sum of the unconditional means of the real interest rate and the inflation rate $(\delta = \overline{r} + \overline{\pi})$. The component of the short-term rate related to the second factor may be considered as the one-period inflation expectation:

$$s_{2,t} = E_t(\pi_{t+1} - \overline{\pi}) = \rho(\pi_t - \overline{\pi}) = \rho\tilde{\pi}_t \tag{3.38}$$

where $\tilde{\pi}_t$ denotes deviation of inflation from the steady-state value.

---

[22] Inflation is measured as the annual change in the log CPI. This measure is preferred because the quarter-on-quarter annualised change in the log CPI is extremely volatile, often with negative readings. Our measure should be interpreted as capturing the underlying or smoothed one-period inflation rate. Inflation is measured as year-on-year changes in the CPI in deviations from its mean, due to the definition of the factors as having zero mean.

From equations (3.36) and (3.38) the value of the second factor in $t + 1$ is:

$$s_{2,t+1} = E_{t+1}(\tilde{\pi}_{t+2}) = \rho\tilde{\pi}_{t+1} = \rho(\rho\tilde{\pi}_t + u_{t+1}) = \rho s_{2,t} + \rho u_{t+1} \qquad (3.39)$$

Comparing equations (3.22) and (3.39), we have the following identification between the parameters of the second factor and the inflation process:

$$\rho = \varphi_2$$
$$\rho u_{t+1} = \sigma_2 \varepsilon_{2,t+1} \qquad (3.40)$$

Using equations (3.38) to (3.40), the following relationship between the inflation and the second factor is obtained:

$$\tilde{\pi}_t = \frac{1}{\varphi_2} s_{2,t} \qquad (3.41)$$

An advantage of this identification procedure is that *ex-ante* real interest rates can be derived. The major drawback of this technique is that it implies the second factor to explain simultaneously the inflation as well as the long-term rates, which in some periods may evidence significantly different volatilities. Consequently, during the periods of higher volatility of the long-term rates, the estimated inflation tends to present a more irregular behaviour than the true inflation.

Secondly, the procedure sketched above is based on the assumption in equation (3.36), which is not necessarily the optimal model for forecasting inflation. In fact, this model is too simple concerning its lag structure and also does not allow for the inclusion of other macroeconomic information that market participants may use to form their expectations of inflation. For example, information about developments in monetary aggregates, commodity prices, exchange rates, wages and unit labour costs, etc., may be used by market participants to forecast inflation and, thus, may be reflected in the bond pricing process. However, a more complex model would certainly not allow a simple identification of the factor.

One way to overcome these problems is by using a joint model for the term structure and the inflation, where the latter still shares a common factor with the interest rates but is also determined by a second specific factor.[23] Thus, inflation can be modelled as a function of two factors:

$$\pi_t = \frac{1}{n}(A_\pi + B_\pi^{\mathrm{T}} s_{\pi,t}) \qquad (3.42)$$

where $\Delta_{\pi t} = (\Delta_{2t}, s_{1\pi,t})^{\mathrm{T}}$ and

$$s_{1\pi,t+1} = \varphi_{1\pi} s_{1\pi,t} + \sigma_{1\pi}\varepsilon_{1\pi,t+1} \qquad (3.43)$$

Comparing to the model developed in Fung *et al.* (1999), this model offers the advantage of not restricting the factor loadings to the values of the parameters of the term structure loadings, as well as providing an additional factor to explain the inflation moves.

---

[23] In this case, the loading of the second factor in the inflation equation is independent from the loading in term structure equations, as no explicit relationship is assumed between the yields and the inflation and, consequently, there are no recursive restrictions between the yields and the inflation.

Therefore, the second term structure factor does not have to be liable simultaneously for the long-term interest rates and the inflation, avoiding more volatile estimates for the inflation in periods of higher volatility of the long-term rates.

In order to overcome the problems detected in the first identification model, the leading indicator properties of $s_{2,t}$ for inflation were also analysed, by setting up a VaR model with p lags:[24]

$$x_t = A_1 x_{t-1} + \cdots + A_p x_{t-p} + \mu + u_t \tag{3.44}$$

where x_t is (2×1) and each of the A_i is a (2×2) matrix of parameters with generic element denoted by $[a_{k,j}^i]$ and $u_t \sim IN(0, \Sigma)$. The vector x_t is defined as $x_t = (\pi_t, s_{2,t})^T$.

Testing whether $s_{2,t}$ has leading indicator properties for inflation corresponds to testing the hypothesis $H_0 : a_{1,2}^1 = \cdots = a_{1,2}^p = 0$. This is a test for Granger causality, i.e., a test of whether past values of the factor along with past values of inflation better "explain" inflation than past values of inflation alone. This of course does not imply that bond yields cause inflation. Instead it means that $s_{2,t}$ is possibly reflecting bond market's expectations as to where inflation might be headed.

In assessing the leading indicator properties of $s_{2,t}$, the Granger causality test can be supplemented with an impulse-response analysis. The vector MA(∞) representation of the VaR is given by:

$$x_t = \mu + u_t + \Psi_1 u_{t-1} + \Psi_2 u_{t-2} + \cdots \tag{3.45}$$

The matrix Ψ_z will then correspond to:

$$\frac{\partial x_{t+z}}{\partial u_t} = \Psi_z \tag{3.46}$$

that is, the row i, column j element of Ψ_z identifies the consequences of a one-unit increase in the jth variable's innovation at date $t (u_{j,t})$ for the value of the ith variable at time $t + z (x_{i,t+z})$, holding all other innovations at all dates constant.

A plot of the row i, column j element of $\Psi_z (\partial x_{i,t+z}/\partial u_{j,t})$, as a function of z is the impulse-response function. It describes the response of $(x_{i,t+z})$ to a one-time impulse in $x_{j,t}$, with all other variables dated t or earlier held constant. Supposing that the date t value of the first variable in the autoregression $s_{2,t}$ is higher than expected, so that $u_{1,t}$ is positive, then we have:[25]

$$\frac{\partial \hat{E}(x_{i,t+z}|s_{2,t}, x'_{t+1}, x'_{t+2}, \ldots, x'_{t-p})}{\partial s_{2,t}} = \frac{\partial x_{i,t+z}}{\partial u_{1,t}} \tag{3.47}$$

Thus if $s_{2,t}$ is a leading indicator of inflation, a revision in market expectations of inflation $\partial \hat{E}(x_{i,t+z}|s_{2,t}, x'_{t-1}, x'_{t-2}, \ldots, x'_{t-p})$ should be captured by the marginal impact of a shock to the innovation process in the equation for $s_{2,t}$.

---

[24] See, e.g., Hamilton (1994), chap. 11.
[25] We use a Cholesky decomposition of the variance–covariance of the innovations to identify the shocks. We order inflation first in the VaR to reflect the idea that whereas inflation does not respond, contemporaneously, to shocks to expectations, these may be affected by contemporaneous information on inflation.

3.6 ECONOMETRIC METHODOLOGY AND APPLICATIONS

As the factors that determine the dynamics of the yield curve are non-observable and the parameters are unknown, a Kalman filter and a maximum likelihood procedure were chosen for the estimation of the model.[26] In a brief description, the Kalman filter is an algorithm that computes the optimal estimate for the state variables at a moment t using the information available up to $t - 1$.

The starting point for the derivation of the Kalman filter is to write the model in state-space form, which includes an observation or measurement equation and a state or transition equation, respectively:

$$\underset{(r \times 1)}{Y_t} = \underset{(r \times n)}{A} \cdot \underset{(n \times 1)}{X_t} + \underset{(r \times k)}{H} \cdot \underset{(k \times 1)}{S_t} + \underset{(r \times 1)}{w_t} \qquad (3.48)$$

$$\underset{(k \times 1)}{S_t} = \underset{(k \times 1)}{C} + \underset{(k \times k)}{F} \cdot \underset{(k \times 1)}{S_{t-1}} + \underset{(k \times k)}{G} \cdot \underset{(k \times 1)}{v_t} \qquad (3.49)$$

where r is the number of variables to estimate, n is the number of observable exogenous variables, k is the number of non-observable or latent exogenous variables (the factors), and w_t and v_t are i.i.d. residuals, distributed as $w_t \sim N(0, R)$ and $v_t \sim N(0, Q)$.

The variance matrices are written as:

$$\underset{(r \times r)}{R} = E(w_t w_t') \qquad (3.50)$$

$$\underset{(k \times k)}{Q} = E(v_{t+1} v_{t+1}') \qquad (3.51)$$

As previously mentioned, two non-identified models were estimated, with two and three factors, and using two different databases in the former case. Considering the shorter database, the two-factor model was estimated using the files on the CD-Rom "va2fgrse" and "v2mlgrse", containing respectively the Kalman filter and the maximum likelihood procedure, written in Matlab code. Conversely, for the three-factor model the files used were "va3fgrse" and "v3mlgrse". The longer database was used only to estimate the two-factor models, by the files "va2fgrsb" and "v2mlgrsb".

Though there are some packages containing automatic procedures to run the Kalman filter (namely TSP), Matlab gives the chance to easily get, from the same file, the econometric results and the yield, forward, volatility and term premium curves, while imposing the required restrictions on the parameters.

According to equation (3.13), the measurement or observation equation in our two- and three-factor non-identified models may be written as:

$$\begin{bmatrix} y_{1,t} \\ y_{2,t} \\ \vdots \\ y_{l,t} \end{bmatrix} = \begin{bmatrix} a_{1,t} \\ a_{2,t} \\ \vdots \\ a_{l,t} \end{bmatrix} + \begin{bmatrix} b_{1,1} & b_{2,1} & \cdots & b_{k,1} \\ b_{1,2} & b_{2,2} & \ddots & b_{k,2} \\ \vdots & \vdots & \ddots & \vdots \\ b_{1,l} & b_{2,l} & \cdots & b_{k,l} \end{bmatrix} \begin{bmatrix} s_{1,t} \\ \vdots \\ s_{k,t} \end{bmatrix} + \begin{bmatrix} w_{1,t} \\ w_{2,t} \\ \vdots \\ w_{l,t} \end{bmatrix} \qquad k = 2 \text{ or } 3$$

$$(3.52)$$

---

[26] The maximum likelihood procedure is usually adopted when the parameters are unknown. Routines are provided for these algorithms.

where $y_{1,t}, y_{2,t}, \ldots, y_{l,t}$ are the l zero-coupon yields at time t with maturities $j = 1, 2, \ldots, u$ periods and $w_{1,t}, w_{2,t}, \ldots, w_{l,t}$ are the normally distributed i.i.d. errors, with null mean and standard deviation equal to e_j^2, of the measurement equation for each interest rate considered, $a_j = A_j/j, b_{k,j} = B_{k,j}/j$.[27]

Following equation (3.22), the transition or state equation is:

$$
\begin{bmatrix} s_{1,t+1} \\ \vdots \\ s_{k,t+1} \end{bmatrix} = \begin{bmatrix} \varphi_1 & 0 & 0 \\ 0 & \ddots & 0 \\ 0 & 0 & \varphi_k \end{bmatrix} \begin{bmatrix} s_{1,t} \\ \vdots \\ s_{k,t} \end{bmatrix} + \begin{bmatrix} \sigma_1 & 0 & 0 \\ 0 & \ddots & 0 \\ 0 & 0 & \sigma_k \end{bmatrix} \begin{bmatrix} v_{1,t+1} \\ \vdots \\ v_{k,t+1} \end{bmatrix} \tag{3.53}
$$

$v_{1,t+1}, \ldots, v_{k,t+1}$ being orthogonal shocks with null mean and variances equal to $\sigma_1^2, \ldots, \sigma_k^2$, respectively. As in the estimation of the models, the information on the homoskedasticity of yields is also exploited. The observation equation may be rewritten as follows:

$$
\begin{bmatrix} y_{1,t} \\ y_{2,t} \\ \vdots \\ y_{l,t} \\ \mathrm{Var}_t(y_{1,t+1}) \\ \mathrm{Var}_t(y_{2,t+1}) \\ \vdots \\ \mathrm{Var}_t(y_{l,t+1}) \end{bmatrix} = \begin{bmatrix} a_{1,t} \\ a_{2,t} \\ \vdots \\ a_{l,t} \\ a_{l+1,t} \\ a_{l+2,t} \\ \vdots \\ a_{2l} \end{bmatrix} + \begin{bmatrix} b_{1,1} & \cdots & b_{k,1} \\ b_{1,2} & \vdots & b_{k,2} \\ \vdots & \ddots & \vdots \\ b_{1,l} & \cdots & b_{k,l} \\ 0 & 0 & 0 \\ 0 & 0 & 0 \\ \vdots & \vdots & \vdots \\ 0 & 0 & 0 \end{bmatrix} \begin{bmatrix} s_{1,t} \\ \vdots \\ s_{k,t} \end{bmatrix} + \begin{bmatrix} v_{1,t} \\ v_{2,t} \\ \vdots \\ v_{l,t} \\ v_{l+1,t} \\ v_{l+2,t} \\ \vdots \\ v_{2l,t} \end{bmatrix} \tag{3.54}
$$

where $a_{l+j,t} = (B_{1,j}^2\sigma_1^2 + B_{2,j}^2\sigma_2^2)/n^2$ and $2l$ is the number of variables to estimate (r in equation (3.48)). In this way we adjust simultaneously the yield curve and the volatility curve, avoiding implausible estimates for the latter, generated by parameters that assure adequate estimations for the yields.

Regarding equations (3.48) and (3.49), in this model A is a column vector with elements $a_{j,t}$ for the first l rows ($l = 9$) and $(B_{1,j}^2\sigma_1^2 + B_{2,j}^2\sigma_2^2)/n^2$ for the next l rows; X_t is a $2l$-dimension column vector of one's ($r = 1$), C is a column vector of zeros and F is a $k \times k$ diagonal matrix, with typical element $F_{i,i} = \varphi_i$.

In all these cases, the starting values for the parameters were computed as those minimising the squared sum of residuals between the estimated yields (with the factors being zero) and the mean observed yields.[28]

When the link between the second factor and the inflation is considered in line with (3.41), the observation equation becomes:[29]

---

[27] Therefore, the parameter l in the state-space model is equal to 9 and there are 18 equations in the measurement equation of the model. Besides the recursive restrictions, the parameters were estimated subject to the usual signal restrictions.

[28] This minimisation was performed using the Excel Solver add-in.

[29] In this case, only the two-factor model is fitted.

$$
\begin{bmatrix} y_{1,t} \\ y_{2,t} \\ \vdots \\ y_{l,t} \\ \mathrm{Var}_t(y_{1,t+1}) \\ \mathrm{Var}_t(y_{2,t+1}) \\ \vdots \\ \mathrm{Var}_t(y_{l,t+1}) \\ \tilde{\pi}_t \end{bmatrix}
=
\begin{bmatrix} a_{1,t} \\ a_{2,t} \\ \vdots \\ a_{l,t} \\ a_{l+1,t} \\ a_{l+2,t} \\ \vdots \\ a_{2l} \\ 0 \end{bmatrix}
+
\begin{bmatrix} b_{1,1} & b_{2,1} \\ b_{1,2} & b_{2,2} \\ \vdots & \vdots \\ b_{1,l} & b_{2,l} \\ 0 & 0 \\ 0 & 0 \\ \vdots & \vdots \\ 0 & 0 \\ 0 & b_\pi \end{bmatrix}
\begin{bmatrix} s_{1,t} \\ s_{2,t} \end{bmatrix}
+
\begin{bmatrix} \upsilon_{1,t} \\ \upsilon_{2,t} \\ \vdots \\ \upsilon_{l,t} \\ \upsilon_{l+1,t} \\ \upsilon_{l+2,t} \\ \vdots \\ \upsilon_{2l,t} \\ \upsilon_\pi \end{bmatrix}
\qquad (3.55)
$$

This model is estimated with the files "va2fgrin" and "v2mlgrin" on the CD-Rom, containing respectively the Kalman filter and the maximum likelihood procedure, also written in Matlab code. Conversely, when the inflation is modelled as motivated by two factors, as in (3.42), the observation equation is:

$$
\begin{bmatrix} y_{1,t} \\ y_{2,t} \\ \vdots \\ y_{l,t} \\ \mathrm{Var}_t(y_{1,t+1}) \\ \mathrm{Var}_t(y_{2,t+1}) \\ \vdots \\ \mathrm{Var}_t(y_{l,t+1}) \\ \tilde{\pi}_t \end{bmatrix}
=
\begin{bmatrix} a_{1,t} \\ a_{2,t} \\ \vdots \\ a_{l,t} \\ a_{l+1,t} \\ a_{l+2,t} \\ \vdots \\ a_{2l} \\ 0 \end{bmatrix}
+
\begin{bmatrix} b_{1,1} & b_{2,1} & 0 \\ b_{1,2} & b_{2,2} & 0 \\ \vdots & \vdots & \vdots \\ b_{1,l} & b_{2,l} & 0 \\ 0 & 0 & 0 \\ 0 & 0 & 0 \\ \vdots & \vdots & \vdots \\ 0 & 0 & 0 \\ 0 & b_{2\pi} & b_{1\pi} \end{bmatrix}
\begin{bmatrix} s_{1,t} \\ s_{2,t} \\ s_{1\pi,t} \end{bmatrix}
+
\begin{bmatrix} \upsilon_{1,t} \\ \upsilon_{2,t} \\ \vdots \\ \upsilon_{l,t} \\ \upsilon_{l+1,t} \\ \upsilon_{l+2,t} \\ \vdots \\ \upsilon_{2l,t} \\ \upsilon_\pi \end{bmatrix}
\qquad (3.56)
$$

In this case, the transition equation becomes:

$$
\begin{bmatrix} s_{1,t+1} \\ s_{2,t+1} \\ s_{1\pi,t+1} \end{bmatrix}
=
\begin{bmatrix} \varphi_1 & 0 & 0 \\ 0 & \varphi_2 & 0 \\ 0 & 0 & \varphi_{1\pi} \end{bmatrix}
\begin{bmatrix} s_{1,t} \\ s_{2,t} \\ s_{1\pi,t} \end{bmatrix}
+
\begin{bmatrix} \sigma_1 & 0 & 0 \\ 0 & \sigma_2 & 0 \\ 0 & 0 & \sigma_{1\pi} \end{bmatrix}
\begin{bmatrix} \varepsilon_{1,t+1} \\ \varepsilon_{2,t+1} \\ \varepsilon_{1\pi,t+1} \end{bmatrix}
\qquad (3.57)
$$

The routines for this model are not included, given that they are very similar to the previous ones. For instance, the model in equations (3.56) and (3.57) is similar to the one in equations (3.53) and (3.54), adding to this an observation equation for the variable $\tilde{\pi}_t$ or its determining factor.

All the Matlab routines used have a similar structure: after the introductory comments, a set of general procedures is defined. These start with the definition of the log-likelihood function, followed by the loading of the sample data. Afterwards, the original parameters and the matrices are defined, as well as some self-explanatory procedures. The following block of the routine is focused on the definition of the transformed parameters. These are created in the next block of the routine ("Defining the Original Parameters"), in order to allow us to define the original parameters as functions of the former, imposing constraints on the original parameter values such as the mean-reversion coefficients of the factors (φ_i) to be between zero and one, the volatilities of the factors (σ_i) and the variances of the errors in the observation errors to be positive and one of the market prices of risk to be negative,[30] so as to impose the risk-premium curve to be mostly positive. In this block, the starting values of the factors for the Kalman filter are also settled to zero.

The matrices containing several factor loadings for the different maturities in equations (3.24) and (3.25) are defined next, as well as the recursive restrictions on those factor loadings. In the routine block entitled "Defining the matrices for the estimation", all the matrices to write the Kalman filter in the state-space form are settled. We start by computing the factor loadings for the maturities considered in the sample.[31] Then the column vector A is formed, with rows 10 to 18 containing the volatilities as in equation (3.29).[32] The 19th row is zero, as the inflation only depends on the second factor and does not have an independent term. The matrix H, containing the factor loadings in the observation equations, is formed next. Given that the volatilities are constant, rows 10 to 18 are null. The 19th row contains the link between the inflation and the second factor, as in equation (3.41).

Subsequently, the matrix F containing the mean-reversion parameters of the factors is formed. As the factors are assumed to be independent, only the elements in the main diagonal are non-zero. After creating the matrices with the variances of the errors of the observation and the state equations, the volatility and the term premium curves are computed for the maturities considered in the sample.

The estimation of the Kalman filter is performed afterwards. It departs from assuming that the starting value of the state vector S is obtained from a normal distribution with mean $\hat{S}_0$ and variance P_0. $\hat{S}_0$ can be seen as a guess concerning the value of S using all information available up to and including $t = 0$. As the residuals are orthogonal to the state variables, $\hat{S}_0$ cannot be obtained using the data and the model. P_0 is the uncertainty about the prior on the values of the state variables.

The next step is to obtain a first estimate for the mean and the variance of the state variables. Concerning the former, from $\hat{S}_0$ and equation (3.49), the optimal estimator for S_1 will be:

$$\hat{S}_{1|0} = C + F\hat{S}_0 \qquad (3.58)$$

Conversely, the variance–covariance matrix will be updated as follows:

$$
\begin{aligned}
P_{1|0} &= E[(S_1 - \hat{S}_{1|0})(S_1 - \hat{S}_{1|0})'] \\
&= E[(C + FS_0 + Gv_1 - C - FS_0)(C + FS_0 + Gv_1 - C - FS_0)'] \\
&= E[(Fv_0 + Gv_1)(v_0'F' + v_1'G')] \\
&= E(Fv_0v_0'F') + E(Gv_1v_1'G') \\
&= FP_{1|0}F' + GQ_1G' \qquad (3.59)
\end{aligned}
$$

Given that $\mathrm{vec}(ABC) = (C' \otimes A) \cdot \mathrm{vec}(B)$, $P_{1|0}$ may be obtained from:[33]

---

[30] In this case, we opted for the second factor.

[31] The element in brackets is the column number in the matrices A and H of the observation equations, which corresponds to the maturity in months added by one, given that the first column of each of those matrices is the initial factor loadings (a_0 and $b_{k,0}$).

[32] The expression in equation (3.29) is multiplied by 1200 in order to annualise the yields and express them as percentages.

[33] In the Matlab routines, we start by updating the variance–covariance matrix in the vector form.

$$\text{vec}(P_{1|0}) = \text{vec}(FP_{1|0}F') + \text{vec}(GQ_1G')$$

$$= (F \otimes F) \cdot \text{vec}(P_{1|0}) + (G \otimes G) \cdot \text{vec}(Q_1)$$

$$= \left[I_{(r^2 \times r^2)} - (F \otimes F) \right]^{-1} [(G \otimes G) \cdot \text{vec}(Q_1)] \qquad (3.60)$$

This block of the routine is concluded by assuming that the starting value of the log-likelihood function is zero. The following block, entitled "Derivation of the KF", starts by the estimation of the independent variables, based on the assumption that w_t is independent from X_t and from all prior information on y and x (denoted by ζ_{t-1}). Therefore, the forecast of y_t conditional on X_t and ζ_{t-1} can be obtained directly from (3.48):

$$E(y_t|X_t, \zeta_{t-1}) = AX_t + H\hat{S}_{t|t-1} \qquad (3.61)$$

The several estimates from equation (3.61) are stored in a matrix defined as YE in the routines, where the number of rows corresponds to the number of observation equations and the number of columns is the number of observations added by one. Given that w_t is also independent from S_t and $\hat{S}_{t|t-1}$, from equations (3.48) and (3.61), the forecast error corresponds to:

$$y_t - E(y_t|X_t, \zeta_{t-1}) = (AX_t + HS_t + w_t) - (AX_t + H\hat{S}_{t|t-1}) = H(S_t - \hat{S}_{t|t-1}) + w_t \qquad (3.62)$$

From (3.62) the conditional variance–covariance matrix of the estimation error of the observation vector will be:[34]

$$E\{[y_t - E(y_t|X_t, \zeta_{t-1})][y_t - E(y_t|X_t, \zeta_{t-1})]'\}$$

$$= E\{[H(S_t - \hat{S}_{t|t-1}) + w_t][H(S_t - \hat{S}_{t|t-1}) + w_t]'\}$$

$$= HE[(S_t - \hat{S}_{t|t-1})(S_t - \hat{S}_{t|t-1})']H' + E(w_t w_t')$$

$$= HP_{t|t-1}H' + R \qquad (3.63)$$

After the updates of the mean and variance–covariance matrices of the dependent variables, the log-likelihood function is computed. In our Kalman filter exercise, the likelihood function is defined as follows:[35]

$$f(y_t|I_{t-1}) = (2\pi)^{-1/2}|HP_{t|t-1}H' + R|^{-1/2}$$

$$\times \exp\left[-\tfrac{1}{2}(y_t - A - H\hat{S}_{t|t-1})'(HP_{t|t-1}H' + R)^{-1}(y_t - A - H\hat{S}_{t|t-1}) \right] \qquad (3.64)$$

---

[34] Notice that from equations (3.48) and (3.61), the forecast error corresponds to:
$$y_t - E(y_t|X_t, \zeta_{t-1}) = (AX_t + HS_t + w_t) - (AX_t + H\hat{S}_{t|t-1}) = H(S_t - \hat{S}_{t|t-1}) + w_t$$

[35] As the latter depends on the residuals of the observation equations, these are previously defined in the Matlab routines.

As usual, the optimisation procedure will be performed as a minimisation problem. Thus, the negative of the log-likelihood function is computed:

$$-\log L(Y_T) = -\sum_{t=1}^{T} \log f(y_t | I_{t-1}) \tag{3.65}$$

It can be shown that the distribution of S_t given y_t, X_t and ζ_{t-1} is $N(\hat{S}_{t|t}, P_{t|t})$, where $\hat{S}_{t|t}$ and $P_{t|t}$ are respectively the optimal forecast of S_t given $P_{t|t}$ and the mean square error of this forecast, corresponding to the following updating equations of the Kalman filter. After the initial estimate of the dependent variables, the mean and the variance–covariance matrices of the Kalman filter may be updated as follows:

$$\hat{S}_{t|t} = \hat{S}_{t|t-1} + P_{t|t-1}H'(HP_{t|t-1}H' + R)^{-1}[y_t - (AX_t + H_{t|t-1})] \tag{3.66}$$

$$P_{t|t} = P_{t|t-1} - P_{t|t-1}H'(HP_{t|t-1}H' + R)^{-1}HP_{t|t-1} \tag{3.67}$$

Following this update, a new estimate for these matrices can be obtained, generalising (3.58) and (3.59):[36]

$$\hat{S}_{t+1|t} = C + F\hat{S}_{t|t}$$

$$= C + F\{\hat{S}_{t|t-1} + P_{t|t-1}H'(HP_{t|t-1}H' + R)^{-1}[y_t - (AX_t + H_{t|t-1})]\}$$

$$= C + F\hat{S}_{t|t-1} + FP_{t|t-1}H'(HP_{t|t-1}H' + R)^{-1}[y_t - (AX_t + H_{t|t-1})] \tag{3.68}$$

$$P_{t+1|t} = FP_{t|t}F' + GQ_tG'$$

$$= F[P_{t|t-1} - P_{t|t-1}H'(HP_{t|t-1}H' + R)^{-1}HP_{t|t-1}]F' + GQ_tG'$$

$$= FP_{t|t-1}F' - FP_{t|t-1}H'(HP_{t|t-1}H' + R)^{-1}HP_{t|t-1}F' + GQ_tG' \tag{3.69}$$

At the end of each update of the Kalman filter, the volatility and the term premium curves are computed. Considering that only Gaussian models were fitted, these curves move only when different values for the parameters are considered, as they do not depend on the factor values. Finally, concluding the routines, there are two blocks where the results are stored in matrices and files and charts for the yields, volatility curves, factors and inflation (in the identified models) are produced. The Matlab routine written to run the Kalman filter for the two-factor identified model is presented next.

```
% This is va2fgrin, a 2-factor Vasicek model, with an identified
% factor, for Germany spot curve estimated using the Kalman Filter
% By Jorge Barros Luis
% Estimation on 1m, 1y, 2y, 3y, 4y, 5y, 7y, 10y
% ============================GENERAL PROCEDURES====================
% computing the log-likelihood function defined below
function lf=va2fgrin(para);
```

---

[36] The matrix $FP_{t|t-1}H'(HP_{t|t-1}H' + R)^{-1}$ is usually known as the gain matrix, since it determines the update in $\hat{S}_{t+1|t}$ due to the estimation error of y_t. Equation (3.68) is known as a Ricatti equation.

```
% loading data
load c:\matlab\datgerin.txt;
% creating the original parameters to be estimated
% r11 to r1919 are the variances of the residuals in observation
% equations
% s10 and s20 are the starting values of the factors (subtracted by the
% respective means)
global delta phi1 phi2 sgm1 sgm2 lmda1 lmda2 r11 r22 r33 r44 r55 r66 r77
r88 r99 r1010 r1111 r1212 r1313 r1414 r1515 r1616 r1717 r1818 r1919 s10
s20;
global AAr HH1r HH2r A H F R Q S10 Q0 p10 vp10 z;
% transposing the data column vector
Y=datgerin';
% computing the number of observations
obs=length(Y(1,:));
% creating a row vector of 1's with No. of columns equal to the number
% of observations
X=ones(1,obs);
% computing the longest term for the restrictions on the parameters (in
% months)
NN=10*12+1;
%=========DEFINING THE TRANSFORMED OR UNRESTRICTED PARAMETERS==========
% these parameters are defined as to impose restrictions on the
% original parameters (e.g. sigma's have to be positive, phi's have to
% be between 0 and 1,
% one of the lambda's has to be negative in order to have positive term
% premia and the variances of the residuals have to be positive)
% persistence parameters (phi1 and phi2)
a1=para(1); a2=para(2);
% volatilities (sigma 1 and sigma2)
b1=para(3); b2=para(4);
% lambda's (the market price of risks), defined as the product between
% the lambda's and the sigma's in the chapter
c1=para(5); c2=para(6);
% variances of the residuals in observation equation errors
d1=para(7); d2=para(8); d3=para(9); d4=para(10); d5=para(11);
d6=para(12); d7=para(13); d8=para(14); d9=para(15);
d10=para(16); d11=para(17); d12=para(18); d13=para(19); d14=para(20);
d15=para(21); d16=para(22); d17=para(23); d18=para(24); d19=para(25);
% conditional mean of short-term interest rate;
e1=para(26);
%=================DEFINING THE ORIGINAL PARAMETERS=================
% conditional mean of short-term interest rate;
delta=exp(e1);
% constrain persistence parameters (phi's) to be positive and <1;
phi1=0.999/(1+exp(-a1));
phi2=0.999/(1+exp(-a2));
% constrain volatilities (sigma's) to be positive;
sgm1=exp(b1);
sgm2=exp(b2);
% constrain the 2st market price of risk (lamda2) to be negative;
lmda1=c1;
lmda2=-exp(c2);
% constrain variances of the observation equation errors
```

```
r11=exp(d1);
r22=exp(d2);
r33=exp(d3);
r44=exp(d4);
r55=exp(d5);
r66=exp(d6);
r77=exp(d7);
r88=exp(d8);
r99=exp(d9);
r1010=exp(d10);
r1111=exp(d11);
r1212=exp(d12);
r1313=exp(d13);
r1414=exp(d14);
r1515=exp(d15);
r1616=exp(d16);
r1717=exp(d17);
r1818=exp(d18);
r1919=exp(d19);
% initial values for the state variables;
s10=0;
s20=0;
%========================================================================
% creating a row vector of the original parameters
P=zeros(1,6);
P(1,1)=phi1;
P(1,2)=phi2;
P(1,3)=sgm1;
P(1,4)=sgm2;
P(1,5)=lmda1;
P(1,6)=lmda2;
%===========DEFINING ZERO ROW VECTORS WITH DIMENSION=NN===============
%Matrices of observation equations in (3.48)
AAr=zeros(1,NN);
HH1r=zeros(1,NN);
HH2r=zeros(1,NN);
%=============Recursive Restrictions on the Factor Loadings============
for n=2:NN
% Equation (3.24)
AAr(n)=delta+AAr(n-1)+0.5*(lmda1^2+lmda2^2-(lmda1+HH1r(n-1)*sgm1)^2-
(lmda2+HH2r(n-1)*sgm2)^2);
% Equation (3.25)
HH1r(n)=1+phi1*HH1r(n-1);
HH2r(n)=1+phi2*HH2r(n-1);
end
%==============Defining the matrices for estimation===================
% Estimated factor loadings for the maturities considered in the sample
% 1m
A1=AAr(2);
H11=HH1r(2);
H12=HH2r(2);
% 3m
A2=AAr(4);
H21=HH1r(4);
```

```
H22=HH2r(4);
% 1y
A3=AAr(13);
H31=HH1r(13);
H32=HH2r(13);
% 2y
A4=AAr(25);
H41=HH1r(25);
H42=HH2r(25);
% 3y
A5=AAr(37);
H51=HH1r(37);
H52=HH2r(37);
% 4y
A6=AAr(49);
H61=HH1r(49);
H62=HH2r(49);
% 5y
A7=AAr(61);
H71=HH1r(61);
H72=HH2r(61);
% 7y
A8=AAr(85);
H81=HH1r(85);
H82=HH2r(85);
% 10y
A9=AAr(121);
H91=HH1r(121);
H92=HH2r(121);
% creating a column vector (18 rows) of A's (independent term of the
% observation equation in (3.48))
A=zeros(19,1);
A(1,1)=A1/1;
A(2,1)=A2/3;
A(3,1)=A3/12;
A(4,1)=A4/24;
A(5,1)=A5/36;
A(6,1)=A6/48;
A(7,1)=A7/60;
A(8,1)=A8/84;
A(9,1)=A9/120;
A(10,1)=1200/(1^2)*(H11^2*sgm1^2+H12^2*sgm2^2);
A(11,1)=1200/(3^2)*(H21^2*sgm1^2+H22^2*sgm2^2);
A(12,1)=1200/(12^2)*(H31^2*sgm1^2+H32^2*sgm2^2);
A(13,1)=1200/(24^2)*(H41^2*sgm1^2+H42^2*sgm2^2);
A(14,1)=1200/(36^2)*(H51^2*sgm1^2+H52^2*sgm2^2);
A(15,1)=1200/(48^2)*(H61^2*sgm1^2+H62^2*sgm2^2);
A(16,1)=1200/(60^2)*(H71^2*sgm1^2+H72^2*sgm2^2);
A(17,1)=1200/(84^2)*(H81^2*sgm1^2+H82^2*sgm2^2);
A(18,1)=1200/(120^2)*(H91^2*sgm1^2+H92^2*sgm2^2);
A(19,1)=0;
% creating a 18*2 matrix of H's (coefficient matrix of observation
% equation in (3.48))
H=zeros(19,2);
```

```
H(1,1)=H11/1;
H(1,2)=H12/1;
H(2,1)=H21/3;
H(2,2)=H22/3;
H(3,1)=H31/12;
H(3,2)=H32/12;
H(4,1)=H41/24;
H(4,2)=H42/24;
H(5,1)=H51/36;
H(5,2)=H52/36;
H(6,1)=H61/48;
H(6,2)=H62/48;
H(7,1)=H71/60;
H(7,2)=H72/60;
H(8,1)=H81/84;
H(8,2)=H82/84;
H(9,1)=H91/120;
H(9,2)=H92/120;
H(10,1)=0;
H(10,2)=0;
H(11,1)=0;
H(11,2)=0;
H(12,1)=0;
H(12,2)=0;
H(13,1)=0;
H(13,2)=0;
H(14,1)=0;
H(14,2)=0;
H(15,1)=0;
H(15,2)=0;
H(16,1)=0;
H(16,2)=0;
H(17,1)=0;
H(17,2)=0;
H(18,1)=0;
H(18,2)=0;
H(19,1)=0;
H(19,2)=1/phi2;
% creating a 2*2 matrix of F's (coefficient matrix of state equations
% in (3.49))
F=zeros(2,2);
F(1,1)=phi1;
F(2,2)=phi2;
% creating the variance-covariance matrix of the observation equation
% errors in (3.48)
R=zeros(19,19);
R(1,1)=r11;
R(2,2)=r22;
R(3,3)=r33;
R(4,4)=r44;
R(5,5)=r55;
R(6,6)=r66;
R(7,7)=r77;
R(8,8)=r88;
```

```
R(9,9)=r99;
R(10,10)=r1010;
R(11,11)=r1111;
R(12,12)=r1212;
R(13,13)=r1313;
R(14,14)=r1414;
R(15,15)=r1515;
R(16,16)=r1616;
R(17,17)=r1717;
R(18,18)=r1818;
R(19,19)=r1919;
% creating the variance-covariance matrix of the state equation errors
in (3.49)
Q=zeros(2,2);
Q(1,1)=sgm1^2;
Q(2,2)=sgm2^2;
% creating the matrix of the volatility curve in Equation (3.29), in %
V=zeros(9,obs+1);
V(1,1)=1/(1^2)*(H11^2*sgm1^2+H12^2*sgm2^2)*1200^2;
V(2,1)=1/(3^2)*(H21^2*sgm1^2+H22^2*sgm2^2)*1200^2;
V(3,1)=1/(12^2)*(H31^2*sgm1^2+H32^2*sgm2^2)*1200^2;
V(4,1)=1/(24^2)*(H41^2*sgm1^2+H42^2*sgm2^2)*1200^2;
V(5,1)=1/(36^2)*(H51^2*sgm1^2+H52^2*sgm2^2)*1200^2;
V(6,1)=1/(48^2)*(H61^2*sgm1^2+H62^2*sgm2^2)*1200^2;
V(7,1)=1/(60^2)*(H71^2*sgm1^2+H72^2*sgm2^2)*1200^2;
V(8,1)=1/(84^2)*(H81^2*sgm1^2+H82^2*sgm2^2)*1200^2;
V(9,1)=1/(120^2)*(H91^2*sgm1^2+H92^2*sgm2^2)*1200^2;
% creating the matrix of the term premium in Equation (3.30), in %
T=zeros(9,obs+1);
T(1,1)=(0.5*(lmda1^2+lmda2^2)-
0.5*((lmda1+H11*sgm1)^2+(lmda2+H12*sgm2)^2))*1200;
T(2,1)=(0.5*(lmda1^2+lmda2^2)-
0.5*((lmda1+H21*sgm1)^2+(lmda2+H22*sgm2)^2))*1200;
T(3,1)=(0.5*(lmda1^2+lmda2^2)-
0.5*((lmda1+H31*sgm1)^2+(lmda2+H32*sgm2)^2))*1200;
T(4,1)=(0.5*(lmda1^2+lmda2^2)-
0.5*((lmda1+H41*sgm1)^2+(lmda2+H42*sgm2)^2))*1200;
T(5,1)=(0.5*(lmda1^2+lmda2^2)-
0.5*((lmda1+H51*sgm1)^2+(lmda2+H52*sgm2)^2))*1200;
T(6,1)=(0.5*(lmda1^2+lmda2^2)-
0.5*((lmda1+H61*sgm1)^2+(lmda2+H62*sgm2)^2))*1200;
T(7,1)=(0.5*(lmda1^2+lmda2^2)-
0.5*((lmda1+H71*sgm1)^2+(lmda2+H72*sgm2)^2))*1200;
T(8,1)=(0.5*(lmda1^2+lmda2^2)-
0.5*((lmda1+H81*sgm1)^2+(lmda2+H82*sgm2)^2))*1200;
T(9,1)=(0.5*(lmda1^2+lmda2^2)-
0.5*((lmda1+H91*sgm1)^2+(lmda2+H92*sgm2)^2))*1200;
%==================== Starting the Kalman Filter ====================
% creating the matrix of the unobservable factors (2*obs+1, as the
% starting values are included)
S10=zeros(2,obs+1);
% assuming starting values for the factors
S10(1,1)=s10;
S10(2,1)=s20;
```

```
% length of the vector of the initial values for the factors;
rr=length(S10(:,1));
% Unconditional variance of the state vector (in vector form)
% Equation (3.60)
vp10=inv(eye(rr^2)-kron(F,F))*reshape(Q,rr*rr,1);
% Unconditional variance of the state vector (in matrix form)
% Equation (3.59)
p10=reshape(vp10,rr,rr)';
% Initial value for the likelihood function
lf=0;
%===================== Derivation of the KF ==========================
for t=1:obs
% Forecasting Yt|t-1 (equation (3.61))
y10=(A*X(:,t)+H*S10(:,t))*1200;
% Creating matrix of estimated Y
YE(:,t:t)=y10;
% covariance of Yt-Yt|t-1 (equation (3.63))
O10=H*p10*H'+R;
kk=length(R(:,1));
%================= Calculate the likelihood function ================
% Forecast error (equation (3.62))
res=Y(:,t)-y10;
% log likelihood function (equation (3.64))
ff=-0.5*log(2*pi*det(O10))-0.5*res'*inv(O10)*res;
% Sum of the negative of the log likelihood function (equation (3.65))
lf=lf-ff;
%======== Continuing updating the state vector and covariances ========
% Update St|t-1, in order to get the expected value of the state
% vector, given the information available up to t (equation (3.66))
S=S10(:,t)+p10*H'*inv(O10)*(Y(:,t)-y10);
% Covariance of St|t (equation (3.67))
p=p10-p10*H'*inv(O10)*H*p10;
% Forecast St+1|t (equation (3.68))
S10(:,t+1)=F*S;
% Update Pt+1|t (equation (3.69))
p10=F*p*F'+Q;
%==================Calculate the volatility curve =====================
V(1,t+1)=1/(1^2)*(H11^2*sgm1^2+H12^2*sgm2^2)*1200^2;
V(2,t+1)=1/(3^2)*(H21^2*sgm1^2+H22^2*sgm2^2)*1200^2;
V(3,t+1)=1/(12^2)*(H31^2*sgm1^2+H32^2*sgm2^2)*1200^2;
V(4,t+1)=1/(24^2)*(H41^2*sgm1^2+H42^2*sgm2^2)*1200^2;
V(5,t+1)=1/(36^2)*(H51^2*sgm1^2+H52^2*sgm2^2)*1200^2;
V(6,t+1)=1/(48^2)*(H61^2*sgm1^2+H62^2*sgm2^2)*1200^2;
V(7,t+1)=1/(60^2)*(H71^2*sgm1^2+H72^2*sgm2^2)*1200^2;
V(8,t+1)=1/(84^2)*(H81^2*sgm1^2+H82^2*sgm2^2)*1200^2;
V(9,t+1)=1/(120^2)*(H91^2*sgm1^2+H92^2*sgm2^2)*1200^2;
%================== Calculate the term premium curve ================
T(1,t+1)=(0.5*(lmda1^2+lmda2^2)-
0.5*((lmda1+H11*sgm1)^2+(lmda2+H12*sgm2)^2))*1200;
T(2,t+1)=(0.5*(lmda1^2+lmda2^2)-
0.5*((lmda1+H21*sgm1)^2+(lmda2+H22*sgm2)^2))*1200;
T(3,t+1)=(0.5*(lmda1^2+lmda2^2)-
0.5*((lmda1+H31*sgm1)^2+(lmda2+H32*sgm2)^2))*1200;
```

```
T(4,t+1)=(0.5*(lmda1^2+lmda2^2)-
0.5*((lmda1+H41*sgm1)^2+(lmda2+H42*sgm2)^2))*1200;
T(5,t+1)=(0.5*(lmda1^2+lmda2^2)-
0.5*((lmda1+H51*sgm1)^2+(lmda2+H52*sgm2)^2))*1200;
T(6,t+1)=(0.5*(lmda1^2+lmda2^2)-
0.5*((lmda1+H61*sgm1)^2+(lmda2+H62*sgm2)^2))*1200;
T(7,t+1)=(0.5*(lmda1^2+lmda2^2)-
0.5*((lmda1+H71*sgm1)^2+(lmda2+H72*sgm2)^2))*1200;
T(8,t+1)=(0.5*(lmda1^2+lmda2^2)-
0.5*((lmda1+H81*sgm1)^2+(lmda2+H82*sgm2)^2))*1200;
T(9,t+1)=(0.5*(lmda1^2+lmda2^2)-
0.5*((lmda1+H91*sgm1)^2+(lmda2+H92*sgm2)^2))*1200;
end
%======================== Transposing matrices ========================
YT=Y';
% Yield matrix
YE1=YE(1:9,:);
% Volatility matrix
YE2=YE(10:18,:);
YE3=YE(19:19,:);
YET=YE1';
VET=YE2;
IET=YE3';
% Observation equation matrices
AArT=AAr';
HH1rT=HH1r';
HH2rT=HH2r';
L=[AArT,HH1rT,HH2rT];
%VT=V';
%TT=T';
S10T=S10';
%============================== Plots ================================
% Yields
Figure(1)
plot(YET)
% Volatilities
Figure(2)
plot(VET)
% Factors
Figure(3)
plot(S10T)
% Estimated inflation
Figure(4)
plot(IET)
%=========================== Saving files ========================
% Estimated Yields
save c:\matlab\V2YETgri YET -ascii;
% Estimated Inflation
save c:\matlab\V2IETgri IET -ascii;
% Factors
save c:\matlab\V2S10gri S10T -ascii;
% Factor loadings
save c:\matlab\V2loadgi L -ascii;
% Volatilities
```

```
save c:\matlab\V2Volgri VET -ascii;
% Term premium
save c:\matlab\V2tprgri TT -ascii;
```

This routine runs the Kalman filter for any given set of parameters. In order to use it in Matlab, an instruction must be written in the software editor comprising the name of the file and the vector of the restricted parameters between brackets, as follows:

va2fgrin([4.035,4.066,-6.465,-6.822,3.098,1.492,-0.690,-0.170,-1.780,-1.236,-0.681,

0.610,-0.083,-0.147, -1.068,0.415,-0.317,-0.079,-0.378,0.735,0.805,0.511,0.392,

-0.561,-2.794,-5.302])

Though running the Kalman filter for given sets of parameters may be interesting to assess the behaviour of the model, a more relevant exercise is the estimation of the optimal set of parameters, which corresponds to the one that maximises the sum of the log-likelihood function or its negative as in equation (3.65). This estimation is performed in separate files, which run on the files used to estimate the Kalman filter.

The starting values of the restricted parameters are inserted in the row after the comment "defining parameters". The single output of these files is an additional file containing the estimated parameters, which is created at the end of the Matlab file. The file corresponding to the Kalman filter file previously inserted is structured as follows:

```
load c:\matlab\datgerin.txt;
echo on;
% creating the original parameters to be estimated
% r11 to r1818 are the variances of the residuals in observation
% equations
% s10 and s20 are the starting values of the factors (subtracted by the
% respective means)
global delta phi1 phi2 sgm1 sgm2 lmda1 lmda2 r11 r22 r33 r44 r55 r66 r77
r88 r99 r1010 r1111 r1212 r1313 r1414 r1515 r1616 r1717 r1818 r1919 s10
s20;
global AAr HH1r HH2r A H F R Q S10 Q0 p10 vp10 z;
% defining data matrix
dat=datgerin;
global dat;
% defining parameters
para=[4.0346916,4.0660162,-6.465255,-6.8215072,3.0979817,1.4923502,-
0.69015894,-0.17029679,-1.7801797,-1.2362226,-0.68102726,0.60983616,-
0.082530108,-0.14685034,-1.0676112,0.41457897,-0.31653961,-0.079408822,-
0.37790821,0.73490396,0.80506935,0.51061064,0.39230219,-0.56051416,-
2.7940033,-5.302371]
global para;
%options about the minimisation function used below (see Matlab manual)
options(1)=1;
options(2)=0.001;
options(3)=0.001;
options(14)=100000;
% defining the optimisation problem (minimise -log-likelihood function)
z=fmins('va2fgrin',para,options);
% saving a file with the parameters;
save c:\matlab\v2pgerin z -ascii;
```

The estimation procedure may be summarised as in Figure 3.5.

The statistical significance of the parameters was tested by computing the usual t-ratios, where the standard deviations were obtained from the variance–covariance matrix of the estimators (see e.g. Hamilton (1994, p. 389) for details), using a numerical procedure. The files used concerning the two-factor models mentioned above are also provided on

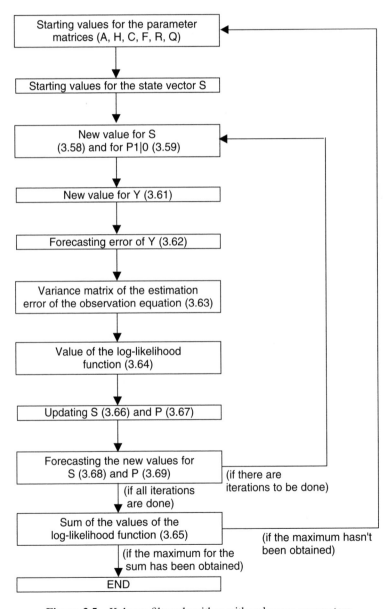

Figure 3.5   Kalman filter algorithm with unknown parameters

the CD-Rom – "v2trgrse", "v2trgrsb" and "v2trgrin", respectively – for the non-identified models using the shorter and longer databases and for the identified model.[37]

The latter is inserted next. The routine starts by reading the data file, which included a file with the original parameters estimated. The derivatives required are computed by arithmetic approximation, being the increment equal to 0.00001. Then the first and the second derivatives are computed and a matrix S containing the second derivatives. The t-ratios are the elements of the main diagonal of the matrix $S2 = \text{inv}(S)/\text{obs}$. Finally, three files are saved, containing respectively the t-ratios, the standard deviations and the matrix $S2$.

```
% This is v2trgrin, a code for the estimation of t-ratios in a
two-factor identified Vasicek model for Germany estimated spot rates
% By Jorge Barros Luis
% loading data
load c:\matlab\datgerin.txt;
% defining the variables
global delta phi1 phi2 sgm1 sgm2 lmda1 lmda2 r11 r22 r33 r44 r55 r66 r77
r88 r99 s10 s20;
global AAr HH1r HH2r A H F R Q S10 Q0 p10 vp10 z;
% transposing the data column vector
Y=datgerin';
% computing the number of observations
obs=length(Y(1,:));
%loading the parameter vector
load v2pgerin.txt;
para=v2pgerin;
%definition of the variations
d=0.00001
%variations for the second derivatives;
incphi1=[d,0,0,0,0,0,0,0,0,0,0,0,0,0,0,0,0,0,0,0,0,0,0,0,0,0,0];
incphi2=[0,d,0,0,0,0,0,0,0,0,0,0,0,0,0,0,0,0,0,0,0,0,0,0,0,0,0];
incsgm1=[0,0,d,0,0,0,0,0,0,0,0,0,0,0,0,0,0,0,0,0,0,0,0,0,0,0,0];
incsgm2=[0,0,0,d,0,0,0,0,0,0,0,0,0,0,0,0,0,0,0,0,0,0,0,0,0,0,0];
inclmda1=[0,0,0,0,d,0,0,0,0,0,0,0,0,0,0,0,0,0,0,0,0,0,0,0,0,0,0];
inclmda2=[0,0,0,0,0,d,0,0,0,0,0,0,0,0,0,0,0,0,0,0,0,0,0,0,0,0,0];
incdelta=[0,0,0,0,0,0,0,0,0,0,0,0,0,0,0,0,0,0,0,0,0,0,0,0,0,0,d];
%parameters after the first variation;
upphi1=para+incphi1;
dwphi1=para-incphi1;
upphi2=para+incphi2;
dwphi2=para-incphi2;
upsgm1=para+incsgm1;
dwsgm1=para-incsgm1;
upsgm2=para+incsgm2;
dwsgm2=para-incsgm2;
uplmda1=para+inclmda1;
dwlmda1=para-inclmda1;
uplmda2=para+inclmda2;
dwlmda2=para-inclmda2;
updelta=para+incdelta;
```

---

[37] Obviously, these files have to be run after the Kalman filter and maximum likelihood estimations.

```
dwdelta=para-incdelta;
uph1uph2=para+incphi1+incphi2;
uph1usg1=para+incphi1+incsgm1;
uph1usg2=para+incphi1+incsgm2;
uph1ulm1=para+incphi1+inclmda1;
uph1ulm2=para+incphi1+inclmda2;
uph1udel=para+incphi1+incdelta;
uph2usg1=para+incphi2+incsgm1;
uph2usg2=para+incphi2+incsgm2;
uph2ulm1=para+incphi2+inclmda1;
uph2ulm2=para+incphi2+inclmda2;
uph2udel=para+incphi2+incdelta;
usg1usg2=para+incsgm1+incsgm2;
usg1ulm1=para+incsgm1+inclmda1;
usg1ulm2=para+incsgm1+inclmda2;
usg1udel=para+incsgm1+incdelta;
usg2ulm1=para+incsgm2+inclmda1;
usg2ulm2=para+incsgm2+inclmda2;
usg2udel=para+incsgm2+incdelta;
ulm1ulm2=para+inclmda1+inclmda2;
ulm1udel=para+inclmda1+incdelta;
ulm2udel=para+inclmda2+incdelta;
uph1dph2=para+incphi1-incphi2;
uph1dsg1=para+incphi1-incsgm1;
uph1dsg2=para+incphi1-incsgm2;
uph1dlm1=para+incphi1-inclmda1;
uph1dlm2=para+incphi1-inclmda2;
uph1ddel=para+incphi1-incdelta;
uph2dsg1=para+incphi2-incsgm1;
uph2dsg2=para+incphi2-incsgm2;
uph2dlm1=para+incphi2-inclmda1;
uph2dlm2=para+incphi2-inclmda2;
uph2ddel=para+incphi2-incdelta;
usg1dsg2=para+incsgm1-incsgm2;
usg1dlm1=para+incsgm1-inclmda1;
usg1dlm2=para+incsgm1-inclmda2;
usg1ddel=para+incsgm1-incdelta;
usg2dlm1=para+incsgm2-inclmda1;
usg2dlm2=para+incsgm2-inclmda2;
usg2ddel=para+incsgm2-incdelta;
ulm1dlm2=para+inclmda1-inclmda2;
ulm1ddel=para+inclmda1-incdelta;
ulm2ddel=para+inclmda2-incdelta;
dph1dph2=para-incphi1-incphi2;
dph1dsg1=para-incphi1-incsgm1;
dph1dsg2=para-incphi1-incsgm2;
dph1dlm1=para-incphi1-inclmda1;
dph1dlm2=para-incphi1-inclmda2;
dph1ddel=para-incphi1-incdelta;
dph2dsg1=para-incphi2-incsgm1;
dph2dsg2=para-incphi2-incsgm2;
dph2dlm1=para-incphi2-inclmda1;
dph2dlm2=para-incphi2-inclmda2;
dph2ddel=para-incphi2-incdelta;
```

```
dsg1dsg2=para-incsgm1-incsgm2;
dsg1dlm1=para-incsgm1-inclmda1;
dsg1dlm2=para-incsgm1-inclmda2;
dsg1ddel=para-incsgm1-incdelta;
dsg2dlm1=para-incsgm2-inclmda1;
dsg2dlm2=para-incsgm2-inclmda2;
dsg2ddel=para-incsgm2-incdelta;
dlm1dlm2=para-inclmda1-inclmda2;
dlm1ddel=para-inclmda1-incdelta;
dlm2ddel=para-inclmda2-incdelta;
dph1uph2=para-incphi1+incphi2;
dph1usg1=para-incphi1+incsgm1;
dph1usg2=para-incphi1+incsgm2;
dph1ulm1=para-incphi1+inclmda1;
dph1ulm2=para-incphi1+inclmda2;
dph1udel=para-incphi1+incdelta;
dph2usg1=para-incphi2+incsgm1;
dph2usg2=para-incphi2+incsgm2;
dph2ulm1=para-incphi2+inclmda1;
dph2ulm2=para-incphi2+inclmda2;
dph2udel=para-incphi2+incdelta;
dsg1usg2=para-incsgm1+incsgm2;
dsg1ulm1=para-incsgm1+inclmda1;
dsg1ulm2=para-incsgm1+inclmda2;
dsg1udel=para-incsgm1+incdelta;
dsg2ulm1=para-incsgm2+inclmda1;
dsg2ulm2=para-incsgm2+inclmda2;
dsg2udel=para-incsgm2+incdelta;
dlm1ulm2=para-inclmda1+inclmda2;
dlm1udel=para-inclmda1+incdelta;
dlm2udel=para-inclmda2+incdelta;
%computation of the second partial derivatives (the elements of the main
diagonal of S);
d2phi1=((v2ungrin(upphi1)-v2ungrin(para))-(v2ungrin(para)-
v2ungrin(dwphi1)))/d^2
d2phi2=((v2ungrin(upphi2)-v2ungrin(para))-(v2ungrin(para)-
v2ungrin(dwphi2)))/d^2
d2sgm1=((v2ungrin(upsgm1)-v2ungrin(para))-(v2ungrin(para)-
v2ungrin(dwsgm1)))/d^2
d2sgm2=((v2ungrin(upsgm2)-v2ungrin(para))-(v2ungrin(para)-
v2ungrin(dwsgm1)))/d^2
d2lmda1=((v2ungrin(uplmda1)-v2ungrin(para))-(v2ungrin(para)-
v2ungrin(dwlmda1)))/d^2
d2lmda2=((v2ungrin(uplmda2)-v2ungrin(para))-(v2ungrin(para)-
v2ungrin(dwlmda2)))/d^2
d2delta=((v2ungrin(updelta)-v2ungrin(para))-(v2ungrin(para)-
v2ungrin(dwdelta)))/d^2
%computation of the cross derivatives (the elements out of the main
diagonal of S);
dph1ph2=(v2ungrin(uph1uph2)-v2ungrin(uph1dph2)-
v2ungrin(dph1uph2)+v2ungrin(dph1dph2))/4*d^2
dph1sg1=(v2ungrin(uph1usg1)-v2ungrin(uph1dsg1)-
v2ungrin(dph1usg1)+v2ungrin(dph1dsg1))/4*d^2
```

```
dph1sg2=(v2ungrin(uph1usg2)-v2ungrin(uph1dsg2)-
v2ungrin(dph1usg2)+v2ungrin(dph1dsg2))/4*d^2
dph1lm1=(v2ungrin(uph1ulm1)-v2ungrin(uph1dlm1)-
v2ungrin(dph1ulm1)+v2ungrin(dph1dlm1))/4*d^2
dph1lm2=(v2ungrin(uph1ulm2)-v2ungrin(uph1dlm2)-
v2ungrin(dph1ulm2)+v2ungrin(dph1dlm2))/4*d^2
dph1delt=(v2ungrin(uph1udel)-v2ungrin(uph1ddel)-
v2ungrin(dph1udel)+v2ungrin(dph1ddel))/4*d^2
dph2sg1=(v2ungrin(uph2usg1)-v2ungrin(uph2dsg1)-
v2ungrin(dph2usg1)+v2ungrin(dph2dsg1))/4*d^2
dph2sg2=(v2ungrin(uph2usg2)-v2ungrin(uph2dsg2)-
v2ungrin(dph2usg2)+v2ungrin(dph2dsg2))/4*d^2
dph2lm1=(v2ungrin(uph2ulm1)-v2ungrin(uph2dlm1)-
v2ungrin(dph2ulm1)+v2ungrin(dph2dlm1))/4*d^2
dph2lm2=(v2ungrin(uph2ulm2)-v2ungrin(uph2dlm2)-
v2ungrin(dph2ulm2)+v2ungrin(dph2dlm2))/4*d^2
dph2delt=(v2ungrin(uph2udel)-v2ungrin(uph2ddel)-
v2ungrin(dph2udel)+v2ungrin(dph2ddel))/4*d^2
dsg1sg2=(v2ungrin(usg1usg2)-v2ungrin(usg1dsg2)-
v2ungrin(dsg1usg2)+v2ungrin(dsg1dsg2))/4*d^2
dsg1lm1=(v2ungrin(usg1ulm1)-v2ungrin(usg1dlm1)-
v2ungrin(dsg1ulm1)+v2ungrin(dsg1dlm1))/4*d^2
dsg1lm2=(v2ungrin(usg1ulm2)-v2ungrin(usg1dlm2)-
v2ungrin(dsg1ulm2)+v2ungrin(dsg1dlm2))/4*d^2;
dsg1delt=(v2ungrin(usg1udel)-v2ungrin(usg1ddel)-
v2ungrin(dsg1udel)+v2ungrin(dsg1ddel))/4*d^2
dsg2lm1=(v2ungrin(usg2ulm1)-v2ungrin(usg2dlm1)-
v2ungrin(dsg2ulm1)+v2ungrin(dsg2dlm1))/4*d^2
dsg2lm2=(v2ungrin(usg2ulm2)-v2ungrin(usg2dlm2)-
v2ungrin(dsg2ulm2)+v2ungrin(dsg2dlm2))/4*d^2
dsg2delt=(v2ungrin(usg2udel)-v2ungrin(usg2ddel)-
v2ungrin(dsg2udel)+v2ungrin(dsg2ddel))/4*d^2
dlm1lm2=(v2ungrin(ulm1ulm2)-v2ungrin(ulm1dlm2)-
v2ungrin(dlm1ulm2)+v2ungrin(dlm1dlm2))/4*d^2
dlm1delt=(v2ungrin(ulm1udel)-v2ungrin(ulm1ddel)-
v2ungrin(dlm1udel)+v2ungrin(dlm1ddel))/4*d^2
dlm2delt=(v2ungrin(ulm2udel)-v2ungrin(ulm2ddel)-
v2ungrin(dlm2udel)+v2ungrin(dlm2ddel))/4*d^2
%Matrix S
S=1/obs*[d2phi1 dph1ph2 dph1sg1 dph1sg2 dph1lm1 dph1lm2 dph1delt;
dph1ph2 d2phi2 dph2sg1 dph2sg2 dph2lm1 dph2lm2 dph2delt; dph1sg1 dph2sg1
d2sgm1 dsg1sg2 dsg1lm1 dsg1lm2 dsg1delt; dph1sg2 dph2sg2 dsg1sg2 d2sgm2
dsg2lm1 dsg2lm2 dsg2delt; dph1lm1 dph2lm1 dsg1lm1 dsg2lm1 d2lmda1
dlm1lm2 dlm1delt; dph1lm2 dph2lm2 dsg1lm2 dsg2lm2 dlm1lm2 d2lmda2
dlm2delt; dph1delt dph2delt dsg1delt dsg2delt dlm1delt dlm2delt
d2delta];
%T-ratios
S2=inv(S)/obs;
tratios=[para(1)/sqrt(S2(1,1));para(2)/sqrt(S2(2,2));para(3)/
sqrt(S2(3,3));para(4)/sqrt(S2(4,4));para(5)/sqrt(S2(5,5));para(6)/
sqrt(S2(6,6));para(16)/sqrt(S2(7,7))];
stdev=[sqrt(S2(1,1));sqrt(S2(2,2));sqrt(S2(3,3));sqrt(S2(4,4));
sqrt(S2(5,5));sqrt(S2(6,6));sqrt(S2(7,7))];
save c:\matlab\v2trgrin tratios -ascii;
```

```
save c:\matlab\v2sdgrin stdev -ascii;
save c:\matlab\v2sgrin S2 -ascii;
```

3.7 ESTIMATION RESULTS

Before the estimation results, it is worthwhile to present the most significant stylised facts concerning the data. The properties of the German yield curve are summarised in Tables 3.1 and 3.2. A number of features are worth noting. Firstly, between 1986 and 1998, the term structure is negatively sloped at the short end, in contrast with the more familiar concave appearance observed for the USA market (see Backus *et al.* (1997)). Secondly, yields are very persistent, with monthly autocorrelations above 0.98 for all maturities.[38] Thirdly, yields are highly correlated along the curve, but correlation is not equal to one, with lower correlations obtained for the ends of the yield curve. This suggests that non-parallel shifts of the yield curve are important. Therefore, one-factor models seem to be insufficient to explain the German term structure of interest rates. Lastly, as expected, the volatility curve of the yields is downward sloping.

The first estimations to be performed were those concerning the forward regressions. These regressions were run using a TSP routine with Newey–West standard errors.[39] Figure 3.6 (simple test) and Figure 3.7 (forward regressions) show the results of the tests

Table 3.1 Properties of German government bond yields in 1986–1988

Maturity	1	3	12	24	36	48	60	84	120
Mean	5.732	5.715	5.681	5.823	6.020	6.203	6.359	6.587	6.793
St. Dev.	2.267	2.224	2.087	1.882	1.686	1.524	1.398	1.228	1.095
Skewness	0.450	0.449	0.490	0.522	0.519	0.487	0.432	0.282	0.049
Kurtosis	−1.258	−1.267	−1.139	−1.051	−0.975	−0.871	−0.737	−0.426	0.001
Autocorrelation	0.991	0.992	0.991	0.990	0.989	0.989	0.988	0.987	0.983

Normality Tests

Maturity	1	3	12	24	36	48	60	84	120
$\chi^2(2)$	15.5558	15.6717	14.6832	14.2669	13.1898	11.1065	8.3923	3.2515	0.0627
$P(X > x)$	0.0004	0.0004	0.0006	0.0008	0.0014	0.0039	0.0151	0.1968	0.9691

Correlation matrix

y1	1.000	0.998	0.969	0.936	0.913	0.891	0.867	0.816	0.743
y3		1.000	0.982	0.955	0.934	0.912	0.889	0.839	0.765
y12			1.000	0.993	0.980	0.964	0.944	0.898	0.829
y24				1.000	0.996	0.986	0.972	0.935	0.875
y36					1.000	0.997	0.988	0.961	0.911
y48						1.000	0.997	0.980	0.940
y60							1.000	0.992	0.962
y84								1.000	0.989
y120									1.000

---

[38] Interest rates are close to being non-stationary.
[39] This routine is not included on the CD-Rom, as this is a trivial exercise.

Table 3.2 Properties of German government bond yields in 1972–1988

Maturity	12	24	36	48	60	72	84	96	120
Mean	6.348	6.609	6.856	7.051	7.202	7.321	7.414	7.487	7.594
St. Dev.	2.290	2.053	1.891	1.770	1.674	1.598	1.535	1.483	1.401
Skewness	0.545	0.349	0.224	0.151	0.108	0.084	0.075	0.077	0.112
Kurtosis	−0.513	−0.671	−0.677	−0.636	−0.575	−0.495	−0.397	−0.281	−0.006
Autocorrelation	0.981	0.985	0.985	0.985	0.985	0.985	0.985	0.984	0.981

Normality Tests

Maturity	12	24	36	48	60	72	84	96	120
$\chi^2(2)$	19.28	12.44	8.76	6.59	5.01	3.64	2.39	1.37	0.67
$P(X > x)$	0.000	0.002	0.013	0.037	0.082	0.162	0.302	0.505	0.715

Correlation matrix

y12	1.000	0.986	0.964	0.942	0.919	0.896	0.874	0.853	0.812
y24		1.000	0.993	0.979	0.962	0.943	0.924	0.906	0.870
y36			1.000	0.996	0.986	0.973	0.958	0.943	0.912
y48				1.000	0.997	0.990	0.980	0.968	0.943
y60					1.000	0.998	0.992	0.984	0.964
y72						1.000	0.998	0.994	0.979
y84							1.000	0.999	0.989
y96								1.000	0.995
y120									1.000

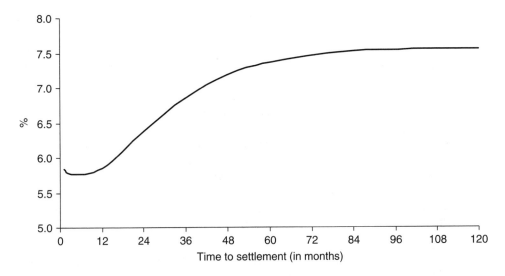

Figure 3.6 Simple test of the pure expectations theory of interest rates. Forward rate average curve in 1986–1998

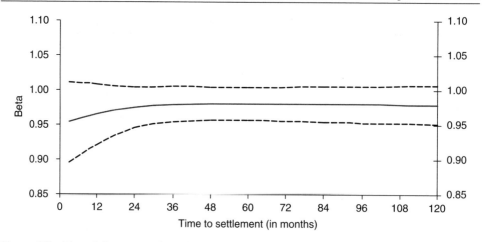

Figure 3.7 Test of the expectations theory of interest rates. Forward regression coefficient in 1986–1998

Table 3.3 Parameter estimates in the forward regressions

M	3	12	24	36	48	60	84	120
β	0.953	0.965	0.975	0.980	0.981	0.981	0.980	0.979
$\sigma(\beta)$	0.029	0.022	0.015	0.013	0.012	0.012	0.013	0.014
α	−0.003	0.005	0.020	0.029	0.034	0.038	0.043	0.046
$\sigma(\alpha)$	0.007	0.019	0.025	0.030	0.033	0.036	0.040	0.043

of the expectations theory of the term structure, in line with equations (3.33) and (3.34). In Table 3.3, the parameter estimates are exhibited.

The pure expectations theory is easily rejected: as shown in Figure 3.6 and Table 3.3, average one-period short-term forward rates vary with maturity, which contradicts equation (3.33) with $\Lambda_n = 0$.[40] However, as shown in Figure 3.7, forward regressions generate slope coefficients close to one for all maturities, with relatively small standard errors,[41] suggesting that the assumption of constant term premiums might be a reasonable approximation.

The results[42] of the term structure estimation are shown in Figure 3.8a and b (average yield curves), Figure 3.9a and b (volatility curves), Figure 3.10a and b (term premium curves), Figure 3.11a and b (one-period forward curves), Figure 3.12a and b (expected short-term interest rate curves), Figure 3.13a and b (time-series yields), Figure 3.14a and b (time-series inflation), Figure 3.15a and b (factor loadings) and Figure 3.16a–f (time-series factors). The parameters and their standard errors are reported in Tables 3.4 and 3.5.[43]

---

[40] In the steady state, it is expected that short-term interest rates remain constant. Thus the one-period forward curve should be flat under the absence of risk premium.

[41] Newey–West standard errors.

[42] Many of the charts which follow need to be viewed in colour to be fully understood. Each of the following figures are included as an Excel file with suitably titled filenames on the CD-Rom.

[43] The inflation rate used in the identified models was obtained from Datastream.

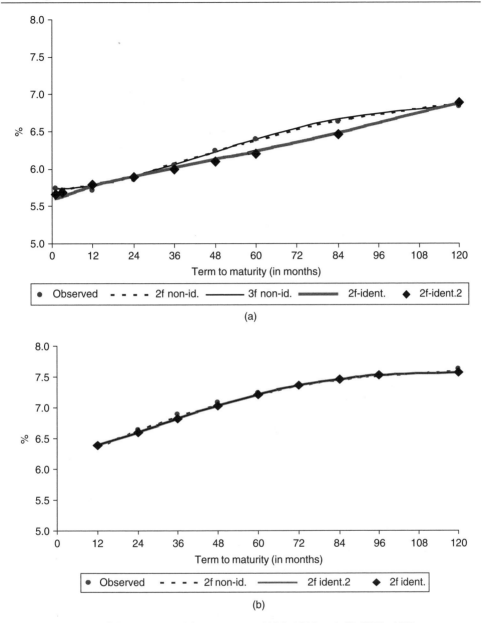

Figure 3.8 Average yield curves: (a) 1986–1998 and (b) 1972–1998

According to Figures 3.8a and b, 3.9a and b, all estimates reproduce very closely both the average yield and the volatility curves, though worse results are obtained for 1986–1998 when the second factor is identified with inflation as in equation (3.55) or equation (3.56).[44] This result must be associated with the link between the behaviour of the second factor and the inflation, which implies a worse fitting for the long-term interest rates.

---

[44] The results with the alternative identified model (in equation (3.56)) are labelled "2f-ident.2".

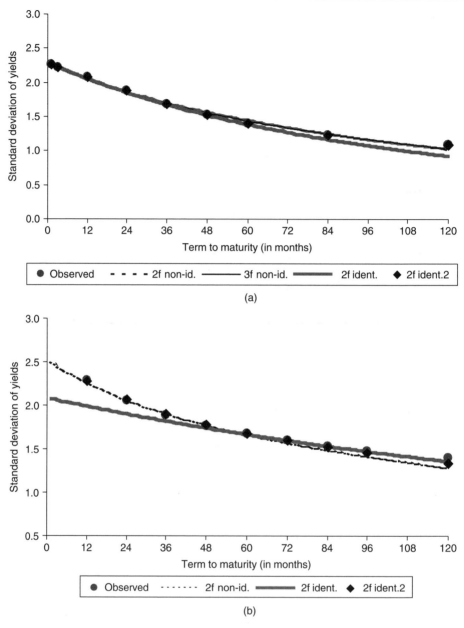

Figure 3.9   Volatility curves: (a) 1986–1998 and (b) 1972–1998

Concerning the term premium and the one-period forward, Figures 3.10a and b, 3.11a and b show again that the results obtained differ in the shorter sample, depending on using identified or non-identified models. The estimates obtained with the identified model in equation (3.55) point to lower risk premium in the maturities between 2 and 7 years, while the risk premium is higher at both ends of the curve. This model still presents an estimate for the 8-year risk premium around 1.7 in both samples, though it converges

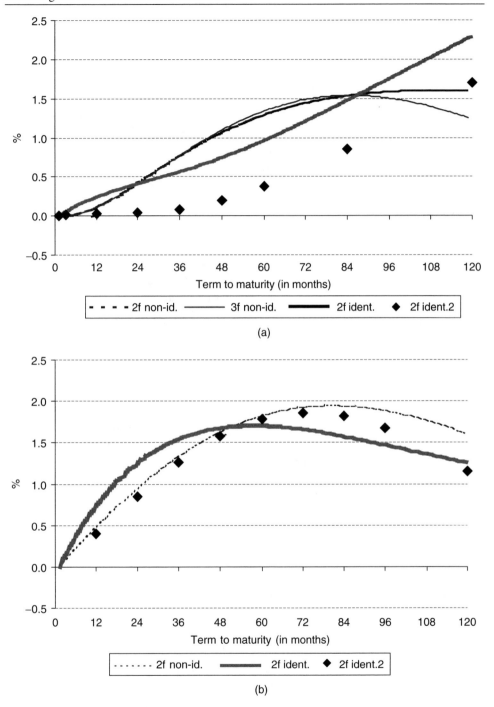

Figure 3.10   Term premium curves: (a) 1986–1998 and (b) 1972–1998

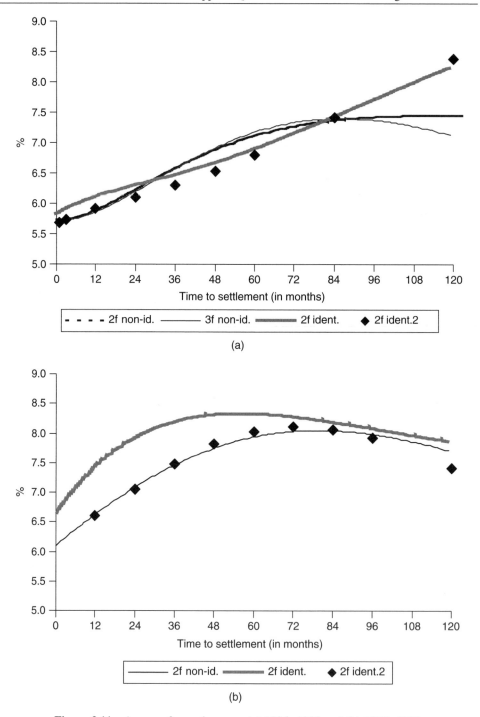

Figure 3.11   Average forward curves: (a) 1986–1998 and (b) 1972–1998

monotonically to a positive value, around 4% in maturities higher than 20 years.[45] In the non-identified models, the term premium rises rapidly up to 1.5 in the 5-year maturity, converging to around 1.6 and 1.25 in the 10-year maturity, respectively using the two- and the three-factor model.[46]

Accordingly, the expected short-term interest rates exhibit differences between the identified and the non-identified models, as well as between the samples (Figure 3.12a and b). The most remarkable feature is the positive slope in the identified models and using the shorter sample, namely with the model in (3.56). In the longer sample, the short-term interest rate is roughly constant in all models, as the shape of the one-period forward and the term premium curves are similar.

Regarding the time-series results, Figure 3.13a and b show the observed and the estimated yields for several maturities considered, while in Figure 3.14a and b the observed and the estimated inflation are shown (according to the models in (3.55) and (3.56)). It can be concluded that all estimates reproduce very closely both the yields across the maturity spectrum and the inflation.[47] However, the fit for the yields is poorer in two subperiods: the first in Spring 1994, where predicted short-term rates are above actual rates and predicted long-term rates are below actual rates;[48] the second in 1998, when long bond yields fell as a consequence of the Russian and Asian crises, whilst short rates remained stable. Therefore, the estimated long-term interest rates remained higher than the actual rates.

The identified model in (3.56) provides more accurate estimates for the inflation, as it uses a specific factor for this variable, instead of the inflation being explained only by the second factor of the term structure.

Focusing on the parameter estimates (Table 3.4), the factors are very persistent, as the estimated φ's are close to one and exhibit low volatility.[49] It is the second factor that contributes positively to the term premium ($\sigma_2\lambda_2$) and exhibits higher persistency. The market price of risk of this factor becomes higher when it is identified with inflation. Conversely, its volatility decreases. All variables are statistically significant, as the parameters evidence very low standard deviations (Table 3.5). This result confirms the general assertion about the high sensitivity of the results to the parameter estimates.[50]

As was seen in the previous charts, the results obtained with the three-factor model and using the shorter sample exhibit some differences to those obtained with the two-factor

---

[45] Notice that the identified model in (3.56) provides lower estimates for the risk premium as the market price of risk of the first factor is higher, giving a lower contribution for the risk premium.

[46] The term premium estimate for the 10-year maturity using the two-factor non-identified model is in line with other estimates obtained for different term structures. See, e.g., De Jong (1997), where an estimate of 1.65 for the 10-year term premium in the US term structure is presented.

[47] The quality of the fit for the yields contrasts sharply with the results found for the US by Gong and Remolona (1997c). In fact, in the latter it was concluded that at least two different two-factor heteroskedastic models are needed to model the whole US term structures of yields and volatilities: one to fit the medium/short end of the curves and another to fit the medium/long terms. The lowest time-series correlation coefficients between the observed and the estimated figures is 0.87, for the 10-year maturity, and the cross-section correlation coefficients are, in most days of the sample, above 0.9.

[48] The surprising behaviour of bond yields during 1994 is discussed in detail in Campbell (1995) with reference to the US market.

[49] Nevertheless, given that the standard deviations are low, the unit root hypothesis is rejected and, consequently, the factors are stationary. The comments of Jerome Henry on this issue are acknowledged.

[50] Very low standard deviations for the parameters have usually been obtained in former Kalman filter estimates of term structure models, as in Babbs and Nowman (1998), Gong and Remolona (1997a), Remolona et al. (1998), and Geyer and Pichler (1996).

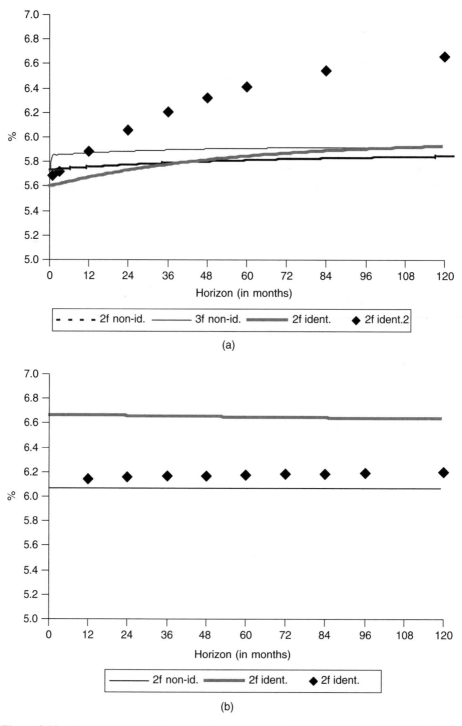

Figure 3.12   Average expected short-term interest rates: (a) 1986–1998 and (b) 1972–1998

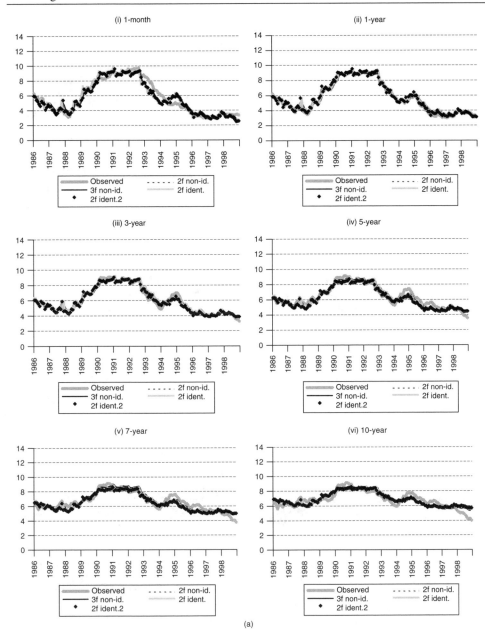

Figure 3.13 Time-series yield estimation results: (a) 1986–1998 and (b) 1972–1998

model. In order to opt between the two- and the three-factor model, a decision must be made based on the estimation accuracy of the models. Consequently, a hypothesis test is performed, considering that both models are nested and the two-factor model corresponds to the three-factor version imposing $\varphi_3 = \sigma_3 = 0$.

This test consists of computing the usual likelihood ratio test $l = -2(\ln v - \ln v^*) \sim \chi^2(q)$, v and v^* being the sum of the likelihood functions respectively of the two- and

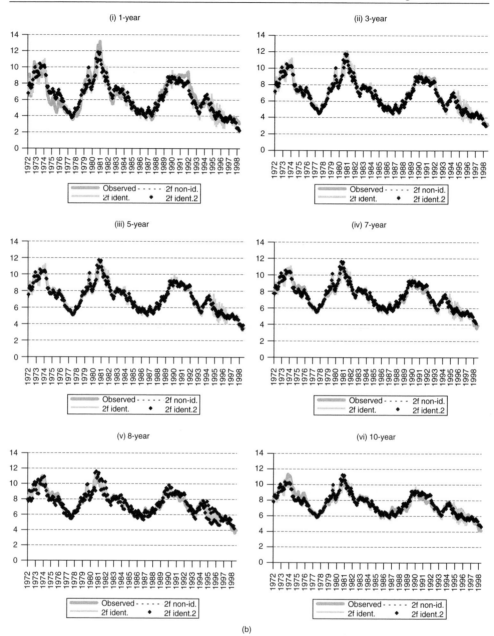

Figure 3.13 (*continued*)

the three-factor models and q the number of restrictions (in this case two restrictions are imposed). The values for $\ln v$ and $\ln v^*$ were -306.6472 and -304.5599, implying that $l = 4.1746$. As $\chi^2(2)_{0.95} = 5.991$, the null hypothesis is not rejected and the two-factor model is chosen. This conclusion is also suggested by the results already presented, due to the fact that the three-factor model does not seem to increase significantly the

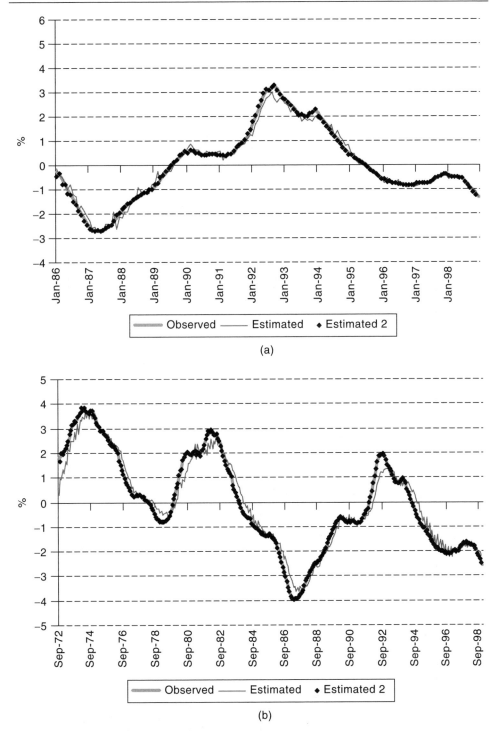

Figure 3.14   Observed and estimated yearly inflation: (a) 1986–1998 and (b) 1972–1998

Table 3.4 Parameter estimates

	δ	σ_1	φ_1	$\lambda_1\sigma_1$	σ_2	φ_2	$\lambda_2\sigma_2$
1986–1998							
2f non-id.	0.00489	0.00078	0.95076	0.22192	0.00173	0.98610	−0.09978
3f non-id.	0.00494	0.00114	0.97101	1.13983	0.00076	0.97543	−1.71811
2f ident.	0.00498	0.00156	0.98163	3.09798	0.00109	0.98216	−4.44754
2f ident.2	0.00566	0.00154	0.98169	3.20068	0.00111	0.98225	−4.45554
1972–1998							
2f non-id.	0.00508	0.00127	0.96283	0.10340	0.00165	0.99145	−0.10560
2f ident.	0.00547	0.00159	0.99225	2.30797	0.00070	0.99259	−5.29858
2f ident.2	0.00526	0.00141	0.95572	0.09198	0.00160	0.99298	−0.09869

	$\sigma_{1\pi}$	$\varphi_{1\pi}$	$\lambda_{1\pi}\sigma_{1\pi}$	$\lambda_{2\pi}\sigma_{1\pi}$	$B_{1\pi}$	$B_{2\pi}$	σ_3	φ_3	$\lambda_3\sigma_3$
1986–1998									
2f non-id.	–	–	–	–	–	–	–	–	–
3f non-id.	–	–	–	–	–	–	0.001317	0.989882	0.006502
2f ident.	–	–	–	–	–	–	–	–	–
2f ident.2	6.89340	0.99773	1.72529	1.55172	0.00004	−0.05438	–	–	–
1972–1998									
2f non-id.	–	–	–	–	–	–	–	–	–
2f ident.	–	–	–	–	–	–	–	–	–
2f ident.2	0.00931	0.99748	0.08405	−2.65631	0.25683	0.06685	–	–	–

Table 3.5 Standard deviation estimates

	δ	σ_1	φ_1	$\lambda_1\sigma_1$	σ_2	φ_2	$\lambda_2\sigma_2$
1986–1998							
2f non-id.	0.00009	0.00001	0.00142	0.00648	0.00003	0.00100	0.00084
2f ident.	0.00001	0.00001	0.00000	0.00000	0.00071	0.00100	0.00005
2f ident.2	0.00001	0.00001	0.00000	0.00000	0.00071	0.00100	0.00005
1972–1998							
2f non-id.	0.00001	0.00001	0.00000	0.00000	0.00249	0.00084	0.00013
2f ident.	0.00000	0.00000	0.00000	0.00000	0.00000	0.00000	0.00000
2f ident.2	0.00000	0.00000	0.00000	0.00000	0.00000	0.00000	0.00000

	$\sigma_{1\pi}$	$\varphi_{1\pi}$	$\lambda_{1\pi}\sigma_{1\pi}$	$\lambda_{2\pi}\sigma_{1\pi}$	$B_{1\pi}$	$B_{2\pi}$	σ_3	φ_3	$\lambda_3\sigma_3$
1986–1998									
2f non-id.	–	–	–	–	–	–	–	–	–
2f ident.	–	–	–	–	–	–	–	–	–
2f ident.2	0.12343	0.00154	0.00653	0.00000	0.00000	0.00004	–	–	–
1972–1998									
2f non-id.	–	–	–	–	–	–	–	–	–
2f ident.	–	–	–	–	–	–	–	–	–
2f ident.2	0.00000	0.00000	0.00000	0.00000	0.00864	0.00025	–	–	–

fitting quality. Consequently, the factor analysis and the identification are focused on the two-factor model.

In what concerns to the factor loadings (Figure 3.15a and b), the first factor – less persistent and volatile – is relatively more important for the short end of the curve, while the second assumes that role in the long end of the curve.[51]

The results already presented illustrate two ways of assessing the identification problem. A third one, as previously mentioned, is to analyse the correlation between the factors and the variables with which they are supposed to be related – the real interest rate and the expected inflation – including the analysis of the leading indicator properties of the second factor concerning the inflation rate.

The comparison between the unobservable factors, on the one hand, and a proxy for the real interest rate and the inflation rate, on the other hand, shows (in Figure 3.16a–d) that the correlation between the factors and the corresponding economic variables is high. In fact, using *ex-post* real interest rates as proxies for the *ex-ante* real rates, the correlation coefficients between one-month and three-month real rates, on the one side, and the first factor, on the other side, are around 0.75 and 0.6 respectively in the shorter and in the longer sample.[52] Using the identified models, that correlation coefficient decreases to 0.6 and 0.7 in the shorter sample, respectively using the models in (3.55) and (3.56), while

---

[51] Excluding the identified two-factor models for the shorter sample.

[52] This finding contrasts with the results in Gerlach (1995) for Germany, between January 1967 and January 1995. However, it is in line with the conclusion of Mishkin (1990b) that US short rates have information content regarding real interest rates.

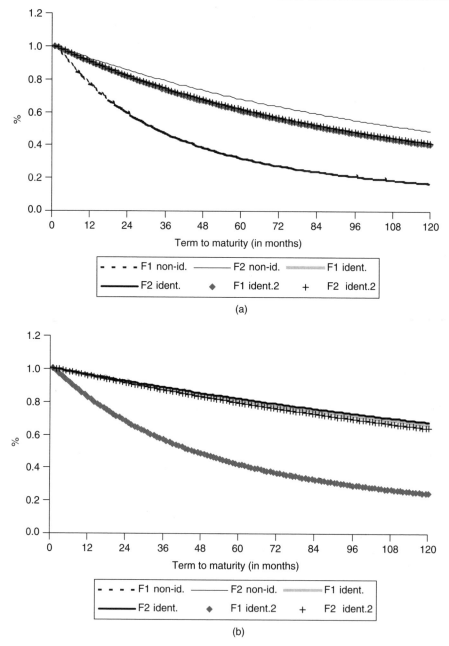

Figure 3.15 Factor loadings in the two-factor models: (a) 1986–1998 and (b) 1972–1998

in the larger sample it increases to 0.75 using the model in (3.55) and slightly decreases to 0.56 with the model in (3.56).

The correlation coefficients between the second factor and the inflation are close to 0.6 and 0.7 in the same samples. When the identified model in (3.55) is used, the second factor basically reproduces the inflation behaviour in the shorter sample, with the correlation

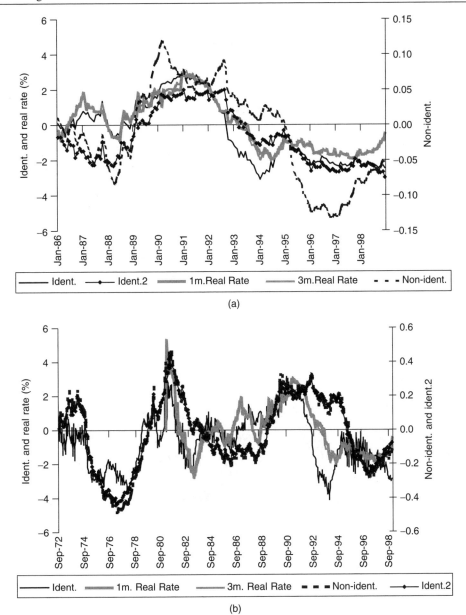

Figure 3.16 Time-series evolution: (a) first factor, 1986–1998; (b) first factor, 1972–1998; (c) second factor, 1986–1998; (d) second factor, 1972–1998; (e) inflation factor, 1986–1998; (f) inflation factor, 1972–1998

coefficient achieving figures above 0.98 in both samples. As the model in (3.56) includes a specific factor, the inflation, the correlation between the second factor and that variable decreases to around 0.5 in the shorter sample and remains close to 0.7 in the larger one.

In Figure 3.16e and f, the behaviour of the specific inflation factor vis-à-vis the observed inflation is presented. This factor in both samples is highly correlated to the inflation,

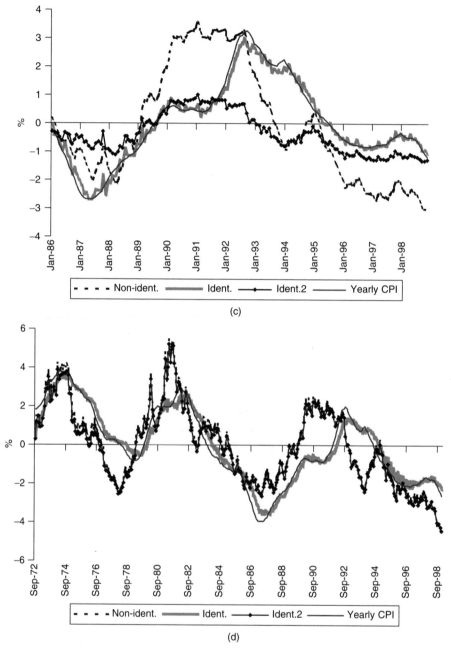

Figure 3.16   (*continued*)

which implies that the correlation between the second factor and the inflation rate becomes lower.

One of the most striking results obtained is that the second factor appears to be a leading indicator of inflation, according to Figure 3.16c and d. This is in line with the pioneer findings of Fama (1975) regarding the forecasting ability of the term structure

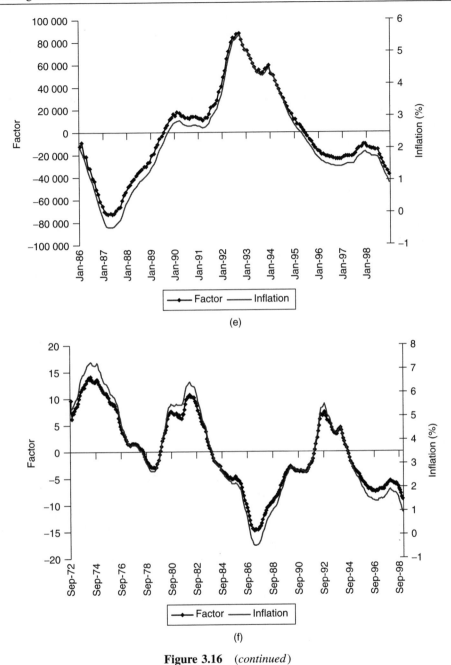

(e)

(f)

Figure 3.16 (*continued*)

on future inflation. It is also consistent with the idea that inflation expectations drive long-term interest rates, given that the second factor is relatively more important for the dynamics of interest rates at the long end of the curve, as previously stated.

If z_{2t} is a leading indicator for π_t, then the highest (positive) correlation should occur between lead values of π_t and z_{2t}. Table 3.6 shows cross-correlation between π_t and z_{2t}

in the larger sample. The shaded figures are the correlation coefficients between z_{2t} and lags of π_t. The first figure in each row is k and the next corresponds to the correlation between π_{t-k} and z_{2t} (negative k means lead). The next to the right is the correlation between π_{t-k-1} and z_{2t}, etc.

According to Table 3.6, the highest correlation (in bold) is at the fourth lead of inflation. Additionally, that correlation increases with leads of inflation up to four and steadily declines for lags of inflation.

Table 3.7 presents the Granger causality test and Figure 3.17 the impulse-response functions. The results strongly support the conjecture that $z_{2,t}$ has leading indicator properties for inflation. At the 5% level of confidence one can reject that $z_{2,t}$ does not Granger cause inflation. This is confirmed by the impulse-response analysis.

A positive shock to the innovation process of z_{2t} is followed by a statistically significant increase in inflation, as illustrated by the first panel in Figure 3.17, where the confidence interval of the impulse-response function does not include zero. However a positive shock to the innovation process of inflation does not seem to be followed by a statistically significant increase in z_{2t}, according to the last panel in Figure 3.17, where the confidence interval includes zero. These results suggest that an innovation to the inflation process does not contain "news" for the process of expectation formation. This is in line with the forward-looking interpretation of shocks to z_{2t} as reflecting "news" about the future course of inflation.

Table 3.6 Cross-correlations of series π_t and z_{2t} (monthly data from 1972:09 to 1998:12)

k					
−25:	0.3974759	0.4274928	0.4570631	0.4861307	0.5129488	0.5394065
−19:	0.5639012	0.5882278	0.6106181	0.6310282	0.6501370	0.6670820
−13:	0.6829368	0.6979626	0.7119833	0.7235875	0.7324913	0.7385423
−7:	0.7432024	0.7453345	0.7457082	**0.7458129**	0.7443789	0.7411556
−1:	0.7368274	0.7311008	0.7144727	0.6954511	0.6761649	0.6561413
5:	0.6360691	0.6159540	0.5949472	0.5726003	0.5478967	0.5229193
11:	0.4960254	0.4706518	0.4427914	0.4156929	0.3870690	0.3590592
17:	0.3311699	0.3011714	0.2720773	0.2425888	0.2126804	0.1829918
23:	0.1527293	0.1226024	0.0927202	0.0636053	0.0362558	0.0085952
29:	−0.0167756	−0.0421135	−0.0673895	−0.0911283	−0.1139021	−0.1356261

Note: Correlation between π_{t-k} and z_{2t} (i.e., negative k means lead).

Table 3.7 Granger causality tests

Inflation does not Granger cause z_{2t}		
Variable	F-Statistic	Significance
π_t	5.8	0.03[a]
z_{2t} does not Granger cause inflation		
Variable	F-Statistic	Significance
z_{2t}	6.12	0.03[a]

[a] Means rejection at 5% level.

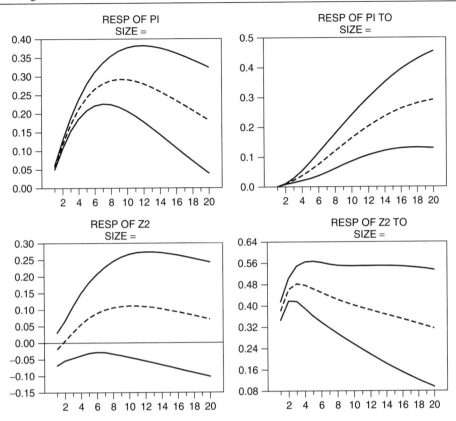

Figure 3.17   Impulse-response functions and two standard error bands

Overall, considering the results for the factor loadings and the relationship between the latent factors and the economic variables, the short-term interest rates are mostly driven by the real interest rates. In parallel, the inflation expectations exert the most important influence on the long-term rates, as is usually assumed. Similar results concerning the information content of the German term structure, namely in the longer terms, regarding future changes in inflation rate were obtained in several previous papers, namely Schich (1996), Gerlach (1995) and Mishkin (1991), using different samples and testing procedures.[53]

---

[53] The Mishkin (1991) and Jorion and Mishkin (1991) results on Germany are contradictory as, according to Mishkin (1991), the short end of the term structure does not contain information on future inflation for all OECD countries studied, except for France, the UK and Germany. Conversely, Jorion and Mishkin (1991) conclude that the predictive power of the shorter rates about future inflation is low in the USA, Germany and Switzerland.

Fama (1990) and Mishkin (1990a,b) present identical conclusions concerning the information content of US term structure regarding future inflation and state that the US dollar short rates have information content regarding future real interest rates and the longer rates contain information on inflation expectations. Mishkin (1990b) also concludes that for several countries the information on inflation expectations is weaker than for the United States. Mehra (1997) presents evidence of a cointegration relation between the nominal yield on a 10-year Treasury bond and the actual US inflation rate. Koedijk and Kool (1995), Mishkin (1991), and Jorion and Mishkin (1991) supply some evidence on the information content of the term structure concerning inflation rate in several countries.

Fleming and Remolona (1998) also found that macroeconomic announcements of the CPI and the PPI affect mostly the long end of the term structure of interest rates, using high frequency data. Nevertheless, it is also important to have in mind that, according to Schich (1999), the information content of the term structure on future inflation is time-varying and depends on the country considered.

The relationship between the factors and the referred variables is consistent with the time-series properties of the factors and those variables. Actually, as observed in Clarida *et al.* (1998), the $I(1)$ hypothesis is rejected in Dickey–Fuller tests for the German inflation rate and short-term interest rate, while, as previously stated, the factors are stationary.

3.8 CONCLUSIONS

The identification of the factors that determine the time-series and cross-section behaviour of the term structure of interest rates is one of the most challenging research topics in finance. In this chapter, it was shown that a two-factor constant volatility model describes quite well the dynamics and shape of the German yield curve between 1986 and 1998.

The data supports the expectations theory with constant term premiums and thus the term premium structure can be calculated and short-term interest rate expectations derived from the adjusted forward rate curve. The estimates obtained for the term premium curve are not inconsistent with the figures usually conjectured. Nevertheless, poorer results are obtained if the second factor is directly linked to the inflation rate, given that restrictions on the behaviour of that factor are imposed, generating less plausible shapes and figures for the term premium curve.

We identified within the sample two periods of poorer model performance, both related to world-wide gyrations in bond markets (Spring 1994 and 1998), which were characterised by sharp changes in long-term interest rates while short-term rates remained stable.

As to the evolution of bond yields in Germany during 1998, it seems that it is more the (low) level of inflation expectations as compared to the level of real interest rates that underlies the dynamics of the yield curve during that year. However, there still remains substantial volatility in long bond yields to be explained. This could be related to the spillover effects of international bond market developments on the German bond market in the aftermath of the Russian and Asian crises.

It was also shown that one of those factors seems to be related to the *ex-ante* real interest rate, while a second factor is linked to inflation expectations. This conclusion is much in accordance with the empirical literature on the subject and is a relevant result for modelling the yield curve using information on macroeconomic variables.

Therefore, modelling the yield curve behaviour, namely for VaR purposes, seems to be reasonably approached by simulations of (*ex-post*) real interest rates and lagged inflation rate. In addition, the results obtained suggest that a central bank has a decisive role concerning the bond market moves, given that it influences both the short and the long ends of the yield curve, respectively by influencing the real interest rate and the inflation expectations. Accordingly, the second factor may also be used as an indicator of monetary policy credibility.

REFERENCES

Aït-Sahalia, Y. (1996), "Testing Continuous-Time Models of the Spot Interest Rate", *Review of Financial Studies*, **9**, 427–470.

Babbs, S. H. and K. B. Nowman (1998), "An Application of Generalized Vasicek Term Structure Models to the UK Gilt-edged Market: a Kalman Filtering analysis", *Applied Financial Economics*, **8**, 637–644.

Backus, D., S. Foresi, A. Mozumdar and L. Wu (1997), "Predictable Changes in Yields and Forward Rates", *mimeo*.

Backus, D., S. Foresi and C. Telmer (1998), "Discrete-Time Models of Bond Pricing", NBER working paper no. 6736.

Balduzzi, P., S. R. Das, S. Foresi and R. Sundaram (1996), "A Simple Approach to Three Factor Affine Term Structure Models", *Journal of Fixed Income*, **6** December, 43–53.

Bliss, R. (1997), "Movements in the Term Structure of Interest Rates", Federal Reserve Bank of Atlanta, *Economic Review*, Fourth Quarter.

Bolder, D. J. (2001), "Affine Term-Structure Models: Theory and Implementation", Bank of Canada, working paper 2001-15.

Breeden, D. T. (1979), "An Intertemporal Asset Pricing Model with Stochastic Consumption and Investment Opportunities", *Journal of Financial Economics*, **7**, 265–296.

Buhler, W., M. Uhrig-Homburg, U. Walter and T. Weber (1999), "An Empirical Comparison of Forward-Rate and Spot-Rate Models for Valuing Interest-Rate Options", *The Journal of Finance*, **LIV**, 1, February.

Campbell, J. Y. (1995), "Some Lessons from the Yield Curve", *Journal of Economic Perspectives*, **9**, 3, 129–152.

Campbell, J. Y., A. W. Lo and A. C. MacKinlay (1997), *The Econometrics of Financial Markets*, Princeton University Press, Princeton, NJ.

Cassola, N. and J. B. Luís (1996), "The Term Structure of Interest Rates: a Comparison of Alternative Estimation Methods with an Application to Portugal", Banco de Portugal, working paper no. 17/96, October 1996.

Cassola, N. and J. B. Luís (2003), "A Two-Factor Model of the German Term Structure of Interest Rates", *Applied Financial Economics*, forthcoming.

Chen, R. and L. Scott (1993a), "Maximum Likelihood Estimations for a Multi-Factor Equilibrium Model of the Term Structure of Interest Rates", *Journal of Fixed Income*, **3**, 14–31.

Chen, R. and L. Scott (1993b), "Multi-Factor Cox–Ingersoll–Ross Models of the Term Structure: Estimates and Test from a Kalman Filter", working paper, University of Georgia.

Clarida, R. and M. Gertler (1997), "How the Bundesbank Conducts Monetary Policy", in Romer, C. D. and D. H. Romer (eds), *Reducing Inflation: Motivation and Strategy*, NBER Studies in Business Cycles, Vol. 30.

Clarida, R., J. Gali and M. Gertler (1998), "Monetary Policy Rules in Practice – Some International Evidence", *European Economic Review*, **42**, 1033–1067.

Cox, J., J. Ingersoll and S. Ross (1985a), "A Theory of the Term Structure of Interest Rates", *Econometrica*, **53**, 385–407.

Cox, J., J. Ingersoll and S. Ross (1985b), "An Intertemporal General Equilibrium Model of Asset Prices", *Econometrica*, **53**, 363–384.

Deacon, M. and A. Derry (1994), "Deriving Estimates of Inflation Expectations from the Prices of UK Government Bonds", Bank of England, working paper 23.

De Jong, F. (1997), "Time-Series and Cross-section Information in Affine Term Structure Models", Center for Economic Research.

Doan, T. A. (1995), *RATS 4.0 User's Manual*, Estima, Evanston, IL.

Duffie, D. and R. Kan (1996), "A Yield Factor Model of Interest Rates", *Mathematical Finance*, **6**, 379–406.

Fama, E. F. (1975), "Short Term Interest Rates as Predictors of Inflation", *American Economic Review*, **65**, 269–282.

Fama, E. F. (1990), "Term Structure Forecasts of Interest Rates, Inflation and Real Returns", *Journal of Monetary Economics*, **25**, 59–76.

Fleming, M. J. and E. M. Remolona (1998), "The Term Structure of Announcement Effects", *mimeo*.

Fung, B. S. C., S. Mitnick and E. Remolona (1999), "Uncovering Inflation Expectations and Risk Premiums from Internationally Integrated Financial Markets", Bank of Canada, working paper 99-6.

Gerlach, S. (1995), "The Information Content of the Term Structure: Evidence for Germany", BIS working paper no. 29, September.

Geyer, A. L. J. and S. Pichler (1996), "A State-Space Approach to Estimate and Test Multifactor Cox–Ingersoll–Ross Models of the Term Structure", *mimeo.*

Gong, F. F. and E. M. Remolona (1997a), "A Three-factor Econometric Model of the US Term Structure", FRBNY *Staff Reports*, **19**, January.

Gong, F. F. and E. M. Remolona (1997b), "Inflation Risk in the U.S. Yield Curve: The Usefulness of Indexed Bonds", Federal Reserve Bank, New York, June.

Gong, F. F. and E. M. Remolona (1997c), "Two Factors Along the Yield Curve", *The Manchester School Supplement*, pp. 1–31.

Hamilton, J. D. (1994), *Time Series Analysis*, Princeton University Press, Princeton, NJ.

Jorion, P. and F. Mishkin (1991), "A Multicountry Comparison of Term-structure Forecasts at Long Horizons", *Journal of Financial Economics*, **29**, 59–80.

Koedijk, K. G. and C. J. M. Kool (1995), "Future Inflation and the Information in International Term Structures", *Empirical Economics*, **20**, 217–242.

Litterman, R. and J. Scheinkman (1991), "Common Factors Affecting Bond Returns", *Journal of Fixed Income*, **1**, June, 49–53.

Luís, J. B. (2001), *Essays on Extracting Information from Financial Asset Prices*, PhD thesis, University of York.

Mehra, Y. P. (1997), "The Bond Rate and Actual Future Inflation", Federal Reserve Bank of Richmond, working paper 97-3, March.

Mishkin, F. (1990a), "What Does the Term Structure Tell Us About Future Inflation", *Journal of Monetary Economics*, **25**, 77–95.

Mishkin, F. (1990b), "The Information in the Longer Maturity Term Structure About Future Inflation", *Quarterly Journal of Economics*, **55**, 815–828.

Mishkin, F. (1991), "A Multi-country Study of the Information in the Shorter Maturity Term Structure About Future Inflation", *Journal of International Money and Finance*, **10**, 2–22.

Nelson, C. R. and A. F. Siegel (1987), "Parsimonious Modelling of Yield Curves", *Journal of Business*, **60**, 4.

Remolona, E., M. R. Wickens and F. F. Gong (1998), "What was the Market's View of U.K. Monetary Policy? Estimating Inflation Risk and Expected Inflation with Indexed Bonds", FRBNY *Staff Reports*, **57**, December.

Ross, S. A. (1976), "The Arbitrage Theory of Capital Asset Pricing", *Journal of Economic Theory*, **13**, 341–360.

Schich, S. T. (1996), "Alternative Specifications of the German Term Structure and its Information Content Regarding Inflation", Deutsche Bundesbank, D.P. 8/96.

Schich, S. T. (1999), "What the Yield Curves Say About Inflation: Does It Change Over Time?", OECD *Economic Department Working Papers*, No. 227.

Svensson, L. E. O. (1994), "Estimating and Interpreting Forward Interest Rates: Sweden 1992–4", CEPR *Discussion Paper Series*, No. 1051.

Vasicek, O. (1977), "An Equilibrium Characterisation of the Term Structure", *Journal of Financial Economics*, **5**, 177–188.

Zin, S. (1997), "Discussion of Evans and Marshall", *Carnegie-Rochester Conference on Public Policy*, November.

Forecasting and Trading Currency Volatility: An Application of Recurrent Neural Regression and Model Combination*

CHRISTIAN L. DUNIS AND XUEHUAN HUANG

ABSTRACT

In this chapter, we examine the use of nonparametric Neural Network Regression (NNR) and Recurrent Neural Network (RNN) regression models for *forecasting* and *trading* currency volatility, with an application to the GBP/USD and USD/JPY exchange rates. Both the results of the NNR and RNN models are *benchmarked* against the simpler GARCH alternative and implied volatility. Two simple model combinations are also analysed.

The intuitively appealing idea of developing a nonlinear nonparametric approach to forecast FX volatility, identify mispriced options and subsequently develop a trading strategy based upon this process is implemented for the first time on a comprehensive basis. Using daily data from December 1993 through April 1999, we develop alternative FX volatility forecasting models. These models are then tested *out-of-sample* over the period April 1999–May 2000, not only in terms of *forecasting accuracy*, but also in terms of *trading efficiency*. In order to do so, we apply a realistic volatility trading strategy using FX option straddles once mispriced options have been identified.

Allowing for transaction costs, most trading strategies retained produce positive returns. RNN models appear as the best single modelling approach yet, somewhat surprisingly, a model combination which has the best overall performance in terms of forecasting accuracy fails to improve the RNN-based volatility trading results.

Another conclusion from our results is that, for the period and currencies considered, the currency option market was inefficient and/or the pricing formulae applied by market participants were inadequate.

4.1 INTRODUCTION

Exchange rate volatility has been a constant feature of the International Monetary System ever since the breakdown of the Bretton Woods system of fixed parities in 1971–73. Not surprisingly, in the wake of the growing use of derivatives in other financial markets, and

---

* This chapter previously appeared under the same title in the *Journal of Forecasting*, **21**, 317–354 (2002). © John Wiley & Sons, Ltd. Reproduced with permission.

Applied Quantitative Methods for Trading and Investment. Edited by C.L. Dunis, J. Laws and P. Naïm
© 2003 John Wiley & Sons, Ltd   ISBN: 0-470-84885-5

following the extension of the seminal work of Black–Scholes (1973) to foreign exchange by Garman–Kohlhagen (1983), currency options have become an ever more popular way to hedge foreign exchange exposures and/or speculate in the currency markets.

In the context of this wide use of currency options by market participants, having the best volatility prediction has become ever more crucial. True, the only unknown variable in the Garman–Kohlhagen pricing formula is precisely the future foreign exchange rate volatility during the life of the option. With an "accurate" volatility estimate and knowing the other variables (strike level, current level of the exchange rate, interest rates on both currencies and maturity of the option), it is possible to derive the theoretical arbitrage-free price of the option. Just because there will never be such thing as a unanimous agreement on the future volatility estimate, market participants with a better view/forecast of the evolution of volatility will have an edge over their competitors.

In a rational market, the equilibrium price of an option will be affected by changes in volatility. The higher the volatility perceived by market participants, the higher the option's price. Higher volatility implies a greater possible dispersion of the foreign exchange rate at expiry: all other things being equal, the option holder has logically an asset with a greater chance of a more profitable exercise. In practice, those investors/market participants who can reliably predict volatility should be able to control better the financial risks associated with their option positions and, at the same time, profit from their superior forecasting ability.

There is a wealth of articles on predicting volatility in the foreign exchange market: for instance, Baillie and Bollerslev (1990) used ARIMA and GARCH models to describe the volatility on hourly data, West and Cho (1995) analysed the predictive ability of GARCH, AR and nonparametric models on weekly data, Jorion (1995) examined the predictive power of implied standard deviation as a volatility forecasting tool with daily data, Dunis *et al.* (2001b) measured, using daily data, both the 1-month and 3-month forecasting ability of 13 different volatility models including AR, GARCH, stochastic variance and model combinations with and without the adding of implied volatility as an extra explanatory variable.

Nevertheless, with the exception of Engle *et al.* (1993), Dunis and Gavridis (1997) and, more recently, Laws and Gidman (2000), these papers evaluate the out-of-sample forecasting performance of their models using traditional statistical accuracy criteria, such as root mean squared error, mean absolute error, mean absolute percentage error, Theil-U statistic and correct directional change prediction. Investors and market participants however have trading performance as their ultimate goal and will select a forecasting model based on financial criteria rather than on some statistical criterion such as root mean squared error minimisation. Yet, as mentioned above, seldom has recently published research applied any financial utility criterion in assessing the out-of-sample performance of volatility models.

Over the past few years, Neural Network Regression (NNR) has been widely advocated as a new alternative modelling technology to more traditional econometric and statistical approaches, claiming increasing success in the fields of economic and financial forecasting. This has resulted in many publications comparing neural networks and traditional forecasting approaches. In the case of foreign exchange markets, it is worth pointing out that most of the published research has focused on exchange rate forecasting rather than on currency volatility forecasts. However, financial criteria, such as Sharpe ratio, profitability, return on equity, maximum drawdown, etc., have been widely used to measure and quantify the out-of-sample forecasting performance. Dunis (1996) investigated the application of NNR to intraday foreign exchange forecasting and his results were evaluated by means of a trading strategy. Kuan and Liu (1995) proposed two-step Recurrent Neural Network (RNN) models to forecast exchange rates and their results were evaluated using traditional statistical accuracy criteria. Tenti (1996) applied RNNs to predict the USD/DEM exchange rate, devising a trading strategy to assess his results, while Franses and Van Homelen (1998) use NNR models to predict four daily exchange rate returns relative to the Dutch guilder using directional accuracy to assess out-of-sample forecasting accuracy. Overall, it seems however that neural network research applied to exchange rates has been so far seldom devoted to FX volatility forecasting.

Accordingly, the rationale for this chapter is to investigate the predictive power of alternative nonparametric forecasting models of foreign exchange volatility, both from a *statistical* and an *economic* point of view. We examine the use of NNR and RNN regression models for *forecasting* and *trading* currency volatility, with an application to the GBP/USD and USD/JPY exchange rates. The results of the NNR and RNN models are *benchmarked* against the simpler GARCH (1,1) alternative, implied volatility and model combinations: in terms of model combination, a simple average combination and the Granger–Ramanathan (1984) optimal weighting regression-based approach are employed and their results investigated.

Using daily data from December 1993 through April 1999, we develop alternative FX volatility forecasting models. These models are then tested out-of-sample over the period April 1999–May 2000, not only in terms of forecasting accuracy, but also in terms of *trading efficiency*. In order to do so, we apply a realistic volatility trading strategy using FX option straddles once mispriced options have been identified.

Allowing for transaction costs, most trading strategies retained produce positive returns. RNN models appear as the best single modelling approach but model combinations, despite their superior performance in terms of forecasting accuracy, fail to produce superior trading strategies.

Another conclusion from our results is that, for the period and currencies considered, the currency option market was inefficient and/or the pricing formulae applied by market participants were inadequate.

Overall, we depart from existing work in several respects.

Firstly, we develop alternative nonparametric FX volatility models, applying in particular an RNN architecture with a loop back from the output layer implying an error feedback mechanism, i.e. we apply a *nonlinear error-correction* modelling approach to FX volatility.

Secondly, we apply our nonparametric models to *FX volatility*, something that has not been done so far. A recent development in the literature has been the application of nonparametric time series modelling approaches to volatility forecasts. Gaussian kernel regression is an example, as in West and Cho (1995). Neural networks have also been found useful in modelling the properties of nonlinear time series. As mentioned above, if there are quite a few articles on applications of NNR models to foreign exchange, stock and commodity markets,[1] there are rather few concerning financial markets volatility

---

[1] For NNR applications to commodity forecasting, see, for instance, Ntungo and Boyd (1998) and Trippi and Turban (1993). For applications to the stock market, see, amongst others, Deboeck (1994) and Leung *et al.* (2000).

forecasting in general.[2] It seems therefore that, as an alternative technique to more traditional statistical forecasting methods, NNR models need further investigation to check whether or not they can add value in the field of foreign exchange volatility forecasting.

Finally, unlike previous work, we do not limit ourselves to forecasting accuracy but extend the analysis to the all-important *trading efficiency*, taking advantage of the fact that there exists a large and liquid FX implied volatility market that enables us to apply sophisticated volatility trading strategies.

The chapter is organised as follows. Section 4.2 describes our exchange rate and volatility data. Section 4.3 briefly presents the GARCH (1,1) model and gives the corresponding 21-day volatility forecasts. Section 4.4 provides a detailed overview and explains the procedures and methods used in applying the NNR and RNN modelling procedure to our financial time series, and it presents the 21-day volatility forecasts obtained with these methods. Section 4.5 briefly describes the model combinations retained and assesses the 21-day out-of-sample forecasts using traditional statistical accuracy criteria. Section 4.6 introduces the volatility trading strategy using FX option straddles that we follow once mispriced options have been identified through the use of our most successful volatility forecasting models. We present detailed trading results allowing for transaction costs and discuss their implications, particularly in terms of a qualified assessment of the efficiency of the currency options market. Finally, Section 4.7 provides some concluding comments and suggestions for further work.

4.2 THE EXCHANGE RATE AND VOLATILITY DATA

The motivation for this research implies that the success or failure to develop profitable volatility trading strategies clearly depends on the possibility to generate accurate volatility forecasts and thus to implement adequate volatility modelling procedures.

Numerous studies have documented the fact that logarithmic returns of exchange rate time series exhibit "volatility clustering" properties, that is periods of large volatility tend to cluster together followed by periods of relatively lower volatility (see, amongst others, Baillie and Bollerslev (1990), Kroner *et al.* (1995) and Jorion (1997)). Volatility forecasting crucially depends on identifying the typical characteristics of volatility within the restricted sample period selected and then projecting them over the forecasting period.

We present in turn the two databanks we have used for this study and the modifications to the original series we have made where appropriate.

4.2.1 The exchange rate series databank and historical volatility

The return series we use for the GBP/USD and USD/JPY exchange rates were extracted from a historical exchange rate database provided by Datastream. Logarithmic returns, defined as $\log(S_t/S_{t-1})$, are calculated for each exchange rate on a daily frequency basis. We multiply these returns by 100, so that we end up with percentage changes in the exchange rates considered, i.e. $s_t = 100 \log(S_t/S_{t-1})$.

---

[2] Even though there are no NNR applications yet to foreign exchange volatility forecasting, some researchers have used NNR models to measure the stock market volatility (see, for instance, Donaldson and Kamstra (1997) and Bartlmae and Rauscher (2000)).

Our exchange rate databank spans from 31 December 1993 to 9 May 2000, giving us 1610 observations per exchange rate.[3] This databank was divided into two separate sets with the first 1329 observations from 31 December 1993 to 9 April 1999 defined as our in-sample testing period and the remaining 280 observations from 12 April 1999 to 9 May 2000 being used for out-of-sample forecasting and validation.

In line with the findings of many earlier studies on exchange rate changes (see, amongst others, Engle and Bollerslev (1986), Baillie and Bollerslev (1989), Hsieh (1989), West and Cho (1995)), the descriptive statistics of our currency returns (not reported here in order to conserve space) clearly show that they are nonnormally distributed and heavily fat-tailed. They also show that mean returns are not statistically different from zero. Further standard tests of autocorrelation, nonstationarity and heteroskedasticity show that logarithmic returns are all stationary and heteroskedastic. Whereas there is no evidence of autocorrelation for the GBP/USD return series, some autocorrelation is detected at the 10% significance level for USD/JPY returns.

The fact that our currency returns have zero unconditional mean enables us to use *squared returns* as a measure of their variance and *absolute returns* as a measure of their standard deviation or volatility.[4] The standard tests of autocorrelation, nonstationarity and heteroskedasticity (again not reported here in order to conserve space) show that squared and absolute currency returns series for the in-sample period are all nonnormally distributed, stationary, autocorrelated and heteroskedastic (except USD/JPY squared returns which were found to be homoskedastic).

Still, as we are interested in analysing alternative volatility forecasting models and whether they can add value in terms of forecasting *realised* currency volatility, we must adjust our statistical computation of volatility to take into account the fact that, even if it is only the matter of a constant, in currency options markets, volatility is quoted in annualised terms. As we wish to focus on 1-month volatility forecasts and related trading strategies, taking, as is usual practice, a 252-trading day year (and consequently a 21-trading day month), we compute the 1-month volatility as the moving annualised standard deviation of our logarithmic returns and end up with the following historical volatility measures for the 1-month horizon:

$$\sigma_t = \frac{1}{21} \sum_{t-20}^{t} (\sqrt{252} \times |s_t|)$$

where $|s_t|$ is the absolute currency return.[5] The value σ_t is the realised 1-month exchange rate volatility that we are interested in forecasting as accurately as possible, in order to see if it is possible to find any mispriced option that we could possibly take advantage of.

The descriptive statistics of both historical volatility series (again not reported here in order to conserve space) show that they are nonnormally distributed and fat-tailed. Further statistical tests of autocorrelation, heteroskedasticity and nonstationarity show that they exhibit strong autocorrelation but that they are stationary in levels. Whereas

---

[3] Actually, we used exchange rate data from 01/11/1993 to 09/05/2000, the data during the period 01/11/1993 to 31/12/1993 being used for the "pre-calculation" of the 21-day realised historical volatility.

[4] Although the unconditional mean is zero, it is of course possible that the conditional mean may vary over time.

[5] The use of absolute returns (rather than their squared value) is justified by the fact that with zero unconditional mean, averaging absolute returns gives a measure of standard deviation.

GBP/USD historical volatility is heteroskedastic, USD/JPY realised volatility was found to be homoskedastic.

Having presented our exchange rate series databank and explained how we compute our historical volatilities from these original series (so that they are in a format comparable to that which prevails in the currency options market), we now turn our attention to the implied volatility databank that we have used.

4.2.2 The implied volatility series databank

Volatility has now become an observable and traded quantity in financial markets, and particularly so in the currency markets. So far, most studies dealing with implied volatilities have used volatilities backed out from historical premium data on traded options rather than over-the-counter (OTC) volatility data (see, amongst others, Latane and Rendleman (1976), Chiras and Manaster (1978), Lamoureux and Lastrapes (1993), Kroner *et al.* (1995) and Xu and Taylor (1996)).

As underlined by Dunis *et al.* (2000), the problem in using exchange data is that call and put prices are only available for given strike levels and fixed maturity dates. The corresponding implied volatility series must therefore be *backed out* using a specific option pricing model. This procedure generates two sorts of potential biases: material errors or mismatches can affect the variables that are needed for the solving of the pricing model, e.g. the forward points or the spot rate, and, more importantly, the very specification of the pricing model that is chosen can have a crucial impact on the final "backed out" implied volatility series.

This is the reason why, in this chapter, we use *data directly observable on the marketplace*. This original approach seems further warranted by current market practice whereby brokers and market makers in currency options deal in fact *in volatility terms* and not in option premium terms any more.[6] The volatility time series we use for the two exchange rates selected, GBP/USD and USD/JPY, were extracted from a *market quoted implied volatilities* database provided by Chemical Bank for data until end-1996, and updated from Reuters "Ric" codes subsequently. These at-the-money forward, market-quoted volatilities are in fact obtained from brokers by Reuters on a daily basis, at the close of business in London.

These implied volatility series are nonnormally distributed and fat-tailed. Further statistical tests of autocorrelation and heteroskedasticity (again not reported here in order to conserve space) show that they exhibit strong autocorrelation and heteroskedasticity. Unit root tests show that, at the 1-month horizon, both GBP/USD and USD/JPY implied volatilities are stationary at the 5% significance level.

Certainly, as noted by Dunis *et al.* (2001b) and confirmed in Tables A4.1 and A4.3 in Appendix A for the GBP/USD and USD/JPY, an interesting feature is that the mean level of implied volatilities stands well above average historical volatility levels.[7] This tendency of the currency options market to overestimate actual volatility is further documented

---

[6] The market data that we use are *at-the-money forward volatilities*, as the use of either in-the-money or out-of-the-money volatilities would introduce a significant bias in our analysis due to the so-called "smile effect", i.e. the fact that volatility is "priced" higher for strike levels which are not at-the-money. It should be made clear that these implied volatilities are not simply backed out of an option pricing model but are instead directly quoted from brokers. Due to arbitrage they cannot diverge too far from the theoretical level.

[7] As noted by Dunis *et al.* (2001b), a possible explanation for implied volatility being higher than its historical counterpart may be due to the fact that market makers are generally options sellers (whereas end users are

by Figures A4.1 and A4.2 which show 1-month actual and implied volatilities for the GBP/USD and USD/JPY exchange rates. These two charts also clearly show that, for each exchange rate concerned, actual and implied volatilities are moving rather closely together, which is further confirmed by Tables A4.2 and A4.4 for both GBP/USD and USD/JPY volatilities.

4.3 THE GARCH (1,1) BENCHMARK VOLATILITY FORECASTS

4.3.1 The choice of the benchmark model

As the GARCH model originally devised by Bollerslev (1986) and Taylor (1986) is well documented in the literature, we just present it very briefly, as it has now become widely used, in various forms, by both academics and practitioners to model conditional variance. We therefore do not intend to review its many different variants as this would be outside the scope of this chapter. Besides, there is a wide consensus, certainly among market practitioners, but among many researchers as well that, when variants of the standard GARCH (1,1) model do provide an improvement, it is only marginal most of the time. Consequently, for this chapter, we choose to estimate a GARCH (1,1) model for both the GBP/USD and USD/JPY exchange rates as it embodies a compact representation and serves well our purpose of finding an adequate *benchmark* for the more complex NNR models.

In its simple GARCH (1,1) form, the GARCH model basically states that the conditional variance of asset returns in any given period depends upon a constant, the previous period's squared random component of the return *and* the previous period's variance.

In other words, if we denote by σ_t^2 the conditional variance of the return at time t and ε_{t-1}^2 the squared random component of the return in the previous period, for a standard GARCH (1,1) process, we have:

$$\sigma_t^2 = \omega + \alpha\varepsilon_{t-1}^2 + \beta\sigma_{t-1}^2 \tag{4.1}$$

Equation (4.1) yields immediately the 1-step ahead volatility forecast and, using recursive substitution, Engle and Bollerslev (1986) and Baillie and Bollerslev (1992) give the n-step ahead forecast for a GARCH (1,1) process:

$$\sigma_{t+n}^2 = \omega[1 + (\alpha + \beta) + \cdots + (\alpha + \beta)^{n-2}] + \omega + \alpha\varepsilon_t^2 + \beta\sigma_t^2 \tag{4.2}$$

This is the formula that we use to compute our GARCH (1,1) n-step ahead out-of-sample forecast.

4.3.2 The GARCH (1,1) volatility forecasts

If many researchers have noted that no alternative GARCH specification could consistently outperform the standard GARCH (1,1) model, some such as Bollerslev (1987), Baillie

---

more often option buyers): there is probably a tendency among option writers to include a "risk premium" when pricing volatility. Kroner *et al.* (1995) suggest another two reasons: (i) the fact that if interest rates are stochastic, then the implied volatility will capture both asset price volatility and interest rate volatility, thus skewing implied volatility upwards, and (ii) the fact that if volatility is stochastic but the option pricing formula is constant, then this additional source of volatility will be picked up by the implied volatility.

and Bollerslev (1989) and Hsieh (1989), amongst others, point out that the Student-t distribution fits the daily exchange rate logarithmic returns better than conditional normality, as the former is characterised by fatter tails. We thus generate GARCH (1,1) 1-step ahead forecasts with the Student-t distribution assumption.[8] We give our results for the GBP/USD exchange rate:

$$\log(S_t / S_{t-1}) = \varepsilon_t$$

$$\varepsilon_t | \varphi_{t-1} \sim N(0, \sigma_t^2)$$

$$\sigma_t^2 = 0.0021625 + 0.032119\varepsilon_{t-1}^2 + 0.95864\sigma_{t-1}^2$$

$$(0.0015222) \quad (0.010135) \quad (0.013969) \qquad\qquad (4.3)$$

where the figures in parentheses are asymptotic standard errors. The t-values for α and β are highly significant and show strong evidence that σ_t^2 varies with ε_{t-1}^2 and σ_{t-1}^2. The coefficients also have the expected sign. Additionally, the conventional Wald statistic for testing the joint hypothesis that $\alpha = \beta = 0$ clearly rejects the null, suggesting a significant GARCH effect.

The parameters in equation (4.3) were used to estimate the 21-day ahead volatility forecast for the USD/GBP exchange rate: using the 1-step ahead GARCH (1,1) coefficients, the conditional 21-day volatility forecast was generated each day according to equation (4.2) above. The same procedure was followed for the USD/JPY exchange rate volatility (see Appendix B4.3).

Figure 4.1 displays the GARCH (1,1) 21-day volatility forecasts for the USD/GBP exchange rate both in- and out-of-sample (the last 280 observations, from 12/04/1999 to

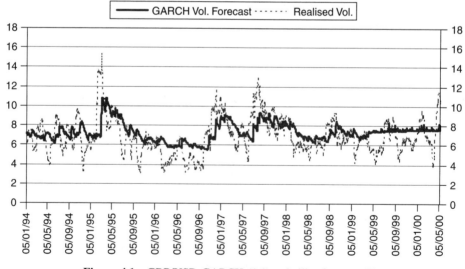

Figure 4.1   GBP/USD GARCH (1,1) volatility forecast (%)

---

[8] Actually, we modelled conditional volatility with both the normal and the t-distribution. The results are only slightly different. However, both the Akaike and the Schwarz Bayesian criteria tend to favour the t-distribution. We therefore selected the results from the t-distribution for further tests (see Appendix B for the USD/GBP detailed results).

09/05/2000). It is clear that, overall, the GARCH model fits the realised volatility rather well during the in-sample period. However, during the out-of-sample period, the GARCH forecasts are quite disappointing. The USD/JPY out-of-sample GARCH (1,1) forecasts suffer from a similar inertia (see Figure C4.1 in Appendix C).

In summary, if the GARCH (1,1) model can account for some statistical properties of daily exchange rate returns such as leptokurtosis and conditional heteroskedasticity, its ability to accurately predict volatility, despite its wide use among market professionals, is more debatable. In any case, as mentioned above, we only intend to use our GARCH (1,1) volatility forecasts as a benchmark for the nonlinear nonparametric neural network models we intend to apply and test whether NNR/RNN models can produce a substantial improvement in the out-of-sample performance of our volatility forecasts.

4.4   THE NEURAL NETWORK VOLATILITY FORECASTS

4.4.1   NNR modelling

Over the past few years, it has been argued that new technologies and quantitative systems based on the fact that most financial time series contain nonlinearities have made traditional forecasting methods only second best. NNR models, in particular, have been applied with increasing success to economic and financial forecasting and would constitute the state of the art in forecasting methods (see, for instance, Zhang *et al.* (1998)).

It is clearly beyond the scope of this chapter to give a complete overview of artificial neural networks, their biological foundation and their many architectures and potential applications (for more details, see, amongst others, Simpson (1990) and Hassoun (1995)).[9]

For our purpose, let it suffice to say that NNR models are a tool for determining the relative importance of an input (or a combination of inputs) for predicting a given outcome. They are a class of models made up of layers of elementary processing units, called neurons or nodes, which elaborate information by means of a nonlinear transfer function. Most of the computing takes place in these processing units.

The input signals come from an input vector $A = (x^{[1]}, x^{[2]}, \ldots, x^{[n]})$ where $x^{[i]}$ is the activity level of the ith input. A series of weight vectors $W_j = (w_{1j}, w_{2j}, \ldots, w_{nj})$ is associated with the input vector so that the weight w_{ij} represents the strength of the connection between the input $x^{[i]}$ and the processing unit b_j. Each node may additionally have also a *bias input* θ_j modulated with the weight w_{0j} associated with the inputs. The total input of the node b_j is formally the dot product between the input vector A and the weight vector W_j, minus the weighted input bias. It is then passed through a nonlinear transfer function to produce the output value of the processing unit b_j:

$$b_j = f\left(\sum_{i=1}^{n} x^{[i]} w_{ij} - w_{0j} \theta_j\right) = f(X_j) \qquad (4.4)$$

---

[9] In this chapter, we use exclusively the multilayer perceptron, a multilayer feedforward network trained by error backpropagation.

In this chapter, we have used the sigmoid function as activation function:[10]

$$f(X_j) = \frac{1}{1 + e^{-X_j}} \tag{4.5}$$

Figure 4.2 allows one to visualise a single output NNR model with one hidden layer and two hidden nodes, i.e. a model similar to those we developed for the GBP/USD and the USD/JPY volatility forecasts. The NNR model inputs at time t are $x_t^{[i]}(i = 1, 2, \ldots, 5)$. The hidden nodes outputs at time t are $h_t^{[j]}(j = 1, 2)$ and the NNR model output at time t is $\tilde{y}_t$, whereas the actual output is y_t.

At the beginning, the modelling process is initialised with random values for the weights. The output value of the processing unit b_j is then passed on to the single output node of the output layer. The NNR error, i.e. the difference between the NNR forecast and the actual value, is analysed through the *root mean squared error*. The latter is systematically minimised by adjusting the weights according to the level of its derivative with respect to these weights. The adjustment obviously takes place in the direction that reduces the error.

As can be expected, NNR models with two hidden layers are more complex. In general, they are better suited for discontinuous functions; they tend to have better generalisation capabilities but are also much harder to train. In summary, NNR model results depend crucially on the choice of the number of hidden layers, the number of nodes and the type of nonlinear transfer function retained.

In fact, the use of NNR models further enlarges the forecaster's toolbox of available techniques by adding models where no specific functional form is *a priori* assumed.[11]

Following Cybenko (1989) and Hornik *et al.* (1989), it can be demonstrated that specific NNR models, if their hidden layer is sufficiently large, can approximate any continuous

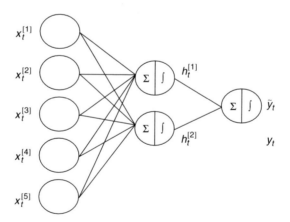

Figure 4.2   Single output NNR model

---

[10] Other alternatives include the hyperbolic tangent, the bilogistic sigmoid, etc. A linear activation function is also a possibility, in which case the NNR model will be linear. Note that our choice of a sigmoid implies variations in the interval]0, +1[. Input data are thus normalised in the same range in order to present the learning algorithm with compatible values and avoid saturation problems.

[11] Strictly speaking, the use of an NNR model implies assuming a functional form, namely that of the *transfer function*.

function.[12] Furthermore, it can be shown that NNR models are equivalent to *nonlinear nonparametric models*, i.e. models where no decisive assumption about the generating process must be made in advance (see Cheng and Titterington (1994)).

Kouam *et al.* (1992) have shown that most forecasting models (ARMA models, bilinear models, autoregressive models with thresholds, nonparametric models with kernel regression, etc.) are embedded in NNR models. They show that each modelling procedure can in fact be written in the form of a network of neurons.

Theoretically, the advantage of NNR models over other forecasting methods can therefore be summarised as follows: as, in practice, the "best" model for a given problem cannot be determined, it is best to resort to a modelling strategy which is a generalisation of a large number of models, rather than to impose *a priori* a given model specification.

This has triggered an ever-increasing interest for applications to financial markets (see, for instance, Trippi and Turban (1993), Deboeck (1994), Rehkugler and Zimmermann (1994), Refenes (1995) and Dunis (1996)).

Comparing NNR models with traditional econometric methods for foreign exchange rate forecasting has been the topic of several recent papers: Kuan and Liu (1995), Swanson and White (1995) and Gençay (1996) show that NNR models can describe in-sample data rather well and that they also generate "good" out-of-sample forecasts. Forecasting accuracy is usually defined in terms of small mean squared prediction error or in terms of directional accuracy of the forecasts. However, as mentioned already, there are still very few studies concerned with financial assets volatility forecasting.

4.4.2 RNN modelling

RNN models were introduced by Elman (1990). Their only difference from "regular" NNR models is that they include a loop back from one layer, either the output or the intermediate layer, to the input layer. Depending on whether the loop back comes from the intermediate or the output layer, either the preceding values of the hidden nodes or the output error will be used as inputs in the next period. This feature, which seems welcome in the case of a forecasting exercise, comes at a cost: RNN models will require more connections than their NNR counterparts, thus accentuating a certain lack of transparency which is sometimes used to criticise these modelling approaches.

Using our previous notation and assuming the output layer is the one looped back, the RNN model output at time t depends on the inputs at time t and on the output at time $t - 1$:[13]

$$\tilde{y}_t = F(x_t, \tilde{y}_{t-1}) \tag{4.6}$$

There is no theoretical answer as to whether one should preferably loop back the intermediate or the output layer. This is mostly an empirical question. Nevertheless, as looping back the output layer implies an error feedback mechanism, such RNN models can successfully be used for nonlinear error-correction modelling, as advocated by Burgess and Refenes

---

[12] This very feature also explains why it is so difficult to use NNR models, as one may in fact end up fitting the noise in the data rather than the underlying statistical process.

[13] With a loop back from the intermediate layer, the RNN output at time t depends on the inputs at time t and on the intermediate nodes at time $t - 1$. Besides, the intermediate nodes at time t depend on the inputs at time t and on the hidden layer at time $t - 1$. Using our notation, we have therefore: $\tilde{y}_t = F(x_t, h_{t-1})$ and $h_t = G(x_t, h_{t-1})$.

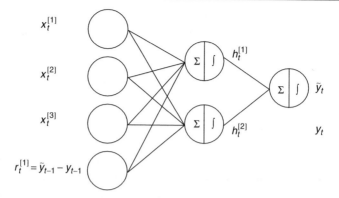

Figure 4.3   Single output RNN model

(1996). This is why we choose this particular architecture as an alternative modelling strategy for the GBP/USD and the USD/JPY volatility forecasts. Our choice seems further warranted by claims from Kuan and Liu (1995) and Tenti (1996) that RNN models are superior to NNR models when modelling exchange rates.

Figure 4.3 allows one to visualise a single output RNN model with one hidden layer and two hidden nodes, again a model similar to those developed for the GBP/USD and the USD/JPY volatility forecasts.

4.4.3   The NNR/RNN volatility forecasts

4.4.3.1   Input selection, data scaling and preprocessing

In the absence of an indisputable theory of exchange rate volatility, we assume that a specific exchange rate volatility can be explained by that rate's recent evolution, volatility spillovers from other financial markets, and macroeconomic and monetary policy expectations.

In the circumstances, it seems reasonable to include, as potential inputs, exchange rate volatilities (including that which is to be modelled), the evolution of important stock and commodity prices, and, as a measure of macroeconomic and monetary policy expectations, the evolution of the yield curve.[14]

As explained above (see footnote 10), all variables were normalised according to our choice of the sigmoid activation function. They had been previously transformed in logarithmic returns.[15]

Starting from a traditional linear correlation analysis, variable selection was achieved via a forward stepwise neural regression procedure: starting with both lagged historical and implied volatility levels, other potential input variables were progressively added, keeping the network architecture constant. If adding a new variable improved the level of explained variance over the previous "best" model, the pool of explanatory variables was updated. If there was a failure to improve over the previous "best" model after several

---

[14] On the use of the yield curve as a predictor of future output growth and inflation, see, amongst others, Fama (1990) and Ivanova *et al.* (2000).

[15] Despite some contrary opinions, e.g. Balkin (1999), stationarity remains important if NNR/RNN models are to be assessed on the basis of the level of explained variance.

attempts, variables in that model were alternated to check whether no better solution could be achieved. The model chosen finally was then kept for further tests and improvements.

Finally, conforming with standard heuristics, we partitioned our total data set into three subsets, using roughly 2/3 of the data for training the model, 1/6 for testing and the remaining 1/6 for validation. This partition in training, test and validation sets is made in order to control the error and reduce the risk of overfitting. Both the training and the following test period are used in the model tuning process: the training set is used to develop the model; the test set measures how well the model interpolates over the training set and makes it possible to check during the adjustment whether the model remains valid for the future. As the fine-tuned system is not independent from the test set, the use of a third validation set which was not involved in the model's tuning is necessary. The validation set is thus used to estimate the actual performance of the model in a deployed environment.

In our case, the 1329 observations from 31/12/1993 to 09/04/1999 were considered as the in-sample period for the estimation of our GARCH (1,1) benchmark model. We therefore retain the first 1049 observations from 31/12/1993 to 13/03/1998 for the training set and the remainder of the in-sample period is used as test set. The last 280 observations from 12/04/1999 to 09/05/2000 constitute the validation set and serve as the out-of-sample forecasting period. This is consistent with the GARCH (1,1) model estimation.

4.4.3.2   Volatility forecasting results

We used two similar sets of input variables for the GBP/USD and USD/JPY volatilities, with the same output variable, i.e. the realised 21-day volatility. Input variables included the lagged actual 21-day realised volatility (Realised21$_{t-21}$), the lagged implied 21-day volatility (IVOL21$_{t-21}$), lagged absolute logarithmic returns of the exchange rate ($|r|_{t-i}$, $i = 21, \ldots, 41$) and lagged logarithmic returns of the gold price (DLGOLD$_{t-i}$, $i = 21, \ldots, 41$) or of the oil price (DLOIL$_{t-i}$, $i = 21, \ldots, 41$), depending on the currency volatility being modelled.

In terms of the final model selection, Tables D4.1a and D4.1b in Appendix D give the performance of the best NNR and RNN models over the validation (out-of-sample) data set for the USD/GBP volatility. For the same input space and architecture (i.e. with only one hidden layer), RNN models marginally outperform their NNR counterparts in terms of directional accuracy. This is important as trading profitability crucially depends on getting the direction of changes right. Tables D4.1a and D4.1b also compare models with only one hidden layer and models with two hidden layers while keeping the input and output variables unchanged: despite the fact that the best NNR model is a two-hidden layer model with respectively ten and five hidden nodes in each of its hidden layers, on average, NNR/RNN models with a single hidden layer perform marginally better while at the same time requiring less processing time.

The results of the NNR and RNN models for the USD/JPY volatility over the validation period are given in Tables D4.2a and D4.2b in Appendix D. They are in line with those for the GBP/USD volatility, with RNN models outperforming their NNR counterparts and, in that case, the addition of a second hidden layer rather deteriorating performance.

Finally, we selected our two best NNR and RNN models for each volatility, NNR (44-10-5-1) and RNN (44-1-1) for the GBP/USD and NNR (44-1-1) and RNN (44-5-1) for the USD/JPY, to compare their out-of-sample forecasting performance with that of our GARCH (1,1) benchmark model. This evaluation is conducted on both statistical and financial criteria in the following sections. Yet, one can easily see from Figures E4.1 and E4.2 in Appendix E that, for both the GBP/USD and the USD/JPY volatilities, these out-of-sample forecasts do not suffer from the same degree of inertia as was the case for the GARCH (1,1) forecasts.

4.5   MODEL COMBINATIONS AND FORECASTING ACCURACY

4.5.1   Model combination

As noted by Dunis *et al.* (2001a), today most researchers would agree that individual forecasting models are misspecified in some dimensions and that the identity of the "best" model changes over time. In this situation, it is likely that a combination of forecasts will perform better over time than forecasts generated by any individual model that is kept constant.

Accordingly, we build two rather simple model combinations to add to our three existing volatility forecasts, the GARCH (1,1), NNR and RNN forecasts.[16]

The simplest forecast combination method is the simple average of existing forecasts. As noted by Dunis *et al.* (2001b), it is often a hard benchmark to beat as other methods, such as regression-based methods, decision trees, etc., can suffer from a deterioration of their out-of-sample performance.

We call COM1 the simple average of our GARCH (1,1), NNR and RNN volatility forecasts with the actual implied volatility (IVOL21). As we know, implied volatility is itself a popular method to measure market expectations of future volatility.

Another method of combining forecasts suggested by Granger and Ramanathan (1984) is to regress the in-sample historical 21-day volatility on the set of forecasts to obtain appropriate weights, and then apply these weights to the out-of-sample forecasts: it is denoted GR. We follow Granger and Ramanathan's advice to add a constant term and not to constrain the weights to add to unity. We do not include both ANN and RNN forecasts in the regression as they can be highly collinear: for the USD/JPY, the correlation coefficient between both volatility forecasts is 0.984.

We tried several alternative specifications for the Granger–Ramanathan approach. The parameters were estimated by ordinary least squares over the in-sample data set. Our best model for the GBP/USD volatility is presented below with t-statistics in parentheses, and the R-squared and standard error of the regression:

$$\text{Actual}_{t,21} = -5.7442 + 0.7382 \text{RNN44}_{t,21} + 0.6750 \text{GARCH}\ (1, 1)_{t,21} + 0.3226 \text{IVOL}_{t,21}$$

$$(-6.550) \qquad\quad (7.712) \qquad\qquad\qquad (8.592) \qquad\qquad\qquad (6.777)$$

$$R^2 = 0.2805 \qquad \text{S.E. of regression} = 1.7129 \qquad\qquad\qquad\qquad (4.7a)$$

---

[16] More sophisticated combinations are possible, even based on NNR models as in Donaldson and Kamstra (1996), but this is beyond the scope of this chapter.

For the USD/JPY volatility forecast combination, our best model was obtained using the NNR forecast rather than the RNN one:

$$\text{Actual}_{t,21} = -9.4293 + 1.5913\text{NNR44}_{t,21} + 0.06164\text{GARCH }(1,1)_{t,21} + 0.1701\text{IVOL}_{t,21}$$

$$(-7.091) \qquad\qquad (7.561) \qquad\qquad\qquad (0.975) \qquad\qquad\qquad\qquad (2.029)$$

$$R^2 = 0.4128 \qquad \text{S.E. of regression} = 4.0239 \qquad\qquad\qquad\qquad (4.7\text{b})$$

As can be seen, the RNN/NNR-based forecast gets the highest weight in both cases, suggesting that the GR forecast relies more heavily on the RNN/NNR model forecasts than on the others. Figures F4.1 and F4.2 in Appendix F show that the GR and COM1 forecast combinations, as the NNR and RNN forecasts, do not suffer from the same inertia as the GARCH (1,1) out-of-sample forecasts do. The Excel file "CombGR_JPY" on the accompanying CD-Rom documents the computation of the two USD/JPY volatility forecast combinations and that of their forecasting accuracy.

We now have five volatility forecasts on top of the implied volatility "market forecast" and proceed to test their out-of-sample forecasting accuracy through traditional statistical criteria.

4.5.2 Out-of-sample forecasting accuracy

As is standard in the economic literature, we compute the Root Mean Squared Error (RMSE), the Mean Absolute Error (MAE) and Theil U-statistic (Theil-U). These measures have already been presented in detail by, amongst others, Makridakis *et al.* (1983), Pindyck and Rubinfeld (1998) and Theil (1966), respectively. We also compute a "correct directional change" (CDC) measure which is described below.

Calling σ the actual volatility and $\hat{\sigma}$ the forecast volatility at time τ, with a forecast period going from $t+1$ to $t+n$, the forecast error statistics are respectively:

$$\text{RMSE} = \sqrt{(1/n)\sum_{\tau=t+1}^{t+n}(\hat{\sigma}_\tau - \sigma_\tau)^2}$$

$$\text{MAE} = (1/n)\sum_{\tau=t+1}^{t+n}|\hat{\sigma}_\tau - \sigma_\tau|$$

$$\text{Theil-U} = \sqrt{(1/n)\sum_{\tau=t+1}^{t+n}(\hat{\sigma}_\tau - \sigma_\tau)^2} \bigg/ \left[\sqrt{(1/n)\sum_{\tau=t+1}^{t+n}\hat{\sigma}_\tau^2} + \sqrt{(1/n)\sum_{\tau=t+1}^{t+n}\sigma_\tau^2}\right]$$

$$\text{CDC} = (100/n)\sum_{\tau=t+1}^{t+n}D_\tau$$

where $D_\tau = 1$ if $(\sigma_\tau - \sigma_{\tau-1})(\hat{\sigma}_\tau - \sigma_{\tau-1}) > 0$ else $D_\tau = 0$

The RMSE and the MAE statistics are scale-dependent measures but give us a basis to compare our volatility forecasts with the realised volatility. The Theil-U statistic is independent of the scale of the variables and is constructed in such a way that it necessarily lies between zero and one, with zero indicating a perfect fit.

For all these three error statistics retained the lower the output, the better the forecasting accuracy of the model concerned. However, rather than on securing the lowest statistical forecast error, the profitability of a trading system critically depends on *taking the right position* and therefore getting the direction of changes right. RMSE, MAE and Theil-U are all important error measures, yet they may not constitute the best criterion from a profitability point of view. The CDC statistic is used to check whether the direction given by the forecast is the same as the actual change which has subsequently occurred and, for this measure, the higher the output the better the forecasting accuracy of the model concerned. Tables 4.1 and 4.2 compare, for the GBP/USD and the USD/JPY volatility respectively, our five volatility models and implied volatility in terms of the four accuracy measures retained.

These results are most interesting. Except for the GARCH (1,1) model (for all criteria for the USD/JPY volatility and in terms of directional change only for the GBP/USD volatility), they show that our five volatility forecasting models offer much more precise indications about future volatility than implied volatilities. This means that our volatility forecasts may be used to identify mispriced options, and a profitable trading rule can possibly be established based on the difference between the prevailing implied volatility and the volatility forecast.

The two NNR/RNN models and the two combination models predict correctly directional change at least over 57% of the time for the USD/JPY volatility. Furthermore, for both volatilities, these models outperform the GARCH (1,1) benchmark model on all

Table 4.1   GBP/USD volatility models forecasting accuracy

GBP/USD Vol.	RMSE	MAE	Theil-U	CDC
IVOL21	1.98	1.63	0.13	49.64
GARCH (1,1)	1.70	1.48	0.12	48.57
NNR (44-10-5-1)	1.69	1.42	0.12	50.00
RNN (44-1-1)	1.50	1.27	0.11	52.86
COM1	1.65	1.41	0.11	65.23
GR	1.67	1.37	0.12	67.74

Table 4.2   USD/JPY volatility models forecasting accuracy[17]

USD/JPY Vol.	RMSE	MAE	Theil-U	CDC
IVOL21	3.04	2.40	0.12	53.21
GARCH (1,1)	4.46	4.14	0.17	52.50
NNR (44-1-1)	2.41	1.88	0.10	59.64
RNN (44-5-1)	2.43	1.85	0.10	59.29
COM1	2.72	2.29	0.11	56.79
GR	2.70	2.13	0.11	57.86

---

[17] The computation of the COM1 and GR forecasting accuracy measures is documented in the Excel file "CombGR_JPY" on the accompanying CD-Rom.

evaluation criteria. As a group, NNR/RNN models show superior out-of-sample forecasting performance on any statistical evaluation criterion, except directional change for the GBP/USD volatility for which they are outperformed by model combinations. Within this latter group, the GR model performance is overall the best in terms of statistical forecasting accuracy. The GR model combination provides the best forecast of directional change, achieving a remarkable directional forecasting accuracy of around 67% for the GBP/USD volatility.

Still, as noted by Dunis (1996), a good forecast may be a necessary but it is certainly not a sufficient condition for generating positive trading returns. Prediction accuracy is not the ultimate goal in itself and should not be used as the main guiding selection criterion for system traders. In the following section, we therefore use our volatility forecasting models to identify mispriced foreign exchange options and endeavour to develop profitable currency volatility trading models.

4.6 FOREIGN EXCHANGE VOLATILITY TRADING MODELS

4.6.1 Volatility trading strategies

Kroner *et al.* (1995) point out that, since expectations of future volatility play such a critical role in the determination of option prices, better forecasts of volatility should lead to a more accurate pricing and should therefore help an option trader to identify over- or underpriced options. Therefore a profitable trading strategy can be established based on the difference between the prevailing market implied volatility and the volatility forecast. Accordingly, Dunis and Gavridis (1997) advocate to superimpose a volatility trading strategy on the volatility forecast.

As mentioned previously, there is a narrow relationship between volatility and the option price. An option embedding a high volatility gives the holder a greater chance of a more profitable exercise. When trading volatility, using at-the-money forward (ATMF) straddles, i.e. combining an ATFM call with an ATFM put with opposite deltas, results in taking no forward risk. Furthermore, as noted, amongst others, by Hull (1997), both the ATMF call and put have the same vega and gamma sensitivity. There is no directional bias.

If a large rise in volatility is predicted, the trader will buy both call and put. Although this will entail paying two premia, the trader will profit from a subsequent movement in volatility: if the foreign exchange market moves far enough either up or down, one of the options will end deeply in-the-money and, when it is sold back to the writing counterparty, the profit will more than cover the cost of both premia. The other option will expire worthless. Conversely, if both the call and put expire out-of-the-money following a period of stability in the foreign exchange market, only the premia will be lost.

If a large drop in volatility is predicted, the trader will sell the straddle and receive the two option premia. This is a high-risk strategy if his market view is wrong as he might theoretically suffer unlimited loss, but, if he is right and both options expire worthless, he will have cashed in both premia.

4.6.2 The currency volatility trading models

The trading strategy adopted is based on the currency volatility trading model proposed by Dunis and Gavridis (1997). A long volatility position is initiated by buying the 1-month

ATMF foreign exchange straddle if the 1-month volatility forecast is above the prevailing 1-month implied volatility level by more than a certain threshold used as a confirmation filter or reliability indicator. Conversely, a short ATMF straddle position is initiated if the 1-month volatility forecast is below the prevailing implied volatility level by more than the given threshold.

To this effect, the first stage of the currency volatility trading strategy is, based on the threshold level as in Dunis (1996), to band the volatility predictions into five classes, namely, "large up move", "small up move", "no change", "large down move" and "small down move" (Figure 4.4). The change threshold defining the boundary between small and large movements was determined as a confirmation filter. Different strategies with filters ranging from 0.5 to 2.0 were analysed and are reported with our results.

The second stage is to decide the trading entry and exit rules. With our filter rule, a position is only initiated when the 1-month volatility forecast is above or below the prevailing 1-month implied volatility level by more than the threshold. That is:

- If $D_t > c$, then buy the ATMF straddle
- If $D_t < -c$, then sell the ATFM straddle

where D_t denotes the difference between the 1-month volatility forecast and the prevailing 1-month implied volatility, and c represents the threshold (or filter).

In terms of exit rules, our main test is to assume that the straddle is held until expiry and that no new positions can be initiated until the existing straddle has expired. As, due to the drop in time value during the life of an option, this is clearly not an optimal trading strategy, we also consider the case of American options which can be exercised at any time until expiry, and thus evaluate this second strategy assuming that positions are only held for five trading days (as opposed to one month).[18]

As in Dunis and Gavridis (1997), profitability is determined by comparing the level of implied volatility at the inception of the position with the prevailing 1-month realised historical volatility at maturity.

It is further weighted by the amount of the position taken, itself a function of the difference between the 1-month volatility forecast and the prevailing 1-month implied volatility level on the day when the position is initiated: intuitively, it makes sense to assume that, if we have a "good" model, the larger $|D_t|$, the more confident we should be about taking the suggested position and the higher the expected profit. Calling G this gearing of position, we thus have:[19]

$$G = |D_t|/|c| \tag{4.8}$$

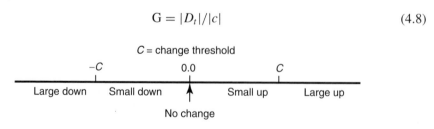

Figure 4.4 Volatility forecasts classification

[18] For the "weekly" trading strategy, we also considered closing out European options before expiry by taking the opposite position, unwinding positions at the prevailing implied volatility market rate after five trading days: this strategy was generally not profitable.

[19] Laws and Gidman (2000) adopt a similar strategy with a slightly different definition of the gearing.

Profitability is therefore defined as a volatility net profit (i.e. it is calculated in volatility points or "*vols*" as they are called by options traders[20]). Losses are also defined as a volatility loss, which implies two further assumptions: when short the straddle, no stop-loss strategy is actually implemented and the losing trade is closed out at the then prevailing volatility level (it is thus reasonable to assume that we overestimate potential losses in a real world environment with proper risk management controls); when long the straddle, we approximate true losses by the difference between the level of implied volatility at inception with the prevailing volatility level when closing out the losing trade, whereas realised losses would only amount to the premium paid at the inception of the position (here again, we seem to overestimate potential losses). It is further assumed that volatility profits generated during one period are not reinvested during the next. Finally, in line with Dunis and Gavridis (1997), transaction costs of 25 bp per trade are included in our profit and loss computations.

4.6.3 Trading simulation results

The currency volatility trading strategy was applied from 31 December 1993 to 9 May 2000. Tables 4.3 and 4.4 document our results for the GBP/USD and USD/JPY monthly trading strategies both for the in-sample period from 31 December 1993 to 9 April 1999 and the out-of-sample period from 12 April 1999 to 9 May 2000. The evaluation discussed below is focused on out-of-sample performance.

For our trading simulations, four different thresholds ranging from 0.5 to 2.0 and two different holding periods, i.e. monthly and weekly, have been retained. A higher threshold level implies requiring a higher degree of reliability in the signals and obviously reduces the overall number of trades.

The profitability criteria include the cumulative profit and loss with and without gearing, the total number of trades and the percentage of profitable trades. We also show the average gearing of the positions for each strategy.

Firstly, we compare the performance of the NNR/RNN models with the benchmark GARCH (1,1) model. For the GBP/USD monthly volatility trading strategy in Table 4.3, the GARCH (1,1) model generally produces higher cumulative profits not only in-sample but also out-of-sample. NNR/RNN models seldom produce a higher percentage of profitable trades in-sample or out-of-sample, although the geared cumulative return of the strategy based on the RNN (44-1-1) model is close to that produced with the benchmark model. With NNR/RNN models predicting more accurately directional change than the GARCH model, one would have intuitively expected them to show a better trading performance for the monthly volatility trading strategies.

This expected result is in fact achieved by the USD/JPY monthly volatility trading strategy, as shown in Table 4.4: NNR/RNN models clearly produce a higher percentage of profitable trades both in- and out-of-sample, with the best out-of-sample performance being that based on the RNN (44-5-1) model. On the contrary, the GARCH (1,1) model-based strategies produce very poor trading results, often recording an overall negative cumulative profit and loss figure.

---

[20] In market jargon, "vol" refers to both implied volatility and the measurement of volatility in percent per annum (see, amongst others, Malz (1996)). Monetary returns could only be estimated by comparing the actual profit/loss of a straddle once closed out or expired against the premium paid/received at inception, an almost impossible task with OTC options.

Table 4.3   GBP/USD monthly volatility trading strategy

1 Threshold = 0.5   Trading days = 21

Sample Observation Period	In-sample (1-1329) (31/12/1993-09/04/1999)					Out-of-sample (1330-1610) (12/04/1999-09/05/2000)				
Models	NNR(44-10-5-1)	RNN(44-1-1)	GARCH(1,1)	COM1	GR	NNR(44-10-5-1)	RNN(44-1-1)	GARCH(1,1)	COM1	GR
P/L without gearing	58.39%	54.47%	81.75%	54.25%	81.40%	5.77%	5.22%	12.90%	10.35%	11.98%
P/L with gearing	240.44%	355.73%	378.18%	182.38%	210.45%	16.60%	35.30%	42.91%	16.41%	19.44%
Total trades	59	59	61	58	61	12	12	11	10	10
Profitable trades	67.80%	70.00%	77.05%	70.69%	83.61%	50.00%	58.33%	72.73%	70.00%	80.00%
Average gearing	2.83	4.05	3.87	2.35	2.13	1.55	2.17	2.39	1.46	1.44

2 Threshold = 1.0   Trading days = 21

Sample Observation Period	In-sample (1-1329) (31/12/1993-09/04/1999)					Out-of-sample (1330-1610) (12/04/1999-09/05/2000)				
Models	NNR(44-10-5-1)	RNN(44-1-1)	GARCH(1,1)	COM1	GR	NNR(44-10-5-1)	RNN(44-1-1)	GARCH(1,1)	COM1	GR
P/L without gearing	61.48%	57.52%	82.61%	64.50%	60.24%	7.09%	12.74%	12.08%	8.33%	9.65%
P/L with gearing	134.25%	190.80%	211.61%	116.99%	88.26%	8.65%	20.23%	20.79%	10.53%	11.03%
Total trades	51	51	58	45	47	7	8	9	5	6
Profitable trades	72.55%	69.09%	84.48%	80.00%	78.72%	85.71%	87.50%	66.67%	80.00%	83.33%
Average gearing	1.68	2.21	2.08	1.53	1.32	1.18	1.61	1.48	1.19	1.13

3 Threshold = 1.5   Trading days = 21

Sample Observation Period	In-sample (1-1329) (31/12/1993-09/04/1999)					Out-of-sample (1330-1610) (12/04/1999-09/05/2000)				
Models	NNR(44-10-5-1)	RNN(44-1-1)	GARCH(1,1)	COM1	GR	NNR(44-10-5-1)	RNN(44-1-1)	GARCH(1,1)	COM1	GR
P/L without gearing	53.85%	61.13%	66.24%	62.26%	39.22%	9.26%	8.67%	8.93%	10.36%	8.69%
P/L with gearing	74.24%	114.88%	113.04%	80.65%	49.52%	11.16%	11.75%	11.32%	11.00%	9.92%
Total trades	40	40	52	31	24	4	6	6	3	2
Profitable trades	80.00%	71.43%	80.77%	83.87%	83.33%	100.00%	83.33%	83.33%	100%	100.00%
Average gearing	1.28	1.62	1.43	1.24	1.19	1.12	1.31	1.22	1.05	1.14

4 Threshold = 2.0   Trading days = 21

Sample Observation Period	In-sample (1-1329) (31/12/1993-09/04/1999)					Out-of-sample (1330-1610) (12/04/1999-09/05/2000)				
Models	NNR(44-10-5-1)	RNN(44-1-1)	GARCH(1,1)	COM1	GR	NNR(44-10-5-1)	RNN(44-1-1)	GARCH(1,1)	COM1	GR
P/L without gearing	69.03%	63.04%	60.57%	48.35%	20.97%	4.39%	7.80%	10.54%	4.39%	-
P/L with gearing	103.33%	98.22%	85.19%	63.05%	24.25%	5.37%	8.71%	11.29%	4.70%	-
Total trades	24	33	31	16	8	1	4	4	1	0
Profitable trades	82.76%	78.57%	79.49%	94.12%	88.89%	100.00%	100.00%	100.00%	100%	-
Average gearing	1.35	1.40	1.24	1.25	1.16	1.22	1.09	1.06	1.06	-

Note: Cumulative P/L figures are expressed in volatility points.

Secondly, we evaluate the performance of model combinations. It is quite disappointing as, for both monthly volatility trading strategies, model combinations produce on average much lower cumulative returns than alternative strategies based on NNR/RNN models for the USD/JPY volatility and on either the GARCH (1,1) or the RNN (44-1-1) model for the GBP/USD volatility. As a general rule, the GR combination model fails to clearly outperform the simple average model combination COM1 during the out-of-sample period, something already noted by Dunis *et al.* (2001b).

Overall, with the monthly holding period, RNN model-based strategies show the strongest out-of-sample trading performance: in terms of geared cumulative profit, they come first in four out of the eight monthly strategies analysed, and second best in the remaining four cases. The strategy with the highest return yields a 106.17% cumulative profit over the out-of-sample period and is achieved for the USD/JPY volatility with the RNN (44-5-1) model and a filter equal to 0.5.

The results of the weekly trading strategy are presented in Tables G4.1 and G4.2 in Appendix G. They basically confirm the superior performance achieved through the use of RNN model-based strategies and the comparatively weak results obtained through the use of model combination.

Table 4.4 USD/JPY monthly volatility trading strategy

1 Threshold = 0.5   Trading days = 21

Sample Observation Period	In-sample (1-1329) (31/12/1993-09/04/1999)					Out-of-sample (1330-1610) (12/04/1999-09/05/2000)				
Models	NNR(44-1-1)	RNN(44-5-1)	GARCH(1,1)	COM1	GR	NNR(44-1-1)	RNN(44-5-1)	GARCH(1,1)	COM1	GR
P/L without gearing	31.35%	16.42%	−26.42%	19.15%	19.73%	16.21%	20.71%	−8.57%	16.19%	3.21%
P/L with gearing	151.79%	144.52%	6.93%	152.36%	82.92%	63.61%	106.17%	−4.42%	75.78%	11.50%
Total trades	62	62	60	60	61	13	13	12	12	13
Profitable trades	54.84%	51.61%	38.33%	53.33%	60.66%	76.92%	84.62%	50.00%	66.67%	61.54%
Average gearing	3.89	3.98	3.77	2.41	2.36	2.86	3.91	5.73	2.63	1.86

2 Threshold = 1.0   Trading days = 21

Sample Observation Period	In-sample (1-1329) (31/12/1993-09/04/1999)					Out-of-sample (1330-1610) (12/04/1999-09/05/2000)				
Models	NNR(44-1-1)	RNN(44-5-1)	GARCH(1,1)	COM1	GR	NNR(44-1-1)	RNN(44-5-1)	GARCH(1,1)	COM1	GR
P/L without gearing	25.83%	44.59%	−9.71%	40.60%	64.35%	20.70%	21.32%	−1.94%	13.53%	26.96%
P/L with gearing	67.66%	105.01%	43.09%	76.72%	122.80%	52.81%	45.81%	42.14%	21.41%	46.53%
Total trades	58	58	57	51	52	12	12	12	11	12
Profitable trades	62.07%	56.90%	36.84%	58.82%	69.23%	83.33%	83.33%	41.67%	63.64%	83.33%
Average gearing	2.01	2.16	1.97	1.58	1.55	1.97	1.94	3.03	1.41	1.66

3 Threshold = 1.5   Trading days = 21

Sample Observation Period	In-sample (1-1329) (31/12/1993-09/04/1999)					Out-of-sample (1330-1610) (12/04/1999-09/05/2000)				
Models	NNR(44-1-1)	RNN(44-5-1)	GARCH(1,1)	COM1	GR	NNR(44-1-1)	RNN(44-5-1)	GARCH(1,1)	COM1	GR
P/L without gearing	47.07%	23.62%	40.93%	46.63%	84.17%	19.65%	25.54%	1.87%	5.09%	23.80%
P/L with gearing	92.67%	75.69%	86.60%	75.70%	109.49%	40.49%	73.19%	31.31%	10.65%	32.91%
Total trades	51	51	46	37	42	10	10	12	6	10
Profitable trades	64.71%	55.77%	52.17%	59.46%	73.81%	80.00%	80.00%	33.33%	50%	90.00%
Average gearing	1.71	1.72	1.60	1.33	1.35	1.54	1.94	2.21	1.37	1.41

4 Threshold = 2.0   Trading days = 21

Sample Observation Period	In-sample (1-1329) (31/12/1993-09/04/1999)					Out-of-sample (1330-1610) (12/04/1999-09/05/2000)				
Models	NNR(44-1-1)	RNN(44-5-1)	GARCH(1,1)	COM1	GR	NNR(44-1-1)	RNN(44-5-1)	GARCH(1,1)	COM1	GR
P/L without gearing	52.52%	28.98%	39.69%	27.89%	75.99%	34.35%	33.70%	0.11%	7.74%	3.09%
P/L with gearing	202.23%	72.21%	49.77%	35.77%	94.30%	60.33%	64.76%	−5.11%	12.35%	5.48%
Total trades	37	37	41	21	26	10	10	12	3	7
Profitable trades	59.46%	61.54%	56.10%	61.90%	80.77%	90.00%	90.00%	33%	100%	71%
Average gearing	1.67	1.59	1.39	1.25	1.26	1.54	1.68	1.54	1.54	1.23

Note: Cumulative P/L figures are expressed in volatility points.

Finally, allowing for transaction costs, it is worth noting that all the trading strategies retained produce positive returns, except some based on the GARCH (1,1) benchmark model for the USD/JPY volatility. RNN models appear as the best single modelling approach for short-term volatility trading. Somewhat surprisingly, model combination, the overall best performing approach in terms of forecasting accuracy, fails to improve the RNN-based volatility trading results.

4.7 CONCLUDING REMARKS AND FURTHER WORK

The rationale for this chapter was to develop a nonlinear nonparametric approach to forecast FX volatility, identify mispriced options and subsequently develop a trading strategy based upon this modelling procedure.

Using daily data from December 1993 through April 1999, we examined the use of NNR and RNN regression models for *forecasting* and subsequently *trading* currency volatility, with an application to the GBP/USD and USD/JPY exchange rates.

These models were then tested *out-of-sample* over the period April 1999–May 2000, not only in terms of *forecasting accuracy*, but also in terms of *trading performance*. In order to do so, we applied a realistic volatility trading strategy using FX option straddles once mispriced options had been identified.

Allowing for transaction costs, most of the trading strategies retained produced positive returns. RNN models appeared as the best single modelling approach in a short-term trading context.

Model combination, despite its superior performance in terms of forecasting accuracy, failed to produce superior trading strategies. Admittedly, other combination procedures such as decision trees, neural networks, as in Donaldson and Kamstra (1996) or Shadbolt and Taylor (2002), and unanimity or majority voting schemes as applied by Albanis and Batchelor (2001) should be investigated.

Further work is also needed to compare the results from NNR and RNN models with those from more "refined" parametric or semiparametric approaches than our GARCH (1,1) benchmark model, such as Donaldson and Kamstra (1997), So et al. (1999), Bollen et al. (2000), Flôres and Roche (2000) and Beine and Laurent (2001).

Finally, applying dynamic risk management, the trading strategy retained could also be refined to integrate more realistic trading assumptions than those of a fixed holding period of either 5 or 21 trading days.

However, despite the limitations of this chapter, we were clearly able to develop reasonably accurate FX volatility forecasts, identify mispriced options and subsequently simulate a profitable trading strategy. In the circumstances, the unambiguous implication from our results is that, for the period and currencies considered, the currency option market was inefficient and/or the pricing formulae applied by market participants were inadequate.

ACKNOWLEDGEMENTS

We are grateful to Professor Ken Holden and Professor John Thompson of Liverpool Business School and to an anonymous referee for helpful comments on an earlier version of this chapter. The usual disclaimer applies.

APPENDIX A

Table A4.1 Summary statistics – GBP/USD realised and implied 1-month volatility (31/12/1993–09/04/1999)

Sample observations	:	1 to 1329	
Variable(s)	:	**Historical vol.**	**Implied vol.**
Maximum	:	15.3644	15.0000
Minimum	:	2.9448	3.2500
Mean	:	6.8560	8.2575
Std. Dev.	:	1.9928	1.6869
Skewness	:	0.69788	0.38498
Kurtosis − 3	:	0.81838	1.1778
Coeff. of variation	:	0.29067	0.20429

Table A4.2 Correlation matrix of realised and implied volatility (GBP/USD)

	Realised vol.	Implied vol.
Realised vol.	1.0000	0.79174
Implied vol.	0.79174	1.0000

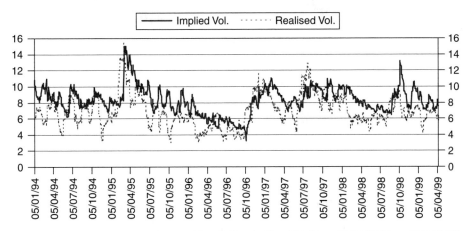

Figure A4.1 GBP/USD realised and implied volatility (%) from 31/12/1993 to 09/04/1999

Table A4.3 Summary statistics – USD/JPY realised and implied 1-month volatility (31/12/1993–09/04/1999)

Sample observations	:	1 to 1329	
Variable(s)	:	**Historical vol.**	**Implied vol.**
Maximum	:	33.0446	35.0000
Minimum	:	4.5446	6.1500
Mean	:	11.6584	12.2492
Std. Dev.	:	5.2638	3.6212
Skewness	:	1.4675	0.91397
Kurtosis − 3	:	2.6061	2.1571
Coeff. of variation	:	0.45150	0.29563

Table A4.4 Correlation matrix of realised and implied volatility (USD/JPY)

	Realised vol.	Implied vol.
Realised vol.	1.0000	0.80851
Implied vol.	0.80851	1.0000

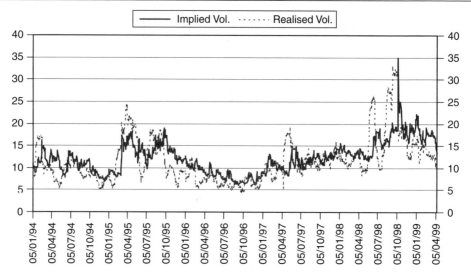

Figure A4.2   USD/JPY realised and implied volatility (%) from 31/12/1993 to 09/04/1999

APPENDIX B

B.4.1   GBP/USD GARCH (1,1) assuming a *t*-distribution and Wald test

GBP/USD GARCH (1,1) assuming a *t*-distribution
converged after 30 iterations

Dependent variable is DLUSD
1327 observations used for estimation from 3 to 1329

Regressor	Coefficient	Standard error	T-Ratio[Prob]
ONE	0.0058756	0.010593	0.55466[0.579]
DLUSD(−1)	0.024310	0.027389	0.88760[0.375]

R-Squared	0.0011320	$\bar{R}$-Squared	−0.0011330
S.E. of regression	0.45031	F-stat. $F(3,1323)$	0.49977[0.682]
Mean of dependent variable	0.0037569	S.D. of dependent variable	0.45006
Residual sum of squares	268.2795	Equation log-likelihood	−749.6257
Akaike info. criterion	−754.6257	Schwarz Bayesian criterion	−767.6024
DW-statistic	1.9739		

Parameters of the Conditional Heteroskedastic Model
Explaining H-SQ, the Conditional Variance of the Error Term

	Coefficient	Asymptotic standard error
Constant	0.0021625	0.0015222
E-SQ(−1)	0.032119	0.010135
H-SQ(−1)	0.95864	0.013969
D.F. of t-dist.	5.1209	0.72992

H-SQ stands for the conditional variance of the error term.
E-SQ stands for the square of the error term.

Wald test of restriction(s) imposed on parameters

Based on GARCH regression of DLUSD on:
ONE   DLUSD(−1)
1327 observations used for estimation from 3 to 1329

Coefficients A1 to A2 are assigned to the above regressors respectively.
Coefficients B1 to B4 are assigned to ARCH parameters respectively.
List of restriction(s) for the Wald test:
b2 = 0; b3 = 0

Wald statistic	CHSQ(2) = 16951.2[0.000]

B.4.2 GBP/USD GARCH (1,1) assuming a normal distribution and Wald test

GBP/USD GARCH (1,1) assuming a normal distribution
converged after 35 iterations

Dependent variable is DLUSD
1327 observations used for estimation from 3 to 1329

Regressor	Coefficient	Standard error	T-Ratio[Prob]
ONE	0.0046751	0.011789	0.39657[0.692]
DLUSD(−1)	0.047043	0.028546	1.6480[0.100]

R-Squared	0.0011651	$\bar{R}$-Squared	−0.0010999
S.E. of regression	0.45030	F-stat. $F(3,1323)$	0.51439[0.672]
Mean of dependent variable	0.0037569	S.D. of dependent variable	0.45006
Residual sum of squares	268.2707	Equation log-likelihood	−796.3501
Akaike info. criterion	−800.3501	Schwarz Bayesian criterion	−810.7315
DW-statistic	2.0199		

Parameters of the Conditional Heteroskedastic Model
Explaining H-SQ, the Conditional Variance of the Error Term

	Coefficient	Asymptotic standard error
Constant	0.0033874	0.0016061
E-SQ(−1)	0.028396	0.0074743
H-SQ(−1)	0.95513	0.012932

H-SQ stands for the conditional variance of the error term.
E-SQ stands for the square of the error term.

Wald test of restriction(s) imposed on parameters

Based on GARCH regression of DLUSD on:
ONE   DLUSD(−1)
1327 observations used for estimation from 3 to 1329

Coefficients A1 to A2 are assigned to the above regressors respectively.
Coefficients B1 to B3 are assigned to ARCH parameters respectively.
List of restriction(s) for the Wald test:
b2 = 0; b3 = 0

Wald statistic	CHSQ(2) = 16941.1[0.000]

B.4.3   USD/JPY GARCH (1,1) assuming a t-distribution and Wald test

USD/JPY GARCH (1,1) assuming a t-distribution
converged after 26 iterations

Dependent variable is DLYUSD
1327 observations used for estimation from 3 to 1329

Regressor	Coefficient	Standard error	T-Ratio[Prob]
ONE	0.037339	0.015902	2.3480[0.019]
DLYUSD(−1)	0.022399	0.026976	0.83032[0.407]

R-Squared	0.0010778	$\bar{R}$-Squared	−0.0011874
S.E. of regression	0.79922	F-stat. $F(3,1323)$	0.47580[0.699]
Mean of dependent variable	0.0056665	S.D. of dependent variable	0.79875
Residual sum of squares	845.0744	Equation log-likelihood	−1385.3
Akaike info. criterion	−1390.3	Schwarz Bayesian criterion	−1403.3
DW-statistic	1.8999		

Parameters of the Conditional Heteroskedastic Model
Explaining H-SQ, the Conditional Variance of the Error Term

	Coefficient	Asymptotic standard error
Constant	0.0078293	0.0045717
E-SQ(−1)	0.068118	0.021094
H-SQ(−1)	0.92447	0.023505
D.F. of t-dist.	4.3764	0.54777

H-SQ stands for the conditional variance of the error term.
E-SQ stands for the square of the error term.

Wald test of restriction(s) imposed on parameters

Based on GARCH regression of DLYUSD on:
ONE   DLYUSD(−1)
1327 observations used for estimation from 3 to 1329

Coefficients A1 to A2 are assigned to the above regressors respectively.
Coefficients B1 to B4 are assigned to ARCH parameters respectively.
List of restriction(s) for the Wald test:
b2 = 0; b3 = 0

Wald Statistic	CHSQ(2) = 11921.3[0.000]

APPENDIX C

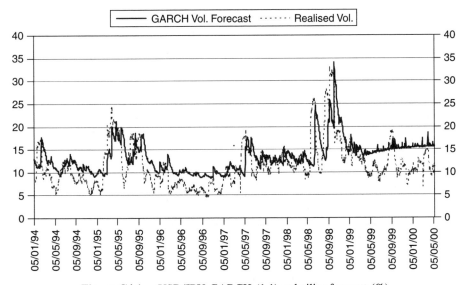

Figure C4.1   USD/JPY GARCH (1,1) volatility forecast (%)

APPENDIX D

Table D4.1a   GBP/USD NNR test results for the validation data set

	NNR (44-1-1)	NNR (44-5-1)	NNR (44-10-1)	NNR (44-10-5-1)	NNR (44-15-10-1)
Explained variance	1.4%	5.9%	8.1%	12.5%	15.6%
Average relative error	0.20	0.20	0.20	0.20	0.21
Average absolute error	1.37	1.39	1.40	1.41	1.44
Average direction error	33.3%	32.3%	31.5%	30.5%	31.5%

Table D4.1b   GBP/USD RNN test results for the validation data set

	RNN (44-1-1)	RNN (44-5-1)	RNN (44-10-1)	RNN (44-10-5-1)	RNN (44-15-10-1)
Explained variance	13.3%	9.3%	5.5%	6.8%	12.0%
Average relative error	0.18	0.19	0.19	0.20	0.20
Average absolute error	1.25	1.29	1.33	1.38	1.42
Average direction error	30.1%	32.6%	32.6%	30.8%	32.3%

NNR/RNN (*a-b-c*) represents different neural network models, where:
   a = number of input variables;
   b = number of hidden nodes;
   c = number of output nodes.
Realised_Vol(t) = f[IVol($t-21$), Realised_Vol($t-21$), $|r|(t-21,\ldots,t-41)$, DLGOLD($t-21,\ldots,t-41$)].

Table D4.2a   USD/JPY NNR test results for the validation data set

	NNR (44-1-1)	NNR (44-5-1)	NNR (44-10-1)	NNR (44-10-5-1)	NNR (44-15-10-1)
Explained variance	5.1%	5.4%	5.4%	2.5%	2.9%
Average relative error	0.16	0.16	0.16	0.16	0.16
Average absolute error	1.88	1.87	1.86	1.85	1.84
Average direction error	30.1%	30.8%	30.8%	32.6%	32.3%

Table D4.2b   USD/JPY RNN test results for the validation data set

	RNN (44-1-1)	RNN (44-5-1)	RNN (44-10-1)	RNN (44-10-5-1)	RNN (44-15-10-1)
Explained variance	8.4%	8.5%	8.0%	3.2%	3.0%
Average relative error	0.16	0.16	0.16	0.16	0.16
Average absolute error	1.86	1.85	1.84	1.85	1.85
Average direction error	30.1%	29.4%	29.4%	31.5%	30.1%

NNR/RNN (*a-b-c*) represents different neural network models, where:
   a = number of input variables;
   b = number of hidden nodes;
   c = number of output nodes.
Realised_Vol(t) = f[IVol($t-21$), Realised_Vol($t-21$), $|r|(t-21,\ldots,t-41)$, DLOIL($t-21,\ldots,t-41$)].

APPENDIX E

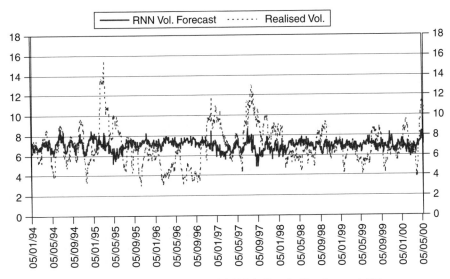

Figure E4.1   GBP/USD RNN (44-1-1) volatility forecast (%)

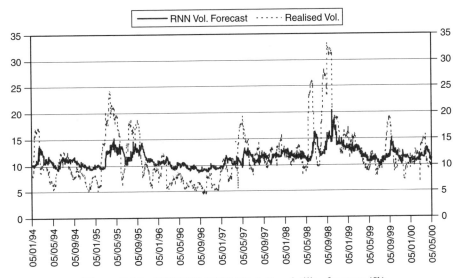

Figure E4.2   USD/JPY RNN (44-5-1) volatility forecast (%)

APPENDIX F

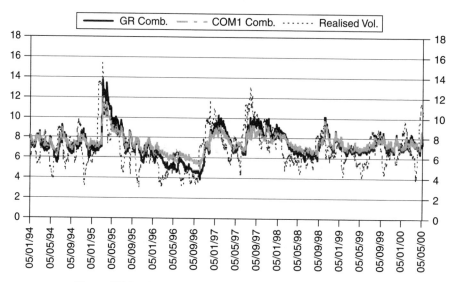

Figure F4.1   GBP/USD volatility forecast combinations (%)

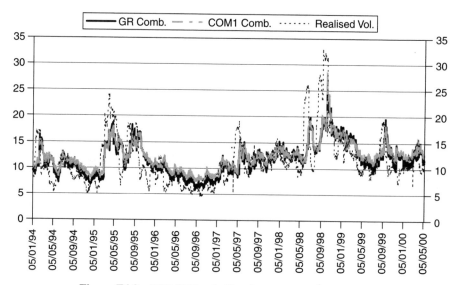

Figure F4.2   USD/JPY volatility forecast combinations (%)

APPENDIX G

Table G4.1 GBP/USD weekly volatility trading strategy

1 Threshold = 0.5   Trading days = 5

Sample Observation Period	In-sample (1-1329) (31/12/1993-09/04/1999)					Out-of-sample (1330-1610) (12/04/1999-09/05/2000)				
Models	NNR(44-10-5-1)	RNN(44-1-1)	GARCH(1,1)	COM1	GR	NNR(44-10-5-1)	RNN(44-1-1)	GARCH(1,1)	COM1	GR
P/L without gearing	162.15%	160.00%	262.41%	189.82%	313.55%	15.37%	13.30%	-12.85%	8.30%	30.08%
P/L with gearing	626.62%	852.70%	889.04%	597.16%	792.87%	36.46%	58.98%	-2.39%	20.92%	53.64%
Total trades	221	221	224	210	232	39	43	40	35	33
Profitable trades	66.97%	68.07%	81.70%	72.86%	91.38%	53.85%	60.47%	30.00%	45.71%	72.73%
Average gearing	2.86	4.20	2.71	2.54	2.19	1.72	2.58	1.82	1.62	1.63

2 Threshold = 1.0   Trading days = 5

Sample Observation Period	In-sample (1-1329) (31/12/1993-09/04/1999)					Out-of-sample (1330-1610) (12/04/1999-09/05/2000)				
Models	NNR(44-10-5-1)	RNN(44-1-1)	GARCH(1,1)	COM1	GR	NNR(44-10-5-1)	RNN(44-1-1)	GARCH(1,1)	COM1	GR
P/L without gearing	166.15%	147.13%	213.13%	167.03%	243.71%	20.09%	12.02%	7.87%	11.11%	18.57%
P/L with gearing	333.20%	420.39%	434.96%	300.56%	366.44%	27.01%	20.87%	12.80%	14.27%	23.42%
Total trades	166	166	153	147	138	21	27	17	13	14
Profitable trades	73.49%	72.00%	84.31%	77.55%	94.93%	76.19%	55.56%	58.82%	76.92%	85.71%
Average gearing	1.82	2.35	1.73	1.61	1.42	1.24	1.64	1.31	1.16	1.21

3 Threshold = 1.5   Trading days = 5

Sample Observation Period	In-sample (1-1329) (31/12/1993-09/04/1999)					Out-of-sample (1330-1610) (12/04/1999-09/05/2000)				
Models	NNR(44-10-5-1)	RNN(44-1-1)	GARCH(1,1)	COM1	GR	NNR(44-10-5-1)	RNN(44-1-1)	GARCH(1,1)	COM1	GR
P/L without gearing	128.90%	137.62%	176.30%	122.22%	129.73%	16.49%	7.06%	7.08%	7.08%	4.39%
P/L with gearing	198.76%	278.91%	268.10%	173.28%	158.83%	19.49%	10.52%	8.56%	7.61%	5.21%
Total trades	113	113	94	82	61	10	18	4	4	2
Profitable trades	74.34%	69.70%	93.62%	82.93%	95.08%	90.00%	50.00%	100.00%	100%	100.00%
Average gearing	1.49	1.81	1.45	1.38	1.21	1.12	1.27	1.19	1.07	1.14

4 Threshold = 2.0   Trading days = 5

Sample Observation Period	In-sample (1-1329) (31/12/1993-09/04/1999)					Out-of-sample (1330-1610) (12/04/1999-09/05/2000)				
Models	NNR(44-10-5-1)	RNN(44-1-1)	GARCH(1,1)	COM1	GR	NNR(44-10-5-1)	RNN(44-1-1)	GARCH(1,1)	COM1	GR
P/L without gearing	95.08%	115.09%	118.43%	62.47%	45.67%	3.26%	7.25%	4.67%	3.26%	-
P/L with gearing	131.34%	194.33%	158.35%	79.39%	52.97%	3.99%	9.27%	5.65%	3.48%	-
Total trades	68	68	56	36	18	1	10	2	1	0
Profitable trades	82.35%	72.44%	94.64%	88.89%	94.44%	100.00%	80.00%	100%	100%	-
Average gearing	1.34	1.55	1.31	1.29	1.14	1.22	1.14	1.16	1.07	-

Note: Cumulative P/L figures are expressed in volatility points.

Table G4.2   USD/JPY weekly volatility trading strategy

1 Threshold = 0.5   Trading days = 5

Sample Observation Period	In-sample (1-1329) (31/12/1993-09/04/1999)					Out-of-sample (1330-1610) (12/04/1999-09/05/2000)				
Models	NNR(44-1-1)	RNN(44-5-1)	GARCH(1,1)	COM1	GR	NNR(44-1-1)	RNN(44-5-1)	GARCH(1,1)	COM1	GR
P/L without gearing	−10.17%	−11.66%	208.63%	77.06%	387.38%	63.95%	78.77%	−82.07%	39.23%	69.31%
P/L with gearing	−79.31%	−32.08%	1675.67%	517.50%	1095.73%	251.14%	372.70%	−359.44%	111.86%	206.43%
Total trades	251	251	242	232	229	50	50	53	48	50
Profitable trades	51.00%	50.60%	54.13%	55.17%	78.60%	76.00%	86.00%	18.87%	60.42%	78.00%
Average gearing	3.76	3.88	3.67	2.67	2.42	3.22	3.73	5.92	2.18	2.35

2 Threshold = 1.0   Trading days = 5

Sample Observation Period	In-sample (1-1329) (31/12/1993-09/04/1999)					Out-of-sample (1330-1610) (12/04/1999-09/05/2000)				
Models	NNR(44-1-1)	RNN(44-5-1)	GARCH(1,1)	COM1	GR	NNR(44-1-1)	RNN(44-5-1)	GARCH(1,1)	COM1	GR
P/L without gearing	18.73%	30.43%	234.66%	142.37%	308.50%	52.70%	63.01%	−75.61%	31.71%	76.88%
P/L with gearing	0.43%	102.50%	897.30%	331.50%	578.10%	88.19%	135.49%	−162.97%	49.88%	124.63%
Total trades	213	213	201	168	165	39	43	53	30	37
Profitable trades	52.11%	54.17%	54.23%	58.93%	82.42%	76.92%	81.40%	24.53%	66.67%	94.59%
Average gearing	2.16	2.16	2.15	1.68	1.65	1.77	1.98	2.96	1.52	1.56

3 Threshold = 1.5   Trading days = 5

Sample Observation Period	In-sample (1-1329) (31/12/1993-09/04/1999)					Out-of-sample (1330-1610) (12/04/1999-09/05/2000)				
Models	NNR(44-1-1)	RNN(44-5-1)	GARCH(1,1)	COM1	GR	NNR(44-1-1)	RNN(44-5-1)	GARCH(1,1)	COM1	GR
P/L without gearing	34.15%	54.46%	251.07%	104.67%	282.96%	64.00%	55.83%	−65.02%	5.33%	52.59%
P/L with gearing	60.28%	164.86%	643.47%	203.58%	399.48%	108.52%	81.09%	−102.88%	11.99%	77.99%
Total trades	157	157	144	98	104	33	35	50	13	22
Profitable trades	54.78%	56.21%	63.89%	60.20%	86.54%	81.82%	80.00%	24.00%	69%	100.00%
Average gearing	1.83	1.75	1.78	1.45	1.35	1.56	1.51	2.00	1.38	1.42

4 Threshold = 2.0   Trading days = 5

Sample Observation Period	In-sample (1-1329) (31/12/1993-09/04/1999)					Out-of-sample (1330-1610) (12/04/1999-09/05/2000)				
Models	NNR(44-1-1)	RNN(44-5-1)	GARCH(1,1)	COM1	GR	NNR(44-1-1)	RNN(44-5-1)	GARCH(1,1)	COM1	GR
P/L without gearing	−6.13%	14.08%	247.22%	71.30%	154.88%	49.61%	53.90%	−43.71%	9.23%	30.33%
P/L with gearing	−35.86%	63.43%	514.30%	105.49%	202.86%	71.66%	86.20%	−52.64%	14.94%	40.28%
Total trades	117	117	113	47	50	21	23	47	6	11
Profitable trades	51.28%	52.94%	70.80%	65.96%	86.00%	90.48%	86.96%	28%	83%	100%
Average gearing	1.58	1.66	1.56	1.28	1.25	1.46	1.52	1.74	1.55	1.30

REFERENCES

Albanis, G. T. and R. A. Batchelor (2001), 21 Nonlinear Ways to Beat the Market. In *Developments in Forecast Combination and Portfolio Choice*, Dunis C, Moody J, Timmermann A (eds); John Wiley: Chichester.

Baillie, R. T. and T. Bollerslev (1989), The Message in Daily Exchange Rates: A Conditional Variance Tale. *Journal of Business and Economic Statistics* **7**: 297–305.

Baillie, R. T. and T. Bollerslev (1990), Intra-day and Inter-market Volatility in Foreign Exchange Rates. *Review of Economic Studies* **58**: 565–585.

Baillie, R. T. and T. Bollerslev (1992), Prediction in Dynamic Models with Time-Dependent Conditional Variances. *Journal of Econometrics* **52**: 91–113.

Balkin, S. D. (1999), Stationarity Concerns When Forecasting Using Neural Networks, Presentation at the INFORMS Conference, Philadelphia, PA.

Bartlmae, K. and F. A. Rauscher (2000), Measuring DAX Market Risk: A Neural Network Volatility Mixture Approach, Presentation at the FFM2000 Conference, London, 31 May–2 June.

Beine, M. and S. Laurent (2001), Structural Change and Long Memory in Volatility: New Evidence from Daily Exchange Rates. In *Developments in Forecast Combination and Portfolio Choice*, Dunis, C., Moody, J. and Timmermann, A. (eds); John Wiley: Chichester.

Black, F. and M. Scholes (1973), The Pricing of Options and Corporate Liabilities. *Journal of Political Economy* **81**: 637–654.

Bollen, P. B., S. F. Gray and R. E. Whaley (2000), Regime-Switching in Foreign Exchange Rates: Evidence from Currency Option Prices. *Journal of Econometrics* **94**: 239–276.

Bollerslev, T. (1986), Generalized Autoregressive Conditional Heteroskedasticity. *Journal of Econometrics* **31**: 307–327.

Bollerslev, T. (1987), A Conditional Heteroskedastic Time Series Model for Speculative Prices and Rates of Return. *Review of Economics and Statistics* **69**: 542–547.

Burgess, A. N. and A. N. Refenes (1996), The Use of Error Feedback Terms in Neural Network Modelling of Financial Time Series. In *Forecasting Financial Markets*, Dunis, C. (ed.); John Wiley: Chichester.

Cheng, B. and D. M. Titterington (1994), Neural Networks: A Review from a Statistical Perspective. *Statistical Science* **9**: 2–54.

Chiras, D. P. and S. Manaster (1978), The Information Content of Option Prices and a Test of Market Efficiency. *Journal of Financial Economics* **6**: 213–234.

Cybenko, G. (1989), Approximation by Superposition of a Sigmoidal Function. *Mathematical Control, Signals and Systems* **2**: 303–314.

Deboeck, G. J. (1994), *Trading on the Edge–Neural, Genetic and Fuzzy Systems for Chaotic Financial Markets*; John Wiley: New York.

Donaldson, R. G. and M. Kamstra (1996), Forecast Combining with Neural Networks. *Journal of Forecasting* **15**: 49–61.

Donaldson, R. G. and M. Kamstra (1997), An Artificial Neural Network–GARCH Model for International Stock Return Volatility. *Journal of Empirical Finance* **4**: 17–46.

Dunis, C. (1996), The Economic Value of Neural Network Systems for Exchange Rate Forecasting. *Neural Network World* **1**: 43–55.

Dunis, C. and M. Gavridis (1997), Volatility Trading Models: An Application to Daily Exchange Rates. *Working Papers in Financial Economics*, BNP Global Markets Research **1**: 1–4.

Dunis, C., J. Laws and S. Chauvin (2000), FX Volatility Forecasts: A Fusion-Optimisation Approach. *Neural Network World* **10**: 187–202.

Dunis, C., J. Moody and A. Timmermann (eds) (2001a), *Developments in Forecast Combination and Portfolio Choice*; John Wiley: Chichester.

Dunis, C., J. Laws and S. Chauvin (2001b), The Use of Market Data and Model Combination to Improve Forecasting Accuracy. In *Developments in Forecast Combination and Portfolio Choice*, Dunis, C., Moody, J. and Timmermann, A. (eds); John Wiley: Chichester.

Elman, J. L. (1990), Finding Structures in Time. *Cognitive Sciences* **14**: 179–211.

Engle, R. F. and T. Bollerslev (1986), Modelling the Persistence of Conditional Variances. *Econometric Reviews* **5**: 1–50.

Engle, R. F., C. H. Hong, A. Kane and J. Noh (1993), Arbitrage Valuation of Variance Forecasts with Simulated Options. In *Advances in Futures and Options Research*, Chance, D. M. and Tripp, R. R. (eds); JIA Press: Greenwich, CT.

Fama, E. F. (1990), Term Structure Forecasts of Interest Rates, Inflation and Real Returns. *Journal of Monetary Economics* **25**: 59–76.

Flôres, R. G. Jr and B. B. Roche (2000), Volatility Modelling in the Forex Market: An Empirical Evaluation. In *Advances in Quantitative Asset Management*, Dunis, C. (ed.); Kluwer: Boston.

Franses, P. H. and P. Van Homelen (1998), On Forecasting Exchange Rates Using Neural Networks. *Applied Financial Economics* **8**: 589–596.

Garman, M. B. and S. W. Kohlhagen (1983), Foreign Currency Option Values. *Journal of International Money and Finance* **2**: 231–237.

Gençay, R. (1996), Non-linear Prediction of Security Returns with Moving Average Rules. *Journal of Forecasting* **15**: 165–174.

Granger, C. W. and R. Ramanathan (1984), Improved Methods of Combining Forecasts. *Journal of Forecasting* **3**: 197–204.

Hassoun, M. H. (1995), *Fundamentals of Artificial Neural Networks*; MIT Press: Cambridge, MA.

Hornik, K., M. Stinchcombe and H. White (1989), Multilayer Feedforward Networks Are Universal Approximators. *Neural Networks* **2**: 359–366.

Hsieh, D. A. (1989), Modeling Heteroscedasticity in Daily Foreign Exchange Rates. *Journal of Business and Economic Statistics* **7**: 307–317.

Hull, J. C. (1997), *Options, Futures and Other Derivative Securities*; Prentice Hall, Englewood Cliffs, NJ.

Ivanova, D., K. Lahiri and F. Seitz (2000), Interest Rate Spreads as Predictors of German Inflation and Business Cycles. *International Journal of Forecasting* **16**: 39–58.

Jorion, P. (1995), Predicting Volatility in the Foreign Exchange Market. *Journal of Finance* **50**: 507–528.

Jorion, P. (1997), *Value at Risk: The New Benchmark for Controlling Market Risk*; McGraw-Hill: New York.

Kouam, A., F. Badran and S. Thiria (1992), Approche Méthodologique pour l'Etude de la Prévision à l'Aide de Réseaux de Neurones, *Actes de Neuro-Nîmes*.

Kroner, K. F., K. P. Kneafsey and S. Claessens (1995), Forecasting Volatility in Commodity Markets. *Journal of Forecasting* **14**: 77–95.

Kuan, C. M. and T. Liu (1995), Forecasting Exchange Rates Using Feedforward and Recurrent Neural Networks. *Journal of Applied Economics* **10**: 347–364.

Lamoureux, C. G. and W. D. Lastrapes (1993), Forecasting Stock-Return Variances: Toward an Understanding of Stochastic Implied Volatilities. *Review of Financial Studies* **6**: 293–326.

Latane, H. A. and R. J. Rendleman (1976), Standard Deviations of Stock Price Ratios Implied in Option Prices. *Journal of Finance* **31**: 369–381.

Laws, J. and A. Gidman (2000), Forecasting Stock Market Volatility and the Application of Volatility Trading Models. *CIBEF Research Paper*, Liverpool Business School.

Leung, M. T., H. Daouk and A.-S. Chen (2000), Forecasting Stock Indices: A Comparison of Classification and Level Estimation Models. *International Journal of Forecasting* **16**: 173–190.

Makridakis, S., S. C. Wheelwright and V. E. McGee (1983), *Forecasting: Methods and Applications*; John Wiley: New York.

Malz, A. M. (1996), Using Option Prices to Estimate Realignment Probabilities in the European Monetary System. In *Forecasting Financial Markets*, Dunis, C. (ed.); John Wiley: Chichester.

Ntungo, C. and M. Boyd (1998), Commodity Futures Trading Performance Using Neural Network Models Versus ARIMA Models. *Journal of Futures Markets* **8**: 965–983.

Pindyck, R. S. and D. L. Rubinfeld (1998), *Econometric Models and Economic Forecasts*; McGraw-Hill: New York.

Refenes, A. N. (1995), *Neural Networks In the Capital Markets*; John Wiley: Chichester.

Rehkugler, H. and H. G. Zimmermann (eds) (1994), *Neuronale Netze in der Ökonomie – Grundlagen und finanzwirtschaftliche Anwendungen*; Verlag Franz Vahlen: München.

Shadbolt, J. and J. G. Taylor (eds) (2002), *Neural Networks and the Financial Markets – Predicting, Combining and Portfolio Optimisation*; Springer-Verlag: London.

Simpson, P. K. (1990), *Artificial Neural Systems–Foundations, Paradigms, Applications, and Implementations*; Pergamon Press: New York.

So, M. K. P., K. Lam and W. K. Li (1999), Forecasting Exchange Rate Volatility Using Autoregressive Random Variance Model. *Applied Financial Economics* **9**: 583–591.

Swanson, N. R. and H. White (1995), A Model-Selection Approach to Assessing the Information in the Term-Structure Using Linear Models and Neural Networks. *Journal of Business and Economic Statistics* **13**: 265–275.

Taylor, S. J. (1986), *Modelling Financial Time Series*; John Wiley: Chichester.

Tenti, P. (1996), Forecasting Foreign Exchange Rates Using Recurrent Neural Networks. *Applied Artificial Intelligence* **10**: 567–581.

Theil, H. (1966), *Applied Economic Forecasting*; North-Holland: Amsterdam.

Trippi, R. and E. Turban (eds) (1993), *Neural Networks in Finance and Investing – Using Artificial Intelligence to Improve Real-World Performance*; Probus: Chicago.

West, K. D. and D. Cho (1995), The Predictive Ability of Several Models of Exchange Rate Volatility. *Journal of Econometrics* **69**: 367–391.

Xu, X. and S. J. Taylor (1996), Conditional Volatility and the Informational Efficiency of the PHLX Currency Options Market. In *Forecasting Financial Markets*, Dunis, C. (ed.); John Wiley: Chichester.

Zhang, G., B. E. Patuwo and M. Y. Hu (1998), Forecasting with Artificial Neural Networks: The State of the Art. *International Journal of Forecasting* **14**: 35–62.

5

Implementing Neural Networks, Classification Trees, and Rule Induction Classification Techniques: An Application to Credit Risk

GEORGE T. ALBANIS

ABSTRACT

There are many commercial data mining softwares available in the market that can be applied to financial applications. Although these softwares apply very powerful modelling tools, the user will have always to consider a financial cost in acquiring them. Apart from these commercial softwares, there are other data mining tools that are available in the public domain for free. A few of these freely available tools are quick and easy to use and they do not require data files to be prepared in special formats. However, they may have less powerful capabilities compared to commercial softwares. In this study, we demonstrate how to implement two freely available softwares on neural networks and decision trees, respectively, and one commercial software for constructing decision trees and rule induction classifiers. Our implementations demonstrate that there are very flexible tools for academics, young quantitative finance professionals and profit speculators who would like to know more in implementing data mining applications.

5.1 INTRODUCTION

There are a host of very powerful and popular commercial data mining softwares available in the market that can be applied to financial applications. A few popular softwares in this area are CART 4.0, See5, AC2, SPSS Answer Tree. Implementing a variety of state of the art modelling tools, these softwares have very powerful capabilities when applied to a spectrum of different financial applications. However, commercial softwares are not available for free. There is always a financial cost in acquiring commercial softwares and more often an additional cost in acquiring a licence for each individual user of these softwares.

Apart from these commercial softwares, there are a host of other data mining softwares that are freely available in the public domain such as C4.5, EC4.5, CN2, MLC++. Although

Dr George Albanis is a quantitative analyst in Hypovereinsbank – HVB Group. The opinions expressed herein are not those of Hypovereinsbank – HVB Group. (Email: albanis_george@hotmail.com)

Applied Quantitative Methods for Trading and Investment. Edited by C.L. Dunis, J. Laws and P. Naïm
© 2003 John Wiley & Sons, Ltd ISBN: 0-470-84885-5

most of the freely available softwares have severely limited capabilities compared to commercial softwares, a few others can be really competitive in terms of predictive accuracy and processing speed. We have to mention, however, that many of the most powerful freely available data mining softwares have been developed and compiled in various operating systems. It is possible that a particular operating system may require additional tools to be installed to enable the installation of freely available softwares. On the other hand, the user may not always find sufficient technical support in installing freely available softwares. Instead, he has to be aware of a variety of technical issues related to operating system capabilities, system memory limitations, and programming libraries related to different softwares. Therefore, the time effort of installing and using either commercial or freely available softwares may be an important factor in triggering the interest of the user and influencing him in choosing between softwares with similar capabilities.

Despite the above technical limitations of freely available data mining softwares, there are a few freely available data mining softwares on the web that are easy to learn and apply for modelling financial applications, without requiring the user to be a technical expert on either the particular data mining algorithm or the operating system. These tools do not require special installations and they do not require individual licences. They are quick and easy to use and they do not require data files to be prepared in special formats. They can be ideal tools for demonstrating a particular modelling tool to a classroom by quickly running a few examples for the students. They can also be useful for analysts in the industry who are considering purchasing commercial data mining softwares, but before they do so, they would like to have an initial understanding of what these tools can do.

For this purpose, we demonstrate in this chapter how to apply two freely available data mining softwares as well as one commercial data mining software. The two freely available data mining softwares that we choose to implement are the Neural Network for Classification in Excel and the Classification Tree in Excel both developed by Angshuman Saha.[1] On the other hand, the commercial software that we choose to apply in this study is See5 for Windows developed by Rulequest Research.

We used three criteria in selecting these tools:

1. Time effort in installing the particular software.
2. Time effort in applying the software in a particular application without the need for the user to be a technical expert.
3. Flexibility in using the particular software in generally used operating systems.

Statistical classification is also known as supervised learning. Supervised learning is a form of learning from a sample of previously known examples. Each example is described by a set of data observations and a class label. Given that the examples are known to come from one of C_{jt} distinct classes ($j = 1, 2, \ldots, k$) of observations, we wish to find functions of these observations that will distinguish the classes, and that will enable us to assign a new example to one of these classes on the basis of m measured characteristics associated with each particular example.

We use two different datasets in our study. The first one is the Australian credit approval dataset that has been studied before by several researchers (Quinlan, 1987, 1993;

---

[1] See www.geocities.com/adotsaha for more information about Angshuman Saha and learn more about his recent software developments.

Michie *et al.*, 1994). The aim is to devise a classification rule for assessing credit card applications. The second dataset is the German credit dataset that also has been used before in previous studies (Michie *et al.*, 1994). The aim is to devise again a classification rule for assessing the credit quality of German borrowers. But note that, more generally, the methods demonstrated in this chapter can be applied to a wealth of trading and investment problems, such as the determination of outperforming/underperforming stocks, bond rating, etc.

All three softwares were found really attractive in terms of predictive accuracy, ease of installation, and flexibility in implementing the particular software in generally used operating systems. However, the freely available softwares were found to be slower than See5 in terms of processing speed. This should be a particular concern in applying large datasets consisting of several thousands of records. See5 will be more flexible in handling large datasets due to its powerful capabilities.

The remainder of this chapter is organised as follows: in Section 5.2, we discuss the data that we used in this study. In Section 5.3, we provide a brief overview on neural networks and demonstrate how to implement a neural network model for classification in Excel. In Section 5.4, we provide a brief overview on decision trees and demonstrate how to implement a classification tree in Excel. In Section 5.5, we demonstrate how to implement the commercial software See5 using a demo version of this software. Finally, Section 5.6 provides some conclusions.

5.2   DATA DESCRIPTION

We have used two datasets for the purpose of this study. The first one is the Australian credit approval dataset. The second one is the German credit dataset. Both datasets are available in the public domain and can be found in Michie *et al.* (1994).

The Australian credit approval dataset refers to credit card applications. The aim is to find a classification rule for assessing credit card applicants. The dataset consists of two classes, 14 predictor variables and 690 data records. This dataset has been studied in the past by Quinlan (1987, 1993) and Michie *et al.* (1994). However, the interpretation of their results has been very difficult because classes and predictor variables have been coded due to the confidentiality of the data. For this reason, it is not possible to assess the relative costs of errors. Also, it is not possible to assess the relative costs of odds to good and bad customers. But it is still a very interesting dataset for having a good mix of categorical and continuous predictor variables. There are also a few missing values: 37 cases (5%) had one or more missing values. The missing values were replaced by the mode for categorical predictor variables or by the mean for continuous predictor variables. A more detailed description of this dataset can be found in the file "Australia_Credit.doc".

The German credit dataset has also been used in previous studies (Michie *et al.*, 1994). The original dataset was provided by Professor Hofmann (Universität Hamburg). This original dataset contains categorical/symbolic attributes. However, Strathclyde University converted this file to numerical attributes for algorithms that cannot handle categorical attributes. We can see both of these files in the Excel workbook "German.xls". On the preprocessed dataset containing numerical attributes, several indicator variables have been added to make it more suitable for algorithms that favour numerical attributes. Since we applied the Australian credit approval dataset with categorical attributes, we chose to apply the German credit dataset with numerical attributes only. The preprocessed dataset consists of two classes, 24 numerical attributes and 1000 data records. To perform our implementation, we have chosen to use 700 randomly selected data records as this is mostly a demonstration exercise. The aim is to find a classification rule for assessing the credit quality of German borrowers. The attributes of the original dataset include status of existing current account, credit history, savings account/bonds, length of employment, age, job, instalment rate in percentage of disposable income, marital status and sex, reason for loan request, duration of current account, length of time at present residence, and credit account.

The providers of this dataset suggest the use of a cost matrix. It is worse to class a customer as good quality when he is a bad quality borrower than it is to class a customer as bad quality when he is a good quality borrower. More detailed information about the German credit dataset can be found in the file "German_Credit.doc".

5.3 NEURAL NETWORKS FOR CLASSIFICATION IN EXCEL

This tool can be used to build multilayer neural network-based classification models in Excel. For those not familiar with artificial neural networks (ANNs), we give below a brief overview.

5.3.1 Artificial neural networks

Neural networks have been used extensively in classification applications. The first neural network architecture was the original perceptron developed by Rosenblatt (1962). Rosenblatt demonstrated that if two datasets are linearly separable, then a neural network perceptron model would be able to separate them. A few years later, Minsky and Papert (1969) demonstrated that this algorithm might not converge if there is no separating hyperplane.

Multilayer feedforward neural networks (MLNNs) consist of a number of neurons that are logically structured into a number of different layers. There is an input layer, an output layer, and one or more hidden layers between the input and output layers (Masters, 1993, 1995). The computational nodes of these layers are correspondingly called input neurons, hidden neurons and output neurons. The neurons in the input layer supply signals that are used as inputs to the second layer. The output signals of the second layer, are used as inputs to the third layer, and so on.

Most ANNs apply some form of "learning rule" which modifies the weights of the connections according to the input patterns. There are various types of learning rules used by neural networks. A very popular one is the delta rule. The delta rule is often utilised by the most common class of ANNs, so-called backpropagation neural networks (BPNNs). According to the delta rule, learning is a supervised process that occurs each time the network is presented with a new input pattern. On each input presentation, the network makes a prediction as to what might be the actual output. If the prediction is far from the actual value, the network makes an appropriate adjustment to its connection weights. Backpropagation follows a gradient descent within the solution's vector space towards a global minimum along the steepest vector of the error surface. The global minimum can be described as the theoretical solution with the lowest possible error. The error surface itself is a hyperparaboloid which is not typically a very smooth function. More often, the solution space can have many irregularities with numerous "pits" and "hills" which may cause the network to settle down in a local minimum rather than the best overall solution.

To determine the nature of the error space and find the best solution, the neural network will have to run a number of times that may vary according to different applications. It is possible to specify additional input parameters to assist the neural network in controlling the "rate of learning" and the "momentum" of learning. The speed of learning is the rate of convergence between the current solution and the global minimum. Momentum helps the network to overcome local minima in the error surface and reach the global minimum.

Figure 5.1 illustrates the layout of a three-layer feedforward neural network. The first layer on the left is the input layer, the second layer in the middle is the hidden layer and the third layer on the right is the output layer. This neural network is fully connected as every neuron in each layer is connected to every neuron in the forward layer. The mathematical functions of the hidden neurons are to intervene between the external input and the network output. Adding one or more hidden layers, the network is able to extract higher-order statistics. This might be particularly valuable when the size of the input layer is large (Haykin, 1994).

Classification of an individual input vector $x'_{it} = (x_{i1t}, x_{i2t}, \ldots, x_{imt})$ into one of different classes can be viewed as a mathematical process of transforming the m input units into output units $y_{i1t}, y_{i2t}, \ldots, y_{ikt}$ that define the class allocation of the unknown vector. For example, in case of two classes, $y_{i1t} = 1$ and $y_{i2t} = 0$ if the individual input vector is to be allocated to class 1 or class 2, respectively.

A few excellent reviews on neural networks are provided by Ripley (1992), Cheng and Titterington (1994), Zhang et $al.$ (1998) and Dunis and Jalilov (2002).

5.3.2 Technical implementation of neural network for classification in Excel

To implement the neural network classification model, we have to open in Excel the main Excel workbook entitled "NNClassAust.xls". We first enter the data in the worksheet entitled "Data", starting from the cell "AC105". The observations for each particular data record should be in rows and the variables should be in columns. Above each column, there is a drop box that allows us to choose the appropriate data type. To treat a column in the data as a categorical predictor, we have to choose the data label "Cat". To treat a column in the data as a continuous predictor, we have to choose the data label "Cont". To

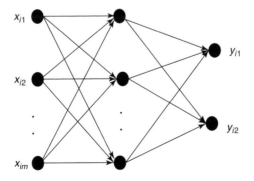

Figure 5.1 A three-layer feedforward neural network

treat a column in the data as a class variable, we have to choose the data label "Output". Finally, to exclude a column from the analysis, we have to choose the data label "Omit". The application offers the facility to omit different predictor variables while running different models. The predictor variables do not need to be in contiguous columns. This feature may save us a lot of time if we want to exclude predictor variables that are redundant in improving the classification performance of the model.

The application can handle at most 50 predictor variables, but only 40 could be categorical. The neural network will be able to process categorical data if they are converted to dummy variables. For example, a categorical variable with two categories in the data can be replaced by two binary variables taking values 0 or 1. The application will convert all categorical to binary variables automatically before the data are processed into the network. Therefore, the number of predictor variables including dummy variables should not be greater than 50. The number of rows in the data should be greater than 10 but should not exceed 10 000. Although the application will be able to build a model for a minimum number of 11 data cases, it is likely that the generalisation performance of the model will not be satisfactory if the number of rows in the data is not representative of the general population. On the other hand, the model may overfit the data if the number of rows in the data is not sufficiently larger than the number of predictor variables.

To perform a classification task, we need to specify only one class variable. The class variable will be treated by the application as categorical. If there is a missing value in a continuous predictor variable, the application will replace it by the column median. On the other hand, if there is a missing value in a categorical predictor variable, the application will replace it by the most frequently occurring category. We have to ensure that the class variable does not have any missing values. If there is a missing value in the class variable, the application will not run and an error message will appear to inform us that we have to delete those data observations where the class variable is missing. The application requires that each category in a categorical predictor variable should have at least two observations. Category labels are case insensitive – for example, category labels such as credit, CREDIT will be treated by the application as members of the same category.

After importing the data in the "Data" worksheet, we have to specify the neural network input parameters in the worksheet entitled "UserInput". On the top left-hand side of this worksheet, we can specify input parameters such as the number of predictor variables ("Number of Inputs"), the number of hidden layers ("Number of Hidden Layers"), the learning parameter ("Learning Parameter"), the momentum ("Momentum"), and the number of rows in the data ("Total #Rows in your Data"). The application can handle up to two hidden layers. The learning parameter and the momentum can take any value between 0 and 1. We can specify these parameters by typing numbers in the cells marked in green next to the parameter headings.

On the bottom left-hand side of the "UserInput" worksheet, we can specify how to use the data in building the neural network architecture. For example, we have the option to use all the data in building the model by selecting the option "Use whole data" next to the heading "Training/Validation Set". But, if we use all the data as the training set, we will be unable to assess the generalisation performance of the model in a different dataset. An alternative will be to split our data into training set and validation set by selecting the option "Partition data into training/validation set". Furthermore, we have two options to select our validation set. We can randomly select a number of data records from the dataset as a test set by selecting option 1 next to the heading "Please Choose One

Option". Alternatively, we can specify that the last few rows in our data should be used as a validation set by selecting option 2. If we are selecting option 2, we have to ensure that all class categories are present in both the training and the validation set. If any of the class categories is not present in the training data, the generalisation performance of the model in new examples is not going to be very satisfactory. On the other hand, if any of the class categories are not present in the validation set, we will not be able to assess the generalisation performance of the neural network in new data. During the training process, we might want to present the input vectors into the neural network in random order by selecting the option "YES" in the corresponding toolbox next to the heading "Present Inputs in Random Order while Training?". Alternatively, if we select "NO", the input patterns will be presented into the model in normal order one after the other.

To train the network, we need to generate a matrix of starting weights. By default, the application generates the starting weights randomly. However, we also have the option to specify a different matrix of starting weights. We have three choices in saving the network weights during the training stage: (a) we can choose to save those weights resulting in the least training error; (b) we can choose to save those weights resulting in the least validation error; and (c) we can choose to save those weights corresponding to the last training cycle. We can select any of these options in the corresponding toolbox next to the heading "Saving Network Weights". Once we have made our selection, the application will save the weights while building the neural network model.

We have the option to save the new model in a separate workbook by clicking "YES" in the corresponding toolbox next to the heading "Save Model in a Separate Workbook?" at the bottom left-hand side of the "UserInput" worksheet. Alternatively, we can specify "NO" if we do not want to save the model in a new workbook.

On the top right-hand side of the "UserInput" worksheet, we can specify the number of neurons for the hidden layers by typing numbers under the headings "Hidden 1" and "Hidden 2". We can also specify the range of initial weights by typing a number next to the headings "Initial Wt Range (0 +/− w): w =". The application can handle up to 20 neurons on each hidden layer. The initial weights should be in the range between 0 and 1.

We can specify the number of training cycles that we want to use while training our neural network by typing a number in the corresponding toolbox next to the heading "No. of Training Cycles". The application can handle up to 500 training cycles. However, this is not a problem since we have the option to save the weights after we have reached 500 training cycles. Then, we can use these weights to run the model for another 500 cycles and so on. We can train the neural network using either a sequential mode or a batch mode by selecting the option "Sequential" or "Batch", respectively, in the appropriate toolbox.

After selecting the neural network inputs in the "UserInput" worksheet, we can start building the neural network by clicking the button "Build Model" that is located to the bottom right-hand side in the "UserInput" worksheet. After clicking this button, a message box will appear on the screen to inform us that the application has saved a matrix of weights on a previous implementation and it can use those as starting weights in training the neural network. If we select "OK" on this message box, another message box will appear on the screen to inform us that we have the choice to use either the existing matrix of weights or to start with a new matrix of random weights that the application will generate for us. If we select "YES", the application will use the matrix of weights that was saved in memory from the previous implementation. If we select "NO", the application will generate a new matrix of weights to start training the network. When we make our selection, the application will start training the neural network. During the training process, we will be able to see graphically on the screen the model performance on both the training and the validation set. When the last training cycle is complete, a message box will appear on the screen to inform us that the application has saved the new model in a new workbook in the current Excel window if we have previously selected this option in the "UserInput" worksheet. The new workbook in which the application has saved the data will appear if we select "OK" on the message box. If we have not previously selected the option to save the results in a new workbook, the results will be displayed on the main workbook in which the application is running.

After the building of the neural network is complete, we will be able to view the output of the model in different worksheets on either the main workbook or a new workbook if we have previously selected this option in the "UserInput" worksheet. Let us assume that we have selected the option to save the classification results in a new workbook. The new workbook saved by the application will contain three worksheets. The worksheet entitled "Model" contains information about the neural network weights that represent the neural network parameters. On the top part of this worksheet, we can find information about the percentage of data records that were classified incorrectly by the model on both the training and the validation sets as one can see in cells "AE102" and "AJ102", respectively. We can also see the number of hidden layers that were used in building the neural network as well as the number of neurons for each hidden layer, respectively, in the cells marked in yellow. We can use this worksheet as a calculator in applying the neural network to classify new data records. For example, if we enter a new vector of predictor variables in the range "AG112:AT112" of those cells marked in green, the application will display the class predicted by the model in cell "AF108". Further below on this worksheet, we can see two classification matrices displaying the classification results for both the training and test sets. The elements across the diagonal of a matrix are the number of data records that were classified by the application correctly, whereas the off-diagonal elements are the number of data records that were classified by the application incorrectly. Overall, the Neural Network for Classification in Excel produced very satisfactory classification results, classifying correctly over 75% of the data cases in both the training and the test sets. The classification results will vary on each different implementation depending on which option we choose about the matrix of starting weights. If we apply a different matrix of starting weights on each different implementation, we will get different classification results. Obviously, we can improve the classification performance of the model even further by changing the network parameters in the "UserInput" worksheet. However, this is only a demonstration on how to apply the model rather than optimising its classification performance.

The second worksheet entitled "Training Data" contains the data that we used to run the application. Immediately after the column of the last predictor variable, there is an additional column giving information about the class predicted by the application. By comparing this column against column "C" which shows the actual class for each data record, we can see which data records were classified by the application correctly and which columns were classified incorrectly. Next to the column showing the predicted class, we can see the scores predicted by the model for the class categories – one score for each class category, respectively. Each data record, in either the training or the validation set, is assigned by the model to the class with the highest score. In the worksheet "Model Parameters" of the new workbook we can find a copy of the input parameters that we entered in the worksheet "UserInput" of the main workbook "NNClassAust.xls".

The main workbook "NNClassAust.xls" contains the same worksheets as those saved by the application on the new workbook plus a few other worksheets. As we can see, the worksheet "Calc" of the main workbook contains the same information as the worksheet "Model" of the new workbook. The worksheet "Output" shows the percentage misclassification error for each training cycle on both the training and the validation set. On the right-hand side of this worksheet, we can see the graphs that we have already seen while building the neural network during the training phase.

In the worksheet entitled "Profile", we can see the profile plots generated by the application for the fitted model. The profile plot is an indicator of the nature of the relationship between the individual predictor variables and the response variable. For example, let us assume that we are looking at the profile of two predictor variables $P1$, $P2$ against the class variable C. Initially, we look at the profile plot of predictor variable $P1$ against C by changing the predictor variable $P2$ between 2 and -2. Then, we look at the profile plot of predictor variable $P2$ against C by changing the predictor variable $P1$ between 2 and -2. If the profile plots generated by these two scenarios have different shapes, then we can conclude that there is an interaction between $P1$ and $P2$, as the effect of one predictor variable on the class variable C is not the same for different values of the other predictor variable. If the class variable has j categories, the model will predict scores for all j categories – one score for each class category, respectively. The final category predicted by the model will be the one having the highest score. If we have m predictor variables, each of the j score functions can be represented as m-dimensional surfaces. We finally plot j profiles – one plot for each class category, respectively. The plots taken together provide an indication on how the scores vary with the predictor variable. In the "Profile" worksheet, we can specify which predictor variable to vary in cell "I6" as well as the number of data points generated in cell "I5". In cells "K6" and "M6", we can also specify the range of values in which the other predictors should be held fixed while varying the predictor variable that we have selected in cell "I6". In the range of cells "J15:V15" that are marked in green, we can type different values for the predictor variables. In cell "I15" we can choose the value that should remain fixed. If we now press the button "Create Profile", the graph will display one profile plot for each class category. The "X" axis shows the values of the predictor variable we have chosen to vary, whereas the "Y" axis shows the corresponding score given by the network for that category. If the predictor variable that we have chosen is a categorical variable, the input parameters related to the number of data points and the range of values to be held fixed will be ignored. The graph will then show the scores for each category of the predictor variable we have chosen to vary.

In the worksheet "LiftChart", the application generates a lift chart for the fitted model after selecting a category in cell "E4" and pressing the button "Create Lift Chart". The lift chart tells us what is the discriminatory power of the fitted model. For example, if we have a class variable with two categories, the model will predict two scores – one score for each category, respectively. If the model is a "good" model, then if we select one class category and look at its score, we would expect that observations receiving high scores are the ones that actually belong to the selected category. If we sort the data of the selected category from high score to low score, we can take a subset of the top observations, and count what percentage of observations for the selected category we have captured. The lift chart for the selected category shows the percentage of the non-selected category against the percentage of the selected category as we proceed from the first data point to the total number of data points. The lift chart tells us what is the percentage of non-j observations that the model also captures by mistake if we want to capture 90% of the truly category j observations. The lift curve starts at 0% and ends at 100%. The better the model, the higher the lift curve will be from the diagonal line joining the points 0% and 100%. The best possible scenario is when we capture 100% of category j and 0% of non-j category.

The implementation for the German credit dataset is similar. As an exercise, the user can try to run the application using the Excel workbook "NNClassGerm.xls".

5.4 CLASSIFICATION TREE IN EXCEL

This tool can be used to build tree-based classification models in Excel. It is an implementation of the C4.5 algorithm developed by Quinlan (1996). For those not familiar with tree-based classification models, we give below a brief overview.

5.4.1 Decision trees

Decision trees are hierarchical, sequential classification structures that recursively partition a set of data records. Many variants of decision trees have been proposed in the literature over the last decades. Two very well known variants are axis-parallel trees and oblique decision trees. Axis-parallel trees apply tests at each internal node of the form $x_{it} > k$ where x_{it} is one of the attributes and k is a constant. Applying these tests results in partitioning the attribute space in the form of hyper-rectangles that are parallel to the feature axis. Oblique decision trees apply tests at each internal node of the form (Murthy, 1997):

$$\sum_{i=1}^{m} \alpha_{it} X_{it} + \alpha_{m+1} = 0$$

where m is the number of the attributes and α_{it} are real-valued coefficients. These tests are equivalent to hyperplanes at an oblique orientation of the axis.

If the underlying concept is defined by a polygonal partitioning of the attribute space, then axis-parallel trees would not be an ideal tool in performing classification. Oblique decision trees would then be more flexible in modelling the underlying concept.

Most of the existing decision tree algorithms use a greedy top-down approach to build a decision tree. According to this approach if all training examples at the current node v of the tree belong to class C_{jt}, then a leaf node is created in the tree with the class C_{jt} and the algorithm halts. Otherwise, a score is assigned to each one of the set of possible splits, S, based on a specific goodness measure. The best split s' with the highest score is then used as the test at the current node. New leaf nodes will be created in the tree according to the distinct outcomes of s'. Edges between the current and leaf nodes are labelled with outcomes of s'. The algorithm partitions the training data using s' into the leaf nodes. A new data observation is classified by passing it through the tree starting from the root node. The test at each internal node along the path is applied to the values of the predictor variables to determine the next edge along which this example should go down. The label at the leaf node at which the data observation ends up is labelled as its predicted class. The tree misclassifies a data observation if the predicted classification is not the same as the data's class label.

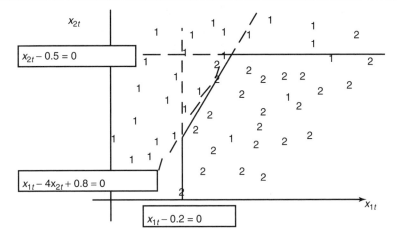

Figure 5.2   An imaginary decision tree with oblique splits

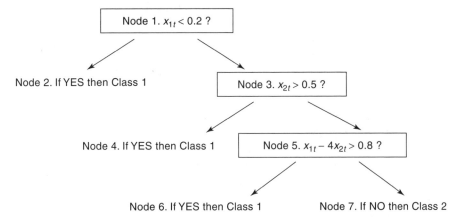

Figure 5.3   A sequential representation of a decision tree with oblique splits

Figure 5.2 gives a graphical illustration of a decision tree that classifies data observations into two classes 1, 2 using two predictor variables: x_{1t} and x_{2t}. A hypothetical sequential representation of this tree is given in Figure 5.3. To classify a new data observation at the top or root of the tree, we first test whether the value of x_{1t} is less than 0.2. If the value of x_{1t} is less than 0.2, the data observation is assigned to class 1. If the value of x_{1t} is greater than 0.2, then we test if the value of x_{2t} is greater than 0.5. If the value of x_{2t} is greater than 0.5, the data observation is assigned to class 1, if it is less than 0.5, then we test if the linear combination $x_{1t} - 4x_{2t}$ is greater than 0.8 and so on. Following a path going down the tree, we are testing conditions of the predictor variables recursively at the nodes of the tree, and decide which path to follow depending on whether or not the conditions of the predictor variables are satisfied.

When building a decision tree, we have to decide which variable we should use at each internal node, which internal node should be split, and what would be the nature of the split. The usual approach to solve these problems is to use an "impurity" index at each node of the tree. The "impurity" index is a measure of the differences between the probabilities of belonging to each class. Several impurity measures have been suggested in the literature. These include among others the Information Index, the Gini Index, Max Minority, Sum Minority, etc. A very effective impurity index is also the Twoing Rule that was proposed by Breiman *et al.* (1984). This impurity index is given as follows (Murthy, 1997; Albanis and Batchelor, 2001):

$$\text{TV} = \left(\frac{|N_L|}{n}\right)\left(\frac{|N_R|}{n}\right)\left(\sum_{i=1}^{k}\left|\frac{\text{CL}_L}{|N_L|} - \frac{\text{CR}_H}{|N_R|}\right|\right)^2$$

where TV is the twoing value, $|N_L|$ is the number of vectors on the left of a split at node v, $|N_R|$ is the number of vectors on the right of a split at node v, n is the total number of vectors at node v, CL_L is the number of vectors in category L on the left of the split, and CR_H is the number of vectors in category H on the right of the split.

We could continue to partition the nodes of a decision tree until all the leaf nodes are contained in a particular class. However, this procedure would lead to a very large tree that is likely to overfit the training data and as a result will have poor generalisation performance to new data. One way to solve this problem would be to stop the growth of the decision tree by adopting a stopping rule. A possible stopping rule would be to stop the growth of the tree when the maximum reduction in impurity is less than some threshold. Obviously, a small threshold would lead to many small leaf nodes, whereas a large threshold would lead to only a few leaf nodes. However, this approach has a disadvantage if the growth of the tree is sequential. In that case, a split is possible at a node of the tree only if the reduction in impurity exceeds some value, independently of what is going to happen at a lower node of the tree as a result of the split. An alternative stopping rule to avoid this problem would be to build a large tree that overfits the data, and then to prune this tree using some pruning criterion (Hand, 1997). A more detailed overview of decision trees can be found in Murthy (1997).

A system that had a very important impact on machine learning research in recent years is the C4.5 algorithm. The C4.5 algorithm is actually an extension of the ID3 algorithm that was developed by Quinlan (1983, 1986). The ID3 system constructs decision trees using a set of predefined examples. The domain of each attribute in these examples represents a small number of either symbolic or attribute values. To construct a tree, an attribute is selected as the root of the tree and several new branches are constructed according to the different values of the selected attribute. This tree is then applied to classify the data in the training set. If the examples at a particular leaf node of the tree belong to the same class, the leaf node is labelled with this class. If a particular leaf node of the tree is not assigned to a class, then the node is labelled with a different attribute that does appear on the path of the tree and new branches are created for possible values of the new attribute. The new tree is then used to classify the training set. This process is repeated until all leaf nodes are associated with a particular class. This algorithm, however, might be more appropriate with symbolic attributes rather than using a range of numerical attributes. This problem was further addressed with the C4.5 algorithm, which allows us to test an inequality of numerical attributes such that $x_{it} \leq k$ with two corresponding possible branches. The information gain of such a test can be computed by sorting the examples on the values of the attribute being considered. For example, if there are only a finite number of attributes, the algorithm will search for $m - 1$ possible splits on this particular attribute. It is obvious that if the examples are not sorted, the search process might be a particularly expensive task in terms of computational resources. However, if the examples are sorted, the search process can be performed in one pass updating the class distributions to the left and right of the threshold. For each possible threshold, an information gain can be computed that can be used in the process of selecting the next test (Holseimer and Siebes, 1991).

5.4.2   Technical implementation of classification tree in Excel

To implement the tree-based classification model, we have to open in Excel the main Excel workbook entitled "CTree01Aust.xls". Then, we have to enter the data in the worksheet entitled "Data", starting from cell "L24". The observations for each particular example in the data should be in rows and the variables should be in columns. Above each column, there is a drop box that allows us to choose the appropriate data type. The names for the different variable types are similar to those that we used for the neural network model. We recall that the data label for a categorical predictor should be declared as "Cat", the data label for a continuous predictor should be declared as "Cont", and the data label for the class variable should be declared as "Output". To exclude a column from the analysis, we have to select the data label "Omit". This application also offers the additional feature to omit different predictor variables while running different models.

The model can handle up to 50 predictor variables. To perform a classification task, the model requires only one class variable. The class variable will be treated by the application as categorical. Each of the categorical predictor variables, including the class variable, should have at most 20 different categories. The number of rows in the data should be greater than 10 but should not exceed 10 000. To reduce the possibility of overfitting, the number of rows should be sufficiently larger than the number of predictor variables. The data rows should be in order one after the other without any blank spaces. We have also to ensure that the class variable does not have any missing values. If there is a missing value in the class variable, the application will not run and an error message will appear to inform us that we have to delete those data observations where the class variable is missing. If there is a missing value in a continuous variable, the application will replace it by the column median. If there is a missing variable in a categorical predictor variable, the application will replace it by the most frequently occurring category. Category labels are case insensitive.

After the data entry in the "Data" worksheet is complete, we have to specify the classification tree inputs in the worksheet entitled "UserInput". The first option on this worksheet is to adjust the number of categories of a categorical predictor. We can select this option if some categorical predictors in our data have more categories than others. This is a very useful feature if we consider that as the application is building the tree, it creates the child nodes by splitting the parent nodes. The predictor variable to be used for this split is based on a certain criterion. If some categorical predictors in our data have more categories than others, this criterion has an inherent bias towards choosing predictors with more categories.

We should have the facility to decide whether to stop splitting a node and declare the node as a leaf node. To control this process, the application allows us to determine the minimum node size, the maximum purity, and the maximum depth of the tree by selecting the corresponding boxes. If we select the "Minimum Node Size" criterion, we should enter in cell "H24" a valid size expressed as a percentage of total observations.

A valid minimum node size should be strictly greater than 0% and less than 100%. The higher this value, the smaller will be the final tree. If we select the option "Maximum Purity", once again we should enter in cell "H26" a value between 0% and 100%. The higher the value of the maximum purity, the larger will be the tree. It is true that we could continue to split the nodes of a decision tree until all the leaf nodes contained tests on only a single class vector of predictor variables. However, this procedure would lead to a very large tree that is likely to model random variation in the training data rather than modelling the true underlying structure of the data. One way to solve this problem is to stop splitting a node if its depth is equal to or greater than a specified threshold. The depth of a node is equal to its parent node depth+1. The root node has a depth of 1. We can determine the maximum depth of the tree by selecting the option "Maximum Depth" and entering a value greater than 1 and less than 20 in cell "H30". The higher the value of the maximum depth criterion, the larger will be the tree (Murthy, 1997). If none of the above three criterions are selected, the application will use default values. The default value for the minimum node size is 5, the default value for the maximum purity is 100%, and the default value for the maximum depth of the tree is 20.

If the values of a predictor variable are identical for all records in a specific node, the values of that predictor variable will not be used to split the node while building the classification tree. However, if all predictor variables have values that are identical for all records in a tree node, there will be no other split in that node. On the other hand, if the predictor variables have values that are very different for all records in a tree node, there will be more than one split in that node. If we continue to partition the nodes of the decision tree, it is likely that the classification tree will be very large with many leaf nodes. It is then more likely that such a tree would overfit the training data and would have poor generalisation performance in classifying new data. One way to solve this problem would be to prune the tree using some pruning criterion. We can choose to prune the classification tree by selecting the option "YES" in the corresponding toolbox in cell "J38". On the other hand, we can select the option "NO" if we do not wish to prune the classification tree.

If we continue to partition the nodes of the decision tree and we select no pruning, it is more likely that the classification tree will overfit the data. One way to test the generalisation performance of the classification tree is to split our data into training and test sets. We have two options to determine how we would like to test the classification tree. We can randomly select a number of data records from the dataset as a test set by selecting option 1 in the corresponding toolbox in cell "H43" and then specifying the percentage of data cases in cell "H45". If we are selecting this option, the number of data records randomly selected should be between 1 and 50% of the original dataset. Alternatively, we have the option to specify that only a few of the last data records should be used as a test set by selecting option 2 in cell "H43" and then specifying the number of data records in cell "H46". If we are selecting this option, we have to ensure that all the class categories are present in the training and test data.

Before we build and test the classification tree, we have the option to save it in a separate workbook by selecting the option "YES" in the corresponding toolbox next to the heading "Save Model in a Separate Workbook?". Alternatively, we can select the option "NO" if we do not want to save the tree in a new workbook.

After selecting the classification tree inputs in the "UserInput" worksheet, we can start building the classification tree by pressing the button "Build Tree". This button is located to the bottom right-hand side in the "UserInput" worksheet. After pressing this button, we have to wait for a few minutes. During this time, the application will use the training data to build the classification tree that it will use in turn to classify the data records in the test set. As soon as the classification of all data records in the test set is complete, a message box will appear on the screen to inform us that the application has saved the new model in a new workbook in the current Excel window if we have previously selected this option in the "UserInput" worksheet. The new workbook in which the application has saved the data will appear on the screen if we select "OK" on the message box. If we have not previously selected the option to save the results in a new workbook, the results will be displayed on the main workbook in which the application is running.

Let us assume that we have selected the option to save the classification results in a new workbook. The new workbook will contain six worksheets. The worksheet entitled "Result" displays information about the input data, descriptive information about the classification tree, and classification results in the training and test sets. On the top left-hand side of the worksheet, we can find information about the number of data records that were used for training and testing, the number of predictor variables, the number of class categories, the majority class, and the percentage of incorrect classifications if the majority class is used as the predicted class. On the right-hand side of this worksheet, we can find information about the classification tree such as the total number of nodes, the number of leaf nodes and the number of different levels in the classification tree. Further below, we can see the misclassification rate in both the training and test sets as well as the time taken by the application to grow the classification tree, prune the growing tree and then use the final tree to classify the data records in the test set. At the bottom part of this worksheet, we can see the classification matrices displaying information on the classification results in both the training and test sets. The elements across the diagonal of a matrix are the number of data records that were classified by the application correctly, whereas the off-diagonal elements are the number of data records that were classified by the application incorrectly. Overall, the classification tree in Excel produced very satisfactory classification results, classifying correctly over 90% of data cases in the training set and over 80% of data cases in the test set. Obviously, we can improve the classification performance of the model even further by changing the model parameters in the "UserInput" worksheet. However, as we mentioned in the previous section, this is only a demonstration on how to apply the model rather than optimising its classification performance.

The second worksheet entitled "Tree" provides a visual display of the classification tree. The classification tree is also displayed in the worksheet "Tree" of the main workbook "CTree01Aust.xls". If we enter the values of the predictor variables starting in cell "H10" and moving downwards on this worksheet, the application will display the predicted class in cell "H7". If we further select a cell in any of the nodes and press the button "View Node", we can see detailed information about this node in the worksheet entitled "NodeView". The worksheet "NodeView" also allows us to see the class distribution and other information for any node by selecting the appropriate node number in cell "F7". In the worksheet "Nodes" of the new workbook saved by the application, we can find more detailed information about the structure of the classification tree such as the number of nodes, the number of branches, and the number of leaf nodes. In the worksheet "UserInput" of the new workbook we can find a copy of the tree input parameters that we entered in the worksheet "UserInput" of the main workbook "CTree01Aust.xls". Finally, in the worksheet "Data" of the new workbook, we can find a copy of the data. Next to the last column of our data, we can find an additional column that gives information about the class predicted by the application. If we compare this column against column "C" showing the actual class for each data record, we can see which data records were classified correctly and which data records were classified incorrectly by the application.

Although the application offers some really handy features, there are some areas for improvement. The implementation of the C4.5 algorithm developed by Quinlan (1993, 1996) offers the facility of generating rules from the tree. However, this feature is not available in this application. Certainly, many of the commercial softwares that implement the C4.5 algorithm or different algorithms may include this facility. We should also mention that the C4.5 algorithm and its improved version C5.0 replace missing values while growing the decision tree rather than before starting to build the tree. This might improve the classification performance of the model. Furthermore, the application assumes similar misclassification costs for all categories and does not offer the facility to adjust misclassification costs. The implementation for the German credit dataset is similar. As an exercise, the reader can try to run the application using the Excel workbook "CTree01Germ.xls".

5.5   SEE5 CLASSIFIER

See5 for Windows is a data mining tool extracting informative patterns from data, assembling them into classifiers, and using them to make predictions. See5 is based on the C4.5 algorithm incorporating several facilities such as variable misclassification costs, handling of several different data types, winnowing of attributes, user-friendly graphic interfaces, sampling and cross-validation features. See5 is a very powerful tool as it can handle large databases consisting of hundreds of thousands of records and many predictor variables. See5 constructs classifiers as decision trees or sets of if–then rules that are generally easy to understand. In the next subsections, we show how to prepare data files for using See5 and illustrate the options for using the system.[2]

5.5.1   Data inputs

All the files that See5 reads or writes for an application have names of the form "filestem. extension", where filestem denotes the application and extension denotes the contents of the file. Two files are essential for all See5 applications: the "names" file and the "data" file. The "names" file describes the attributes and classes.

The file "Australia.names" looks like this:

```
pos,neg.

A1:    a,b.
A2:    continuous.
A3:    continuous.
A4:    g,gg,p.
A5:    ff,d,i,k,j,aa,m,c,w, e, q, r,cc, x.
A6:     ff,dd,j,bb,v,n,o,h,z.
A7:    continuous.
A8:    t, f.
```

---

[2] See www.rulequest.com for documentation and tutorials about the See5 classifier.

```
A9:      t, f.
A10:     continuous.
A11:          t, f.
A12:      s, q, p.
A13:     continuous.
A14:     continuous.
```

Regarding the format of this file, tabs and spaces are permitted inside a name or value. We can also include special characters such as comma, colon, period and vertical bar "|" in names and values by using the escape character "\". For example, the name "John, Stewart, and Co." could be written as "John\, Stewart\, and Co\.". If we use the vertical bar "|" before some text, the remainder of the text will be ignored. Therefore, we can use this feature if we want to include comments. Blank lines are ignored by the application.

The first line of the "Australia.names" file refers to the class categories. In this example, the class categories are "pos" (positive) and "neg" (negative). The predictor variables ("A1", "A2", "A3", etc.) are defined immediately after the class variable in the order they appear in the dataset. See5 can handle several different types of predictor variables including continuous variables, categorical variables, times, timestamps, and case labels. In the "Australia.names" file above, "A1" is a categorical variable taking the values "a" and "b", whereas "A2" and "A3" are continuous variables.

In general, the application handles two types of predictor variables: explicitly defined variables and implicitly defined variables. Explicitly defined variables are defined directly in the data. The name of an explicitly defined variable is followed by a colon ":" and a description of the values taken by the variable. Explicitly defined variables can be categorical, continuous, dates (i.e. yyyy/mm/dd or yyyy-mm-dd), clock times (i.e. hh:mm:ss), timestamps handling both dates and times (i.e. yyyy/mm/dd hh:mm:ss) and label variables that can be used to identify a particular case. See5 offers also the facility to handle ordered variables denoted as a comma-separated list of names. The values can be prefaced by the comment "[ordered]" to indicate that they are ordered (i.e. mark: [ordered] low, average, high). Otherwise, they will be considered by the application as unordered. If we type the word "ignore", the values of the attribute will be ignored.

Implicitly defined variables are defined by particular formulas. The name of an implicitly defined variable is followed by "=" and then the particular formula. The formula can be written using parentheses and may refer to other predictor variables that have already been defined. The formula can handle numbers, dates, times, and categorical attribute values enclosed in quotes. Several common operators and functions can be used in the formula such as $+, -, *, /, \char`^$ (raising number to power of ...), $>, >=, <, <=, =, <>$ or $! =$ (not equal), and, or, $\sin(\ldots)$, $\tan(\ldots)$, $\log(\ldots)$, $\exp(\ldots)$, $\text{int}(\ldots)$. The value of an implicitly defined variable will be either continuous or true/false.

Optionally, we can select in the "Australia.names" file the way that See5 constructs classifiers. For example, if we type the comment "attributes included:" followed by a comma-separated list of attribute names, the application will restrict the predictor variables used in constructing the classifiers to those already named. On the other hand, if we type the comment "attributes excluded", the application will not use any of the named attributes in constructing the classifiers.

The second essential file for running the application is the data file denoted as "Australia.data". This file provides information about the training data that the application will use in constructing classifiers. Each data record in this file consists of values defining the explicitly defined variables. Since we have declared the class categories "pos" and "neg" in the first line of the "Australia.names" file, the class variable will be the last column in the "Australia.data" file immediately after the predictor variables. The values of the predictor variables must be separated by commas. Missing values can be denoted as either "?" or "N/A".

Apart from the "names" and "data" files, we can define three other optional files. To test the classifier in a different data set, we can use a test file named "Australia.test". This file will consist of new data records that we can use to evaluate the generalisation performance of the classifier. We can also use another test file named "Australia.cases". This file is almost the same as the test file with the only difference that the class category for each data record in this file can be omitted. Finally, we can use a costs file named "Australia.costs". On this file, we have the option to adjust the misclassification costs if we want to penalise for incorrect classifications in a particular class. In the next subsection we will describe how to use the application in constructing a certain classifier.

5.5.2   Implementing See5 for Windows

To implement a demo version of the See5 software, we will need first to install it onto our PC desktop. To perform this installation, we need the compressed file named "See5-demo.zip" from the CD-Rom. After decompressing "See5-demo.zip", we need to extract its files into a new directory of our choice. On this new directory, we should be able to find a file named "setup.exe". If we use the mouse to hit this file twice, we will initiate the process for installing See5. During the installation process, we have to follow the instructions and specify where we would like to save the component files for See5. However, if we do not specify a directory and select the option "Next", the application will install See5 in the directory "C:\Program Files\See5-Demo". When the installation process is complete, we can browse through the directory See5-Demo. In this directory, we will find a subdirectory named "Samples". In this subdirectory, we need to transfer the data files that we are going to need for our application. These files are also available on the CD-Rom.

After transferring the data files in the subdirectory "Samples", we can start using See5 by selecting "Start/Programs" in the main Windows menu and then selecting the icon "See5-demo". After selecting this icon, the main window for the See5 classifier will appear on the screen. This main window consists of six buttons. The first button from left to right is named "Locate Data". Pressing this button and browsing through the subdirectory "Samples", we can select the input file "Australia.data". After selecting this file and pressing the button "Open", the main application window for See5 will display information about the input files as we can see in Figure 5.4. The second button from left to right on the main application window is named "Construct Classifier". Pressing this button, a new window will appear on the screen named "Classifier Construction Options" as we can see in Figure 5.5. Using this new window, we can specify the type of classifier that we want to construct. If we press the "Defaults" button at the very bottom on this window, the application will use default values to construct a classifier and will produce an output report similar to the one in Table 5.1. The top part of this report displays information about the version of the See5 software, the date and time we run the application, and the names for the class categories. We also read that See5 has used 400 cases from the training data to construct the decision tree.

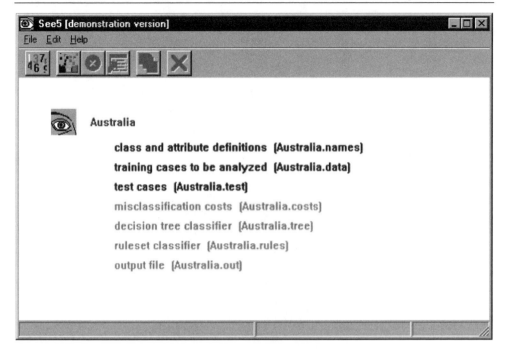

Figure 5.4   See5 classifier main window – locate data

The decision tree employs each data record's predictor values to map it into a leaf associated with one of the classes. Every leaf node of the tree is followed by numbers of the form (N) or (N/M). N is the number of training cases that are mapped to a given leaf node, whereas M is the number of these training cases that were classified incorrectly by the leaf node. As we can see in the output report in Table 5.1, using the "Defaults" option results in a very simplified tree. The predictor variable "A8" is the only variable appearing in the decision tree. This indicates that "A8" might be particularly important for the classification decision. However, if we exclude this variable from the dataset, this might result in a more complex decision tree which might be less accurate than the decision tree in Table 5.1.[3]

At the bottom part of the See5 output, we can see the classification results of the decision tree in both the training and test sets. The size of the tree is equal to its number of leaves. The column "Errors" shows the number and percentage of data cases that were classified incorrectly by the tree. See5 classified correctly over 80% of data cases in both the training and the test sets using default parameters only to construct the decision tree. However, a number of other options to improve further the classification performance of the model are also available.

---

[3] The user may want to assess the importance of the predictor variable "A8" in the classification decision. To this end, we have excluded this variable from the dataset, creating the "Australia2.data" file which does not include this variable in the list of predictor variables.

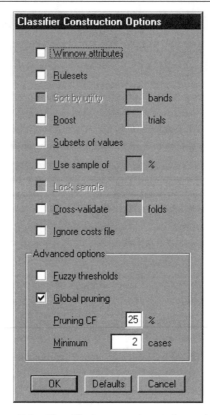

Figure 5.5   Classifier construction options window

5.5.3   Rulesets

A very useful feature of the See5 classifier is its ability to generate classifiers in the form of unordered collections of simple if–then rules. This is the second option in the "Classifier Construction Options" window. If we select the option "Rulesets", See5 will construct a ruleset as we can see in Table 5.2. If we do not select any other options, the ruleset will be very simplified as we can see in Table 5.2. Once again, the predictor variable "A8" is the only variable appearing in the ruleset. If we exclude this variable from the dataset, this will produce a different ruleset which might be more complex than the current ruleset but not necessarily more accurate.[4]

Each rule on a ruleset consists of a rule number to identify the rule. Next to the rule number, we can see statistics of the form (N, lift X) or (N/M, lift X). These statistics are used to summarise the performance of the rule. N shows the number of training cases covered by the rule, whereas M shows how many of these training cases belong to a class different from the class predicted by the rule. X shows the estimated accuracy of the rule (the figure in square brackets, e.g. [0.928] in Table 5.2) divided by the prior probability of the rule's class. The application estimates the rule's accuracy using the ratio

---

[4] As an exercise the user can try to run the "Australia2.data" which does not include "A8" in the list of predictor variables.

Table 5.1 Classification output of See5 using default settings to construct a decision tree

See5 [Release 1.16] Mon Oct 07 22:49:38 2002

Read 400 cases (14 attributes) from Australia.data

Decision tree:

A8 = t: pos (193/13)
A8 = f: neg (207/37)

Evaluation on training data (400 cases):

Decision Tree	
Size	Errors
2	50(12.5%) ≪

(a)	(b)	<-classified as
180	37	(a): class pos
13	170	(b): class neg

Evaluation on test data (290 cases):

Decision Tree	
Size	Errors
2	50(17.2%) ≪

(a)	(b)	<-classified as
126	40	(a): class pos
10	114	(b): class neg

Time: 0.1 secs

$(N - M + 1)/(N + 2)$. The lift X is calculated by dividing the rule's estimated accuracy by the relative frequency of the predicted class in the training set. After the statistics line, we can see one or more conditions that must be satisfied if a rule is applicable. On the last line of each rule we can see the class predicted by the rule. Next to the predicted class we can see in brackets a value between 0 and 1 indicating a confidence level on the prediction.

If we use a ruleset to classify a new case, it may happen that several of the rules might be applicable as all of their conditions might be satisfied. It is obvious, however, that if the applicable rules predict different classes, there will be an implicit conflict. See5 handles this problem by adopting a voting strategy. According to this strategy, each applicable rule votes for its predicted class with a voting weight equal to its confidence value. Then, the votes are counted up, and the class with the highest total vote is chosen as the final prediction. If no rule is applicable, the application uses a default class. In the example below, we use the default option where rules are ordered by class and then sub-ordered by confidence. We can specify an alternative ordering based on contribution to predictive accuracy if we select the "Sort by utility" option. According to this ordering, the rule that most reduces the error rate appears first and the rule that contributes least appears last.

Table 5.2   Classification output of See5 using default settings to construct a ruleset

See5 [Release 1.16]   Mon Oct 07 23:14:19 2002

Options:
Rule-based classifiers

Read 400 cases (14 attributes) from Australia.data

Rules:

Rule 1: (193/13, lift 1.7)
   A8 = t
   -> class pos [0.928]

Rule 2: (207/37, lift 1.8)
   A8 = f
   -> class neg [0.818]

Default class: pos

Evaluation on training data (400 cases):

Rules		
No	Errors	
2	50(12.5%)	≪

(a)	(b)	<-classified as
180	37	(a): class pos
13	170	(b): class neg

Evaluation on test data (290 cases):

Rules		
No	Errors	
2	50(17.2%)	≪

(a)	(b)	<-classified as
126	40	(a): class pos
10	114	(b): class neg

Time: 0.2 secs

5.5.4   Boosting

Another useful feature of See5 is boosting (Schapire, 1990; Freund and Schapire, 1996). If we select the option named "Boost" and we type a number in the box next to this option, the application will generate a committee of several classifiers (either decision trees or rulesets) rather than just one. The number of classifiers constructed by the application will be equal to the number that we type in the relevant box. Here is a brief description of how boosting works: in the first run, the application generates a decision tree or ruleset using

Table 5.3   Classification output of See5 using boosting to construct decision trees

---

See5 [Release 1.16]   Mon Oct 07 23:56:58 2002

Options: 3 boosting trials

Read 400 cases (14 attributes) from Australia.data

- - - - -   Trial 0: - - - - -

Decision tree:

A8 = t: pos (193/13)
A8 = f: neg (207/37)

- - - - -   Trial 1: - - - - -

Decision tree:

A8 = t: pos (183.5/22.7)
A8 = f: neg (216.5/64.7)

- - - - -   Trial 2: - - - - -

Decision tree:

A10 > 3: neg (78.2/15.3)
A10 <= 3:
:...A3 <= 0.21: neg (34.2/12.6)
    A3 > 0.21: pos (287.6/85.8)

Evaluation on training data (400 cases):

Trial	Decision Tree	
	Size	Errors
0	2	50(12.5%)
1	2	50(12.5%)
2	3	117(29.3%)
boost		50(12.5%) ≪

(a)	(b)	<-classified as
180	37	(a): class pos
13	170	(b): class neg

Evaluation on test data (290 cases):

Trial	Decision Tree	
	Size	Errors
0	2	50(17.2%)
1	2	50(17.2%)
2	3	71(24.5%)
boost		50(17.2%) ≪

(a)	(b)	<-classified as
126	40	(a): class pos
10	114	(b): class neg

Time: 0.1 secs

the training data. It is quite possible that the first classifier will misclassify some cases in the data. The application will then construct a second classifier focusing on classifying those cases that were incorrectly classified in the first run. As a result, it is expected that the second classifier will be different than the first classifier. But, it is also possible that the second classifier might misclassify some data cases as well. The application will then construct a third classifier focusing on classifying those cases that were incorrectly classified in the second run and so on. This process will be terminated if the most recent classifiers are either very accurate or inaccurate. In classifying new cases, each classifier votes for its predicted class. Then, the votes are counted to determine the final class. If we select "Boost" and we specify three trials, then the application will construct one decision tree for each trial separately as we can see in Table 5.3. Alternatively, if we apply boosting and we select "Rulesets", the application will produce a different ruleset on each trial as we can see in Table 5.4.[5]

See5 is quite fast in constructing classifiers. However, the training process might be slow if boosting is applied and the data set consists of thousands of records. To avoid this problem, See5 incorporates a facility to speed up the training of the classifier. If we select the option "Use sample of $x\%$" in the "Classifier Construction Options" window, the application will use a random sample of $x\%$ of the data to train the classifier. If $x\%$ is less than or equal to 50%, the application will use another disjoint sample of the data equal to $x\%$ to evaluate the classifier. On the other hand, if $x\%$ is greater than 50%, the application will use the remaining data that were not used for training to evaluate the classifier. By default, the random sample will change every time that a classifier is constructed. Therefore, if we run See5 with sampling a number of times, we will get different classification results. We can avoid this re-sampling, if we select the "Lock sample" option on the "Classifier Construction Options" window. Selecting a random sample of data to train the classifier will speed up the classification process but it may affect the classification performance.

5.5.5 Winnowing attributes

More often, the decision trees and rulesets constructed by See5 do not use all of the predictor variables. The "Australia.data" file has 14 predictor variables but only a few of them appear in the tree and the ruleset. This ability to pick up and choose among the predictor variables is an important advantage of data mining techniques. If there are several alternatives for each test in the tree or ruleset, only a few of them might contain information that can be used in constructing the classifier (Littlestone, 1988). See5 offers the facility to pre-select a subset of the attributes that it will then use in constructing either a decision tree or a ruleset. We can utilise this feature if we select the option "Winnow attributes" at the very top in the "Classifier Construction Options" window.

5.5.6 Categorical value subsets

Tests on categorical predictor variables will result in a separate branch in the tree for each different value of a categorical predictor variable. If the categorical predictor variables

---

[5] Our results show no improvement with the "boosting" option as we did not attempt to optimise its use here, but just to illustrate its potential application. Note that, with the "Australia2" dataset, using this option yields an error rate of 6.5% on training and 19.7% on test, while the default yields an error rate of respectively 14.5% and 24.10% on the training and test sets.

Table 5.4   Classification output of See5 using boosting to construct rulesets

See5 [Release 1.16]   Sat Oct 26 20:43:22 2002

  Options: 3 boosting trials

Read 400 cases (14 attributes) from Australia.data

- - - - - Trial 0:- - - - Rules:

Rule 0/1: (193/13, lift 1.7) A8 = t -> class pos [0.928]
Rule 0/2: (207/37, lift 1.8) A8 = f -> class neg [0.818]

Default class: pos

- - - - - Trial 1:- - - - - Rules:

Rule 1/1: (183.5/22.8, lift 1.5) A8 = t -> class pos [0.872]
Rule 1/2: (216.5/64.8, lift 1.6) A8 = f -> class neg [0.699]

Default class: pos

- - - - - Trial 2:- - - - - Rules:

Rule 2/1: (287.6/85.8, lift 1.2) A3 > 0.21 A10 <= 3 -> class pos [0.700]
Rule 2/2: (78.2/15.3, lift 1.9) A10 > 3 -> class neg [0.797]
Rule 2/3: (35.9/12.6, lift 1.5) A3 <= 0.21 -> class neg [0.641]

Default class: pos

Evaluation on training data (400 cases):

Trial	Rules		
	No	Errors	
0	2	50(12.5%)	
1	2	50(12.5%)	
2	3	117(29.3%)	
boost		50(12.5%)	≪

(a)	(b)	<-classified as
180	37	(a): class pos
13	170	(b): class neg

Evaluation on test data (290 cases):

Trial	Rules		
	No	Errors	
0	2	50(17.2%)	
1	2	50(17.2%)	
2	3	71(24.5%)	
boost		50(17.2%)	≪

(a)	(b)	<-classified as
126	40	(a): class pos
10	114	(b): class neg

Time: 0.2 secs

consist of many different categories, the tests on different values for each categorical predictor variable will result in many separate branches in the tree. This may have the effect of fragmenting the data during construction of the decision tree. We can reduce the possibility of fragmentation in the data by selecting the "Subsets of values" option in the "Classifier Construction Options" window. If we select this option, the application will group values of the categorical predictor variables into subsets. Then, each subtree will be associated with a subset rather than with a single value. This option is recommended when a dataset has important categorical variables with more than four or five values.

5.5.7 Softening thresholds

The decision tree separates the training data into their corresponding classes by successive partitioning of the variables. Each predictor variable is compared against some threshold. For example, let us assume that the leaf node of a decision tree tests whether the value of a predictor variable is less than or equal to 9. If it is less than or equal to 9, the case is assigned to a certain class. If it is greater than 9, then more conditions will be tested before reaching a decision about the class of that case. One of the disadvantages of this approach is that thresholds might be quite sharp. A case with hypothetical values 8.97, 8.98 or 8.99 might fall in a different class than cases with hypothetical values 9.01, 9.02 or 9.03. For some classification problems, it might be acceptable to use sharp thresholds. For example, there are specific bands for a credit assessment. For other applications, however, it might not be ideal to use sharp thresholds. To deal with this problem, See5 has an option to "soften" sharp thresholds in testing conditions on the values of the predictor variables. If we select the option "Fuzzy thresholds" on the "Classifier Construction Options" window, then each threshold is broken into three bounds: lower bound, upper bound and a central value v. If the value of the predictor variable is below the lower bound, the single branch corresponding to the condition "$<=$" will be used for the classification. If the value of the predictor variable is above the upper bound, the single branch corresponding to the condition "$>$" will be used for the classification. On the other hand, if the value of the predictor variable lies between the lower bound and the upper bound, both branches of the tree will be used for classification and the results will be combined. The values of lower and upper bounds will be determined by the application after analysing the sensitivity of the classification to small changes in the threshold. Soft thresholds might not improve the classifier's accuracy on the test set. Furthermore, soft thresholds affect only decision tree classifiers but not rulesets.

5.5.8 Cross-validation trials

To test the classification performance of the classifier we can use either sampling or a separate test file. Either way we choose, the classifier is evaluated on new data cases that have not been used previously in training the classifier. However, it is likely that this estimate might not be very accurate if the datasets that we use in training and testing the classifier are not very large. The most common solution to test the performance of the classifier if the training set is small is the leave-one-out method (Masters, 1993, 1995). According to this method, a single element is held out from the training set and the remaining $n - 1$ elements are used to build the classification rule that is then used to classify the element that was left out. In the next step, this single element is returned into the training set and a different element is removed. The classifier is then retrained using the remaining $n - 1$ elements and it is tested on the new element that was left out. By repeating this process for any individual element in the training set, every known element is used for both training and testing. The proportion of elements that are misclassified from each class gives a direct estimate of the actual error rate in that class. The advantage of the leave-one-out method is that the test set is almost as large as the training set. This means that the estimate of the error rate is approximately unbiased. A close relative of the leave-one-out method is the rotation method. According to this method, a number m of mutually exclusive subsets are defined. The $m - 1$ subsets are used to build the classification rule which is then used to classify the subset that was left out. Repeating this procedure m times, all observations are tested out-of-sample. We can apply m-fold cross-validation procedures in testing the classifiers constructed by See5 by selecting the option "Cross-validate folds" on the "Classifier Construction Options" window. The application will perform a number of cross-validation trials equal to the number we specify in the box next to the option we have selected.

5.5.9   Costs file

On many classification applications, we might need to adjust the classification costs. On other applications, the classification costs might be treated as equal. We can ignore the classification costs file by selecting the option "Ignore costs file".

5.5.10   Advanced options

At the bottom part of the "Classifier Construction Options" window, we can see a few advanced options concerning the classifier generation process. See5 constructs decision trees as follows. Initially, a large tree is constructed to fit the data. Then, this tree is pruned by the application to remove those branches that are predicted to have a high error rate. Applying this process to every subtree, the application decides whether to replace each subtree by a leaf node or not. Then, a global pruning stage looks at the performance of the tree as a whole. If we do not select the default "Global pruning" option, the second pruning stage will not be applied. This might result in larger decision trees and rulesets. The "Pruning CF" option affects the way that error rates are estimated. The smaller the value we specify for this option, the higher the level of pruning on the initial tree. The "Minimum cases" option controls the degree to which the initial tree can fit the data. The default value is two cases. Values higher than the default might lead to an initial tree that fits the training data only approximately.

5.5.11   Construct classifier

After making our selections in the "Classifier Construction Options" window and clicking the "OK" button at the bottom left-hand side, the classifier-generating process will begin. We can interrupt this process by pressing the "Stop" button on the main application window. If we do not select this button, the classifier-generating process will continue running. When this process is complete, a new window will appear on the screen reporting the classification output. On this report we can see either the decision tree or the rulesets depending on which one we use, the classification results in the training set, and the classification results in either the test set or the cross-validation trials depending on which option we select. If we close the output window, we can re-display the output from the last classifier construction by pressing the fourth button from left to right on the main application window named "Review Output".

After building the classifier, the application offers the facility to use the classifier interactively to predict the class for new data cases. To start the interactive interpreter, we need to press the fifth button from left to right on the main application window named "Use classifier". This will link the interactive interpreter to the most recent classifier that has been constructed by the current application. It will then prompt for information about the case to be classified. It is possible that the values of all predictor variables may not be needed. The values of the predictor variables will depend on the case itself. After entering all the relevant information, the most probable class will be shown.

See5 also shows how training or test data relate to a classifier and vice versa. We can use this facility by pressing the button named "Cross-Reference" on the main application window. After pressing this button a new window will appear on the screen showing the most recent classifier for the current application and how this classifier relates to cases in the data, test or cases file. On the left-hand side of this window, we can see the classifier. On the right-hand side, we can see a list of cases. Each case has a [?] tag. This tag is red if the case is misclassified. Each case has also a number and the actual class to which the case belongs. If we click the tag [?] in front of a case number or label, the application will display on the left-hand side of the screen those parts of the classifier relevant to that case. The values of those predictor variables that play no part in classifying the particular case are displayed in a lighter tone. The "Reset" button can be used at any time to restore the window to its initial state. The "Save" button preserves the details of the displayed classifier and case list as an ASCII file selected through a dialogue box.

All the functions that we discussed above can also be initiated from the File menu. The Edit menu facilitates changes to the names and costs files after an application's files have been located. On-line help is available through the Help menu.

Taking into account the options we presented above, it is obvious that See5 offers a lot of flexibility in constructing classification models. See5 is also faster in terms of processing speed compared to the freely available softwares that we presented in the previous two sections. This will be an important advantage if the dataset consists of several thousands of records.

As an exercise, the user can try to run the application using the data file "German.data". This dataset is quite interesting because we have to adjust the classification costs for the two classes. As opposed to the neural network and classification tree in Excel, See5 offers the facility to adjust the classification costs by editing the file "German.costs" and adjusting the numbers accordingly.

Overall, all the classification models produced very satisfactory classification results using the "Australia" dataset. The neural network for classification in Excel classified correctly over 75% of the data cases in both the training and the test sets. The classification tree in Excel classified correctly over 90% of data cases in the training set and over 80% of data cases in the test set. On the other hand, See5 classified correctly over 80% of data cases in both the training and the test sets using default parameters only to construct the classifiers. Selecting appropriate parameters for each of the different options in See5, we may be able to improve further the classification performance of the models. Therefore, we will not attempt to compare further the classification performance of our models with existing academic results: as we mentioned in the previous sections, this is only a demonstration on how to apply the models rather than optimising their classification performance.

5.6 CONCLUSIONS

In this chapter, we demonstrated how to implement two freely available and one commercial softwares for data mining applications in finance. The freely available softwares that we implemented are the Neural Network for Classification in Excel and the Classification Tree in Excel. The commercial software is See5 for Windows. See5 for Windows is a data mining tool extracting informative patterns from data, assembling them into classifiers and using them to classify new data.

To implement the softwares we used two datasets that are available in the public domain. The first dataset is known as the Australian credit approval dataset. The aim was to construct a classification rule for assessing the quality of credit card applicants. The second dataset is known as the German credit dataset. The aim on this one was to construct a classification rule for assessing the credit quality of German borrowers.

Beyond these examples, the methods demonstrated in this chapter can be applied to many other quantitative trading and investment problems, such as the determination of outperforming/underperforming stocks, bond rating, etc.

All three softwares were found really attractive in terms of predictive accuracy, ease of installation and flexibility in implementing the particular software in generally used operating systems. However, the freely available softwares were found to be slower than See5 in terms of processing speed. This should be of particular concern if a dataset consists of several thousands of records. Furthermore, See5 will be more flexible to handle large datasets because it has been designed to handle thousands of records.

Despite the above technical limitations, freely available data mining softwares can be downloaded from the web for free and they do not require individual licences to be bought. They are quick and easy to use and they do not require data files to be prepared in special formats. They can be ideal tools for demonstrating data mining applications in a classroom by quickly running a few examples with the students. They can also be useful tools for analysts and profit speculators in the financial industry who are considering purchasing commercial data mining softwares, but before they do so would like to have an initial understanding about the general capabilities of these tools.

There are several other freely available softwares on the web that might be more flexible in dealing with large datasets and might be more accurate than the tools that we implemented in this chapter. However, more often freely available softwares have been developed and compiled in different operating systems and they may require additional installations in supporting the software on different operating environments. Besides, the user may not always find sufficient technical support in installing freely available softwares. In that case, he should be aware of a variety of technical issues related to operating system capabilities, system memory limitations and programming libraries related to different softwares.

REFERENCES

Albanis, G. T. and R. A. Batchelor (2001), "21 Nonlinear Ways to Beat the Stock Market", in: C. Dunis and A. Timmerman (eds), *Developments in Forecast Combination and Portfolio Choice*, Kluwer Academic Publishers, Dordrecht.

Breiman, L., J. H. Friedman, E. A. Olshen and C. J. Stone (1984), *Classification and Regression Trees*, Wadsworth and Brooks, Monterey, CA.

Cheng, B. and D. M. Titterington (1994), "Neural Networks: A Review from a Statistical Perspective", *Statistical Science*, **9**(1), 2–54.

Dunis, C. and J. Jalilov (2002), "Neural Network Regression and Alternative Forecasting Techniques for Predicting Financial Variables", *Neural Network World*, **2**, 113–139.

Freund, Y. and R. Schapire (1996), "Experiments with a New Boosting Algorithm", Thirteenth International Conference on Machine Learning, Bari, Italy.

Hand, D. J. (1997), *Construction and Assessment of Classification Rules*, John Wiley, Chichester, UK.

Haykin, S. (1994), *Neural Networks – A Comprehensive Foundation*, MacMillan College Publishing, New York.

Holseimer, M. and A. Siebes (1991), "Data Mining – the Search for Knowledge in Databases", Report CS-R9406. CWI, P.O. Box 94079 GB, Amsterdam, The Netherlands.

Littlestone, N. (1988), "Learning Quickly when Irrelevant Attributes Abound", *Machine Learning*, **2**(4), 285–318.

Masters, T. (1993), *Practical Neural Network Recipes in C++*, Academic Press, New York.

Masters, T. (1995), *Advanced Algorithms for Neural Networks, A C++ Sourcebook*, Academic Press, New York.

Michie, D., D. Spiegelhafter and C. C. Taylor (1994), *Machine Learning, Neural and Statistical Classification*, Ellis Horwood Series in Artificial Intelligence, New York.

Minsky, M. L. and S. A. Papert (1969), *Perceptrons*, MIT Press, Cambridge, MA.

Murthy, K. V. S. (1997), "On Growing Better Decision Trees from Data", PhD Dissertation, Johns Hopkins University, Baltimore, MD.

Quinlan, J. R. (1983), "Learning Efficient Classification Procedures and their Application to Chess and Games", in: R. S. Michalski, J. G. Garbonell and T. M. Mitchell (eds), *Machine Learning, an Artificial Intelligence Approach*, Vol. 1, Morgan Kaufmann, San Mateo, CA.

Quinlan, J. R. (1986), "Induction of Decision Trees", *Machine Learning*, **1**, 81–106.

Quinlan, J. R. (1987), "Simplifying Decision Trees", *International Journal of Man–Machine Studies*, **27**, December, 221–234.

Quinlan, J. R. (1993), *C4.5: Programs for Machine Learning*, Morgan Kaufmann, San Mateo, CA.

Quinlan, J. R. (1996), "Improved Use of Continuous Attributes in C4.5", *Journal of Artificial Intelligence Research*, **4**, 77–90.

Ripley, B. D. (1992), "Statistical Aspects of Neural Networks", in: O. E. Barndorff-Nielsen, J. L. Jensen and W. S. Kendall (eds), *Networks and Chaos – Statistical and Probabilistic Aspects*, Chapman and Hall, London.

Rosenblatt, F. (1962), *Principles of Neurodynamics*, Spartan Books, Washington, DC.

Schapire, R. (1990), "The Strength of Weak Learnability", *Machine Learning*, **5**(2), 197–227.

Zhang, G., B. E. Patuwo and M. Y. Hu (1998), "Forecasting with Artificial Neural Networks: the State of the Art", *International Journal of Forecasting*, **14**, 35–62.

6

Switching Regime Volatility:
An Empirical Evaluation

BRUNO B. ROCHE AND MICHAEL ROCKINGER

ABSTRACT

Markov switching models are one possible method to account for volatility clustering. This chapter aims at describing, in a pedagogical fashion, how to estimate a univariate switching model for daily foreign exchange returns which are assumed to be drawn in a Markovian way from alternative Gaussian distributions with different means and variances. An application shows that the US dollar/Deutsche Mark exchange rate can be modelled as a mixture of normal distributions with changes in volatility, but not in mean, where regimes with high and low volatility alternate. The usefulness of this methodology is demonstrated in a real life application, i.e. through the performance comparison of simple hedging strategies.

6.1 INTRODUCTION

Volatility clustering is a well known and well documented feature of financial markets rates of return. The seminal approach proposed by Engle (1982), with the ARCH model, followed several years later by Bollerslev (1986), with the GARCH models, led to a huge literature on this subject in the last decade. This very successful approach assumes that volatility changes over time in an autoregressive fashion. There are several excellent books and surveys dealing with this subject. To quote a few, Bollerslev et al. (1992, 1993), Bera and Higgins (1993), Engle (1995) and Gouriéroux (1997) provide a large overview of the theoretical developments, the generalisation of the models and the application to specific markets. ARCH models provide a parsimonious description for volatility clustering where volatility is assumed to be a deterministic function of past observations.

However, ARCH models struggle to account for the stylised fact that volatility can exhibit discrete, abrupt and somehow fairly persistent changes. In the late 1980s, Hamilton (1989) proposed an alternative methodology, the Markovian switching model, which encountered great success. Although initiated by Quandt (1958) and Goldfeld and Quandt (1973, 1975) to provide a description of markets in disequilibrium, this approach has not encountered a great interest until the works of Hamilton (1989) on business cycles modelling, and of Engel and Hamilton (1990) on exchange rates. The main feature of this approach is that it involves multiple structures and allows returns to be drawn from distinct distributions.

Applied Quantitative Methods for Trading and Investment.   Edited by C.L. Dunis, J. Laws and P. Naïm
© 2003 John Wiley & Sons, Ltd   ISBN: 0-470-84885-5

The change of regime between the distributions is determined in a Markovian manner. It is driven by an unobservable state variable that follows a first-order Markov chain which can take values of {0, 1}. The value of that variable is dependent upon its past values. The switching mechanism thus enables complex dynamic structures to be captured and allows for frequent changes at random times. In that way, a structure may persist for a period of time and then be replaced by another structure after a switch occurs.

This methodology is nowadays very popular in the field of nonlinear time series models and it has experienced a wide number of applications in the analysis of financial time series. Although the original Markov switching models focused on the modelling of the first moment with application to economic and financial time series, see e.g. Hamilton (1988, 1989), Engel and Hamilton (1990), Lam (1990), Goodwin (1993), Engel (1994), Kim and Nelson (1998), among others, a growing body of literature is developing with regard to the application of this technique and its variant to volatility modelling. To quote again a few among others, Hamilton and Lin (1996), Dueker (1997) and Ramchand and Susmel (1998). Gray (1996) models switches in interest rates. Chesnay and Jondeau (2001) model switches of multivariate dependency.

In this chapter we present the switching methodology in a pedagogical framework and in a way that may be useful for the financial empiricist. In Section 6.2 the notations and the switching model are introduced. In Section 6.3 we develop the maximum likelihood estimation methodology and show how the switching model can be estimated. This methodology is applied in Section 6.4 to the US dollar (USD)/Deutsche Mark (DEM) exchange rate for the period 1 March 1995 to 1 March 1999. In that section it is shown how estimation results are to be interpreted, and how endogenously detected changes between states can improve the performances of simple real life hedging strategies. Section 6.5 concludes and hints at further lines of research.

6.2 THE MODEL

We assume, in this chapter, that foreign exchange returns[1] are a mixture of normal distributions. This means that returns are drawn from a normal distribution where the mean and variance can take different values depending on the "state" a given return belongs to. Since there is pervasive evidence that variance is persistent, yet little is known about its mean, it is useful to consider the more restrictive mixture model where just the variance can switch. This leads us to introduce the following model, based on Hamilton (1994):

$$R_t = \mu + [\sigma_1 S_t + \sigma_0(1 - S_t)]\varepsilon_t$$

where ε_t are independent and identically distributed normal innovations with mean 0 and variance 1. S_t is a Markov chain with values 0 and 1, and with transition probabilities $p = [p_{00}, p_{01}, p_{10}, p_{11}]$ such that:

$$\Pr[S_t = 1|S_{t-1} = 1] = p_{11} \qquad \Pr[S_t = 0|S_{t-1} = 1] = p_{01}$$
$$\Pr[S_t = 1|S_{t-1} = 0] = p_{10} \qquad \Pr[S_t = 0|S_{t-1} = 0] = p_{00}$$

where $p_{11} + p_{01} = 1$ and $p_{10} + p_{00} = 1$.

---

[1] Returns are calculated as the difference in the natural logarithm of the exchange rate value S_t for two consecutive observations: $R_t = 100[\ln(S_t) - \ln(S_{t-1})]$. This corresponds to continuously compounded returns.

Let

$$\rho_j = \Pr[S_1 = j] \; \forall j$$

be the unconditional probability of being in a certain state at time 1 and let $\rho = [\rho_0, \rho_1]'$.

If λ designates the vector of all remaining parameters $\lambda = [\mu, \sigma_1, \sigma_0]'$ then we can define $\theta = [\lambda', p', \rho']'$ the vector of all parameters.[2]

In the following we use the notation

$$\underline{R}_t = [R_t, R_{t-1}, \ldots, R_1]$$

to designate the vector of realisations of past returns.

It is also useful to introduce the density of R_t conditional on regime S_t: $f(R_t|S_t)$. For the model considered, in the case where ε_t is normally distributed, this density can be written as:[3]

$$f(R_t|S_t; \theta) = \frac{1}{\sqrt{2\pi}} \frac{1}{\sigma_1 S_t + \sigma_0(1 - S_t)} \exp\left\{ -\frac{1}{2}\left(\frac{R_t - \mu}{\sigma_1 S_t + \sigma_0(1 - S_t)}\right)^2 \right\} \qquad (6.1)$$

This illustrates that for a given parameter vector θ and for a given state S_t, the density of returns can be written in a straightforward manner. Expression (6.1) shows that the conditional density depends only on the current regime S_t and not on past ones. It should also be noted that, due to the Markovian character of the regimes, the information contained in $\underline{R}_{t-1}$ is summarised in S_t.

6.3 MAXIMUM LIKELIHOOD ESTIMATION

The likelihood is

$$L = f(\underline{R}_T; \theta) = f(R_T|\underline{R}_{T-1}; \theta)f(R_{T-1}|\underline{R}_{T-2}; \theta) \cdots f(R_2|\underline{R}_1; \theta)f(R_1; \theta) \qquad (6.2)$$

and we wish to obtain the maximum likelihood estimate

$$\theta \in \arg\max(\theta) \ln f(R_T; \theta)$$

In order to apply a maximum likelihood procedure on (6.2), it is necessary to introduce the states S_t so that expression (6.1) can be used. To see how this can be done suppose that θ is given and consider a typical element of the likelihood which can be developed by using obvious probabilistic rules:

$$f(R_t|\underline{R}_{t-1}; \theta) \equiv \frac{f(\underline{R}_t; \theta)}{f(\underline{R}_{t-1}; \theta)}$$

$$f(R_t|\underline{R}_{t-1}; \theta) = \frac{\displaystyle\sum_{S_t=0}^{1} f(\underline{R}_t, S_t; \theta)}{f(\underline{R}_{t-1}; \theta)}$$

---

[2] Notice that there is a link between ρ and p, as we will see later on.
[3] Notice that densities (associated with continuous random variables) are written as $f(\cdot)$ and probabilities (associated with discrete random variables) as $\Pr[\cdot, \cdot]$.

$$f(R_t|\underline{R}_{t-1};\theta) = \frac{\sum_{S_t=0}^{1} f(R_t|\underline{R}_{t-1}, S_t;\theta) f(\underline{R}_{t-1}, S_t;\theta)}{f(\underline{R}_{t-1};\theta)}$$

Moreover:

$$f(R_t|\underline{R}_{t-1}, S_t;\theta) = \sum_{S_t=0}^{1} f(R_t|S_t;\theta) \Pr[S_t|R_{t-1};\theta] \tag{6.3}$$

where the last equality follows from (i) the Markovian character of the problem whereby the knowledge of S_t summarises the entire history $\underline{R}_{t-1}$ so that $f(R_t|R_{t-1}, S_t;\theta) = f(R_t|S_t;\theta)$ and (ii) $f(\underline{R}_{t-1}, S_t;\theta)/f(\underline{R}_{t-1};\theta) = \Pr[S_t|R_{t-1};\theta]$.

We also have:

$$\Pr[S_t|\underline{R}_{t-1};\theta] = \sum_{S_{t-1}=0}^{1} \frac{\Pr[S_t, S_{t-1}, \underline{R}_{t-1};\theta]}{f(\underline{R}_{t-1};\theta)}$$

$$\Pr[S_t|\underline{R}_{t-1};\theta] = \sum_{S_{t-1}=0}^{1} \frac{\Pr[S_t|S_{t-1}, \underline{R}_{t-1};\theta] \Pr[S_{t-1}, \underline{R}_{t-1};\theta]}{f(\underline{R}_{t-1};\theta)} \tag{6.4}$$

$$\Pr[S_t|\underline{R}_{t-1};\theta] = \sum_{S_{t-1}=0}^{1} \Pr[S_t|S_{t-1};\theta] \Pr[S_{t-1}, \underline{R}_{t-1};\theta]$$

The last equality follows from the fact that $\Pr[S_t|S_{t-1}, \underline{R}_{t-1};\theta] = \Pr[S_t|S_{t-1};\theta]$ by the assumption that states evolve according to a first-order Markov process.

Using Bayes' formula it follows that:

$$\Pr[S_{t-1}|\underline{R}_{t-1};\theta] = \frac{\Pr[S_{t-1}, \underline{R}_{t-1};\theta]}{f(\underline{R}_{t-1};\theta)}$$

$$\Pr[S_{t-1}|\underline{R}_{t-1};\theta] = \frac{f(R_{t-1}, S_{t-1}, \underline{R}_{t-2};\theta)}{\sum_{S_{t-1}=0}^{1} f(\underline{R}_{t-1}, S_{t-1};\theta)} \tag{6.5}$$

$$\Pr[S_{t-1}|\underline{R}_{t-1};\theta] = \frac{f(R_{t-1}|S_{t-1};\theta) \Pr[S_{t-1}|\underline{R}_{t-2};\theta]}{\sum_{S_{t-1}=0}^{1} f(R_{t-1}|S_{t-1};\theta) \Pr[S_{t-1}|\underline{R}_{t-2};\theta]}$$

Henceforth, at time $t-1$, $f(R_{t-1}|S_{t-1};\theta)$, which is defined in equation (6.1) shows up in natural fashion. If we assume that we know $\Pr[S_{t-1}|\underline{R}_{t-2};\theta]$ then it becomes possible using equation (6.5) to compute $\Pr[S_{t-1}|\underline{R}_{t-1};\theta]$ and from equation (6.4) to derive the conditional probability of S_t given $\underline{R}_{t-1}$. $\Pr[S_t|\underline{R}_{t-1};\theta]$ can therefore be computed, for all t, in a recursive fashion.

The starting value for the probabilities $\Pr[S_1 = j|R_0;\theta] = \Pr[S_1 = j;\theta] = \rho_j$ can be either estimated directly as additional parameters in the maximum likelihood estimation, or approximated by the steady state probabilities which have to verify

$$\Pr[S_1 = i; \theta] = \sum_{j=0}^{1} \Pr[S_1 = j; \theta] p_{ij}$$

$$\Rightarrow \Pr[S_t = 1; \theta] = \frac{1 - p_{00}}{2 - p_{11} - p_{00}} \quad \text{and} \quad \Pr[S_t = 0; \theta] = \frac{1 - p_{11}}{2 - p_{11} - p_{00}} \qquad (6.6)$$

One realises, at this stage, that the likelihood for a given θ can be obtained by iterating on equation (6.3) which involves the computation of (6.4). As a by-product, the computation of (6.4) involves (6.5) which are the filtered probabilities of being in a given state conditional on all currently available information $\Pr[S_t | R_t; \theta]$. Also forecasts of states can be easily obtained by iterating on the transition probabilities.

Using standard numerical methods, this procedure allows for a fast computation of the estimates.

6.4   AN APPLICATION TO FOREIGN EXCHANGE RATES

Before we develop in detail one application of the switching model to the foreign exchange markets, we wish to start this section with a brief overview of the functioning of these markets as they offer notable features.

6.4.1   Features of the foreign exchange interbank market

It is interesting to note that, in contrast to other exchange markets, the interbank foreign exchange (also called forex) market has no geographical limitations, since currencies are traded all over the world, and there is no trading-hours scheme, indeed currencies are traded around the clock. It is, truly, a 24 hours, 7 days-a-week market.

Another notable feature is that, in contrast to other exchange markets too, forex traders negotiate deals and agree transactions over the telephone with trading prices and volumes not being known to third parties. The tick quotes are provided by market-makers and conveyed to the data subscribers' terminal. They are meant to be indicative, providing a general indication of where an exchange rate stands at a given time. Though not necessarily representing the actual rate at which transactions really take place, these indicative quotes are felt as being fairly accurate and matching the true prices experienced in the market. Moreover, in order to avoid dealing with the bid–ask bounce, inherent to most high-frequency data (see, for instance, chapter 3 in Campbell *et al.* (1997)), use was made, for the estimation of the switching model, of the bid series only, generally regarded as a more consistent set of observations.

In the following we will use, as an illustration, the USD/DEM exchange rate. The tick-by-tick quotes have been supplied by Reuters via Olsen & Associates. We will use daily quotes which are arbitrarily taken at each working day at 10pm GMT (corresponding approximately to the closing of Northern American markets). We obviously could have used a different time of the day and/or different frequencies.

It is interesting to note that, in this high-frequency dataset, there are significant intraday, intraweek and intrayear seasonal patterns (see Figures 6.1 and 6.2), explained respectively by the time zone effect (in the case of the USD/DEM rate, the European and the US time

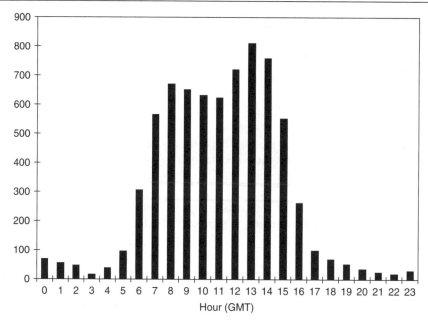

Figure 6.1 Intraday pattern USD/DEM (average number of transactions per hour)

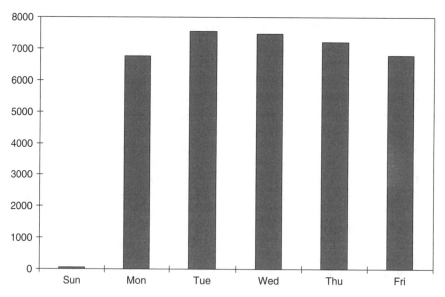

Figure 6.2 Intraweek pattern USD/DEM (average number of transactions per day of the week)

zones are the most active ones), the low activity exhibited during weekends and some universal public holidays (e.g. Christmas, New Year). Some other factors such as the release of economic indicators by, amongst others, central banks may also induce seasonality in foreign exchange markets. Seasonalities are also investigated by Guillaume *et al.* (1997).

Further descriptions of questions related to intraday data in forex markets can be found in Baillie and Bollerslev (1989), Goodhart and Figliuoli (1991), Müller *et al.* (1997) and Schnidrig and Würtz (1995), among others.

6.4.2 Descriptive statistics

In our empirical application of switching models, as previously said, we will use daily observations of the USD/DEM exchange rate. We obtain these by sampling from the tick-by-tick data, extracting those recorded at 10pm GMT, from October 1995 to October 1998, corresponding to 775 observations overall.

Table 6.1 displays the basic descriptive statistics for the USD/DEM foreign exchange returns, for the tick-by-tick and daily data.

There is an enormous difference between the first two moments of the series, confirming the dramatic effect of time aggregation (see Ghysels *et al.* (1998)). As indicated in Table 6.1, daily returns data is negatively skewed, yet in a non-significant way. This suggests that there exist some strong negative values but not enough to be statistically meaningful.

The series exhibits leptokurtosis (which means that the distribution of the data has thicker tails than a normal one) and heteroskedasticity (or volatility clustering) as shown by the Ljung–Box test on the squared returns. This latter observation is a well known feature of financial rates of return: large price changes in magnitude, irrespective of sign, are likely to be followed by large price movements; small price changes in magnitude are likely to be followed by small price movements. Finally, the assumption of normality of the data can be rejected at any level of significance as indicated by the Jarque–Bera and Kolmogorov–Smirnov tests.

It is well known from the literature on mixture of distributions that a mixture of normal distributions can be leptokurtic. This suggests that daily USD/DEM exchange rate returns are good candidates for being explained by switching among distributions.

Table 6.1 Descriptive statistics of the daily and tick-by-tick returns

	No. of observations	Mean	Variance	Skewness	Kurtosis	Acf(1)	Acf(2)
Tick-by-tick	5 586 417	2.8E-08	4.17E-08	−0.09	13.34	−46.3%	0.4%
Daily	775	2.0E-04	2.84E-05	−0.23	4.17		

Ljung–Box (20 lags)	critical value at 5% = 31.4
Daily returns	25.33
Squared daily returns	43.82*

Normality tests of daily returns	
Jarque–Bera	58.68*
Kolmogorov–Smirnov	0.0607*

*Denotes parameter estimates statistically significant at the 1% level.

6.4.3 Model empirical results

We obtain the estimates for the Markov switching model in a recursive way via maximum likelihood, under normality for the errors and supposing two volatility regimes.

We are using the Gauss software for estimating the model variables. The program is made up of six parts which are fully described in the Appendix. While the first three sections deal with data loading, preparation and the inclusion of the relevant libraries, sections four and five compute the maximum likelihood estimation of the model's parameters. The software proposes several optimisation algorithms. We choose the algorithm proposed by Berndt, Hall, Hall and Hausman (BHHH). The last section computes the filtered probabilities as described in equation (6.5) and the smoothed probabilities (i.e. the probabilities of being in a given state conditional on all currently available information at $t - 1$: $\Pr[S_t | R_{t-1}; \theta]$). Full details of the program are given in Appendix A.

Table 6.2 shows the estimates for the USD/DEM model. All coefficients are significant at the 5% level. The probability of staying in the higher volatility regime (i.e. $S_t = 0$) is 0.8049, which means that, on average, it lasts for about five days $(1/(1 - 0.8049) = 5.13$; see also Hamilton (1989)).

6.4.4 Model evaluation strategy

Model evaluation is carried out in two ways. Firstly, we test whether the model residuals are normal and non-correlated; we also test if standardised returns follow a normal distribution. This approach provides a common ground for statistically assessing the model performance. Our evaluation criterion consists in a thorough analysis of the residuals (i.e. the analysis and testing of the normality assumptions). For the latter, to make things easily reproducible, we have used the two common Jarque–Bera and Kolmogorov–Smirnov tests. Secondly, our evaluation also comprises checking the switching volatility model through its performance in a close to real life hedging strategy.

6.4.5 Residuals analysis

We carry out a brief analysis of the residuals of the computed model. Strictly speaking, the term "residuals" is used here for the series of standardised returns (i.e. the returns series divided by the forecast volatilities). If the volatility captures well the fluctuations of the market, and the model's assumptions are valid, such residuals are expected to be normal.

Table 6.2 Markov switching model: empirical results

	Value	Std. error	t-Statistics	$\Pr(>t)$
μ	0.0345	0.0171	2.023	0.0215
σ_0	0.6351	0.0281	22.603	0.0000
σ_1	0.2486	0.0313	7.934	0.0000
p_{00}	0.8049	0.0620	12.976	0.0000
p_{11}	0.6348	0.0927	6.848	0.0000

Table 6.3 Model residuals – basic statistics and normality tests

	Daily returns	Model residuals
Mean	0.0043	0.0485
Std. dev.	0.9944	1.0804
Skewness	−0.2455	−0.1344
Exc. kurtosis	1.2764	1.2228
Sample size	775	

Ljung–Box (20 lags)	critical value at 5% = 31.4	
Std. residuals	25.33	23.6
Squared std. residuals	43.82*	16.9

Normality tests		
Jarque–Bera	58.68*	49.18*
Kolmogorov–Smirnov	0.061*	0.057*

*Denotes parameter estimates statistically significant at the 1% level.

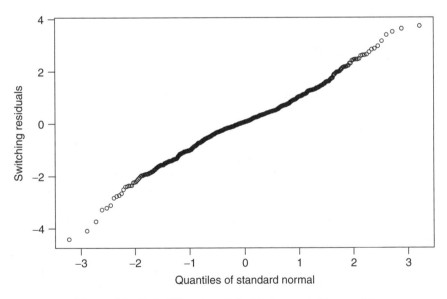

Figure 6.3 Probability plot of the Markov switching model

Table 6.3 presents the basic summary statistics and normality tests for the standardised log-returns and the standardised residuals/returns computed from the model. Figure 6.3 shows the normal score plot for the standardised returns from the model.

Here the normal score plot is used to assess whether the standardised residuals data have a Gaussian distribution. If that is the case, then the plot will be approximately a straight line. The extreme points have more variability than points towards the centre. A plot that is bent down on the left and bent up on the right means that the data have longer tails than the Gaussian.

The striking feature is that the model captures fairly well the heteroskedasticity of the underlying time series (as shown by the Ljung–Box test on the squared residuals) and, therefore, achieves homoskedasticity.

Having said that, the switching model residuals do not follow a normal distribution. Both the Jarque–Bera and the Kolmogorov–Smirnov normality tests enable us to reject the hypothesis that the residuals follow a normal distribution. Although this does not invalidate the switching model, this highlights the fact that nonlinearities still exist in the residuals that the switching model did not manage to capture.

6.4.6 Model evaluation with a simple hedging strategy

In this section we show how filtered volatility estimates can be combined with technical trend-following systems to improve the performance of these systems.

The negative relationship between the performance of trend-following trading systems and the level of volatility in foreign exchange markets is a well known empirical finding. In other words, trending periods in the forex markets tend to occur in relatively quiet (i.e. low volatility) periods.

We here compare hedging strategies using trend-following systems with similar systems combined with Markov switching filtered volatility.

6.4.6.1 Trend-following moving average models

As described by Müller (1995), trend-following systems based on moving average models are well known technical solutions, easy to use, and widely applied for actively hedging foreign exchange rates.

The moving average (MA) is a useful tool to summarise the past behaviour of a time series at any given point in time. In the following example, MAs are used in the form of momenta, that is the difference of the current time series values and an MA. MAs can be defined with different weighting functions of their summation. The choice of the weighting function has a key influence on the success of the MA in its application.

Among the MAs, the exponentially weighted moving average (EMA) plays an important role. Its weighting function declines exponentially with the time distance of the past observations from now. The sequential computation of EMAs along a time series is simple as it relies upon a recursion formula. For time series with a strong random element, however, the rapidly increasing shape of the exponential function leads to strong weights of the very recent past and hence for short-term noise structures of the time series. This is a reason why other MA weighting functions have been found worthy of interest in empirical applications. The following subsection presents two families of MA weighting functions. Both families can be developed with repeated applications of the MA/EMA operator.

6.4.6.2 Moving average definitions

A moving average of the time series x is a weighted average of the series of elements of the past up to now:

$$\text{MA}_{x,w;n} \equiv \frac{\sum\limits_{j=-\infty}^{n} w_{n-j} x_j}{\sum\limits_{j=-\infty}^{n} w_{n-j}} \tag{6.7}$$

where w_k is a series of weights independent of n.

A fundamental property of a moving average is its range r (or centre of gravity of the weighted function w_k):

$$r \equiv \frac{\sum\limits_{k=0}^{\infty} w_k k}{\sum\limits_{k=0}^{\infty} w_k} \tag{6.8}$$

The range r of a discrete time series is in units of the time series index, but unlike this integer index it can be any positive real number.

EMAs have the following declining weights:

$$w_k \equiv \left(\frac{r}{r+1}\right)^k \tag{6.9}$$

where r is the centre of gravity. In the case of daily time series, $r = (d-1)/2$ ($d =$ number of days in moving average).

An EMA can be computed by a recursion formula. If its value $\text{EMA}_x(r, t_{n-1})$ of the previous series element x_{n-1} is known, one can easily compute the value at t_n:

$$\text{EMA}_x(r, t_n) = \mu \text{EMA}_x(r, t_{n-1}) + (1-\mu)x_n \quad \text{with} \quad \mu = \frac{r}{r+1} \tag{6.10}$$

or expressed in number of days in the moving average:

$$\mu = 1 - \frac{2}{d+1} \quad \text{i.e.} \quad r = \frac{d-1}{2} \tag{6.11}$$

The recursion needs an initial value to start with. There is usually no information before the first series element x_1, which is the natural choice for this initialisation:

$$\text{EMA}_x(r, t_1) = x_1 \tag{6.12}$$

The error made with this initialisation declines with the factor $[r/(r+1)]^{n-1}$.

In many applications, the EMA will neither be used at t_1 nor in the initial phase after t_1 which is called the built-up time. After the built-up time, when the EMA is used, one expects to be (almost) free of initialisation errors.

6.4.6.3 Trading rules with EMA trading models

MA models summarise the past behaviour of a time series at any given point in time. This information is used to identify trends in financial markets in order to subsequently take positions according to the following rule:

$$\text{If } x(t_n) > \text{EMA}_x(r, t_n) \text{ go long (or stay long)}$$

$$\text{If } x(t_n) < \text{EMA}_x(r, t_n) \text{ go short (or stay short)}$$

with $x(t_n)$ the spot exchange rate at time t. Commission costs of 0.00025 DEM are charged for each trade. A trade is defined as being long and going short or vice versa.

An EMA model is defined by its type (i.e. MA or EMA) and, in the latter case, its centre of gravity (or number of MA days). There are obviously an infinite number of different combinations. Our analysis here is arbitrarily limited to one EMA type (i.e. 50 days or $\mu = 0.96$).

6.4.6.4 Trading rules of EMA trading models with volatility filters

It is a well known empirical finding that trend-following systems tend to perform poorly when markets become volatile. One possible explanation lies in the fact that, most of the time, high volatility periods correlate with periods when prices change direction.

The previous rules are thus combined with the following new rules:

$$\text{If volatility} > \text{volatility threshold } T, \text{ then reverse position}$$

$$\text{(i.e. go long if current position is short and vice versa)}$$

$$\text{If volatility} < \text{volatility threshold } T, \text{ keep position as indicated}$$

$$\text{by the underlying MA model}$$

6.4.6.5 Trading results

Table 6.4 shows the numerical results. Strategies based on the EMA model without volatility filtering are leading to approximately zero profit (if commission costs are not included), denoting the inability of the EMA model considered here to detect profitable trends. The volatility filter trading strategy based on filtered probabilities on the other hand is improving considerably the performance of the model. It is interesting to note that, despite the higher frequency of the trades (253 vs. 65), the performance after transaction costs is still significantly higher. Lastly, in terms of the risk/reward ratio, the latter model achieves a remarkable performance, although the average profit per annum is average.

The file "Hedging System Simulation.xls" on the CD-Rom contains the raw forex data as well as the Markovian switching volatility and the moving average computations. The file is split into three worksheets.

Table 6.4 Summary results of trading strategies (including transaction costs)

	Without volatility filter	With volatility filter
Total profit (%)	−4.9%	15.4%
Average profit per annum	−1.6%	5.1%
Maximum drawdown[a]	19.4%	10.4%
Number of trades	65	253
Risk/reward ratio[b]	−0.08	0.49

[a] Drawdowns are defined as the difference between the maximum profit potentially realised to date and the profit (or loss) realised to date. The maximum drawdown is therefore the maximum value of the drawdowns observed in history. It is an estimate of the maximum loss the strategy would have incurred.
[b] Defined as the ratio maximum drawdown/average profit per annum.

The first worksheet ("USDDEM EMA System") contains the basic computation of the EMA model and the trading model simulation. Columns A and B contain the date and the mid forex rate respectively. Column C contains the EMA computation. The EMA centre of gravity is input in cell C3. Column E contains the switching volatility figures. The computation of these figures is given in the third worksheet ("Backup", column N); the formula is based on the filtered probabilities, i.e. $\Pr[S_t = 0 | R_t]\sigma_0 + \Pr[S_t = 1 | R_t]\sigma_1$. Column F computes the trading signal as described in Sections 6.4.6.3 and 6.4.6.4 above. The volatility threshold is input in cell C4. Columns G to N contain the trading simulation formulas; in particular, columns I, J, K and L contain the profit and loss calculations, while columns M and N compute the drawdowns. The profit and loss figures are computed "open" in column I (i.e. how much profit/loss is potentially realised by the strategy each day) and "closed" in column J (i.e. how much profit/loss is effectively realised at the close of each trade). Columns K and L are merely cumulative computations of column J and I and give the cumulative profit and loss figures effectively and potentially realised respectively. The computation of the drawdowns (i.e. the differences between the maximum profit potentially realised to date and the profit or loss realised to date) are computed in columns M and N. Lastly, the trading summary statistics are computed in cells I2 to I6.

The second worksheet ("Graph") contains the graph showing the open profit and loss. The third worksheet ("Backup") contains the raw data, i.e. columns A to D contain the forex data from Reuters (at 22:00 GMT) with the bid and ask quotes.

Cells C3 and C4 allow the user to simulate the performance of different scenarios depending on the EMA operator and the volatility threshold value respectively selected. The summary results of the trading strategy are displayed in cells I2:I6.

Figure 6.4 displays the daily profit and loss trajectories for the two hedging strategies analysed in this chapter. During the first period (until mid-1997), the EMA without volatility filter dominates the other strategy. As of mid-1997, the volatility filter strategy clearly outperforms in terms of profit and risk. The chart also shows that the equity curve of the volatility filter strategy is less volatile, thus leading to lower risk. The figure also suggests a somewhat poor performance for the EMA strategy without volatility filter.

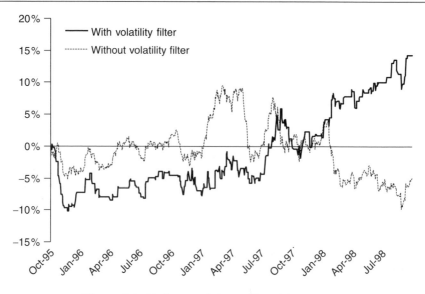

Figure 6.4   Daily cumulative profit and loss curves

6.5   CONCLUSION

In this chapter we have studied the behaviour of a Markovian switching volatility model for the USD/DEM daily foreign exchange series.

The analysis of the residuals shows that the heteroskedasticity of the initial dataset has been removed although the residuals series still presents high excessive kurtosis and fails to pass two standard normality tests.

When applied within a hedging framework, the filtered probabilities computed with the Markovian switching model enable us to improve the performance of trend-following systems both in terms of risk and absolute profits. This empirical result denotes that foreign exchange markets do not follow trends in a systematic way and that volatility modelling could be one interesting approach to classify market trend dynamics.

As a further extension, an economic interpretation of these results should be considered. The existence of long-lasting trending and jagged periods in very liquid markets are issues that deserve more attention.

REFERENCES

Baillie, R. and T. Bollerslev (1989), "Intra-Day and Inter-Market Volatility in Exchange Rates", *Review of Economic Studies*, **58**, 565–85.

Bera, A. K. and M. L. Higgins (1993), "ARCH Models: Properties, Estimation and Testing", *Journal of Economic Surveys*, **7**, 305–66.

Bollerslev, T. (1986), "Generalized Autoregressive Conditional Heteroskedasticity", *Journal of Econometrics*, **31**, 307–27.

Bollerslev, T., R. Chou and K. Kroner (1992), "ARCH Modeling in Finance: A Review of the Theory and Empirical Evidence", *Journal of Econometrics*, **52**, 5–59.

Bollerslev, T., R. Engle and D. Nelson (1993), "ARCH Models", in R. F. Engle and D. McFadden (eds), *Handbook of Econometrics*, Vol. 4, North-Holland, Amsterdam.

Campbell, J. Y., A. W. Lo and A. C. MacKinlay (1997), *The Econometrics of Financial Markets*, Princeton University Press, Princeton, NJ.

Chesnay, F. and E. Jondeau (2001), "Does Correlation Between Stock Returns Really Increase During Turbulent Periods", *Economic Notes*, **30** (1), 53–80.

Dueker, M. J. (1997), "Markov Switching in GARCH Processes and Mean-Reverting Stock Market Volatility", *Journal of Business & Economic Statistics*, **15**, 26–34.

Engel, C. (1994), "Can the Markov Switching Model Forecast Exchange Rates?", *Journal of International Economics*, **36**, 151–65.

Engel, C. and J. D. Hamilton (1990), "Long Swings in the Dollar: Are They in the Data and Do Markets Know It?", *American Economic Review*, **80**, 689–713.

Engle, R. (1982), "Autoregressive Conditional Heteroskedasticity with Estimates of the Variances of U.K. Inflation", *Econometrica*, **50**, 987–1008.

Engle, R. (1995), *ARCH Selected Readings*, Oxford University Press, Oxford.

Ghysels, E., C. Gouriéroux and J. Jasiak (1998), "High Frequency Financial Time Series Data: Some Stylized Facts and Models of Stochastic Volatility", Chapter III.7 in C. Dunis and B. Zhou (eds), *Nonlinear Modelling of High Frequency Financial Time Series*, John Wiley, Chichester.

Goldfeld, S. M. and E. Quandt (1973), "A Markov Model for Switching Regressions", *Journal of Econometrics*, **1**, 3–16.

Goldfeld, S. M. and E. Quandt (1975), "Estimation in a Disequilibrium Model and the Value of Information", *Journal of Econometrics*, **3**, 325–48.

Goodhart, C. and L. Figliuoli (1991), "Every Minute Counts in Financial Markets", *Journal of International Money and Finance*, **10**, 23–52.

Goodwin, T. H. (1993), "Business-Cycle Analysis with a Markov Switching Model", *Journal of Business & Economic Statistics*, **11**, 331–39.

Gouriéroux, C. (1997), *ARCH Models and Financial Applications*, Springer-Verlag, New York.

Gray, S. F. (1996), "Modeling the Conditional Distribution of Interest Rates as a Regime-Switching Process", *Journal of Financial Economics*, **42**, 27–62.

Guillaume, D., M. Dacorogna, R. Davé, U. Müller, R. Olsen and O. Pictet (1997), "From the Bird's Eye to the Microscope: A Survey of New Stylized Facts of the Intra-Daily Foreign Exchange Markets", *Finance and Stochastics*, **1**, 95–129.

Hamilton, J. D. (1988), "Rational-Expectations Econometric Analysis of Changes in Regimes: An Investigation of the Term Structure of Interest Rates", *Journal of Economic Dynamics and Control*, **12**, 385–423.

Hamilton, J. D. (1989), "A New Approach to the Economic Analysis of Nonstationary Timeseries and the Business Cycle", *Econometrica*, **57**, 357–84.

Hamilton, J. D. (1994), *Time Series Analysis*, Princeton University Press, Princeton, NJ.

Hamilton, J. D. and G. Lin (1996), "Stock Market Volatility and the Business Cycle", *Journal of Applied Econometrics*, **11**, 573–93.

Kim, C. J. and C. R. Nelson (1998), "Business Cycle Turning Points, a New Coincident Index, and Tests of Duration Dependence Based on a Dynamic Factor Model with Regime Switching", *Review of Economics and Statistics*, **80**, 188–201.

Lam, P. S. (1990), "The Hamilton Model with a General Autoregressive Component", *Journal of Monetary Economics*, **26**, 409–32.

Müller, U. (1995), "Specially Weighted Moving Averages with Repeated Application of the EMA Operator", Internal Paper, O&A Research Group.

Müller, U., M. Dacorogna, D. Davé, R. Olsen, O. Pictet and J. Von Weizsäcker (1997), "Volatilities of Different Time Resolutions – Analyzing the Dynamics of Market Components", *Journal of Empirical Finance*, **4** (2 & 3), 213–40.

Quandt, R. E. (1958), "The Estimation of Parameters of a Linear Regression System Obeying Two Separate Regimes", *Journal of the American Statistical Association*, **53**, 873–80.

Ramchand, L. and R. Susmel (1998), "Volatility and Cross Correlation Across Major Stock Markets", *Journal of Empirical Finance*, **5**, 397–416.

Schnidrig, R. and D. Würtz (1995), "Investigation of the Volatility and Autocorrelation Function of the USD/DEM Exchange Rate on Operational Time Scales', Proceedings of the High Frequency Data in Finance Conference (HFDF-I), Zürich.

APPENDIX A: GAUSS CODE FOR MAXIMUM LIKELIHOOD FOR VARIANCE SWITCHING MODELS

The code is made up of a core program (MLS.PRG) that contains sub-procedures (i) proc1 that computes the maximum likelihood theta (θ) and (ii) proc2 that computes the filtered and smoothed probabilities.

The comments are framed with the following signs: /* comment */.

MLS.PRG

```
/* MLS.PRG Maximum likelihood code for model with changing variances */

/* Part I : load the libraries and source files */
/* ------------------------------------------------------------------ */

library maxlik,pgraph;
#include maxlik.ext;
maxset;
graphset;
#include maxprtm.src;

/* external source file see details here below */
#include smooth.src;

/* Part II : load the log returns data vector rt */
/* ------------------------------------------------------------------ */

open fin=filename for read;
x=readr(fin, nb_of_obs_in_the_rt_vector);
T=rows(x);
dat=x[1:T-1,1];
rt=100*x[1:T-1,2];

/* Part III : initialisation of parameters */
/* ------------------------------------------------------------------ */
A=0.0;
S1=0.6;
S2=0.4;
p=0.8;   p=-ln((1-p)/p);
q=0.2;   q=-ln((1-q)/q);

b0=A|S1|S2|p|q;
let b0={
  0.001
  1.36
  0.60
  2.00
  3.00
}; b0=b0';

x=rt;
T=rows(x);

output file=out.out reset;
output file=out.out off;
```

```
/* Part IV :  this procedure computes the vector of likelihood evaluated theta (θ) */
/* ------------------------------------------------------------------------- */

proc (1)=switch(theta,Rt);
local A,S1,S2,p,q,PrSt,St,j,ft,aux,p0,x,BP,mu,sig,K,auxo,rho;
local l,maxco,auxn, fRtSt, PrStRtM, PrStRt, fRt, t, BigT, PStat,const;

A=theta[1];
S1=ABS(theta[2]);
S2=ABS(theta[3]);
x=theta[4];   p=exp(x)/(1+exp(x));
x=theta[5];   q=exp(x)/(1+exp(x));

BP=(p~(1-p))|((1-q)~q);
mu=A;
sig=S1|S2;
K=2;
BigT=rows(rt);

rho=(1-q)/(2-p-q);
Pstat=rho~(1-rho);

const=1/sqrt(2*Pi);
fRtSt=const*(1./sig').*exp(-0.5*( ((Rt-mu)./sig')^2 ));
PrStRtM=Pstat|zeros(BigT-1,K);
PrStRt=zeros(BigT,K);
fRt=zeros(BigT,1);

t=2;
do until t>=BigT+1;
   aux=fRtSt[t-1,.].*PrStRtM[t-1,.];
   PrStRt[t-1,.]=aux/(sumc(aux')');
   PrStRtM[t,.]=PrStRt[t-1,.]*BP;
   t=t+1;
endo;

fRt[1,.]=fRtSt[1,.]*Pstat';
fRt[2:BigT]=sumc( (fRtSt[2:BigT,.].*PrStRtM[2:BigT,.])' );

retp(ln(fRt[1:BigT]));
endp;

/* Part V : maximum likelihood Evaluation(BHHH optimisation algorithm) */
/* ------------------------------------------------------------------- */
_max_Algorithm=5; /* 5= BHHH Algorithm */
_max_CovPar=2;    /* Heteroskedastic-consistent */
_max_GradMethod=0;
_max_LineSearch=5; /* 5= BHHH Algorithm */

{th,f,g,h,retcode}=maxlik(x,0,&switch,b0);
output file=out.out reset;

call maxprtm(th,f,g,h,retcode,2);

/* Part VI : call the routine smooth.src that computes the filtered probabilities
(fpe) and the smooth probabilities (spe) */
/* ------------------------------------------------------------------------- */

{fpe,spe}=smooth(th[1]|th,x);
output file=out.out off;
```

```
/* Part VII : this procedure computes filtered & smoothed probability estimates */
/* -------------------------------------------------------------------- */

proc (2)=smooth(th,y);
local mu1,mu2,p,q,s1,s2,rho,pa,pfx,its,p1,ind,thn,yxx,fk,t,spe,pax,qax,n;

/* Data initialisation */
/* -------------------------------------------------------------------- */

        mu1 = th[1];
        mu2 = th[2];
        s1 = abs(th[3]);
        s2 = abs(th[4]);
        p = th[5]; p=exp(p)/(1+exp(p));
        q = th[6]; q=exp(q)/(1+exp(q));
        n = rows(y);
        rho = (1-q)/(2-p-q);
        pa = rho|(1 - rho);
        p1 = zeros(4,1);

/* pax=filtered probas */
/* -------------------------------------------------------------------- */

        pax = zeros(n,4);
        (S_t|S_t-1)=(1,1)~(2,1)~(1,2)~(2,2)~(S_t=1)~(S_t-1=1);

/* qax smoothed probas, same structure as pax */
/* -------------------------------------------------------------------- */

        pfx = zeros(n,1);     @ likelihoods from filter @

/* Calculate probability weighted likelihoods for each obs */
/* -------------------------------------------------------------------- */

        yxx = (1/s1)*exp(-0.5*((y-mu1)/s1)^2 ) ~ (1/s2)*exp(-0.5*((y-mu2)/s2)^2 );
        yxx = (p*yxx[.,1])~((1-p)*yxx[.,2])~((1-q)*yxx[.,1])~(q*yxx[.,2]);

/*  Next call basic filter, store results in pax, pfx  */
/* -------------------------------------------------------------------- */

        its = 1;
        do until its > n;
            p1[1] = pa[1]*yxx[its,1];
            p1[2] = pa[1]*yxx[its,2];
            p1[3] = pa[2]*yxx[its,3];
            p1[4] = pa[2]*yxx[its,4];
            pfx[its] = sumc(p1);
            p1 = p1/pfx[its,1];
            pax[its,.] = p1';
            pa[1,1] = p1[1,1] + p1[3,1];
            pa[2,1] = p1[2,1] + p1[4,1];
            its = its+1;
        endo;

/* Smoothed probability estimate */
/* -------------------------------------------------------------------- */

        spe = pax[1,.]~pax[1,.];
        spe[1,2]=0; spe[1,4]=0; spe[1,5]=0; spe[1,7]=0;
        t = 2;
        do until t > n;
          spe = (((yxx[t,1]*spe[.,1:4])+(yxx[t,3]*spe[.,5:8]))~
              ((yxx[t,2]*spe[.,1:4])+(yxx[t,4]*spe[.,5:8])))/pfx[t,1];
```

```
           spe = spe | (pax[t,.] ~ pax[t,.]);
           spe[t,2]=0; spe[t,4]=0; spe[t,5]=0; spe[t,7]=0;
           t=t+1;
        endo;

        spe = spe[.,1:4] + spe[.,5:8];

/* Calculate filtered and smoothed probs that st=1 (col. 5) and st-1 =1 (col. 6) */
/* ---------------------------------------------------------------- */

        pax=[pr(st=1|st-1=1) ~ pr(st=2|st-1=1) ~ pr(st=1|st-1=2) ~ pr(st=2|st-1=2)]
        pax = pax ~ (pax[.,1] + pax[.,3]) ~ (pax[.,1] + pax[.,2]);
        qax = spe ~ (spe[.,1] + spe[.,3]) ~ (spe[.,1] + spe[.,2]);

        retp(pax,qax);

endp;
```

7

Quantitative Equity Investment Management with Time-Varying Factor Sensitivities*

YVES BENTZ

ABSTRACT

Factor models are widely used in modern investment management. They enable invest-ment managers, quantitative traders and risk managers to model co-movements among assets in an efficient way by concentrating the correlation structure of asset returns into a small number of factors. Because the factor sensitivities can be estimated by regression techniques these factors can be used to model the asset returns. Unfortunately, the corre-lation structure is not constant but evolves in time and so do the factor sensitivities. As a result, the sensitivity estimates have to be constantly updated in order to keep up with the changes.

This chapter describes three methods for estimating time-varying factor sensitivities. The methods are compared and numerous examples are provided. The first method, based on rolling regressions, is the most popular but also the least accurate. We show that this method can suffer from serious biases when the sensitivities change over time. The second method is based on a weighted regression approach which overcomes some of the limitations of the first method by giving more importance to recent observations. Finally, a Kalman filter-based stochastic parameter regression model is described that optimally estimates non-stationary factor exposures. The three methods have been implemented in the software provided on the CD-Rom so that readers can use and compare them with their own data and applications.

7.1 INTRODUCTION

Are you satisfied with the accuracy of your factor sensitivity estimates? If not, perhaps the following situation will sound familiar... After days of careful analysis, John had constructed a long–short portfolio of stocks. John's boss, however, felt uncomfortable about the position as he feared that the expected outperformance, i.e. the alpha, may take time to materialise and be perturbed by unwanted risk exposures. John updated the risk model with the latest estimates of factor sensitivities and ran the optimiser in order to immunise the position against these exposures. After monitoring the profit and loss over

---

* The information presented and opinions expressed herein are solely those of the author and do not necessarily represent those of Credit Suisse First Boston.

Applied Quantitative Methods for Trading and Investment. Edited by C.L. Dunis, J. Laws and P. Naïm
© 2003 John Wiley & Sons, Ltd ISBN: 0-470-84885-5

a few days, it became clear that the position was exposed to general market movements. In fact the alpha was dominated by a market beta.

What went wrong? The optimiser? The trading strategy? Actually, neither of them. The true underlying factor sensitivities had not been constant over the estimation period and, as a result, the OLS[1] sensitivity estimates that John used for the risk model were seriously misleading.

While factor sensitivities are known to vary over time, prevailing methods such as rolling regressions can be severely biased because they estimate past average factor exposures rather than forecast where these exposures are going to be in the future. In contrast, the adaptive procedure described in this chapter models and predicts the variations of factor sensitivities instead of merely smoothing past sensitivities. It can therefore be used to take advantage of the dynamics driving the relationships between stock and factor returns. As a result, risk models can be more accurate, investment strategies can be better immunised against unwanted risk, and risk–return profiles can be significantly improved.

While prevailing methods are often too simple to be correct, powerful adaptive procedures are often too complicated to be usable. This chapter presents in simple terms the essentials of dealing with time-varying factor sensitivities. It describes and compares the various methods of modelling time-varying risk exposures. Particular emphasis is given to an elegant, rich and powerful estimation method based on the Kalman filter.

The software and spreadsheets supplied on the CD-Rom provide the reader with intuitive examples of the various procedures and show how most of the complexity can be handed over to the computer program. The reader may wish to use the estimation tool pack provided on their own data in order to estimate time-varying regression coefficients. The software is provided for educational purposes only.

7.1.1 Who should read this chapter and what are its possible applications?

This chapter is aimed at all those using linear regression models with economic and financial time series. This includes areas such as investment analysis, quantitative trading, hedging, index tracking, investment performance attribution, style management and risk measurement. In particular, this chapter is targeted at everyone who has heard of adaptive models, stochastic parameter models or Kalman filtering but could not or did not want to invest the time and effort in order to implement such models.

This chapter consists of four main sections. Section 7.2 is a short review of factor models and factor sensitivities. It introduces the notations used in the rest of the chapter. The following sections describe three different methods for estimating the factor exposures. The first method, presented in Section 7.3, is based on a rolling regression procedure and uses OLS estimation. The procedure is straightforward and can be implemented in a simple spreadsheet. It does not require any complex estimation procedure and can use the widely available linear regression models. The shortcomings of the method are demonstrated. The second method, presented in Section 7.4, is based on weighted least squares estimation. The procedure rests on a slightly more complex set of equations but overcomes a number of weaknesses of the OLS procedure. The third method, presented in Section 7.5, consists of an adaptive procedure based on the Kalman filter. This stochastic

---

[1] Ordinary least squares estimation is the usual linear regression estimation procedure used on rolling windows to compute betas and other factor sensitivities.

parameter regression model is shown to be the most accurate and robust procedure of the three, yielding optimal estimates of factor sensitivities and modelling their time structure. Finally, Section 7.6 concludes the Chapter.

7.2 FACTOR SENSITIVITIES DEFINED

The estimation and use of factor sensitivities play an important role in equity investment management. Investment diversification, portfolio hedging, factor betting[2] or immunisation,[3] index tracking, performance attribution, style management all necessitate at some stage an accurate estimation of factor sensitivities. The factors can be the overall market (some broad stock market index), some industrial sector, some investment style grouping (index of growth stocks) or other variables that underlie the correlation structure of stock returns such as macroeconomic factors (e.g. inflation, GDP growth), statistical factors (usually obtained by principal component analysis), or returns of other asset classes (e.g. crude oil, gold, interest rates, exchange rates).[4]

The sensitivity of a stock[5] to a factor is usually defined as the expected stock return corresponding to a unit change in the factor. If $Y(t)$ is the return[6] of the stock at time t and $X(t)$ is the simultaneous return (or change) of the factor, then β in the following equation can be viewed as the factor sensitivity:

$$Y(t) = \alpha + \beta X(t) + \varepsilon(t) \qquad (7.1)$$

where α is a constant representing the average extra-factor performance of the stock and $\varepsilon(t)$ is a random variable with zero mean (by construction), constant variance and zero covariance with $X(t)$.

If both the stock and the factor returns $Y(t)$ and $X(t)$ can be observed in the market (and they usually can), then α and β can be estimated by regression techniques. Once the β coefficient has been estimated, it is possible to immunise the investment against movements in the factor by selling β amount of a tradable proxy for the factor for every unit of the investment. For instance, if the factor is the UK stock market, one can sell β pounds of FTSE 100 index futures for each pound invested. The expected return of the hedged position would then be α.

More generally, several factor sensitivities can be estimated simultaneously. In order to estimate joint sensitivities, equation (7.1) is generalised to more than one factor:

$$Y(t) = \alpha + \sum_{i=1}^{N} \beta_i X_i(t) + \varepsilon(t)$$

$$= X(t)\beta + \varepsilon(t) \qquad (7.2)$$

---

[2] For instance, an investor could construct a portfolio that would be sensitive to one factor only (e.g. default risk) and immune to all other factors.

[3] For instance, an investor could construct a portfolio that would not be sensitive to one factor (e.g. long-term interest rates risk) but remain sensitive to all other factors.

[4] Not all factors may be relevant for all factor models. For example, using macroeconomic factors makes little sense when modelling daily or hourly returns.

[5] Sensitivity estimation is obviously not restricted to stocks but can also apply to other assets, portfolios of assets or investment strategies.

[6] As factor sensitivities may not have a flat term structure, β is a function of the horizon over which returns are calculated, i.e. betas based on monthly, weekly, daily and hourly returns may all be different from each other.

where $Y(t)$ is the return of the investment at time t. $X_i(t)$ are the returns of the i factors. α is a constant representing the average extra-factor return of the investment. It is the sensitivity coefficient β_0 to the constant factor $X_0(t) = 1$. β_i is a parameter that represents the joint sensitivity of the investment return to changes in factor i. $\varepsilon(t)$ is a random variable with zero mean (by construction), constant variance (by assumption) and zero covariance with the factor returns.

The joint sensitivity coefficients β_i measure "clean" sensitivities, accounting for the sole effect of one variable X_i while controlling for the other effects. Hence, if the joint sensitivity of Y to X_1 has a value of S, Y is expected to change by S when X_1 changes by 1, if all the other variables $X_2, \ldots, X_n$ remain constant. β_i is the partial derivative $\partial \hat{Y}(X_i)/\partial X_i$ of the expectation $\hat{Y}$ of Y with respect to X_i.

7.3 OLS TO ESTIMATE FACTOR SENSITIVITIES: A SIMPLE, POPULAR BUT INACCURATE METHOD

Estimating factor sensitivities can be simple or complex, depending on the assumptions made about the relationships between stock and factor returns. The most popular method with practitioners and, unfortunately, also the least accurate is standard linear regression, also known as ordinary least squares (OLS) estimation. It is simple, easy to implement and widely available in statistical software packages. OLS minimises the mean squared error (MSE) of the linear model described in equation (7.2). The problem has a simple closed form solution which consists of a matrix inversion and a few matrix multiplications.

Equation (7.2) can be rewritten using a more concise matrix notation, as:

$$\mathbf{Y} = \mathbf{X}\boldsymbol{\beta} + \boldsymbol{\varepsilon} \tag{7.3}$$

where $\mathbf{Y}$ is a $T \times 1$ vector of the asset returns, $\mathbf{X}$ a $T \times (N+1)$ vector of the factor returns, $\boldsymbol{\beta}$ a $(N+1) \times 1$ vector of factor sensitivities and $\boldsymbol{\varepsilon}$ a $T \times 1$ vector of random variables with zero mean, i.e.

$$\mathbf{Y} = \begin{bmatrix} Y_1 \\ Y_2 \\ \cdots \\ Y_T \end{bmatrix}, \quad \mathbf{X} = \begin{bmatrix} 1 & X_{11} & \cdots & X_{1N} \\ 1 & X_{21} & \cdots & \cdots \\ \cdots & \cdots & X_{tj} & \cdots \\ 1 & X_{T1} & \cdots & X_{TN} \end{bmatrix}, \quad \boldsymbol{\beta} = \begin{bmatrix} \alpha \\ \beta_1 \\ \cdots \\ \beta_N \end{bmatrix}, \quad \boldsymbol{\varepsilon} = \begin{bmatrix} \varepsilon_1 \\ \varepsilon_2 \\ \cdots \\ \varepsilon_T \end{bmatrix}$$

with expectation $\mathrm{E}(\boldsymbol{\varepsilon}) = \mathbf{0}$ and variance–covariance matrix $\sigma^2(\boldsymbol{\varepsilon}) = \sigma^2 \mathbf{I}$. Here Y_t is the tth observation of the investment return; X_{ti} is the tth observation of the ith factor return X_i; β_i is the sensitivity of $\mathbf{Y}$ to factor X_i; ε_t is the error term at time t.

The expression of the OLS estimator $\hat{\boldsymbol{\beta}}$ of $\boldsymbol{\beta}$ can then be shown to be:

$$\hat{\boldsymbol{\beta}} = (\mathbf{X}'\mathbf{X})^{-1}\mathbf{X}'\mathbf{Y} \tag{7.4}$$

and its estimated variance–covariance matrix is $s^2(\hat{\boldsymbol{\beta}})$:

$$s^2(\hat{\boldsymbol{\beta}}) = \mathrm{MSE} \, (\mathbf{X}'\mathbf{X})^{-1} \tag{7.5}$$

with MSE being the mean squared error of the regression model:

$$\text{MSE} = \frac{1}{T-2} \sum_{t=1}^{T} (Y(t) - \hat{Y}(t))^2 \qquad \hat{Y}(t) = \sum_{i=0}^{N} \beta_i X_i(t) \qquad (7.6)$$

OLS estimates of the factor sensitivities are unconditional, i.e. they are *average* sensitivities over the observation sample. Any variation of the betas over the sample is not modelled and the resulting error is attributed to sampling, i.e. to the $\boldsymbol{\varepsilon}$ term in equation (7.3). Therefore, when using OLS, the modeller implicitly assumes that the factor sensitivities are constant over the data sample. Hence, in the case of a deterministic relationship where beta would change over time in a predictable way, OLS would estimate an average beta over the sample with a large prediction error $\boldsymbol{\varepsilon}$.

The problem is illustrated in Figure 7.1. The sensitivity $\partial Y / \partial X$ of a *dependent variable* (say Y) to an *independent* one (say X) is represented on the vertical axis. The actual sensitivity is not constant but varies over time. Linear regression measures an average (or unconditional) effect over the estimation data set. In the case of Figure 7.1, this average sensitivity is close to zero and would probably not be statistically significant. However, the actual sensitivity is far from small. For instance, at time t, the true factor sensitivity is strongly negative although the unconditional model's prediction is slightly positive.

Parameter estimation is clearly biased here. At time t, the expected value of beta is quite different from the true value. The model wrongly attributes to the stochastic residual $\boldsymbol{\varepsilon}$ an effect that is in fact largely deterministic. The importance of the estimation error depends on the variance of the actual sensitivity over the sample (the more volatile the sensitivity, the more likely sensitivity measured at a particular time differs from the average sensitivity) and the size of the estimation window.

The example given in the "Sensitivity_estimation.xls" file illustrates standard linear regression (OLS) using Microsoft Excel's native LINEST function.[7] The data set consists

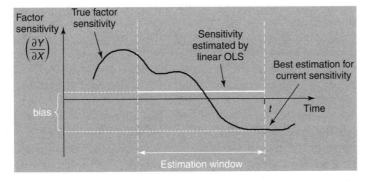

Figure 7.1 Actual sensitivity (in black) and unconditional sensitivity measured by linear OLS estimation (in white). When the true sensitivity is not constant but conditional on time, OLS estimation, which measures an unconditional (average) sensitivity over time, is biased. The amplitude of the bias depends on the variance of the true sensitivity and the length of the estimation window

---

[7] A more user-friendly linear regression tool is also available through the "Analysis Tool pack" add-in that comes with Excel.

of 100 observations of two observable variables, Y and X, representing daily percentage returns. X and Y are related by a simple time-varying relationship that is mostly deterministic (90% of the variance in Y is related to X):

$$Y(t) = \beta(t) \times X(t) + \varepsilon(t) \tag{7.7}$$

where $\beta(t)$ is a linear function of time; $\varepsilon(t)$ is a Gaussian random variable ($\mu = 0\%$, $\sigma = 0.1\%$). The actual beta (generated in column B and plotted in white in Figure 7.1) increases linearly over the period, starting at -0.49, turning positive at time $t = 50$ and finishing at 0.50.

Cell K3 contains the Excel formula for the beta estimated over the entire data set, i.e. "=LINEST(\$E\$3:\$E\$102,\$C\$3:\$C\$102,TRUE,FALSE)". Its value is -0.04. If this value is used to predict Y based on X using the same data set, the R-square is 2%. Cell K4 contains the formula for the beta estimated over the last 50 observations only. Its value is 0.23 and the corresponding R-square (using these 50 observations) is 61%.[8] Given all the information available at time $t = 100$ (i.e. 100 observations of X and Y), which one is the right value of beta to use at time $t = 100$? And at time $t = 101$?

Actually, neither of the two values is satisfactory as they correspond to past averages of betas rather than current values or predictions of beta. The true value of beta at time $t = 100$ is 0.5 and the best value to use when a new value of X and Y becomes available at $t = 101$ would be 0.51. Unfortunately OLS is unsuitable when beta changes over time because it averages out the variations of beta rather than models its time structure. Furthermore it is backward looking rather than predictive. In other terms, OLS is insensitive to the order of the observations. One could scramble the data, OLS would still yield the same estimate of beta. The potentially useful information contained in the data chronology is not used.

Intuitively, one can see that the estimates are highly sample-dependent. If beta changes rapidly, estimates using short time periods should be better than estimates using longer periods. Unfortunately, by reducing the estimation period, one increases sampling error. The best window size should correspond to an optimal trade-off between sampling error and beta variation. On the one hand, if the estimation period is too short, there are not enough observations to separate the information from the noise, resulting in large *sampling variance*. On the other hand, if the estimation period is too long, the current beta may significantly differ from its average, resulting in a *biased model*. This is known as the bias/variance dilemma.[9]

Based on this perception, many practitioners use rolling regressions. This consists of applying a linear regression model to a rolling window of observations. The window is an ordered subsample of the time series. Figure 7.2 illustrates the rolling window approach.

An example of rolling regression is given in column H of the spreadsheet. The corresponding (out-of-sample) R-square is 39.2%.

The provided sensitivity estimation tool pack in the "SEToolPack.XLS" file can also be used to estimate rolling regressions. In order to do so, select "Sensitivity estimation" from

---

[8] Note that these R-square figures are *in-sample* and do not reflect the out-of-sample performance of the model. At time $t = 75$ for instance, the 25 last observations (i.e. 76 → 100) are not yet available. And yet we use the $t = 100$ estimate of beta in order to compute this R-square.

[9] This issue becomes even more important and difficult to resolve when measuring joint sensitivities that change at different speeds. Which window size should then be used?

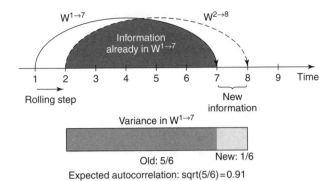

Figure 7.2 Rolling regressions. Sensitivities are estimated over a rolling window (here $W^{1\to7}$) of the n last observations (here $n = 7$). Then, the estimation window is moved forward by a rolling step of p observations (here $p = 1$) and a new set of factor sensitivities is estimated (here on $W^{2\to8}$). The procedure goes on until the last observation in the data set is reached. Unless $p = n$, consecutive windows are not independent. Actually, $(n - p)/n$ of the variance in a window is shared with an adjacent window and only p/n of the variance is new information

```
┌─────────────────────────────────────────────────────────┐ ? X
│ SENSITIVITY ESTIMATION TOOL PACK                          │
│                                                           │
│  Data Inputs:                                             │
│                                                           │
│   Dependent variable        $C$2:$C$117          ▤       │
│   Independent variables      $A$2:$B$117          ▤       │
│   ☑ Labels in first row                                   │
│                                                           │
│  Models for sensitivity calculations:                     │
│                                                           │
│    ○ Linear rolling regression (unweighted/weighted least squares) │
│    ○ Recursive linear regression (weighted/unweighted least squares) │
│    ● Stochastic parameter regression (Kalman filtering)   │
│                                                           │
│    ☑ Include constant in regression equation              │
│    ☐ Standardize sensitivities (inputs are normalised)    │
│                                                           │
│  Output Ranges  (Upper left Corner):   ┌──────┐ ┌────────┐│
│                                        │ Help │ │ Cancel ││
│   Estimated senisitivities  $J$2 ▤     └──────┘ └────────┘│
│   Standard errors (optional) $T$2 ▤    ┌──────────────────┐│
│                                        │       OK         ││
│  Copyright © Yves Bentz. 2001. All rights reserved. └──────────────────┘│
└─────────────────────────────────────────────────────────┘
```

Figure 7.3 Using the sensitivity estimation tool pack to estimate rolling regressions

the tools menu. In the main menu (Figure 7.3) enter the Y and X ranges into the corresponding edit boxes (dependent and independent variables respectively), select the range where you want the computed sensitivities to be saved to (output range),[10] select "Linear rolling regression" option and press "OK" to go to the next dialogue box (Figure 7.4). In the "Rolling regression" dialogue box, select "no weighting" and a window size.

---

[10] The sensitivity estimation tool pack can be used with any worksheet and is not restricted to the example sheet provided. For instance, it can be used with the "stock beta estimation" sheet or any proprietary data collected by the reader in other workbooks.

Model1: Rolling Regression

Total number of data points selected: 116

Size of the Rolling Window 16

Weighting options

- No Weighting (Uniform Weighting)
- Linear Weighting (first:0 ; last:1)

Weight Decay Rate (%)

- Linear Weighting
- Exponential Weighting

Lin: W(t) − W(t-1)
Exp: 1-W(t) / W(t-1)

3

Help

Exit All

Cancel

- Custom weight   Enter Range

OK

Figure 7.4 The rolling regression menu of the tool pack

The example provided in the spreadsheet consists of two factors, X_1 and X_2 and 115 observations. The dependent variable Y is generated by a time-varying linear relationship of the factors. The sensitivities and the additive stochastic noise are stored in columns AF to AI of the example sheet. They have been constructed so that each represents a different type of time series. The sensitivity to X_1 is a continuous function of time, the sensitivity to X_2 is constant except for a large level shift occurring half-way through the sample and alpha is a slowly growing value. These time series are represented by the white lines in the graph included in the spreadsheet (Figure 7.5). The grey lines correspond to the rolling regression estimates. The first n observations, where n is the window size, are used to estimate the regression coefficients at time n. "Ini. Period" will therefore appear in the first n rows.

Rolling regressions, although popular, are still unsuitable for time-varying sensitivity estimation. They give the illusion that they can handle conditional betas while in reality they are biased estimators of time-varying sensitivities. This is because OLS linear regression estimates an average sensitivity over each rolling window. If actual sensitivities vary over time (e.g. follow a trend) they will depart from their average.

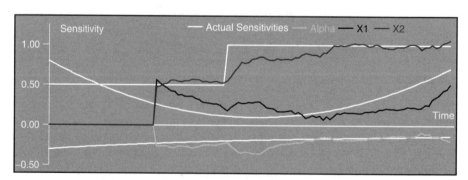

Figure 7.5 Rolling regression example. The data set is provided in the "Example" sheet of "SEToolPack.xls" file. It consists of 115 observations. The white lines correspond to the actual sensitivities. The grey lines are the sensitivities estimated by the rolling regression model provided in the tool pack. The size of the rolling window is 32 observations

Figure 7.2 shows that sensitivities computed from adjacent windows are highly correlated because they are estimated from data sets that share $n - p$ observations, n being the
window size and p the rolling shift between two consecutive windows. Autocorrelation in
rolling sensitivities increases with the window size n. This autocorrelation is *independent*
of the behaviour of the actual sensitivities. Even for random sensitivities, autocorrelation
in estimated sensitivities is expected to be $\sqrt{(n - p)/p}$ (the correlation squared is the
percentage of variance common to two adjacent windows, i.e. $(n - p)/p$). The measured
effect of a particular event persists as long as it remains in the rolling estimation window.
The consequences of this persistence are threefold:

- **"Ghost" effects**. If a significant event occurs on one particular day, it will remain in
the sensitivity series for p further days, where p is the length of the rolling window.
The apparent sensitivity persistence is a measurement artefact and does not necessarily
relate to a true sensitivity shock. The amplitude of the effect depends on both the size
of the rolling window and the variance of the actual sensitivity. Figure 7.6 illustrates
the shadow effect. The *estimation bias* is a function of the difference between the
two sensitivity levels, their respective durations and the length of the rolling window.
Measured sensitivity remains at this level for another 15 days although actual sensitivity
has returned to its normal level. This is the *shadow effect*. Rolling regression measures
an effect that may have long disappeared.

- **The difference between two consecutive sensitivity estimates is only determined
by two observations**. That is the observation entering the rolling window (i.e. the
most recent data point) and the observation leaving the rolling window (i.e. the most

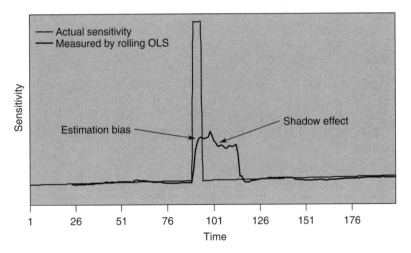

Figure 7.6 Estimation bias and shadow effect in rolling estimation. In this controlled experiment, the actual sensitivity of Y to X is represented by the thin line. It has been chosen constant
over most of the data set at some level (LL) except for a very short period of 5 days during
which it takes an unusually high value (HL). This may be caused, for instance, by incorrect market expectations motivated by unfounded rumours. Sensitivity is estimated by OLS regression
over a rolling window. The window is 20 days long. Sensitivity estimates are represented by the
bold line. Rolling estimation clearly underestimates actual sensitivity. At the end of the fifth day
of HL, the estimate reaches its maximum value of $(5 \times HL + 15 \times LL)/20$

remote data point). While it is legitimate that the most recent observation affects this difference, there is no reason why the most remote point should have more influence than any other observation in the window, especially because the size of the window has been chosen somewhat arbitrarily.

- **Sensitivity estimates lag actual sensitivity**. Because rolling regression measures an average sensitivity over the estimation period, estimated betas lag actual betas, especially when the latter trend. The lag depends on the length of the rolling window. This effect is clearly visible in Figure 7.5. The beta to variable X_2 slowly adapts to the level shift while the beta to X_1 seems to lag the actual beta by about 20 observations.

7.4 WLS TO ESTIMATE FACTOR SENSITIVITIES: A BETTER BUT STILL SUB-OPTIMAL METHOD

One of the major limitations of rolling OLS is that all observations are given equal weight, irrespective of their distance in time. Hence, the most recent observation is given the same "credibility" as the most remote observation in the window. A natural improvement of the rolling window procedure would be to give observations different weights based on their position in the time series. This procedure is known as weighted least squares (WLS) estimation and can better deal with variations of sensitivities (see, among others, Pindyck and Rubinfeld (1998)). Remote observations are attributed less weight than recent observations.

The criterion to be minimised, WSSR, is the weighted sum of squared residuals rather than the ordinary sum of squared residuals, SSR. WSSR is defined by:

$$\text{WSSR}(\boldsymbol{\beta}) = \sum_{t=1}^{T} w(t)(\hat{Y}_\beta(t) - Y(t))^2 = (\mathbf{Y} - \mathbf{X}\boldsymbol{\beta})'\mathbf{W}(\mathbf{Y} - \mathbf{X}\boldsymbol{\beta}) \tag{7.8}$$

where $\mathbf{W}$ is a diagonal matrix containing the weights $w(t)$, i.e.

$$\mathop{\mathbf{W}}_{T \times T} = \begin{bmatrix} w(1) & 0 & \ldots & 0 \\ 0 & w(2) & \ldots & \ldots \\ \ldots & \ldots & \ldots & 0 \\ 0 & \ldots & 0 & w(T) \end{bmatrix}$$

The weighted least squares estimator $\hat{\boldsymbol{\beta}}_w$ is:

$$\hat{\boldsymbol{\beta}}_w = (\mathbf{X}'\mathbf{W}\mathbf{X})^{-1}\mathbf{X}'\mathbf{W}\mathbf{Y} \tag{7.9}$$

and the estimated variance–covariance matrix of $\hat{\boldsymbol{\beta}}_w$ is $s^2(\hat{\boldsymbol{\beta}}_w)$:

$$s^2(\hat{\boldsymbol{\beta}}_w) = \text{MSE}_w(\mathbf{X}'\mathbf{W}\mathbf{X})^{-1} \tag{7.10}$$

with MSE_w being the weighted squared error of the regression model:

$$\text{MSE}_w = \frac{\text{WSSR}}{\displaystyle\sum_{t=1}^{T} w(t) - 2} \tag{7.11}$$

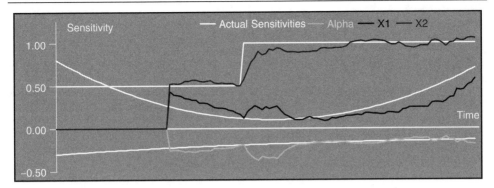

Figure 7.7 Weighted regression example. The size of the rolling window is still 32 observations. However, here the observations have been weighted using a linear function of time and a decay rate of 3%

Not surprisingly, when $\mathbf{W} = \mathbf{I}$, i.e. when all observations have equal weight, equations (7.8) to (7.10) can be condensed into the OLS equation. The most popular functions, which are provided by the tool pack, are linear or exponential but other functions such as sigmoids can be considered. A decay rate determines the speed at which the weight of an observation decreases with time.[11]

In order to use the sensitivity estimation tool pack, select one of the weighting options in the rolling regression menu (Figure 7.3). For instance, select a linear weighting and enter a weight decay of 3%. Figure 7.7 shows the result of the estimation.

Weighted least squares estimation induces less autocorrelation in the estimates than ordinary least squares estimation. Depending on the decay rate, shadow effects, lag and persistence problems are considerably reduced.

However, WLS does not provide a way to model the sensitivities time series. It still measures past (weighted) average sensitivities rather than predicting future ones. In addition, all sensitivity coefficients in the regression equation are identically affected by the weighting, regardless of their rate of change as the weights only depend on the position of the observation in the time series. Consequently, constant sensitivities suffer from large weight discount rates while highly variable sensitivities suffer from small decay rates. There is no single weight discount rate that is adapted to all factor sensitivity coefficients when their variances differ and some trade-off has to be made.

7.5 THE STOCHASTIC PARAMETER REGRESSION MODEL AND THE KALMAN FILTER: THE BEST WAY TO ESTIMATE FACTOR SENSITIVITIES

The procedures that have been described so far involve a single regression equation with constant betas. These procedures use ordinary or weighted least squares in order to repeatedly estimate new model coefficients from adjacent windows of observations.

The stochastic parameter model, however, is based on a conceptually different approach (see Gouriéroux *et al.* (1997), or Harvey (1989)). The beta coefficients are not assumed

---

[11] Although this rate is usually set *a priori*, one could also estimate it, for instance by minimising the WSSR.

constant and are optimally adjusted when new information becomes available. The dynamics of the betas are modelled in a second equation. Very much like a GARCH model,[12] the stochastic parameter regression model is based on a system of equations. Hence, the linear regression equation (7.2) can be rewritten into a simple time-varying regression by letting $\boldsymbol{\beta}$ follow a given time process, for example an autoregressive process:[13]

$$\mathbf{Y}_t = \mathbf{X}_t \boldsymbol{\beta}_t + \boldsymbol{\varepsilon}_t \tag{7.12}$$

and

$$\boldsymbol{\beta}_t = \boldsymbol{\Phi}\boldsymbol{\beta}_{t-1} + \boldsymbol{\eta}_t \qquad \text{for } t = 1, \ldots, T \tag{7.13}$$

where $\boldsymbol{\Phi}$ is a non-random $K \times K$ matrix, K being the number of factors; $\boldsymbol{\eta}_t$ is a vector of serially uncorrelated disturbances with zero mean. It is not observable.

The addition of the second equation (7.13) allows beta to vary in time according to a process that can be modelled. However, $\boldsymbol{\Phi}$ and $\boldsymbol{\eta}_t$ are not observable and need to be estimated. Simple estimation procedures such as OLS which can only handle single equations cannot be used here but fortunately, the problem can be resolved as it can easily be put into a state space form. The Kalman filter can then be used to update the parameters of the model. Moreover, the same Kalman filter can be employed with a large variety of time processes for the sensitivities without adding much computational complexity.[14]

Originally developed by control engineers in the 1960s (see Kalman (1960)) for application concerning spacecraft navigation and rocket tracking, state space models have since attracted considerable attention in economics, finance, and the social sciences and have been found to be useful in many non-stationary problems and particularly for time series analysis. A state space model consists of a system of equations aimed at determining the state of a dynamic system from observed variables (usually time series) contaminated by noise. Time, or the ordering of observations, plays an important role in such models. Two identical state space models applied to the same data are likely to produce different estimates if observations are presented to the models in different orders (i.e. scrambling observations alters model estimates). It is therefore not surprising that they are usually used for modelling time series. The state of the dynamic system, described by "state variables", is assumed to be linearly related to the observed input variables.

The stochastic coefficient regression model expressed in a state space form can be defined by a system of two equations. The first equation (e.g. equation (7.12)) is referred to as the *observation equation* and relates the dependent variable, $\mathbf{Y}_t$, to the independent variables by the unobservable states (in the case of equation (7.12), the state is simply the vector of sensitivities $\boldsymbol{\beta}_t$). More generally, the observation equation takes the following form:

$$\mathbf{Y}_t = \mathbf{H}_t(\mathbf{s}_t + \mathbf{d}) + \boldsymbol{\varepsilon}_t \qquad \text{for } t = 1, \ldots, T \tag{7.14}$$

---

[12] See for instance Bollerslev (1986).

[13] Equation 7.13 describes one example of a time process that can be used for modelling the sensitivities time series. This particular process corresponds to a simple AR1. The Kalman filter approach can be used with many more processes.

[14] If $\boldsymbol{\eta}_t$ has zero variance and $\boldsymbol{\Phi} = \mathbf{I}$, then $\boldsymbol{\beta}_t$ is constant and equation (7.12) is just the familiar equation of a linear regression. The estimates of $\boldsymbol{\beta}_t$ are those of a recursive regression (OLS linear regression using all the observations from $i = 1$ to t) and the estimate of $\boldsymbol{\beta}_T$ is identical to the OLS estimate of a linear regression. If the variance of $\boldsymbol{\eta}_t$ is larger than zero, however, sensitivity coefficients are allowed to change over time.

where $\mathbf{Y}_t$ is the dependent observable variable (e.g. an asset return) at time t. $\mathbf{s}_t$ is a K vector that describes the state of the factor sensitivities of the asset returns at time t. $\mathbf{d}$ is a K non-random vector that can account for the long-term mean in sensitivities. $\mathbf{H}_t$ is a K vector that contains the factor values at time t. $\boldsymbol{\varepsilon}_t$ is a serially uncorrelated perturbation with zero mean and variance R_t, i.e.: $E(\boldsymbol{\varepsilon}_t) = \mathbf{0}$ and $\text{Var}(\boldsymbol{\varepsilon}_t) = R_t$, R_t being non-random. It is not observable.

The exact representation of $\mathbf{H}_t$ and $\mathbf{s}_t$ will depend on model specification. For the autoregressive model described by equations (7.12) and (7.13), which is also the most popular, $\mathbf{H}_t$ and $\mathbf{s}_t$ simply correspond to $\mathbf{X}_t$ and $\boldsymbol{\beta}_t$ respectively. However, this is not the case for more complex models such as the random trend model which requires more state variables ($K = 2N$, N being the number of factors). In general, the elements of $\mathbf{s}_t$ are not observable. However, their time structure is assumed to be known. The evolution through time of these unobservable states is a first-order Markov process described by a *transition equation*:

$$\mathbf{s}_t = \boldsymbol{\Phi}\mathbf{s}_{t-1} + \mathbf{c}_t + \boldsymbol{\eta}_t \qquad \text{for } t = 1, \ldots, T \qquad (7.15)$$

where $\boldsymbol{\Phi}$ is a non-random $K \times K$ state transition matrix; $\mathbf{c}_t$ is a non-random K vector; $\boldsymbol{\eta}_t$ is an $m \times 1$ vector of serially uncorrelated disturbances with zero mean and covariance $\mathbf{Q}_t$; $E(\boldsymbol{\eta}_t) = \mathbf{0}$ and $\text{Var}(\boldsymbol{\eta}_t) = \mathbf{Q}_t$, $\mathbf{Q}_t$ being non-random. It is not observable.

The initial state vector $\mathbf{s}_0$ has a mean of $\mathbf{s}$ and a covariance matrix $\mathbf{P}_0$, i.e.:

$$E(\mathbf{s}_0) = \mathbf{s} \quad \text{and} \quad \text{Var}(\mathbf{s}_0) = \mathbf{P}_0$$

Furthermore, the disturbances $\boldsymbol{\varepsilon}_t$ and $\boldsymbol{\eta}_t$ are uncorrelated with each other in all time periods, and uncorrelated with the initial state, i.e.:

$$E(\boldsymbol{\varepsilon}_t, \boldsymbol{\eta}_t') = \mathbf{0} \text{ for all elements } \eta_t \text{ of } \boldsymbol{\eta}_t, \quad \text{and} \quad \text{for } t = 1, \ldots, T$$

and

$$E(\boldsymbol{\varepsilon}_t, \mathbf{s}) = \mathbf{0} \quad \text{and} \quad E(\boldsymbol{\eta}_t, \mathbf{s}) = \mathbf{0} \quad \text{for } t = 1, \ldots, T$$

The system matrices $\boldsymbol{\Phi}$, $\mathbf{P}$ and $\mathbf{Q}$, the vectors $\boldsymbol{\eta}$, $\mathbf{c}$ and $\mathbf{d}$ and the scalar R are non-random although some of them may vary over time (but they do so in a predetermined way). Furthermore, the *observation noise* $\boldsymbol{\varepsilon}_t$ and the *system noise* $\boldsymbol{\eta}_t$ are Gaussian white noises.

The most popular processes used for time-varying sensitivities are the random walk model and the random trend model.

The random walk model dictates that the best estimate of future sensitivities is the current sensitivity. To specify this model, vectors $\mathbf{d}$ and $\mathbf{c}$ are set to zero and the system matrices for the random walk model are given by equations (7.16):[15]

$$\mathbf{s}_t = [\beta_{t,1}, \beta_{t,2}, \ldots, \beta_{t,N}]'$$
$$\mathbf{H}_t = [1, F_{t,1}, \ldots, F_{t,N-1}] \qquad (7.16)$$
$$\boldsymbol{\Phi} = \mathbf{I}$$

---

[15] Hence the random walk specification of the stochastic regression model can be expressed as a system of two equations: (1) $\mathbf{Y}_t = \mathbf{X}_t\boldsymbol{\beta}_t + \boldsymbol{\varepsilon}_t$ and (2) $\boldsymbol{\beta}_t = \boldsymbol{\beta}_{t-1} + \boldsymbol{\eta}_t$.

where $\mathbf{\Phi}$ is $N \times N$, $\mathbf{H}_t$ is $1 \times N$ and $\mathbf{s}_t$ is $N \times 1$, N being the number of independent variables, including the constant.

The random trend model dictates that the best estimate of future sensitivities is the current sensitivity plus the trend. In the presence of a trend, sensitivities at $t + 1$ are not equally likely to be above or under the value at t. A simple model which allows the sensitivities to trend is the random trend model. A sensitivity coefficient β_{it} follows a random trend if:

$$\beta_t = \beta_{t-1} + \delta_{t-1} + \eta_{t,1}$$
$$\delta_t = \delta_{t-1} + \eta_{t,2}$$

(7.17)

where β_t represents the sensitivity vector at time t and δ_t is the random trend in the sensitivity vector at time t.[16]

In a state space form, the system in (7.17) can be written as:

$$\begin{pmatrix} \beta_t \\ \delta_t \end{pmatrix} = \mathbf{\Phi}_0 \begin{pmatrix} \beta_{t-1} \\ \delta_{t-1} \end{pmatrix} + \begin{pmatrix} \eta_{t,1} \\ \eta_{t,2} \end{pmatrix}$$

(7.18)

where the individual sensitivity random trend state transition matrix is given by $\mathbf{\Phi}_0 = \begin{bmatrix} 1 & 1 \\ 0 & 1 \end{bmatrix}$.

To specify this model, vectors $\mathbf{d}$ and $\mathbf{c}$ are set to zero and the collection of factor sensitivities and trends are expressed as:

$$\mathbf{s}(t) = [\beta_1(t), \delta_1(t), \beta_2(t), \delta_2(t), \dots, \beta_N(t), \delta_N(t)]'$$

(7.19)

$$\mathbf{H}(t) = [1, 0, 1, 0, \dots, 1, 0]$$

(7.20)

$$\mathbf{\Phi} = \begin{bmatrix} \mathbf{\Phi}_0 & \mathbf{0} & \cdots & \mathbf{0} \\ \mathbf{0} & \mathbf{\Phi}_0 & & \mathbf{0} \\ \vdots & & \ddots & \\ \mathbf{0} & \mathbf{0} & & \mathbf{\Phi}_0 \end{bmatrix}$$

(7.21)

where the dimensions of the state of sensitivities has been doubled to include trends in the sensitivities, i.e. $\mathbf{\Phi}$ is $2N \times 2N$, $\mathbf{s}_t$ is $2N \times 1$ and $\mathbf{H}_t$ is $1 \times 2N$.

Other time processes such as the random coefficient model (Schaefer *et al.*, 1975) or the mean-reverting coefficient model (Rosenberg, 1973) can also be used within this modelling framework.

The objective of state space modelling is to estimate the unobservable states of the dynamic system in the presence of noise. The Kalman filter is a recursive method of doing this, i.e. filtering out the observation noise in order to optimally estimate the state vector at time t, based on the information available at time t (i.e. observations up to and including Y_t). What makes the operation difficult is the fact that the states (e.g. the sensitivities) are not constant but change over time. The assumed amount of observation noise versus system noise is used by the filter to optimally determine how much of the variation in Y_t should be attributed to the system, and how much is caused by observation

---

[16] Hence the random trend specification of the stochastic regression model can be expressed as a system of three equations: (1) $\mathbf{Y}_t = \mathbf{X}_t \beta_t + \varepsilon_t$, (2) $\beta_t = \beta_{t-1} + \delta_{t-1} + \eta_{t,1}$ and (3) $\delta_t = \delta_{t-1} + \eta_{t,2}$.

noise. The filter consists of a system of equations which allows us to update the estimate of the state s_t when new observations become available.

Equations (7.22) to (7.31) describe the Kalman filter.[17] These equations are important to the more technical readers who want to develop and implement the model. Other readers may want to skip these equations and directly move to the more intuitive example given later.

The first two equations define the state $\hat{s}_{t|t}$ (equation (7.22)) and the state error covariance matrix $\mathbf{P}_{t|t}$ (equation (7.23)):

$$\hat{s}_{t|t} = \mathrm{E}(s_t | Y_1, \ldots, Y_t) \tag{7.22}$$

$$\mathbf{P}_{t|t} = \mathrm{E}((s_t - \hat{s}_{t|t})(s_t - \hat{s}_{t|t})') = \mathrm{Var}(s_t - \hat{s}_{t|t}) \tag{7.23}$$

where the notation $\hat{a}_{b|c}$ denotes an estimate of a at time b conditional on the information available at time c.

The predicted state of sensitivities $\hat{s}_{t|t-1}$ and the corresponding forecasting error covariance matrix $\mathbf{P}_{t|t-1} = \mathrm{E}((s_t - \hat{s}_{t|t-1})(s_t - \hat{s}_{t|t-1})')$ are given by the *prediction equations* (7.24) and (7.25):

$$\hat{s}_{t|t-1} = \mathbf{\Phi}\hat{s}_{t-1|t-1} + \mathbf{c}_t \tag{7.24}$$

$$\mathbf{P}_{t|t-1} = \mathbf{\Phi}\mathbf{P}_{t-1|t-1}\mathbf{\Phi}' + \mathbf{Q}_t \tag{7.25}$$

and the predicted dependent variable is given by equation (7.26):

$$\hat{\mathbf{Y}}_{t|t-1} = \mathbf{H}_t\hat{s}_{t|t-1} + \mathbf{d} \tag{7.26}$$

The *forecast error* $\mathbf{e}_t$ at time t and its variance f_t can be calculated by equations (7.27) and (7.28) respectively:

$$\mathbf{e}_t = \mathbf{Y}_t - \hat{\mathbf{Y}}_{t|t-1} \tag{7.27}$$

$$f_{t|t-1} = \mathbf{\Phi}\mathbf{P}_{t|t-1}\mathbf{\Phi}' + R_t \tag{7.28}$$

The new information is represented by the prediction error, $\mathbf{e}_t$. It can be the result of several factors: random fluctuations in returns, changes in underlying states, or error in previous state estimates. Given this new information, the estimate $\hat{s}_{t|t}$ of the state vector and its covariance $\mathbf{P}_{t|t}$ can now be updated through the *updating equations* (7.29) and (7.30) respectively. The Kalman filter uses the new information for adjusting the estimates of the underlying states, where the new information is simply the prediction error of the returns. The Kalman gain matrix, $\mathbf{K}_t$, optimally adjusts the state estimates in order to reflect the new information:

$$\hat{s}_{t|t} = \hat{s}_{t|t-1} + \mathbf{K}_t\mathbf{e}_t \tag{7.29}$$

$$\mathbf{P}_{t|t} = (\mathbf{I} - \mathbf{K}_t\mathbf{H}_t')\mathbf{P}_{t|t-1} \tag{7.30}$$

The Kalman gain matrix is calculated from the observation noise variance R_t and the predicted state error covariance $\mathbf{P}_{t|t-1}$ with the recursive equation (7.31):

$$\mathbf{K}_t = \mathbf{\Phi}\mathbf{P}_{t|t-1}\mathbf{H}_t'(\mathbf{H}_t\mathbf{P}_{t|t-1}\mathbf{H}_t' + R_t)^{-1} \tag{7.31}$$

---

[17] Further explanations can be found in Harvey (1989) or Gouriéroux *et al.* (1997).

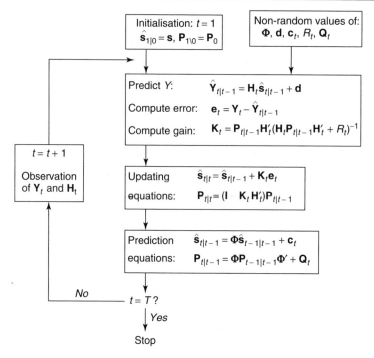

Figure 7.8 Flowchart of the Kalman filter

In order to clarify the sequence of the Kalman filter equations, Figure 7.8 presents a flowchart for the filter.

The recursive nature of the Kalman filter is a major computational advantage. It enables the model to update the conditional mean and covariance estimates of the states at time t based on the sole estimate obtained at time $t - 1$. Although it takes into account the entire history, it does not need an expanding memory.

For an intuitive understanding of the principles involved, let us consider the example of the time-varying sensitivity (which follows a random walk) of a dependent variable Y_t to a single independent variable X_t. The familiar regression equation is:

$$Y_t = b_t X_t + \varepsilon_t \qquad \text{for } t = 1, \dots, T \qquad (7.32)$$

which can be represented in a state space form, using the random walk specification:

$$\begin{aligned} Y_t &= b_t X_t + \varepsilon_t \\ b_t &= b_{t-1} + \eta_t \end{aligned} \qquad \text{for } t = 1, \dots, T \qquad (7.33)$$

with $\text{Var}(\varepsilon_t) = R$ and $\text{Var}(\eta_t) = Q$. We can recognise the observation and transition equations (7.14) and (7.15) with $\mathbf{s}_t = b_t$, $\mathbf{H}_t = X_t$, $\mathbf{\Phi} = 1$, $\mathbf{d} = 0$, $\mathbf{c}_t = 0$.

Upon presentation of a new observation X_t of X, the model expects to observe a value $b_{t|t-1} X_t$ of Y based on its predicted state[18] $b_{t|t-1}$. However, the observed value Y_t of the

---

[18] As the sensitivity coefficient b is assumed to follow a random walk the predicted state is equal to the last estimate $b_{t-1|t-1}$ of the state resulting from all available information at time $t - 1$.

dependent variable Y is likely to be different from the model's expectation. This forecast error may result from two sources:

- Some unpredictable force temporarily affects the dependent variable. This random noise should not affect the state.
- The true value of the sensitivity of Y to X has changed (structural change). This is not a temporary disturbance and affects the state.

The purpose of the Kalman filter is to attribute some share of the prediction error to each of these two sources, i.e. separate the signal from the noise. The relative magnitude of the system noise variance Q and the observation noise variance R is therefore an important parameter of the model. The following equations correspond to the various stages of the Kalman filter for the random walk specification.[19]
The prediction equations:

$$\hat{b}_{t|t-1} = \hat{b}_{t-1|t-1}$$

$$P_{t|t-1} = P_{t-1|t-1} + Q \tag{7.34}$$

The updating equations:

$$\hat{b}_{t|t} = \hat{b}_{t|t-1} + k_t(Y_t - \hat{b}_{t|t-1}X_t)$$

$$P_{t|t} = (1 - k_t)P_{t|t-1} \tag{7.35}$$

$$k_t = \frac{P_{t|t-1}X_t^2}{P_{t|t-1}X_t^2 + R}$$

The sensitivity estimate $\hat{b}_{t|t}$ is updated by taking into account the forecast error. The fraction of forecast error that is added to the previous estimate of b is the Kalman gain k_t. Its value is in the interval [0,1], with zero corresponding to $Q = 0$ and one corresponding to $R = 0$. The Kalman gain depends on the relative value of observation and system noises and on the estimated variance of the state. For small values of k_t (large observation noise R compared to system noise Q and/or small uncertainty about the state estimate), considerable credibility is given to the previous sensitivity and as a result to remote observations. The sensitivity coefficient b_t evolves smoothly over time.

In contrast, if k_t takes larger values (i.e. large system noise Q compared to observation noise R and/or large uncertainty about the state estimate), then more credibility is given to recent observations and therefore less weight is given to recent sensitivity estimates. In this case, the sensitivity coefficient b_t evolves quickly over time and its volatility increases.

In order to understand well the effect of the ratio between system and observation noise variance, let us consider an example where the sensitivity coefficient, beta, is constant over the data set except for a short time period (5 days) during which it takes an unusually high value. This pattern may be created, for example, by incorrect market expectations motivated by unfounded rumours. A Kalman filter is used to estimate the time-varying sensitivity. Three different signal to noise ratios (Q/R) are applied. For a ratio of 1

---

[19] The notation $\hat{a}_{b|c}$ denotes an estimate of a at time b conditional on the information available at time c.

(Figure 7.9), the model rapidly adapts to the jump in sensitivity. However, this quick reaction comes at a cost of increased volatility in the beta estimates and of a large standard error. If the signal to noise ratio is decreased to a value of 0.1 (Figure 7.10), the *beta* estimates become smoother and the confidence bands narrower. The model seems to be more reliable, although it does not adapt quickly enough to the shift in beta occurring at time $t = 90$. If Q/R is set to a small value, such as 0.02 (Figure 7.11), beta estimates become very smooth and the confidence bands become very small. However, with such a small ratio, the model does not manage to properly track the sensitivity when it jumps to a high level. It is also interesting to see how the standard error, i.e. $P_{t|t}$, decreases after a few observations. This is because the initial value of $P_{t|t-1}$ (i.e. $P_{1|0}$) was deliberately chosen to be large so that the system could rapidly adjust the value of *beta* in order to match the observations.

This model is available in the sensitivity estimation tool pack. Select "Stochastic parameter regression" in the main menu to enter the submenu displayed in Figure 7.12. Select "Random walk". Make sure that the "Estimate parameters" check box is unchecked.

The stochastic parameter regression menu proposes both a random walk model and a random trend model for the underlying sensitivities. The system and observation noise variance can be set by the user (option B), in which case a reference to the cells containing the values has to be entered in the corresponding text box.[20] The system noise variances can also be set to a multiple of the observation noise variance (option A). In this case, the user sets the desired signal to noise ratio in the edit box. An alternative way is to let the system estimate the optimal values of the parameters from the data. The estimation

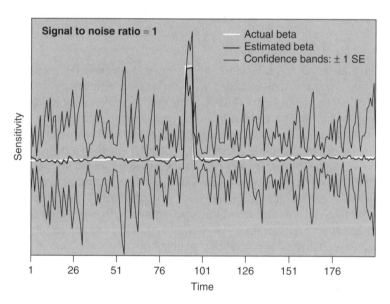

Figure 7.9 Actual versus estimated beta. The system noise to observation noise ratio, Q/R, is 1. This ratio allows the Kalman filter to rapidly adapt to the jump in sensitivity. However, this quick reaction comes at a cost of increased volatility in the *beta* estimates and of a very large standard error

---

[20] Unless the user has a good prior knowledge of the values to be entered in these cells (on the "Example" sheet, range "F2:F5"), we do not recommend using this option.

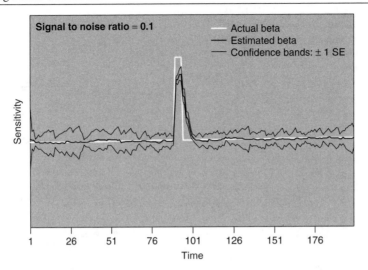

Figure 7.10 Actual versus estimated beta. Q/R is now 0.1. The beta estimates are smoother and their standard errors smaller. However, the model seems to adapt more slowly to the sensitivity jump

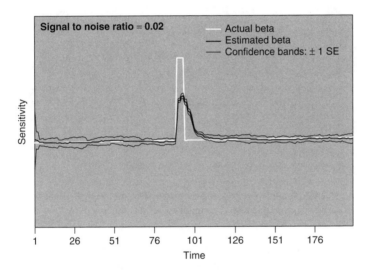

Figure 7.11 Actual versus estimated beta. For $Q/R = 0.02$, beta estimates are very smooth and their standard errors are much smaller. This is because variations in co-movements of X_t and Y_t are attributed to fluke rather than to true variations in beta

procedure is described later in the chapter. Figure 7.13 shows the results of the random walk model for a signal to noise ratio of 1.

While models 1 and 2 use values for the R and Q variances that are constant over the data set, model 3 ("Intervention analysis") enables users to apply their own time-varying R and Q values. This is achieved by specifying the range containing additive noise variances (i.e. R and Q time series). This enables the user to force the model to

Model 3: Stochastic Parameter Regression (Kalman Filtering)   [?] [X]

Model for Sensitivity Time Structure:

Variances of sensitivity levels (Q) are:

    A ◉ All set equal to   [1] ⬍

⦿ Random Walk (1)

    B ○ R & Q Set manually in Range   [$F$2:$F$5] 📊

Variances of sensitivity levels and trends (Q) are:

    A ○ All set equal to: *Trend* [1] ⬍   *Level* [1] ⬍

○ Stochastic Trend (2)

    B ◉ R & Q Set manually in Ranges   [$F$2:$G$5] 📊

    ○ Random Walk Model (1)   ⦿ Random Trend Model (2)

○ Intervention Analysis (3)   *Intervention Time series* [$N$3:$Q$117] 📊

☐ Estimate Parameters (Initial values set in A or B)   [Estimation Options]

Output range   [$F$2] 📊   [Help] [Exit All] [Cancel] [OK]
for parameters

Figure 7.12   The stochastic parameter regression menu of the tool pack

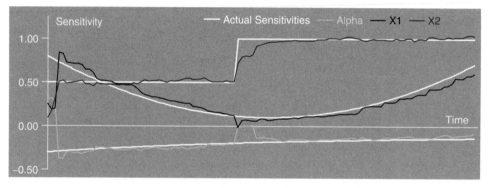

Figure 7.13   Stochastic parameter regression example. The underlying sensitivities are assumed to follow a random walk (model 1) and the signal to noise ratio is set to 1

rapidly adapt to important events (by increasing Q during this period) or, on the contrary, to make the model insensitive to irrelevant events (by increasing R during this period). For instance, if the system noise variance Q is increased for variable X_2 at time $t = 52$ (cell "Q54" is set to a large number (e.g. 50)), the model adapts rapidly to the level shift in β_2 and models almost perfectly the actual factor sensitivities. The result of this model is displayed in Figure 7.14.[21]

---

[21] Model 3 should only be used to force the model to take prior knowledge into account. In general columns N to Q in the "Example" sheet should be set to zero unless the user wants to modulate the adaptation speed of the model by increasing the credibility attributed to some observations (by putting a positive number for the additive Q values) or by decreasing this credibility (by putting a positive number for the additive R value). The values to be entered are discretionary and depend on the user's perception of the event's importance. The bigger the value the more it will alter the model's adaptation speed for the corresponding period.

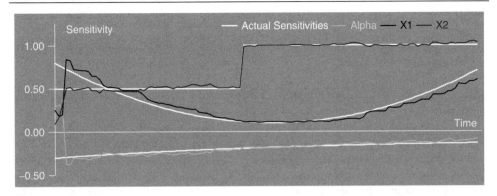

Figure 7.14 Example of the stochastic parameter regression using model 3. The underlying sensitivities are assumed to follow a random walk with system noise added at $t = 52$ (time of level shift in b_2). The signal to noise ratio is still set to 1. The fit is almost perfect as the model is forced to adapt to the level shift

The reader should now be familiar with the functioning of the Kalman filter. This adaptive procedure optimally computes the current state of the model (i.e. the factor sensitivities and their covariance matrix) given the previous state and some hyper-parameters such as system and observation noise variances. Two important questions remain unanswered: (i) how do we determine the initial state of the model?, (ii) how do we best set the values for the hyper-parameters?

The initial distribution of the state vector (mean s and covariance P_0) can be set in several ways. The simplest is to use prior knowledge. For instance, one can start with a prior value of 1 for a stock's beta, and a prior value of 0 for the sensitivity of the return to exchange rates. A popular alternative is to estimate sensitivities (and their covariance matrix) from a subsample of the data by OLS. However, this may use too many observations from the data sample and we have already shown the shortcomings of OLS estimation in cases where sensitivities are not constant. The model provided in the tool pack uses a diffuse prior (see Harvey (1989)). A diffuse prior corresponds to an infinite covariance matrix P_0 (i.e. $P_0^{-1} = 0$) so that no credibility is given to the initial state estimate, letting the Kalman filter estimate the states from the data. Practically, however, a large initial covariance matrix is used rather than an infinite one. P_0 is given by equation (7.36):

$$P_0 = \kappa I \qquad (7.36)$$

κ being equal to a large but finite number (e.g. 100 000). In the case of a diffuse prior, the mean of the initial state distribution, s, is irrelevant as long as it is finite. We use a value of zero for all state variables. The use of a diffuse prior can be viewed as a way to let the filter estimate the initial values from the first observations.

Because a diffuse prior is used, little information needs to be supplied by the user. Once the time series model for the sensitivities and the values for the *hyper-parameters* Φ, Q, R, d and c have been chosen, the adaptive model optimally estimates the sensitivities. The values for these parameters can be set by the user but they can also be estimated from the data. The model provided in the tool pack supports an optimisation algorithm in order to find the "best" parameters.[22]

Given the hyper-parameters, the Kalman filter derives recursive values for the factor sensitivities and their covariance. Hence, the model provides predictions of the dependent variable and residuals can be computed, conditional on the hyper-parameter values. A suitable maximisation routine can then be used to maximise the likelihood of observing the data.

Maximum likelihood estimation consists of finding an estimate of the unknown parameter vector θ such that it maximises the likelihood of generating the data that were actually observed. In other words, given the sample of observations Y_t, finding a solution for θ that maximises the joint density probability function $\mathcal{L}(\mathbf{Y}, \theta)$. As observations are not independent in a time series model, the joint density function is not the usual product of probability density function corresponding to each observation. Instead, conditional probability density functions are used to write the joint density function:

$$\mathcal{L}(\mathbf{Y}, \theta) = \prod_{t=1}^{T} p(Y_t | Y_1, Y_2, \ldots, Y_{t-1}) \tag{7.37}$$

The disturbances and the initial state vector following a multivariate normal distribution by assumption, the conditional density functions $p(Y_t | Y_1, Y_2, \ldots, Y_{t-1})$ are also normal. The means $\hat{Y}_{t|t-1}$ and variances $f_{t|t-1}$ of these normal distributions are given by the Kalman filter equations (7.26) and (7.28). The model having Gaussian residuals e_t, the logarithm of the likelihood function $\mathcal{L}(\mathbf{Y}, \theta)$ – i.e. the log-likelihood function $\log \mathcal{L}(\mathbf{Y}, \theta)$ – can be written in terms of the prediction errors e_t and their variances $f_{t|t-1}$ that have been defined in equations (7.27) and (7.28):

$$\log \mathcal{L}(\theta | Y_1, Y_2, \ldots, Y_T) = -\frac{T}{2} \ln(2\pi) - \frac{1}{2} \sum_{t=1}^{T} \ln(f_{t|t-1}) - \frac{1}{2} \sum_{t=1}^{T} \frac{e_t^2}{f_{t|t-1}} \tag{7.38}$$

The maximum likelihood estimate $\hat{\theta}$ of the parameter vector θ is the value of θ that maximises log-likelihood, i.e.:

$$\hat{\theta} = \arg \max_{\theta} \log \mathcal{L}(\theta | Y_1, Y_2, \ldots, Y_T) \tag{7.39}$$

The Kalman filter algorithm and equation (7.38) are used to compute the log-likelihood for a given value of θ. A numerical optimiser is employed to find the vector θ of hyper-parameters that maximises the log-likelihood function.

The log-likelihood function in equation (7.38) is a non-linear function of the hyper-parameters and, unfortunately, there is no analytical solution θ_{MLE} to the equation

$$\frac{\partial \log \mathcal{L}}{\partial \theta} = 0 \tag{7.40}$$

---

[22] "Best" according to criteria such as prediction mean square error or a likelihood function.

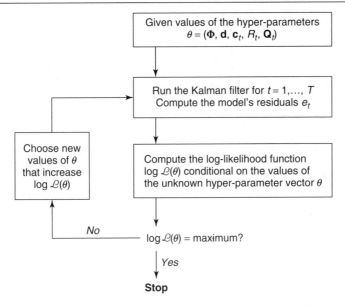

Figure 7.15   The maximum likelihood estimation procedure

A numerical optimisation method for finding the maximum likelihood parameters is therefore employed. This iterative procedure is represented in Figure 7.15.

The critical stage of this procedure is the algorithm used to determine the parameter vector that maximises log-likelihood. There are numerous methods for maximising such a non-linear function. However, they are unequal in terms of convergence speed and dependence on initial parameter values. The optimiser used by the tool pack is based on a quasi-Newton method (see for instance Greene (1977, p. 204)). It usually converges to a minimum within a few iterations.

By checking the "Estimate parameters" check box, the software optimises the R and Q parameters and saves them in the range indicated in the text box. The "Estimation option" button enables the user to select the optimisation criterion (Figure 7.16), mean squared error or log-likelihood.

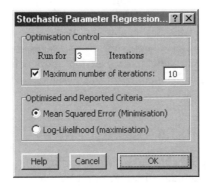

Figure 7.16   The optimisation menu for the stochastic parameter regression. System and observation noise variances can be estimated from the data

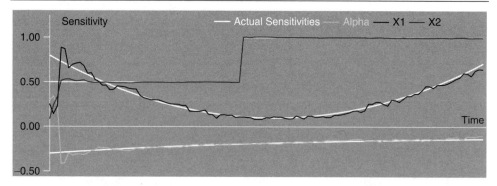

Figure 7.17 This is the result of the stochastic parameter regression using model 3 with optimised parameters. The underlying sensitivities are assumed to follow a random walk with system noise added at $t = 52$ (time of level shift in b_2). The R and Q values have been computed by maximum likelihood estimation

Once the hyper-parameters of the model are estimated, the procedure runs the Kalman filter one last time to compute the sensitivities. The R and Q values are saved on the spreadsheet. The result of the optimised model is displayed in Figure 7.17.

Given the optimised hyper-parameters, the stochastic parameter model can be expressed as:

$$Y(t) = \alpha(t) + \beta_1(t)X_1(t) + \beta_2(t)X_2(t) + \varepsilon(t)$$

$$\text{where} \quad \alpha(t) = \alpha(t - 1) + \eta_1(t), \text{Var}(\eta_1) = 1.11\text{E-}04 \text{ (cell "F3")}$$

$$\beta_1(t) = \beta_1(t - 1) + \eta_2(t), \text{Var}(\eta_2) = 6.02\text{E-}04 \text{ (cell "F4")}$$

$$\beta_2(t) = \beta_2(t - 1) + \eta_3(t), \text{Var}(\eta_3) = 8.73\text{E-}08 \text{ (cell "F5")}$$

$$\text{Var}(\varepsilon) = 1.30\text{E-}08 \text{ (cell "F2")}$$

For instance for $t = 50$, we have:

$$Y = -0.19 + 0.11X_1 + 0.50X_2 + \varepsilon \text{ (cells J52:L52)}$$

The reader will find it a useful and rewarding exercise to play with the provided example. Experimenting with different hyper-parameter values or injecting additional system noise through the intervention analysis will enable the user to get a good understanding of the functioning of the Kalman filter. Comparing the estimates from the various models (i.e. unweighted rolling regression, weighted regression and stochastic parameter regression) will give the reader a good understanding of the strengths and weaknesses of the various approaches.

7.6 CONCLUSION

This chapter has described three methods for estimating time-varying factor models. The third approach, based on Kalman filtering, is clearly superior to rolling regressions or time-weighted regressions. As the reader would probably have realised when using the software provided, the computational complexity of the Kalman filter can easily be handed over to a computer program. As a result, the stochastic parameter regression model can be used as easily as the less accurate rolling regression approach.

The advantage of adaptive models such as the stochastic parameter regression model resides in its capability to estimate the dynamics of the underlying factor sensitivities. This enables one to predict ahead risk exposures rather than merely measure their past average. Given the many applications of factor modelling and time series regression analysis in equity management, stochastic parameter regression models should prove a useful addition to the asset manager's toolbox.

REFERENCES

Bollerslev, T. (1986), "Generalised Autoregressive Conditional Heteroskedasticity", *Journal of Econometrics*, **31**, 307–327.

Gouriéroux, C., A. Monfort and G. Gallo (1997), *Time Series and Dynamic Models*, Cambridge University Press, Cambridge.

Greene, W. H. (1977), *Econometric Analysis*, 3rd edition, Prentice Hall, Englewood Cliffs, NJ.

Harvey, A. C. (1989), *Forecasting, Structural Time Series Models and the Kalman Filter*, Cambridge University Press, Cambridge.

Kalman, R. E. (1960), "A New Approach to Linear Filtering and Prediction Problems", *Journal of Basic Engineering, Transactions ASMA*, Series D, **82** (1), 35–45.

Pindyck, R. S. and D. L. Rubinfeld (1998), *Econometric Models and Economic Forecasts*, 4th edition, McGraw-Hill, New York.

Rosenberg, B. (1973), "Random Coefficients Models: The Analysis of a Cross Section of Time Series by Stochastically Convergent Parameter Regression", *Annals of Social and Economic Measurement*, **2** (4), 399–428.

Schaefer, S., R. Brealey, S. Hodges and H. Thomas (1975), "Alternative Models of Systematic Risk", in E. Elton and M. Gruber (eds), *International Capital Markets: An Inter and Intra Country Analysis*, North-Holland, Amsterdam, pp. 150–161.

8

Stochastic Volatility Models: A Survey with Applications to Option Pricing and Value at Risk*

MONICA BILLIO AND DOMENICO SARTORE

ABSTRACT

This chapter presents an introduction to the current literature on stochastic volatility models. For these models the volatility depends on some unobserved components or a latent structure.

Given the time-varying volatility exhibited by most financial data, in the last two decades there has been a growing interest in time series models of changing variance and the literature on stochastic volatility models has expanded greatly. Clearly, this chapter cannot be exhaustive, however we discuss some of the most important ideas, focusing on the simplest forms of the techniques and models used in the literature.

The chapter is organised as follows. Section 8.1 considers some motivations for stochastic volatility models: empirical stylised facts, pricing of contingent assets and risk evaluation. While Section 8.2 presents models of changing volatility, Section 8.3 focuses on stochastic volatility models and distinguishes between models with continuous and discrete volatility, the latter depending on a hidden Markov chain. Section 8.4 is devoted to the estimation problem which is still an open question, then a wide range of possibility is given. Sections 8.5 and 8.6 introduce some extensions and multivariate models. Finally, in Section 8.7 an estimation program is presented and some possible applications to option pricing and risk evaluation are discussed.

Readers interested in the practical utilisation of stochastic volatility models and in the applications can skip Section 8.4.3 without hindering comprehension.

8.1 INTRODUCTION

In the last two decades there has been a growing interest in time series models of changing variance, given the time-varying volatility exhibited by most financial data. In fact, the empirical distributions of financial time series differ substantially from distributions obtained from sampling independent homoskedastic Gaussian variables. Unconditional density functions exhibit leptokurtosis and skewness; time series of financial returns show

---

* We gratefully acknowledge help from Michele Gobbo, Massimiliano Caporin and Andrea Giacomelli.

Applied Quantitative Methods for Trading and Investment. Edited by C.L. Dunis, J. Laws and P. Naïm
© 2003 John Wiley & Sons, Ltd ISBN: 0-470-84885-5

evidence of volatility clustering; and squared returns exhibit pronounced serial correlation whereas little or no serial dependence can be detected in the return process itself.

These empirical regularities suggest that the behaviour of financial time series may be captured by a model which recognises the time-varying nature of return volatility, as follows:

$$y_t = \mu_t + \sigma_t \varepsilon_t \qquad \varepsilon_t \sim IID(0, 1), \quad t = 1, 2, \ldots, T$$

where y_t denotes the return on an asset. A common way of modelling σ_t is to express it as a deterministic function of the squares of lagged residuals. Econometric specifications of this form are known as ARCH models and have achieved widespread popularity in applied empirical research (see Bollerslev et al. (1992, 1993), Bera and Higgins (1993)).

Alternatively, volatility may be modelled as an unobserved component following some latent stochastic process, such as an autoregression. The resulting models are called stochastic volatility (SV) models and have been the focus of considerable attention in recent years (Taylor, 1994; Ghysels et al., 1996; Shephard, 1996). These models present two main advantages over ARCH models. The first one is their solid theoretical background, as they can be interpreted as discretised versions of stochastic volatility continuous-time models put forward by modern finance theory (see Hull and White (1987)). The second is their ability to generalise from univariate to multivariate series in a more natural way, as far as their estimation and interpretation are concerned. On the other hand, SV models are more difficult to estimate than ARCH models, due to the fact that it is not easy to derive their exact likelihood function. For this reason, a number of econometric methods have been proposed to solve the problem of estimation of SV models.

The literature on SV models has expanded greatly in the last 10 years, reaching considerable proportions; this chapter cannot therefore be exhaustive. We prefer to discuss some of the most important ideas, focusing on the simplest forms of the techniques and models used in the literature, referring the reader elsewhere for generalisations and technicalities. In the organisation of the structure of the present chapter, we have been inspired by the paper of Shephard (1996), who gave a very interesting survey on SV models updated to 1995.

To start, we will consider some motivations for stochastic volatility models: empirical stylised facts, pricing of contingent assets and risk evaluation.

8.1.1 Empirical stylised facts

To illustrate the models and to develop the examples we will work with three European stock indexes: the FTSE100, the CAC40 and the MIB30, which are market indexes for the London, Paris and Milan equity markets. These series run from 4 January 1999 to 12 August 2002, yielding 899 daily observations.

Throughout we will work with the compounded return[1] on the series

$$y_t = \log(x_t/x_{t-1})$$

---

[1] An advantage of using a return series is that it helps in making the time series stationary, a useful statistical property (see footnote 4).

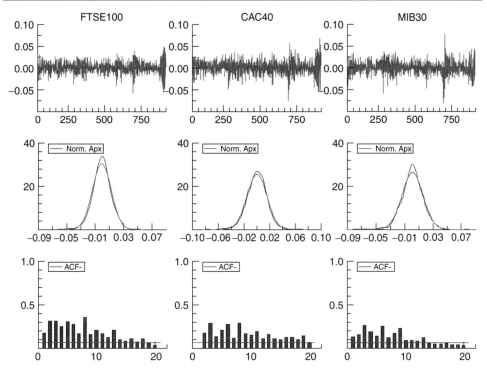

Figure 8.1 Summaries of the daily returns on three European stock indexes: the FTSE100, the CAC40 and the MIB30. Summaries are: time series of returns, non-parametric density estimate and normal approximation, correlogram of squared returns

where x_t is the value of the stock index. Figure 8.1 displays some summaries of these three series. The raw time series of y_t suggests that there are periods of volatility clustering: days of large movements are followed by days with the same characteristics. This is confirmed by the use of a correlogram on y_t^2, also reported in Figure 8.1, which shows significant correlations existing at quite extended lag lengths. This suggests that y_t^2 may follow a process close to an ARMA(1,1), for a simple AR process cannot easily combine the persistence in shocks with the low correlation. A correlogram of y_t shows little activity and so is not given in this figure.

Figure 8.1 also gives a density estimate of the unconditional distribution of y_t together with the corresponding normal approximation.[2] This suggests that y_t is leptokurtic. This is confirmed by Table 8.1, which reports an estimate of the excess of kurtosis with respect to the normal distribution, which is significantly positive.

Table 8.1 also reports the Jarque–Bera test for normality and the asymmetry coefficients evidencing that the distributions are negatively skewed, partially due to the period of analysis, and for all three the null hypothesis of normality is clearly rejected.

These stylised facts can be summarised as follows: non-significant serial correlation in the levels of returns; volatility clustering, which implies a significant and positive serial correlation in the squares y_t^2; heavy tails and persistence of volatility.

---

[2] The graphs are produced with the Ox software using some of its basic commands and default options. See also Section 8.7.1.

Table 8.1 Summary statistics for the daily returns in Figure 8.1. In parentheses: the p-value of the Jarque–Bera test

	FTSE100	CAC40	MIB30
Mean	−0.03634	−0.000219	−0.04313
Standard deviation	0.001463	0.015630	0.001689
Asymmetry	−0.2574	−0.223998	−0.23383
Excess of kurtosis	1.547015	4.624507	2.268374
Jarque–Bera test	97 (0.00)	106 (0.00)	197 (0.00)

Finally, there is some evidence that stock markets share periods of high volatility. This suggests that multivariate models will be important.

8.1.2 Pricing contingent assets

Consider an asset C, with expiring date $t + \tau$, which is a function of a generic underlying security S. Assume now that S can be described by the following geometric diffusion process:

$$dS = \mu S dt + \sigma S dz$$

so that $d \log S = (\mu - \sigma^2/2)\, dt + \sigma dz$. Economists term such an asset C as "contingent" or "derivative". A primary example of a derivative is an option, which gives the owner the ability but not the obligation to trade the underlying security at a given price K, called the strike price, in the future. European call options are the most known: the owner can buy the underlying asset at the strike price K only when the call expires, i.e. at date $t + \tau$. Its value at the expiration date will be:

$$C_t + \tau = \max(S_{t+\tau} - K, 0)$$

Its purchase value at time t is as yet unknown, but can be determined in different ways. One of these consists of calculating the discounted expected value of the option at time $t + \tau$.

$$\exp(-r\tau) E_{S_{t+\tau}|S_t}[\max(S_{t+\tau} - K, 0)]$$

where r is the risk-free interest rate. However, this completely ignores the fact that this is a risky asset and traders expect higher returns than on riskless assets. This is the reason why the discounted expected value is not considered by the market as a correct method to evaluate an asset. To avoid this inconvenience it is opportune to introduce a utility function into the pricing of options, letting the dealers choose the risk–expected gain combination they prefer.

It turns out that the added complexity of a utility function can be avoided by assuming continuous and costless trading. This statement can be shown by creating a particular portfolio, which by construction is made up of owning θ of the underlying shares and by borrowing a single contingent asset C. If the investor properly selects θ at each time, the stochastic component of the process disappears and ensures the portfolio has a riskless dynamic, making its return a deterministic function of time (see Black and

Scholes (1973)). As time passes, the portfolio will have to be continually adjusted to maintain risklessness, hence the need for continuous costless trading.

The return of this portfolio must be equal to the riskless interest rate r because the portfolio itself is risk-free, otherwise traders will have an arbitrage opportunity. This condition is necessary to obtain the stochastic differential equation followed by the contingent asset:

$$\frac{\partial C}{\partial t} + \frac{1}{2}\frac{\partial^2 C}{\partial S \partial S}\sigma^2 S^2 + r\frac{\partial C}{\partial S}S = rC \quad \text{with end condition } C = \max(S - K, 0)$$

This equation is quite easy to solve and does not depend on the mean parameter μ nor on the risk preferences of the traders. Whatever the risk preferences may be, the evaluation of the option does not change. When solving the equation, risk-neutral preferences are used to simplify calculations. With instantaneous variance σ^2, the following Black–Scholes valuation formula is obtained:

$$C_t^{\text{BS}}(\sigma^2) = S_t \Phi(d) - K e^{-r\tau} \Phi(d - \sigma\sqrt{\tau}) \quad \text{where} \quad d = \frac{\log(S_t/K) + (r + \sigma^2/2)\tau}{\sigma\sqrt{\tau}}$$

Note that σ^2 is the only unknown parameter: S_t and r are observed, while τ and K are usually given by institutional norms. The price depends strictly on σ^2 which is more important than the drift, as is often the case in finance, so that the price of the option can be considered an indicator of the volatility of the underlying asset.

Empirically, the Black–Scholes formula can be used in two ways: either by estimating σ^2 (the historical volatility) and then calculating the option price or by using real prices to determine a value for σ^2 (called implied volatility).

This type of analysis has a considerable shortcoming: the basic assumption that stock returns follow a geometric diffusion process is a poor one, as indicated in Figure 8.1, and can affect the valuation formula, reducing the precision of the option pricing. This realisation has prompted theoretical work into option pricing theory under various changing volatility regimes. The leading paper in this field is Hull and White (1987), to which we will return later.

8.1.3 Risk evaluation

VaR (Value at Risk) is the maximum amount that is expected to be lost over some target period, i.e. the maximum likely loss. It is a statistical risk measure and represents a percentile of the probability distribution of the variable of interest.

Generally speaking, VaR can be analytically defined as follows. Let x_t be a random variable of interest measure and $F_x(x_t)$ its cumulative distribution function:

$$a = \text{Prob}(x_t \leq \overline{x}_t) = F_x(\overline{x}_t) = \int_{-\infty}^{\overline{x}_t} f(x_t)\, dx_t$$

VaR is the percentile defined by the relation:

$$\text{VaR}_x(1 - a) = x_t^* = F_{x_t}^{-1}(a)$$

where $(1 - a)$ is the VaR confidence level, for instance 95% or 99%, and $F_{x_t}^{-1}(a)$ is the inverse of the cumulative distribution function.

Given its generality, the VaR method can be applied for different types of risk measurement, such as market risk, credit risk, operational risk and commodity risk (see Alexander (1996)). Moreover, for its versatility, VaR allows us to obtain an intuitive risk measure, to define homogeneous risk measures that permit a comparison among different financial instruments, to determine limiting positions and to construct risk-adjusted profitability measures.

Let us concentrate on its application to market risk. Market risk means the possibility that an unexpected variation of market factors (interest rates, exchange rates, stock prices, etc.) causes an increase or a reduction in the value of a position or in the value of a financial portfolio. VaR, in this context, is the maximum expected loss of a marketable financial instruments portfolio which could be experienced, for a specified time horizon period and a specified confidence level.

We now consider a general portfolio model which allows us to set all the hypotheses discriminating a risk measurement model like VaR in a systematic manner, by paying particular attention to the role of the volatility.

Let x_τ be a random variable which represents the value of a portfolio in a future period τ. It is defined by the following relation:

$$x_\tau = \sum_{i=1}^{N} w_{i,t} P_{i,\tau}$$

where the random variables $P_{i,\tau}$ represent the future value of the N assets in the portfolio and $w_{i,t}$ are their weights at time t. If we suppose that the N assets will be subjected to K risk market factors $\chi_{j,\tau}$, the future value of the portfolio can be expressed as a function of the K stochastic risk factors by the following pricing formula:

$$x_\tau = \sum_{i=1}^{N} w_{i,t} P_{i,\tau}(\chi_{1,\tau}, \ldots, \chi_{K,\tau})$$

The hypothesis characterising the model therefore concerns: the endogenous variable choice; the pricing formula; the risk factors definition and their distributions; the risk factors volatility; the risk factors mapping; the confidence level and the choice of the time horizon.

In the literature, the following approaches are suggested to estimate the VaR (Best, 1998): parametric methods; historical simulation; Monte Carlo simulation; stress testing. Concerning the parametric methods and the Monte Carlo simulation, it is crucial to properly describe the volatility dynamics of the risk factors to obtain correct estimates of the VaR (see, for example, Lehar et al. (2002)).

8.2 MODELS OF CHANGING VOLATILITY

Following Cox (1981) and Shephard (1996) models of changing volatility can be usefully partitioned into observation-driven and parameter-driven models. They both can be generally expressed using the following parametric framework:

$$y_t | z_t \sim N(\mu_t, \sigma_t^2)$$

where μ_t is often set equal to zero (as we do not intend to focus on that feature of the model).

In the first class, i.e. in observation-driven models, z_t is a function of lagged values of y_t. The autoregressive conditional heteroskedasticity (ARCH) models introduced by Engle (1982) are the most representative example of observation-driven models. They describe the variance as a linear function of the squares of past observations:

$$\sigma_t^2 = \alpha_0 + \alpha_1 y_{t-1}^2 + \cdots + \alpha_p y_{t-p}^2$$

and so the model is defined by the conditional density (one-step-ahead forecast density):

$$y_t | Y^{t-1} \sim N(0, \sigma_t^2)$$

where Y^{t-1} is the set of observations up to time $t - 1$. This allows today's variance to depend on the variability of recent observations and then one type of shock alone drives both the series itself and its volatility.

The use of models described by their one-step-ahead forecast offers remarkable advantages that are worth being highlighted. First, the likelihood expression can be simply obtained by combining these densities, making the estimation and testing easy to handle, at least in principle. Second, conditional densities imply the use of conditional moments which are used widely to specify finance theory, although this is conditional on economic agents', if not econometricians', information. Finally, the observation-driven models parallel the autoregressive and moving average ones which are commonly used for models of changing means.

In the second class, i.e. in parameter-driven (or parameter dynamic latent variable or state space) models, z_t is a function of an unobserved or latent component. The log-normal stochastic volatility model created by Taylor (1986) is the simplest and best-known example:

$$y_t | h_t \sim N(0, \exp(h_t)) \qquad h_t = \alpha + \beta h_{t-1} + \eta_t, \qquad \eta_t \sim NID(0, \sigma_\eta^2) \qquad (8.1)$$

where h_t represents the log-volatility, which is unobserved but can be estimated using the observations. With respect to the previous class, these models are driven by two types of shock, one of which influences the volatility (i.e. conditional variance equations). These models parallel the Gaussian state space models of means dealt with by Kalman (1960).

In spite of this, a shortcoming of parameter-driven volatility models is that they generally lack analytic one-step-ahead forecast densities $y^t | Y^{t-1}$, unlike the models of the mean which fit into the Gaussian state space form. Hence either an approximation or a numerically intensive method is required to deal with these models.

Although SV models are harder to handle statistically than the corresponding observation-driven models, there are still some good reasons for investigating them. We will see that their properties are easier to find, understand, manipulate and generalise to the multivariate case. They also have simpler analogous continuous time representations, which is important given that much modern finance employs diffusions. An example of this is the work by Hull and White (1987) which uses a log-normal SV model, replacing the discrete time AR(1) for h_t with an Ornstein–Uhlenbeck process.

8.3   STOCHASTIC VOLATILITY MODELS

For these models the volatility depends on some unobserved components or a latent structure. One interpretation for the latent h_t is to represent the random and uneven flow of new
information, which is very difficult to model directly, into financial markets (Clark, 1973).
The most popular of these parameter-driven stochastic volatility models, from Taylor
(1986), puts

$$\begin{cases} y_t = \varepsilon_t \exp(h_t/2) \\ h_t = \alpha + \beta h_{t-1} + \eta_t \end{cases} \tag{8.2}$$

where ε_t and η_t are two independent Gaussian white noises, with variances 1 and σ_η^2,
respectively. Due to the Gaussianity of η_t, this model is called a log-normal SV model.

Another possible interpretation for h_t is to characterise the regime in which financial
markets are operating and then it could be described by a discrete valued variable. The
most popular approach to modelling changes in regime is the class of Markov switching
models introduced by Hamilton (1989) in the econometrics literature. In that case the
simplest model is:[3]

$$\begin{cases} y_t = \varepsilon_t \exp(h_t/2) \\ h_t = \alpha + \beta s_t \end{cases} \tag{8.3}$$

where s_t is a two-state first-order Markov chain which can take values 0, 1 and is independent of ε_t. The value of the time series s_t, for all t, depends only on the last value
s_{t-1}, i.e. for $i, j = 0, 1$:

$$P(s_t = j | s_{t-1} = i, s_{t-2} = i, \ldots) = P(s_t = j | s_{t-1} = i) = p_{ij}$$

The probabilities $(p_{ij})_{i,j=0,1}$ are called transition probabilities of moving from one state
to the other. Obviously, we get that:

$$p_{00} + p_{01} = p_{10} + p_{11} = 1$$

and these transition probabilities are collected in the transition matrix $\mathbf{P}$:

$$\mathbf{P} = \begin{bmatrix} p_{00} & 1 - p_{11} \\ 1 - p_{00} & p_{11} \end{bmatrix}$$

which fully describes the Markov chain.

A two-state Markov chain can easily be represented by a simple AR(1) process as
follows:

$$s_t = (1 - p_{00}) + (-1 + p_{00} + p_{11})s_{t-1} + v_t \tag{8.4}$$

where $v_t = s_t - E(s_t | s_{t-1}, s_{t-2}, \ldots)$. Although v_t can take only a finite set of values, on
average v_t is zero. The innovation v_t is thus a martingale difference sequence. Given the

---

[3] The representation $y_t = \sigma_{s_t} \varepsilon_t$, with $\sigma_0 = \exp(\alpha/2)$ and $\sigma_1 = \exp((\alpha + \beta)/2)$, is clearly equivalent. To identify
the regime 1 as the high volatility regime, we set $\beta > 0$.

autoregressive representation of the Markov chain, it is possible to rewrite the volatility equation of model (8.3) in the following way:

$$h_t = \alpha + \beta s_t$$
$$= \alpha + \beta[(1 - p_{00}) + (-1 + p_{00} + p_{11})s_{t-1} + v_t]$$
$$= \alpha(2 - p_{00} - p_{11}) + \beta(1 - p_{00}) + (-1 + p_{00} + p_{11})h_{t-1} + \beta v_t$$

The SV model with discrete volatility has therefore the same structure as model (8.2) but with a noise that can take only a finite set of values:

$$\begin{cases} y_t = \varepsilon_t \exp(h_t/2) \\ h_t = a + bh_{t-1} + \omega_t \end{cases} \quad (8.5)$$

We describe the basic properties of both types of model in the following sections.

8.3.1   SV models with continuous volatility

We consider ε_t and η_t independent, Gaussian white noises. The properties of model (8.2) are discussed in Taylor (1986, 1994) (see also Shephard (1996)). Broadly speaking, given the product process nature of the model, these properties are easy to derive, but estimation is substantially harder than for the corresponding ARCH models.

As η_t is Gaussian, h_t is a standard Gaussian autoregression. It will be stationary (covariance[4] and strictly[5]) if $|\beta| < 1$ with:

$$\mu_h = E(h_t) = \frac{\alpha}{1 - \beta}$$

$$\sigma_h^2 = \text{Var}(h_t) = \frac{\sigma_\eta^2}{1 - \beta^2}$$

As ε_t is always stationary, y_t will be stationary if and only if h_t is stationary, y_t being the product of two stationary processes. Using the properties of the log-normal distribution, all the moments exist if h_t is stationary and in particular the kurtosis is:

$$\frac{E(y_t^4)}{(E(y_t^2))^2} = 3 \exp(\sigma_h^2) \geq 3$$

which shows that the SV model has fatter tails than the corresponding normal distribution and all the odd moments are zero.

---

[4] A stochastic process y_t is covariance stationary if the degree of covariance amongst its observations depends only on the time gap between them, i.e. $\text{Cov}(y_t, y_{t+r}) = \gamma(r)$ for all t.
[5] For some processes there will exist no moments, even in cases where the corresponding unconditional distributions are perfectly well-behaved. The strict stationarity of y_t is then defined as follows: $F(y_{t+r}, y_{t+r+1}, \ldots, y_{t+r+p}) = F(y_t, y_{t+1}, \ldots, y_{t+p})$ for all p and r.

The dynamic properties of y_t are easy to find. First, as ε_t is iid, y_t is a martingale difference[6] and is a white noise[7] if $|\beta| < 1$. As h_t is a Gaussian AR(1):

$$\text{Cov}(y_t^2, y_{t-r}^2) = E(y_t^2 y_{t-r}^2) - (E(y_t^2))^2$$

$$= E(\exp(h_t + h_{t-r})) - (E(\exp(h_t)))^2$$

$$= \exp(2\mu_h + \sigma_h^2)(\exp(\sigma_h^2 \beta^r) - 1)$$

and so:

$$\rho_{y_t^2}(r) = \frac{\text{Cov}(y_t^2, y_{t-r}^2)}{\text{Var}(y_t^2)} = \frac{\exp(\sigma_h^2 \beta^r) - 1}{3\exp(\sigma_h^2) - 1} \simeq \frac{\exp(\sigma_h^2) - 1}{3\exp(\sigma_h^2) - 1} \beta^r$$

Hence, the memory of the y_t is defined by the memory of the latent h_t, in this case an AR(1). Moreover, note that if $\beta < 0$, $\rho_{y_t^2}(r)$ can be negative, unlike the ARCH models. This is the autocorrelation function of an ARMA(1,1) process, thus the SV model behaves in a manner similar to the GARCH(1,1) model. Finally, note that there is no need for non-negativity constraints nor for bounded kurtosis constraints on the coefficients. This is a great advantage with respect to GARCH models.

Insights on the dynamic properties of the SV model can also be obtained by squaring and taking logs, getting:

$$\begin{cases} \log(y_t^2) = h_t + \log(\varepsilon_t^2) \\ h_t = \alpha + \beta h_{t-1} + \eta_t \end{cases} \tag{8.6}$$

a linear process, which adds the iid $\log(\varepsilon_t^2)$ to the AR(1) h_t. As a result $\log(y_t^2) \sim$ ARMA(1,1). If ε_t is Gaussian, then $\log(\varepsilon_t^2)$ has a mean of -1.27 and variance 4.93, but its distribution is far from being normal, as it is heavily skewed with a long left-hand tail, caused by taking the logs of very small numbers, an operation which generates outliers. The autocorrelation function for $\log(y_t^2)$ is:

$$\rho_{\log(y_t^2)}(r) = \frac{\beta^r}{1 + 4.93/\sigma_h^2}$$

8.3.2 SV models with discrete volatility

We consider a two-state Markov chain s_t independent of ε_t, which is a Gaussian white noise.

Assuming stationarity,[8] the unconditional probabilities to be in the regime $0 (P(s_t = 0)$ $= \pi_0)$ or 1 $(P(s_t = 1) = \pi_1)$ are defined as follows:

$$\begin{cases} \pi_0 = p_{00}\pi_0 + (1 - p_{11})\pi_1 \\ \pi_1 = (1 - p_{00})\pi_0 + p_{11}\pi_1 \end{cases}$$

---

[6] y_t being a martingale difference stipulates that $E|y_t| < \infty$ and that $E(y_t|y_{t-1}, y_{t-2}, \ldots) = 0$. All martingale differences have zero means and are uncorrelated over time. If the unconditional variance of the martingale difference is constant over time, then the series is also a white noise.

[7] This means $E(y_t) = \mu$, $\text{Var}(y_t) = \sigma^2$ and $\text{Cov}(y_t, y_{t+r}) = 0$ for all $r \neq 0$. Often μ will be taken to be zero. These unconditional moment conditions are sometimes strengthened to include y_t being independent, rather than uncorrelated, over time. This will be called strong white noise, a special case of which is independent and identically distributed (iid).

[8] An ergodic Markov chain is a covariance stationary process. For some basic properties of Markov chains, see Hamilton (1994, chap. 22).

with $\pi_0 + \pi_1 = 1$, or in a vector form:

$$\begin{cases} \pi = \mathbf{P}\pi \\ \mathbf{1}'\pi = 1 \end{cases}$$

where $\mathbf{1} = (1, 1)'$. Thus, they are:

$$\pi_0 = \frac{1 - p_{11}}{2 - p_{00} - p_{11}}$$

$$\pi_1 = \frac{1 - p_{00}}{2 - p_{00} - p_{11}}$$

From the definition of b in equation (8.5), we can note that when $p_{00} + p_{11} > 1$ the h_t process is likely to persist in its current state and it would be positively serially correlated. Its unconditional moments are:

$$E(h_t) = \alpha + \beta E(s_t)$$

$$= \alpha + \beta\pi_1$$

$$\text{Var}(h_t) = \beta^2\pi_1(1 - \pi_1)$$

Under stationarity,[9] as for the SV model with continuous volatility, all the moments exist, all the odd moments are zero and the kurtosis is:

$$\frac{E(y_t^4)}{(E(y_t^2))^2} = 3\frac{(\pi_0 + \exp(2\beta)\pi_1)}{(\pi_0 + \exp(\beta)\pi_1)^2} \geq 3$$

Moreover, as ε_t is iid, y_t is a martingale difference and its dynamic properties are described by the covariances of squares:

$$\begin{aligned} \text{Cov}(y_t^2, y_{t-r}^2) &= E(y_t^2 y_{t-r}^2) - (E(y_t^2))^2 \\ &= E(\exp(h_t + h_{t-r})) - (\exp(\alpha)\pi_0 + \exp(\alpha + \beta)\pi_1)^2 \\ &= \exp(2\alpha)P(s_t = 0, s_{t-r} = 0) + \exp(2\alpha + \beta)P(s_t = 0, s_{t-r} = 1) \\ &\quad + \exp(2\alpha + \beta)P(s_t = 1, s_{t-r} = 0) + \exp(2\alpha + 2\beta)P(s_t = 1, s_{t-r} = 1) \\ &\quad - (\exp(\alpha)\pi_0 + \exp(\alpha + \beta)\pi_1)^2 \end{aligned}$$

where the vector of unconditional joint probabilities $P(s_t, s_{t-r})$ can be computed as follows:

$$P(s_t, s_{t-r}) = P(s_t|s_{t-r})P(s_{t-r})$$

$$= \mathbf{P}^r\pi$$

---

[9] For this see Francq and Zakoïan (2001) and Francq et al. (2001).

with:

$$\mathbf{P}^r = \begin{bmatrix} \dfrac{(1-p_{11}) + \lambda^r(1-p_{00})}{2-p_{00}-p_{11}} & \dfrac{(1-p_{11}) + \lambda^r(1-p_{11})}{2-p_{00}-p_{11}} \\[3mm] \dfrac{(1-p_{00}) + \lambda^r(1-p_{00})}{2-p_{00}-p_{11}} & \dfrac{(1-p_{00}) + \lambda^r(1-p_{11})}{2-p_{00}-p_{11}} \end{bmatrix}$$

and $\lambda = -1 + p_{00} + p_{11}$.

Finally, it is useful to note that h_t is itself a Markov chain which can take the values α and $\alpha + \beta$ with the same transition matrix $\mathbf{P}$.

8.4   ESTIMATION

The difficulties in estimating SV models lie in the latent nature of the volatility. Inference may be difficult, because the distribution of $y_t|Y^{t-1}$ is specified implicitly rather than explicitly and the likelihood function appears as a multivariate integral the size of which is equal to the number of observations multiplied by the size of the latent variables, which is 1 for the described models.

Like most non-Gaussian parameter-driven models, there are many different ways of performing estimation: some involve estimating or approximating the likelihood, others use the method of moments procedures (see Ghysels *et al.* (1996) and Shephard (1996)).

Let us first of all clearly state the problem of computing the likelihood function for the general class of parametric dynamic latent variable or non-linear and/or non-Gaussian state space models.

8.4.1   A general filter for non-Gaussian parameter-driven models

Both SV models (with continuous and discrete volatility) fit in the following framework:

$$\begin{cases} y_t = \phi_t(h_t, \varepsilon_t; \theta) & \text{measurement equation} \\ h_t = \varphi_t(h_{t-1}, \eta_t; \theta) & \text{transition equation} \end{cases} \tag{8.7}$$

where ε_t and η_t are independent white noises, with marginal distributions which may depend on θ, the vector of parameters. Let H^t and Y^t denote $(h_1, h_2, \ldots, h_t)'$ and $(y_1, y_2, \ldots, y_t)'$, respectively.

There are serious difficulties in computing the likelihood function; in fact, with T the number of observations, we have:

$$f(Y^T, H^T; \theta) = \prod_{t=1}^{T} f(y_t|Y^{t-1}, H^t; \theta) f(h_t|Y^{t-1}, H^{t-1}; \theta)$$

and the likelihood function is:

$$\ell_T(\theta) \equiv f(Y^T; \theta) = \int \prod_{t=1}^{T} f(y_t|Y^{t-1}, H^t; \theta) f(h_t|Y^{t-1}, H^{t-1}; \theta) \prod_{t=1}^{T} dh_t \tag{8.8}$$

which is an integral whose size is equal to the number of observations multiplied by the dimension of the unobserved variable h_t, and thus it is practically unfeasible.

It is however possible to derive a general algorithm which allows the formal computation of the likelihood function by decomposing the calculation of integral (8.8) into a sequence of integrals of lower dimension.

Let $f(h_{t-1}|Y^{t-1})$ be the input of the iteration,[10] $t = 1, 2, \ldots, T$. First of all, we can decompose the joint conditional density of h_t, h_{t-1} into the product of the transition density by the input density:

$$\text{step 1} \qquad f(h_t, h_{t-1}|Y^{t-1}) = f(h_t|h_{t-1})f(h_{t-1}|Y^{t-1})$$

By marginalisation we obtain the prediction density of h_t:

$$\text{step 2} \qquad f(h_t|Y^{t-1}) = \int f(h_t, h_{t-1}|Y^{t-1}) \, dh_{t-1} = \int f(h_t|h_{t-1})f(h_{t-1}|Y^{t-1}) \, dh_{t-1}$$

Let us now consider the joint density of y_t, h_t. It can be decomposed into the product of the measurement density and the prediction density:

$$\text{step 3} \qquad f(y_t, h_t|Y^{t-1}) = f(y_t|h_t)f(h_t|Y^{t-1})$$

and, again, by marginalisation we obtain the one-step-ahead forecast density of y_t:

$$\text{step 4} \qquad f(y_t|Y^{t-1}) = \int f(y_t, h_t|Y^{t-1}) \, dh_t = \int f(y_t|h_t)f(h_t|Y^{t-1}) \, dh_t$$

which is particularly useful, since by the combination of these densities it is possible to obtain the likelihood function. Finally, by conditioning we obtain the filtering density (output):

$$\text{step 5} \qquad f(h_t|Y^t) = \frac{f(y_t, h_t|Y^{t-1})}{f(y_t|Y^{t-1})} = \frac{f(y_t|h_t)f(h_t|Y^{t-1})}{\int f(y_t|h_t)f(h_t|Y^{t-1}) \, dh_t}$$

which ends the iteration.

The previous algorithm allows us to obtain several important elements. Step 2 gives the estimation of h_t given all the information available until $t - 1$ (prediction density). Step 5 provides the estimation of h_t given all the information currently available (filtering density). Finally step 4, by providing the one-step-ahead forecast density, allows us to compute the likelihood function.

Unfortunately, only in very special cases is it possible to obtain analytic recursive algorithms[11] from this general filtering algorithm: the Kalman filter in the Gaussian and linear case and the Hamilton filter in the Markovian and discrete case.

In the Gaussian and linear cases, the initial input $f(h_1|Y^0)$ and the measurement and transition densities are assumed to be Gaussian and at each step of the algorithm Gaussianity is preserved, then also all the outputs are Gaussian. The normal distribution is

---

[10] For the first iteration ($t = 1$) it is possible to consider the unconditional distribution of h_t, $f(h_1)$. For the sake of simplicity we omit the dependence on the parameter θ.

[11] See also Shephard (1994) for another particular case in which h_t is set to be a random walk and $\exp(\eta_t)$ a highly contrived scaled beta distribution. This delivers a one-step-ahead prediction distribution which has some similarities to the ARCH models.

completely described by its first two moments and then the algorithm can be rewritten by relating means and variances of the different densities involved. This is the Kalman filter.

For the switching regime models introduced by Hamilton (1989), which represent the Markovian and discrete case, the integrals which appear at steps 2 and 4 become a simple sum over the possible regimes, and then the whole algorithm is analytically tractable.

In all the other cases, it is necessary to consider approximated solutions or simulation-based methods. Examples of approximations are the extended Kalman filter (Anderson and Moore, 1979; Harvey, 1989; Fridman and Harris, 1998), the Gaussian sum filter (Sorenson and Alspach, 1971), the numerical integration (Kitagawa, 1987), the Monte Carlo integration (Tanizaki and Mariano, 1994, 1998), or the particle filter (Gordon *et al.*, 1993); Kitagawa, 1996; Pitt and Shephard, 1999a). The simulation-based solutions are certainly more time-consuming and demanding in terms of computing, but they are definitely more general. We will see these methods in greater detail later.

However, for the two presented models (8.2) and (8.3), the general filter introduced here is useful for estimation. In fact, for the linearised version (8.6), the Kalman filter allows a quasi-maximum likelihood estimation of the parameters and the discrete version (8.3) is a particular case of switching regime models for which the Hamilton filter gives the likelihood function.

8.4.1.1 The Kalman filter for quasi-maximum likelihood (QML) estimation of continuous SV models

We can consider the log-transformation (8.6) of the continuous SV model. As $\log(\varepsilon_t^2) \sim$ iid, we obtain a linear state space model.

Let $LY^\tau = (\log(y_1^2), \log(y_2^2), \ldots, \log(y_\tau^2))'$, $\hat{h}_{t/\tau} = E(h_t|LY^\tau) = E(h_t|Y^\tau)$ and $Q_{t/\tau} = \mathrm{MSE}(h_t|LY^\tau) = \mathrm{MSE}(h_t|Y^\tau)$. The Kalman filter (see, for example,[12] Harvey (1989)) computes these quantities recursively for $t = 1, \ldots, T$:

$$\hat{h}_{t/t-1} = \alpha + \beta \hat{h}_{t-1/t-1}$$

$$Q_{t/t-1} = \beta^2 Q_{t-1/t-1} + \sigma_\eta^2$$

$$e_{t/t-1} = \log(y_t^2) - \hat{h}_{t/t-1}$$

$$F_{t/t-1} = Q_{t/t-1} + \pi^2/2$$

$$\hat{h}_{t/t} = \hat{h}_{t/t-1} + K_t e_{t/t-1}$$

$$Q_{t/t} = (1 - K_t)^2 Q_{t/t-1}$$

where $K_t = Q_{t/t-1} F_{t/t-1}^{-1}$ is the Kalman gain. However, as $\log(\varepsilon_t^2)$ is not Gaussian, the Kalman filter can be used to provide the best linear unbiased estimator of h_t given Y^t.

Moreover, if (8.6) were a Gaussian state space model, the Kalman filter would provide the exact likelihood function. In fact, a by-product of the filter are the innovations $e_{t/t-1}$,

---

[12] See also Carraro and Sartore (1987).

which are the one-step-ahead forecast errors and their corresponding mean square errors, $F_{t/t-1}$. Together they deliver the likelihood (ignoring constants):

$$\ell_T(\theta) = -\frac{1}{2}\sum_{t=1}^{T} \log F_{t/t-1} - \frac{1}{2}\sum_{t=1}^{T} \frac{e^2_{t/t-1}}{F_{t/t-1}}$$

As the state space is linear but not Gaussian, the filter gives a quasi-likelihood function which can be used to obtain a consistent estimator $\hat{\theta}$ and asymptotically normal inference (see Ruiz (1994)).

This way of estimating h_t is used by Melino and Turnbull (1990), after estimating θ by the generalised method of moments (see Section 8.4.3.1). Harvey *et al.* (1994) examine the QML estimator.

8.4.1.2 The Hamilton filter for maximum likelihood estimation of discrete SV models

The discrete SV model (8.3) is a non-linear and non-Gaussian state space model. In the two-regimes case, the transition equation can be written in a linear form (see (8.5)) and the measurement equation can be linearised by the log transformation, but both the equations are non-Gaussian. However, the joint process (y_t, h_t) is Markovian and thus the general filter presented in Section 8.4.1 gives an analytic recursion, since the integrals become simple sums over the possible values of h_t. The input is the filtered probability[13] $P(h_{t-1}|Y^{t-1})$ and the algorithm gives the prediction probability, the one-step-ahead forecast density and the subsequent filtered probability:

$$P(h_t|Y^{t-1}) = \sum_{h_{t-1}} P(h_t|h_{t-1})P(h_{t-1}|Y^{t-1})$$

$$f(y_t|Y^{t-1}) = \sum_{h_t} f(y_t|h_t)P(h_t|Y^{t-1})$$

$$P(h_t|Y^t) = \frac{f(y_t|h_t)P(h_t|Y^{t-1})}{\sum_{h_t} f(y_t|h_t)P(h_t|Y^{t-1})}$$

The combination of the one-step-ahead forecast densities:

$$\ell_T(\theta) = \prod_{t=1}^{T} f(y_t|Y^{t-1})$$

provides the likelihood function, the maximisation of which gives the maximum likelihood estimators of the parameters.

---

[13] The initial probability $P(h_0|Y^0)$ can be taken equal to the unconditional (ergodic) probability $P(h_0) = \pi$.

8.4.2 A general smoother for non-Gaussian parameter-driven models

We might also want to obtain the estimation of h_t given all the information available, that is conditional on Y^T. Such a procedure is called smoothing and as before it is possible to derive a formal backward algorithm which delivers the smoothed densities $f(h_t|Y^T)$.

Let $f(h_{t+1}|Y^T)$ be the input of the iteration,[14] $t = T - 1, T - 2, \ldots, 2, 1$. We can decompose the joint density of h_{t+1}, h_t, conditional on the information set Y^t, in the product of the transition density by the filtered density (available from the filter):

$$\text{step 1} \qquad f(h_{t+1}, h_t|Y^t) = f(h_{t+1}|h_t) f(h_t|Y^t)$$

By conditioning with the prediction density obtained from the filter, we obtain the following conditional density:

$$\text{step 2} \qquad f(h_t|h_{t+1}, Y^t) = \frac{f(h_{t+1}, h_t|Y^t)}{f(h_{t+1}|Y^t)}$$

The joint density of h_{t+1}, h_t, conditional on the information set Y^T, is given by the product of the conditional density $f(h_t|h_{t+1}, Y^T)$ by the input of the algorithm $f(h_{t+1}|Y^T)$. The information set h_{t+1}, Y^T is included in the information set $h_{t+1}, Y^t, \varepsilon_{t+1}^T, \eta_{t+2}^T$, where $\varepsilon_{t+1}^T = (\varepsilon_{t+1}, \ldots, \varepsilon_T)'$ and $\eta_{t+2}^T = (\eta_{t+2}, \ldots, \eta_T)'$. Given that $\varepsilon_{t+1}^T, \eta_{t+2}^T$ is independent of h_t, h_{t+1}, Y^t, we can conclude that $f(h_t|h_{t+1}, Y^T) = f(h_t|h_{t+1}, Y^t)$ (computed at step 2) and then:

$$\text{step 3} \qquad f(h_{t+1}, h_t|Y^T) = f(h_t|h_{t+1}, Y^T) f(h_{t+1}|Y^T) = f(h_t|h_{t+1}, Y^t) f(h_{t+1}|Y^T)$$

Finally, by marginalisation we obtain the smoothed density of h_t (output):

$$\text{step 4} \qquad f(h_t|Y^T) = \int f(h_{t+1}, h_t|Y^T)\, dh_{t+1} = \int f(h_t|h_{t+1}, Y^t) f(h_{t+1}|Y^T)\, dh_{t+1}$$

Again, only in the linear and Gaussian case, and in the Markovian and discrete case is it possible to obtain an analytic backward recursion: the Kalman smoother and the Kim smoother (Kim, 1994).

8.4.2.1 The Kalman smoother for continuous SV models

Let $\hat{h}_{t+1/T} = E(h_{t+1}|LY^T) = E(h_{t+1}|Y^T)$ and $Q_{t+1/T} = \text{MSE}(h_{t+1}|LY^T) = \text{MSE}(h_{t+1}|Y^T)$. The Kalman smoother[15] computes these quantities recursively for $t = T - 1, T - 2, \ldots, 2, 1$:

$$\hat{h}_{t/T} = \hat{h}_{t/t} + \beta Q_{t/t} Q_{t+1/t}^{-1} (\hat{h}_{t+1/T} - \hat{h}_{t+1/t})$$

$$Q_{t/T} = Q_{t/t} + \beta^2 Q_{t/t}^2 Q_{t+1/t}^{-2} (Q_{t+1/T} - Q_{t+1/t})$$

where $\hat{h}_{t/t}, Q_{t/t}, \hat{h}_{t+1/t}, Q_{t+1/t}$ are stored from the Kalman filter.

---

[14] For the first iteration ($t = T - 1$), the input is simply the final output of the filter $f(h_T|Y^T)$.
[15] See also de Jong (1989).

For the log transformation of the continuous SV model (8.6), the Kalman smoother is useful in estimating the unobserved log-volatility, in fact it provides the best linear unbiased estimator of h_t given $(y_1, y_2, \ldots, y_T)'$.

8.4.2.2 The Kim smoother for discrete SV models

The input is the smoothed probability $P(h_{t+1}|Y^T)$ and the recursion is simply:

$$P(h_t|Y^T) = \sum_{s_{t+1}} \frac{P(h_{t+1}|h_t)P(h_t|Y^t)P(h_{t+1}|Y^T)}{P(h_{t+1}|Y^t)}$$

where $P(h_t|Y^t)$ and $P(h_{t+1}|Y^t)$ are stored from the Hamilton filter.

8.4.3 Other estimation methods for continuous SV models

For the discrete SV model the Hamilton filter allows us to obtain the maximum likelihood estimator of the parameters. On the contrary, for the continuous SV models, the Kalman filter provides only an approximation of the likelihood function. Let us review some other possible estimation methods useful for the continuous SV model.

Like most non-Gaussian parameter-driven models, there are many different ways to perform estimation. Some involve estimating the likelihood; others use method of moments procedures.

8.4.3.1 Method of moments

The simplest approach is the method of moments, based on matching empirical and theoretical moments. In the SV case there are many possible moments to use in estimating the parameters of the model. This is because y_t^2 behaves like an ARMA(1,1) model and moving average models do not allow sufficient statistics which are of a smaller dimension than T. This suggests that the use of a finite number of moment restrictions is likely to lead to loss of information. Examples include those based on y_t^2, y_t^4, $y_t^2 y_{t-r}^2$, although there are many other possibilities. As a result, we may well want to use more moments than there are parameters to estimate, implying that they will have to be pooled. A reasonably sensible way of doing this is via the Generalised Method of Moments (GMM).

We can consider, for example, the vector g_T of the first r autocovariances of y_t^2 or of $\log(y_t^2)$ as moment constraints. There are more moments than parameters and the issue is how to weight all the available information. The GMM approach of Hansen (1992) suggests minimising the quadratic form $g_T' W_T g_T$ by varying the parameters θ and the weighting matrix W_T should reflect the relative importance given to matching each of the chosen moments. Applications of this method to SV models are the seminal work of Melino and Turnbull (1990) and the extensive study of Andersen and Sørensen (1996).

The main advantage of the GMM approach comes from the fact that it does not require distributional assumptions. However, this is not useful for the SV model since it is a fully specified parametric model. On the contrary, as argued by Shephard (1996), there are a number of drawbacks to the GMM estimation of the SV model. First of all, GMM can only be used if h_t is stationary; if β is close to one (as we will find for many high-frequency financial data sets), we can expect GMM to work poorly. Second, parameter estimates are not invariant to the parameterisation and the model (8.2) is not fundamentally more interesting than

$$\begin{cases} y_t = \varepsilon_t \gamma \ \exp(h_t/2) \\ h_t = \beta h_{t-1} + \eta_t \end{cases}$$

Third, as already observed, the squares y_t^2 behave like an ARMA(1,1) model; if σ_η^2 is small (as we will find in practice), $\rho_{y_t^2}(r)$ will be small but positive for many r. This implies that for many series the number of moments to be considered will have to be very high to capture the low correlation in the volatility process. Finally, GMM does not deliver an estimate (filtered or smoothed) of h_t, consequently a second form of estimation will be required.

The GMM and QML approaches are the simplest way of estimating the SV models and they are about equally efficient, with the relative performance being dependent on the specific parameter values (see Andersen and Sørensen (1997)).

8.4.3.2 Simulation-based methods

All the other estimation approaches are based on simulation techniques. In the last 10 years there has been a growing interest in simulation-based[16] methods which propose several ways of resolving the inference problem for this class of models (see Billio (1999, 2002b)). In fact, it is clear that one can easily recursively simulate (path simulations) from the system (8.2) for any given value of parameters, θ.

A first approach relies on simulation-based methods which are relatively simple to implement, but which are less efficient than the maximum likelihood approach: see, for example, the simulated method of moments (Duffie and Singleton, 1993), the indirect inference method (Gouriéroux et al., 1993) or the efficient method of moments (Gallant and Tauchen, 1996; Gallant et al., 1997). A second approach considers the problem of the computation (or of the approximation) of the likelihood and then of the maximum likelihood estimator through importance sampling methods (Danielsson and Richard, 1993; Danielsson, 1994; Durbin and Koopman, 1997). In a Bayesian framework, a third approach considers Markov Chain Monte Carlo (MCMC) techniques based on the data augmentation principle, which yields samples out of the joint posterior distribution of the latent volatility and all model parameters, and allows the parameter estimates and the latent volatility dynamics to be obtained (Jacquier et al., 1994; Kim et al., 1998; Chib et al., 2002). Finally, a fourth approach utilises MCMC methods to compute (or approximate) the maximum likelihood estimator (see the simulated expectation maximisation (Shephard, 1993; Geyer, 1994, 1996; Billio et al., 1998).

In practice, the choice between these different simulation-based approaches depends on several criteria, such as efficiency and computing time. Unfortunately, in general there is a trade-off between these criteria. Methods like the simulated maximum likelihood and the simulated likelihood ratio have several advantages in the estimation of SV models. Since they are likelihood methods, the classical theory of maximum likelihood carries over to the simulated case and standard likelihood ratio tests can be constructed. MCMC-based approaches are certainly more time-consuming, but also allow estimation of the latent volatility dynamics by simulating from the smoothing/posterior distribution of h_t.

---

[16] Simulation techniques make use of sequences of pseudo-random numbers which are generated by a computer procedure.

Let us briefly introduce part of these methods and their application to SV models.

8.4.3.2.1 Indirect inference approach

The so-called indirect inference methodology was recently introduced in the literature by Smith (1993), Gouriéroux *et al.* (1993), Gallant and Tauchen (1996) for a simulation-based inference on generally intractable structural models through an auxiliary model, conceived as easier to handle. This methodology allows the use of somewhat misspecified auxiliary models, since the simulation process in the well-specified structural model and the calibration of the simulated paths against the observed one through the same auxiliary model will provide an automatic misspecification bias correction. There are several ways of implementing this idea.[17]

The original approach is the indirect inference method of Gouriéroux *et al.* (1993). Consider an auxiliary model $f_a(y_t|Y^{t-1}; \pi)$ for the observed data (for example[18] the general linear state space model obtained by the log transformation (8.6)). Let $\hat{\pi}_T = \Pi_T(Y^T)$ denote the QML estimator of π based on f_a as a function $\Pi_T(\cdot)$ of the observed data set Y^T. The indirect inference estimator of structural parameters θ is given by:

$$\hat{\theta}_{\mathrm{II}} = \arg \min_{\theta} [\hat{\pi}_T - \tilde{\pi}_{NT}(\theta)]' W_T [\hat{\pi}_T - \tilde{\pi}_{NT}(\theta)]$$

where W_T is a weighting matrix and $\tilde{\pi}_{NT}(\theta)$ is the π estimator obtained on a simulated path of $\tilde{Y}^{NT}$ for a given value of θ (i.e. that is given by the binding function $\tilde{\pi}_{NT}(\theta) = \lim_{N\to\infty} \Pi_{NT}(\tilde{Y}^{NT})$, which is approximated by $\Pi_{NT}(\tilde{Y}^{NT})$ for large N). This approach may be very computationally demanding as one needs to evaluate the binding function $\tilde{\pi}_{NT}(\theta)$ for each value of θ appearing in the numerical optimisation algorithm.

The estimator of Gallant and Tauchen (1996) circumvents the need to evaluate the binding function by using the score vector $\partial f_a(y_t|Y^{t-1}; \pi)/\partial \pi$ (score generator) to define the matching conditions. If the auxiliary model $f_a(y_t|Y^{t-1}; \pi)$ is chosen flexibly with a suitable non-parametric interpretation, then the estimator achieves the asymptotic efficiency of maximum likelihood and has good power properties for detecting misspecification (Gallant and Long, 1997; Tauchen, 1997), hence the term Efficient Method of Moments (EMM). EMM delivers consistent estimates of the structural parameter vector under weak conditions on the choice of the auxiliary model. However, extrapolating from the generalised method of moments evidence, it is natural to conjecture that the quality of inference may hinge on how well the auxiliary model approximates the salient features of the observed data. This intuition is formalised by Gallant and Long (1997), who show that a judicious selection of the auxiliary model, ensuring that the quasi-scores asymptotically span the true score vector, will result in full asymptotic efficiency.[19]

---

[17] For all these methods, it is necessary to recycle the random numbers used in the calculation when θ changes, in order to have good numerical and statistical properties of the estimators based on these simulations.

[18] Another possible auxiliary model is an ARMA(p, q) on the logarithms of the squared data (see Monfardini (1998)).

[19] In fact, as the score generator approaches the true conditional density, the estimated covariance matrix for the structural parameter approaches that of maximum likelihood. This result embodies one of the main advantages of EMM, since it prescribes a systematic approach to the derivation of efficient moment conditions for estimation in a general parametric setting.

Andersen *et al.* (1999) perform an extensive Monte Carlo study of EMM estimation of a stochastic volatility model. They examine the sensitivity to the choice of auxiliary model using ARCH, GARCH and EGARCH models for the score as well as non-parametric extensions. EMM efficiency approaches that of maximum likelihood for larger sample sizes, while inference is sensitive to the choice of auxiliary model in small samples, but robust in larger samples.[20]

The indirect inference theory, however, crucially depends on the correct specification assumption concerning the structural model. There is now an emerging literature (see, for example, Dridi and Renault (2000) and Dridi (2000)) which focuses on procedures more robust to the structural model specification. In particular, Dridi and Renault (2000) propose an extension to the indirect inference methodology to semiparametric settings and show how the semiparametric indirect inference works on basic examples using SV models.

8.4.3.2.2 *Importance sampling*

A more direct way of performing inference is to compute the likelihood by integrating out the latent h_t process. As previously seen, the integral (8.8) has no closed form and it has to be computed numerically. However, the likelihood function naturally appears as the expectation of the function $\prod_{t=1}^{T} f(y_t|Y^{t-1}, H^t; \theta)$ with respect to the p.d.f. P defined by[21] $\prod_{t=1}^{T} f(h_t|Y^{t-1}, H^{t-1}; \theta)$, from which it is easy to recursively draw. Therefore, an unbiased simulator of the whole likelihood function $\ell_T(\theta)$ is $\prod_{t=1}^{T} f(y_t|Y^{t-1}, {}^n\tilde{H}^t; \theta)$ where ${}^n\tilde{H}^t$ are recursively drawn from the auxiliary p.d.f. P. The likelihood is then approximated by the empirical mean:

$$\frac{1}{N} \sum_{n=1}^{N} \prod_{t=1}^{T} f(y_t|Y^{t-1}, {}^n\tilde{H}^t; \theta)$$

and this simulated likelihood can be numerically maximised. However, this basic simulator may be very slow, in the sense that the simulator may have a very large variance and then some accelerating technique is needed. One solution is to consider the general method of importance sampling based on a sequence of conditional p.d.f.s $q(h_t|Y^T, H^{t-1}1)$. Let us denote this probability distribution by Q and the corresponding expectation by E_Q. We have:

$$\ell_T(\theta) = E_P \left[\prod_{t=1}^{T} f(y_t|Y^{t-1}, H^t; \theta) \right]$$

$$= E_Q \left[\prod_{t=1}^{T} \frac{f(y_t|Y^{t-1}, H^t; \theta) f(h_t|Y^{t-1}, H^{t-1}; \theta)}{q(h_t|Y^T, H^{t-1}; \theta)} \right]$$

---

[20] Care must be taken, however, to avoid over-parameterisation of the auxiliary model, as convergence problems may arise if the quasi-score is extended to the point where it begins to fit the purely idiosyncratic noise in the data.

[21] It is important to note that this p.d.f. is neither $f(H^T; \theta)$, except when y_t does not cause h_t, nor $f(H^T|Y^T; \theta)$.

Therefore, an unbiased simulator of $\ell_T(\theta)$ is:

$$E_Q\left[\prod_{t=1}^{T} \frac{f(y_t|Y^{t-1}, {}^n\tilde{H}^t;\theta)f({}^n\tilde{h}_t|Y^{t-1}, {}^n\tilde{H}^{t-1};\theta)}{q({}^n\tilde{h}_t|Y^T, {}^n\tilde{H}^{t-1};\theta)}\right]$$

where ${}^n\tilde{H}^T$ is drawn in Q. The problem is then how to choose the importance function: the natural answer is by reducing the Monte Carlo variance. It is easy to calculate the theoretical optimal choice $f(H^T|Y^T;\theta) = \prod_{t=1}^{T} f(h_t|Y^T, H^{t-1})$ (i.e. the smoothing density of h_t), for which one simulation is sufficient, but it is clearly not computable. Then it is possible to consider the smoothing density of an approximating model, or to fix a parametric family of importance functions, choosing the member that minimises the Monte Carlo variance (which is eventually computed in an approximated way). For the SV model (8.2), the first solution is proposed by Sandmann and Koopman (1998) by using as approximating model the linearised version (8.6). In the aim of the second solution, Danielsson and Richard (1993) propose a sequentially optimised importance sampling, which Danielsson (1994) applies to the SV model.[22] In both cases, the simulated maximum likelihood estimates of model parameters are obtained by numerical optimisation of the logarithm of the simulated likelihood.[23]

8.4.3.2.3 Bayesian approach

In the Bayesian setting, there are also serious difficulties in estimating the SV model. In general, the posterior density $f(\theta|Y^T)$ and the posterior expectation of θ cannot be computed in a closed form. Again, this complex setting requires a simulation-based approach. The data augmentation principle, which considers the latent variable h_t as nuisance parameters, and the utilisation of Gibbs sampling (Gelfand and Smith, 1990), by iterating simulations from $f(H^T|Y^T, \theta)$ (data augmentation step) and $f(\theta|Y^T, H^T)$ (parameter simulation step), allow simulation from the joint posterior distribution $f(H^T, \theta|Y^T)$, derivation of the distribution of interest as the marginal distribution of θ and approximation of the posterior expectation by a sample average. When conditional distributions cannot be directly simulated, the corresponding steps in the Gibbs algorithm are replaced by Metropolis–Hastings steps.[24] Moreover, the prior modelling on the parameters is usually quasi-non-informative.

One way of considering this approach is to regard it as an empirical Bayes procedure, reporting the mean of the posterior distributions as an estimator of θ. This is the approach followed by Jacquier et al. (1994) who show that empirical Bayes outperforms QML and GMM in the SV case.

In Jacquier et al. (1994) the posterior distribution of the parameters was sampled by MCMC methods using a one-move approach (i.e. the latent variables h_t were sampled each at time from $f(h_t|Y^T, H^{-t}, \alpha, \beta, \sigma_\eta^2)$, where H^{-t} denotes all the elements of H^T excluding h_t). Although this algorithm is conceptually simple, it is not particularly efficient from a simulation perspective, as is shown by Kim et al. (1998), who develop an alternative,

---

[22] The details will not be dealt with here as they are quite involved, even for the simplest model.
[23] As for non-efficient methods, numerical and statistical accuracy is obtained by recycling the random numbers used in the calculation for each parameter value.
[24] Such hybrid algorithms are validated in Tierney (1994).

more efficient, multi-move MCMC algorithm. The efficiency gain in the Kim *et al.* (1998) algorithm arises from the joint sampling of H^T in one block conditioned on everything else in the model. Finally, Chib *et al.* (2002) develop efficient Markov Chain Monte Carlo algorithms for estimating generalised models of SV defined by heavy-tailed Student-*t* distributions, exogenous variables in the observation and volatility equations, and a jump component in the observation equation (see Section 8.5.1).

8.4.3.2.4 *An MCMC approach to maximum likelihood estimation*

Although the Bayesian approach is straightforward to state and computationally attractive, it requires the elicitation of a prior, which is often regarded by some econometricians as being difficult in dynamic models. Even if this is not an insurmountable problem, alternatives are available which allow us to perform maximum likelihood estimation using MCMC methods.

The first possibility is the Simulated Expectation Maximisation (SEM) algorithm proposed by Shephard (1993). The EM algorithm exploits the following decomposition of the log-likelihood function:

$$\log f(Y^T; \theta) = \log f(Y^T, H^T; \theta) - \log f(H^T | Y^T; \theta)$$

$$= E[\log f(Y^T, H^T; \theta) | Y^T] - E[\log f(H^T | Y^T; \theta) | Y^T]$$

and iterates:

$$\theta^{i+1} = \arg\max_{\theta} E_{\theta^i}[\log f(Y^T, H^T; \theta) | Y^T]$$

This is an increasing algorithm such that the sequence θ^i converges to the ML estimator. The problem is that, although $\log f(Y^T, H^T; \theta)$ has in general a closed form, the same is not true for its conditional expectation. In the SEM algorithm this expectation is replaced by an approximation based on simulations. Thus, the problem is now to be able to draw in the conditional distribution of H^T given Y^T and θ. Shephard (1993), in the context of a non-linear state space model, uses the Hastings–Metropolis algorithm to solve this problem, and applies it to the SV model.

Another possible approach is the Simulated Likelihood Ratio (SLR) method proposed by Billio *et al.* (1998). The general principle is:

$$\frac{f(Y^T; \theta)}{f(Y^T; \bar{\theta})} = E_{\bar{\theta}}\left[\frac{f(Y^T, H^T; \theta)}{f(Y^T, H^T; \bar{\theta})} \middle| Y^T \right] \tag{8.9}$$

where $\bar{\theta}$ is an arbitrary fixed value of the parameters. Obviously:

$$\arg\max_{\theta} f(Y^T; \theta) = \arg\max_{\theta} \frac{f(Y^T; \theta)}{f(Y^T; \bar{\theta})}$$

and with $^n\tilde{H}^T, n = 1, 2, \ldots, N$, simulated paths in the conditional distribution $f(H^T | Y^T; \theta)$, the SLR method amounts to maximising:

$$\frac{1}{N} \sum_{n=1}^{N} \frac{f(^{n}\tilde{H}^{T}, Y^{T}; \theta)}{f(^{n}\tilde{H}^{T}, Y^{T}; \overline{\theta})}$$

with respect to θ. The method can be implemented by simulating the conditional distribution[25] $f(H^{T}|Y^{T}; \overline{\theta})$. As already noted, it is impossible to simulate directly this distribution, thus a Hastings–Metropolis approach is suggested.

Contrary to the SEM approach, the SLR method allows for the computation of the likelihood surface and then of likelihood ratio test statistics. It needs only one optimisation run and not a sequence of optimisations; it is possible to store the simulated paths, and then only one simulation run is required. Moreover, as the simulation is made for only one value of the parameter, the objective function will be smooth with respect to θ, even if simulations involve rejection methods.

Billio *et al.* (1998) apply the SLR method also to the SV model (8.2).

8.5   EXTENSIONS OF SV MODELS

The basic SV models can be generalised in a number of directions. Straightforward generalisations might allow ε_{t} to have heavy-tailed Student-t distributions and exogenous variables in the observation and volatility equations.

Moreover, the ARCH in mean model of Engle *et al.* (1987) can be extended to the SV framework, by specifying $y_{t} = \mu_{0} + \mu_{1}\exp(h_{t}) + \varepsilon_{t}\exp(h_{t}/2)$. This model allows y_{t} to be moderately serially correlated, but in the discrete SV model the Hamilton filter no longer works, because y_{t}, h_{t} are not jointly Markovian.

8.5.1   Extensions of continuous SV models

In the context of continuous SV models, Harvey *et al.* (1994) concentrated their attention on models based on Student-t error; Mahieu and Schotman (1998) analysed the possibility of using a mixture distribution. Jacquier *et al.* (1995) have computed the posterior density of the parameters of a Student-t-based SV model. This particular type of model in fact can be viewed as an Euler discretisation of a Student-t-based Levy process but with additional stochastic volatility effects; further articles are available in (continuous-time) mathematical options and risk assessment literature.[26] By building on the work of Kim *et al.* (1998), Chib *et al.* (2002) develop efficient Markov Chain Monte Carlo algorithms for estimating these models. They also consider a second type of model which contains a jump component[27] in the observation equation to allow for large, transient movements.

---

[25] The resulting Monte Carlo approximation of (8.9) could be only locally good around $\overline{\theta}$, and so Geyer (1996) suggests updating $\overline{\theta}$ to the maximiser of the Monte Carlo likelihood and repeating the Monte Carlo procedure using the new $\overline{\theta}$. By updating $\overline{\theta}$ a few times, one should obtain better approximations of the relative likelihood function near the true maximum likelihood estimate.

[26] Leading references include Eberlein (2001) and Eberlein and Prause (2001). The extension to allow for stochastic volatility effects is discussed in Eberlein and Prause (2001) and Eberlein *et al.* (2001).

[27] Jump models are quite popular in continuous-time models of financial asset pricing. See, for example, Merton (1976), Ball and Torous (1985), Bates (1996), Duffie *et al.* (2000).

Moreover, a natural framework for extension of continuous SV models might be based on adapting the Gaussian state space so that:

$$\begin{cases} y_t = \varepsilon_t \exp(z_t' h_t / 2) \\ h_t = T_t h_{t-1} + \eta_t \qquad \eta_t \sim N(0, \mathrm{H}_t) \end{cases}$$

and then on allowing h_t to follow a more complicated ARMA process. Another simple example would be:

$$z_t = \begin{pmatrix} 1 \\ 1 \end{pmatrix} \qquad h_t = \begin{pmatrix} \beta & 0 \\ 0 & 1 \end{pmatrix} h_{t-1} + \eta_t, \qquad \eta_t \sim N \left\{ 0, \begin{pmatrix} \sigma_{\eta_1}^2 & 0 \\ 0 & \sigma_{\eta_2}^2 \end{pmatrix} \right\}$$

Now, the second component of h_t is a random walk, allowing the permanent level of the volatility to slowly change. This is analogous to the Engle and Lee (1992) decomposition of shocks into permanent and transitory. A model along the same lines has been suggested by Harvey and Shephard (1993), who allow (ignoring the cyclical AR(1) component):

$$z_t = \begin{pmatrix} 1 \\ 0 \end{pmatrix} \qquad T_t = \begin{pmatrix} 1 & 1 \\ 0 & 1 \end{pmatrix} \qquad \mathrm{H}_t = \begin{pmatrix} 0 & 0 \\ 0 & \sigma_{\eta_2}^2 \end{pmatrix}$$

This uses the Kitagawa and Gersch (1984) smooth trend model in the SV context, which in turn is close to putting a cubic spline through the data. This may provide a good summary of historical levels of volatility, but it could be poor as a vehicle for forecasting as confidence intervals for forecasted volatilities h_{t+r} may grow very quickly with r.

Another suggestion is to allow h_t to be a fractional process, giving the long-memory SV model. For financial time series, there is strong evidence that the effect of a shock to volatility persists (i.e. is not absorbed) for a long number of periods (see e.g. Andersen and Bollerslev (1997), Lobato and Savin (1998), Harvey (1998), Bollerslev and Jubinski (1999), Bollerslev and Mikkelsen (1999), Bollerslev and Wright (2000) and Ray and Tsay (2000)), thus the concept of long memory seems suitable and has been suggested by Breidt *et al.* (1998). A covariance stationary time series y_t has long memory if:

$$\sum_{r=0}^{\infty} |\mathrm{Cov}(y_t, y_{t-r})| = \infty$$

with $\mathrm{Var}(y_t) < \infty$. Basically, it says that the autocovariances do decay as the lag increases but very slowly, usually hyperbolically.

Currently there exist four approaches to estimate the long-memory SV model. The quasi-maximum likelihood estimator of Breidt *et al.* (1998), the GMM approach of Wright (1999), the widely used semiparametric, log-periodogram estimator of Geweke and Porter-Hudak (1983) (see e.g. Andersen and Bollerslev (1997), Ray and Tsay (2000), Wright (2000), Deo and Hurvich (2001) and the recent developments of Hurvich and Ray (2001), Hurvich *et al.* (2001)) and the Bayesian estimator based on the Markov Chain Monte Carlo sampler (Chan and Petris, 1999) and eventually the wavelet representation of the log-squared returns (Jensen, 1999, 2000, 2001).

The quasi-MLE of the long-memory SV model is known to be strongly consistent, but requires the order of the short-memory autoregressive and moving average parameters to be correctly identified, as does the GMM estimator. The difference between the quasi-MLE and GMM is that when the fractional order of integration is smaller than 1/4, the asymptotic properties in addition to consistency are known for the GMM estimator. Unlike the quasi-MLE of a short-memory stochastic volatility model whose asymptotic properties are known (Harvey *et al.*, 1994; Ruiz, 1994), these other asymptotic properties are not yet known for the quasi-MLE of the long-memory SV model. However, in simulation experiments, Wright (1999) finds that neither estimator's finite-sample properties dominate the other; the GMM estimator of the long-memory parameter generally produces smaller standard errors but with a significant downward bias. From these simulations Wright (1999) admonishes developing alternative estimators of the long-memory SV model that are more efficient and less biased. In fact, even if Deo and Hurvich (2001) find the asymptotic properties for the log-periodogram estimator of volatility to be similar to those proved by Robinson (1995) for the same estimator in the mean, correct inference about the degree of long-memory relies on the number of Fourier frequencies in the regression growing at a rate that is dependent on the value of the unknown long-memory parameter. It thus seems that neither the quasi-MLE nor the log-periodogram estimator of the long-memory volatility model lend themselves nicely to the construction of confidence intervals or hypothesis testing of the long-memory parameter estimate.

Finally, it could be useful to allow the SV model to capture the non-symmetric response to shocks. This feature can be modelled by allowing ε_{t-1} and η_t to be correlated. If ε_{t-1} and η_t are negatively correlated, and if $\varepsilon_{t-1} > 0$, then $y_{t-1} > 0$ and h_t is likely to fall. Hence, a large effect of y_{t-1}^2 on the estimated h_t will be accentuated by a negative sign on y_{t-1}, while its effect will be partially ameliorated by a positive sign. This correlation was suggested by Hull and White (1987) and estimated using GMM by Melino and Turnbull (1990) and Scott (1991). A simple quasi-maximum likelihood estimator has been proposed by Harvey and Shephard (1996). Jacquier *et al.* (1995) have extended their single-move MCMC sampler to estimate this effect.

8.5.2 Extensions of discrete SV models

In the discrete case, the basic model might be extended by considering different Markov chains, which can allow the decomposition of shocks into permanent and transitory as in the continuous case:

$$\begin{cases} y_t = \varepsilon_t \exp(z_t' h_t / 2) \\ h_t = \mu + TS_t \end{cases} \tag{8.10}$$

where S_t represents a vector of Markov chains. However, the vector of Markov chains can easily be represented by a single Markov chain with a sufficient number of states and then the model (8.10) formally reduces to the basic model (8.3).

Finally, the two SV models can be combined by allowing the continuous latent volatility to be governed by a first-order Markov chain. In that case, the estimation is very difficult. So *et al.* (1998) therefore propose Bayesian estimators which are constructed by Gibbs sampling.

8.6 MULTIVARIATE MODELS

Most macroeconomics and finance is about how variables interact, thus a multivariate approach is very important. For multivariate stochastic volatility models this means that it is essential to capture changing cross-covariance patterns. Multivariate modelling of covariance is rather new and difficult because it is afflicted by extreme problems of lack of parsimony. From a modelling point of view, the multivariate SV models are easier to extend than the ARCH models, but the estimation problem remains.

8.6.1 Multivariate continuous SV models

Some multivariate continuous SV models are easy to state. Harvey *et al.* (1994) applied quasi-likelihood Kalman filtering techniques on:

$$y_{it} = \varepsilon_{it} \exp(h_{it}/2) \qquad i = 1, \ldots, M, \qquad \varepsilon_t = (\varepsilon_{1t}, \ldots, \varepsilon_{Mt})' \sim NIID(0, \Sigma_\varepsilon) \qquad (8.11)$$

where Σ_ε is a correlation matrix and $h_t = (h_{1t}, \ldots, h_{Mt})'$ a multivariate random walk, although more complicated linear dynamics could be handled. The approach again relies on linearising, this time with loss of information, by writing $\log y_{it}^2 = h_{it} + \log \varepsilon_{it}^2$. The vector of $\log \varepsilon_{it}^2$ is iid, all with means -1.27, and a covariance matrix which is a known function of Σ_ε. Consequently, Σ_ε and the parameters indexing the dynamics of h_t can be estimated.

It is worthwhile pointing out two aspects of this model. If rank constraints are imposed on h_t, common trends and cycles will be allowed into the process describing the volatility. Furthermore, the model is similar to Bollerslev's (1990) model which is characterised by constant conditional correlation. Hence the model is better defined as one of changing variances rather than of changing correlation. Consequently, it fails to represent important features of the data and so it is of limited interest.

Perhaps a more attractive multivariate SV model can be obtained by introducing factors. The simplest one-factor model is:

$$\begin{cases} y_t = \lambda f_t + w_t, & w_t \sim NIID(0, \Sigma_w) \\ f_t = \varepsilon_t \exp(h_t/2), & h_t = \beta h_{t-1} + \eta_t, & \eta_t \sim NIID(0, \sigma_\eta^2) \end{cases}$$

where y_t is perturbed by w_t and explained by the scaled univariate SV model f_t. Typically Σ_w will be assumed diagonal, perhaps driven by independent SV models.

The lack of an obvious linearising transformation for these models prevents us from effectively using Kalman filtering methods. MCMC methods do not suffer this drawback and are explored in Jacquier *et al.* (1995) and Pitt and Shephard (1999b).

8.6.2 Multivariate discrete SV models

The multivariate extension of the discrete stochastic volatility model (8.3) is easy to state. We can consider the multivariate framework (8.11) and allow each component of $h_t = (h_{1t}, \ldots, h_{Mt})'$ to follow a two-state Markov chain, i.e.

$$\begin{cases} y_{it} = \varepsilon_{it} \exp(h_{it}/2), & i = 1, \ldots, M, & \varepsilon_t = (\varepsilon_{1t}, \ldots, \varepsilon_{Mt})' \sim NIID(0, \Sigma_\varepsilon) \\ h_{it} = \alpha + \beta s_{it} \end{cases}$$

In order to apply the Hamilton filter and to obtain the likelihood function, it is useful to define a new Markov chain S_t with 2^M states, which represents the M Markov chains governing the dynamics of h_t.

If the M Markov chains are independent, the transition probabilities of S_t are simply obtained by multiplying the probabilities that drive the different Markov chains. Accordingly, the transition probability matrix will be $\mathbf{Q} = \mathbf{P}_1 \otimes \mathbf{P}_2 \otimes \cdots \otimes \mathbf{P}_M$, where $\otimes$ indicates the Kronecker product and $\mathbf{P}_i$ the transition matrix of $s_{it}, i = 1, 2, \ldots, M$. In that case, the number of states rises exponentially with the dimension of h_t, but the number of parameters describing the Markov chains grows linearly with M and is $2M$.

A more general specification does not make any *a priori* assumptions about the relations between the different Markov chains. The transition probabilities of the composite Markov chain S_t are then given by:

$$q_{ij} = (S_t = j | S_{t-1} = i), \qquad i, \ j = 1, 2, \ldots, 2^M$$

which requires $2^M(2^M - 1)$ parameters. To understand the dimension of the problem, with $M = 2$ (and two states), the independent case requires four parameters, while the general specification requires 12 parameters.

Clearly the general specification becomes quickly unfeasible but, in some applications, the independent case is not useful to understand the causality between the volatility of different assets. Billio (2002a) proposes considering several correlated cases with a number of parameters comprised between $2M$ and $2^M(2^M - 1)$ by exploiting the concept of Granger causality.

As for the continuous SV model, a more interesting multivariate extension can be obtained by introducing a latent factor structure where the latent factors are characterised by discrete stochastic volatility. Unfortunately, in that case the joint process of the observable variable y_t and of the latent Markov chains is no longer Markovian, and then the Hamilton filter no longer works. For the estimation it is thus necessary to use some approximation or to use simulation-based methods (see Billio and Monfort (1998), Kim and Nelson (1999)).

8.7 EMPIRICAL APPLICATIONS

To provide simple illustrations of the usefulness of SV models, the two basic models are estimated and their output is used to develop standard option pricing and to calculate the VaR of an asset or a portfolio.

8.7.1 The Volatility program

There do not exist statistical packages to easily and directly estimate[28] SV models and thus the necessary routines have been developed with Ox (version 3.20), a programming

---

[28] Linear state space models can be estimated with the Kalman filter in EViews, with the Gauss package FANPAC or the Ox package SSFPack (see also STAMP). Thus the linearised version (8.6) could be estimated with a quasi-maximum likelihood approach. For the switching regime models, see also MSVAR, an Ox package developed by H.M. Krolzig and designed for the econometric modelling of univariate and multiple time series subject to shifts in regime (http://www.economics.ox.ac.uk/research/hendry/krolzig/).

language created mainly by Jurgen A. Doornik.[29] These routines can also be used within the package GiveWin.

The files required for running the Volatility program[30] are "volatilitymain.ox", the main program file, "volatility.oxo", a compiled file containing the definition of the functions, and the header file "volatility.h", containing the lists of global variables and functions. In Ox or GiveWin it is sufficient to load the main program file, to select the appropriate options and then to run the program (for the details of the commands and options see the enclosed readme.txt file).

Depending on which commands are commented out (// in front of the command) the program can:

- Estimate a basic continuous or discrete SV model on a user provided series;
- Simulate a basic continuous or discrete SV model;
- Estimate a basic continuous or discrete model on a user provided series and then simulate an alternative path with the estimated parameters.

It shall be stressed that GiveWin is not needed to estimate the models but only to display graphs. This program can easily be used with the freeware version of Ox in conjunction with any text editor, however we recommend the use of OxEdit since it integrates with Ox; both packages can be downloaded from Doornik's website (see footnote 29). All the graphic windows presented in this chapter are taken from GiveWin.

The first line of code in Figure 8.2, just before the "main" command, imports the "volatility.oxo" file, which contains the functions, recalls the Database class and other Ox packages such as the graphic, the probabilistic and the maximisation ones.[31]

The program is then organised as follows:

- In a first step the time series of interest is requested in an Excel spreadsheet. The user has to indicate the exact path of the file to be loaded (other data formats can be used, see the readme.txt file for additional details). Data passed to the programs must be the price levels, the necessary transformations are directly carried out by the estimation routines.
- In a second step the model is chosen, estimated and, if desired, simulated.
- Finally, the outputs of the model are printed and graphed to the screen and saved.

---

[29] Ox is an object-oriented matrix programming language with a comprehensive mathematical and statistical function library whose major features are speed, extensive library and well-designed syntax, leading to programs which are easy to maintain. In particular, this program takes advantage of the concept of class: it is possible to create new classes based on existing ones and to use their functions, therefore avoiding the need to rewrite them for the new class. In our case, the program is built on the Database class, which is the class designed for handling databases, samples, names of variables, etc. The Database class is used as a starting point for the more specific class of Stochastic Volatility Model: the functions, both to estimate and to simulate the models and to store the results, are totally rewritten, while the functions that manage the time series are part of the Database class. More information on Ox can be found at http://www.nuff.ox.ac.uk/users/doornik/. See also Doornik (2001).

[30] Updated versions of the program will be available for download at the address www.greta.it (under the Working Papers section). The package is free of charge for academic and research purposes. For commercial use, please contact the author (mgobbo@greta.it).

[31] Of course, it is possible to modify the program by adding functions belonging to the loaded Database class or to other different classes. In this case, the class containing the desired functions must be loaded by adding a line of code (#import "...") before the "main" command.

```
#import "volatility"

main()
{
        decl stochobj = new Stochastic();                    // create object

        stochobj.Load("c:/programs/stocvol/series.xls");     // load series
        stochobj.Info();                                     // database info

        stochobj.Select(Y_VAR, { "FTSE100", 0, 0 } );        // variable selection

        stochobj.SetSelSample(-1, 1, -1, 1);                 // full sample
        MaxControl(-100, 100);                               // maximization control

        stochobj.Estimate(0, 2, <-0.28; 0.54; 0.15>);        // estimate the model

        stochobj.Simulation(0, 0, 1500, 0);                  // simulate the model

        stochobj.SeriesEst("c:/programs/stocvol/FTSE100E.xls"); // save estimated data to file

        stochobj.SeriesSim("c:/programs/stocvol/FTSE100S.xls"); // save simulated data to file

        stochobj.Graph(0, "c:/programs/stocvol/FTSE100.ps");    // save graph to file

        delete stochobj;
}
```

Figure 8.2   The main program "volatilitymain.ox" loaded with GiveWin with the full list of commands

The available variables in the Excel file "series.xls" are the daily stock indexes analysed in Section 8.1.1, i.e. the FTSE100, the CAC40 and the MIB30 indexes. In the example developed in this chapter attention will be focused on the modelling of the FTSE100 index.

In the first part of the program, these variables are loaded in Excel format. Thus the full sample of FTSE100 is selected in order to start the analysis and perform the estimation. The command "Estimate" is quite complex and requires inputs by the user: the type of model, the choice of the initialisation of the parameter values and their values if the user wants to define them (see Figure 8.3 and the readme.txt file).

8.7.1.1   Estimation

The package allows the analysis of the two basic models, i.e. the log-normal SV model (8.2), called ARSV in the program, which is estimated by quasi-maximum likelihood with the Kalman filter, and the two-regime switching model (8.3), called SRSV, which is estimated by maximum likelihood with the Hamilton filter.

The first model is:

$$\begin{cases} y_t = \mu + \varepsilon_t \exp(h_t/2) \\ h_t = \alpha + \beta h_{t-1} + \eta_t \end{cases}$$

with ε_t and η_t independent Gaussian white noises. Their variances are 1 and σ_η^2, respectively. The volatility equation is characterised by the constant parameter α, the autoregressive parameter β and the variance σ_η^2 of the volatility noise. The mean is either imposed equal to zero or estimated with the empirical mean of the series (see equation (8.12)).

```
main ()
{
    ...
    // load data file into object, the example consider Excel file
    // recall that in Ox are available different load commands
    // depending on file type see for further information Ox references
    stochobj.Load("c:/programs/stocvol/series.xls");
    ...
    // select the variable of interest from the database
    // remember to insert the same names as in the database, in the
    // example we consider the FTSE100 series
    stochobj.Select(Y_VAR, { "FTSE100", 0, 0 } );
    ...
    // estimation command, input required:
    // a -> model type 0: ARSV, 1:SRSV
    // b -> starting values 0:random, 1:user, 2:data driven
    // c -> set of initial parameters value, 0:if b=0 or 2,
    //        if b=1 -> 3x1:if a=2, 5x1:if a=1
    // in the example ARSV, user provided starting values
    stochobj.Estimate(0, 2, <-0.28; 0.54; 0.15>);
    ...
    delete stochobj;
}
```

Figure 8.3   The "Load", "Select" and "Estimate" commands

Since the specification of the conditional volatility is an autoregressive process of order one, the stationarity condition is $|\beta| < 1$. Moreover, the volatility σ_η must be strictly positive. In the estimation procedure the following logistic and logarithm reparameterisations:

$$\beta = 2\left(\frac{\exp(b)}{1 + \exp(b)}\right) - 1 \qquad \sigma_\eta = \exp(s_\eta)$$

have been considered in order to satisfy the above constraints.

The second model is a particular specification of the regime switching model introduced by Hamilton. Precisely the distribution of the returns is described by two regimes with the same mean but different variances and by a constant transition matrix:

$$y_t = \begin{cases} \mu + \sigma_0 \varepsilon_t & \text{if } s_t = 0 \\ \mu + \sigma_1 \varepsilon_t & \text{if } s_t = 1 \end{cases} \qquad \mathbf{P} = \begin{bmatrix} p_{00} & 1 - p_{11} \\ 1 - p_{00} & p_{11} \end{bmatrix}$$

where[32] s_t is a two-state Markov chain independent of ε_t, which is a Gaussian white noise with unit variance. The parameters of this model are the mean μ, the low and high standard deviation σ_0, σ_1 and the transition probabilities p_{00}, p_{11} (also called regime persistence probabilities). As for the log-normal SV model, the logarithm and the logistic transformations ensure the positiveness of the volatilities and constrain the transition probabilities to assume values in the (0,1) interval.

Before starting the estimation it is necessary to transform the raw time series, expressed in level, into logarithmic returns[33] and to set the starting values of the parameters in

---

[32] According to the model (8.3), $\sigma_0 = \exp(\alpha/2)$ and $\sigma_1 = \exp((\alpha + \beta)/2)$.

[33] In the Excel file "series.xls" there are 899 observations of the daily stock indexes analysed in Section 8.1.1. In the estimation we therefore consider 898 daily return observations.

the maximisation algorithm.[34] Moreover, for the log-normal SV model the returns are modified as follows:

$$y_t^* = \log(y_t - \overline{y}_t)^2 + 1.27 \tag{8.12}$$

where $\overline{y}_t$ is the empirical mean. Thus, for the log-normal SV model the mean is not estimated but is simply set equal to the empirical mean.

While these transformations are automatically done by the estimation procedure, the setting of the starting parameter values requires a choice by the user from the following options.

- *Random initialisation*: a range of possible values of the parameters is fixed, where necessary, and a value is randomly extracted. This method is useful when the user has no idea about the possible value of the parameters but wants to better investigate the parametric space. The drawback of this option is that the optimisation algorithm may be quite time-consuming, because it needs more iterations to converge and the probability that it does not converge to the global maximum increases and then several optimisation runs (with different random starting values) may be required.
- *Data-driven initialisation*: the starting values of the parameters are calculated considering the time series analysed. For example, the sample mean is used as an approximation of the mean of the switching regime model and the empirical variance multiplied by appropriate factors is used for the high and low variance. This alternative helps the user to speed up the convergence even if he has no opinion on the possible values of the parameters.
- *User initialisation*: the starting values of the parameters are directly inserted by the user.

In the example, the data-driven initialisation has been selected.

During the estimation it is possible to control each step of the algorithm through the command MaxControl (see the readme.txt file for more information). The estimation output is then given by the estimated values of the parameters, their standard errors and relative significance test statistics.[35]

Figure 8.4 shows the final output of the log-normal SV model for the FTSE100 index. In this example the numerical optimisation ends after 76 iterations, which take 8.32 seconds,[36] and the log-likelihood[37] is -1153.7. The volatility of the FTSE100 index is very persistent, in fact the autoregressive coefficient of the volatility equation (β) is equal to 0.956. In practice, for financial time series this coefficient is very often bigger than 0.9.

Figure 8.5 exemplifies the graphic output, which consists of the estimated volatility for the FTSE100 index along with the historical return series. The estimated volatility is obtained by using the Kalman smoother $\hat{h}_{t/T} = E(h_t|Y^{*T})$, which is however not immediately useful. In fact, we are interested in $E(\sigma_t|Y^T) = E(\exp(h_t/2)|Y^T)$, but $E(\exp(h_t/2)|Y^T) \neq \exp(E(h_t/2|Y^T))$. Thus, we consider a first-order Taylor expansion

---

[34] Recall that data transformations are directly carried out by the programs that require input price levels.

[35] The standard errors are calculated following Ruiz (1994) for the log-normal SV model and as the inverse of the information matrix for the switching regime model. In both cases the z-statistics asymptotically follow an $N(0,1)$ distribution.

[36] On a Pentium III 933 MHz.

[37] For the log-normal SV model the log-likelihood is computed with the Kalman filter for the transformed series y_t^*, see equation (8.12).

```
---- Database information ----
Sample:    1 - 899 (899 observations)
Frequency: 1
Variables: 3

Variable        #obs  #miss        min       mean        max     std.dev
FTSE100          899      0     3777.1     5879.6     6930.2       623.5
CAC40            899      0     3023.7     5091.7     6922.3      892.33
MIB30            899      0      23564      37752      51093      6472.4

Starting values
parameters
   -0.00037495       0.020098       -5.9420
gradients
       -1628.7        0.56669        0.50753
Initial function =        -8311.86544015


Position after 76 BFGS iterations
Status: Strong convergence
parameters
     -0.39130         3.7872         -3.1959
gradients
  4.5475e-007 -2.2737e-007 -2.2737e-008
function value =          -1153.70477274


Stochastic Volatility Model, version 1.00
Strong convergence

                     parameters value      standard error           z-statistic
costant                   -0.391298            0.195784               -1.99862
AR part                    0.955684            0.0220615              43.3191
standard deviation         0.19665             0.0578519               3.3992
elapsed time 8.32 secs                   loglikelihood -1153.7
forecasted volatility 0.0189846
```

Figure 8.4 Estimation output of the log-normal SV model for the FTSE100 index

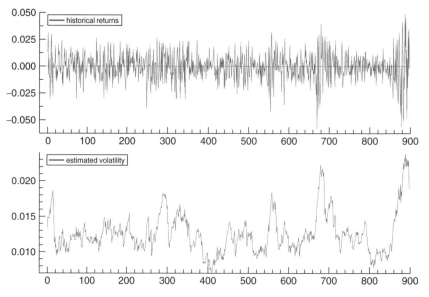

Figure 8.5 Historical returns and estimated volatility for the FTSE100 index obtained with the log-normal SV model

of $\exp(h_t/2)$ around $\hat{h}_{t/T}$, and compute the conditional mean and estimate the volatility in the following way:

$$\hat{\sigma}_{t/T} = E\left(\exp\left(\frac{h_t}{2}\right)|Y^T\right) \cong \exp\left(\frac{\hat{h}_{t/T}}{2}\right) + \frac{1}{8}\exp\left(\frac{\hat{h}_{t/T}}{2}\right)Q_{t/T}$$

This computation is performed directly by the program and Figure 8.5 presents the estimated volatility.

Figure 8.6 shows the final output[38] of the switching regime model for the FTSE100 index. In this case the numerical optimisation ends after 26 iterations, which take 7.65 seconds, and the log-likelihood[39] is -2680.18. For this model we can judge the persistence

```
---- Database information ----
Sample:    1 - 899 (899 observations)
Frequency: 1
Variables: 3

Variable        #obs  #miss        min       mean        max     std.dev
FTSE100          899      0     3777.1     5879.6     6930.2       623.5
CAC40            899      0     3023.7     5091.7     6922.3      892.33
MIB30            899      0      23564      37752      51093      6472.4

Starting values
parameters
  -0.00036337      -0.69315      -0.69315      -4.6792      -4.0521
gradients
       433.59        6.8030      -0.17620      -19.442      -54.401
Initial function =         2626.32194786

Position after 26 BFGS iterations
Status: Strong convergence
parameters
  -0.00017494        4.9389        3.2807      -4.5279      -3.7532
gradients
   5.3524e-005   0.00000 -4.5475e-008  4.3201e-006 -8.6402e-007
function value =          2680.17860015

Stochastic Volatility Model, version 1.00
Strong convergence

                         parameters value      standard error      z-statistic
mean                        -0.000174935         0.000387296        -0.451684
low persistence prob.          0.992889          0.00435136          228.179
high persistence prob.         0.963762          0.0227076           42.4422
low volatility reg.            0.0108036          0.000399697         27.0294
high volatility reg.           0.0234427          0.00231372          10.132
elapsed time   7.65 secs                 loglikelihood -2680.18
forecasted volatility 0.0196862
```

Figure 8.6 Estimation output of the switching regime model for the FTSE100 index

---

[38] It is important to underline that the z-statistics for the transition probabilities are not useful for testing $p_{ii} = 0$, $p_{ii} = 1$, $i = 0, 1$. In fact, these tests are not standard since they imply testing for the presence of two regimes (see Davies (1977, 1987) and Hansen (1992, 1996)).

[39] In this case the log-likelihood is computed with the Hamilton filter for the return series and thus it is not directly comparable with the log-likelihood of the log-normal SV model.

of the volatility by the value taken by the transition (or persistence) probabilities p_{00}, p_{11}. They are very high (0.99 and 0.96), confirming the high persistence of the volatility of the FTSE100 index. Moreover, the levels of the high and low volatility are perfectly in line with the values of the volatility estimated with the log-normal SV model.

In Figure 8.7 the graphic output of the switching regime model is presented. It consists of the historical return series, the weighted or estimated volatility and the estimated switches between regimes.[40]

To estimate the volatility we consider the output of the Kim smoother. Since $\sigma_t = \exp(\alpha/2)(1 - s_t) + \exp((\alpha + \beta)/2)s_t = \sigma_0(1 - s_t) + \sigma_1 s_t$, we can compute:

$$\hat{\sigma}_{t/T} = E(\sigma_t|Y^T) = \sigma_0 P(s_t = 0|Y^T) + \sigma_1 P(s_t = 1|Y^T) \tag{8.13}$$

where

$$P(s_t = 0|Y^T) = P(h_t = \alpha|Y^T) \quad \text{and} \quad P(s_t = 1|Y^T) = P(h_t = \alpha + \beta|Y^T)$$

Finally, it is possible to save the estimated volatility. Since the visualisation of the graphs is possible only with the commercial version of Ox, if this is not available the program allows only the saving of the estimated volatility series. The "SeriesEst" command allows the saving of the following series in an Excel format:[41] historical returns,

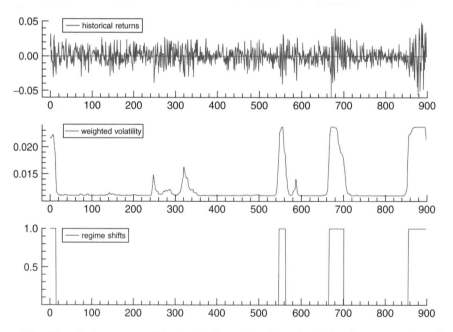

Figure 8.7 Historical returns, weighted volatility and estimated switches between regimes for the FTSE100 index obtained with the regime switching model

---

[40] The regime is 0 if $P(h_t = \alpha|Y^T) \geq 0.5$ and 1 otherwise.

[41] In the output file, for the ARSV model, Var1 indicates the historical returns and Var2 the estimated volatilities. For the SRSV, Var1 indicates the historical returns, Var2 the estimated volatilities, Var3 and Var4 the smoothed and filtered probabilities of the high volatility regime and Var5 the regime shifts.

```
...
// simulation command, input required:
// a -> simulate? 0:yes 1:no
// b -> simulated model 0:ARSV, 1:SRSV
// c -> length of simulated series
// d -> parameters for the simulation:
//        3x1 if b=0   ex. <-0.28; 0.54; 0.15>
//        5x1 if b=1   ex. <-0.01; 0.8; 0.8; 0.2; 0.4>
//        if 0 use the last estimated values, check that model type of
//        simulation and estimation correspond
// in the example, simulate ARSV with last estimated parameters
stochobj.Simulation(0, 0, 2500, 0);

// save data to file
// historical returns; estimated volatility;
// conditional probability of high regime; regime shifts.
stochobj.SeriesEst("c:/programs/stocvol/FTSE100E.xls");

// save data to file
// simulated returns; simulated volatility;
// conditional probability of high regime; regime shifts.
stochobj.SeriesSim("c:/programs/stocvol/FTSE100S.xls");

// Graph command, input required
// a -> 0: visualize, 1: don't visualize
// save graph to file, path of the destination
stochobj.Graph(0, "c:/programs/stocvol/graphs.ps");
...
```

Figure 8.8   The "Simulation", "SeriesEst", "SeriesSim" and "Graph" commands

estimated volatilities and for the switching regime model the smoothed and filtered probabilities of the high volatility regime and the regime shifts. Moreover, the graphs can be directly saved in a postscript format with the "Graph" command. In both cases the user should provide a path including the name and extension of the destination file. The "Graph" command includes also an additional control variable to choose whether or not to plot the series (see Figure 8.8).

8.7.1.2   Simulation

The Volatility program also allows simulation of both the models. The "Simulation" command gives the possibility to choose the type of model, the values of the parameters and the length of the simulated series. If the user wants to simulate the model characterised by the parameters just estimated, the last input of the "Simulation" command must be set to 0, otherwise it has to be replaced by the column vector of the desired parameters.

The graphic output of the simulation is composed of the simulated series and their volatilities. A final possibility is to plot both the estimation and simulation phases (see Figures 8.9 and 8.10). In particular, for the switching regime model the program plots the simulated volatility, which jumps between the low and high level, and the smoothed (weighted) simulated volatility, which is computed in the same way as the estimated volatility (see equation (8.13)).

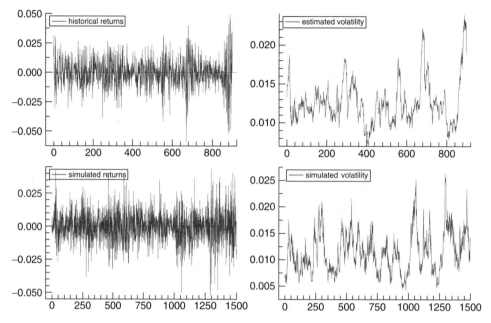

Figure 8.9   Estimation and simulation graphic output of the log-normal SV model

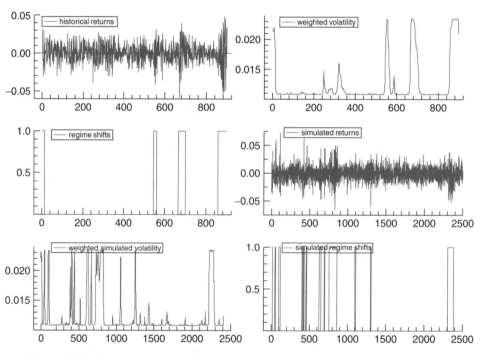

Figure 8.10   Estimation and simulation graphic output of the switching regime model

Finally, it is possible to save the simulated volatility. The "SeriesSim" command allows the saving of the following series in an Excel format:[42] simulated returns, simulated volatilities and for the switching regime model the smoothed probabilities of the high volatility regime and the regime shifts.

8.7.1.3 Forecasting

The final output given by the Volatility program is the forecasted volatility for the following period. The Kalman and Hamilton filters also give the prediction density of h_{t+1}, then it is possible to forecast the next value of the volatility.

For the log-normal SV model, we consider a first-order Taylor expansion of $\exp(h_t/2)$ around $\hat{h}_{T+1/T}$ and by taking the conditional expectation we forecast the volatility in the following way:

$$\hat{\sigma}_{T+1/T} = E\left(\exp\left(\frac{h_{T+1}}{2}\right)\bigg|Y^T\right) \cong \exp\left(\frac{\hat{h}_{T+1/T}}{2}\right) + \frac{1}{8}\exp\left(\frac{\hat{h}_{T+1/T}}{2}\right)Q_{T+1/T}$$

With regard to the switching regime model, since $\sigma_t = \sigma_0(1 - s_t) + \sigma_1 s_t$, we can forecast the volatility as follows:

$$\hat{\sigma}_{T+1/T} = E(\sigma_{T+1}|Y^T) = \sigma_0 P(s_{T+1} = 0|Y^T) + \sigma_1 P(s_{T+1} = 1|Y^T)$$

where

$$P(s_{T+1} = 0|Y^T) = P(h_{T+1} = \alpha|Y^T) \qquad P(s_{T+1} = 1|Y^T) = P(h_{T+1} = \alpha + \beta|Y^T)$$

are the prediction probabilities[43] obtained with the last iteration of the Hamilton filter.

The forecasted volatility is evidenced in the output and it is saved as the last value of the estimated volatility.[44]

Let us now consider some practical utilisations of the estimated volatilities.

8.7.2 Option pricing

As seen in Section 8.1.2, the option price in the Black and Scholes framework can be expressed as a conditional expectation given the current price of the underlying asset:

$$C_t^{BS} = \exp(-r\tau)E_{S_{t+\tau}|S_t}[\max(S_{t+\tau} - K, 0)]$$

---

[42] For the ARSV model, Var1 indicates the simulated returns and Var2 the simulated volatilities. For the SRSV, Var1 indicates the simulated returns, Var2 the simulated volatilities, Var3 the smoothed probabilities of the high volatility regime and Var4 the regime shifts.

[43] It is possible to obtain the prediction probabilities by multiplying the transition matrix $\mathbf{P}$ by the filtered probabilities (which are saved in the estimation output file as Var4), i.e.

$$\begin{bmatrix} P(s_{t+1} = 0|Y^t) \\ P(s_{t+1} = 1|Y^t) \end{bmatrix} = \mathbf{P}\begin{bmatrix} P(s_t = 0|Y^t) \\ P(s_t = 1|Y^t) \end{bmatrix}$$

[44] In the estimation output file, in the last row the non-zero value for the estimated volatility is the forecasted volatility, while the non-zero value for the filtered probability is the prediction probability of the high volatility regime (see footnote 43). All the other variables are set equal to zero.

where the dynamic of the asset is described by a geometric diffusion process and the expectation is taken with respect to the risk-neutral probability measure.

Since the Black and Scholes formula can be expressed as a function only of the volatility, great effort has been made in modelling its behaviour. While Black and Scholes assume that it is constant over the life of the option, a series of models proposed in the late 1980s supposes that it varies through time in a deterministic or stochastic way, in an attempt to capture the empirical features of the option prices. In fact, an analysis of the volatility implied in the market option prices (the so-called implied volatility) highlights that the volatility is neither constant through time nor independent of the strike price (the so-called "smile" and "sneer" effect) (see Rubinstein (1985)).

A very simple approach consists of using the volatility estimated with stochastic volatility models as input to the Black and Scholes formula. In that case, it is sufficient to consider the forecasted volatility $\hat{\sigma}_{t/t-1}$ as the volatility parameter in the formula to obtain the option price:

$$C_t = C_t^{BS}(\hat{\sigma}_{t/t-1})$$

In the following we review some stochastic volatility models for the option pricing, which consider the volatility as an exogenous stochastic process.

The path-breaking work on stochastic volatility models applied to option pricing is the paper by Hull and White (1987). The authors assume that both the underlying security S and the variance σ^2 follow a geometric diffusion process:

$$dS = \mu S dt + \sigma S dz$$
$$d\sigma^2 = \phi \sigma^2 dt + \xi \sigma^2 d\omega$$

where the correlation ρ between the two Brownian motions dz, $d\omega$ is a constant with modulus less than one. Hull and White take $\rho \equiv 0$. Scott (1987) considers the case in which the volatility follows an Ornstein–Uhlenbeck process and also imposes the restriction $\rho \equiv 0$. Finally, Heston (1993) proposes the familiar mean-reverting square root process for the volatility:

$$dS = \mu S dt + \sigma S dz$$
$$d\sigma^2 = \gamma(\phi - \sigma^2)dt + \xi \sigma d\omega$$

where ϕ is the long-run average variance and he takes the assumption $\rho \neq 0$.

Introducing stochastic volatility into the definition of the stochastic differential equation of the underlying asset creates several complications. A dynamic portfolio with only one option and one underlying asset is not sufficient to create a riskless investment strategy. The problem arises since the stochastic differential equation for the option contains two sources of uncertainty. Unfortunately, it is impossible to eliminate volatility market risk premium and correlation parameters from the partial differential equation using only one option and one underlying asset. Moreover, these parameters are difficult to estimate[45] and extensive use of numerical techniques is required to solve the two-dimensional partial differential equation.

---

[45] An exception occurs when the volatility is a deterministic function of the asset price or time. In this case it is possible to easily find a solution to the partial differential equation.

In the Hull and White (1987) formula, the option price is determined assuming that the volatility market risk premium is zero and there is zero correlation between the two Brownian motions describing the underlying asset and the volatility, i.e. the volatility is uncorrelated with the asset price. With these assumptions and using a risk-neutral valuation procedure, they show that the price of an option with stochastic volatility is the Black and Scholes price integrated over the distribution of the mean volatility:

$$C_t^{HW} = \int C_t^{BS}(\overline{\sigma}^2) g(\overline{\sigma}^2 | \sigma_t^2) d\overline{\sigma}^2$$

where

$$\overline{\sigma}^2 = \frac{1}{\tau} \int_t^{t+\tau} \sigma^2(u) du$$

and $g(\overline{\sigma} | \sigma_t^2)$ is the conditional probability density of the mean variance $\overline{\sigma}^2$ over the period τ.

In the more general case of non-zero correlation, the framework becomes more complex, allowing only numerical solutions.

It can be observed that continuous time stochastic volatility provides an attractive and intuitive explanation for observed volatility patterns and for observed biases in implied volatility. Precisely, smiles, skews, upward and downward term structures of implied volatility arise naturally from a stochastic volatility model. However the fact that stochastic volatility models fit empirical patterns does not mean that those models are correct and the biases in market prices may be the result of other factors, not considered, such as liquidity problems.

A work related to that of Hull and White is Naik (1993). While in the Hull and White specification the volatility follows a continuous diffusion process, Naik analyses the case where the instantaneous variance of an asset is subject to random discontinuous shifts. In particular, the volatility is described with a right-continuous Markov chain process: it remains in the same state for a random amount of time and then shifts to another state with transition probabilities determined by a matrix. In the case of a two-state volatility process the transition matrix is simply:

$$\mathbf{P} = \begin{bmatrix} p_{00} & 1 - p_{11} \\ 1 - p_{00} & p_{11} \end{bmatrix}$$

Assuming that the underlying process is continuous, the risk of a shift in volatility is diversifiable, and therefore not priced, and that the two processes are uncorrelated, the option valuation equation can be expressed in a closed form as follows:

$$C_t^N(\sigma_1) = \int_0^\tau C_t^{BS}(\overline{\sigma}^2(x)) g(x | \sigma_1) dx$$

where σ_1 indicates the high volatility level, $\overline{\sigma}^2(x) = [\sigma_1^2 x + \sigma_0^2(\tau - x)]/\tau, 0 \le x \le \tau$ and $g(x | \sigma_1)$ denotes the unconditional density of the time spent by the volatility process in the high volatility state, given the current high volatility state. In the same way it is possible to determine the option price conditional on the current low volatility state ($C_t^N(\sigma_0)$ with σ_0 the low volatility level).

As in the Hull and White model, the option price is the expectation of the Black and Scholes formula computed for the average future volatility, given the current state. Since two regimes are considered, the final option price can be obtained by a weighted average of the two conditional values $C_t^N(\sigma_1)$ and $C_t^N(\sigma_0)$.

This analysis can be extended by considering multiple states and correlation between changes of the underlying and shifts in volatility, but unfortunately in these cases the option price can be obtained only via numerical methods. In this kind of procedure a discrete time Markov chain is used as an approximation of the volatility process.

We briefly present two examples of this approach, due to Billio and Pelizzon (1997) and Bollen (1998) (see also Bollen *et al.* (2000)). Both these works are based on the hypothesis that the returns of the underlying asset follow a switching regime model. The distribution is characterised by a mixture of distributions with different variance, where the weights depend on a hidden Markov chain process which represents possible different volatility regimes of the market. To obtain the numerical solution, the basic idea is to approximate the distribution through a multinomial approach, considering a binomial tree for each of the two distributions characterised by different variance.

Following Cox *et al.* (1979), the future value of the underlying process can be expressed as:

$$S_{t+\Delta t} = \begin{cases} uS_t & p \\ dS_t & 1-p \end{cases}$$

One possible specification of the parameters that guarantees asymptotic normality and convergence to the desired mean and variance of the continuously compounded returns is $u = \exp(\sqrt{\sigma^2 \Delta t + r^2 \Delta t^2})$, $d = u^{-1}$ and $p = (e^{r\Delta t} - d)/(u - d)$. In this case the process is fully characterised by the parameter representing the variance σ^2, since the step size Δt and the risk-free interest rate r are given. Once the variance is estimated it is possible to construct a tree to represent the possible future paths of the variable and hence the distribution of returns (at maturity).

If a regime switching model is considered, the distribution of the returns is simply a mixture of the distributions characterising each state. Therefore a discrete process can be used to approximate the continuous time process, and hence the distribution of returns, in each state. In this case, two binomial distributions are used as an approximation of the mixture of the two distributions:

$$S_{t+\Delta t} = \begin{cases} u_1 S_t | s_t = 1 & p_{11} \\ u_0 S_t | s_t = 0 & p_{00} \\ d_0 S_t | s_t = 0 & 1 - p_{00} \\ d_1 S_t | s_t = 1 & 1 - p_{11} \end{cases}$$

where s_t denotes the regime.

In this case it is necessary to invoke the risk-neutral hypothesis to determine the values of the parameters that are $u_1 = \exp(\sqrt{\sigma_1^2 \Delta t + r^2 \Delta t^2})$, $d_1 = u_1^{-1}$, $p_{11} = (e^{r\Delta t} - d_1)/(u_1 - d_1)$ for the high volatility regime and $u_0 = \exp(\sqrt{\sigma_0^2 \Delta t + r^2 \Delta t^2})$, $d_0 = u_0^{-1}$ and $p_{00} = (e^{r\Delta t} - d_0)/(u_0 - d_0)$ for the low volatility regime. This model is usually called a quadrinomial tree (or lattice). The inner two branches correspond to the low volatility regime while the outer ones correspond to the high volatility regime. Each set of probabilities $(p_{ii}, 1 - p_{ii})$ must be interpreted as the branch probability conditional on the regime i, with $i = 0, 1$.

Although the quadrinomial tree represents both distributions accurately, its branches do not recombine efficiently, exhibiting an exponential growth of the computational time as the number of steps increases.

Bollen (1998) proposes a method to overcome this problem and develops a pentanomial tree. The definition of the parameters is modified to yield both the possibility to recombine the tree and the convergence of the discrete process to the mixture of distributions. This is obtained by approximating each regime density by a trinomial distribution instead of the binomial one. The modified tree has five evenly spaced branches because the step sizes of the two regimes are in the ratio 1:2 ($u_1 = \exp(\sqrt{\sigma_1^2 \Delta t + r^2 \Delta t^2})$, $u_0 = \exp(\frac{1}{2}\sqrt{\sigma_1^2 \Delta t + r^2 \Delta t^2})$ and the middle branch is shared by the two regimes:

$$S_{t+\Delta t} = \begin{cases} u_1 S_t | s_t = 1 & p_{1,u} \\ u_0 S_t | s_t = 0 & p_{0,u} \\ S_t & p_m \\ d_0 S_t | s_t = 0 & p_{0,d} \\ d_1 S_t | s_t = 1 & p_{1,d} \end{cases}$$

where $p_{s_t,u}$, $p_{s_t,d}$ are the probabilities to go up and down conditional on the regime s_t and p_m is the probability to remain at the same level price S_t.

Once the tree is generated, the option value is calculated operating backward from the terminal values, i.e. the payoffs, to the valuation time. In the regime switching approaches, for simplicity two conditional option values are calculated at each step, where the conditioning information is the regime at the valuation time t:

$$\begin{cases} C_t(s_t = 0) = [p_{00}C_{t+1}(s_{t+1} = 0) + (1 - p_{00})C_{t+1}(s_{t+1} = 1)]e^{-r\Delta t} \\ C_t(s_t = 1) = [(1 - p_{11})C_{t+1}(s_{t+1} = 0) + p_{11}C_{t+1}(s_{t+1} = 1)]e^{-r\Delta t} \end{cases}$$

At the valuation time the value of the option is obtained as a weighted average of the two conditional option values, where the weights depend on the knowledge of the current regime. If the regime is unknown, the unconditional probabilities:

$$\frac{1 - p_{11}}{2 - p_{00} - p_{11}} \qquad \frac{1 - p_{00}}{2 - p_{00} - p_{11}}$$

are used.

Let us take an example of the pentanomial approach by considering the parameters estimated in Section 8.7.1.1.

We deal with a European call option on the FTSE100 index quoted at LIFFE on 22 August 2000 (when the FTSE100 index quoted 6584.82), with maturity June 2001 and strike price 5900. The risk-free interest rate r is approximated with three-month Libor[46] and the time to maturity in terms of trading days is 213. In this example $\Delta t = 1$.

---

[46] London Interbank Offered Rate.

Taking the estimated volatilities of Section 8.7.1.1, the parameters of the pentanomial model can be computed as follows:

$$p_{1,u} = \frac{e^r - e^{-\sqrt{\sigma_1^2 + r^2}}}{e^{\sqrt{\sigma_1^2 + r^2}} - e^{-\sqrt{\sigma_1^2 + r^2}}}$$

$$u_1 = e^{\sqrt{\sigma_1^2 + r^2}}$$

$$p_{0,u} = \frac{e^r - e^{-\frac{1}{2}\sqrt{\sigma_1^2 + r^2}} - p_m\left(1 - e^{-\frac{1}{2}\sqrt{\sigma_1^2 + r^2}}\right)}{e^{\frac{1}{2}\sqrt{\sigma_1^2 + r^2}} - e^{-\frac{1}{2}\sqrt{\sigma_1^2 + r^2}}}$$

$$u_0 = e^{\frac{1}{2}\sqrt{\sigma_1^2 + r^2}}$$

$$d_0 = e^{-\frac{1}{2}\sqrt{\sigma_1^2 + r^2}}$$

$$p_m = 1 - 4\left(\frac{\sqrt{\sigma_0^2 + r^2}}{\sqrt{\sigma_1^2 + r^2}}\right)^2$$

$$d_1 = e^{-\sqrt{\sigma_1^2 + r^2}}$$

$$p_{0,d} = 1 - p_{0,u} - p_m$$

$$p_{1,d} = 1 - p_{1,u}$$

Once the tree is generated, the payoffs are calculated with the usual procedure (see Appendix A for details). The conditional option values $C_t(s_t = 0)$, $C_t(s_t = 1)$ are obtained using the estimated transition probabilities, while the final value of the option is a weighted average where the weights are the unconditional probabilities:

$$\frac{1 - p_{11}}{2 - p_{00} - p_{11}} \qquad \frac{1 - p_{00}}{2 - p_{00} - p_{11}}$$

The pentanomial option value is therefore 1055.14, while the market value was 1047.5.

8.7.3 Value at risk

VaR is a very intuitive measure to evaluate market risk because it indicates the maximum potential loss at a given level of confidence (a) for a portfolio of financial assets over a specified time horizon (h).

In practice, the value of a portfolio is expressed as a function of K risk factors, $x_\tau = \sum_{i=1}^{N} w_{i,t} P_{i,\tau}(\chi_{1,\tau}, \ldots, \chi_{K,\tau})$. The factors influencing the portfolio value are usually identified with some market variables such as interest rates, exchange rates or stock indexes. If their distribution is known in a closed form, we need to estimate the distribution of the future value of the portfolio conditional on the available information and the VaR is then the solution to:

$$a = \int_{-\infty}^{\text{VaR}(h,a)} f(x_{t+h}) \, dx$$

Different parametric models can be used to forecast the portfolio return distribution. The simple way to calculate VaR involves assuming that the risk factor returns follow a multivariate normal distribution conditional on the available information. If the portfolio return is linearly dependent on them, its probability distribution is also normal and the VaR is simply the quantile of this analytic distribution. If the linear assumption is inappropriate, the portfolio return can be approximated as a quadratic function of the risk factor returns.

An alternative way to handle the non-linearity is to use Monte Carlo simulation. The idea is to simulate repeatedly the random processes governing the risk factors. Each simulation gives us a possible value for the portfolio at the end of our time horizon. If enough of these simulations are considered, it is possible to infer the VaR, as the relevant quantile of the simulated distribution.

Since market risk factors usually have fatter tails than the normal distribution, it is also possible to use historical simulation rather than a parametric approach. The idea behind this technique is to use the historical distribution of returns to the assets in the portfolio to simulate the portfolio's VaR, on the hypothetical assumption that we held this portfolio over the period of time covered by our historical data set. Thus, the historical simulation involves collecting historic asset returns over some observation period and using the weights of the current portfolio to simulate the hypothetical returns we would have had if we had held our current portfolio over the observation period. It is then assumed that this historical distribution of returns is also a good proxy for the portfolio return distribution it will face over the next holding period and VaR is calculated as the relevant quantile of this distribution.

The advantage of the parametric approach is that the factors variance–covariance matrix can be updated using a general model of changing or stochastic volatility. The main disadvantage is that the factor returns are usually assumed to be conditionally normal, losing the possibility to take into account non-linear correlations among them. Historical simulation has the advantage of reflecting the historical multivariate probability distribution of the risk factor returns, avoiding ad hoc assumptions. However the method suffers a serious drawback. Its main disadvantage is that it does not incorporate volatility updating. Moreover, extreme quantiles are difficult to estimate, as extrapolation beyond past observations is impossible. Finally, quantile estimates tend to be very volatile whenever a large observation enters the sample and the database is not sufficiently large.

The advantage of the parametric approach to update the volatility suggests the simplest utilisation of the SV models for the VaR computation. Having chosen the asset or portfolio distribution (usually the normal one), it is possible to use the forecasted volatility to characterise the future return distribution. Thus, $\hat{\sigma}_{T+1/T}$ can be used to calculate the VaR over the next period.

A different approach using the SV model is to devolatilise the observed returns series and to revolatilise it with an appropriate forecasted value, obtained with a particular model of changing volatility. This approach is considered in several recent works (Barone-Adesi et al., 1998; Hull and White, 1998) and is a way of combining different methods and partially overcoming the drawbacks of each.

To make the historical simulation consistent with empirical findings, the log-normal SV model and the regime switching model may be considered to describe the volatility behaviour. Past returns are standardised by the estimated volatility to obtain standardised residuals. Statistical tests can confirm that these standardised residuals behave approximately as an iid series which exhibits heavy tails. Historical simulation can then be used. Finally, to adjust them to the current market conditions, the randomly selected standardised residuals are multiplied by the forecasted volatility obtained with the SV model.

Table 8.2 VaR at different confidence levels for the FTSE100 index return

Confidence level	Log-normal SV model	Regime switching model
0.1	2.5442	2.7503
0.05	3.9298	3.5874
0.01	5.3417	4.6502

For example, Table 8.2 shows the results obtained with the FTSE100 index return by considering 1 000 000 historical simulations[47] (see Appendix B for details). Clearly, this approach allows a wide range of stochastic and changing volatility models, such as ARCH–GARCH models, to be considered. Moreover, it must be pointed out that instead of using historical simulation, an appropriate standard distribution can also be considered to model the transformed returns and then several probability distributions can be assumed for the unconditional returns (McNeil and Frey, 2000; Eberlein *et al.*, 2001).

Another example of a parametric approach to VaR calculation considers the hypothesis that a regime switching model governs the asset returns (Billio and Pelizzon, 2000):

$$y_t = \begin{cases} \mu + \sigma_0 \varepsilon_t & s_t = 0 \\ \mu + \sigma_1 \varepsilon_t & s_t = 1 \end{cases}$$

where $\varepsilon_t \sim N(0,1)$ is independent of s_t.

To calculate the VaR it is necessary to determine the value of the conditional distribution for which the cumulative density is a, i.e.

$$a = \sum_{s_{t+h}=0,1} P(s_{t+h}|I_t) \int_{-\infty}^{\text{VaR}(h,a)} f_{s_{t+h}}(y_{t+h}|I_t)\, dy$$

where $f_{s_{t+h}}(y_{t+h}|I_t)$ is the probability density of y_{t+h} when the regime is s_{t+h} and conditional on the available information set I_t (usually containing past returns), $P(s_{t+h}|I_t)$ is the prediction probability obtained by the Hamilton filter.

Given the parameters estimated in Section 8.7.1.1 for the switching regime model and the prediction probabilities at time $t + h$ (obtained by the product of the transition matrix, for $h - 1$ steps, and the conditional probabilities $P(s_{t+1}|I_t)$ given by the Hamilton filter), the VaR is the relevant quantile of the mixture distribution.

The model can be generalised to the case of N risky assets providing an explicit link between the return on the asset and the return on the market index, thus by explicitly modelling the correlation between different assets. The Multivariate Switching Regime Beta Model (Billio and Pelizzon, 2000) is a sort of market model or better a single factor model in the Arbitrage Pricing Theory framework where the return of a single stock i is characterised by the regime switching of the market index and the regime switching of the specific risk of the asset. It can be written as:

$$\begin{cases} y_{mt} = \mu_m(s_t) + \sigma_m(s_t)\varepsilon_t & \varepsilon_t \sim IIN(0,1) \\ y_{1t} = \mu_1(s_{1t}) + \beta_1(s_t, s_{1t})y_{mt} + \sigma_1(s_{1t})\varepsilon_{1t} & \varepsilon_{1t} \sim IIN(0,1) \\ y_{2t} = \mu_2(s_{2t}) + \beta_2(s_t, s_{2t})y_{mt} + \sigma_2(s_{2t})\varepsilon_{2t} & \varepsilon_{2t} \sim IIN(0,1) \\ \quad \vdots \\ y_{Nt} = \mu_N(s_{Nt}) + \beta_N(s_t, s_{Nt})y_{mt} + \sigma_N(s_{Nt})\varepsilon_{Nt} & \varepsilon_{Nt} \sim IIN(0,1) \end{cases}$$

---

[47] Each operation takes about 12 seconds.

where y_{mt} is the market return, the market regime variable s_t and the single stock regime variables s_{jt}, $j = 1, \ldots, N$ are independent Markov chains, ε_t and ε_{jt}, $j = 1, \ldots, N$, are independently distributed.

Using this approach it is possible to take into account the correlation between different assets. In fact, the variance–covariance matrix between the two assets i and j is:

$$\boldsymbol{\Sigma}(s_t, s_{it}, s_{jt}) = \begin{bmatrix} \beta_i^2(s_t, s_{it})\sigma_m^2(s_t) + \sigma_i^2(s_{it}) & \beta_i(s_t, s_{it})\beta_j(s_t, s_{jt})\sigma_m^2(s_t) \\ \beta_i(s_t, s_{it})\beta_j(s_t, s_{jt})\sigma_m^2(s_t) & \beta_j^2(s_t, s_{jt})\sigma_m^2(s_t) + \sigma_j^2(s_{jt}) \end{bmatrix}$$

then the correlation between different assets depends on the extent to which each asset is linked, through the factor loading β, to the market index.

To calculate VaR for a portfolio based on N assets it is sufficient to use the approach presented above. In particular, considering two assets and assuming that the number of regimes is two for all three Markov chains we have:

$$a = \sum_{s_{t+h}=0,1} \sum_{s_{i,t+h}=0,1} \sum_{s_{j,t+h}=0,1} P(s_{t+h}, s_{i,t+h}, s_{j,t+h}|I_t) \int_{-\infty}^{\text{VaR}(h,a)} f_{s_{t+h}, s_{i,t+h}, s_{j,t+h}}(y|I_t)\, dy$$

where $f_{s_{t+h}, s_{i,t+h}, s_{j,t+h}}(y|I_t)$ is the probability density of the portfolio return y when the regimes are $s_{t+h}, s_{i,t+h}, s_{j,t+h}$ and conditional on the available information set I_t. This distribution has mean $\mathbf{w}'\boldsymbol{\mu}(s_{t+h}, s_{i,t+h}, s_{j,t+h})$ and variance $\mathbf{w}'\boldsymbol{\Sigma}(s_{t+h}, s_{i,t+h}, s_{j,t+h})\mathbf{w}$ where $\mathbf{w}$ is the vector of the percentage of wealth invested in the two assets and $\boldsymbol{\mu}(s_{t+h}, s_{i,t+h}, s_{j,t+h})$ is the vector of risky asset mean returns, i.e.

$$\boldsymbol{\mu}(s_{t+h}, s_{i,t+h}, s_{j,t+h}) = \begin{cases} \mu_i(s_{i,t+h}) + \beta_i(s_{t+h}, s_{i,t+h})\mu_m(s_{t+h}) \\ \mu_j(s_{j,t+h}) + \beta_j(s_{t+h}, s_{j,t+h})\mu_m(s_{t+h}) \end{cases}$$

The drawback of this approach is that it requires the estimation of a number of parameters that grows exponentially with the number of assets. In fact, the number of possible regimes generated by this model is 2^{N+1}.

One possible solution is to consider the idiosyncratic risk distributed as $IIN(0, \sigma_i^2)$ (without a specific Markov chain dependency) and to characterise the systematic risk with more than one source of risk. This approach is in line with the Arbitrage Pricing Theory model where the risky factors are characterised by switching regime processes. Formally, we can write this model as:

$$\begin{cases} F_{jt} = \alpha_j(s_{jt}) + \theta_j(s_{jt})\varepsilon_{jt} & \varepsilon_{jt} \sim IIN(0,1), \quad j = 1, 2, \ldots, K \\ y_{it} = \mu_i + \sum_{j=1}^{K} \beta_{ij}(s_{jt})F_{jt} + \sigma_i \varepsilon_{it} & \varepsilon_{it} \sim IIN(0,1), \quad i = 1, 2, \ldots, N \end{cases}$$

where F_{jt} is the value of factor j at time t ($j = 1, 2, \ldots, K$), $\beta_{ij}(s_{jt})$ is the factor loading of the asset i on factor j, s_{jt}, $j = 1, 2, \ldots, K$, are independent Markov chains, and ε_{jt}, $j = 1, 2, \ldots, K$, and ε_{jt}, $j = 1, 2, \ldots, N$, are independently distributed.

This model is more parsimonious, in fact the introduction of an extra asset implies that only $K + 2$ parameters need to be estimated. This approach is valid when the number of assets in the portfolio is high and the specific risk is easily eliminated by diversification.

8.8 CONCLUDING REMARKS

We have tried to develop an introduction to the current literature on stochastic volatility models. Other than the classical log-normal model introduced by Taylor (1986), we have also presented the discrete volatility model in which the latent stochastic structure of the volatility is described by a Markov chain.

Both models (with continuous and discrete volatility) fit in the framework of a non-linear and non-Gaussian state space model, thus the estimation and smoothing problems are developed along the same lines. Only for the discrete case does the general algorithm introduced allow us to compute the likelihood function and then to obtain maximum likelihood estimates. In the continuous case, approximations or simulations must be introduced.

Some extensions and multivariate models are also presented, however there is still a great deal of work to be done.

Finally, the estimation program presented considers the two basic models and allows an estimation of the latent volatility. Some possible applications are suggested and discussed.

APPENDIX A: APPLICATION OF THE PENTANOMIAL MODEL

The example considers a European call option on the FTSE100 index, with maturity June 2001 and strike price 5900 traded at LIFFE on 22 August 2000. Three-month Libor is used as an approximation of the risk-free interest rate r. The FTSE100 index quoted 6584.82 and Libor was 6.22%.

The FTSE100 index being a weighted average of the prices of 100 stocks, the dividend effect must be considered. In the example, this parameter is considered constant[48] and equal to $q = 3\%$. The time to maturity in terms of trading days is 213 and the step size is the single trading day ($\Delta t = 1$).

Taking the estimated volatilities of Section 8.7.1.1 ($\hat{\sigma}_0 = 0.0108036$ and $\hat{\sigma}_1 = 0.0234427$), the parameters of the pentanomial model can be computed as follows:

$$p_{1,u} = \frac{e^{r-q} - e^{-\sqrt{\hat{\sigma}_1^2 + (r-q)^2}}}{e^{\sqrt{\hat{\sigma}_1^2 + (r-q)^2}} - e^{-\sqrt{\hat{\sigma}_1^2 + (r-q)^2}}} = 0.4968$$

$$u_1 = e^{\sqrt{\hat{\sigma}_1^2 + (r-q)^2}} = 1.0237$$

$$u_0 = e^{\frac{1}{2}\sqrt{\hat{\sigma}_1^2 + (r-q)^2}} = 1.0118$$

$$p_{0,u} = \frac{e^{r-q} - e^{-\frac{1}{2}\sqrt{\hat{\sigma}_1^2 + (r-q)^2}} - p_m\left(1 - e^{-\frac{1}{2}\sqrt{\hat{\sigma}_1^2 + (r-q)^2}}\right)}{e^{\frac{1}{2}\sqrt{\hat{\sigma}_1^2 + (r-q)^2}} - e^{-\frac{1}{2}\sqrt{\hat{\sigma}_1^2 + (r-q)^2}}}$$
$$= 0.4277$$

$$d_0 = e^{-\frac{1}{2}\sqrt{\hat{\sigma}_1^2 + (r-q)^2}} = 0.9883$$

$$d_1 = e^{-\sqrt{\hat{\sigma}_1^2 + (r-q)^2}} = 0.9768$$

$$p_m = 1 - 4\left(\frac{\sqrt{\hat{\sigma}_0^2 + (r-q)^2}}{\sqrt{\hat{\sigma}_1^2 + (r-q)^2}}\right)^2 = 0.1504$$

$$p_{0,d} = 1 - p_{0,u} - p_m = 0.4219$$

$$p_{1,d} = 1 - p_{1,u} = 0.5032$$

---

[48] During the period of analysis the dividend yield was nearly constant. For details, see http://www.londonstockexchange.com.

Given u_1, u_0, d_0, d_1, the possible one-step-ahead values for the FTSE100 index can be calculated as follows:

$$S_{t+1} \rightarrow \begin{cases} \rightarrow & u_1 S_t = 6741.01 \\ \rightarrow & u_0 S_t = 6662.45 \\ & S_t = 6584.82 \\ \rightarrow & d_0 S_t = 6508.11 \\ \rightarrow & d_1 S_t = 6432.25 \end{cases}$$

and the tree is recursively generated.

The payoffs at maturity are calculated with the usual formula:

$$C_T = \max(S_T - K, 0)$$

and the values of the option in the previous periods are obtained operating backwards. In particular:

• At time $T - 1$, the conditional values of the option at the ith node, $C_{T-1}^i(s_{T-1} = 0)$, $C_{T-1}^i(s_{T-1} = 1)$, are given by

$$\begin{cases} C_{T-1}^i(s_{T-1} = 0) = [(1 - p_{0,u} - p_m)C_T^{i-1} + p_m C_T^i + p_{0,u} C_T^{i+1}]e^{-r} \\ C_{T-1}^i(s_{T-1} = 1) = [(1 - p_{1,u})C_T^{i-2} + p_{1,u} C_T^{i+2}]e^{-r} \end{cases}$$

Note that the nodes ± 1 consider the option values obtained with u_0 and d_0, while the nodes ± 2 consider u_1 and d_1. The calculation is repeated for all the nodes at time $T - 1$ and we obtain two sets of conditional option values $C_{T-1}^i(s_{T-1} = 0)$, $C_{T-1}^i(s_{T-1} = 1)$.

• At time $T - 2$
  – for each node i, the values of the option are obtained conditional on the regime in $T - 1$:

$$\begin{cases} C_{T-2/T-1}^i(s_{T-1} = 0) = [(1 - p_{0,u} - p_m)C_{T-1}^{i-1}(s_{T-1} = 0) + p_m C_{T-1}^i(s_{T-1} = 0) + p_{0,u}C_{T-1}^{i+1}(s_{T-1} = 0)] \\ C_{T-2/T-1}^i(s_{T-1} = 1) = [(1 - p_{0,u} - p_m)C_{T-1}^{i-1}(s_{T-1} = 1) + p_m C_{T-1}^i(s_{T-1} = 1) + p_{0,u}C_{T-1}^{i+1}(s_{T-1} = 1)] \end{cases}$$

  – using the estimated transition probabilities ($\hat{p}_{00} = 0.992889$, $\hat{p}_{11} = 0.963762$), they are then discounted considering the possibility that a switch occurs between time $T - 1$ and $T - 2$:

$$\begin{cases} C_{T-2}^i(s_{T-2} = 0) = [\hat{p}_{00}C_{T-2/T-1}^i(s_{T-1} = 0) + (1 - \hat{p}_{00})C_{T-2/T-1}^i(s_{T-1} = 1)]e^{-r} \\ C_{T-2}^i(s_{T-2} = 1) = [(1 - \hat{p}_{11})C_{T-2/T-1}^i(s_{T-1} = 0) + \hat{p}_{11}C_{T-2/T-1}^i(s_{T-1} = 1)]e^{-r} \end{cases}$$

Again we obtain two sets of conditional option values $C_{T-2}^i(s_{T-2} = 0)$, $C_{T-2}^i(s_{T-2} = 1)$.
• This computation is iterated for $T - 3, T - 4, \ldots, t$.

At the evaluation time t, we obtain two conditional values $C_t(s_t = 0)$, $C_t(s_t = 1)$, which are respectively 1047.61 and 1093.54. Finally, the value of the option is calculated as a weighted average of these two values, where the weights depend on the knowledge of the current regime. If the regime is unknown, the estimated unconditional probabilities

$$\hat{p}_0 = \frac{1 - \hat{p}_{11}}{2 - \hat{p}_{00} - \hat{p}_{11}} \qquad \hat{p}_1 = \frac{1 - \hat{p}_{00}}{2 - \hat{p}_{00} - \hat{p}_{11}}$$

can be used.

The pentanomial option value is therefore 1055.14 while the market value was 1047.5. Another possibility, probably better from a methodological point of view as it uses all the available information, is to consider the filtered probabilities obtained as output of the estimation step, i.e. $P(s_t = 0|Y^t) = 0.98636043$ and $P(s_t = 1|Y^t) = 0.01363957$. In that case, the pentanomial option value is 1048.24.

As an exercise, readers may wish to replicate the following examples:

1. European put option quoted on 23/10/2000, strike price: 7000, FTSE100: 6315.9, Libor: 6.1475%, days to maturity: 39, option price: 700.
   Results: Conditional option values: 756.15 and 679.89. Option value considering unconditional probabilities: 692.4.
2. European put option quoted on 03/11/2000, strike price: 5500, FTSE100: 6385.44, Libor: 6.12625%, days to maturity: 160, option price: 117.
   Results: Conditional option values: 143.29 and 101.08. Option value considering unconditional probabilities: 108.

APPENDIX B: APPLICATION TO VALUE AT RISK

Consider a portfolio which perfectly replicates the composition of the FTSE100 index. Given the estimated volatility of the stochastic volatility models, the VaR of this portfolio can be obtained following the procedure proposed in Barone-Adesi *et al.* (1998).

The historical portfolio returns are rescaled by the estimated volatility series to obtain the standardised residuals $u_t = y_t/\sigma_t, t = 1, \ldots, T$ (in our case $T = 898$, see footnote 33). The historical simulation can be performed by bootstrapping the standardised returns to obtain the desired number of residuals $u_j^*, j = 1, \ldots, M$, where M can be arbitrarily large. To calculate the next period returns, it is sufficient to multiply the simulated residuals by the forecasted volatility $\hat{\sigma}_{T+1/T}$:

$$y_j^* = u_j^* \hat{\sigma}_{T+1/T}$$

The VaR for the next day, at the desired level of confidence h, is then calculated as the Mhth element of these returns sorted in ascending order.

REFERENCES

Alexander, C. (1996), *The Handbook of Risk Management and Analysis*, John Wiley, New York.
Andersen, T. G. and T. Bollerslev (1997), "Heterogeneous information arrivals and return volatility dynamics: uncovering the long run in high frequency returns", *Journal of Finance*, **52**, 975–1005.
Andersen, T. G. and B. E. Sørensen (1996), "GMM estimation of a stochastic volatility model: a Monte Carlo study", *Journal of Business and Economic Statistics*, **14**, 328–352.

Andersen, T. G. and B. E. Sørensen (1997), "GMM and QML asymptotic standard deviations in stochastic volatility models: a comment on Ruiz (1994)", *Journal of Econometrics*, **76**, 397–403.

Andersen, T. G., H. Chung and B. E. Sørensen. (1999), "Efficient method of moments estimation of a stochastic volatility model: a Monte Carlo study", *Journal of Econometrics*, **91**, 61–87.

Anderson, B. and J. Moore (1979), *Optimal Filtering*, Prentice Hall, New York.

Ball, C. and W. Torous (1985), "On jumps in common stock prices and their impact on call option pricing", *Journal of Finance*, **40**, 155–173.

Barone-Adesi, G., F. Burgoin and K. Giannopoulos (1998), "Don't look back", *Risk*, **11**, 100–104.

Bates, D. S. (1996), "Jumps and stochastic volatility: exchange rate processes implicit in Deutsche mark options", *The Review of Financial Studies*, **9**, 69–107.

Bera, A. and M. Higgins (1993), "Arch models: properties, estimation and testing", *Journal of Economic Surveys*, **7**, 305–366.

Best, P. (1998), *Implementing Value at Risk*, John Wiley & Sons, New York.

Billio, M. (1999), Simulation based methods for non linear state space models, Ph.D. thesis, Paris Dauphine.

Billio, M. (2002a), "Correlated Markov chain", Working Paper, GRETA, Venice.

Billio, M. (2002b), "Simulation based methods for financial time series", *Atti della XLI Riunione Scientifica of Italian Statistical Society*, Università di Milano-Bicocca, 5–7 June.

Billio, M. and A. Monfort (1998), "Switching state space models: likelihood, filtering and smoothing", *Journal of Statistical Planning and Inference*, **68/1**, 65–103.

Billio, M. and L. Pelizzon (1997), "Pricing options with switching volatility", in *Money, Finance, Banking and Insurance*, C. Hipp (ed.), Verlang.

Billio, M. and L. Pelizzon (2000), "Value-at-Risk: a multivariate switching regime approach", *Journal of Empirical Finance*, **7**, 531–554.

Billio, M., A. Monfort and C. P. Robert (1998), "The simulated likelihood ratio (SLR) method", *Document de Travail du CREST 9828*, Paris.

Black, F. and M. Scholes (1973), "The pricing of options and corporate liabilities", *Journal of Political Economy*, **81**, 637–654.

Bollen, N. (1998), "Valuating option in regime switching models", *Journal of Derivatives*, **6**, 38–49.

Bollen, N., S. Gray and R. Whaley (2000), "Regime-switching in foreign exchange rates: evidence from currency options", *Journal of Econometrics*, **94**, 239–276.

Bollerslev, T. (1990), "Modelling the coherence in short-run nominal exchange rates: a multivariate generalized ARCH approach", *Review of Economics and Statistics*, **72**, 498–505.

Bollerslev, T. and D. Jubinski (1999), "Equity trading volume and volatility: latent information arrivals and common long-run dependencies", *Journal of Business and Economic Statistics*, **17**, 9–21.

Bollerslev, T. and H. O. Mikkelsen (1999), "Long-term equity anticipation securities and stock market volatility dynamics", *Journal of Econometrics*, **92**, 75–99.

Bollerslev, T. and J. Wright (2000), "Semiparametric estimation of long-memory volatility dependencies: the role of high-frequency data", *Journal of Econometrics*, **98**, 81–106.

Bollerslev, T., R. Chow and K. Kroner (1992), "Arch modelling in finance: a review of the theory and empirical evidence", *Journal of Econometrics*, **52**, 5–59.

Bollerslev, T., R. F. Engle and D. Nelson (1993), "Arch models", in *Handbook of Econometrics*, R. Engle and D. McFadden (eds), North-Holland, Amsterdam, vol. IV.

Breidt, F. J., N. Crato and P. de Lima (1998), "On the detection and estimation of long memory in stochastic volatility", *Journal of Econometrics*, **83**, 325–348.

Carraro, C. and D. Sartore (1987), "Square root iterative Kalman filter: theory and applications to regression models", *Annales d'Economie et de Statistique*, **6/7**.

Chan, N. H. and G. Petris (1999), "Bayesian analysis of long memory stochastic volatility models", Technical Report, Department of Statistics, Carnegie Mellon University.

Chib, S., F. Nardari and N. Shephard (2002), "Markov Chain Monte Carlo methods for stochastic volatility models", *Journal of Econometrics*, **108/2**, 281–316.

Clark, P. K. (1973), "A subordinated stochastic process model with fixed variance for speculative prices", *Econometrica*, **41**, 135–156.

Cox, D. R. (1981), "Statistical analysis of time series: some recent developments", *Scandinavian Journal of Statistics*, **8**, 93–115.

Cox, J. C., S. A. Ross and M. Rubinstein (1979), "Option pricing: a simplified approach", *Journal of Financial Economics*, **7**, 229–263.

Danielsson, J. (1994), "Stochastic volatility in asset prices: estimation with simulated maximum likelihood", *Journal of Econometrics*, **61**, 375–400.

Danielsson, J. and J. Richard (1993), "Accelerated Gaussian importance sampler with application to dynamic latent variable models", *Journal of Applied Econometrics*, **8**, 153–173.

Davies, R. B. (1977), "Hypothesis testing when a nuisance parameter is present only under the alternative", *Biometrika*, **64**, 247–254.

Davies, R. B. (1987), "Hypothesis testing when a nuisance parameter is present only under the alternative", *Biometrika*, **74**, 33–43.

de Jong, P. (1989), "Smoothing and interpolation with the state space model", *Journal of the American Statistical Association*, **84**, 1085–1088.

Deo, R. S. and C. M. Hurvich (2001), "On the log periodogram regression estimator of the memory parameter in long memory stochastic volatility models", *Econometric Theory*, **17**, 686–710.

Doornik, J. A. (2001), *Ox: An Object-Oriented Matrix Language* (4th edition), Timberlake Consultants Press, London.

Dridi, R. (2000), "Simulated asymptotic least squares theory", Working Paper 396, London School of Economics–Suntory Toyota, Econometrics.

Dridi, R. and E. Renault (2000), "Semi-parametric indirect inference", Working Paper 392, London School of Economics–Suntory Toyota, Econometrics.

Duffie, D. and K. Singleton (1993), "Simulated moments estimation of Markov models of asset prices", *Econometrica*, **61**, 929–952.

Duffie, D., J. Pan and K. Singleton (2000), "Transform analysis and asset pricing for affine jump-diffusions", *Econometrica*, **68**, 1343–1376.

Durbin, J. and S. Koopman (1997), "Monte Carlo maximum likelihood estimation for non Gaussian state space models", *Biometrika*, **84**, 669–684.

Eberlein, E. (2001), "Application of generalized hyperbolic Lévy motion to finance", in *Lévy Processes–Theory and Applications*, O. E. Barndorff-Nielsen, T. Mikosch and S. Resnick (eds), Birkhauser Boston, MA, pp. 319–337.

Eberlein, E. and K. Prause (2001), "The generalized hyperbolic model: financial derivatives and risk measures", in *Proceedings of the Year 2000 Congress of the European Mathematical Society*.

Eberlein, E., J. Kallsen and J. Kristen (2001), "Risk management based on stochastic volatility", FDM Preprint 72, University of Freiburg.

Engle, R. F. (1982), "Autoregressive conditional heteroskedasticity with estimates of the variance of the United Kingdom inflation", *Econometrica*, **50**, 987–1007.

Engle, R. F. and G. G. J. Lee (1992), "A permanent and transitory component model of stock return volatility", UCSD Economics Discussion Papers 92-44, University of California at San Diego.

Engle, R. F., D. M. Lilien and R. P. Robins (1987), "Estimating time-varying risk premium in the term structure: the ARCH-M model", *Econometrica*, **55**, 391–407.

Francq, C. and J. M. Zakoïan (2001), "Stationarity of multivariate Markov-switching ARMA models", *Journal of Econometrics*, **102**, 339–364.

Francq, C., M. Roussignol and J. M. Zakoïan (2001), "Conditional heteroskedasticity driven by hidden Markov chains", *Journal of Time Series Analysis*, **22/2**, 197–220.

Fridman, M. and L. Harris (1998), "A maximum likelihood approach for non-Gaussian stochastic volatility models", *Journal of Business and Economic Statistics*, **16**, 284–291.

Gallant, A. and J. Long (1997), "Estimating stochastic differential equations efficiently by minimum chi-square", *Biometrika*, **84**, 125–141.

Gallant, A. and G. Tauchen (1996), "Which moments to match?", *Econometric Theory*, **12**, 657–681.

Gallant, A., D. Hsieh and G. Tauchen (1997), "Estimation of stochastic volatility models with diagnostics", *Journal of Econometrics*, **81**, 159–192.

Gelfand, A. and A. Smith (1990), "Sampling based approaches to calculating marginal densities", *Journal of the American Statistical Association*, **85**, 398–409.

Geweke, J. and S. Porter-Hudak (1983), "The estimation and application of long-memory time series models", *Journal of Time Series Analysis*, **4**, 221–238.

Geyer, C. (1994), "On the convergence of Monte Carlo maximum likelihood calculations", *Journal of the Royal Statistical Society,* B **65**, 261–274.

Geyer, C. (1996), "Estimation and optimization of functions", in *Markov Chain Monte Carlo in Practice*, W. Gilks, S. Richardson and D. Spiegelhalter (eds), Chapman and Hall, London, pp. 241–258.

Ghysels, E., A. Harvey and E. Renault (1996), "Stochastic volatility", in: *Statistical Methods in Finance*, C. Rao and G. Maddala (eds), North-Holland, Amsterdam.

Gordon, N., D. Salmond and A. Smith (1993), "A novel approach to non-linear and non Gaussian Bayesian state estimation", *IEE Proceedings*, **F140**, 107–133.

Gouriéroux, C., A. Monfort and E. Renault (1993), "Indirect inference", *Journal of Applied Econometrics*, **8**, 85–118.

Hamilton, J. D. (1989), "A new approach to the economic analysis of nonstationary time series and the business cycle", *Econometrica*, **57/2**, 357–384.

Hamilton, J. D. (1994), *Time Series Analysis*, Princeton University Press, Princeton, NJ.

Hansen, B. E. (1992), "The likelihood ratio test under nonstandard conditions: testing the Markov switching model of GNP", *Journal of Applied Econometrics*, **7**, S61–S82.

Hansen, B. E. (1996), "Erratum: The likelihood ratio test under nonstandard conditions: testing the Markov switching model of GNP", *Journal of Applied Econometrics*, **11/2**, 195–198.

Harvey, A. C. (1989), *Forecasting, Structural Time Series Models and the Kalman Filter*, Cambridge University Press, Cambridge.

Harvey, A. C. (1998), "Long-memory in stochastic volatility", in *Forecasting Volatility in the Financial Market*, J. Knight and S. Sachell (eds), Butterworth-Heinemann, London.

Harvey, A. C. and N. Shephard (1993), "Estimation and testing stochastic variance models", London School of Economics–Suntory Toyota, Econometrics, no. 93–268.

Harvey, A. C. and N. Shephard (1996), "Estimation of an asymmetric model of asset prices", *Journal of Business and Economic Statistics*, **14/4**, 429–434.

Harvey, A. C., E. Ruiz and N. Shephard (1994), "Multivariate stochastic variance models", *Review of Economic Studies*, **61**, 247–264.

Heston, S. (1993), "A closed-form solution for option with stochastic volatility with application to bond and currency options", *The Review of Financial Studies*, **6**, 327–343.

Hull, J. and A. White (1987), "The pricing of options on assets with stochastic volatilities", *Journal of Finance*, **42**, 281–300.

Hull, J. and A. White (1998), "Incorporating volatility updating into the historical simulation method for Value-at-Risk", *The Journal of Risk*, **1**, 5–19.

Hurvich, C. M. and B. K. Ray (2001), "The local Whittle estimator of long memory stochastic signal volatility", Working Paper, Department of Statistics and Operations Research, New York University, http://www.stern.nyu.edu/sor/research/wp01.html.

Hurvich, C. M., E. Moulines and P. Soulier (2001), "Estimation of long memory in stochastic volatility", Preprint 153, Université d'Evry-Val d'Essonne, http://www.tsi.enst.fr/~soulier/paper.html.

Jacquier, E., N. G. Polson and P. Rossi (1994), "Bayesian analysis of stochastic volatility models", *Journal of Business and Economic Statistics*, **12**, 371–417.

Jacquier, E., N. G. Polson and P. Rossi (1995), "Models and Priors for Multivariate Stochastic Volatility", CIRANO Working Papers 95-18.

Jensen, M. J. (1999), "An approximate wavelet MLE of short and long memory parameters", *Studies in Nonlinear Dynamics and Econometrics*, **3**, 239–353.

Jensen, M. J. (2000), "An alternative maximum likelihood estimator of long-memory processes using compactly supported wavelets", *Journal of Economic Dynamics and Control*, **24**, 361–387.

Jensen, M. J. (2001), "Bayesian inference of long-memory stochastic volatility via wavelets", Working Paper 01–02, Department of Economics, University of Missouri-Columbia.

Kalman, R. E. (1960), "A new approach to linear filtering and prediction problems", *Journal of Basic Engineering, Transactions ASMA*, Series D **82**, 35–45.

Kim, C. J. (1994), "Dynamic linear models with Markov-switching", *Journal of Econometrics*, **60**, 1–22.

Kim, C. J. and C. R. Nelson (1999), *State-Space Models with Regime Switching*, MIT Press, Cambridge, MA.

Kim, S., N. Shephard and S. Chib (1998), "Stochastic volatility: likelihood inference and comparison with arch models", *Review of Economic Studies*, **65**, 361–393.

Kitagawa, G. (1987), "Non-Gaussian state space modeling of nonstationary time series" (with discussion), *Journal of the American Statistical Association*, **82**, 400, 1032–1063.

Kitagawa, G. (1996), "Monte Carlo filter and smoother for non-Gaussian non linear state space models", *Journal of Computational and Graphical Statistics*, **5**, 1–25.

Kitagawa, G. and W. Gersch (1984), "A smoothness priors-state space modeling of time series with trend and seasonality", *Journal of the American Statistical Association*, **79**, 378–389.

Lehar, A., M. Scheicher and C. Schittenkopf (2002), "Garch vs stochastic volatility: option pricing and risk management", *Journal of Banking and Finance*, **26**(2& 3), 323–345.

Lobato, I. and N. E. Savin (1998), "Real and spurious long-memory properties of stock-market data", *Journal of Business and Economic Statistics*, **16**, 261–268.

Mahieu, R. and P. Schotman (1998), "An empirical application of stochastic volatility models", *Journal of Applied Econometrics*, **16**, 333–359.

McNeil, A. J. and R. Frey (2000), "Estimation of tail-related risk measures for heteroskedastic financial time series: an extreme value approach", *Journal of Empirical Finance*, **7**, 271–300.

Melino, A. and S. M. Turnbull (1990), "Pricing foreign currency options with stochastic volatility", *Journal of Econometrics*, **45**, 239–265.

Merton, R. C. (1976), "Option pricing when underlying stock returns are discontinuous", *Journal of Financial Economics*, **3**, 125–144.

Monfardini, C. (1998), "Estimating stochastic volatility models through indirect inference", *Econometrics Journal*, **1**, 113–128.

Naik, V. (1993), "Option valuation and hedging strategies with jumps in the volatility of asset returns", *Journal of Finance*, **48**, 1969–1984.

Pitt, M. and N. Shephard (1999a), "Filtering via simulation: auxiliary particle filter", *Journal of the American Statistical Association*, **94**, 590–599.

Pitt, M. and N. Shephard (1999b), "Time varying covariances: a factor stochastic volatility approach" with discussion, in *Bayesian Statistics*, J. Bernardo, J. O. Berger, A. P. Dawid and A. F. M. Smith (eds), Oxford University Press, Oxford, Vol. 6, pp. 547–570.

Ray, B. K. and R. Tsay (2000), "Long-range dependence in daily stock volatilities", *Journal of Business and Economic Statistics*, **18**, 254–262.

Robinson, P. M. (1995), "Log-periodogram regression of time series with long range dependence", *Annals of Statistics*, **23**, 1043–1072.

Rubinstein, M. (1985), "Nonparametric tests of alternative option pricing models using all reported trades and quotes on the 30 most active CBOE options classes from August 23, 1976 through August 21, 1978", *The Journal of Finance*, **40**, 455–480.

Ruiz, E. (1994), "Quasi maximum likelihood estimation of stochastic volatility models", *Journal of Econometrics*, **63**, 289–306.

Sandmann, G. and S. Koopman (1998), "Estimation of stochastic volatility models via Monte Carlo maximum likelihood", *Journal of Econometrics*, **87**, 271–301.

Scott, L. O. (1987), "Option pricing when the variance changes randomly: theory, estimation and an application", *Journal of Financial and Quantitative Analysis*, **22**, 419–438.

Scott, L. (1991), "Random variance option pricing", *Advances in Future and Options Research*, **5**, 113–135.

Shephard, N. (1993), "Fitting non-linear time series models, with applications to stochastic variance models", *Journal of Applied Econometrics*, **8**, 135–152.

Shephard, N. (1994), "Local scale model: state space alternative to integrated GARCH processes", *Journal of Econometrics*, **60**, 181–202.

Shephard, N. (1996), "Statistical aspects of ARCH and stochastic volatility", in *Time Series Models with Econometric, Finance and Other Applications*, D. R. Cox, D. V. Hinkley and O. E. Barndorff-Nielsen (eds), Chapman and Hall, London, pp. 1–677.

Smith, A. A. (1993), "Estimating non linear time series models using simulated vector autoregressions", *Journal of Applied Econometrics*, **8**, S63–S84.

So, M. K. P., K. Lam and W. K. Lee (1998), "A stochastic volatility model with Markov switching", *Journal of Business and Economic Statistics*, **16**, 244–253.

Sorenson, H. and D. Alspach (1971), "Recursive Bayesian estimation using Gaussian sums", *Automatica*, **7**, 465–479.

Tanizaki, H. and R. Mariano (1994), "Prediction, filtering and smoothing in non-linear and non-normal cases using Monte Carlo integration", *Journal of Applied Econometrics*, **9**, 163–179.

Tanizaki, H. and R. Mariano (1998), "Nonlinear and nonnormal state-space modeling with Monte Carlo stochastic simulation", *Journal of Econometrics*, **83**(1&2), 263–290.

Tauchen, G. (1997), "New minimum chi-square methods in empirical finance", in *Advances in Economics and Econometrics: Theory and Applications, Seventh World Congress*, D. Kreps and K. Wallis (eds), Cambridge University Press, Cambridge.

Taylor, S. J. (1986), *Modelling Financial Time Series*, John Wiley, Chichester.

Taylor, S. J. (1994), "Modelling stochastic volatility: a review and comparative study", *Mathematical Finance*, **4**, 183–204.

Tierney, L. (1994), "Markov chains for exploring posterior distributions" (with discussion), *Annals of Statistics*, **22**, 1701–1786.

Wright, J. H. (1999), "A new estimator of the fractionally integrated stochastic volatility model", *Economics Letter*, **63**, 295–303.

Wright, J. H. (2000), "Log-periodogram estimation of long memory volatility dependencies with conditionally heavy tailed returns", Board of Governors of the Federal Reserve System, International Finance Discussion Papers no. 685, http://www.bog.frb.fed.us.

9

Portfolio Analysis Using Excel

JASON LAWS

ABSTRACT

This chapter analyses the familiar Markovitz model using Excel. This topic is taught on finance degrees and Masters programmes at Universities all over the world increasingly through the use of Excel. We take time out to explain how the spreadsheet is set up and how simple short cuts can make analysis of this type of problem quick and straightforward. In the first section of the chapter we use a 2 variable example to show how portfolio risk and return vary with the input weights then he goes onto show how to determine the optimal weights, in a risk minimisation sense, using both linear expressions and also using matrix algebra. In the second part of the chapter we extend the number of assets to seven and illustrate using matrix algebra within Excel that Markovitz analysis of an n-asset portfolio is as straightforward as the analysis of a two asset portfolio. We take special care in showing how the correlation matrix can be generated most efficiently and how within the same framework the optimisation objective can be modified without fuss.

9.1 INTRODUCTION

The motivation for this chapter is to show how the Markovitz model of portfolio risk can be modelled in Excel. The goal of this paper is not to provide an in-depth discussion of this model but instead to show how it can be implemented within Excel. Excellent discussions of this model can be found in a wide range of corporate finance or investment text books, including Cuthbertson and Nitzsche (2001). However, it is worthwhile to provide a brief overview of this theory. In essence the underlying rationale is based on the twin facets of expected risk and return, with risk being measured by the variance or standard deviation of expected returns. The efficient frontier of the portfolio is given by:

1. Those assets which offer a higher return for the same risk, or equivalently
2. Those assets which offer a lower risk for the same return.

The precise position an investor takes on the efficient frontier depends on his/her utility function based on the two motives of expected return and risk; in other words the utility function is positively sloped in the return/risk domain. Initially I assume that this utility function is very steep (i.e. the individual is highly risk averse) so his/her desired position is a corner maximum where risk is minimised with respect to just two assets. Later the

Applied Quantitative Methods for Trading and Investment. Edited by C.L. Dunis, J. Laws and P. Naïm
© 2003 John Wiley & Sons, Ltd ISBN: 0-470-84885-5

analysis is further extended to incorporate a large number of assets and/or objectives other than portfolio risk minimisation.

9.2   THE SIMPLE MARKOVITZ MODEL

In the simple Markovitz model portfolio returns, r_p, in a two-asset model are given by:

$$r_p = w_1 r_1 + w_2 r_2 \qquad (9.1)$$

and the corresponding variance of portfolio returns σ_p^2, by:

$$\sigma_p^2 = w_1^2 \sigma_1^2 + w_2^2 \sigma_2^2 + 2 w_1 w_2 \sigma_{12} \qquad (9.2)$$

where w_i represents the weight allocated to asset i in the portfolio ($i = \{1, 2\}$), σ_i^2 represents the variance of the returns on asset i ($i = \{1, 2\}$), r_i represents the historical returns of asset i ($i = \{1, 2\}$) and σ_{12} represents the covariance between the returns on assets 1 and 2. Using the relationship that the correlation coefficient (ρ_{12}) between two assets can be calculated as:

$$\rho_{12} = \frac{\sigma_{12}}{\sigma_1 \sigma_2}$$

then equation (9.2) can be rewritten as:

$$\sigma_p^2 = w_1^2 \sigma_1^2 + w_2^2 \sigma_2^2 + 2 w_1 w_2 \rho_{12} \sigma_1 \sigma_2 \qquad (9.3)$$

This is a much more convenient version of the portfolio variance equation and one that students are often more at ease with as here we use the correlation coefficient which takes the range -1 to $+1$ whereas previously we incorporated the covariance whose size is relative to the individual variances.

As an illustration of this model we will now apply it using two indices of stock prices, namely, the FT World equity index for the UK (WIUTDK$) and the FT World index for European equities which excludes the UK (WIEXUK$). The frequency of the data for this example was chosen as weekly and covers the period January 1996 to end June 2002. The raw data and subsequent analysis for this example in this and the next section are included in the file "Laws001.xls". This file includes several worksheets, the titles of which are self-explanatory.

As highlighted above the Markovitz model is based around asset returns and not "raw prices". The first task therefore is to generate a return series where the weekly return is given by:

$$100 \log_e \left(\frac{P_t}{P_{t-1}} \right) \qquad (9.4)$$

where P_t is the current price level, P_{t-1} is the price level in the previous period and $\log_e$ is the natural log transformation. A screen shot of this initial transformation (contained in the worksheet "Returns") is given in Figure 9.1.

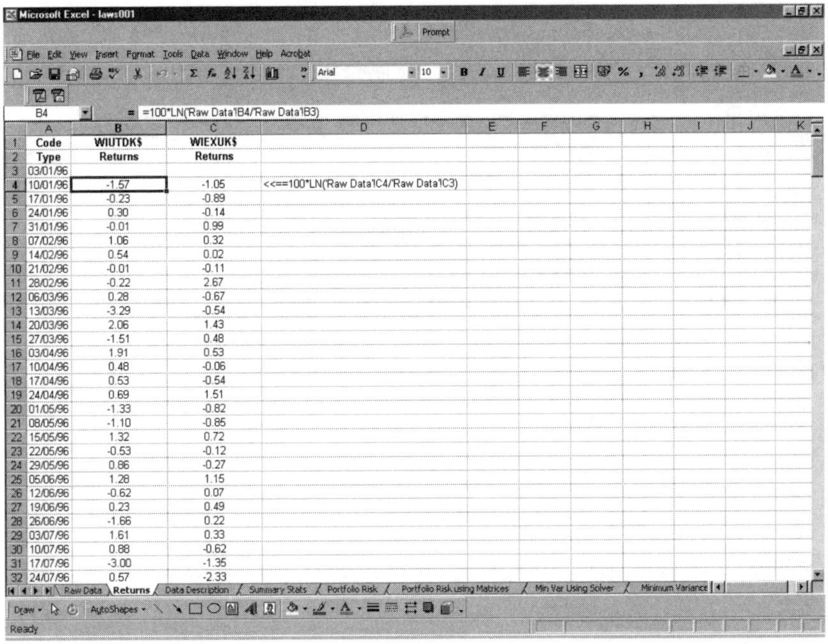

B4 = =100*LN('Raw Data'!B4/'Raw Data'!B3)

	A	B	C	D
1	Code	WIUTDK$	WIEXUK$	
2	Type	Returns	Returns	
3	03/01/96			
4	10/01/96	-1.57	-1.05	<<==100*LN('Raw Data'!C4/'Raw Data'!C3)
5	17/01/96	-0.23	-0.89	
6	24/01/96	0.30	-0.14	
7	31/01/96	-0.01	0.99	
8	07/02/96	1.06	0.32	
9	14/02/96	0.54	0.02	
10	21/02/96	-0.01	-0.11	
11	28/02/96	-0.22	2.67	
12	06/03/96	0.28	-0.67	
13	13/03/96	-3.29	-0.54	
14	20/03/96	2.06	1.43	
15	27/03/96	-1.51	0.48	
16	03/04/96	1.91	0.53	
17	10/04/96	0.48	-0.06	
18	17/04/96	0.53	-0.54	
19	24/04/96	0.69	1.51	
20	01/05/96	-1.33	-0.82	
21	08/05/96	-1.10	-0.85	
22	15/05/96	1.32	0.72	
23	22/05/96	-0.53	-0.12	
24	29/05/96	0.86	-0.27	
25	05/06/96	1.28	1.15	
26	12/06/96	-0.62	0.07	
27	19/06/96	0.23	0.49	
28	26/06/96	-1.66	0.22	
29	03/07/96	1.61	0.33	
30	10/07/96	0.88	-0.62	
31	17/07/96	-3.00	-1.35	
32	24/07/96	0.57	-2.33	

Figure 9.1 Worksheet "Returns" in the file "Laws001.xls"

The Excel instruction necessary to carry out this calculation based on the raw data contained in the worksheet "Raw Data" is shown in the fourth line of the fourth column of this screen shot. Note also that throughout this chapter I have rounded the data correct to two decimal places.

In order to implement the Markovitz model we must first of all find the mean and standard deviation of each of our series. This is easily achieved in Excel using the "AVERAGE" and "STDEV" functions respectively. For completeness we have also calculated the measures of kurtosis and skewness using the "KURT" and "SKEW" functions respectively. These measures are shown in the worksheet "Summary Statistics" and are reproduced in Figure 9.2.

Here we can see that the distributions of both returns series are "peaked" relative to the normal distribution.[1] The negative skewness also indicates that the distribution has an asymmetric tail extending more towards negative values. More importantly, in terms of Markovitz analysis, we can see that the European data has a higher average weekly return over the period than the UK data but a higher standard deviation of returns. The correlation between returns is 0.76, which provides opportunities for risk diversification.

The workbook "Portfolio Risk" implements equation (9.3)[2] above using the WIUTDK$ and WIEXUK$ data. This is achieved by substituting a range of values for w_1 from 0 to 1, where 0 implies that 0% of wealth is invested in the WIUTDK$ index (with 100% being invested in the WIEXUK$ index) and 1 implies that 100% of wealth is invested

---

[1] Since the measure of excess kurtosis (i.e. observed kurtosis minus the normal curve value of 3) is positive. If the kurtosis measure were negative then we would say that the distribution is flat.

[2] In fact it implements the square root of equation (9.3).

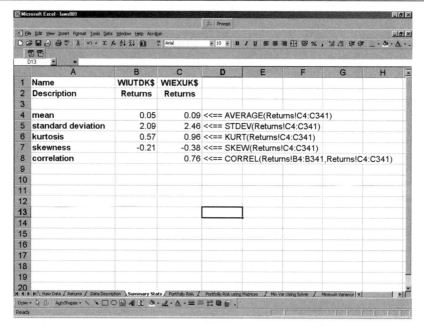

Figure 9.2 Worksheet "Summary Statistics" in the file "Laws001.xls"

in the WIUTDK$ index (with 0% invested in the WIEXUK$ index). The result of this analysis is shown in Figure 9.3.

Note in the explanation of the contents of cells C2 and D2 that use has been made of the "$" sign. The reason for this is that when we copy the formula in cells C2 and D2 down the columns we would like to fix the formula on the cells which contain the returns, standard deviations and correlations in the "Summary Statistics" worksheet,[3] varying only the portfolio weights.

It is evident from these results that as we decrease the proportion of wealth invested in the WIUTDK$ index the portfolio risk declines (as return rises) then begins to rise (as return rises). There is therefore some benefit to be gained from incorporating the WIEXUK$ index into the portfolio.

This is best illustrated using an "XY" chart in Excel. To do this highlight cells C2 to D12 (inclusive) and then click the "Chart Wizard" button. Select the chart type "XY (Scatter)" and any of the subtypes which include a fitted line (Figure 9.4).[4]

You may add a chart title and titles for each axis if you wish. Finally you end up with the graph in Figure 9.5, as depicted in the worksheet "Efficient Frontier". Here we can see that as we decrease the proportion invested in the WIUTDK$ index the portfolio risk

---

[3] A short-cut to locking a calculation on a cell address is to use the F4 key. Pressing the F4 key once places a $ sign before both the letter and the number. Pressing twice places a $ sign just before the number and pressing three times places a $ sign before the letter.

[4] It is more than likely (depending upon your set-up) that Excel will have drawn a chart with risk on the vertical axis and return on the horizontal axis (because our return data was in the first column Excel has assumed this for the y-axis). It is however standard in this type of analysis to plot the data with returns on the vertical axis and risk on the horizontal axis. To correct this simply select the "Series" tab and change the X and Y value locations accordingly.

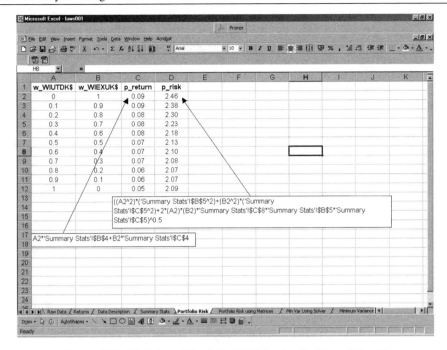

Figure 9.3 Worksheet "Portfolio Risk" in the file "Laws001.xls"

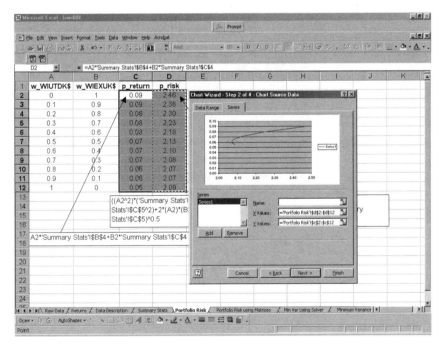

Figure 9.4 The Chart Wizard dialogue box

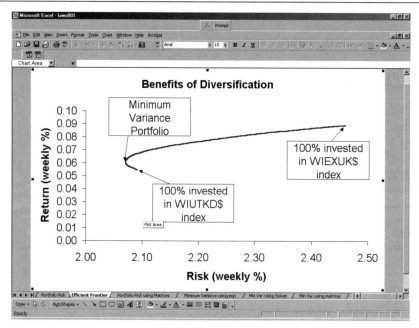

Figure 9.5　Worksheet "Efficient Frontier" in the file "Laws001.xls"

drops and returns rise (initially). If our objective is to minimise portfolio risk then there exists some optimal investment in the WIUTDK$ index. It is possible to find this optimal investment using calculus as follows.

We wish to minimise:

$$\sigma_p^2 = w_1^2\sigma_1^2 + w_2^2\sigma_2^2 + 2w_1w_2\rho_{12}\sigma_1\sigma_2 = w_1^2\sigma_1^2 + (1-w_1)^2\sigma_2^2 + 2w_1(1-w_1)\rho_{12}\sigma_1\sigma_2$$

$$= w_1^2\sigma_1^2 + \sigma_2^2 + w_1^2\sigma_2^2 - 2w_1\sigma_2^2 + 2w_1\rho_{12}\sigma_1\sigma_2 - 2w_1^2\rho_{12}\sigma_1\sigma_2$$

by varying w_1, noting that $w_2 = 1 - w_1$.

This can be achieved by setting the derivative of σ_p^2 (portfolio risk) with respect to w_1 (the proportion invested in asset 1) equal to zero, i.e.

$$\frac{\delta\sigma_p^2}{\delta w_1} = 2w_1\sigma_1^2 + 2(1-w_1)(-1)\sigma_2^2 + 2\rho_{12}\sigma_1\sigma_2 - 4w_1\rho_{12}\sigma_1\sigma_2 = 0$$

$$\Rightarrow w_1\sigma_1^2 + (1-w_1)(-1)\sigma_2^2 + \rho_{12}\sigma_1\sigma_2 - 2w_1\rho_{12}\sigma_1\sigma_2 = 0$$

$$\Rightarrow w_1(\sigma_1^2 + \sigma_2^2 - 2\rho_{12}\sigma_1\sigma_2) = \sigma_2^2 - \rho_{12}\sigma_1\sigma_2$$

$$\Rightarrow w_1 = \frac{\sigma_2^2 - \rho_{12}\sigma_1\sigma_2}{\sigma_1^2 + \sigma_2^2 - 2\rho_{12}\sigma_1\sigma_2} \quad \text{and} \quad w_2 = 1 - w_1 \tag{9.5}$$

Applying this formula to our dataset we find the results of Figure 9.6, as shown in the worksheet "Minimum Variance Using Eqn". Here we can see that there is some optimal mix of the WIUTDK$ (82%) and the WIEXUK$ (18%) indexes that minimises risk at

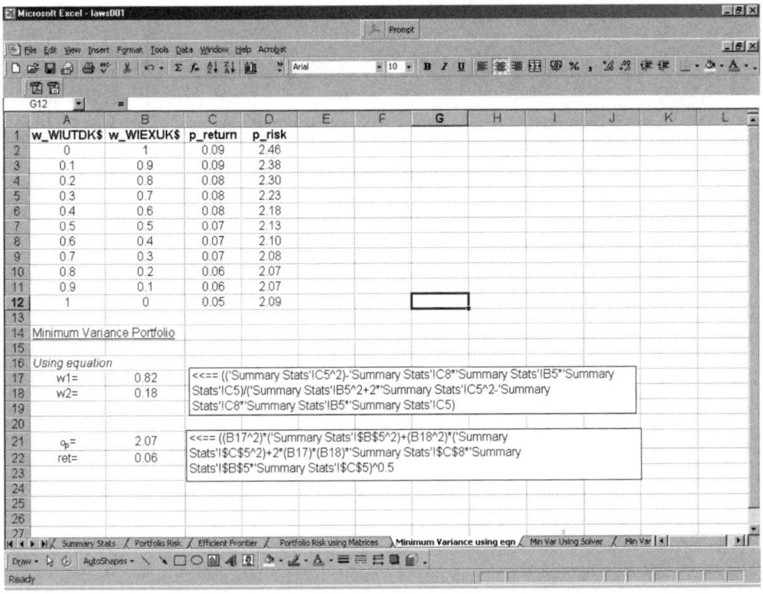

Figure 9.6   Worksheet "Minimum Variance using eqn" in the file "Laws001.xls"

2.07% per week with a return of 0.06% per week.[5] Note the minimum risk is less than that of either of the individual securities.

An alternative way to find this result which doesn't use calculus is to use Excel's in-built optimisation tool – "Solver". To illustrate how this works we have created a duplicate spreadsheet in the worksheet "Min Var Using Solver" and have added an additional line of calculations to allow us to alter the weights (Figure 9.7).

As you can see we have set the initial weights to 0.5 (i.e. 50%) for the WIUTDK$ index which automatically implies 50% for the WIEXUK$ index. Any arbitrary values for the initial weights will be all right. It is important in this respect to remember to set cell B19 equal to 1−A19. Also the values in cells C19 and D19 must be shown according to the formulae determining them rather than just their actual values. To begin using Solver we choose "Tools" then "Solver" from the Excel menu. This produces the dialogue box in Figure 9.8.

Here we set the "Target Cell" as D19 as it contains the calculation for the portfolio standard deviation. We aim to minimise this value (hence we check the radio button "Min") by changing the weight in the WIUTDK$ index (which is located in cell A19). There is no need to impose the constraint that $w_1 + w_2 = 1$ (i.e. A19 + B19 = 1) because, as noted above, w_2 is set automatically to equal $1 - w_1$. We click the "Solve" button to begin the optimisation and get the results of Figure 9.9, as shown in the worksheet "Min Var Using Solver", which as expected is identical to the outcome using the minimum variance formula. Therefore, again we find that there are some benefits, in terms of risk reduction, by changing a portfolio from 100% UK equities to a mix of 82% UK equities and 18% European equities.

---

[5] Note that we can convert these weekly risk and returns to annual risk and returns by multiplying the risk (measured by standard deviation) by the square root of 52 and the returns by 52.

Row	A	B	C	D
1	w_WIUTDK$	w_WIEXUK$	p_return	p_risk
2	0	1	0.09	2.46
3	0.1	0.9	0.09	2.38
4	0.2	0.8	0.08	2.30
5	0.3	0.7	0.08	2.23
6	0.4	0.6	0.08	2.18
7	0.5	0.5	0.07	2.13
8	0.6	0.4	0.07	2.10
9	0.7	0.3	0.07	2.08
10	0.8	0.2	0.06	2.07
11	0.9	0.1	0.06	2.07
12	1	0	0.05	2.09
13				
14	Minimum Variance Portfolio			
15				
16	Using Solver			
17				
18	w_WIUTDK$	w_WIEXUK$	p_return	p_risk
19	0.50	0.50	0.07	2.13

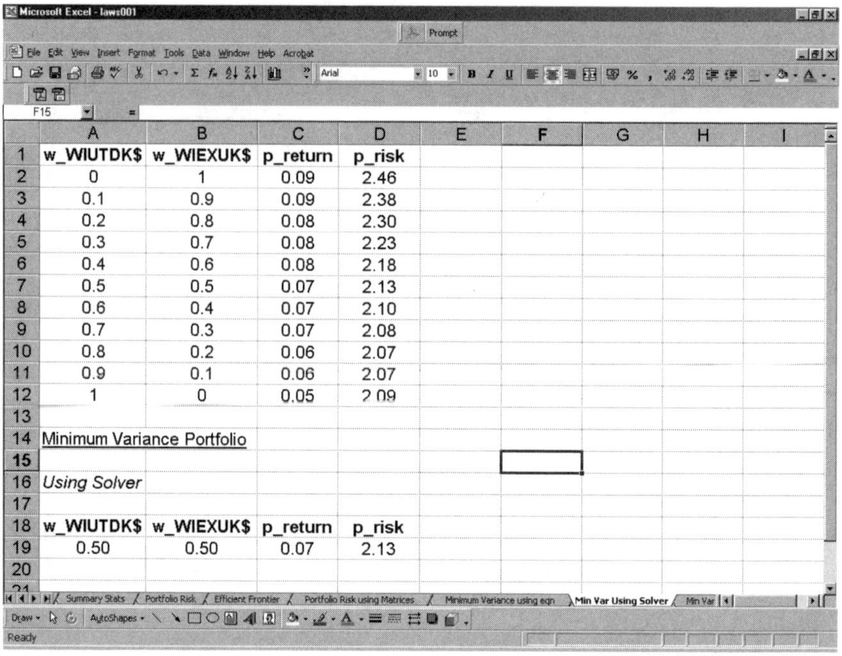

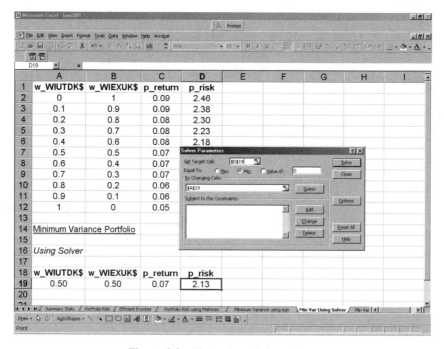

Figure 9.7 Worksheet "Min Var using solver" in the file "Laws001.xls" (pre-Solver)

Row	A	B	C	D
1	w_WIUTDK$	w_WIEXUK$	p_return	p_risk
2	0	1	0.09	2.46
3	0.1	0.9	0.09	2.38
4	0.2	0.8	0.08	2.30
5	0.3	0.7	0.08	2.23
6	0.4	0.6	0.08	2.18
7	0.5	0.5	0.07	
8	0.6	0.4	0.07	
9	0.7	0.3	0.07	
10	0.8	0.2	0.06	
11	0.9	0.1	0.06	
12	1	0	0.05	
13				
14	Minimum Variance Portfolio			
15				
16	Using Solver			
17				
18	w_WIUTDK$	w_WIEXUK$	p_return	p_risk
19	0.50	0.50	0.07	2.13

Figure 9.8 The Solver dialogue box

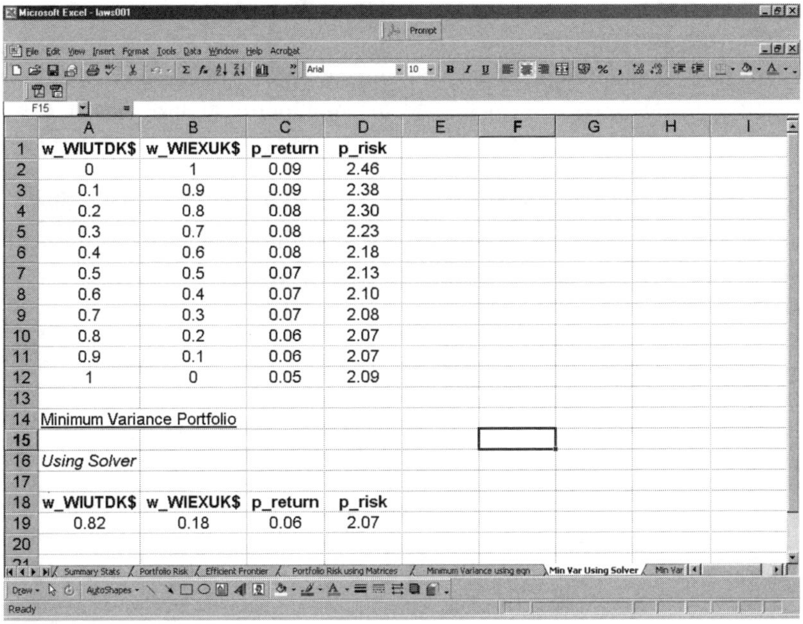

	A	B	C	D
1	w_WIUTDK$	w_WIEXUK$	p_return	p_risk
2	0	1	0.09	2.46
3	0.1	0.9	0.09	2.38
4	0.2	0.8	0.08	2.30
5	0.3	0.7	0.08	2.23
6	0.4	0.6	0.08	2.18
7	0.5	0.5	0.07	2.13
8	0.6	0.4	0.07	2.10
9	0.7	0.3	0.07	2.08
10	0.8	0.2	0.06	2.07
11	0.9	0.1	0.06	2.07
12	1	0	0.05	2.09
13				
14	Minimum Variance Portfolio			
15				
16	Using Solver			
17				
18	w_WIUTDK$	w_WIEXUK$	p_return	p_risk
19	0.82	0.18	0.06	2.07
20				

Figure 9.9 Worksheet "Min Var using solver" in the file "Laws001.xls" (post-Solver)

9.3 THE MATRIX APPROACH TO PORTFOLIO RISK[6]

Equation (9.2) can be rewritten using matrix notation as:

$$\sigma_p^2 = \begin{bmatrix} w_1 & w_2 \end{bmatrix} \times \begin{bmatrix} \sigma_{11} & \sigma_{12} \\ \sigma_{21} & \sigma_{22} \end{bmatrix} \times \begin{bmatrix} w_1 \\ w_2 \end{bmatrix} \tag{9.6}$$

Note that if you multiply the matrices out you end up with equation (9.2). The benefit of using matrix notation is that we are able to generalise the formula to n-assets as follows:

$$\sigma_p^2 = \mathbf{w}'\boldsymbol{\Sigma}\mathbf{w} \tag{9.7}$$

where $\mathbf{w} = (w_1, w_2, \ldots, w_N)$ and $\boldsymbol{\Sigma}$ is a covariance matrix with the variance terms on the diagonal and the covariance terms on the off-diagonal. The returns equation can be summarised by:

$$r_p = \mathbf{w}'\boldsymbol{\mu} \tag{9.8}$$

where $\boldsymbol{\mu}$ is a vector of assets historical returns.

To extend the linear version of the Markovitz equation (9.2) to incorporate more assets becomes particularly cumbersome as in addition to adding a term that incorporates the variance we must also include a term that incorporates the covariance/correlation.[7]

[6] For this and the following sections, the reader must be acquainted with the rudiments of matrix algebra.

[7] For a two-asset portfolio there exists just one unique covariance (σ_{12}), for a three-asset portfolio there are three unique covariances ($\sigma_{12}, \sigma_{13}, \sigma_{23}$) and so on. It follows that for an n-asset portfolio there are $N(N-1)/2$ unique covariances.

In Figure 9.10 we have applied the matrix version of the portfolio risk equation when the mix of assets is 50:50. You will see that the outcome is the same as we found previously.

Just as we have done previously with the linear version of the risk equation we can also use Solver in this environment to find the minimum variance portfolio which we

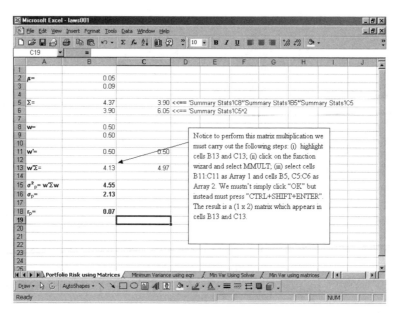

Figure 9.10 Worksheet "Portfolio Risk using Matrices" in the file "Laws002.xls" (pre-Solver)

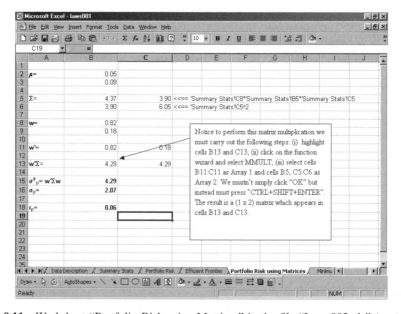

Figure 9.11 Worksheet "Portfolio Risk using Matrices" in the file "Laws002.xls" (post-Solver)

again find is an 82:18 split between UK and European equities.[8] Note that the screen shots of Figures 9.10 and 9.11 are taken from the same worksheet "Portfolio Risk Using Matrices", the only difference is that Figure 9.11 has had Solver applied to find the minimum variance portfolio.

9.4 MATRIX ALGEBRA IN EXCEL WHEN THE NUMBER OF ASSETS INCREASES

From the previous section we can see that modelling portfolio risk within Excel using matrices rather than the linear version of the risk equation appears far more convenient and flexible. The file "Laws002.xls" includes data on equity indices from seven European countries, including the UK and forms the basis of all operations in this section. As before, this file contains a number of worksheets, the titles of which are self-explanatory. We are going to utilise this dataset to show how portfolio analysis for portfolios with more than two assets can be modelled within Excel.

The dataset comprises weekly European equity price indexes data over the period January 1996 to end June 2002. The list of data used is:

WIFIND$ – FTSE WORLD INDEX – FINLAND
WIEIRE$ – FTSE WORLD INDEX – IRELAND
WIITAL$ – FTSE WORLD INDEX – ITALY
WINETH$ – FTSE WORD INDEX – NETHERLANDS
WISPAN$ – FTSE WORLD INDEX – PRICE INDEX
WISWIT$ – FTSE WORLD INDEX – SWITZERLAND
WIUTDK$ – FTSE WORLD INDEX – UNITED KINGDOM

To avoid issues of exchange rate risk all indices are expressed in US dollar terms. The two worksheets "Raw Data" and "Returns" include the original data and the weekly log returns respectively.

As we did previously with the two-asset portfolio example we again calculate the summary statistics of the returns datasets. These are then used as the inputs into the portfolio analysis examples which follow. The summary statistics shown in Figure 9.12 can be found in the "Summary Statistics" worksheet. Here we can see that there is a positive trade-off between risk and return with the historical returns of Finland (in US

---

[8] As an aside it should be noted that the minimum variance formula derived above can also be derived using matrix notation. Should we do this we find that the optimal weight, $\mathbf{w}^*$, in asset 1 is given by:

$$\mathbf{w}^* = \frac{\Sigma^{-1}\mathbf{e}}{\mathbf{e}'\Sigma^{-1}\mathbf{e}}$$

where $\mathbf{e}'$ is a unit vector. An application of this approach to the current dataset can be found in the worksheet "Min Var Using Matrices" where again we find the optimal weights are 82% and 18% for WIUTDK$ and WIEXUK$ respectively. Notice here we utilised two new functions, "MINVERSE" and "TRANSPOSE". As with the "MMULT" function, when we use these functions we must first of all highlight the cells where the output is to be displayed and after completing the necessary fields in the function wizard we must remember to press "CTRL + SHIFT + ENTER" rather than simply clicking "OK".

	WIFIND$	WIEIRE$	WIITAL$	WINETH$	WISPAN$	WISWIT$	WIUTDK$
mean	0.26	0.10	0.13	0.09	0.11	0.08	0.05
sd	5.77	2.93	3.28	2.65	3.19	2.49	2.09
annual mean	13.46	5.42	6.84	4.43	5.83	4.35	2.84
annual sd	41.57	21.13	23.65	19.12	22.97	17.94	15.05
rank (mean)	1	4	2	5	3	6	7
rank (sd)	1	4	2	5	3	6	7

Correlation

	WIFIND$	WIEIRE$	WIITAL$	WINETH$	WISPAN$	WISWIT$	WIUTDK$
WIFIND$	1.00	0.32	0.43	0.47	0.47	0.34	0.48
WIEIRE$	0.32	1.00	0.45	0.53	0.51	0.49	0.58
WIITAL$	0.43	0.45	1.00	0.65	0.66	0.52	0.58
WINETH$	0.47	0.53	0.65	1.00	0.71	0.66	0.72
WISPAN$	0.47	0.51	0.66	0.71	1.00	0.60	0.64
WISWIT$	0.34	0.49	0.52	0.66	0.60	1.00	0.57
WIUTDK$	0.48	0.58	0.58	0.72	0.64	0.57	1.00

Covar Matrix

	WIFIND$	WIEIRE$	WIITAL$	WINETH$	WISPAN$	WISWIT$	WIUTDK$
WIFIND$	33.24	5.43	8.19	7.18	8.66	4.87	5.83
WIEIRE$	5.43	8.59	4.32	4.14	4.79	3.61	3.56
WIITAL$	8.19	4.32	10.76	5.63	6.89	4.21	4.00
WINETH$	7.18	4.14	5.63	7.03	6.03	4.37	3.98
WISPAN$	8.66	4.79	6.89	6.03	10.15	4.76	4.27
WISWIT$	4.87	3.61	4.21	4.37	4.76	6.19	2.96
WIUTDK$	5.83	3.56	4.00	3.98	4.27	2.96	4.36

Figure 9.12   Worksheet "Summary Statistics" in the file "Laws002.xls"

dollar terms) being the highest but with these returns also having the highest historical standard deviation of returns.[9]

Note that it can be quite cumbersome to compute the covariance matrix when the number of assets becomes large as particular care has to be taken when utilising the "COVAR" function to ensure that the correct cells are referred to. When the number of assets gets larger it is advisable to use the following result to construct the covariance matrix.

$$\sigma_{ij} = \frac{\mathbf{E'E}}{N} \tag{9.9}$$

where $\mathbf{E}$ is a vector of excess returns,[10] $\mathbf{E'}$ is its transpose and N is the number of data observations.

It is an easy task to construct a vector of excess returns. The spreadsheet in Figure 9.13 (worksheet "Covariance") shows how it is done for this dataset.

At the bottom of this worksheet is the covariance calculation of Figure 9.14. Note that the calculated covariances are identical to those found above using the "COVAR" function.[11]

---

[9] The data in this example has been selected so that it exhibits a positive relationship between risk and return. Quite often data may be selected that does not conform to this expectation as risk and return data is very sensitive to the choice of sample and to the choice of frequency.

[10] Defined as that period's return minus the mean return.

[11] An alternative method of obtaining the covariance matrix is to use Excel's "OFFSET" function. This function allows you to define a block of cells relative to some initial cell. Its arguments are (initial cells, rows and

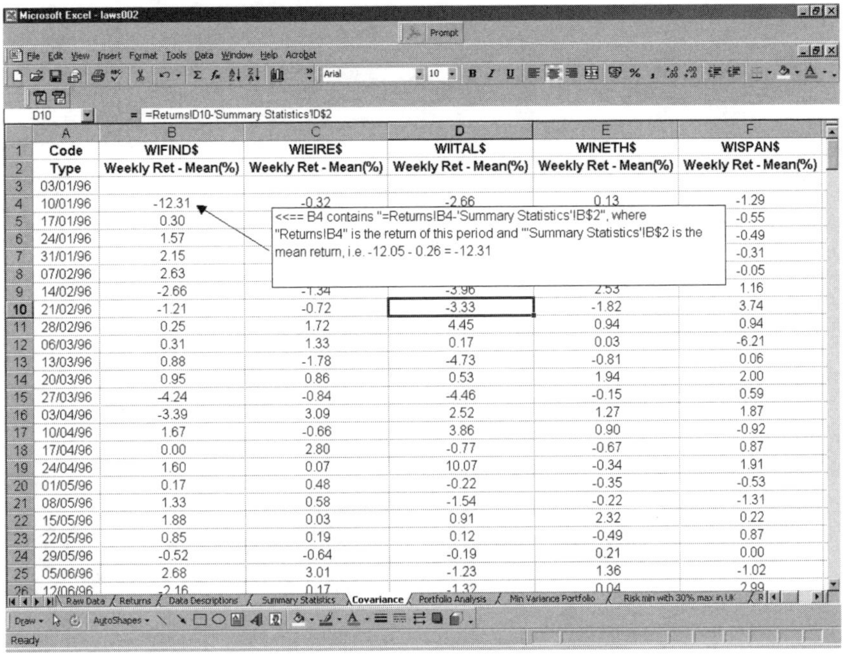

D10 = =Returns!D10-'Summary Statistics'!D$2

	A	B	C	D	E	F
1	Code	WIFIND$	WIEIRE$	WIITAL$	WINETH$	WISPAN$
2	Type	Weekly Ret - Mean(%)	Weekly Ret - Mean(%)	Weekly Ret - Mean(%)	Weekly Ret - Mean(%)	Weekly Ret - Mean(%)
3	03/01/96					
4	10/01/96	-12.31	-0.32	-2.66	0.13	-1.29
5	17/01/96	0.30				-0.55
6	24/01/96	1.57				-0.49
7	31/01/96	2.15				-0.31
8	07/02/96	2.63				-0.05
9	14/02/96	-2.66	-1.34	-3.96	2.53	1.16
10	21/02/96	-1.21	-0.72	-3.33	-1.82	3.74
11	28/02/96	0.25	1.72	4.45	0.94	0.94
12	06/03/96	0.31	1.33	0.17	0.03	-6.21
13	13/03/96	0.88	-1.78	-4.73	-0.81	0.06
14	20/03/96	0.95	0.86	0.53	1.94	2.00
15	27/03/96	-4.24	-0.84	-4.46	-0.15	0.59
16	03/04/96	-3.39	3.09	2.52	1.27	1.87
17	10/04/96	1.67	-0.66	3.86	0.90	-0.92
18	17/04/96	0.00	2.80	-0.77	-0.67	0.87
19	24/04/96	1.60	0.07	10.07	-0.34	1.91
20	01/05/96	0.17	0.48	-0.22	-0.35	-0.53
21	08/05/96	1.33	0.58	-1.54	-0.22	-1.31
22	15/05/96	1.88	0.03	0.91	2.32	0.22
23	22/05/96	0.85	0.19	0.12	-0.49	0.87
24	29/05/96	-0.52	-0.64	-0.19	0.21	0.00
25	05/06/96	2.68	3.01	-1.23	1.36	-1.02
26	12/06/96	-2.16	0.17	-1.32	0.04	2.99

<<== B4 contains "=Returns!B4-'Summary Statistics'!B$2", where "Returns!B4" is the return of this period and "'Summary Statistics'!B$2 is the mean return, i.e. -12.05 - 0.26 = -12.31

Figure 9.13 Worksheet "Covariance" in the file "Laws002.xls" (Excess Return Calculation)

In the worksheet "Portfolio Analysis" we use the matrix approach to portfolio risk:

$$\sigma_p^2 = \mathbf{w}'\mathbf{\Sigma}\mathbf{w} \tag{9.10}$$

to find the variance of an equally weighted portfolio.

To do this we construct a column vector of weights (see cells B5 to B11 in the "Portfolio Analysis" worksheet) which represents the **w** vector above. We then take the transpose of this vector[12] to obtain the $\mathbf{w}'$ vector above. Our covariance matrix ($\mathbf{\Sigma}$) is drawn from the "Summary Statistics" worksheet. The matrix algebra involved in calculating the portfolio risk can be broken down into the following matrix multiplications:

$$(1 \times N) \text{ vector} \times (N \times N) \text{ matrix} \times (N \times 1) \text{ matrix}$$

where here $N = 7$.

Taking the last two operations first the result we obtain is an $(N \times 1)$ matrix. This is the result found in cells B26 to H26 of the "Portfolio Analysis" worksheet. If we then

columns) where rows and columns are the row or column shifts from the original cells. In the spreadsheet "Laws002.xls" there are two worksheets that utilise this function. One is an introductory example entitled "Using Offset" whilst the other is an application of this function to the return databank. Once you are familiar with this function you will find that it is the most convenient way to find the covariance matrix of large asset portfolios.

[12] Using the "TRANSPOSE" function within Excel. This is implemented in the same way as all matrix functions.

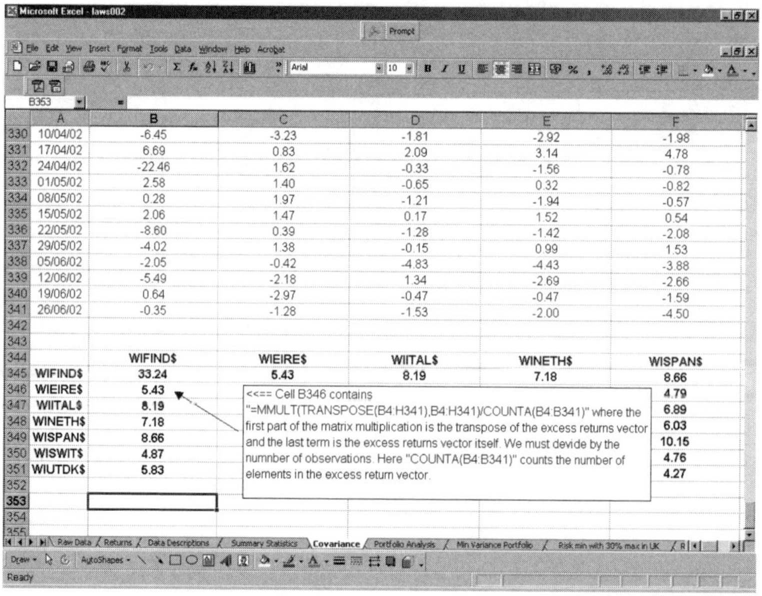

	A	B	C	D	E	F
330	10/04/02	-6.45	-3.23	-1.81	-2.92	-1.98
331	17/04/02	6.69	0.83	2.09	3.14	4.78
332	24/04/02	-22.46	1.62	-0.33	-1.56	-0.78
333	01/05/02	2.58	1.40	-0.65	0.32	-0.82
334	08/05/02	0.28	1.97	-1.21	-1.94	-0.57
335	15/05/02	2.06	1.47	0.17	1.52	0.54
336	22/05/02	-8.60	0.39	-1.28	-1.42	-2.08
337	29/05/02	-4.02	1.38	-0.15	0.99	1.53
338	05/06/02	-2.05	-0.42	-4.83	-4.43	-3.88
339	12/06/02	-5.49	-2.18	1.34	-2.69	-2.66
340	19/06/02	0.64	-2.97	-0.47	-0.47	-1.59
341	26/06/02	-0.35	-1.28	-1.53	-2.00	-4.50
342						
343						
344		WIFIND$	WIEIRE$	WIITAL$	WINETH$	WISPAN$
345	WIFIND$	33.24	5.43	8.19	7.18	8.66
346	WIEIRE$	5.43				4.79
347	WIITAL$	8.19				6.89
348	WINETH$	7.18				6.03
349	WISPAN$	8.66				10.15
350	WISWIT$	4.87				4.76
351	WIUTDK$	5.83				4.27

Figure 9.14 Worksheet "Covariance" in the file "Laws002.xls" (Covariance Calculation)

multiply the first $(1 \times N)$ vector by the result above (an $(N \times 1)$ matrix) we obtain a scalar as a result. That scalar is the portfolio variance and can be found in cell B28 (Figure 9.15). Using this dataset we find that the risk of an equally weighted portfolio is 2.46% per week with a return of 0.12% per week.

Fortunately within Excel it is not necessary to break this calculation down into these individual parts. Cell 34 includes the formulae necessary to combine the two matrix multiplications into one cell, whilst cell C37 includes the formulae necessary to eliminate both the matrix multiplication and also the vector transposition. It is therefore possible to find a portfolio variance in one cell given only a vector of portfolio weights and a covariance matrix. We are now going to utilise this framework and together with Excel's "Solver" tool find the portfolio composition that minimises portfolio variance.

Previously when we used "Solver" in a two-asset environment the weight assigned to the second asset adjusted automatically to changes in the weight of the first asset. Within an N-asset environment this is not possible and instead we have to add a number of constraints within the "Solver" dialogue box. The screen shot in Figure 9.16 includes the required constraints. The significance of the constraints are:

- $B$5:$B$11<=1 – we cannot invest more than 100% of our wealth in any asset.
- $B$5:$B$11>=0 – we cannot be "short" in any asset.
- $E$5=1 – we must invest all of our wealth in these assets.

Again we are minimising portfolio variance (cell B22) but this time rather than varying just one single cell we are varying the contents of the vector of weights (B5:B11). The result shown in the worksheet "Min Variance Portfolio" is given in Figure 9.17.

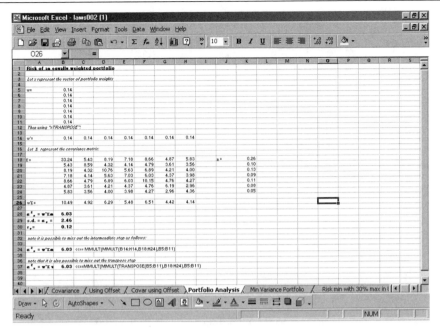

Figure 9.15 Worksheet "Portfolio Analysis" in the file "Laws002.xls"

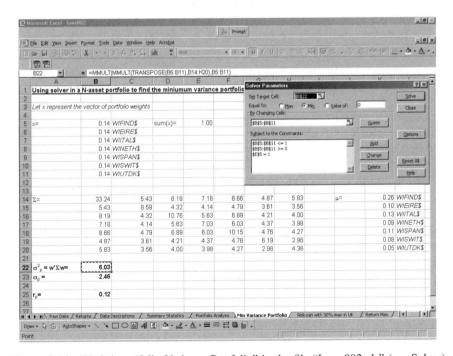

Figure 9.16 Worksheet "Min Variance Portfolio" in the file "Laws002.xls" (pre-Solver)

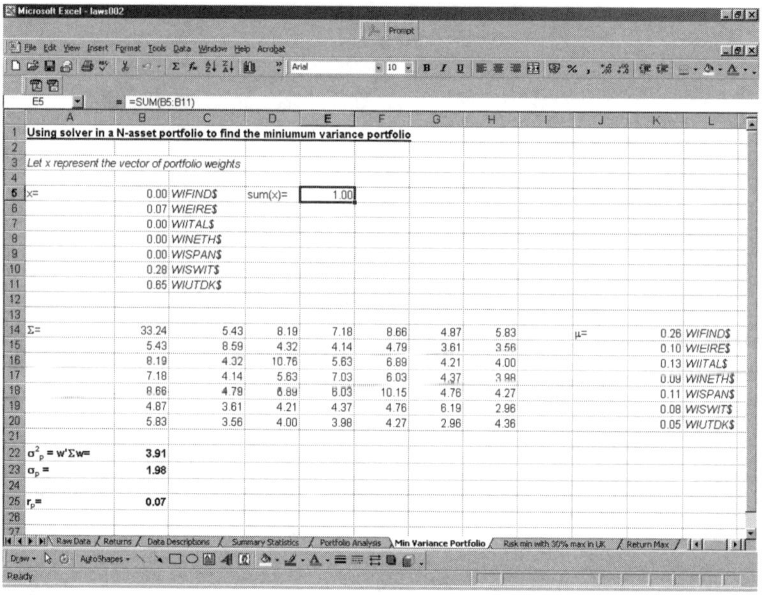

Figure 9.17 Worksheet "Min Variance Portfolio" in the file "Laws002.xls" (post-Solver)

This analysis shows that in order to obtain the minimum variance portfolio we should assign 65% of our wealth to UK equities, 28% to Swiss equities and 7% to Irish equities. Moreover, based on this dataset we should not invest any wealth in Finnish, Italian, Dutch or Spanish equities.

9.5   ALTERNATIVE OPTIMISATION TARGETS

So far we have concentrated our efforts on finding the minimum variance portfolio that fits our dataset. However it can easily be shown that a variety of differing objectives can be modelled within Excel.

As an example, consider the scenario above where we found that a portfolio comprising a 65% investment in UK equities together with a 28% investment in Swiss equities and a 7% investment in Irish equities produced a portfolio with a weekly return of 0.07% and a standard deviation of 1.98% per week. It may be the case that we would like to limit our investment in UK equities to some predetermined figure, say 30%. In order to incorporate this into our analysis we simply add this constraint:

$$\$B\$11 = <0.3$$

where $\$B\$11$ is the cell that includes the proportion of wealth invested in UK equities. The worksheet "Risk min with 30% max in UK" shows the results of this analysis where we find the optimal portfolio consists of 17% Irish equities, 3% Italian equities, 10% Dutch equities, 39% Swiss equities and 30% UK equities. The return of this portfolio is 0.08% per week with a standard deviation of 2.06% per week.

We could also construct the optimisation problem such that we minimise portfolio risk subject to investing at least 5% in each index. This requires us to change the constraint

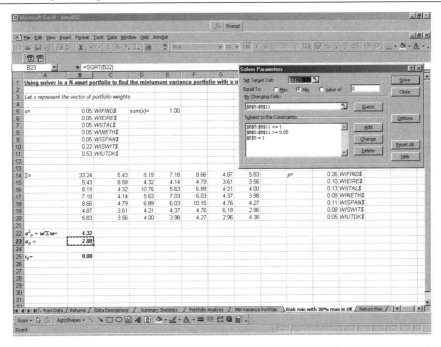

Figure 9.18 Worksheet "Risk min with 30% max in the UK" in the file "Laws002.xls"

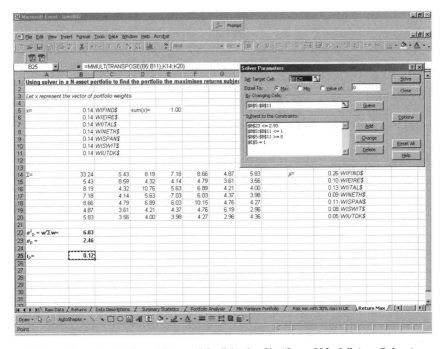

Figure 9.19 Worksheet "Return Max" in the file "Laws002.xls" (pre-Solver)

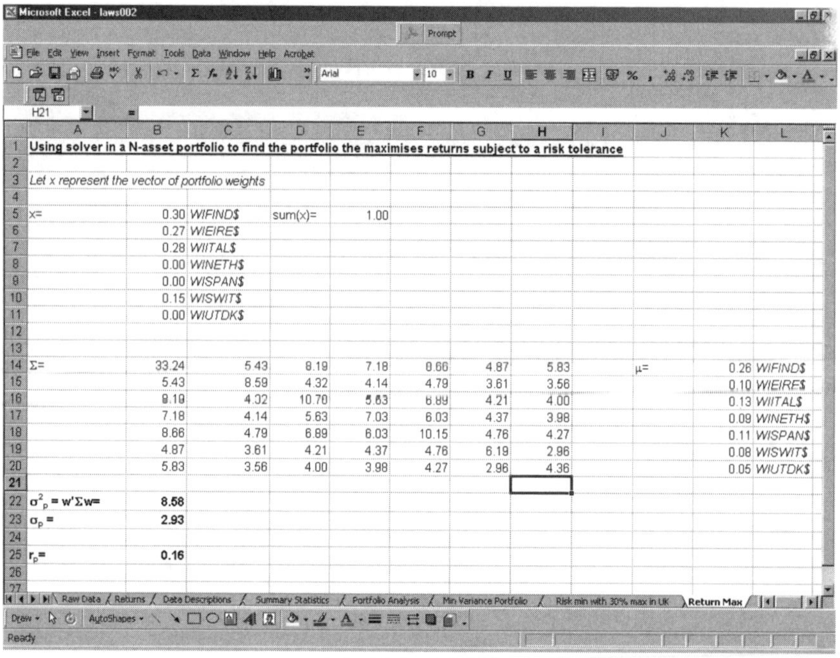

	A	B	C	D	E	F	G	H	I	J	K	L
1	Using solver in a N-asset portfolio to find the portfolio the maximises returns subject to a risk tolerance											
2												
3	*Let x represent the vector of portfolio weights*											
4												
5	x=	0.30	*WIFIND$*	sum(x)=	1.00							
6		0.27	*WIEIRE$*									
7		0.28	*WIITAL$*									
8		0.00	*WINETH$*									
9		0.00	*WISPAN$*									
10		0.15	*WISWIT$*									
11		0.00	*WIUTDK$*									
12												
13												
14	Σ=	33.24	5.43	8.19	7.18	8.66	4.87	5.83		μ=	0.26	*WIFIND$*
15		5.43	8.59	4.32	4.14	4.79	3.61	3.56			0.10	*WIEIRE$*
16		8.19	4.32	10.70	5.63	6.89	4.21	4.00			0.13	*WIITAL$*
17		7.18	4.14	5.63	7.03	6.03	4.37	3.98			0.09	*WINETH$*
18		8.66	4.79	6.89	6.03	10.15	4.76	4.27			0.11	*WISPAN$*
19		4.87	3.61	4.21	4.37	4.76	6.19	2.96			0.08	*WISWIT$*
20		5.83	3.56	4.00	3.98	4.27	2.96	4.36			0.05	*WIUTDK$*
21												
22	**σ^2_p = w'Σw=**	**8.58**										
23	**σ_p =**	**2.93**										
24												
25	**r_p=**	**0.16**										
26												

Figure 9.20 Worksheet "Return Max" in the file "Laws002.xls" (post-Solver)

\$B\$5:\$B\$11>=0 to \$B\$5:\$B\$11>=0.05, i.e. we must invest at least 5% in each index. The set-up (and results) for such a problem are shown in Figure 9.18.

It is also possible to utilise "Solver" to reverse the problem to one of return maximisation subject to a given level of risk tolerance. The worksheet "Return Max" takes the current dataset and attempts to find a portfolio that maximises returns subject to a risk tolerance level of 2.93%.[13] The solver dialogue box is shown completed in Figure 9.19.

Here you can see that the focus of attention is now on cell B25 (where the portfolio return result is calculated) and that an additional constraint:

\$B\$23<=2.93 – portfolio risk is less than 2.93%

has been added. The results are shown in Figure 9.20.

Here we can see that a mix of investments of Finnish equities (30%), Irish equities (27%), Italian equities (28%) and Swiss equities (15%) produces a portfolio offering a return of 0.16% per week with a target maximum standard deviation of 2.93% per week.

9.6 CONCLUSION

As stated at the outset the aim of this chapter was to illustrate how Markovitz-type portfolio analysis can be implemented within Excel. This is best achieved by looking at the problem in its matrix format rather than its linear format and then implementing the

[13] Note that an investment in Irish equities alone produces a risk of 2.93% per week with a return of 0.10% per week.

calculations using Excel's matrix algebra functions. If the problem is set up correctly it is then possible to use Excel's "Solver" function to optimise the portfolio subject to a variety of constraints and targets.

BIBLIOGRAPHY

Benninga, S. (2000), *Financial Modeling*, MIT Press, Cambridge, MA.

Cuthbertson, K. and D. Nitzsche (2001), *Investments: Spot and Derivative Markets*, John Wiley, Chichester.

Jackson, M. and M. Staunton (2001), *Advanced Modelling in Finance Using Excel and VBA*, John Wiley, Chichester.

Markovitz, H. (1952), "Portfolio Selection", *Journal of Finance*, **7**(1), March, 77–91.

Markovitz, H. (1959), *Portfolio Selection: Efficient Diversification of Investments*, John Wiley, New York.

10

Applied Volatility and Correlation Modelling Using Excel*

FRÉDÉRICK BOURGOIN

ABSTRACT

This chapter implements a range of univariate and multivariate models within Microsoft Excel. This is extremely useful as a large proportion of finance professionals, students and researchers that are familiar with this package. We show how to generate one-step ahead forecasts of volatility using the JP Morgan RiskMetrics model, JP Morgan RiskMetrics model with an optimal decay, a GARCH model with and without a variance reduction technique and finally using the GJR model to account for asymmetric reaction to news. A comparison of forecasts is made and some useful insights to the efficiency of the models is highlighted. In the second part of this chapter, we model the time-varying correlation using different models. As with the univariate approach this includes the JP Morgan RiskMetrics model with and without optimal decay, a GARCH model with and without variance reduction and finally the so-called "Fast GARCH" model of which the author has previously made significant contributions to the literature.

10.1 INTRODUCTION

The practicability of multivariate GARCH models has been the subject of several articles in the past few years, particularly regarding the feasibility of large size problems (Athayde, 2001; Bourgoin, 2000, 2002; Engle and Mezrich, 1995, 1996; Ding and Engle, 1994; Ledoit, 2001; Ledoit *et al.*, 2001). Some models work well only on specific data, like the orthogonal GARCH (Alexander and Chibumba, 1997) with yield curve or term structure of implied volatilities (see Bourgoin (2000) for the reasons). Because all these models require complex optimisation routines and tricks, GARCH models have always required special software like Rats (Regression Analysis of Time Series), Eviews, Matlab, S-Plus, Gauss, Ox or even special C++ code. In this chapter, we will try to provide an understandable way to construct GARCH models, both univariate and multivariate models, using Excel, the most widely used financial application in the market place. Two Excel spreadsheets are provided on the CD-Rom, one for the univariate models and another one for the multivariate models (Bourgoin001.xls, and Bourgoin002.xls, respectively).

---

* The views expressed herein are those of the author and do not necessarily reflect the views of Barclays Global Investors. I retain responsibility for any errors.

Applied Quantitative Methods for Trading and Investment. Edited by C.L. Dunis, J. Laws and P. Naïm
© 2003 John Wiley & Sons, Ltd   ISBN: 0-470-84885-5

10.2 THE BASICS

Let P_t be the price of a security at time t with $t = 1, \ldots, T$ and the continuously compounded returns expressed as $r_t = \ln(P_t/P_{t-1})$ with $\mu_t = E(r_t|F_{t-1})$ where $F(t-1)$ is the information set available at time $t - 1$.

The simplest linear time series model is the ARMA(p, q) process where $r(t)$ follows an autoregressive process, i.e., the past values of $r(t)$ influence future values of $r(t)$ and a moving average component which is formed by the error term, ε_{t-1}. Mathematically we have the following:

$$r_t = \theta_0 + \sum_{i=1}^{p} \phi_i r_{t-i} + \sum_{j=1}^{q} \theta_i \varepsilon_{t-i} \tag{10.1}$$

In the following pages we will not focus our attention on modelling the first moment of the distribution, so we will consider that $E(r_t) = \mu_t = 0$ and that either it has been done before or that it is statistically insignificant. The main purpose of this chapter is to consider the following: $\sigma_t^2 = \text{Var}(r_t|F_{t-1})$ and how to account for the time-varying volatility observed in the financial markets. So the model becomes:

$$r_t = \sigma_t \varepsilon_t \quad \text{where} \quad \sigma_t^2 = f(\varepsilon_{t-1}^2, \ldots, \varepsilon_{t-i}^2; \sigma_{t-1}^2, \ldots, \sigma_{t-j}^2) \quad \text{with} \quad i, j > 0,$$

$$\varepsilon_t \rightarrow N(0, 1)^1 \tag{10.2}$$

We try in this chapter to use only the Excel Solver add-in[2] and no additional optimisation add-in (several packages are available and a lot more flexible and powerful than the Excel Solver[3]), their usage is quite similar to the Solver, readily available as part of Excel.

We use the maximum likelihood estimation technique to evaluate the parameters of the models shown in the chapter.

The likelihood function is the following:

$$L = f(r_{n+1}, r_{n+2}, \ldots, r_T, \Theta) = f(r_t|F_{t-1})f(r_{t-1}|F_{t-2})\ldots f(r_{n+1}|F_n) \tag{10.3}$$

where n is the number of parameters to estimate.

If f follows a normal probability distribution with zero mean and variance σ_t^2, then L becomes:

$$L(r_{n+1}, r_{n+2}, \ldots, r_T, \Theta) = \prod_{t=n+1}^{T} f(r_t|F_{t-1}) = \prod_{t=n+1}^{T} \frac{1}{\sqrt{2\pi\sigma_t^2}} \exp\left(-\frac{r_t^2}{\sigma_t^2}\right) \tag{10.4}$$

For the purpose of the optimisation, we often find it more convenient to work with the natural log of this function, $\ln(L)$, because of the following property: $\ln(ab) = \ln(a) + (b)$.

---

[1] Obviously other probability distributions can be considered like the Student(t), GED(v) or the skewed Student(k, t) distribution but this is beyond the scope of this chapter.

[2] In order to set up the Solver add-in in Excel, start Excel $\Rightarrow$ Tools $\Rightarrow$ Add-ins $\Rightarrow$ Solver Add-in should be checked and then press <OK>, if it doesn't appear in the list, use your MS Office CD-Rom to install the required component.

[3] Palisade Corporation sells the @RiskOptimizer, a more powerful version of the Excel Solver with genetic algorithm and Monte Carlo simulation capabilities, see http://www.palisade.com.

The likelihood function becomes:

$$\ln(L, \Theta) = \sum_{t=n+1}^{T} -\frac{1}{2}\ln(2\pi) - \frac{1}{2}\ln(\sigma_t^2) - \frac{1}{2}\frac{r_t^2}{\sigma_t^2} \tag{10.5}$$

where we can drop $\ln(2\pi)$ as well.

10.3 UNIVARIATE MODELS

The Excel spreadsheets "Bourgoin001.xls" and "Bourgoin002.xls" both have a common set-up:

- Column A and B should have the dates and the security used for analysis, here, the S&P 500 index.
- Column C calculates the log returns for the index.
- Column D specifies the volatility equation.
- Column E calculates the log-likelihood function for each date (when we do an optimisation, which is not the case for the RiskMetrics Volatility model).
- Column F calculates the annualised volatility using the square-root rule.[4]
- The other columns show details on how to set up the Solver in order to perform the optimisation.

10.3.1 The RiskMetrics model

In the RiskMetrics model (J.P. Morgan, 1995), the volatility process specification is the following:

$$\sigma_t^2 = (1 - \lambda)\varepsilon_{t-1}^2 + \lambda\sigma_{t-1}^2 \tag{10.6}$$

The variance at time t depends on the previous squared returns and the previous variance. If we want to forecast the term structure of volatility going forward, we can show that it is constant:

$$E(\sigma_{t+1}^2|F_t) = E((1 - \lambda)\varepsilon_t^2 + \lambda\sigma_t^2) = (1 - \lambda)E(\varepsilon_t^2) + \lambda E(\sigma_t^2)$$
$$= (1 - \lambda)\varepsilon_t^2 + \lambda\sigma_{t|t-1}^2$$
$$E(\sigma_{t+2}^2|F_t) = E((1 - \lambda)\varepsilon_{t+1}^2 + \lambda\sigma_{t+1|t}^2) = (1 - \lambda)E(\varepsilon_{t+1|t}^2) + \lambda E(\sigma_{t+1|t}^2) \tag{10.7}$$
$$= (1 - \lambda)\sigma_{t+1|t}^2 + \lambda\sigma_{t+1|t}^2 = \sigma_{t+1|t}^2$$
$$E(\sigma_{t+h}^2|F_t) = \sigma_{t+1|t}^2$$

[4] Only statistically applicable to the random walk and the RiskMetrics model, it is industry practice to use it regardless of the volatility model. See Tsay (2002) and Diebold *et al.* (1997) for more details.

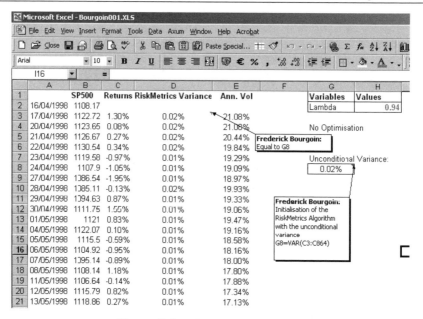

Figure 10.1   The RiskMetrics model

The worksheet "RiskMetrics" in the spreadsheet "Bourgoin001.xls" (see screenshot in Figure 10.1) implements this model on the S&P500 data from April 1998 to August 2001.

The initialisation of the algorithm is quite important regardless of the volatility model used (here RiskMetrics), one should always default the first observation of the volatility to the unconditional standard deviation of the time series ($\sigma_1 = \overline{\sigma}$). This is particularly crucial when complex models are used; bad starting values can lead to a non-convergence of the optimisation process.

Note that the spreadsheet allows λ, the decay factor, to be varied. In practice though, it is set to 0.94 for daily data and 0.97 for monthly data.[5]

10.3.2   The optimal decay factor model

In the previous spreadsheet (RiskMetrics), we didn't use any optimisation as the user gives λ, the decay factor. If we want to find the optimal decay factor for the time series, maximum likelihood estimation is required to find the only parameter necessary, λ. The worksheet "OptimalDecay" in Bourgoin001.xls (see Figure 10.2) shows how it is done.

Remarks:

- The grey background identifies the optimised values or changing cells in every spreadsheet.
- No standard errors are calculated for any models, this is beyond the scope of this chapter.
- The Solver options are shown in Figure 10.3.[6]

---

[5] In practice, we can observe less heteroskedasticity in monthly data than in daily data, that is the reason why the decay has been set higher (standard set by J.P. Morgan (1995)).
[6] These options are accessed from the main Solver window by clicking on "Options".

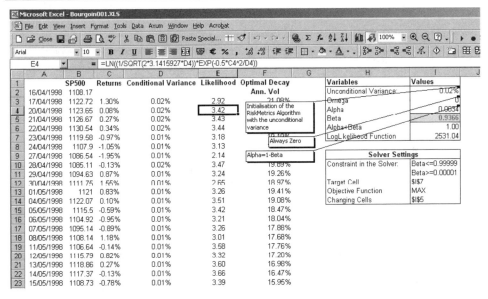

Figure 10.2 Optimal decay

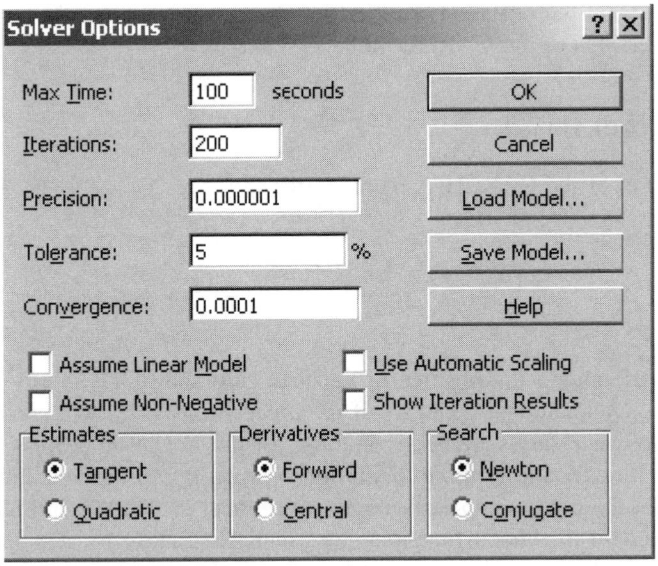

Figure 10.3 Solver settings

- The higher the decay factor (less than 1), the longer the half-life, for example with a decay factor of 0.94, 50% of the weight is in the previous 11 observations, if the decay increases to 0.98, the half-life increases to 34 observations (see RiskMetrics Technical Document, p. 93). When the decay equals 1, we mean revert to the unconditional standard deviation calculation if we initialised the process with $\sigma_0 = \overline{\sigma}$.

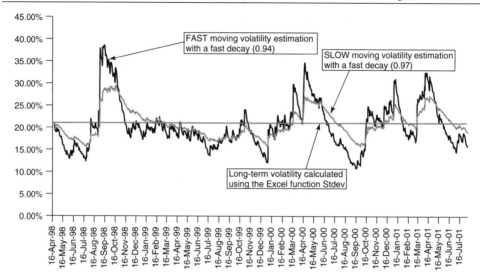

Figure 10.4 Annualised RiskMetrics volatility with varying decay factors

A comparison of different decay factors can be found in the sheet named "DifferentDe-cayChart" in Bourgoin001.xls (Figure 10.4).

As we will see in the next section, the RiskMetrics and optimal decay models are, in fact, simpler versions of the GARCH model.

10.3.3 The GARCH model

The general form of the GARCH(p, q) model is:

$$\sigma_t^2 = \omega + \sum_{i=1}^{p} \alpha_i \varepsilon_{t-i}^2 + \sum_{j=1}^{q} \beta_j \sigma_{t-j}^2 \qquad (10.8)$$

Where all the parameters are positive or equal to zero and $\sum_{i=1}^{\max(p,q)} (\alpha_i + \beta_i) < 1$, this implies that the unconditional volatility of the process exists (we will show this later on) and provides the necessary stationary condition for the stochastic process.

The GARCH model allows more flexibility to be built into the volatility process than RiskMetrics but the extra complexity comes at a price, in that the optimisation is more complex (maximum likelihood functions are usually known to be very flat functions of their parameters, which makes it difficult for optimisers).

We will restrict our analysis to the financial industry standard (Engle and Mezrich, 1995), the GARCH(1,1) with just one lag for the residual and one lag for the conditional variance. As we can see from the above equation, the RiskMetrics equation is embedded in it.[7] We have shown previously that the term structure of volatility forecast is flat for RiskMetrics, here however the GARCH(1,1) allows for a mean-reversion process to take place for the

---

[7] In a GARCH(1,1), the volatility equation becomes: $\sigma_t^2 = \omega + \alpha \varepsilon_{t-1}^2 + \beta \sigma_{t-1}^2$. If we replace ω by 0 and α by $1 - \beta$, then the model falls back to the RiskMetrics equation.

volatility. That is, the volatility mean reverts to a long-term average, the unconditional volatility of the process.

To forecast the volatility, we have to iterate equation (10.8) forward (with $p = 1$ and $q = 1$):

$$\sigma_t^2(1) = E(\sigma_{t+1/t}^2) = \omega + \alpha\varepsilon_t^2 + \beta\sigma_t^2$$

$$\sigma_t^2(2) = E(\omega + \alpha\varepsilon_{t+1}^2 + \beta\sigma_t^2(1)) = \omega + \alpha E(\varepsilon_{t+1}^2) + \beta\sigma_t^2(1)$$

$$= \omega + \alpha E(\sigma_t^2(1)) + \beta\sigma_t^2(1)$$

$$= \omega + (\alpha + \beta)\sigma_t^2(1)$$

$$\sigma_t^2(3) = \omega + (\alpha + \beta)\sigma_t^2(2) = \omega(1 + (\alpha + \beta)) + (\alpha + \beta)^2\sigma_t^2(1)$$

Hence for a forecasting horizon h, we have:

$$\sigma_t^2(h) = \omega\frac{1 - (\alpha + \beta)^{h-1}}{1 - (\alpha + \beta)} + (\alpha + \beta)^{h-1}\sigma_t^2(1) \tag{10.9}$$

When h tends to infinity, we have the following long-term variance of the GARCH(1,1) process:

$$\lim_{h\to\infty} \sigma_t^2(h) = \overline{\sigma}^2 = \frac{\omega}{1 - \alpha - \beta} \tag{10.10}$$

where $\overline{\sigma}$ is the unconditional variance.

The spreadsheet-based application ("DataGARCH" sheet in Bourgoin001.xls) is not very different from the optimal decay sheet; only now omega and alpha are part of the optimisation routine (Figure 10.5).

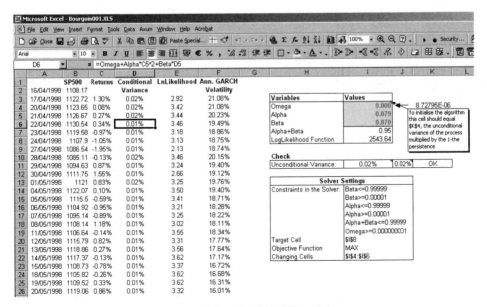

Figure 10.5 The GARCH model

However because we know the long-term volatility $\overline{\sigma}^2$ using historical data and the standard time series approach:

$$\overline{\sigma}^2 = \frac{1}{N}\sum_{t=1}^{N}(r_t - \overline{r})^2 \quad \text{or} \quad \Sigma = \frac{1}{T}E(RR') \tag{10.11}$$

We can replace ω by using equations (10.10) and (10.11) together:

$$\omega = \overline{\sigma}^2(1 - \alpha - \beta) \tag{10.12}$$

ω is then NOT required in the optimisation process! The technique has been pioneered by Engle and Mezrich (1995) and is called the variance targeting technique, so we can make the optimisation routine simpler by reducing the number of parameters from three to two. One should note that on the spreadsheet in Figure 10.6 ("DataGARCH_VT" in Bourgoin001.xls) only alpha and beta are greyed out.

As we can see the likelihood function $I$8 is identical to the normal GARCH model in the previous example, so there seems to be no loss of likelihood in the model and we were able to reduce the number of parameters at the same time.

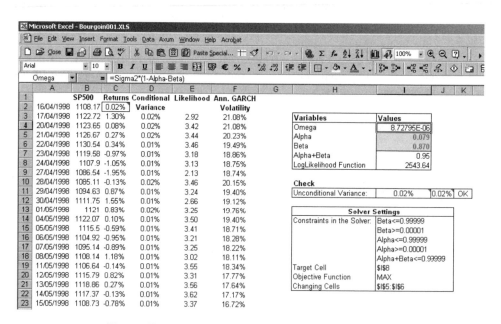

Figure 10.6   The GARCH model with variance targeting

10.3.4   THE GJR model

Since Black (1976) it is well accepted that stocks have an asymmetric response to news. In order to account for these asymmetries encountered in the market, Glosten, Jagannathan and Runkle (GJR; Glosten *et al.*, 1993) extended the framework of the GARCH(1,1) to take this into account. The augmented model can be written as:

$$r_t = \sigma_t \varepsilon_t \qquad \sigma_t^2 = \omega + \alpha \varepsilon_{t-1}^2 + \beta \sigma_{t-1}^2 + \gamma S_{t-1} \varepsilon_{t-1}^2 \qquad S_t = \begin{cases} 0 & \text{if } \varepsilon_t > 0 \\ 1 & \text{if } \varepsilon_t < 0 \end{cases} \quad (10.13)$$

with $\alpha > 0$, $\beta > 0$, $\gamma > 0$ and $\alpha + \beta + \frac{1}{2}\gamma < 1$. When returns are positive, $\gamma S_{t-1} \varepsilon_{t-1}^2$ is equal to zero and the volatility equation collapses to a GARCH(1,1) equation; on the contrary, when returns are negative, the volatility equation is augmented by γ, a positive number, meaning that the impact of this particular negative return is bigger on the estimation of volatility, as shown below:

$$\text{if } \varepsilon_t < 0, \quad \sigma_t^2 = \omega + (\alpha + \gamma)\varepsilon_{t-1}^2 + \beta \sigma_{t-1}^2$$

We can forecast the volatility term structure:

$$\sigma_{\text{GJR},t}^2(h) = \omega \frac{1 - \left(\alpha + \beta + \frac{1}{2}\gamma\right)^{h-1}}{1 - \left(\alpha + \beta + \frac{1}{2}\gamma\right)} + \left(\alpha + \beta + \frac{1}{2}\gamma\right)^{h-1} \sigma_{\text{GJR},t}^2(1) \qquad (10.14)$$

with $\sigma_{\text{GJR},t}^2(1) = \omega + \alpha \varepsilon_t^2 + \beta \sigma_t^2 + \gamma S_t \varepsilon_t^2 / 2$. We can derive the long-term variance process from this model as:

$$\lim_{h \to \infty} \sigma_{\text{GJR},t}^2(h) = \bar{\sigma}^2 = \frac{\omega}{1 - \alpha - \beta - \gamma/2} \qquad (10.15)$$

The spreadsheet-based application (Figure 10.7) is located in "DataGARCHGJR_VT" (Bourgoin001.xls).

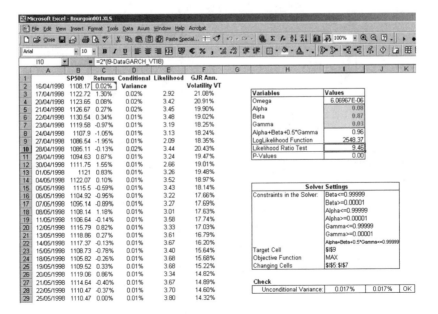

Figure 10.7 The GJR model with variance targeting

Remarks:

- Here we use again the variance targeting process (note that $I$4, omega is not greyed out) in order to facilitate the optimisation process.
- One good way to ensure that the optimisation has good starting values is to give alpha and beta the values of a GARCH(1,1) process with gamma equal to a very low positive value (say 0.01 for example as long as alpha+beta+0.5*gamma is strictly less than 1).
- One should also note that the likelihood function is slightly higher in GJR(1,1) with 2548.37 against 2543.64 for the GARCH(1,1). The likelihood ratio test[8] performed in $I$10 allows us to conclude that this model is capturing some of the unaccounted volatility dynamics of the simple GARCH model.

10.3.5 Model comparison

Since we've calculated several types of volatility model, we can now look at the one-step-ahead volatility forecast over time (Figure 10.8).

Several remarks can be made:

- The GJR model shows clearly that it is more sensitive to the big downward movements of the S&P500. For example, in August 1998, it shows a substantial increase in volatility compared to the GARCH model or any of the weighted-decay models.
- There are clearly two distinct types of model here: the weighted-decay on the one side and the GARCH-type model on the other. This can be shown from the high degree of persistence of the volatility with the weighted-decay models (after a shock their

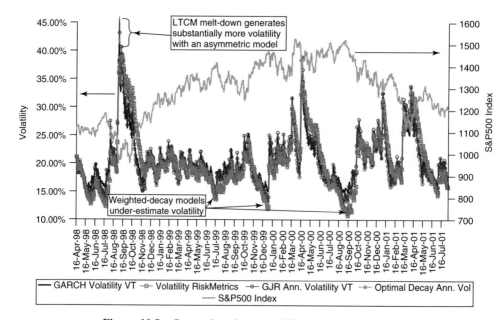

Figure 10.8 Comparison between different volatility models

---

[8] For the likelihood ratio test, refer to Gallant (1997, p. 181).

volatility is consistently higher than the GARCH-type models), because the persistence parameters $\alpha + \beta = 1 = \lambda$ compared to $\alpha + \beta < 1$ for the GARCH model.

- We can also see that during calm periods, the weighted-decay volatilities tend to decrease much more than the GARCH models, this is due to the fact that there is no mean reversion embedded in these models. If we take the extreme case, the volatility will progressively tend to zero if the asset returns are zero in the near future; this has been one of the main criticisms of the RiskMetrics model.

The difference in the volatility estimation not only differs historically, but also when we try to forecast the term structure of volatility in the future (Figure 10.9). As we've shown earlier, the weighted-decay methodology does not provide any insight into the future behaviour of the term structure of volatility since there is no information in its term structure (the term structure of forecast is flat and equal to the one-step-ahead volatility forecast). On the other hand, the GARCH-type model shows us the mean-reversion process to the long-term volatility (the unconditional volatility) happening over time. Here, we can see that the GARCH model mean reverts slightly quicker than the GJR model, but both models show that the volatility is likely to increase in the next 5 months (horizon of forecasting).

In this section, we've seen that it is possible to estimate and forecast volatility using complex volatility models within the Excel framework. However if one wants, for example, to do complicated statistical tests for diagnostic checking, Excel will not be a suitable framework for a proper econometric analysis of financial time series. But for common day-to-day analysis, the practicality and user friendliness is unrivalled.

The next section will introduce the modelling of conditional correlation using the same framework utilised above.

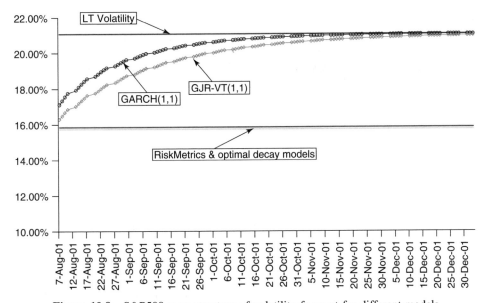

Figure 10.9 S&P500 term structure of volatility forecast for different models

10.4 MULTIVARIATE MODELS

In this section, we will show how to perform multivariate models to calculate conditional correlation estimation and forecast the term structure using Excel. Several models will be considered, the J.P. Morgan RiskMetrics, the optimal decay model and three GARCH models: the full diagonal GARCH, and its simpler derivative with variance targeting, and the superfast GARCH model (Bourgoin, 2002). For convenience purposes and simplicity, we will consider only a two-variable system, more can be added but with additional complexity in the spreadsheet set-up. Each calculation devoted to a specific asset or cross-term (volatility for asset 1, asset 2 and the covariance) will have its own background colour in the workbook Bourgoin002.xls. In this way it is easier to read and understand the spreadsheet.

10.4.1 The RiskMetrics model

Let us consider a two-asset model, where both volatilities and the covariance follow the RiskMetrics (RiskMetrics Technical Document, p. 82) equation:

$$\sigma_{1,t}^2 = (1 - \lambda)\varepsilon_{1,t-1}^2 + \lambda\sigma_{1,t-1}^2$$
$$\sigma_{2,t}^2 = (1 - \lambda)\varepsilon_{2,t-1}^2 + \lambda\sigma_{2,t-1}^2 \qquad (10.16)$$
$$\sigma_{12,t}^2 = (1 - \lambda)\varepsilon_{1,t-1}\varepsilon_{2,t-1} + \lambda\sigma_{12,t-1}^2$$

The initialisation of $\sigma_{1,0}$, $\sigma_{2,0}$, $\sigma_{12,0}$ is set to the unconditional volatilities and covariance.

The model has very appealing attributes in a multivariate framework: it is very quick to calculate for a large size covariance matrix and the covariance is always positive definite by construction as long as λ is the same everywhere in the covariance matrix.[9] But the drawbacks are still the same in a multivariate framework: flat term structure of forecast, too much persistence of shocks and too low volatilities during calm periods.

The spreadsheet of Figure 10.10 ("RiskMetrics" in Bourgoin002.xls) shows the implementation of RiskMetrics for volatilities and correlations for two stock indexes, the French CAC40 and the German DAX30. The volatilities are calculated in exactly the same way as in Bourgoin001.xls, but here we add the cross-term to calculate the covariance. Equation (10.16) is calculated in columns F, G and H respectively. Column I is the resulting correlation by applying the standard textbook formula:

$$\rho_{i,j} = \sigma_{i,j}/(\sigma_i\sigma_j)$$

10.4.2 The optimal decay model

The optimal decay model is a generalisation of the RiskMetrics model where the optimal decay is not predetermined at 0.94. The objective function is the likelihood function. In

---

[9] A matrix is positive definite as long as its minimum eigenvalue is strictly positive. This is crucial for risk management purposes because otherwise a linear combination of assets in the portfolio can yield to a negative portfolio variance. For a more detailed explanation, refer to J.P. Morgan (1997).

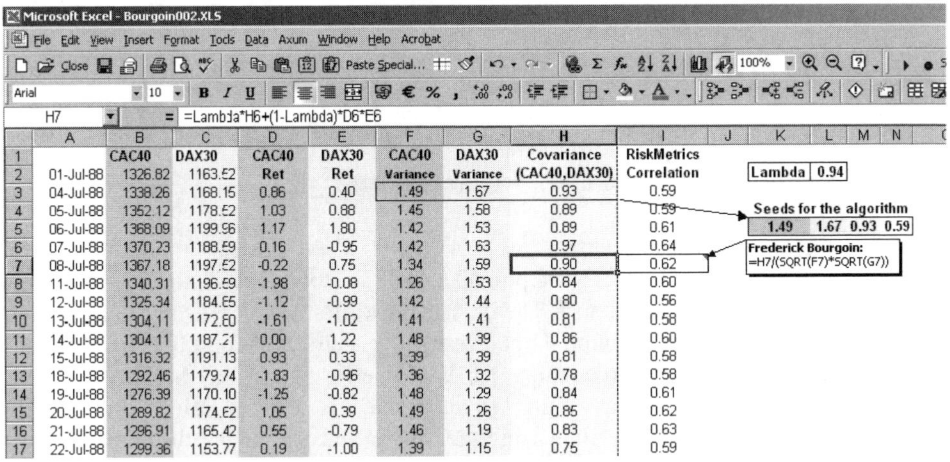

	A	B	C	D	E	F	G	H	I
1		CAC40	DAX30	CAC40	DAX30	CAC40	DAX30	Covariance	RiskMetrics
2	01-Jul-88	1326.82	1163.52	Ret	Ret	Variance	Variance	(CAC40,DAX30)	Correlation
3	04-Jul-88	1338.26	1168.15	0.86	0.40	1.49	1.67	0.93	0.59
4	05-Jul-88	1352.12	1178.52	1.03	0.88	1.45	1.58	0.89	0.59
5	06-Jul-88	1368.09	1199.96	1.17	1.80	1.42	1.53	0.89	0.61
6	07-Jul-88	1370.23	1188.59	0.16	-0.95	1.42	1.63	0.97	0.64
7	08-Jul-88	1367.18	1197.52	-0.22	0.75	1.34	1.59	0.90	0.62
8	11-Jul-88	1340.31	1196.59	-1.98	-0.08	1.26	1.53	0.84	0.60
9	12-Jul-88	1325.34	1184.65	-1.12	-0.99	1.42	1.44	0.80	0.56
10	13-Jul-88	1304.11	1172.60	-1.61	-1.02	1.41	1.41	0.81	0.58
11	14-Jul-88	1304.11	1187.21	0.00	1.22	1.48	1.39	0.86	0.60
12	15-Jul-88	1316.32	1191.13	0.93	0.33	1.39	1.39	0.81	0.58
13	18-Jul-88	1292.46	1179.74	-1.83	-0.96	1.36	1.32	0.78	0.58
14	19-Jul-88	1276.39	1170.10	-1.25	-0.82	1.48	1.29	0.84	0.61
15	20-Jul-88	1289.82	1174.62	1.05	0.39	1.49	1.26	0.85	0.62
16	21-Jul-88	1296.91	1165.42	0.55	-0.79	1.46	1.19	0.83	0.63
17	22-Jul-88	1299.36	1153.77	0.19	-1.00	1.39	1.15	0.75	0.59

Figure 10.10 The RiskMetrics model bivariate

order to write the likelihood function, we need to define the probability distribution, here we will use the multivariate normal distribution:

$$f(x, \mu, \Omega) = \frac{1}{(2\pi)^{n/2}|\Omega|^{1/2}} \exp\left[\frac{-1}{2}(x-\mu)'\Omega^{-1}(x-\mu)\right] \tag{10.17}$$

where μ is the vector of the mean and Ω the covariance matrix for two assets with zero mean, the multivariate normal distribution looks like this:

$$f(x_1, x_2, \sigma_1, \sigma_2, \rho_{12}) = \frac{1}{2\pi\sigma_1\sigma_2(1-\rho_{12}^2)} \exp\left(\frac{-1}{2(1-\rho_{12}^2)}\left[\frac{x_1^2}{\sigma_1^2} - \frac{2\rho_{12}x_1x_2}{\sigma_1\sigma_2} + \frac{x_2^2}{\sigma_2^2}\right]\right) \tag{10.18}$$

The likelihood function for a time-varying covariance matrix is the following:

$$\begin{aligned}
\ln L &= \ln\left(\prod_{i=1}^{T} f(x_{1,i}, x_{2,i}, \Theta)\right) = \sum_{i=1}^{T} \ln(f(x_{1,i}, x_{2,i}, \Theta)) \\
&= \sum_{t=1}^{T} -\ln(2\pi) - \ln(\sigma_{1,t}) - \ln(\sigma_{2,t}) - \frac{1}{2}\ln(1-\rho_{12,t}^2) \\
&\quad - \frac{1}{2(1-\rho_{12,t}^2)}\left[\frac{x_{1,t}^2}{\sigma_{1,t}^2} - \frac{2\rho_{12,t}x_{1,t}x_{2,t}}{\sigma_{1,t}\sigma_{2,t}} + \frac{x_{2,t}^2}{\sigma_{2,t}^2}\right]
\end{aligned} \tag{10.19}$$

The optimisation routine will be to maximise the log-likelihood function with respect to the decay factor:

$$\max \ln L(\lambda) \quad \text{with} \quad 0 < \lambda \leq 1$$

Here the covariance specification is:

$$\sigma_{1,t}^2 = (1 - \hat{\lambda})\varepsilon_{1,t-1}^2 + \hat{\lambda}\sigma_{1,t-1}^2$$

$$\sigma_{2,t}^2 = (1 - \hat{\lambda})\varepsilon_{2,t-1}^2 + \hat{\lambda}\sigma_{2,t-1}^2 \qquad (10.20)$$

$$\sigma_{12,t}^2 = (1 - \hat{\lambda})\varepsilon_{1,t-1}\varepsilon_{2,t-1} + \hat{\lambda}\sigma_{12,t-1}^2$$

where $\hat{\lambda}$ is the optimal decay factor.

The spreadsheet of Figure 10.11 ("OptimalDecay" in Bourgoin002.xls) is identical to the RiskMetrics sheet up to column I. The only major difference here is that we calculate the log-likelihood function (column J) at every time step (equation (10.18)). The sum of the log-likelihood functions (equation (10.19)) is performed in cell M9. Since we are trying to find the optimal lambda, we need to maximise this cell (see Solver settings). The optimal decay factor is obtained after using the Solver and optimising the spreadsheet in cell M8.

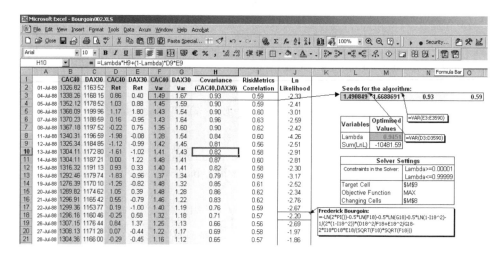

Figure 10.11 The bivariate optimal decay model

10.4.3 The diagonal GARCH model

In the diagonal GARCH model, each variance and covariance term has its own dynamics (set of parameters), so the functional form for the model is:

$$\sigma_{1,t}^2 = \omega_{11} + \alpha_{11}\varepsilon_{1,t-1}^2 + \beta_{11}\sigma_{1,t-1}^2$$

$$\sigma_{2,t}^2 = \omega_{22} + \alpha_{22}\varepsilon_{2,t-1}^2 + \beta_{22}\sigma_{2,t-1}^2 \qquad (10.21)$$

$$\sigma_{12,t}^2 = \omega_{12} + \alpha_{12}\varepsilon_{1,t-1}\varepsilon_{2,t-1} + \beta_{12}\sigma_{12,t-1}^2$$

The spreadsheet of Figure 10.12 ("Full Diagonal GARCH" in Bourgoin002.xls) is more complex because we have to deal with multiple constraints:

$$\alpha_{ij} + \beta_{ij} < 1, \quad \alpha_{ij} > 0, \quad \beta_{ij} > 0 \quad \text{and} \quad \omega_{ii} > 0$$

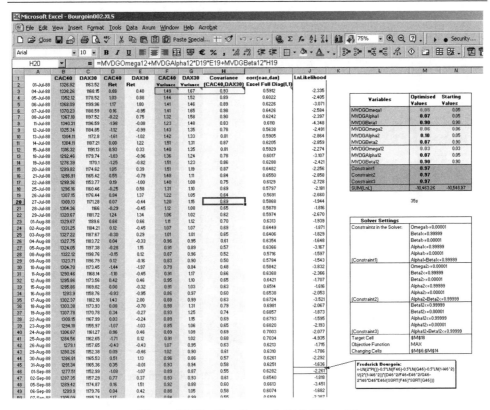

Figure 10.12 The diagonal GARCH model

Note that ω_{ij} is allowed to be negative because otherwise you constrain the long-term correlation to be positive between the two assets.[10]

The spreadsheet is identical to the optimal decay spreadsheet with regard to the log-likelihood function. The optimisation, on the other hand, has multiple constraints (17 in total!) and nine parameters as indicated in the Solver settings. Each variance (1 and 2) and the covariance have their own parameters (alphas, betas and omegas).

Because the optimisation procedure is quite complicated, it might require a long time to run.[11]

10.4.4 The diagonal GARCH model with variance targeting

For this model, we apply the variance targeting technique mentioned in Section 10.3.3 to the multivariate context:

$$\omega_{ij} = \overline{\sigma}_{ij}^2 (1 - \alpha_{ij} - \beta_{ij}) \tag{10.22}$$

Because most of the time the alphas and betas tend to have very similar optimised values between each equation, the complexity arises from the fit of the omegas, using the variance

---

[10] This can be derived easily from the long-term correlation implied by the diagonal model.
[11] It took 35 seconds to run on a PIII-600 MHz with 256 Mb RAM and Windows 2000.

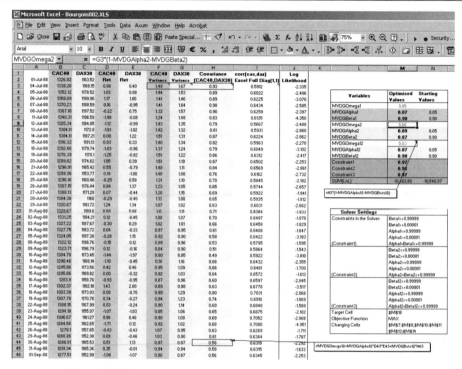

Figure 10.13 The diagonal GARCH model with variance targeting

targeting technique accelerates the optimisation procedure dramatically.[12] In practice, the model appeal is greatly enhanced.

In the spreadsheet of Figure 10.13 ("Full Diagonal GARCH VT" in Bourgoin002.xls), we can see that the spreadsheet is almost identical to the diagonal GARCH model, the only subtle difference is that Omega1, Omega2 and Omega12 are not part of the opti- misation procedure (check cells M41 and M42), they have been replaced by formulas (equation (10.22)) as shown in cell M12. The number of constraints is reduced to 15 from 17 and most importantly the number of parameters is now only six instead of nine.

10.4.5 The scalar GARCH model with variance targeting

This is the most simplified model of the "traditional" type. We consider that all assets under analysis have the same parameters, i.e., $\alpha_{ij} = \overline{\alpha}$ and $\beta_{ij} = \overline{\beta}$, and we use the variance targeting technique in order to eliminate the omegas from the estimation procedure, so the number of parameters to optimise becomes completely independent from the number of variables in the model and equal to two ($\overline{\alpha}$ and $\overline{\beta}$):

$$\sigma_{1,t}^2 = \overline{\sigma}_1^2(1 - \overline{\alpha} - \overline{\beta}) + \overline{\alpha}\varepsilon_{1,t-1}^2 + \overline{\beta}\sigma_{1,t-1}^2$$

$$\sigma_{2,t}^2 = \overline{\sigma}_2^2(1 - \overline{\alpha} - \overline{\beta}) + \overline{\alpha}\varepsilon_{2,t-1}^2 + \overline{\beta}\sigma_{2,t-1}^2 \qquad (10.23)$$

$$\sigma_{12,t}^2 = \overline{\sigma}_{12}^2(1 - \overline{\alpha} - \overline{\beta}) + \overline{\alpha}\varepsilon_{1,t-1}\varepsilon_{2,t-1} + \overline{\beta}\sigma_{12,t-1}^2$$

---

[12] Instead of 35 seconds, the optimisation routine took only 17 seconds, half the time required by the general model with hardly any reduction in the likelihood function.

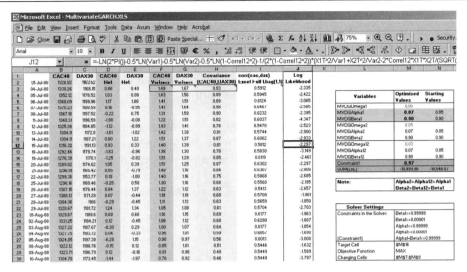

Figure 10.14   The scalar GARCH model with variance targeting

The worksheet of Figure 10.14 ("Scalar GARCH VT" in Bourgoin002.xls) shows how this is done. Only MVDGAlpha1 and MVDGBeta1 are optimised, the omegas are derived from the unconditional variances and the covariance calculated in F3:H3. Here the number of constraints is a lot smaller (five).

We can note a clear drop in the log-likelihood function to $-10\,489.96$, whereas before we had hardly any changes of likelihood at all. Although quite restrictive, the structural constraints of the model (alphas and betas identical across all equations) provide a very appealing model where the number of parameters is *always* two, so the optimiser will be very quick.[13] In this particular case, we can see that the log-likelihood function is lower than the optimal decay ($-10\,481$) but the model guarantees the mean-reversion process, avoiding the underestimation of the volatilities during calm periods.

10.4.6   The fast GARCH model

The purpose of this model is to enable us to calculate conditional correlation in a very fast and easy manner. It was first presented by Bourgoin (2002), and follows in the footsteps of Ding and Engle (1994), Ledoit (1999), Pourahmadi (1999), Bourgoin (2000) and Athayde (2001) to deal with a very large number of assets. For the purpose of clarity, we will only present the model in a 2×2 setting but the application is straightforward to generalise to a very large number of assets.

As we have seen in the previous paragraph it is possible to use the variance targeting process on a scalar GARCH in order to obtain a multivariate model with just two para-meters regardless of the size of the covariance matrix. This is very appealing because the optimisation routine will converge quickly to the results. However the problem would be much simpler if we could avoid the estimation of the levels of persistence, $\bar{\alpha}$ and $\bar{\beta}$.

Here we follow the idea of Athayde (2001) on the estimation of these parameters. If a "natural" index exists for the data, we can calculate a univariate GARCH model and apply

---

[13] The optimisation routine took only 7 seconds to find the solution.

the parameters of persistence to the multivariate scalar GARCH model. On the other hand when there is not a "natural" index for the data, we construct a synthetic index return from an equal-weighted portfolio of all the assets under analysis and perform a univariate GARCH on this synthetic return series. Bourgoin (2002) showed that within a portfolio of equities, bonds or FX, there is not much difference between the persistence parameters (alpha and beta) of each component within the portfolio; hence it is practically equivalent to a scalar GARCH model.

So, as an extension to the previous model, we calculate a single univariate GARCH model for the synthetic index (here a GARCH(1,1) but any model discussed in the volatility section can be used) and apply its persistence parameters "down" to the covariance matrix, like Athayde (2001).

So the model looks like this. From either a synthetic or a real index, we have:

$$\sigma_{index,t}^2 = \omega_{Index} + \hat{\alpha}\varepsilon_{Index,t-1}^2 + \hat{\beta}\sigma_{index,t-1}^2 \qquad (10.24)$$

We then plug in the persistence parameters ($\hat{\alpha}$ and $\hat{\beta}$) "down" into the multivariate equation:

$$\sigma_{1,t}^2 = \overline{\sigma}_1^2(1 - \hat{\alpha} - \hat{\beta}) + \hat{\alpha}\varepsilon_{1,t-1}^2 + \hat{\beta}\sigma_{1,t-1}^2$$

$$\sigma_{2,t}^2 = \overline{\sigma}_2^2(1 - \hat{\alpha} - \hat{\beta}) + \hat{\alpha}\varepsilon_{2,t-1}^2 + \hat{\beta}\sigma_{2,t-1}^2 \qquad (10.25)$$

$$\sigma_{12,t}^2 = \overline{\sigma}_{12}^2(1 - \hat{\alpha} - \hat{\beta}) + \hat{\alpha}\varepsilon_{1,t-1}\varepsilon_{2,t-1} + \hat{\beta}\sigma_{12,t-1}^2$$

The result is an optimisation procedure that runs on a single univariate GARCH(1,1) model. Asymmetric specifications can be used as well, as long as we can specify the long-term covariance terms like in the GJR model.

Now let us look at the set-up required to perform this new model in the spreadsheet example of Figure 10.15 ("Fast GARCH" in Bourgoin002.xls). The first task required is to

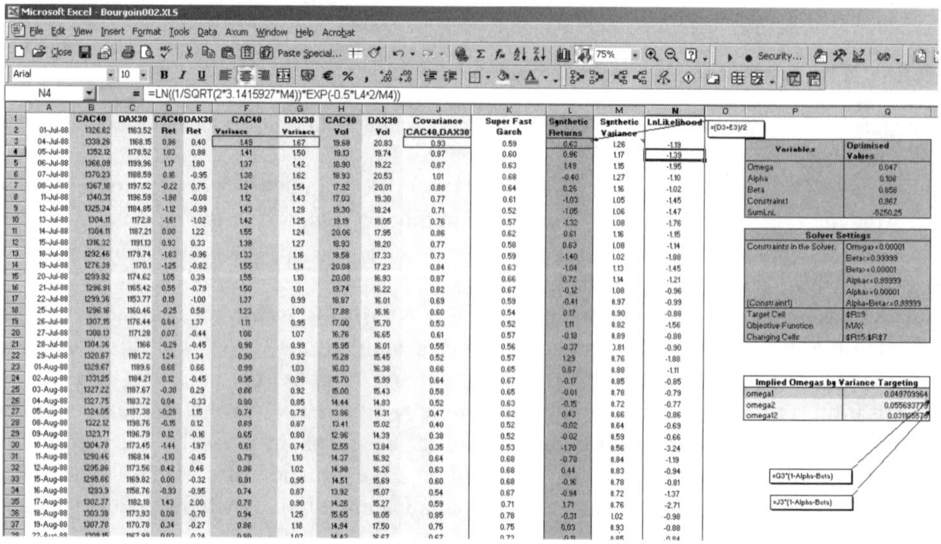

Figure 10.15 The fast GARCH model

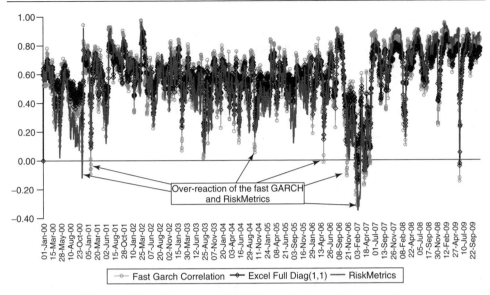

Figure 10.16 Multivariate GARCH correlation model comparison

calculate the returns on an equal-weighted portfolio (column L) and perform a univariate GARCH(1,1) on it (columns M and N for the variance and the log-likelihood function respectively); this is done in the grey cells. The cells Q25:Q27 contain the variance targeting omegas derived from the unconditional covariance matrix and the alpha and beta calculated for the univariate GARCH model. The rest follows through in the same way as the other spreadsheets.

10.4.7 Model comparison

We can plot the time-varying correlation resulting from the various models as in Figure 10.16 ("GraphicalResults" in Bourgoin002.xls). We can see that despite the added complexity and difference in the models, they provide the same patterns over time. We can notice that the fast GARCH and RiskMetrics tend to slightly overestimate and underestimate the correlation during stress times.

10.5 CONCLUSION

We've seen from this chapter that it is possible to calculate GARCH models in Excel, from the most simple one in a univariate setting (RiskMetrics) to a fairly complicated model in a multivariate framework (diagonal GARCH). We've shown that quite quickly when we increase the complexity of the model, the number of parameters and constraints increases dramatically, as well as the time required for the optimisation. In order to deal with the high dimensionality problem, we've shown a new technique called the fast GARCH that is easily implemented in Excel and can provide a solution when the number of assets under analysis becomes large. The spreadsheets show how to perform the statistical analysis, build the maximum likelihood function required for the Solver in order to obtain the parameters for each model and several comparison charts have also been produced. Although it is not recommended to use Excel as an advanced statistical package, the flexibility and insight gained by the spreadsheet-based approach should outweigh the drawbacks, at least in the beginning.

REFERENCES

Alexander, C. and A. M. Chibumba (1997), "Orthogonal GARCH: An Empirical Validation in Equities, Foreign Exchange and Interest Rates", School of Mathematical Sciences Discussion Paper, Sussex University.

Athayde, G. (2001), "Forecasting Relationship between Indexes of Different Countries: A New Approach to the Multivariate GARCH", Forecasting Financial Markets Conference, London, May 2001.

Black, F. (1976), "Studies of Stock Market Volatility Changes", *Proceedings of the American Statistical Association*, Business and Economic Statistics Edition, 177–181.

Bourgoin, F. (2000), "Large Scale Problem in Conditional Correlation Estimation", in *Advances in Quantitative Asset Management*, C. Dunis (ed.), Kluwer Academic, Dordrecht.

Bourgoin, F. (2002), "Fast Calculation of GARCH Correlation", Forecasting Financial Markets Conference, London, May 2001.

Diebold, F. X., A. Hickman, A. Inoue and T. Schuermann (1997), "Converting 1-Day Volatility to h-Day Volatility: Scaling by Sqrt(h) is Worse than You Think", Working Paper, Department of Economics, University of Pennsylvania.

Ding, X. and R. F. Engle (1994), "Large Scale Conditional Covariance Matrix: Modelling, Estimation and Testing", UCSD Discussion Paper.

Engle, R. F. and J. Mezrich (1995), "Grappling with GARCH", *Risk Magazine*, **8** (9), 112–117.

Engle, R. F. and J. Mezrich (1996), "GARCH for Groups", *Risk Magazine*, **9** (8), 36–40.

Gallant, A. R. (1997), *An Introduction to Econometric Theory*, Princeton University Press, Princeton, NJ.

Glosten, L. R., R. Jagannathan and D. Runkle (1993), "Relationship between the Expected Value and the Volatility of the Nominal Excess Returns on Stocks", *Journal of Finance*, **48** (5), 1779–1801.

J. P. Morgan (1995), RiskMetrics© Technical Document, Version 4.0.

J. P. Morgan (1997), RiskMetrics© Monitor Fourth Quarter, pp. 3–11.

Ledoit, O. (1999), "Improved Estimation of the Covariance Matrix of Stock Returns with an Application to Portfolio Selection", UCLA Working Paper.

Ledoit, O., P. Santa-Clara and M. Wolf (2001), "Flexible Multivariate GARCH Modeling with an Application to International Stock Markets", UCLA Working Paper.

Pourahmadi, M. (1999), "Joint Mean–Covariance Models with Applications to Longitudinal Data: Unconstrained Parametrization", *Biometrika*, **86**, 677–690.

Tsay, S. T. (2002), *Analysis of Financial Time Series*, Wiley InterScience, New York.

11

Optimal Allocation of Trend-Following Rules: An Application Case of Theoretical Results

PIERRE LEQUEUX

ABSTRACT

This chapter builds upon previously published results on the statistical properties of trading rules to propose an allocation model for trading rules based on simple moving averages. This model could easily be extended to cover a larger universe of linear trading rules and is presented here purely as a proof of concept. We use theoretical results on volatility, correlation, transactions costs and expected returns of moving averages trading rules within a mean–variance framework to determine what should be the optimal weighting of trading rules to maximise the information ratio, thereby presenting an unbiased methodology of selecting an ex-ante optimal basket of trading rules.

11.1 INTRODUCTION

Moving averages have now been used for many years by both academics and market participants. Whereas the former have usually been using moving averages trading rules as a means of testing for market efficiency (LeBaron, 1991, 1992; Levich and Thomas, 1993; Schulmeister, 1988; Taylor, 1980, 1986, 1990a,b, 1992, 1994), traders have had more profit-motivated goals in mind. It is therefore quite surprising that only a relatively small section of literature has been devoted to the statistical properties of trend-following trading rules. This is clearly one of the most important issues for a market practitioner. Statistical properties of trading rules may give clearer insights in regard of the level of transactions cost, diversification, risk and also return one might expect under various price trend model hypotheses. This chapter first presents some of the mainstream results that have been published by Acar and Lequeux (1995, 1996), Acar *et al.* (1994) and Acar (1994). In the latter part of this chapter we demonstrate how these theoretical results could be used within a mean–variance trading rule allocation model.

11.2 DATA

To illustrate the main findings on the statistical properties of moving averages and also our mean–variance trading rules allocation model we use a sample of five currency pairs USD–JPY, EUR–USD, GBP–USD, USD–CAD and AUD–USD. The data

Applied Quantitative Methods for Trading and Investment.   Edited by C.L. Dunis, J. Laws and P. Naïm
© 2003 John Wiley & Sons, Ltd   ISBN: 0-470-84885-5

Table 11.1   Summary statistics of daily logarithmic returns of exchange rates

	USD–JPY	EUR–USD	GBP–USD	USD–CAD	AUD–USD
Mean	0.03%	−0.03%	0.00%	0.01%	−0.02%
Stdev	0.75%	0.59%	0.46%	0.32%	0.65%
Min	−5.65%	−2.28%	−2.15%	−1.54%	−2.65%
Max	3.22%	2.64%	2.04%	1.61%	4.69%
Skew	−0.84	0.27	0.08	−0.25	0.24
Kurtosis	5.08	1.21	1.17	2.41	2.95
$a(1)$[a]	0.0459	0.0249	0.0526	0.0218	0.0210
$a(2)$	0.0187	−0.0120	−0.0316	−0.0254	−0.0282
$a(3)$	−0.0402	−0.0098	−0.0449	−0.0059	0.0277
$a(4)$	−0.0205	0.0009	0.0053	−0.0162	−0.0297
$a(5)$	0.0079	−0.0181	0.0397	−0.0684	−0.0122
$a(6)$	0.0013	0.0195	−0.0236	−0.0094	0.0148
$a(7)$	−0.0131	−0.0148	−0.0212	−0.0377	−0.0014
$a(8)$	0.0390	−0.0060	0.0208	−0.0355	−0.0248
$a(9)$	−0.0472	−0.0027	0.0021	0.0746	0.0097
$a(10)$	0.0746	0.0335	0.0013	0.0097	−0.0034

[a] $a(n)$ means the autocorrelation coefficient of order n.

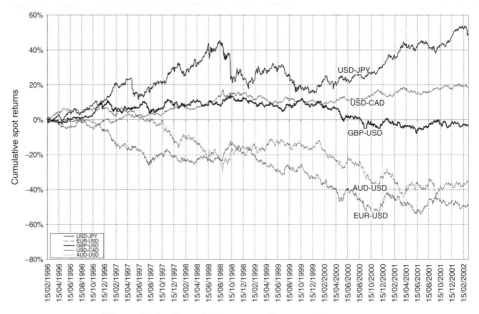

Figure 11.1   Cumulative return of spot exchange rates

covers the period 15/02/1996 to 12/03/2002, a total of 1582 daily observations. For each exchange rate we have the spot foreign exchange rate and the relevant 1-month interest rate series. As is usual in empirical financial research, we use daily spot returns, defined as $\ln(S_t/S_{t-1})$. Each of the exchange rates is sampled at 16:00 GMT. We use a hypothetical transaction cost of −0.03%, which generally represents the operating cost in the interbank market. Table 11.1, taken from cells O1:X17 of the worksheet "Data" of Lequeux001.xls, shows the summary statistics of the daily logarithmic returns for the five exchange rates sampled. As can be seen in Table 11.1, all the series under review are clearly non-normal. This is to be expected for most financial time series (Taylor, 1986).

It is also worth noting that the time series have had a significant mean over the period and that they all exhibit positive serial dependencies of first order. Overall the spot exchange rates studied here have exhibited a trend over the period 1996 to 2002. This is more particularly true for USD–JPY, EUR–USD and AUD–USD, as shown in the worksheet "Cumulative Spot Returns" and reproduced in Figure 11.1.

11.3   MOVING AVERAGES AND THEIR STATISTICAL PROPERTIES

Market efficiency depends upon rational, profit-motivated investors (Arnott and Pham, 1993). Serial dependencies or in more simple terms, trends, have been commonly observed in currency markets (Kritzman, 1989; Silber, 1994) and are linked to market participants' activity and their motivation. Central banks attempt to dampen the volatility of their currency because stability assists trade flows and facilitates the control of inflation level. A central bank might intervene directly in the currency market in times of high volatility, such as the ERM crisis in 1992, or act as a discreet price-smoothing agent by adjusting their domestic interest rate levels. Other participants in the foreign exchange markets, such as international corporations, try to hedge their currency risk and therefore have no direct profit motivation. Arguably they may have the same effect as a central bank on exchange rate levels. The success of momentum-based trading rules in foreign exchange markets is most certainly linked to the heterogeneity of market agents and their different rationales, which render the FX markets inefficient. Autoregressive models such as moving averages are indeed particularly well suited to trade foreign exchange markets, where it is estimated that around 70% of strategies are implemented on the back of some kind of momentum strategies (Billingsley and Chance, 1996). Lequeux and Acar (1998) have demonstrated the added value of using trend-following methods by proposing a transparent active currency benchmark that relies on simple moving averages to time the currency market. The AFX benchmark they proposed had a return over risk ratio exceeding 0.64[1] for the period January 1984 to November 2002, and this compares well to other traditional asset classes. Moving average trading rules are an attractive proposition as a decision rule for market participants because of their simplicity of use and implementation. The daily simple moving average trading rules work as follows: when the rate penetrates from below (*above*) a moving average of a given length m, a buy (*sell*) signal is generated. If the current price is above the m-moving average, then it is left long for the next 24 hours, otherwise it is held short. Figure 11.2 illustrates the working of such a trading rule.

The rate of return generated by a simple moving average of order m is simply calculated as: $R_t = B_{t-1} X_t$ where $X_t = \ln(P_t/P_{t-1})$ is the underlying logarithmic return, P_t the asset price at time t, and B_{t-1} the signal triggered by the trading rule at time $t-1$. B_{t-1} is

---

[1] See http://www.quant.cyberspot.co.uk/AFX.htm for more information on the AFX.

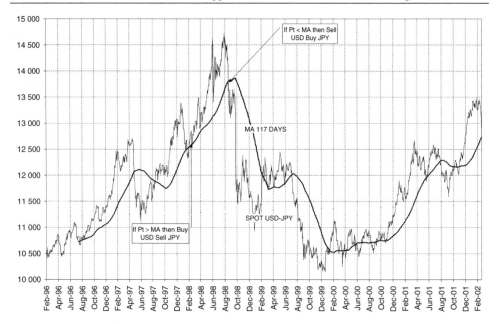

Figure 11.2   Spot USD–JPY and moving average trading rule of 117 days

defined as:

$$
\left\{
\begin{array}{ll}
B_{t-1} = 1 & \text{if } P_{t-1} > \dfrac{1}{m} \displaystyle\sum_{i=1}^{m} P_{t-i} \quad \text{(long position)} \\[3ex]
B_{t-1} = -1 & \text{if } P_{t-1} < \dfrac{1}{m} \displaystyle\sum_{i=1}^{m} P_{t-i} \quad \text{(short position)}
\end{array}
\right\}
$$

11.4   TRADING RULE EQUIVALENCE

In this chapter we consider a slightly modified version of moving averages. Instead of using spot prices the moving average signals generated are based on logarithmic prices. Simple moving averages by construction are autoregressive models with constrained parameters. Therefore the major difference between linear predictors such as simple and weighted moving averages and momentum trading rules resides in the weighting scheme used. Simple moving averages give decreasing weights to past underlying returns whereas momentum rules give an equal weight. Table 11.2 shows the equivalence for the simple moving average. Results for other linear predictors such as weighted, exponential or double moving averages crossover rules can be found in Acar and Lequeux (1998).

As an illustration Table 11.3 shows how trading signals would be generated for a simple moving average trading rule of order 10.

When not strictly identical (as in the case of the momentum method), signals generated by trading rules based on logarithmic prices are extremely similar to the ones generated by rules based on prices. Acar (1994) shows that using Monte Carlo simulations the signals are identical in at least 97% of the cases. Figure 11.3 clearly depicts this by showing the returns generated by simple moving averages trading rules of order 2 to 117

Table 11.2 Return/price signals equivalence

Rule	Parameter(s)	Price sell signals	Equivalent return sell signals
Linear rules		$\ln(C_t) < \displaystyle\sum_{j=0}^{m-1} a_j \ln(C_{t-j})$	$\displaystyle\sum_{j=0}^{m-2} d_j X_{t-j} < 0$
Simple MA	$m \geq 2$	$a_j = 1/m$	$d_j = (m-j-1)$

Table 11.3 Numerical example of signal generation when using prices or logarithmic price returns

Date	Spot price	$X_t =$ $\ln(P_t/P_{t-1})$	$d_j =$ $(m-j-1)$	$\displaystyle\sum_{j=0}^{m-2} d_j X_{t-j}$	$\displaystyle\frac{1}{m}\sum_{j=0}^{m-1} \ln(C_{t-j})$	$\displaystyle\sum_{j=0}^{m-2} d_j X_{t-j} < 0$	$\ln(C_t) < \displaystyle\sum_{j=0}^{m-1} a_j \ln(C_{t-j})$
30/01/2002	13 298						
31/01/2002	13 378	0.005998	1				
01/02/2002	13 387	0.000673	2				
04/02/2002	13 296	−0.00682	3				
05/02/2002	13 333	0.002777	4				
06/02/2002	13 357	0.0018	5				
07/02/2002	13 362	0.000374	6				
08/02/2002	13 481	0.008866	7				
11/02/2002	13 365	−0.00864	8				
12/02/2002	13 290	−0.00563	9	−0.0006	13 355	−1	−1
13/02/2002	13 309	0.001429		−0.00517	13 356	−1	−1
14/02/2002	13 231	−0.00588		−0.01172	13 341	−1	−1
15/02/2002	13 266	0.002642		−0.00226	13 329	−1	−1
18/02/2002	13 259	−0.00053		−0.00556	13 325	−1	−1
19/02/2002	13 361	0.007663		0.000299	13 328	1	1

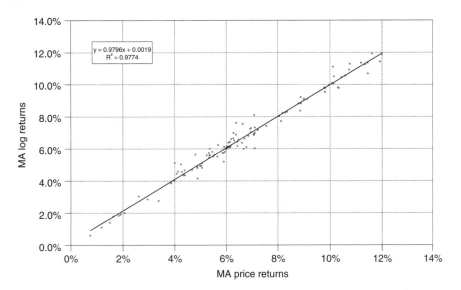

Figure 11.3 Comparison of returns generated by the moving averages using log returns or prices

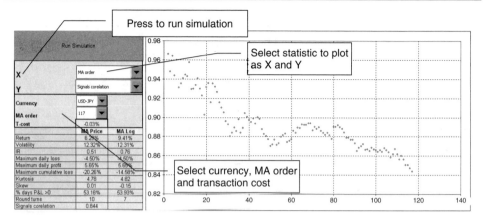

Figure 11.4   Correlation of signals as a function of the moving average order

based both on prices and logarithmic returns for USD–JPY over the period 26/07/1996 to 12/03/2002. The near equivalence is quite obvious. Note that the reader can recreate Figure 11.3 by drawing an XY plot of the data contained in (B3:B118, N3:N118) of the "Results" worksheet of the file "Lequeux001.xls".

Figure 11.4 further illustrates the relationship between logarithmic returns and price-based trading rule signals. The reader can furthermore investigate the various performance statistics of simple moving averages of order 2 to 117 by using the worksheet "MA" in Lequeux001.xls. The user should first select a currency pair and then press the simulation button. All statistics will then be calculated for a moving average of order 2 to 117. The results can then be visualised as an XY plot by selecting the data for X and Y as shown in Figure 11.4. Alternatively the user can select a currency pair and specify the moving average order to compare the differences between logarithmic and price based trading rules.

11.5   EXPECTED TRANSACTIONS COST UNDER ASSUMPTION OF RANDOM WALK

When evaluating the performance of a trading rule taking into account transaction costs is crucial. Whereas this can be done empirically, doing so implies making some assumptions in regard of the underlying dependencies. It may therefore induce a bias in the rule selection process. Acar and Lequeux (1995) demonstrated that over a period of T days, there are an expected number, N, of round turns[2] and therefore a total trading cost (TC), c, equal to cN. The number N of round turns is a stochastic variable, which depends mainly on the individual forecaster F_t rather than on the underlying process. Assuming that the underlying time series, X_t, follows a centred identically and independently distributed normal law, the expected number of round turns generated by a moving average of order m, supposing that a position is opened at the beginning of the period and that the last position is closed at the end day of the period, is given by:

$$E(N) = 1 + (T - 2)\left[\frac{1}{2} - \frac{1}{\pi}\text{arc } \sin(\rho_F)\right]$$

---

[2] A round turn is defined as reversing a position from one unit long to one unit short or vice versa.

where

$$\rho_F = \sum_{i=0}^{m-2} (m - i - 1)(m - i - 2) \Big/ \sum_{i=0}^{m-2} (m - i - 1)^2 \quad \text{if } m \geq 2$$

Subsequently, the expected transaction costs will be $E(\mathrm{TC}) = -cE(N)$, where c is the trading cost per round turn. Table 11.4 indicates the expected number of round turns out of a 250-day year under the random walk assumption. The last column shows the resulting yearly cost in percentage terms for a cost per transaction equal to $c = 0.03\%$.

To further illustrate the relationship between moving average order and number of round turns generated we used the spreadsheet Lequeux001.xls to calculate the number of round turns observed for each of our currency exchange rates and plotted this alongside the ex-ante expected theoretical number of round turns (Figure 11.5). The number of transactions

Table 11.4 Expected number of transactions and cost for simple MAs

Moving average	Expected number of round turns[a]	Expected yearly cost %, $c = 0.03\%$
$S(2)$	125.00	−3.75
$S(3)$	92.52	−2.77
$S(5)$	67.40	−2.02
$S(9)$	48.62	−1.46
$S(17)$	34.92	−1.05
$S(32)$	25.46	−0.76
$S(61)$	18.62	−0.56
$S(117)$	13.68	−0.41

[a] Number of round turns assuming a year of 250 trading days.

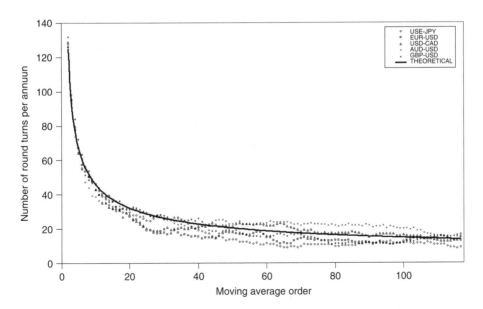

Figure 11.5 Observed and theoretical number of round turns as a function of the MA order

decreases as a function of the order of the moving average. The reader can reproduce this chart by running the simulation and selecting "MA order" for the X variable and "Round turns" for the Y variable in the worksheet "MA". This of course only plots the results for the selected currency pair. To produce the comparison chart the reader must obtain the data for each currency pair, which is stored in column AD, and generate the plot themselves.

The formula is exact for linear rules and just an approximation for non-linear predictors. The shorter-term moving averages generate the most trading signals. Therefore if one takes into account transaction costs it clearly appears that for equally expected gross returns, longer-term rules must be preferred. The number of round turns generated by a moving average trading rule is higher under the random walk assumption than when the underlying series exhibit positive autocorrelation and lower when exhibiting negative autocorrelation. Indeed, the more positive the autocorrelation, the more trends and the fewer transactions there are. However the number of transactions is higher when there are negative autocorrelations and therefore the expected return after transactions costs will be lower. One important implication is that negative autocorrelations will be more difficult to exploit than positive ones when transaction costs are taken into account. This may well explain why there are very few active currency managers relying on contrarian[3] strategies. The theoretical model can help managers who rely on linear predictors such as simple moving averages to factor in ex-ante the cost of implementing their strategy.

11.6 THEORETICAL CORRELATION OF LINEAR FORECASTERS

Another strong argument for using trading rules based on an autoregressive model over a fundamental process is that it is possible to calculate ex-ante the level of correlation between the signals generated by linear trading rules. It is therefore possible to estimate ex-ante what diversification can be provided by a set of linear trading rules. This is clearly not possible when it comes to an exogenous process. It would indeed be very difficult to determine the ex-ante correlation of the returns generated by a trading strategy based for example on interest rate movements or current account announcements. Acar and Lequeux (1996) have shown that under the assumption of a random walk without drift it is possible to derive the correlation of linear trading rule returns. Assuming that the underlying time series, X_t, follows a centred identically and independently distributed normal law, the returns $R_{1,t}$ and $R_{2,t}$ generated by simple moving averages of order m_1 and m_2 exhibit linear correlation, ρ_R, given by:

$$\rho_R(m_1, m_2) = \frac{2}{\pi} \text{arc} \sin \left[\frac{\displaystyle\sum_{i=0}^{\min(m_1,m_2)-2} (m_1 - i - 1)(m_2 - i - 1)}{\sqrt{\displaystyle\sum_{i=0}^{m_1-2} (m_1 - i - 1)^2} \sqrt{\displaystyle\sum_{i=0}^{m_2-2} (m_2 - i - 1)^2}} \right]$$

---

[3] Contrarian strategies are mean-reverting strategies. Therefore these strategies will be at their best when the underlying series exhibit a high level of negative autocorrelation in their returns.

Table 11.5 Simple moving average returns expected correlation[4]

ρ	MA-2	MA-3	MA-5	MA-9	MA-17	MA-32	MA-61	MA-117
MA-2	1	0.705	0.521	0.378	0.272	0.196	0.142	0.102
MA-3		1	0.71	0.512	0.366	0.264	0.19	0.137
MA-5			1	0.705	0.501	0.361	0.26	0.187
MA-9				1	0.699	0.501	0.359	0.258
MA-17					1	0.707	0.504	0.361
MA-32						1	0.705	0.502
MA-61							1	0.704
MA-117								1

Table 11.5 utilises this equation and shows the coefficient correlation between the returns generated by different moving averages when applied to the same underlying market.

Trend-following systems are positively correlated. Zero or negative correlation obviously would require the combination of trading rules of different nature such as trend-following and contrarian strategies. Buy and sell signals and therefore returns of trend-following trading rules are not independent over time under the random walk assumption. This will therefore put a floor on the maximum risk reduction that can be achieved by using them.

11.7 EXPECTED VOLATILITY OF MA

Volatility of returns is an important measure of underlying risk when comparing trading strategies. There are many fallacious statements and feelings regarding short-term versus long-term trading strategies. This usually derives from some sort of confusion between position-to-position and mark-to-market returns. Acar *et al.* (1994) have shown by using a bootstrap approach that the volatility of the returns generated by trading rules is approximately equal to the volatility of the underlying process applied to and is thus independent of the moving average order. To illustrate this relationship Figure 11.6 shows the volatility of the daily returns generated by moving averages of order 2 to 177 and the volatility of USD–JPY spot daily returns over the period 15/02/1996 to 12/03/2002. The reader can reproduce this chart by running the simulation and selecting "MA order" for the X variable and "Volatility" for the Y variable in the worksheet "MA".

As exhibited in Figure 11.6, though the variance of the trading rule returns differs depending on the moving average order, the overall level remains quite independent of the time horizon. The difference in terms of risk would be of no consequence to a market trader, the same level of riskiness as a buy and hold position in the underlying. On a mark-to-market basis active management does not add risk relative to a passive holding of the asset.

---

[4] For instance ρ(MA-2, MA-117) means the rule returns correlation between the simple moving average of order 2 and the moving average of order 117 is equal to 0.102

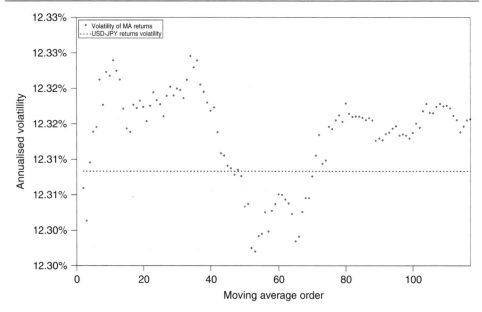

Figure 11.6   Volatility of spot USD–JPY and moving averages trading rule returns of order 2 to 117

11.8   EXPECTED RETURN OF LINEAR FORECASTERS

To depict the relationship between the returns generated by moving averages trading rules we conducted a Monte Carlo experiment. We generated 10 000 simulated series of 400 data points. The random variables were generated using a methodology developed by Zangari (1996)[5] where each random variable r^t results from the mixture of two independent normal distributions of mean zero: one with a probability of occurrence $p = 1$ and a standard deviation of 1 and the other with a probability of success of 0.1 and a standard deviation of 3.

$$r^t = \Phi(0,1) + \Phi(0,3)B(0.1)$$

For each of the series drawn we calculated the return that would have been generated for moving averages of order 2 to 117. We also noted the normalised drift $|\mu m|/\sigma m$ and the first three autocorrelation coefficients of the series drawn. We then regressed the normalised drift and the first three autocorrelation coefficients of the underlying time series against the computed moving average trading rule annualised returns. The results are shown in Figures 11.7 and 11.8.[6]

As illustrated in Figures 11.7 and 11.8, the expected return of moving averages is a function of both drift and price dependencies. Short-term moving average returns will be

---

[5] The simulation can be found in the spreadsheet Lequeux002.xls. Note however that with 10 000 iterations the simulation takes a long time to run. It is possible to change the number of iterations, to say 100, by selecting "Tools", "Macro", "Visual Basic Editor" and changing the line of code "For i = 1 To 10000" to "For i = 1 To 100".

[6] Figure 11.7 can be found in the "Sensitivity to Drift" workbook of Lequeux004.xls. Figure 11.8 can be found in the "Sensitivity of Dependencies" workbook of Lequeux004.xls.

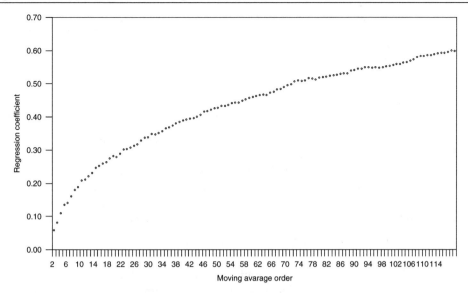

Figure 11.7   Normalised drift and moving average trading rule returns

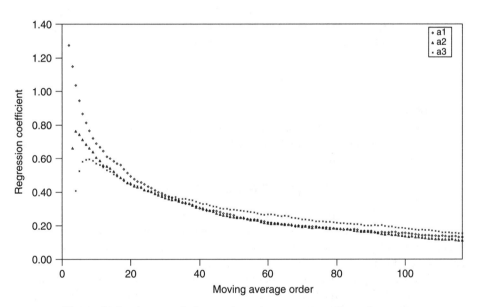

Figure 11.8   Autocorrelations and moving average trading rule returns

far more sensitive to price dependencies rather than drift, whereas the return of longer-term moving averages will be more sensitive to the exchange rate drift. This relationship is well highlighted by Figures 11.7 and 11.8. On the one hand we note that the regression coefficient between the drift of the underlying time series and the delivered return of the moving average trading rule increases with the length of the moving average. On the other hand the coefficients of regression between returns of the moving average trading rule and the first three autocorrelation coefficients of the underlying time series decrease

Table 11.6   Weighting of ρ as a function of the moving average order

Weightings	MA-2	MA-3	MA-5	MA-9	MA-17	MA-32	MA-61	MA-117
A(1)	1.000	0.634	0.426	0.370	0.367	0.339	0.311	0.329
A(2)	0.000	0.366	0.336	0.328	0.318	0.324	0.305	0.282
A(3)	0.000	0.000	0.238	0.302	0.316	0.337	0.384	0.390

with the length of the moving average. Research on the expected return of trend-following strategies has been published. Acar (1994) wrote a seminal paper that proposes a closed form solution to estimate ex-ante the return of a trend-following trading rule. The results are interesting because they provide an unbiased framework for a better understanding of what may drive the returns generated by linear trading rules. Assuming that the rate of return, x_t, follows a Gaussian process, Acar established the mean of the trading rule by:

$$E(r_{t+1}) = \sqrt{2/\pi}\,\sigma\rho e^{(-\mu_f^2/2\sigma_f^2)} + \mu(1 - 2\Phi[-\mu_f/\sigma_f])$$

where $\rho = \mathrm{Corr}(x_{t+1}, f_t)$, Φ is the cumulative function of $N(0,1)$, μ is the expected value and σ is the standard deviation of the underlying return x_t. The expected value and standard deviation of the forecaster f_t are given by μ_f and σ_f. In the case of a random walk with drift model the above formula will simplify as $E(r_{t+1}) = \mu(1 - 2\Phi[-\mu_f/\sigma_f])$. In this case the expected return is a negative function of the volatility. In the special case when there is no drift the expected profit is given by:

$$E(r_{t+1}) = \sqrt{\frac{2}{\pi}}\,\sigma\,\mathrm{Corr}(x_{t+1}, f_t)$$

In our applied example we use an adjusted form of this proposition where $\rho = \sum_{i=1}^{3} w_i \mathrm{Corr}(x_{t+1}, f_t)$, with w_i the weight attributed as a function to the sensitivity of the forecaster to autocorrelation coefficients. The weights were derived from our Zangari simulation and are shown in Table 11.6.[7]

11.9   AN APPLIED EXAMPLE

In the previous sections of this chapter we have highlighted that it is possible to determine ex-ante the transaction cost, the volatility, the estimated returns as well as the correlation between linear individual forecasters such as moving averages. This provides us with the necessary statistical tools to establish a framework for a mean–variance allocation model of trend-following rules. Though we could use a larger sample of linear trading rules such as simple, weighted, exponential moving averages and momentums, we choose to focus only on a subset of trading rules for the sake of computational simplicity. The reader could easily translate this framework to a wider universe of trading rules if required. In the following we try to determine ex-ante what would be the optimal weighting between moving averages of order 2, 3, 5, 9, 32, 61 and 117 to maximise the delivered information ratio. The model has been programmed into a spreadsheet[8] to give the reader the possibility

---

[7] The results may be found in the "Regressions Data" sheet of Lequeux004.xls, A59:I62.
[8] The model can be found in the "Simulation" sheet of the spreadsheet Lequeux005.xls. The results contained in Tables 11.7 and 11.8 may be found in the appropriate workbooks of Lequeux003.xls. The reader can see how they were arrived at by referring to the "Performance Basket" sheet of Lequeux005.xls.

to experiment and also investigate the effect of changing the sampling methodology to estimate the various parameters required to estimate ex-ante returns of our set of moving averages. Figure 11.9 details the workings of the spreadsheet.

Tables 11.7 and 11.8 show the results that were obtained when using this model and when allocating equally between the moving averages of order 2, 3, 5, 9, 32, 61 and 117.

The returns generated by the moving average trading rule allocation model have outperformed the equally weighted basket of moving averages in terms of return divided by risk (IR) for four currencies out of five. It also provides cash flow returns that are closer to normal as denoted by the lower kurtosis of the daily returns (Tables 11.7 and 11.8). Though these may not appear as outstanding results at first, one has to take into account the level of transaction cost incurred. Because of the daily rebalancing necessary the cost of implementation will be far greater for the allocation model than for the equally weighted approach. The fact that the model still manages to outperform the equally weighted basket demonstrates somehow the higher quality of the allocation model.

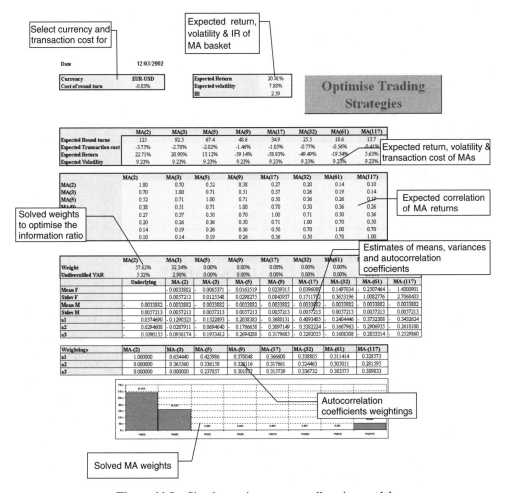

Figure 11.9 Simple moving averages allocation model

Table 11.7   Results for the equally weighted basket of moving averages

	EUR–USD	USD–JPY	GBP–USD	USD–CAD	AUD–USD
Return	1.56%	6.06%	−2.01%	−1.73%	3.77%
Volatility	6.77%	9.01%	5.24%	3.79%	7.64%
IR	0.23	0.67	−0.38	−0.46	0.49
Maximum cumulative drawdown	−11.27%	−11.13%	−13.35%	−16.85%	−10.64%
Normalised maximum cumulative drawdown	−1.66	−1.23	−2.55	−4.45	−1.39
Maximum daily loss	−2.11%	−3.16%	−1.36%	−1.54%	−3.53%
Maximum daily profit	1.96%	5.64%	1.48%	0.90%	2.65%
Skew	0.12	0.87	0.17	−0.78	−0.01
Kurtosis	3.36	12.56	3.26	5.52	5.39

Table 11.8   Results for the mean–variance allocation model

	EUR–USD	USD–JPY	GBP–USD	USD–CAD	AUD–USD
Return	−0.47%	10.29%	1.32%	−0.98%	10.73%
Volatility	9.97%	12.75%	7.58%	5.48%	11.05%
IR	−0.05	0.81	0.17	−0.18	0.97
Maximum cumulative drawdown	−16.52%	−13.54%	−16.17%	−15.34%	−18.68%
Normalised maximum cumulative drawdown	−1.66	−1.06	−2.13	−2.80	−1.69
Maximum daily loss	−2.67%	−3.22%	−1.49%	−1.61%	−4.72%
Maximum daily profit	2.58%	5.65%	2.15%	1.51%	2.65%
Skew	0.08	0.52	0.25	−0.19	−0.25
Kurtosis	0.92	4.36	0.90	1.76	2.65

11.10   FINAL REMARKS

In this chapter we first highlighted some of the statistical properties of trading rules and developed the reason for the interest in these for a market participant. In the latter part of the chapter we went on to provide the reader with an unbiased framework for trading rules allocation under constraint of cost and maximisation of information ratio. The results have shown that in four currency pairs out of five this would have provided better economic value than using an equally weighted basket of trading rules. These results are significant for active currency managers who seek to provide their investors with a balanced risk/return profile in the currency markets whilst using trend-following models. Though the results are encouraging, the challenge remains ahead. How to forecast the drift and serial dependencies remains the essence in any forecasting context and remains the key factor in bettering such a model. It may well be that the answer for forecasting those parameters lies more within a macro-fundamental approach rather than using uniquely the price as an information discounting process.

REFERENCES

Acar, E. (1994), "Expected Return of Technical Forecasters with an Application to Exchange Rates", Presentation at the International Conference on Forecasting Financial Markets: New Advances for Exchange Rates and Stock Prices, 2–4 February 1994, London. Published in *Advanced Trading Rules*, Acar & Satchell (eds), Butterworth-Heinemann, 1998.

Acar, E. and P. Lequeux (1995), "Trading Rules Profits and the Underlying Time Series Properties", Presentation at the First International Conference on High Frequency Data in Finance, Olsen and Associates, Zurich, Switzerland, 29–31 March 1995. Forthcoming in P. Lequeux (ed.), *Financial Markets Tick by Tick*, Wiley, London.

Acar, E. and P. Lequeux (1996), "Dynamic Strategies: A Correlation Study", in C. Dunis (ed.), *Forecasting Financial Markets*, Wiley, London, pp. 93–123.

Acar, E., P. Lequeux and C. Bertin (1994), "Tests de marche aléatoire basés sur la profitabilité des indicateurs techniques", *Analyse Financière*, **4** 82–86.

Arnott, R. D. and T. K. Pham (1993), "Tactical Currency Allocation", *Financial Analysts Journal*, **Sept**, 47–52.

Billingsley, R. and D. Chance (1996), "Benefits and Limitations of Diversification among Commodity Trading Advisors", *The Journal of Portfolio Management*, **Fall**, 65–80.

Kritzman, M. (1989), "Serial Dependence in Currency Returns: Investment Implications", *Journal of Portfolio Management*, **Fall**, 96–102.

LeBaron, B. (1991), "Technical Trading Rules and Regime Shifts in Foreign Exchange", University of Wisconsin, Social Science Research, Working Paper 9118.

LeBaron, B. (1992), "Do Moving Average Trading Rule Results Imply Nonlinearities in Foreign Exchange Markets", University of Wisconsin, Social Science Research, Working Paper 9222.

Lequeux, P. and E. Acar (1998), "A Dynamic Benchmark for Managed Currencies Funds", *European Journal of Finance*, **4**(4), 311–330.

Levich, R. M. and L. R. Thomas (1993), "The Significance of Technical Trading-Rule Profits in the Foreign Exchange Market: A Bootstrap Approach", *Journal of International Money and Finance*, **12**, 451–474.

Schulmeister, S. (1988), "Currency Speculations and Dollar Fluctuations", Banco Nationale del Lavaro, *Quarterly Review*, **167** (Dec), 343–366.

Silber, L. W. (1994), "Technical Trading: When it Works and When it Doesn't", *The Journal of Derivatives*, **Spring**, 39–44.

Taylor, S. J. (1980), "Conjectured Models for Trends in Financial Prices, Tests and Forecasts", *Journal of the Royal Statistical Society*, Series A, **143**, 338–362.

Taylor, S. J. (1986), *Modelling Financial Time Series*, Wiley, Chichester, UK.

Taylor, S. J. (1990a), "Reward Available to Currency Futures Speculators: Compensation for Risk or Evidence of Inefficient Pricing?", *Economic Record* (Suppl.), **68**, 105–116.

Taylor, S. J. (1990b), "Profitable Currency Futures Trading: A Comparison of Technical and Time-Series Trading Rules", in L. R. Thomas (ed), *The Currency Hedging Debate*, IFR Publishing, London, pp. 203–239.

Taylor, S. J. (1992), "Efficiency of the Yen Futures Market at the Chicago Mercantile Exchange", in B. A. Goss (ed.), *Rational Expectations and Efficient Future Markets*, Routledge, London, pp. 109–128.

Taylor, S. J. (1994), "Trading Futures Using the Channel Rule: A Study of the Predictive Power of Technical Analysis with Currency Examples", *Journal of Futures Markets*, **14**(2), 215–235.

Zangari, P. (1996), "An Improved Methodology for Measuring VAR", RiskMetrics Monitor, Reuters/J.P. Morgan.

12

Portfolio Management and Information from Over-the-Counter Currency Options*

JORGE BARROS LUÍS

ABSTRACT

This chapter looks at the informational content of prices in the currency option market. Risk reversals, strangles and at-the-money forward volatilities derived from OTC are used, along with data regarding exchange traded options. Three empirical applications of the literature are presented. The first one is on the EUR/USD, where option prices for several strikes are obtained from currency option spread prices and risk-neutral density functions are estimated using different methods. This application is followed by the analysis of implied correlations and the credibility of the Portuguese exchange rate policy, during the transition to the EMU, and of the Danish exchange rate policy around the Euro referendum in September 2000. This chapter is supported by the necessary application files, produced in Excel, to allow the reader to validate the author results and/or apply the analysis to a different dataset.

12.1 INTRODUCTION

Portfolio and risk management are based on models using estimates for future returns, volatilities and correlations between financial assets. Considering the forward looking features of derivative contracts, option prices have been used intensively in order to extract information on expectations about the underlying asset prices.

Compared to forward and futures contracts, option prices provide an estimate not only for the expected value of the underlying asset price at the maturity date of the contract, but also for the whole density function under the assumption of risk neutrality (the risk-neutral density or RND), based on the theoretical relationship developed in Breeden and Litzenberger (1978). This information is relevant for Value-at-Risk (VaR) exercises, as well as stress tests. However, the completion of these exercises also demands correlation estimates, which can be obtained from option prices only in the case of currency options.

Contrary to interest rates and stock price indexes, currency options are more heavily traded in over-the-counter (OTC) markets.[1] The information from OTC markets usually

---

* This chapter contains material included in the PhD thesis of the author (Luís, 2001).
[1] According to BIS (2001), at the end of June 2001, the OTC market was responsible for 99.5% of the aggregate value of open positions in currency options.

Applied Quantitative Methods for Trading and Investment. Edited by C.L. Dunis, J. Laws and P. Naïm
© 2003 John Wiley & Sons, Ltd ISBN: 0-470-84885-5

comprises Black–Scholes implied volatilities for at-the-money forward options, as well as prices for some option spreads, such as risk-reversals and straddles.

This data provides useful information about the uncertainty, the skewness and the kurtosis of the exchange rate distribution.[2] Furthermore, it allows the estimation of the RND function without knowing option prices for a wide range of strike prices (see, for example, Malz (1997) and McCauley and Melick (1996)). Another advantage of OTC options is that, as they have fixed terms to maturity, instead of fixed maturity dates,[3] the RND functions don't have to be corrected by the effect of time on the distribution parameters.[4]

Concerning correlations between exchange rates, Campa *et al.* (1997) show that in forecasting correlations between the US dollar–German Mark and the US dollar–Japanese yen exchange rates, in a period from January 1989 to May 1995, correlations implied by option prices outperform historically based measures, namely conditional correlations, J.P. Morgan RiskMetrics™ correlations and a GARCH (1,1)-based correlation.

As implied correlations shall be the best estimate for the future correlation between two exchange rates, it must result from using the available information in the most efficient way. Consequently, implied correlations must not be affected by the behaviour of the variance of the exchange rates.[5] OTC currency option market data also allows us to assess the credibility of target zones, by no-arbitrage tests built upon prices of options for any known strikes as in Campa and Chang (1996), and by monitoring implied correlations.

This chapter contains six additional sections. In the next section, the basic issues of currency option spreads valuation are introduced. The estimation of RND functions from option spreads is assessed in the third section. Two other informational contents of currency options are exploited in the fourth and fifth sections, respectively measures of correlation and arbitrage-based credibility tests.

The sixth section contains the empirical applications: the first subsection concerns the estimation of RND functions from currency option spreads, focusing on the EUR/USD expectations between January 1999 and October 2000. As the euro is a recent currency, the limited track record regarding its path and the behaviour of the European Central Bank (ECB) reinforces the importance of analysing the market expectations on the future evolution of its exchange rate vis-à-vis the US dollar. The analysis of the expectations on the US dollar/euro exchange rate is also relevant given that, though the exchange rate is not an intermediate target of the monetary policy followed by the ECB, most international commodities are denominated in that currency.

In the first 22 months of its life, the euro depreciated nearly 30% vis-à-vis the US dollar. This movement was also characterised by significant increases of the historical and implied volatilities of the EUR/USD exchange rate, though with much higher variability in the former case (Figure 12.1, which may be found in the file "chart1.xls"). Two Excel files are provided to illustrate this application, both using 1-month options, one concerning

---

[2] Though one may question the leading indicator properties of the risk-reversals, as their quotes exhibit a high correlation with the spot rate. Using data between January 1999 and October 2000, the contemporaneous correlation with the EUR/USD spot rate is 0.53 and decreases when lags are considered. Dunis and Lequeux (2001) show that the risk-reversals for several currencies do not anticipate spot market movements.

[3] These options are usually traded for maturities of 1, 3, 6 and 12 months.

[4] Some papers have tried to correct this maturity dependence using prices of exchange traded options, namely Butler and Davies (1998), Melick and Thomas (1998) and Clews *et al.* (2000).

[5] Loretan and English (2000) analyse this link between correlation and variances for the case of two stock indexes.

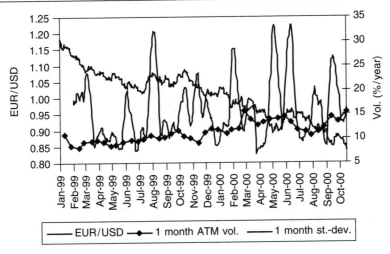

Figure 12.1   EUR/USD: volatility and spot rate

the RND functions estimated by a linear combination of two log-normal distributions ("OTC_EUR_USD") and another related to the RND functions estimated allowing one discrete jump to the underlying asset ("OTC_EUR_USD_jump").

The second subsection focuses on the behaviour of the Portuguese and Danish currencies respectively during the transition until 1998 towards the Economic and Monetary Union (EMU) and the euro referendum in September 2000. In this subsection, implied correlations are computed in the files "correlations_PTE_database" and "correlations_DKK_database", respectively for the Portuguese escudo and the Danish crown.

In order to have a deeper assessment of the prospects regarding the evolution of the two exchange rate policies, several credibility tests developed in Section 12.5 are also performed around the two above-mentioned episodes related to the EMU. Three Excel files are supplied for this application: "credibility_tests_DKK_1m" and "credibility_tests_DKK_1year" regarding the Danish crown and "credibility_tests_PTE_3m" concerning the Portuguese escudo. Finally, the seventh section concludes.

As illustrated in Figure 12.2 (which can be found in the file "credibility_tests_PTE_3m. xls"), the short-term interest rate convergence of the Portuguese escudo vis-à-vis the German Mark increased in mid-1997. Consequently the gap between the spot and the 3-month forward exchange rate started to be filled, while the exchange rate implied volatility diminished. This shift could have been taken by a portfolio or a market risk manager as a signal of the Portuguese participation in the third phase of the EMU on 1 January 1999.

Concerning the Danish crown episode, Figure 12.3 (which can be found in the file "credibility_tests_DKK_1 year.xls") shows that during the months before the Danish referendum (Thursday 28 September 2000) the interest rate spread against the European currency increased, along with the exchange rate volatility. This move could have been interpreted as reflecting an increasing probability attached to the detachment of the Danish currency from the euro, within the Exchange Rate Mechanism of the European Monetary System (ERM-EMS II).

The data used in the EUR/USD application consists of a database comprising bi-monthly quotations of the British Bankers Association (BBA), published by Reuters, between 13

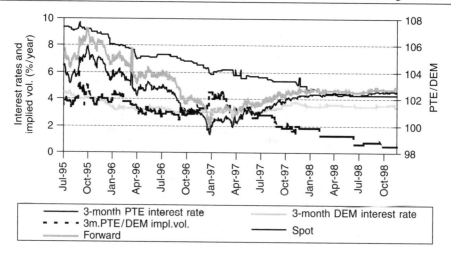

Figure 12.2   DEM/PTE: interest rates and implied volatility

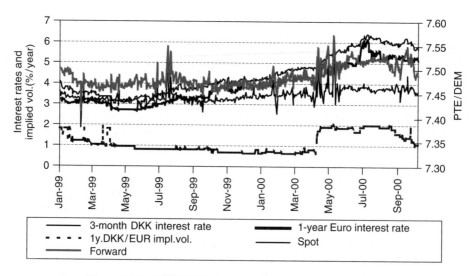

Figure 12.3   EUR/DKK: interest rates and implied volatility

January 1999 and 18 October 2000, for at-the-money forward volatilities and risk-reversal and strangle prices with $\delta = 0.25$ also quoted in volatilities of the USD/euro exchange rate.[6]

Regarding the options on the PTE exchange rates, the data used comprises volatilities (ask quotes) of OTC at-the-money forward options, disclosed by Banco Português do Atlântico,[7] for the exchange rate of German Mark/escudo (DEM/PTE), German Mark/US

---

[6] These quotations are published on the Reuters page BBAVOLFIX1 ("BBA Currency Option Volatility Fixings"). Forward rates were computed based on the covered interest rate parity.

[7] Through the BPAI page of Reuters.

dollar (DEM/USD) and US dollar/escudo (USD/PTE), between 26 July 1996 and 30 April 1998. Maturities of 1, 2, 3, 6 and 12 months were considered. Call-option prices from the Chicago Mercantile Exchange (CME) for the DEM/USD exchange rate were also used, with quarterly maturities between September 1996 and June 1998, from 27 July 1995 to 19 September 1997.

The currency option data for the Danish crown was obtained from Reuters, consisting of implied volatilities used in the pricing of EUR/DKK, USD/DKK and USD/EUR options (ask quotes) and spot exchange and interest rates for the EUR and the DKK, from 4 January 1999 to 10 October 2000.

12.2   THE VALUATION OF CURRENCY OPTIONS SPREADS

According to market conventions, financial institutions quote OTC options in implied volatilities (*vols*), as annual percentages, which are translated to monetary values using the Garman–Kohlhagen (1983) valuation formula. When the strike price corresponds to the forward rate (at-the-money forward options), the formula respectively for call and put-option prices is:[8]

$$C = \exp{(-i_\tau^f \tau)}[FN(d_1) - XN(d_2)] \tag{12.1}$$

$$P = \exp{(-i_\tau^f \tau)}[XN(-d_2) - FN(-d_1)] \tag{12.2}$$

where $d_1 = [\ln(F/X) + (\sigma^2/2)\tau]/\sigma\sqrt{\tau}, d_2 = d_1 - \sigma\sqrt{\tau}, F$ is the forward exchange rate,[9] X is the strike price, $N(d_i)$ $(i = 1, 2)$ represents the value of the cumulative probability function of the standardised normal distribution for d_i, S is the spot exchange rate,[10] i_τ^f is the τ-maturity domestic risk-free interest rate, i_τ^{f*} is the τ-maturity foreign risk-free interest rate and σ^2 is the instantaneous variance of the exchange rate.

Strike prices are usually denominated in the moneyness degree of the option, instead of monetary values. Moneyness is usually measured by the option delta (δ), which is the first derivative of the option price in order to the underlying asset price.[11] Following equations (12.1) and (12.2), the delta values are:

$$\delta_C = \frac{\partial C(X)}{\partial S} = \exp{(-i_\tau^{f*}\tau)}N(d_1) \tag{12.3}$$

$$\delta_P = \frac{\partial P(X)}{\partial S} = -\exp{(-i_\tau^{f*}\tau)}N(-d_1) \tag{12.4}$$

In the OTC currency option market, option spreads are traded along with option contracts. Among these spreads, risk-reversals and strangles are the most commonly traded. Risk reversals are composed of buying a call-option (long call) and selling a put-option (short put), with each option being equally out-of-the-money, i.e., they have the same moneyness.

---

[8] This formula was originally presented in Garman and Kohlhagen (1983) and is based on the assumption of exchange rate log-normality. It is basically an adaptation of the Black–Scholes (1973) formulas, assuming that the exchange rate may be taken as an asset paying a continuous dividend yield equal to the foreign interest rate.

[9] According to the covered interest rate parity, F corresponds to $S \exp{[(i_\tau^f - i_\tau^{f*})\tau]}$.

[10] Quoted as the price of the foreign currency in domestic currency units.

[11] Given that the pay-off of a call-option increases when the underlying asset price increases and the opposite happens to put-options, the delta of a call-option (δ_C) is positive, while the delta of a put-option (δ_P) is negative.

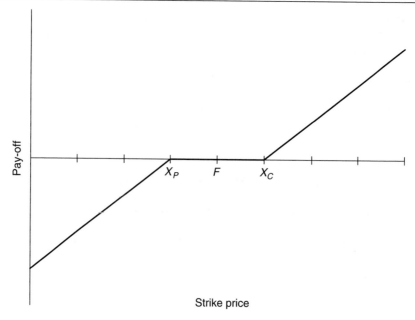

Figure 12.4 Risk-reversal pay-off

Therefore, the forward price will be lower than the strike price of the call-option (X_C) and higher than the strike price of the put-option, corresponding to X_P (see Figure 12.4). Risk-reversals are usually traded for $\delta = 0.25$. For simplification, the volatility of the call-option with $\delta = 0.75$ is regularly used as a proxy for the volatility of the put-option with $\delta = 0.25$.[12] Consequently, the price of a risk-reversal (in *vols*) is:

$$rr_t = \sigma_t^{0.25\delta} - \sigma_t^{0.75\delta} \tag{12.5}$$

with $\sigma^{0.25\delta}$ and $\sigma^{0.75\delta}$ representing the implied volatilities of the call-options with $\delta = 0.25$ and $\delta = 0.75$, respectively. The price of a risk-reversal may be taken as a skewness indicator, being positive when the probability attached to a given increase of the underlying asset price is higher than the probability of a similar decrease.

Strangles (usually also identified as a bottom vertical combination, due to the graphical representation of its pay-off) are option portfolios including the acquisition of a call-option and a put-option with different strike prices but with the same moneyness. Both options being out-of-the-money, the strike price of the call-option is higher than that of the put-option, as in the case of the risk-reversals (see Figure 12.5).[13]

These option spreads are also usually traded for options with $\delta = 0.25$ and their prices are defined as the difference (in *vols*) to a reference volatility, frequently the at-the-money

---

[12] In fact, according to equations (12.3) and (12.4), $\delta_P = \delta_C - \exp\left(-i_t^{f^*}\tau\right)$. With $\delta = 0.25$, $\delta_C = \exp\left(-i_t^{f^*}\tau\right) - 0.25$. For short-term options, the first component of the right-hand side of the previous expression is close to 1, unless the foreign interest rate is significantly high. Thus $\delta_C = 0.75$.

[13] The difference is that the put-option is bought in the strangle case, instead of being sold as happens with the risk-reversal.

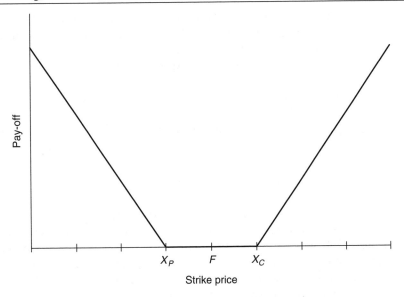

Figure 12.5 Strangle pay-off

forward, as follows:

$$str_t = 0.5(\sigma_t^{0.25\delta} + \sigma_t^{0.75\delta}) - atm_t \tag{12.6}$$

where atm_t is the implied volatility of the at-the-money forward option. The market participants consider $\delta = 0.5$ as a proxy for the delta of the at-the-money forward option.[14]

If the implied volatility is similar for the strike prices of the options included in the strangle, the average of those option volatilities must be close to the implied volatility of the at-the-money forward option and the strangle price will be around zero. Therefore, the strangle price may be considered as a kurtosis indicator, given that it provides information about the smile curvature.

12.3 RND ESTIMATION USING OPTION SPREADS

Using risk-reversal and strangle prices with $\delta = 0.25$ and the at-the-money forward volatility, the volatilities for 0.25 and 0.75 deltas may be computed following equations (12.5) and (12.6):[15]

$$\sigma_t^{0.25\delta} = atm_t + str_t + 0.5rr_t \tag{12.7}$$

$$\sigma_t^{0.75\delta} = atm_t + str_t - 0.5rr_t \tag{12.8}$$

---

[14] From equation (12.3), it is easy to conclude that the delta of an *at-the-money* option is $\delta_t^{0.5\delta} = \exp(-i_\tau^{f*})N [\sigma\sqrt{\tau}/2]$. For short-term options and for the usual volatility values (in the range 10–40% per year), $\delta_t^{0.5\delta} \cong 0.5$, given that the discount factor is close to one and the value at which the cumulative normal distribution function is computed is also close to zero. This implies that the normal distribution value will be around 0.5.

[15] See, e.g., Malz (1996, 1997) or McCauley and Melick (1996).

Given that only three values in the delta-volatility space are available, the RND estimation is not possible. Consequently, one needs to assume a functional specification as a proxy for the volatility curve. Malz (1997) uses the following quadratic polynomial function resulting from a second-order Taylor expansion for $\delta = 0.5$:

$$\sigma_t^\delta(\delta) = \beta_0 atm_t + \beta_1 rr_t(\delta - 0.5) + \beta_2 str_t(\delta - 0.5)^2 \qquad (12.9)$$

Restricting the curve to fit perfectly the three observed points in the delta-volatility space $(\sigma_t^{0.25\delta}, atm_t$ and $\sigma_t^{0.75\delta})$, we get:[16]

$$\sigma_t^\delta(\delta) = atm_t - 2rr_t(\delta - 0.5) + 16str_t(\delta - 0.5)^2 \qquad (12.10)$$

Thus, knowing only the at-the-money forward volatility and the risk-reversal and strangle prices, a curve in delta-volatility space is obtained. Substituting equation (12.3) and/or equation (12.4) in equation (12.10), the relationship between volatility and strike price (volatility smile) is obtained. Next, the option prices are computed from those volatilities, using equations (12.1) and/or (12.2), allowing the RND estimation.

The final step in the estimation procedure will be to extract the RND from the option prices. Different techniques for the estimation of the RND functions from European option prices are found in the relevant literature.[17] Among these, one of the most popular techniques has been the linear combination of two log-normal distributions.[18] It consists of solving the following optimisation problem:

$$\min_{\alpha_1,\alpha_2,\beta_1,\beta_2,\theta} \sum_{i=1}^{N}[\hat{C}(X_i, \tau) - C_i^0]^2 + \sum_{i=1}^{N}[\hat{P}(X_i, \tau) - P_i^0]^2 \qquad (12.11)$$

$$\text{s.t. } \beta_1, \beta_2 > 0 \text{ and } 0 \leq \theta \leq 1$$

which solves to provide solutions for C and P of:

$$\hat{C}(X_i, \tau) = \exp(-i_\tau^f \tau)\int_{X_i}^{\infty}[\theta L(\alpha_1, \beta_1; S_T) + (1-\theta)L(\alpha_2, \beta_2; S_T)](S_T - X_i)dS_T$$

$$= \exp(-i_\tau^f \tau)\theta\left[\exp\left(\alpha_1 + \frac{1}{2}\beta_1^2\right)N\left(\frac{-\ln(X_i) + (\alpha_1 + \beta_1^2)}{\beta_1}\right) - X_iN\left(\frac{-\ln(X_i) + \alpha_1}{\beta_1}\right)\right]$$

$$= \exp(-i_\tau^f \tau)(1-\theta)\left[\exp\left(\alpha_2 + \frac{1}{2}\beta_2^2\right)N\left(\frac{-\ln(X_i) + (\alpha_2 + \beta_2^2)}{\beta_2}\right)\right.$$

$$\left. - X_iN\left(\frac{-\ln(X_i) + \alpha_2}{\beta_2}\right)\right] \qquad (12.12)$$

---

[16] Replacing δ in (12.9) by 0.25, 0.5 and 0.75, respectively, and using simultaneously equations (12.5) and (12.6) (see Malz (1997)).

[17] See for instance Abken (1995), Bahra (1996), Deutsche Bundesbank (1995), Malz (1996) or Söderlind and Svensson (1997).

[18] This technique is due to Ritchey (1990) and Melick and Thomas (1997).

$$\hat{P}(X_i, \tau) = \exp(-i_\tau^f \tau) \int_{-\infty}^{X_i} [\theta L(\alpha_1, \beta_1; S_T) + (1 - \theta) L(\alpha_2, \beta_2; S_T)](X_i - S_T) dS_T$$

$$= \exp(-i_\tau^f \tau) \theta \left[-\exp\left(\alpha_1 + \frac{1}{2}\beta_1^2\right) N\left(\frac{\ln(X_i) - (\alpha_1 + \beta_1^2)}{\beta_1}\right) + X_i N\left(\frac{\ln(X_i) - \alpha_1}{\beta_1}\right) \right]$$

$$= \exp(-i_\tau^f \tau)(1 - \theta) \left[-\exp\left(\alpha_2 + \frac{1}{2}\beta_2^2\right) N\left(\frac{\ln(X_i) - (\alpha_2 + \beta_2^2)}{\beta_2}\right) + X_i N\left(\frac{\ln(X_i) - \alpha_2}{\beta_2}\right) \right]$$

$$(12.13)$$

and where $L(\alpha_i, \beta_i; S_T)$ is the log-normal density function i ($i = 1, 2$), the parameters α_1 and α_2 are the means of the respective normal distributions, β_1 and β_2 are the standard deviations of the latter and θ the weight attached to each distribution. The expressions for α_i and β_i are the following:

$$\alpha_i = \ln F_t + \left(\mu_i - \frac{\sigma_i^2}{2}\right) \tau \tag{12.14}$$

$$\beta_i = \sigma_i \sqrt{\tau} \tag{12.15}$$

where μ is the drift of the exchange rate return. Though this method imposes some structure on the density function and raises some empirical difficulties, it offers some advantages, as it is sufficiently flexible and fast. Therefore it will be used in the following sections.[19]

Alternatively, it will be considered that the exchange rate follows a stochastic process characterised by a mixture of a geometric Brownian motion and a jump process. Following Ball and Torous (1983, 1985) and Malz (1996, 1997), when no more than one jump is expected during the period under analysis, the Poisson jump model presented by Merton (1976) and Bates (1991) may be simplified into a Bernoulli model for the jump component.[20] Therefore, an option price with an underlying asset following such a process is a weighted average of the Black–Scholes (1973) formula given a jump and the Black–Scholes (1973) function value with no jump.

Option price equations considering a discrete jump correspond to:

$$\hat{C}(X_i, \tau) = \exp(-i_\tau^f \tau) \int_{X_i}^{\infty} (\lambda\tau L(\alpha_1^*, \beta_1^*; S_T) + (1 - \lambda\tau)L(\alpha_2^*, \beta_2^*; S_T))(S_T - X_i) dS_T$$

$$= \exp(-i_\tau^f \tau)\lambda\tau \left[\exp\left[\alpha_1^* + \frac{1}{2}\beta_1^{*2} - \ln(1 + k)\right](1 + k)N\left(\frac{-\ln(X_i) + (\alpha_1^* + \beta_1^{*2})}{\beta_1^*}\right) \right.$$

---

[19] For instance, Bliss and Panigirtzoglou (2000) conclude that a smile interpolation method dominates the log-normal mixture technique in what concerns the stability of the results vis-à-vis measurement errors in option prices.
[20] As the US dollar/euro exchange rate is under analysis, the assumption of existing no more than one jump during the lifetime of the option is reasonable.

$$-X_i N\left(\frac{-\ln(X_i)+\alpha_1^*}{\beta_1^*}\right)\Big] + \exp(-i_\tau^f \tau)(1-\lambda\tau)\Big[\exp\Big[\alpha_2^* + \frac{1}{2}\beta_2^{*2}\Big]$$

$$\times N\left(\frac{-\ln(X_i)+(\alpha_2^* + \beta_2^{*2})}{\beta_2^*}\right) - X_i N\left(\frac{-\ln(X_i)+\alpha_2^*}{\beta_2^*}\right)\Big] \tag{12.16}$$

$$\hat{P}(X_i,\tau) = \exp(-i_\tau^f \tau)\int_{-\infty}^{X_i}(\lambda\tau L(\alpha_1^*,\beta_1^*;S_T)+(1-\lambda\tau)L(\alpha_2^*,\beta_2^*;S_T))(X_i-S_T)dS_T$$

$$= \exp(-i_\tau^f \tau)\lambda\tau\Big[-\exp\Big[\alpha_1^* + \frac{1}{2}\beta_1^{*2} - \ln(1+k)\Big](1+k)N\left(\frac{\ln(X_i)-(\alpha_1^* + \beta_1^{*2})}{\beta_1^*}\right)$$

$$+X_i N\left(\frac{\ln(X_i)-\alpha_1^*}{\beta_1^*}\right)\Big] + \exp(-i_\tau^f \tau)(1-\lambda\tau)\Big[-\exp\Big[\alpha_2^* + \frac{1}{2}\beta_2^{*2}\Big]$$

$$\times N\left(\frac{\ln(X_i)-(\alpha_2^* + \beta_2^{*2})}{\beta_2^*}\right) + X_i N\left(\frac{\ln(X_i)-\alpha_2^*}{\beta_2^*}\right)\Big] \tag{12.17}$$

The parameters λ and k are respectively the probability and the magnitude of a jump. The parameters α_i^* and β_i^* correspond to:

$$\alpha_i^* = \ln F_t + \ln(1+k) - \left(\lambda k + \frac{\sigma^2}{2}\right)\tau \tag{12.18}$$

$$\beta_i^* = \sigma\sqrt{\tau} \tag{12.19}$$

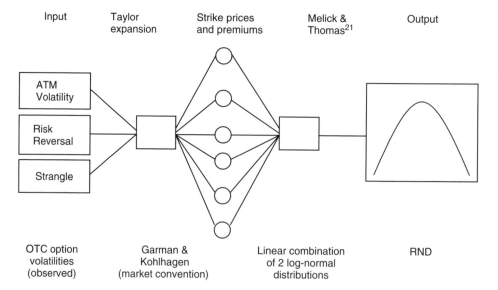

Figure 12.6 Estimation procedure of RND functions from option spreads

Source: Adapted from McCauley and Melick (1996).

---

[21] Using a mixture of two log-normal distributions with no jumps or with up to one jump, following Merton (1976), Bates (1991) or Malz (1996, 1997).

The whole estimation procedure, including both RND estimation techniques, can then be briefly presented using Figure 12.6, based on that presented in McCauley and Melick (1996).

12.4   MEASURES OF CORRELATION AND OPTION PRICES

The implied volatilities of options on cross exchange rates provide enough information to compute implied correlations between the exchange rates involved. Assuming no arbitrage opportunities, the exchange rate between currencies X and Y at time t, denoted by $S_{1,t}$, may be written as:

$$S_{1,t} = S_{2,t} S_{3,t} \tag{12.20}$$

where $S_{2,t}$ and $S_{3,t}$ are the exchange rates, respectively, between X and a third currency Z and between Z and Y.

Let $s_{i,t} = \ln(S_{i,t})$, with $i = 1, 2, 3$. Thus:

$$s_{1,t} = s_{2,t} + s_{3,t} \tag{12.21}$$

Denoting the daily exchange rate variation $s_{i,t} - s_{i,t-1}$ by $v_{i,t}$, we have:

$$v_{1,t} = v_{2,t} + v_{3,t} \tag{12.22}$$

Let $\sigma_{i,t,T}$ (with $i = 1, 2, 3$) be the standard deviation of daily returns over a period of time from t to $t + T$ and let $\text{Cov}(v_{2,t,T}, v_{3,t,T})$ be the covariance between $v_{2,t}$ and $v_{3,t}$ over the same period. The variance of $v_{1,t}$ from t to $t + T$ is given by:

$$\sigma_{1,t,T}^2 = \sigma_{2,t,T}^2 + \sigma_{3,t,T}^2 + 2 \ \text{Cov}(v_{2,t,T}, v_{3,t,T}) \tag{12.23}$$

As $\text{Cov}(v_{2,t,T}, v_{3,t,T}) = \rho_{t,T} \sigma_{2,t,T} \sigma_{3,t,T}$, where $\rho_{t,T}$ is the correlation coefficient between $v_{2,t}$ and $v_{3,t}$, solving equation (12.23) in order to $\rho_{t,T}$ we get:

$$\rho_{t,T} = \frac{\sigma_{1,t,T}^2 - \sigma_{2,t,T}^2 - \sigma_{3,t,T}^2}{2\sigma_{2,t,T}\sigma_{3,t,T}} \tag{12.24}$$

In equation (12.24), the correlation coefficient between the daily returns of the exchange rates of two currencies vis-à-vis a third currency may be obtained from the variance of the daily returns of the exchange rates between the three currencies.[22] Accordingly, when t is the current time, it is possible to estimate at t the correlation between future daily returns of two exchange rates, using forecasts of the variances of the daily returns of the exchange rates between the three currencies:[23]

$$\hat{\rho}_{t,T} = \frac{\hat{\sigma}_{1,t,T}^2 - \hat{\sigma}_{2,t,T}^2 - \hat{\sigma}_{3,t,T}^2}{2\hat{\sigma}_{2,t,T}\hat{\sigma}_{3,t,T}} \tag{12.25}$$

---

[22] Notice that it is irrelevant how exchange rates are expressed, since the variance of the growth rate of a variable is equal to the variance of the growth rate of its inverse.

[23] The variances used are $\sigma^2(T - t)$.

There are several ways to estimate the correlation coefficient in equation (12.25), from the information available at time t. The simplest way is to compute the historical correlation over a window of $t - T$ days:

$$\hat{\rho}_{t,T} = \frac{\sum_{j=0}^{T}[(v_{2,t-T+j} - \bar{v}_{2,t-T,T})(v_{3,t-T+j} - \bar{v}_{3,t-T,T})]}{\sqrt{\sum_{j=0}^{T}(v_{2,t-T+j} - \bar{v}_{2,t-T,T})^2 \sum_{j=0}^{T}(v_{3,t-T+j} - \bar{v}_{3,t-T,T})^2}} = \frac{\hat{Cov}(v_{2,t-T,T}, v_{3,t-T,T})}{\hat{\sigma}_{2,t-T,T}\hat{\sigma}_{3,t-T,T}}$$

(12.26)

where $\bar{v}_i$ corresponds to the average rates of return.

Instead of a single past correlation, a moving average of several past correlations can be used as a forecast of future correlation, attaching equal or different weights to each past correlation. Equally weighted moving averages have the disadvantage of taking longer to reveal the impact of a shock to the market and to dissipate that impact.

One of the most currently used weighting techniques is the exponentially weighted moving averages (EWMA), where higher weights are attached to most recent observations in the computation of the standard deviations and the covariance.[24] This methodology offers some advantages over the traditional equally weighted moving averages, namely because volatilities and correlations react promptly to shocks and have less memory, given the higher weight attached to recent data.

Using EWMA, the weighted returns ($\tilde{v}$) are obtained by pre-multiplying the matrix of returns (v) by a diagonal matrix of weights (λ), as follows:

$$\tilde{v} = \lambda v$$

(12.27)

with

$$\lambda = \begin{bmatrix} 1 & 0 & 0 & 0 & \cdots & 0 \\ & \sqrt{\lambda} & 0 & 0 & \cdots & 0 \\ & & \sqrt{\lambda^2} & 0 & \cdots & 0 \\ & & & \ddots & & 0 \\ & & & & \ddots & \vdots \\ & & & & & \sqrt{\lambda^{T-1}} \end{bmatrix} \quad \text{and} \quad v = \begin{bmatrix} v_{t,1} & v_{t,2} & v_{t,3} & \cdots & \cdots & v_{t,k} \\ v_{t-1,1} & v_{t-1,2} & v_{t-1,3} & \cdots & \cdots & v_{t-1,k} \\ v_{t-2,1} & v_{t-2,2} & v_{t-2,3} & \cdots & \cdots & v_{t-2,k} \\ \vdots & \vdots & \vdots & \vdots & \vdots & \vdots \\ \vdots & \vdots & \vdots & \vdots & \vdots & \vdots \\ v_{t-T,1} & v_{t-T,2} & v_{t-T,3} & \cdots & \cdots & v_{t-T,k} \end{bmatrix}$$

where $0 \leq \lambda \leq 1$.

Each column of v corresponds to the returns of each asset price included in the portfolio, while each row corresponds to the time at which the return occurred. Consequently, standard deviations are calculated as:[25]

$$\hat{\sigma}_{i,t,T} = \sqrt{(1-\lambda)\sum_{j=1}^{T}\lambda^{T-j}(v_{i,t-T+j} - \bar{v}_{i,t-T,T})^2}$$

(12.28)

with $i = 2, 3$.

[24] J.P. Morgan RiskMetrics™ methodology uses EWMA to calculate the variances and covariances of financial asset prices, in order to compute the VaR of a financial portfolio.
[25] The term $1/(1 - \lambda)$ corresponds to the asymptotic limit of the sum of the weights, i.e., the sum of the terms of a geometric progression with ratio equal to λ (being $\lambda < 1$).

Identically, the covariance corresponds to:

$$C\hat{o}v(v_{2,t,T}, v_{3,t,T}) = (1 - \lambda) \sum_{j=1}^{T} \lambda^{T-j} (v_{2,t-T+j} - \overline{v}_{2,t-T,T})(v_{3,t-T+j} - \overline{v}_{3,t-T,T})$$

(12.29)

Therefore, the correlation coefficient is:[26]

$$\hat{\rho}_{t,T} = \frac{\sum_{j=1}^{T} \lambda^{T-j} [(v_{2,t-T+j} - \overline{v}_{2,t-T,T})(v_{3,t-T+j} - \overline{v}_{3,t-T,T})]}{\sqrt{\sum_{j=1}^{T} \lambda^{T-j} (v_{2,t-T+j} - \overline{v}_{2,t-T,T})^2 \sum_{j=1}^{T} \lambda^{T-j} (v_{3,t-T+j} - \overline{v}_{3,t-T,T})^2}}$$

(12.30)

The formula in equation (12.30) can be represented in a recursive form. In fact, the standard deviations and the covariance can be computed recursively, in the following way:

$$\hat{\sigma}^2_{i,t,T} = (1 - \lambda)(v_{i,t} - \overline{v}_{i,t-T,T})^2 + \lambda \hat{\sigma}^2_{i,t-1,T}$$

(12.31)

$$C\hat{o}v(v_{2,t,T}, v_{3,t,T}) = (1 - \lambda)(v_{2,t} - \overline{v}_{2,t-T,T})(v_{3,t} - \overline{v}_{3,t-T,T}) + \lambda C\hat{o}v(v_{2,t-1,T}, \overline{v}_{3,t-1,T})$$

(12.32)

Nevertheless, EWMA measures are still past dependent. On the contrary, implied correlations computed from option prices are forward looking measures that should quickly reflect any perceived structural breaks in the data generating process. These correlations may be obtained directly from volatility quotes. Both techniques will be implemented in Section 12.6.

12.5 INDICATORS OF CREDIBILITY OF AN EXCHANGE RATE BAND

Another relevant exercise for portfolio management when financial assets are denominated in currencies managed within target zones is the assessment of the credibility of the exchange rate policy. Several indicators have been used in the past to perform these exercises, namely spot interest rate spreads and spot and forward exchange rates.[27] More recently, information from option prices started to be used for this purpose.

The simplest analysis using currency option prices is that consisting of deriving the RND function and quantifying the probability of reaching the band limits. When there is only information on at-the-money forward options, the RND may be approached using implied volatilities to calculate the standard deviation of the distribution,[28] assuming the log-normality of the exchange rate.

---

[26] In Campa and Chang (1996), the weights are directly attached to correlations in moving periods with a fixed length: $\hat{\rho}_{t,T} = (1 - \lambda) \sum_{j=1}^{n} \lambda^{j-1} \rho_{t-T-(j-1),T}$.

[27] See Svensson (1991).

[28] In the OTC market, the volatilities (in annual percentages) are quoted instead of the option prices.

The credibility of exchange rate bands can be analysed through a more rigorous method, building indicators based on the constraints on option prices implicit in the perfect credibility assumption (see Malz (1996), Campa and Chang (1996) and Campa et al. (1997)).

Consider a fluctuation band with upper and lower bounds denoted by $\overline{S}$ and $\underline{S}$, respectively. First, consider the extreme case of strike prices of a call-option at the upper bound of the band or above it ($X \geq \overline{S}$). Under perfect credibility the call-option is worthless, since it will never expire in-the-money. Conversely, if the strike price of a put-option is at the lower edge of the band or below it ($X \leq \underline{S}$), the put-option is also worthless, since the probability of expiring in-the-money is nil.

It can be shown that the intrinsic value of a call-option – the maximum between zero and the option price if immediately exercised – equals:[29]

$$C(X) = S \exp\left(-i_\tau^{f*}\tau\right) - X \exp\left(-i_\tau^{f}\tau\right) \tag{12.33}$$

For strike prices within the band, the maximum value of the call-option price is given by:

$$C(X \leq \overline{S}) = (\overline{S} - X) \exp\left(-i_\tau^{f}\tau\right) \tag{12.34}$$

This value is reached only when the exchange rate is expected to get to the band ceiling at the expiry date with certainty. This implies that the perfect credibility of the band is rejected whenever the current value of the call-option price, with strike price $X \leq S$, exceeds the maximum value that the option price may take according to equation (12.34), assuming that the future exchange rate is within the band:

$$C(X \leq \overline{S}) > (\overline{S} - X) \exp\left(-i_\tau^{f}\tau\right) \tag{12.35}$$

A tighter constraint on option prices in a fully credible exchange rate band can be defined from the convexity relationship between the option price and the strike price. The argument can be exposed in two steps. First, each unitary increase in the strike price yields a maximum reduction of the value of the call options expiring in-the-money that equals the current value of that unit (when the probability of expiring in-the-money is 1).[30] Second, the higher the strike price, the less probable it is that the call-option expires in-the-money, and hence the smaller the reduction in the call-option price for each unitary increase in the strike price.[31] Thus we have $- \exp\left(-i_\tau^{f}T\right) \leq \partial C(X)/\partial X \leq 0$ and $\partial^2 C(X)/\partial X^2 \geq 0$.

Figure 12.7 illustrates the constraints on the behaviour of options prices in a perfectly credible exchange rate band. Straight line (1) represents the line of maximum slope that passes through $C(\underline{S})$, when the unit rise in the strike price cuts the option price by the present value of that unit. This slope is the symmetric of the discount factor $- \exp\left(-i_\tau^{f}\tau\right)$.[32] Straight line (2) joins the prices of the options with strike prices $\underline{S}$ and $\overline{S}$, being $C(\underline{S})$ and $C(\overline{S})$ respectively equal to $S \exp\left(-i_\tau^{f*}\tau\right) - \underline{S}\exp\left(-i_t^{f}\tau\right)$ and zero.[33]

---

[29] Using compounded interest in continuous time. Campa and Chang (1996) consider discrete compounding.
[30] This happens when the absolute value of the slope of the call-option price function is one, i.e. the cumulative probability is zero.
[31] The minimum reduction is obtained when $C(X)$ is horizontal, i.e. when the slope of the curve is zero and the cumulative probability is one.
[32] The straight line crosses the point F, since its slope equals $-C(\underline{S})/x - \underline{S}$, with x denoting the horizontal intercept. Therefore, equalling that ratio to the value of the slope of line $- \exp\left(-i_t^{f}\tau\right)$ yields $x = F$.
[33] The value of $C(\underline{S})$ is found by substituting X by $\underline{S}$ in equation (12.33).

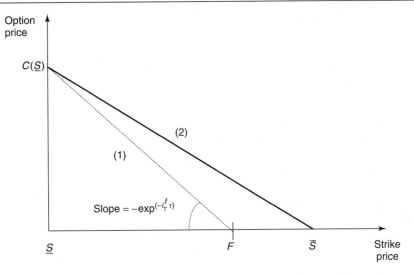

Figure 12.7 Option prices in a perfectly credible band (convexity test)

Since the relationship between the option price and the strike price is strictly convex, if the exchange rate band is fully credible, the call-option price should stand in a convex curve between (1) and (2), that contains points $(\underline{S}, C(\underline{S}))$ and $(\overline{S}, 0)$ for any strike price ranging between $\underline{S}$ and $\overline{S}$. Therefore, the perfect credibility of an exchange rate band can always be rejected provided that a given point in the call-option price function (for $\underline{S} \leq X \leq \overline{S}$) is higher than the corresponding point in line (2). This being the case, given that the call-option price function is strictly convex, the price of a call-option with strike price greater than $\overline{S}$ is positive, which means that the probability the exchange rate exceeds the band upper bound is not zero.

It can be shown that the assessment of the rejection of perfect credibility corresponds to checking whether the following convexity condition holds:[34]

$$C(X) > \frac{\overline{S} - X}{\overline{S} - \underline{S}}[S \exp(-i_\tau^{f^*}\tau) - \underline{S} \exp(-i_\tau^f \tau)] \tag{12.36}$$

As mentioned in Campa and Chang (1996), condition (12.36) is more restrictive than condition (12.35) whenever the forward rate is within the band.[35] In the case of wide

---

[34] See Campa and Chang (1996).
[35] Multiplying and dividing the right-hand term of equation (12.36) by $\exp(i_\tau^f \tau)$ yields:

$$C(X) \geq \frac{\overline{S} - X}{\overline{S} - \underline{S}} \exp(i_\tau^f \tau) \exp(-i_\tau^f \tau)[S \exp(-i_\tau^{f^*}\tau) - \underline{S} \exp(-i_\tau^f \tau)] \Leftrightarrow C(X) \geq \frac{\overline{S} - X}{\overline{S} - \underline{S}} \exp(-i_\tau^f \tau)(F - \underline{S})$$

$$\Leftrightarrow C(X) \geq [(\overline{S} - X) \exp(-i_\tau^f \tau)] \left(\frac{F - \underline{S}}{\overline{S} - \underline{S}} \right)$$

The first factor of the right-hand term in this inequality is the right-hand term of inequality (12.35), so (12.36) is a more restrictive condition when the second factor is smaller than 1 (i.e., when $\underline{S} \leq F \leq \overline{S}$), as in this case the full credibility will be rejected from a lower value.

exchange rate bands – as happened with the ERM of the EMS before the launch of the euro – the results should be expected to point in general to the non-rejection of perfect credibility, so the exercise provides no additional relevant information. However, more interesting exercises can be attempted in these cases – e.g. using equation (12.36) to calculate the smaller possible bandwidth that would have permitted the non-rejection of its perfect credibility – i.e., the minimum size of a perfectly credible band.

Bearing in mind the process of monetary integration in the EU, this exercise allows us to use option prices to identify the band in which a currency could have floated without imposing a realignment within the term to maturity of the option. With the beginning of the EMU becoming closer, the currency would then be expected to float in a progressively narrower interval.

Transforming (12.36) into an identity and using the principle of a band's symmetry around the central parity yields $\underline{S} = S_c/(1 + \alpha)$ and $\overline{S} = (1 + \alpha)S_c$ (where S_c is the central parity). Substituting $\underline{S}$ and $\overline{S}$ for these expressions, the equation resulting from (12.36) can be solved in order to α, given S_c:[36]

$$
\begin{aligned}
\alpha = \{[&-SX \exp(-i_\tau^{f^*}\tau) - S_c^2 \exp(-i_\tau^f \tau) - \sqrt{\{[SX \exp(-i_\tau^{f^*}\tau) + S_c^2 \exp(-i_\tau^f \tau)]^2}} \\
&- 4S_c^2[C(X) - S \exp(-i_\tau^{f^*}\tau)][-C(X) - X \exp(-i_\tau^f \tau)]\}]/2S_c[C(X) \\
&- S \exp(-i_\tau^{f^*}\tau)]\} - 1
\end{aligned}
$$
(12.37)

One can also build a measure of realignment intensity $(G(T))$ between t and T. Intuitively, this measure corresponds to the weighted average of the size of the possible realignments when the exchange rate overcomes the band ceiling:[37]

$$
G(T) = \int_{\overline{S}}^{\infty} (S_T - \overline{S})q(S_T)dS_T
$$
(12.38)

Given that the upper ceiling of the band after a realignment may be higher than the spot rate, this must be considered as a measure of the minimum intensity of realignment. Comparing (12.38) to the call-option definition in (12.1) and making $X = \overline{S}$, the intensity of realignment is equivalent to $\exp(i_\tau^f \tau)C(\overline{S})$, i.e., the capitalised value at the maturity date of the call-option with strike corresponding to the upper bound of the exchange rate band.[38]

Even when there are no options for the strike price $\overline{S}$, it is possible to compute the minimum value of a theoretical option for that strike price, based on the convexity relationship between option prices and strike prices. A lower bound for the intensity of realignment will then be computed according to:[39]

$$
C(\overline{S}) \geq C(X) - \frac{\overline{S} - X}{X - \underline{S}}[S \exp(-i_\tau^{f^*}\tau) - \underline{S} \exp(-i_\tau^f \tau) - C(X)]
$$
(12.39)

---

[36] This corresponds to the lowest value of the solutions to the equation resulting from (12.36).

[37] Therefore, this measure does not consider all possible realignments, as these may occur even when the spot rate is inside the band.

[38] Notice that, in the interval $[\overline{S}, +\infty]$, the maximum of the function is $S_T - X$.

[39] See Campa and Chang (1996).

For at-the-money forward options (when $X = S \exp[(i_\tau^f - i_\tau^{f^*})\tau] = F$), it can be shown that the intensity of realignment will be given as:[40]

$$G(T) \geq C(X) \exp(i_\tau^f \tau) \cdot \frac{\overline{S} - S}{F - \underline{S}} + F - \overline{S} \qquad (12.40)$$

12.6 EMPIRICAL APPLICATIONS

12.6.1 The estimation of RND functions using option spreads: an application to the US dollar/euro exchange rate

According to the evolution of the EUR/USD spot exchange rate and risk-reversals (Figure 12.8), five main periods may be identified. The first one is between the euro launch and mid-July 1999, during which the euro depreciated vis-à-vis the USD from around 1.17 to 1.02 and the risk-reversals got closer to zero. The second period, until mid-October, was marked by the euro appreciation, up to around 1.08, with the risk-reversals becoming positive, i.e. suggesting expectations of further appreciation of the euro vis-á-vis the USD. During the third period, the risk-reversals returned to negative values with the depreciation of the euro until mid-May 2000, achieving a level around 0.895. In the fourth period, the euro recovered to a level around 0.95 at the end of June 2000. Lastly, the European currency started a downward movement until mid-October, only interrupted after the joint exchange rate intervention on 22 September, held by the ECB, the Federal Reserve, the Bank of Japan and the Bank of England. This intervention moved the risk-reversals sharply upwards, again to positive values.

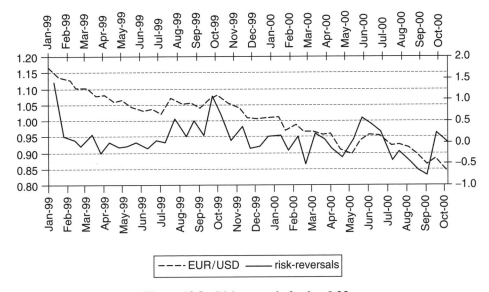

Figure 12.8   Risk-reversals for $\delta = 0.25$

---

[40] See also Campa and Chang (1996).

```
Sub Full_Estimation()
'
' Estimated_Vols Macro
' Macro recorded on 7-12-2002 by Jorge Barros Luís
'
Row = InputBox(Prompt:="First row for the estimation (e.g. 2)",_
Title:="1st Estimation Row")
Row2  = InputBox(Prompt:="Last row for the estimation (e.g. 3)",_
Title:="Last Estimation Row")
NoRows = Row2 - Row
Sheets("Strike_Call").Select
LastRow = Range("a1").End(xlToRight).Address
Range("a1", LastRow).Select
For m = 0 To NoRows
Sheets("Strike_Call").Select
Range("a1").Select
'Estimation of the strikes corresponding to the deltas
    For n = 1 To 19
    SolverReset
    SolverAdd CellRef:=Range(Cells(Row + m, 23 + n - 1), Cells(Row +_
    m, 23 + n - 1)), Relation:=1, FormulaText:=Range(Cells(Row + m, 23_
    + n - 2), Cells(Row + m, 23 + n - 2)) - 0.001
    SolverAdd CellRef:=Range(Cells(Row + m, 22 + n), Cells(Row + m, 22_
    + n)), Relation:=3, FormulaText:="0"
    Range(Cells(Row + m, 1 + n), Cells(Row + m, 1 + n)).Select
    SolverOk SetCell:=Range(Cells(Row + m, 1 + n), Cells(Row + m, 1 +_
    n)), MaxMinVal:=2, ByChange:=Range(Cells(Row + m, 22 + n),_
    Cells(Row + m, 22 + n))
    SolverSolve True
    Next n


    "For n =  21 To NoColumns = 1
    SolverReset
    SolverAdd CellRef:=Range(Cells(Row + m, 23 + n - 1), Cells(Row + m,_ 23
    + n - 1)),
    Relation:=1, FormulaText:=Range(Cells(Row + m,_ 23 + n - 2), Cells(Row +
    m, 23 + n - 2)) - 0.001
    SolverAdd CellRef:=Range(Cells(Row + m, 22 + n), Cells(Row + m, 22_ +
    n)),
    Relation:=3, FormulaText:="0"
    Range(Cells(Row + m, 1 + n), Cells(Row + m, 1 + n)).Select
    SolverOk SetCell:=Range(Cells(Row + m, 1 + n), Cells(Row + m, 1 +_ n)),
    MaxMinVal:=2, ByChange:=Range(Cells(Row + m, 22 + n),_
    Cells(Row + m, 22 + n))
    SolverSolve True
    Next n''
ActiveWindow.LargeScroll ToRight:=-2
'Copy strikes to new sheet
Range(Cells(Row + m, 23), Cells(Row + m, 41)).Select
Selection.Copy
```

Figure 12.9 Visual Basic macro: the estimation of strike prices

```
Sheets("Sheet3").Select
Range("A1").Select
Selection.PasteSpecial Paste:=xlAll, Operation:=xlNone,
SkipBlanks:=False, Transpose:=True
'Copy call option prices to new sheet
Sheets("Call").Select
ActiveWindow.LargeScroll ToRight:=-2
Range(Cells(Row + m, 2), Cells(Row + m, 20)).Select
Application.CutCopyMode = False
Selection.Copy
Sheets("Sheet3").Select
Range("B1").Select
Selection.PasteSpecial Paste:=xlValues, Operation:=xlNone, SkipBlanks:_
=False, Transpose:=True
'Ordering by strike
Columns("A:B").Select
Application.CutCopyMode = False
Selection.Sort Key1:=Range("A1"), Order1:=xlAscending, Header:=xlNo, _
OrderCustom:=1, MatchCase:=False, Orientation:=xlTopToBottom
'Copy of the ordered strikes
Range("A1:A19").Select
Selection.Copy
Sheets("Strikes").Select
Range(Cells(Row + m, 2), Cells(Row + m, 2)).Select
Selection.PasteSpecial Paste:=xlAll, Operation:=xlNone,_
SkipBlanks:=False, Transpose:=True
'Copy of the ordered call-option prices
Sheets("Sheet3").Select
Range("B1:B19").Select
Application.CutCopyMode = False
Selection.Copy
Sheets("Strikes").Select
Range(Cells(Row + m, 23), Cells(Row + m, 23)).Select
Selection.PasteSpecial Paste:=xlAll, Operation:=xlNone,_
SkipBlanks:=False, Transpose:=True
```

Figure 12.9 (*continued*)

The estimations of the RND functions assuming a linear combination of two log-normal distributions were performed in the files "OTC_EUR_USD.xls", using a Visual Basic macro ("Full_Estimation").[41] Figure 12.9 presents the block of the macro concerning the estimation of strike prices.

The macro starts by asking the user to insert the number of the first and last row to be estimated. After computing the number of rows and positioning in the first cell of the sheet "Strike_Call", the strike prices corresponding to the option deltas are estimated.

---

[41] This macro is run directly from the Excel menu and only demands the user to copy previously the first row in each sheet to the rows containing new data to be used for estimation.

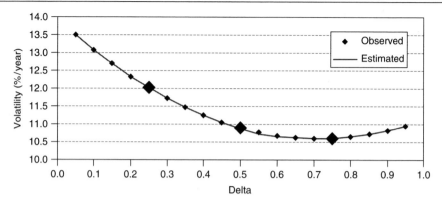

Figure 12.10 Observed and estimated 1-month volatilities at 13/01/99

This step follows equations (12.3) and (12.10) and is carried out for all the call-option deltas between 0.05 and 0.95, with an interval equal to 0.05.

Figure 12.10 illustrates the results obtained in this step for the first sample day, with the larger markers representing the three volatility–delta pairs computed from the risk-reversal, the strangle and the at-the-money volatility figures, with the remaining markers being those resulting from the curve in equation (12.10).[42] Afterwards, the volatility–delta function is transformed into a volatility–strike (smile) curve, by estimating the strikes that minimise the squared differences to the observed volatilities. With the volatility smile and using the pricing formula in (12.1), call-option prices are obtained.

The observed values in Figure 12.10 are computed in the "Delta_Vol" sheet, while the estimated values are obtained in the "Strike_Call" sheet. In this sheet, the first set of columns (up to column T) contains the squared difference between the observed volatility (in order to the delta) and the estimated volatility (in order to the strike price). The estimated strike prices are in the second set of columns of the same sheet (between columns V and AO). The third set of columns in the same sheet (between AQ and BJ) contains the estimated volatility, which results from equation (12.10), being the call-option delta obtained from inserting in equation (12.3) the estimated strike prices in the second set of columns in the sheet "Strike_Call". Lastly, the sum of the squared residuals is presented in column BL.

It can be seen in Figure 12.10 that the estimated volatilities are very close to the observed figures. This result is usually obtained only after some iterations and trials concerning the starting values, given the non-linear features of the target function. Thus, the choice of those starting values is crucial for the final result.

Afterwards, the RND is estimated, being the parameters of the distributions obtained in order to minimise the squared difference between the estimated and the observed call-option prices, as in equations (12.11) to (12.15).[43] Figure 12.11 shows the fitting obtained for the same first sample day concerning call-option prices.

---

[42] The exercise was performed only considering call-option prices, as all relevant formulas (namely (12.5) and (12.6)) were also derived for call options.

[43] The estimated RND parameters are presented in the file "Param.". Again, given the non-linear features of the target function in the optimisation problem, the choice of the starting figures is relevant. In the applications presented on the CD-Rom, the estimated values for the RND parameters at the previous date were used as starting values. In order to estimate only the RND parameters, an additional Visual Basic macro is provided ("RND_Estimation").

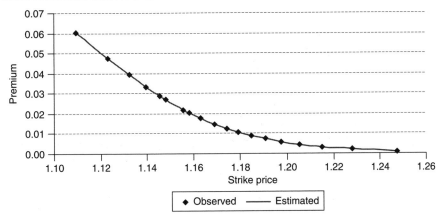

Figure 12.11 Observed and estimated 1-month call-option prices at 13/01/99

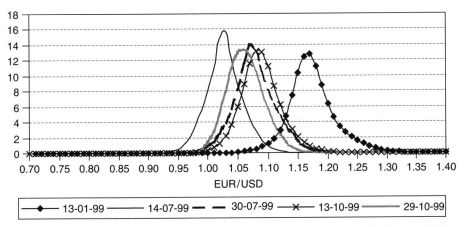

Figure 12.12 1-Month EUR/USD RND functions using two log-normal mixtures (1999)

These prices are subsequently used to estimate the RND functions as illustrated in Figures 12.12 and 12.13, employing the Solver add-in in the sheet "Param.", as shown in Figure 12.14. The usual constraints are imposed, i.e., the weight parameter θ has to be between zero and one, while the standard deviations of the normal distributions have to be positive.

The "PD" sheet contains the cumulative distribution functions, while the "RND" sheet contains the RND functions, computed simply as the arithmetic difference between consecutive values of the cumulative distribution function. The remaining sheets in the files are used to compute several statistics.[44] For the quartiles, sheets "Q25" and "Q75" are used to calculate the difference between the cumulative distribution function for each grid value and the respective percentile. Conversely, the files "q25_Min" and "q75_Min" are used to identify the grid values with those minimum differences.

---

[44] As Excel is being used, these computations are performed on a discrete basis. A thinner grid, in the "Grid" sheet, computed in the interval forward rate $+/-0.05$ is used to compute the mode and the median. The RND values for this thinner grid are computed in the "F_Grid" sheet.

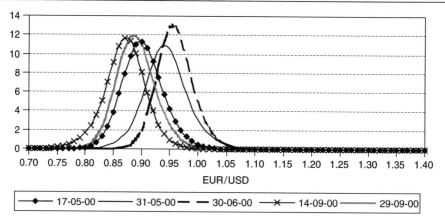

Figure 12.13 1-Month EUR/USD RND functions using two log-normal mixtures (2000)

```
'Estimation of RND parameters
Sheets("Param.").Select
Range("a1").Select
    SolverReset
    SolverAdd CellRef:=Range(Cells(Row + m, 2), Cells(Row + m, 2)),_
    Relation:=3, FormulaText:="0"
    SolverAdd CellRef:=Range(Cells(Row + m, 2), Cells(Row + m, 2)),_
    Relation:=1, FormulaText:="1"
    SolverAdd CellRef:=Range(Cells(Row + m, 4), Cells(Row + m, 4)),_
    Relation:=3, FormulaText:="1/1000"
    SolverAdd CellRef:=Range(Cells(Row + m, 6), Cells(Row + m, 6)),_
    Relation:=3, FormulaText:="1/1000"
    Range(Cells(Row + m, 53), Cells(Row + m, 53)).Select
    SolverOk SetCell:=Range(Cells(Row + m, 53), Cells(Row + m, 53)),_
    MaxMinVal:=2, ByChange:=Range(Cells(Row + m, 2), Cells(Row + m,_
    6))
    SolverSolve True
Sheets("Strikes").Select
Next m
End Sub
```

Figure 12.14 Visual Basic macro: the estimation of RND functions

In line with the spot exchange rate and the risk-reversal evolution, the RND function during the first half of 1999 moved leftwards and the left tail increased. After the recovery of the euro until mid-October 1999, the EUR/USD spot rate fell again and the risk-reversals decreased, though they kept positive most of the time until mid-May 2000. Consequently, the RND functions remained mostly upward biased or symmetrical.

Afterwards, the euro appreciation vis-à-vis the USD until the end of June 2000 brought a significant increase in right tail of the RND. This movement was inverted with the euro depreciation that occurred until mid-September. Following the joint central banks' intervention on 22 September, the RND skewness shifted again to positive values.

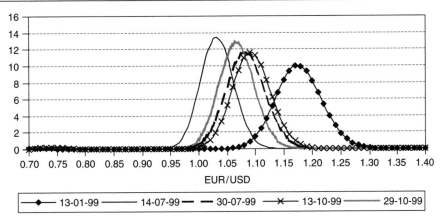

Figure 12.15   1-Month EUR/USD RND functions using a jump distribution (1999)

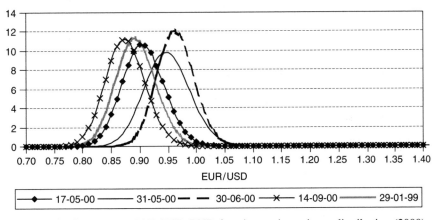

Figure 12.16   1-Month EUR/USD RND functions using a jump distribution (2000)

Concerning the jump distributions, the file "OTC_EUR_USD_jump" (similar to the one previously described) is also presented on the CD-Rom. This file contains similar macros and the results illustrated in Figures 12.15 and 12.16 are similar to those shown in Figures 12.12 and 12.13.

12.6.2   Implied correlations and credibility tests from currency options data: the Portuguese escudo and the Danish crown

Implied correlations from option prices were computed in order to assess the credibility of the Portuguese and Danish exchange rate policies, respectively during the transition until 1998 towards the EMU and the euro referendum in September 2000.[45] In fact, the anticipation by market participants of monetary integration between two currencies shall correspond to a very high (in absolute value) correlation between those two currencies, on the one side, and any third currency, on the other side.

---

[45] The Danish crown was kept under a target zone regime after the euro launch, integrating the ERM II fluctuation band of $+/-2.25\%$ vis-à-vis the euro. From 1 January 2001 on, the Danish crown would be the only currency in the ERM II, as the Greek drachma would be integrated in the euro.

Concerning the Portuguese escudo, implied correlations were computed between the DEM/USD and the USD/PTE, for the period between July 1996 and August 1998, considering in equation (12.20) S_1, S_2 and S_3 respectively as the DEM/PTE, DEM/USD and USD/PTE.[46] For the Danish crown, the implied correlation between the EUR/USD and the USD/DKK was computed, using the exchange rates EUR/DKK, EUR/USD and USD/DKK. The files used, "correlations_PTE_database.xls" and "correlations_DKK_database.xls", are also included on the CD-Rom.

The file "correlations_PTE_database.xls" contains separate sheets for the bid and ask at-the-money implied volatilities, though the implied correlations are computed using only the ask quotations, in the sheet "Corr.ask". In this sheet implied correlations computed from exchange traded options are also presented (though not computed), as well as the spread between the Portuguese escudo and the German Mark forward overnight rate, for settlement on 1 January 1999.[47] The file "correlations_DKK_database.xls" contains all the data and computations in one sheet.

Figure 12.17 shows that the implied correlation between the German Mark and the Portuguese escudo exchange rates, vis-à-vis the US dollar, increased since the end of

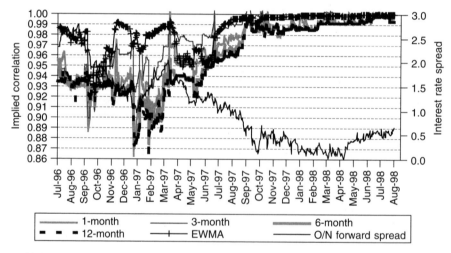

Figure 12.17 Implied and EWMA correlations between the rates of variation of the DEM/USD and PTE/USD (3-month term) and the spread between the Portuguese and German forward overnight interest rates (settlement on 1 January 1999)

---

[46] Following this notation, perfect correlation between S_2 and S_3 corresponds to a correlation coefficient equal to -1. The results will be presented in absolute values.

[47] The forward overnight interest rates with settlement on 1 January 1999 were computed from the estimations of daily spot curves, using the Nelson and Siegel (1987) or the Svensson (1994) models. The former method consists of estimating the parameters $\beta_0, \beta_1, \beta_2$ and τ of the following specification for the spot curve:

$$s_m = \beta_0 + (\beta_1 + \beta_2)[1 - e^{(-m/\tau)}]/(m/\tau) - \beta_2[e^{(-m/\tau)}]$$

The choice of one of these models was done based on a likelihood test, given that the Nelson and Siegel (1987) model corresponds to a restricted version of the Svensson (1994) model.

the first quarter of 1997 until May 1998, in all maturities considered.[48] In March 1998, following the announcement of the 1997 fiscal deficits of EU countries, the implied correlation increased to above 0.99. On the eve of the Brussels summit of 1–3 May 1998, the correlation between the exchange rate variations of DEM/USD and USD/PTE was already between 0.99 and 1.

Therefore, the results from implied correlations are consistent with the general assertion that financial market participants anticipated the inclusion of Portugal in the group of the euro founding members.[49]

The relationship between the behaviour of implied correlations and the expectations of the escudo's participation in the euro area seems to be confirmed by the evolution of the term structure of interest rates. In fact, exchange rate correlations and the spread between the Portuguese escudo and the German Mark forward overnight rate, for settlement on 1 January 1999, show a similar trend.[50]

In order to validate the results obtained for the implied correlations, CME data on German Mark/US dollar option premia were also used. For this purpose, the mismatching between the structure of OTC and that of market data had to be overcome. In fact, as previously mentioned, whilst OTC data involves options with a constant term to maturity and a variable maturity date, the exchange traded options usually have constant maturity date and variable term to maturity.

To have comparable data, given that the database on Portuguese escudo options comprised OTC volatilities for five maturities (1, 2, 3, 6 and 12 months), the term structure of volatility was estimated from OTC data, using the method presented in Nelson and Siegel (1987) for the estimation of the term structure of interest rates.[51] Compared to other methods previously used, such as those in Xu and Taylor (1994), this method provides smooth and flexible spot and forward volatility curves.[52] Furthermore, it is in line with the generally accepted assumption that expectations revert towards a long-term level (corresponding to β_0) as the term increases, though not necessarily in a monotonic way and from the short-term volatility (corresponding to $\beta_0 + \beta_1$), as in Xu and Taylor (1994).[53]

Concerning the term structure of volatilities, the results obtained point to the existence of a positively sloped curve on most days included in the sample, both for DEM/PTE

---

[48] These correlations are computed using ask prices for the implied volatilities. As EMU implies a structural change in the pattern of the correlations, the forecasting ability of implied correlations is not compared with alternative GARCH-type models.

[49] The correlations obtained with the EWMA method revealed identical patterns of evolution, though with slightly higher values and a smoother path.

[50] Reflecting the European Union Treaty and other legal dispositions relative to the introduction of the euro, the conversion rates to the euro of the participating currencies were only known on the last market day before the euro was born, on 1 January 1999. However, as announced on 3 May 1998, the current bilateral central parities of the Exchange Rate Mechanism of the European Monetary System (ERM-EMS) would be used in the calculation of the irrevocable conversion rates to the euro. Admitting that both the announcement of the participating countries and the rule of conversion to the euro were credible, the behaviour of the interest and exchange rates in the transition to the EMU became restricted by the need for full convergence, up to 31 December 1998, between the short-term interest rates prevailing in the EU-11 and between the market bilateral exchange rates and the central parities. Consequently, the convergence of forward interest rates for settlement on 1 January 1999 and the correlation between variations in the EU-11 currency exchange rates vis-à-vis third currencies (say, the US dollar) should increase.

[51] The properties of the term structure of volatility are assessed in Campa and Chang (1995).

[52] The model used in Xu and Taylor (1994) only permits three shapes for the term structure of volatilities.

[53] The slope of the volatility curve depends on the values of β_0 and β_1, while the curvature is related to the values of β_1, β_2 and τ. For further details, see Nelson and Siegel (1987).

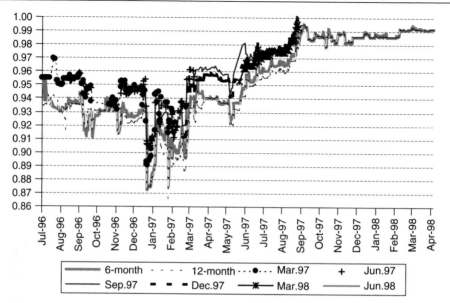

Figure 12.18 Implied correlations between the DEM and the PTE vis-à-vis the USD from OTC and exchange traded options

and USD/PTE exchange rates.[54] Regarding exchange rate correlations, they were slightly below those achieved with OTC volatilities until the third quarter of 1997 (Figure 12.18). In Figure 12.19, implied correlations between EUR/USD and USD/DKK suggest that the market expected a very close future path for the Danish crown and the euro, in line with the prevalent target zone regime.[55]

The anticipation of the Portuguese participation in the EMU is also evident in the progressive reduction of the minimum width of the perfectly credible band vis-à-vis the Deutsche mark, which corresponds to equation (12.37). According to Figure 12.20, this variable fell sharply since January 1997, from values over 3% to less than 0.5%. This behaviour is consistent with the shift in expectations towards a lower depreciation of the escudo vis-à-vis the Deutsche mark, but also with the reduction of market uncertainty about the future values of PTE/DEM.

Performing a similar exercise for the Danish crown, Figure 12.21 shows that the minimum width of the fully credible band remained generally below the ERM bandwidth (2.25%), which means that the necessary condition in (12.36) was fulfilled. The 1-month minimum width fluctuated between 0.25% and 0.5% since January 1999 and until November, when it decreased slightly. In the same period the 1-year minimum width fell from 1.6 to 0.6.

Conversely, between April and May 2000, implied volatilities increased, with the increase of the interest rate spreads between the Danish crown and the euro interest rates, as well as with the steepening of the Danish money market yield curve (Figure 12.22).

---

[54] These results were achieved on 81% and 73% of days, concerning respectively DEM/PTE and USD/PTE exchange rates.

[55] In this case, a high correlation also corresponds to a negative coefficient, as the euro and the Danish crown exchange rates vis-à-vis the US dollar are defined in opposite ways.

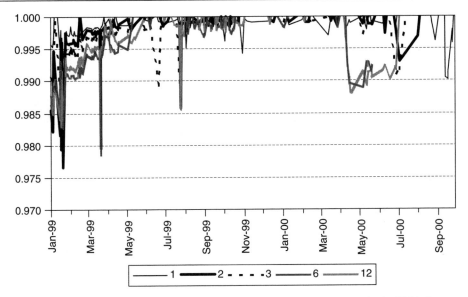

Figure 12.19 Implied correlations between the EUR and the DKK vis-à-vis the USD for several terms (in months)

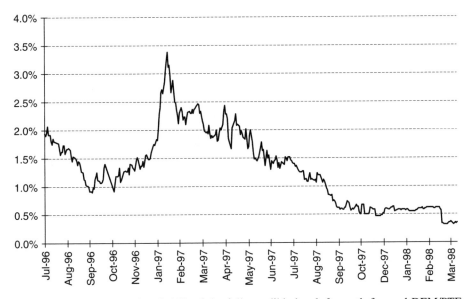

Figure 12.20 Minimum bandwidth of the fully credible band: 3-month forward DEM/PTE

From May and until one month before the referendum, the slopes of the money market yield and implied volatility curves stayed respectively around 1.1 and 1.3 percentage points. Afterwards, the slopes decreased until negative values, which suggests that market participants became more concerned with the short-term effects of the referendum result.

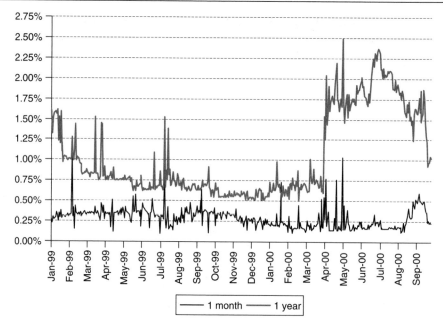

Figure 12.21   Minimum bandwidth of the fully credible band of the EUR/DKK exchange rate

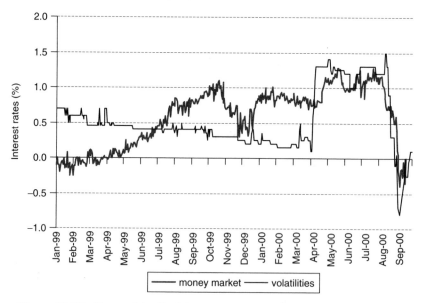

Figure 12.22   Slope of the Danish money market yield and implied volatility

Notwithstanding, some violations of the necessary condition for the target zone credibility occurred during the period studied, namely in mid-May and in the first half of
July 2000, when the 1-year minimum width achieved values between 2.3% and 2.5%.[56]

---

[56] On these occasions, the minimum intensity of realignment computed as in equation (12.40) was 0.004.

This resulted from an interest rate and volatility increase, almost one month after the Central Bank of Denmark repo rate increase by 0.6 percentage points (from 4.1% to 4.7% on 9 June 2000), following the ECB decision to increase the refi rate to 4.25% from 3.75%.

After the referendum, the Central Bank of Denmark increased the repo rate to 5.6%, from 5.1%. This move was followed by a sharp decrease of the 1-year minimum width of the perfectly credible band, from 1.9% to 1%. Then, the market seemed to expect that, notwithstanding the referendum result, the Danish monetary policy would continue to be anchored to the ECB policy, within the ERM II target zone.

The violation of the full credibility condition contrasts with the evolution of the EUR/DKK exchange rate, whose spot rate kept moving in a quite narrow band, while the forward rate was always far from the band ceiling, accomplishing the Svensson (1991) simple credibility test (Figure 12.23).[57]

The files used for the estimations illustrated in Figures 12.20–12.22 are "credibility_tests_PTE_3m.xls", "credibility_tests_DKK_1m.xls" and "credibility_tests_DKK_1y.xls" and are also included on the CD-Rom. All these files have a similar structure: the first three columns contain the data on the interest rates and the spot exchange rates; the forward exchange rates are computed in the fourth column, while the bounds of the ERM-EMS are in the two following columns; the implied (offer) volatilities and the respective call-option prices are presented next; in the following column the minimum intensity of realignment is computed, as in equation (12.40); the credibility tests in equations (12.34) and (12.36) are performed next; finally, the minimum width of the fully credible band in equation (12.37) is calculated.

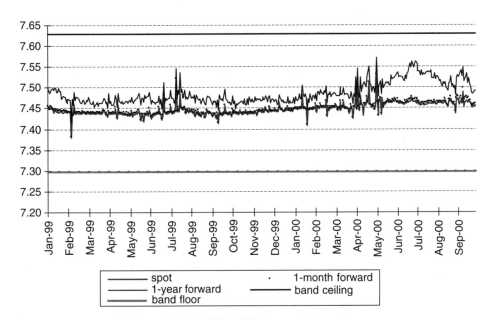

Figure 12.23   EUR/DKK Spot and forward rates

---

[57] This test corresponds to assessing whether the forward rate exceeds the target zone limits.

12.7   CONCLUSIONS

In the OTC currency option market, financial institutions quote regularly at-the-money forward volatilities, as well as risk-reversals and strangles, which provide information respectively on the skewness and kurtosis of the distribution of the underlying asset. The informational content of these prices is supposedly higher than that from exchange traded option prices concerning currency options, as in this case the over-the-counter market involves a significantly higher transactions volume. Besides, using only this information, it is possible to estimate the whole RND function, as well as to test the credibility of a target zone.

Currency option prices also provide relevant information on implied correlations between exchange rates, that can be necessary for portfolio management or risk assessments. Compared to the usual conditional correlations, the former offer the advantage of being forward looking, allowing one to obtain correlation measures from market data in periods in which regime shifts are expected. Considering the EMU, implied correlations permit market expectations to be assessed on the degree of convergence between potential participating currencies.

Three empirical applications of the literature were presented: firstly on the EUR/USD, followed by the analysis of implied correlations and the credibility of the Portuguese exchange rate policy, during the transition to the EMU, and of the Danish exchange rate policy around the euro referendum in September 2000.

As in many other cases found in the literature, the euro depreciation vis-à-vis the US dollar has occurred against the UIP predictions. Simultaneously, market expectations about the future behaviour of the exchange rate also changed markedly, which is reflected by OTC quotes for EUR/USD options. The results obtained confirm the general assertion that the expectations on the euro evolution deteriorated from January 1999 to October 2000, though some improvements happened after the joint exchange rate intervention in September 2000.

Regarding the credibility of the Portuguese exchange rate policy, the results are consistent with the idea that the probability of the escudo's participation in the euro area from the beginning increased persistently over the course of 1997. Additionally, the market attributed a high degree of credibility to the bilateral central parity announced at the 1–3 May 1998 European summit.

On the eve of the summit, market participants were expecting a perfect correlation between the movements of the Deutsche Mark and the Portuguese escudo, vis-à-vis the US dollar. Furthermore, the central moments of the PTE/DEM exchange rate RND function converged to the central parity and the uncertainty regarding the future values of PTE/DEM decreased strongly.

Though the Danish crown and the euro kept almost perfectly correlated during the first three quarters of 2000, the credibility of the ERM target zone was challenged by option market participants before the referendum, mainly in the beginning of July. This change in market expectations followed the widening of the gap between the key interest rates of the Danish crown and the euro. After the referendum, though the integration in the euro was rejected, the credibility of the Danish monetary policy was enhanced, reflected in the decrease of the minimum width of the fully credible band.

REFERENCES

Abken, P. A. (1995), "Using Eurodollar Futures and Options: Gauging the Market's View of Interest Rate Movements", *Federal Reserve Bank of Atlanta Economic Review*, **Mar/Apr**, 10–30.

Bahra, B. (1996), "Implied Risk-Neutral Probability Density Functions from Option Prices: Theory and Application", *Bank of England Economic Bulletin*, **Aug**, 299–309.

Ball, C. and W. N. Torous (1983), "A Simplified Jump Process for Common Stock Returns", *Journal of Financial and Quantitative Analysis*, **18**, March, 53–65.

Ball, C. and W. N. Torous (1985), "On Jumps in Common Stock Prices and Their Impact on Call Option Pricing", *Journal of Finance*, **XL**(1), March, 155–173.

Bates, D. S. (1991), "The Crash of '87: Was It Expected? The Evidence from Options Markets", *Journal of Finance*, **XLVI**(3), July, 1009–1044.

BIS (2001), "The Global OTC Derivatives Market at end-June 2001: Second Part of the Triennial Central Bank Survey of Foreign Exchange and Derivatives Market Activity".

Black, F. and M. Scholes (1973), "The Pricing of Options and Corporate Liabilities", *Journal of Political Economy*, **81** (May/Jun), 637–654.

Bliss, R. R. and N. Panigirtzoglou (2000), "Testing the Stability of Implied Probability Density Functions", *Bank of England Working Paper*, No. 114.

Breeden, D. T. and R. H. Litzenberger (1978), "Prices of State-Contingent Claims Implicit in Option Prices", *Journal of Business*, **51**(4), October, 621–651.

Butler, C. and H. Davies (1998), "Assessing Market Views on Monetary Policy: The Use of Implied Risk-Neutral Probability Distributions", paper presented to the BIS/CEPR Conference "Asset Prices and Monetary Policy", January.

Campa, J. M. and P. H. K. Chang (1995), "Testing the Expectations Hypothesis on the Term Structure of Volatilities in Foreign Exchange Options", *Journal of Finance*, **50**, 529–547.

Campa, J. M. and P. H. K. Chang (1996), "Arbitrage-based Tests of Target-Zone Credibility: Evidence from ERM Cross-Rate Options", *American Economic Review*, **86**(4), September.

Campa, J. M., P. H. K. Chang and R. L. Reider (1997), "ERM Bandwidths for EMU and After: Evidence from Foreign Exchange Options", *Economic Policy*, **24**, April, 55–89.

Clews, R., N. Panigirtzoglou and J. Proudman (2000), "Recent Developments in Extracting Information from Option Markets", *Bank of England Quarterly Bulletin*, **Feb**, 50–60.

Deutsche Bundesbank (1995), "The Information Content of Derivatives for Monetary Policy", *Deutsche Bundesbank Monthly Report*, **Nov**.

Dunis, C. and P. Lequeux (2001), "The Information Content of Risk-Reversals", *Derivatives Uses, Trading and Regulation*, **2**, 98–117.

Garman, M. M. and S. W. Kohlhagen (1983), "Foreign Currency Option Values", *Journal of International Money and Finance*, **2**, December, 231–237.

Loretan, M. and W. B. English (2000), "Evaluating Correlation Breakdowns during Periods of Market Volatility", *BIS Conference Papers*, Vol. 8, Bank for International Settlements, March.

Luís, J. B. (2001), "Essays on Extracting Information from Financial Asset Prices", PhD thesis, University of York.

Malz, A. M. (1996), "Using Option Prices to Estimate Realignment Probabilities in the European Monetary System: the Case of Sterling–Mark", *Journal of International Money and Finance*, **15**(5), 717–748.

Malz, A. M. (1997), "Estimating the Probability Distribution of the Future Exchange Rate from Option Prices", *Journal of Derivatives*, **Winter**, 18–36.

McCauley, R. and W. Melick (1996), "Risk Reversal Risk", *Risk*, **9**(11), November, 54–57.

Melick, W. R. and C. P. Thomas (1997), "Recovering an Asset's Implied PDF from Option Prices: An Application to Crude Oil during the Gulf Crisis", *Journal of Financial and Quantitative Analysis*, **32**(1), March, 91–115.

Melick, W. R. and C. P. Thomas (1998), "Confidence Intervals and Constant-Maturity Series for Probability Measures Extracted from Options Prices", paper presented to the Bank of Canada Conference "Information in Financial Asset Prices", May.

Merton, R. C. (1976), "Option Pricing when Underlying Stock Returns are Discontinuous", *Journal of Financial Economics*, **Jan/Mar**(3), 125–144.

Nelson, C. R. and A. F. Siegel (1987), "Parsimonious Modelling of Yield Curves", *Journal of Business*, **60**(4), 473–489.

Ritchey, R. R. (1990), "Call Option Valuation for Discrete Normal Mixtures", *The Journal of Financial Research*, **XIII**(4), Winter.

Söderlind, P. and L. E. O. Svensson (1997), "New Techniques to Extract Market Expectations from Financial Instruments", *Journal of Monetary Economics*, **40**, 383–429.

Svensson, L. E. O. (1991), "The Simplest Test of Target Zone Credibility", *International Monetary Fund Staff Papers*, **38**, 655–665.

Svensson, L. E. O. (1994), "Estimating and Interpreting Forward Interest Rates: Sweden 1992–4", *CEPR Discussion Paper Series* No. 1051.

Xu, X. and S. J. Taylor (1994), "The Term Structure of Volatility Implied by Foreign Exchange Options", *Journal of Financial and Quantitative Analysis*, **29**(1), March.

13

Filling Analysis for Missing Data: An Application to Weather Risk Management*

CHRISTIAN L. DUNIS AND VASSILIOS KARALIS

ABSTRACT

This chapter examines and analyses the use of alternative methods when confronted with missing data, a common problem when not enough historical data or clean historical data exist: this will typically be the case when trying to develop a decision tool either for a new asset in a given asset class (say a recently issued stock in a given company sector) or for a new asset class as such (for instance weather derivatives).

Weather derivatives are used to illustrate this analysis because most weather derivatives pricing methodologies rely heavily on "clean" weather temperature data. The methodology adopted is to discard certain observed values and treat them as missing data. We then examine and analyse the imputation accuracy of different interpolation techniques and filling methods for missing historical records of temperature data: the Expectation Maximisation (EM) algorithm, the Data Augmentation (DA) algorithm, the Kalman filter (KF), Neural Networks Regression (NNR) models and, finally, Principal Component Analysis (PCA).

These methodologies are benchmarked against simpler techniques like the fallback methodology and a naïve approach whereby missing temperature observations are imputed with the same day value of the previous year. Their performance is evaluated against the actual values of the "missing data" using standard measures of forecasting accuracy widely used in the economic literature.

Overall, it is found that, for the periods and the data series concerned, the results of PCA outperformed the other methodologies in all cases of missing observations analysed.

13.1 INTRODUCTION

This entire book has been devoted to answering this apparently simple question: with the help of different methods, what can we learn about the future from the financial data available from the past? In other words, we have taken data availability for granted.

---

* The opinions expressed herein are those of the authors, and not necessarily those of Girobank.

Applied Quantitative Methods for Trading and Investment. Edited by C.L. Dunis, J. Laws and P. Naïm
© 2003 John Wiley & Sons, Ltd ISBN: 0-470-84885-5

But the absence of data, or of clean data, is a rather common problem facing users of quantitative methods in financial markets.

Admittedly, in recent years, the increasing availability of powerful computers has made it ever easier to collect, store and process higher frequency databanks, at a time when the use of advanced technologies for trading, risk and asset management has grown exponentially among financial institutions. Nevertheless, in a multivariate context, taking into account the fact that most financial markets do not move independently from each other, the nonsynchronicity of such high frequency data arrival clearly poses major practical problems. Similarly, even at daily frequencies, a risk manager will possibly face a dilemma over which data to retain for the marking-to-market and Value-at-Risk (VaR) computation of a portfolio containing assets from different markets when some of these are not trading either because of the time difference or a public holiday.

Such problems will be exacerbated when not enough historical data or clean historical data exist: this will typically be the case when trying to develop a decision tool either for a new asset in a given asset class (say a recently issued stock in a given company sector) or for a new asset class as such (for instance weather derivatives).

The motivation for this chapter is to consider and examine the problem of missing data. Weather data are used to illustrate this analysis because most weather derivatives pricing methodologies rely heavily on "clean" weather temperature data. The methodology adopted is to discard certain observed values and treat them as "missing data". We then examine and analyse the imputation accuracy of different interpolation techniques and filling methods for missing historical records of temperature data. These are the Expectation Maximisation (EM) algorithm, which is a common technique for determining maximum-likelihood estimates, the Data Augmentation (DA) algorithm, an iterative simulation very similar to the EM algorithm and which may be regarded as a stochastic edition of the EM, the Kalman filter (KF), a smoothing algorithm which can be used to estimate missing observations once a model has been represented in state space form, Principal Component Analysis (PCA), an approach adapted to fill in appropriate values for missing observations from data that are available from correlated variables and, finally, Neural Networks Regression (NNR) models which have been used here to identify and possibly benefit from nonlinear correlations between temperature series.

These methodologies are benchmarked against simpler and widely used techniques like the fallback methodology and a naïve approach whereby missing temperature observations are imputed with the same day value of the previous year. This benchmarking is carried out to gauge the potential added value of the different methods retained in the imputation process. The performance of these techniques as predictors of the "pseudo missing" values is evaluated using standard measures of forecasting accuracy widely used in the economic literature, such as mean absolute error, root mean squared error, etc.

Overall, we conclude that, for the periods and the data series concerned, the results of PCA outperformed the other methodologies in all cases of missing observations analysed.

The rest of the chapter is organised as follows. Section 13.2 gives a brief overview of the importance of clean weather data for weather derivatives pricing and discusses the weather data used in this research. Section 13.3 documents the different filling methods retained while Section 13.4 presents our empirical results. Finally, Section 13.5 concludes this chapter.

13.2   WEATHER DATA AND WEATHER DERIVATIVES

13.2.1   The importance of weather data for weather derivatives pricing

The history of the weather derivatives market dates back to 1996, when electricity deregulation in the USA caused the power market to begin changing from series of local monopolies to competitive regional wholesale markets. Energy companies realising the impact of weather on their operations took control of their weather risk and created a new market around it. While a number of pioneering trades were made as early as 1996, the market did not really take off until after September 1999, when the Chicago Mercantile Exchange (CME) embarked on listing and trading standard futures and options contracts on US temperature indexes. Since 2000, the weather risk market has grown significantly and become progressively more diversified across industries, even if this market originally evolved from the energy sector. According to the Second Annual Weather Risk Industry survey commissioned by the Weather Risk Management Association (WRMA), the total market size for weather derivatives increased to an impressive $11.5 billion at the end of 2001 (see PricewaterhouseCoopers (2002)).

Most weather derivatives contracts traded were temperature related (over 82%). These are "heating degree days" (HDDs) and "cooling degree days" (CDDs) contracts. A degree day is the deviation of the average daily temperature (ADT) from a predefined temperature defined as K in the following equations. HDDs and CDDs are the most common degree day measurements. The temperature below K represents the temperature below which heating devices are expected to turn on (HDDs), and above which air conditioners are expected to turn on (CDDs). Since HDDs and CDDs are measuring heating and cooling needs compared to the base temperature, they are calculated according to the following equations:

$$\text{Daily HDDs} = \max(0, (K - \text{ADT})) = \max\left(0, \left(K - \frac{T_{\max} + T_{\min}}{2}\right)\right)$$

$$\text{Daily CDDs} = \max(0, (\text{ADT} - K)) = \max\left(0, \left(\frac{T_{\max} + T_{\min}}{2} - K\right)\right)$$

where $T_{\max}$ and $T_{\min}$ are the maximum and minimum, respectively, recorded temperature during the day.[1] The calculation of daily degree days for longer periods (week, season, year) is based on straightforward summation:

$$\text{HDDs} = \sum_{i}^{n}\left[\max\left(0, \left(K - \frac{T_{\max} + T_{\min}}{2}\right)\right)\right]$$

$$\text{CDDs} = \sum_{i}^{n}\left[\max\left(0, \left(\frac{T_{\max} + T_{\min}}{2} - K\right)\right)\right]$$

In order to demonstrate how a degree day index may be structured to moderate risk, suppose that an energy company through the past 10 years' supply and temperature

---

[1] In the USA, the standard baseline temperature (K) is 65°F (18.3°C), but the 65°F base temperature can fluctuate from one region to another.

analysis has determined the expected cumulative number of HDDs during the heating season. The company is expecting to sell a given amount of energy units according to this number and sets its budgets to this level. Its analysis also suggests that, for each HDD below the 10-year average, demand will decrease by a set number of energy units, creating a marginal loss of \$55 000 versus budget. In such a case the company may purchase a HDD index derivative to achieve protection at a price of \$55 000 for each HDD lower than a given strike (see Corbally and Dang (2001)).

Traditionally, financial derivatives such as options on equities, bonds, forex or commodities are priced using no-arbitrage models such as the Black–Scholes pricing model. In the case of weather derivatives, the underlying asset is a physical quantity (temperature, rain, wind or snow) rather than a traded asset. Given that the underlying weather indexes are not traded, a no-arbitrage model cannot be directly applied to price weather derivatives.

Another approach is used in the insurance industry, known as Historical Burn Analysis (HBA). The central assumption of the method is that the historical record of weather contracts payouts gives a precise illustration of the distribution of potential payouts. As noted by Henderson (2001), if weather risk is calculated as the payouts standard deviation, then the price of the contract will be given by the equation:

$$\text{Price}_{\text{bid/offer}}(t) = D(t, T) \times (\mu \pm \alpha \sigma)$$

where $D(t, T)$ is the discount factor from contract maturity T to the pricing time t, μ is the historical average payout, σ is the historical standard deviation of payouts and α is a positive number denoting the protection seller's risk tolerance.

HBA therefore crucially depends on historical temperature data. Collecting historical data may be somewhat difficult and costly but, even when the data is available, there are several types of errors like missing data or unreasonable readings. Consequently, the data must be "cleaned" – that is, the errors and omissions must be fixed – in order to be used for pricing and risk management purposes.

13.2.2 The weather databank

For this research, we use daily temperature data (cleaned data) for Philadelphia International (WMO: 724080) weather station (the index station) and for its "fallback station" according to the WRMA, the Allentown-Bethlehem (WMO: 725170).[2] This data was obtained from QuantWeather (www.quantweather.com). Furthermore, to perform PCA and NNR, we use temperature data for all the neighbouring stations for which cleaned data are available. In order to create a series of consequent daily temperature observations for $T_{\max}$ (maximum daily temperature), $T_{\min}$ (minimum daily temperature) and the corresponding T_{avg} $((T_{\max} + T_{\min})/2)$ for all the available stations, the databank spans from 1 July 1960 to 31 December 1993 (i.e. 33 years and 12 237 observations). Moreover, to examine the impact of seasonality, this databank was divided into two separate subsets. The first one includes only the "Autumn" (September, October and November) temperature observations and the second one only November temperature observations, totalling

---

[2] Weather stations are identified in several ways. The most common is a six-digit WMO ID assigned by the World Meteorological Organisation. WMO IDs are the primary means of identifying weather stations outside the USA, while in the USA the five-digit Weather Bureau Army Navy identities (WBAN IDs) are widely used.

3094 and 1020 observations respectively. Standard tests like the serial correlation LM test, ADF, Phillips–Perron, ARCH-LM and Jarque–Bera tests (not reported here in order to conserve space) showed that all the series are autocorrelated, stationary, heteroskedastic and not normally distributed.

In order to assess the imputation accuracy of the methodologies, several "holes" were created in the datasets. Arbitrarily, it is assumed that all the missing observations occurred in November 1993. We also supposed that the missing data were *missing at random*. The fallback methodology employs different procedures to handle missing data according to the number of consecutive missing days, with 12 days or more an important breakpoint.[3] Therefore, five different gaps were created including 1, 7, 10 (<12), 20 and 30 (>12) consecutive missing days. Since HDDs and CDDs are calculated as the deviation of the average daily temperature from the standard baseline temperature and, again, in order to conserve space only the imputed values of the average temperature dataset (T_{avg}) are presented and compared later in this chapter.

13.3 ALTERNATIVE FILLING METHODS FOR MISSING DATA

In order to ensure that more complex methodologies do indeed add value in the imputation process, it is essential to benchmark them against simpler and more widely used methods like the naïve approach and the fallback method. We first present these benchmarks before turning to more sophisticated methods.

13.3.1 The naïve approach

The naïve hypothesis retained is to impute the missing temperature observation with the same day value of the previous year. This simple model is formed by:

$$Y_t = Y^*$$

where Y_t is the missing temperature data at period t and Y^* the corresponding imputed value, i.e. the temperature that prevailed on the same day the previous year.

13.3.2 The fallback methodology

The second part of the WRMA confirmation[4] establishes the weather industry's standard for determining and adjusting weather data. It presents an estimation of temperature based on a weather index station, which is usually an agreed region designated in the confirmation by an airport location, WBAN or WMO ID. In the event that weather data is not available for the index station, the WRMA confirmation sets forth the interpolation procedures to be used to determine the missing data under the provision entitled "fallback methodology" (see Raspé (2001), p. 233). The fallback method provides an adjustment based on temperature at a selected alternative weather index station referred to as the "fallback station".

---

[3] See Section 13.3.2 below.
[4] Standard forms of documents and other confirming evidence exchanged between the parties in a weather contract.

13.3.2.1   Fallback terminology

It is important at this point to define some basic terminology of the fallback methodology:

- *Adjustment* indicates the mean of the arithmetic difference of the daily maximum and/or minimum temperature (if the unavailable temperature is a daily maximum and/or minimum respectively) at the fallback station subtracted from the corresponding temperature at the index station during the period in which temperature data is unavailable.
- *Missing data day* denotes any day during the calculation period for which data for the index station is unavailable.
- *Missing data calculation day* means the same day and same month as the relevant missing data day.
- *Leap year exception* stipulates that, in the event that the missing data day is 29 February, the missing data calculation day shall be considered as 1 March.

13.3.2.2   Data missing for less than 12 consecutive days

If temperature data is unavailable for less than 12 consecutive days during the calculation period, the "adjustment" will be computed for each "missing data day" using a period of the 15 days immediately prior to, and the 15 days immediately following, the relevant "missing data day". If there are unavailable temperature data at the fallback station and/or the index station within the 15-day periods prior to and following a "missing data day", then an adjustment period of the first 15 days on which the relevant temperature values are available (out of a maximum of 25 days) on either side of each "missing data day" shall be used to calculate the "adjustment". To illustrate this process consider the case of one missing observation, say Y_0. Let Z be the temperature on the fallback station and Y the temperature being measured. Then the gap between Y and Z is measured over the period t_{-1} to t_{-15} and t_1 to t_{15} and the average gap is calculated over this period and designated as "avg". Thus the interpolated value is $Y_0 = Z_0 + \text{avg}$. Similar methods would apply to the computation of missing data for longer periods.

13.3.2.3   Data missing for 12 or more consecutive days

If there are missing temperature observations for more than 12 consecutive days, the "adjustment" for each "missing data day" will be computed using temperature values from a period of the 15 days prior to (including the relevant "missing data calculation day") and the 15 days after the applicable "missing data calculation day" for the three prior years. If there is no data for the index station and/or the fallback station in the immediate three previous years, the adjustment period will be extended until three years of temperature values can be obtained. In the event that there are unavailable temperatures at the fallback station and/or the index station within the periods of the 15 days prior to a "missing data calculation day" or the 15 following days, then an adjustment period shall be the first 15 days on which the relevant temperature data are available (out of a maximum of 25 days) on either side of each "missing data calculation day".

13.3.3   The expectation maximisation algorithm

The EM algorithm is a common technique for determining maximum-likelihood estimates for parametric models when data are not entirely available. Developed by Dempster *et al.*

(1977), the EM algorithm generated an innovation in the analysis of incomplete data, making it possible to calculate efficient parameter estimates in a wide variety of statistical problems, under the assumption that the data are normally distributed.

13.3.3.1 Maximum-likelihood estimation

The principle of maximum likelihood provides a means of choosing an asymptotically efficient estimator for a parameter or a set of parameters. Consider a random sample of n observations from a normal distribution with mean μ and variance σ^2. The probability density function for each observation is (see e.g. Greene (2000), p. 125):

$$f(x_i) = (2\pi)^{-\frac{1}{2}} \times (\sigma^2)^{-\frac{1}{2}} \times \exp\left[-\frac{1}{2}\frac{(x_i - \mu)^2}{\sigma^2}\right]$$

Since the observations are independent, their joint density is:

$$f(x_1, x_2, \ldots, x_n | \mu, \sigma^2) = \prod_{i=1}^{n} f(x_i) = (2\pi)^{-\frac{n}{2}} \times (\sigma^2)^{-\frac{n}{2}} \times \exp\left[-\frac{1}{2} \times \sum_{i=1}^{n} \frac{(x_i - \mu)^2}{\sigma^2}\right]$$

This equation gives the probability of observing this specific sample. We are now interested in the values of μ and σ^2 that make this sample most probable, in other words, the maximum-likelihood estimates (MLE) θ_{MLE} of μ and σ^2. Since the log function is monotonically increasing and easier to work with, we usually calculate θ_{MLE} by maximising the natural logarithm of the likelihood function:

$$\ln L(\mu, \sigma^2 | x_1, x_2, \ldots, x_n) = -\frac{n}{2} \times \ln(2\pi) - \frac{n}{2} \times \ln(\sigma^2) - \frac{1}{2}\sum_{i=1}^{n}\left[\frac{(x_i - \mu)^2}{\sigma^2}\right]$$

This translates into finding solutions to the following first-order conditions:

$$\frac{\partial \ln L}{\partial \mu} = \frac{1}{\sigma^2} \times \sum_{i=1}^{n}(x_i - \mu) = 0 \qquad \frac{\partial \ln L}{\partial \sigma^2} = -\frac{n}{2\sigma^2} + \frac{1}{2\sigma^4} \times \sum_{i=1}^{n}(x_i - \mu)^2 = 0$$

Finally, the MLE estimates are:

$$\hat{\mu}_{ML} = \frac{1}{n} \times \sum_{i=1}^{n} x_i = \bar{x}_n \quad \text{and} \quad \hat{\sigma}^2_{ML} = \frac{1}{n} \times \sum_{i=1}^{n}(x_i - \bar{x}_n)^2$$

13.3.3.2 The E-step and M-step of the algorithm

When some observations Y_{obs} of the sample are missing, the MLE estimates θ_{MLE} are not obtainable, because the likelihood function is not defined at the missing data points. In order to overcome this problem we apply the EM algorithm which exploits the interdependence between the missing data Y_{mis} and parameters θ_{MLE}. The Y_{mis} enclose information relevant to estimating θ_{MLE}, and θ_{MLE} in turn helps us to compute probable values of Y_{mis}. This relation suggests the following scheme for estimating θ_{MLE} in the presence of

Y_{obs} alone: "fill in" the missing data Y_{mis} based on an initial estimate of θ_{MLE}, re-estimate θ_{MLE} based on Y_{obs} and the filled-in Y_{mis} and iterate until the estimates converge (see Schafer (1997)). In any missing data case, the distribution of the complete dataset Y can be factored as:

$$P(Y|\theta) = P(Y_{\text{obs}}|\theta) \times P(Y_{\text{mis}}|Y_{\text{obs}}, \theta) \tag{13.1}$$

Considering each term in the above equation as a function of θ, we have:

$$l(\theta|Y) = l(\theta|Y_{\text{obs}}) + \log P(Y_{\text{mis}}|Y_{\text{obs}}, \theta) + c \tag{13.2}$$

where $l(\theta|Y) = \log P(Y|\theta)$ indicates the complete data log-likelihood, $l(\theta|Y_{\text{obs}}) = \log L(\theta|Y_{\text{obs}})$ the observed data log-likelihood, and c a random constant. Averaging equation (13.2) over the distribution $P(Y_{\text{mis}}|Y_{\text{obs}}, \theta^{(t)})$, where $\theta^{(t)}$ is an initial estimate of the unknown parameter, we get:

$$Q(\theta|\theta^{(t)}) = l(\theta|Y_{\text{obs}}) + H(\theta|\theta^{(t)}) + c \tag{13.3}$$

where

$$Q(\theta|\theta^{(t)}) = \int (l(\theta|Y) \times P(Y_{\text{mis}}|Y_{\text{obs}}, \theta^{(t)})) \, dY_{\text{mis}}$$

and

$$H(\theta|\theta^{(t)}) = \int (\log P(Y_{\text{mis}}|Y_{\text{obs}}, \theta) \times P(Y_{\text{mis}}|Y_{\text{obs}}, \theta^{(t)})) \, dY_{\text{mis}}$$

A basic conclusion of Dempster et al. (1977) is that if we consider $\theta^{(t+1)}$ as the value of θ that maximises $Q(\theta|\theta^{(t)})$, then $\theta^{(t+1)}$ is an improved estimation compared to $\theta^{(t)}$:

$$l(\theta^{(t+1)}|Y_{\text{obs}}) \geq l(\theta^{(t)}|Y_{\text{obs}})$$

In summary, it is convenient to think of the EM as an iterative algorithm that operates in two steps as follows:

- E-step: The expectation step, in which the function $Q(\theta|\theta^{(t)})$ is calculated by averaging the complete data log-likelihood $l(\theta|Y)$ over $P(Y_{\text{mis}}|Y_{\text{obs}}, \theta^{(t)})$.
- M-step: The maximisation step, in which $\theta^{(t+1)}$ is calculated by maximising $Q(\theta|\theta^{(t)})$.[5]

13.3.4 The data augmentation algorithm

Data augmentation is an iterative simulation algorithm, a special kind of Markov chain Monte Carlo (MCMC). As underlined by Schafer (1997), DA is very similar to the EM algorithm, and may be regarded as a stochastic edition of EM. In many cases with missing values, the observed data distribution $P(\theta|Y_{\text{obs}})$ is difficult to define. However, if Y_{obs} is "augmented" by a preliminary value of Y_{mis}, the complete data distribution $P(\theta|Y_{\text{obs}}, Y_{\text{mis}})$ can be handled.

[5] The EM algorithm was implemented with the SPSS software.

For an initial guess $\theta^{(t)}$ of the parameter, we select a value of the missing data from the conditional distribution of Y_{mis}:

$$Y_{\text{mis}}^{(t+1)} \sim P(Y_{\text{mis}}|Y_{\text{obs}}, \theta^{(t)}) \tag{13.4}$$

Conditioning on $Y_{\text{mis}}^{(t+1)}$, we select a new value of θ from its complete data distribution:

$$\theta^{(t+1)} \sim P(\theta|Y_{\text{obs}}, Y_{\text{mis}}^{(t+1)}) \tag{13.5}$$

Alternating (13.4) and (13.5) from an initial value $\theta^{(0)}$, we obtain a stochastic sequence $\{(\theta^{(t)}, Y_{\text{mis}}^{(t)}): t = 1, 2, \ldots\}$ that converges to a stationary distribution $P(\theta, Y_{\text{mis}}|Y_{\text{obs}})$, the joint distribution of the missing data and parameters given the observed data, and the subsequences $\{\theta^{(t)}: t = 1, 2, \ldots\}$ and $\{Y_{\text{mis}}^{(t)}: t = 1, 2, \ldots\}$ with $P(\theta|Y_{\text{obs}})$ and $P(Y_{\text{mis}}|Y_{\text{obs}})$ their stationary distributions respectively. For a large value of t we can consider $\theta^{(t)}$ as an approximate draw from $P(\theta|Y_{\text{obs}})$; alternatively, we can regard $Y_{\text{mis}}^{(t)}$ as an approximate draw from $P(Y_{\text{mis}}|Y_{\text{obs}})$.

In summary, DA is an iterative algorithm that operates in two steps as follows:

- *I-step*: The imputation step, in which the missing data are imputed by drawing them from their conditional distribution given the observed data and assumed initial values for the parameters $\theta^{(t)}$.
- *P-step*: The posterior step, in which the values for the parameters are simulated by drawing them from their complete data distribution given the most recently imputed values $Y_{\text{mis}}^{(t+1)}$ for the missing data.

The convergence performance of the DA algorithm depends on the amount of missing information (how much information about the parameters is contained in the missing part of the data relative to the observed part). High rates of missing information cause successive iterations to be highly correlated, and a large number of cycles will be needed for the algorithm to converge. Low rates of missing information produce low correlation and rapid convergence.[6]

The EM and DA algorithms provide optimal solutions under the assumption that the data are normally distributed. However, weather temperature data deviate from normality. Nevertheless, in many cases the normal model is useful even when the actual data are non-normal (see Schafer (1997), p. 147). The EM algorithm is used to calculate the missing values on the level of the series. Additionally, it is almost always better to run the EM algorithm before using the DA to impute missing data because running the EM first will provide good starting values for the DA and will help to predict its likely convergence behaviour.

13.3.5   The Kalman filter models

The seminal works of Harvey (1989) and Hamilton (1994) have underlined the advantages of using state space modelling for representing dynamic systems where unobserved

---

[6] The DA algorithm was implemented using Schafer's stand alone NORM software, which can be downloaded at http://www.stat.psu.edu/~jls/misoftwa.html.

variables (the so-called "state" variables) can be integrated within an "observable" model. The advantage of handling problems of missing observations with the state space form is that the missing values can be estimated by a smoothing algorithm like the Kalman filter. The filtering is used to estimate the expected value of the state vector according to the information available at time t, while the intention of smoothing is to include the information made available after time t.

Harvey (1981) has shown that, if the observations are normally distributed, and the present estimator of the state vector is the most accurate, the predictor and the updated estimator will also be the most accurate. In the absence of the normality assumption a similar result holds, but only within the class of estimators and predictors which are linear in the observations.

Several chapters in this book have documented in detail state space models and the Kalman filter so we will avoid giving a new presentation.[7] Let it suffice to say that, based on the principle of parsimony, our initial Kalman filter model was an AR(1) process with a constant mean, implying that extreme temperatures would show some persistence, but they would eventually return to their mean level for the period under review. Nevertheless, comparing the imputation accuracy of alternative models that we tried, we concluded that the best model for the T_{avg} series of the entire dataset is an ARMA(1,2) process, while for the "Autumn" dataset it is an ARMA(2,1) and for the "November" dataset an ARMA(1,1).[8]

13.3.6 The neural networks regression models

Here again, two chapters in this book have documented the use of NNR models for prediction purposes.[9] In the circumstances, let us just say that the starting point for the NNR models was the linear correlations between the T_{max} and T_{min} of the index station considered and the explanatory temperature series. While NNR models endeavour to identify nonlinearities, linear correlation analysis can give an indication of which variables should be included. Variable selection was achieved using a backward stepwise neural regression procedure: starting with lagged historical values of the dependent variable and observations for correlated weather stations, we progressively reduced the number of inputs, keeping the network architecture constant. If omitting a variable did not deteriorate the level of explained variance over the previous best model, the pool of explanatory variables was updated by getting rid of this input (see also Dunis and Jalilov (2002)). The chosen model was then kept for further tests and improvements.

---

[7] See Bentz (2003), Billio and Sartore (2003) and Cassola and Luís (2003).
[8] The Kalman filter models were implemented with EViews 4.0. The model for the entire dataset is an ARMA(1,2) process giving a system of four equations:

$$@signal\ allavg = c(1) + sv1 + c(2)^*sv2 + c(3)^*sv3$$

as the observation equation, plus the three state equations:

$$@state\ sv1 = c(5)^*sv1(-1) + [var = exp(c(4))]$$
$$@state\ sv2 = sv1(-1)$$
$$@state\ sv3 = sv2(-1)$$

[9] See Dunis and Williams (2003) and Dunis and Huang (2003).

Finally, each of the datasets was partitioned into three subsets, using approximately 2/3 of the data for training the model, 1/6 for testing and the remaining 1/6 for validation. The intentions of this partition are the control of the error and the reduction of the risk of overfitting. For instance, the final models for the "November" T_{max} and T_{min} series have one hidden layer with five hidden nodes.[10]

13.3.7 Principal component analysis

PCA is a standard method for extracting the most significant uncorrelated sources of variation in a multivariate system. The objective of PCA is to reduce dimensionality, so that only the most significant sources of information are used. This approach is very useful in highly correlated systems, like weather temperatures from neighbouring stations, because there will be a small number of independent sources of variation and most of them can be described by just a few principal components. PCA has numerous applications in financial markets modelling: the main ones concern factor modelling within the Arbitrage Pricing Theory framework (see Campbell *et al.* (1997)), robust regression analysis in the presence of multicollinearity (again a problem often affecting factor modelling) and yield curve modelling (see Alexander (2001)), although, in this latter case, other techniques seem preferable.[11] It may also be used to overcome the problem of missing data, as we shall see next.

13.3.7.1 Principal components computation[12]

Assume that the data for which the PCA is to be carried out consist of M variables indexed $j = 1, 2, \ldots, M$ and N observations on each variable, $i = 1, 2, \ldots, N$, generating an $N \times M$ matrix $\mathbf{X}$. The input data must be stationary. Furthermore, these stationary data will need to be normalised before the analysis, otherwise the first principal component will be dominated by the input variable with the greatest volatility. Thus, we also assume that each of the M columns of the stationary data matrix $\mathbf{X}$ has mean $\mu = 0$ and variance $\sigma^2 = 1$. This can be achieved by subtracting the sample mean and dividing by the sample standard deviation for each element x_{ij} of matrix $\mathbf{X}$. Consequently we have created a matrix $\mathbf{X}$ of standardised mean deviations. We will transform this matrix to a new set of random variables, which are pairwise uncorrelated. Let $\mathbf{z}_1$ be the new variable with the maximum variance, then the first column vector $\boldsymbol{\alpha}_1$ of M elements is defined as:

$$
\begin{array}{ccccc}
\mathbf{z}_1 & = & \mathbf{X} & \times & \boldsymbol{\alpha}_1 \\
(N \times 1) & = & (N \times M) & \times & (M \times 1)
\end{array}
\tag{13.6}
$$

The new variable $\mathbf{z}_1 (N \times 1)$ is a linear combination of the elements in vector $\boldsymbol{\alpha}_1$. The product $\mathbf{z}_1^T \times \mathbf{z}_1$ is the sum of the squares of $\mathbf{z}_1$ elements.[13]

Substituting equation (13.6) for $\mathbf{z}_1$ we have:

$$
\mathbf{z}_1^T \times \mathbf{z}_1 = (\mathbf{X} \times \boldsymbol{\alpha}_1)^T \times (\mathbf{X} \times \boldsymbol{\alpha}_1) = \boldsymbol{\alpha}_1^T \times (\mathbf{X}^T \times \mathbf{X}) \times \boldsymbol{\alpha}_1
\tag{13.7}
$$

---

[10] The NNR models were implemented using the PREVIA software.
[11] See Cassola and Luís (2003).
[12] Appendix A gives a brief technical reminder on eigenvectors, eigenvalues and PCA.
[13] T indicates matrix transposition.

The unbiased covariance matrix of the data which produced matrix $\mathbf{X}$ is:

$$\frac{1}{N-1} \times \mathbf{X}^T \times \mathbf{X}$$

where $\mathbf{X}^T \times \mathbf{X}$ is $(N-1)$ times the covariance matrix. Consequently, the maximum variance is found by selecting as vector $\boldsymbol{\alpha}_1$ the one that maximises $\boldsymbol{\alpha}_1^T \times (\mathbf{X}^T \times \mathbf{X}) \times \boldsymbol{\alpha}_1$. In addition vector $\boldsymbol{\alpha}_1$ is normalised by the condition that its length equals 1, that is $\boldsymbol{\alpha}_1^T \times \boldsymbol{\alpha}_1 = 1$. In summary, the conditions that determine $\mathbf{z}_1$ are:

- max $\mathbf{z}_1^T \times \mathbf{z}_1$
- $\boldsymbol{\alpha}_1^T \times \boldsymbol{\alpha}_1 = 1$ (vector $\boldsymbol{\alpha}_1$ normalised)

This optimisation problem can be solved analytically with the use of the Lagrange multiplier (λ_1) and vector differentiation. But it can also be solved with Excel Solver.

The second vector $\mathbf{z}_2 = \mathbf{X} \times \boldsymbol{\alpha}_2$ is determined by the following conditions:

- max $\mathbf{z}_2^T \times \mathbf{z}_2$
- $\boldsymbol{\alpha}_2^T \times \boldsymbol{\alpha}_2 = 1$ (vector $\boldsymbol{\alpha}_2$ normalised)
- $\boldsymbol{\alpha}_2^T \times \boldsymbol{\alpha}_1 = 0$ ($\mathbf{z}_2$ uncorrelated with $\mathbf{z}_1$)

The last constraint derives from

$$\text{Cov}(\mathbf{z}_1, \mathbf{z}_2) = 0 \Rightarrow \boldsymbol{\alpha}_1^T \times (\mathbf{X}^T \times \mathbf{X}) \times \boldsymbol{\alpha}_2 = 0 \Rightarrow (\mathbf{X}^T \times \mathbf{X} \times \boldsymbol{\alpha}_2)^T \times \boldsymbol{\alpha}_1 = 0$$

$$\Rightarrow \lambda_2 \times \boldsymbol{\alpha}_2^T \times \boldsymbol{\alpha}_1 = 0 \Rightarrow \boldsymbol{\alpha}_2^T \times \boldsymbol{\alpha}_1 = 0 \quad (\lambda_2 \neq 0)$$

In highly correlated systems, such as weather temperatures, the first two eigenvalues explain more than 90% of the total variance. There is therefore no need to retain more principal components.

13.3.7.2   PCA and missing temperature data

Suppose that the weather station with missing observations is St_1, and assume that $St_2, \ldots, St_5$ are the correlated weather stations. In order to use PCA to fill in the missing observations we execute the following steps.

- *Step 1*: Perform a PCA on St_1 and $St_2, \ldots, St_5$ using all the available data on St_1 to obtain principal components and factor weights ($w_{11}, w_{12}, w_{13}, w_{14}, w_{15}$). The selection of the principal components will depend on how highly correlated the system is. However, they should always be less than the number of variables (<5).
- *Step 2*: Perform one more PCA on $St_2, \ldots, St_5$ using all the available data on these variables and the same number of principal components ($P_1, \ldots, P_4$).
- *Step 3*: Using the factor weights from step 1 and the principal components from step 2 we rebuild a simulated data history on St_1 according to the equation:

$$St_1^* = w_{11}P_1 + \cdots + w_{14}P_4$$

- *Step 4*: The final step is the calibration of our model. The actual data on St_1 that are available should be compared with the ones obtained from step 3 to choose the appropriate mean and standard deviation to "reconstruct" the missing weather station data.[14]

---

[14] Appendix B documents the Excel file "WD_PCA.xls" of the accompanying CD-Rom, which shows the computation of 10 days of missing T_{max} temperature data.

The accuracy of the imputation will depend on the strength of the correlation within the system. As weather temperature data are highly correlated, PCA is intuitively an appropriate methodology for filling missing observations.

For our weather observations, all the datasets are stationary, so PCA can be performed. The correlations between temperature data from neighbouring stations are extremely high, so the proportion of total variation that can be explained by only two eigenvalues is about 96%. For example, the linear model with just two principal components for the "November" T_{max} is:

$$X_{max} = 0.452 \times P_1 + 0.1435 \times P_2$$

The values obtained by the above equation are standardised and therefore need to be multiplied by their standard deviation and added to their mean to transform them back into temperatures. We obtain the values for the "November" T_{min} data in the same way and calculate the consequent T_{avg} temperatures accordingly.

13.4 EMPIRICAL RESULTS

13.4.1 The imputation accuracy measures

We use five standard error statistics to gauge the imputation accuracy of the alternative filling methods retained. These measures are documented in Table 13.1 (for more details, see for instance Makridakis *et al.* (1983)).

Table 13.1 Statistical accuracy measures

Accuracy measure	Formula
Mean absolute error (MAE)	$\text{MAE} = \dfrac{1}{T} \times \left(\displaystyle\sum_{t=1}^{T} |\tilde{y}_t - y_t| \right)$
Mean absolute percentage error (MAPE)	$\text{MAPE} = \dfrac{100}{T} \times \left(\displaystyle\sum_{t=1}^{T} \left| \dfrac{\tilde{y}_t - y_t}{y_t} \right| \right)$
Root mean squared error (RMSE)	$\text{RMSE} = \sqrt{\dfrac{1}{T} \times \left(\displaystyle\sum_{t=1}^{T} (\tilde{y}_t - y_t)^2 \right)}$
Theil's inequality coefficient (Theil-U)	$U = \dfrac{\sqrt{\dfrac{1}{T} \times \left(\displaystyle\sum_{t=1}^{T} (\tilde{y}_t - y_t)^2 \right)}}{\sqrt{\dfrac{1}{T} \times \left(\displaystyle\sum_{t=1}^{T} (\tilde{y}_t)^2 \right)} + \sqrt{\dfrac{1}{T} \times \left(\displaystyle\sum_{t=1}^{T} (y_t)^2 \right)}}$
Mean Error (ME)	$\text{ME} = \dfrac{1}{T} \times \left(\displaystyle\sum_{t=1}^{T} (\tilde{y}_t - y_t) \right)$

13.4.2   The imputation results

In order to conserve space, only the imputed values of the average temperature dataset (T_{avg}) are presented and compared. It is worth noting however that, throughout the calculation procedures and for most of the techniques, the imputations of T_{avg} missing values obtained as the average of the T_{max} and T_{min} imputations for the same missing values are more accurate than those obtained by employing the methodologies directly with the T_{avg} series. Daily temperatures are reported in degrees Fahrenheit. The comparison of the imputation accuracy results for the "November" T_{avg} series of the Philadelphia International index station (724080) is presented in Table 13.2.

These results show that, on all the criteria adopted, PCA substantially outperformed the other methodologies in all cases of missing observations. This means that PCA may be used to avoid mispricing of weather derivatives and to reduce the error in the settlement process. The EM, the Kalman filter and the NNR methods outperform the naïve approach, but are less accurate than the fallback method. In fact, the fallback methodology appears as the second most accurate method. Finally, the worst methodology in terms of imputation accuracy appears to be the DA, whereas the naïve approach is validated as a difficult, and

Table 13.2   Imputation accuracy measures for the "November" dataset

Performance Measure	Naïve	Fallback	PCA	Kalman	NNR	EM	DA
One Missing Month T_{avg} (Average Performance Measures)							
Mean Absolute Error:	8.02	2.45	1.13	6.13	2.63	6.22	8.48
Root Mean Squared Error:	11.30	2.96	1.37	7.90	2.97	7.90	11.58
Theil's Inequality Coefficient:	0.12	0.03	0.01	0.08	0.03	0.08	0.12
Mean Absolute Percentage Error:	15.93%	4.99%	2.35%	12.04%	5.49%	12.24%	17.50%
Mean Error:	−0.98	−1.68	−0.03	−2.73	−2.57	−2.45	−1.88
20 Missing Days T_{avg} (Average Performance Measures)							
Mean Absolute Error:	8.13	2.63	1.00	6.13	2.85	6.25	7.45
Root Mean Squared Error:	11.81	3.22	1.27	8.49	3.18	8.49	11.01
Theil's Inequality Coefficient:	0.12	0.03	0.01	0.09	0.03	0.09	0.11
Mean Absolute Percentage Error:	14.73%	5.14%	1.99%	10.99%	5.71%	11.29%	13.74%
Mean Error:	−4.53	−2.03	−0.25	−4.58	−2.75	−4.15	−4.00
10 Missing Days T_{avg} (Average Performance Measures)							
Mean Absolute Error:	4.55	1.95	0.65	3.20	2.60	3.45	5.30
Root Mean Squared Error:	5.69	2.55	0.88	4.27	2.90	4.26	6.74
Theil's Inequality Coefficient:	0.06	0.03	0.01	0.05	0.03	0.05	0.07
Mean Absolute Percentage Error:	9.85%	4.08%	1.41%	6.68%	5.73%	7.28%	11.56%
Mean Error:	0.75	1.55	0.15	−0.70	−2.40	0.15	0.50
One Missing Week T_{avg} (Average Performance Measures)							
Mean Absolute Error:	5.14	2.57	0.71	3.36	2.71	3.71	4.79
Root Mean Squared Error:	6.36	3.02	1.00	4.59	3.09	4.58	6.07
Theil's Inequality Coefficient:	0.07	0.03	0.01	0.05	0.03	0.05	0.07
Mean Absolute Percentage Error:	10.93%	5.31%	1.53%	6.69%	5.90%	7.54%	9.94%
Mean Error:	2.43	2.29	0.29	−2.07	−2.43	−0.86	−2.07
One Missing Day (T_{avg})							
Mean Absolute Error:	3.00	1.00	0.50	1.50	3.50	3.00	7.50
Root Mean Squared Error:	3.00	1.00	0.50	1.50	3.50	3.00	7.50
Theil's Inequality Coefficient:	0.03	0.01	0.01	0.02	0.04	0.03	0.08
Mean Absolute Percentage Error:	6.90%	2.27%	1.15%	3.45%	8.05%	6.90%	17.24%
Mean Error:	3.00	1.00	0.50	−1.50	−3.05	3.00	7.50

Table 13.3 Deviation of computed from actual HDDs

Missing Days	Actual HDDs	Fallback HDDs	PCA HDDs	Kalman F. HDDs	EM HDDs	DA HDDs	Naive HDDs	NNR HDDs
A Missing Day (11/01/93)	21.50	20.00	21.50	23.00	18.50	14.00	18.50	20.00
A Missing Week (11/01/93–11/07/93)	123.50	107.50	122.00	138.00	129.50	138.00	106.50	131.50
10 Missing Days (11/01/93–11/10/93)	186.50	171.00	185.50	193.50	185.00	181.50	179.00	188.50
20 Missing Days (11/01/93–11/20/93)	293.00	331.00	297.50	378.50	370.00	367.00	377.50	359.50
A Missing Month (11/01/93–11/30/93)	487.50	535.50	488.00	563.50	555.00	538.00	511.00	548.00
Deviation from actual HDDs for a Missing Day:	1.5	0	1.5	3	7.5	3	1.5	
Deviation from actual HDDs for a Missing Week:	16	1.5	14.5	6	14.5	17	8	
Deviation from actual HDDs for 10 Missing Days:	15.5	1	7	1.5	5	7.5	2	
Deviation from actual HDDs for 20 Missing Days:	38	4.5	85.5	77	74	84.5	66.5	
Deviation form actual HDDs for a Missing Month:	48	0.5	76	67.5	50.5	23.5	60.5	

easy to "compute", benchmark to beat.[15] For the two other datasets, the "Entire" dataset and the "Autumn" temperature observations, the results also show that PCA outperformed all the other methodologies in all the cases of missing data.[16]

Furthermore, using the imputed values of the missing temperature data obtained from these techniques, the HDDs for November 1993 have been calculated and compared with actual HDDs. Table 13.3 shows the deviation between computed and actual HDDs. The baseline temperature for the computation of the HDDs is 65°F.

It is again obvious that PCA outperforms all the other methodologies. The deviation of the PCA results from actual HDDs for a missing day is 0, while for 10 missing days it is 1 degree (against 15.5 degrees for the fallback method); for one missing month, it is 0.5 degree, against 48 degrees for the fallback method! On average, the deviation of PCA-based results from actual HDD data is 1.5 degree, while the second best methodology, the fallback method, deviates on average by 23.8 degrees.

13.5 CONCLUDING REMARKS

In this chapter, we set out to examine and analyse the use of alternative methods when confronted with missing data, a common problem when not enough historical data or clean historical data exist.

Because of the need for "clean" weather temperature data in the fast growing weather derivatives markets as pricing methodologies rely heavily on them, we examined the imputation accuracy of different interpolation techniques and filling methods for missing historical temperature records. We would argue that the conclusions based on this analysis would serve as a good guide to the general problem of dealing with missing values.

Overall, for the periods and the data series concerned, the results of PCA outperformed all the other methodologies in all cases of missing observations and consequently in the calculation of HDDs. The only drawback of PCA compared with the second most accurate method, the fallback method, is that PCA requires more correlated weather temperature "clean" data. Nevertheless, if the necessary data are available, PCA should be preferred in replacing missing temperature observations. More generally, PCA provides a very efficient and simple method for filling missing data in the presence of a correlated system of variables. As has been shown, it is also easy to implement, as this can be done in Excel.

---

[15] The poor performance of the EM and DA methods may be linked to the violation of the assumption that the data are normally distributed (see Section 13.3.4 above), which is not the case here.

[16] Complete results are available from the authors.

APPENDIX A

A.1 Eigenvalue and eigenvector

Let A be a linear transformation symbolised by a matrix $\mathbf{A}$. If there is a vector $\mathbf{X} \in \mathfrak{R}^n \neq 0$ such that:

$$\mathbf{A} \times \mathbf{X} = \lambda \times \mathbf{X}$$

for some scalar λ, then λ is called the eigenvalue of $\mathbf{A}$ with corresponding (right) eigenvector $\mathbf{X}$. Eigenvalues are also known as characteristic roots, proper values or latent roots (see Marcus and Minc (1988)).

Eigenvalues are given by the solutions of the characteristic equation of the given matrix:

$$(\mathbf{A} - \lambda \times \mathbf{I}) \times \mathbf{X} = 0$$

where $\mathbf{I}$ is the identity matrix.

A.2 An introduction to PCA

Assume that the data for which the PCA is to be carried out consist of M variables indexed $j = 1, 2, \ldots, M$ and N observations on each variable, $i = 1, 2, \ldots, N$, generating an $N \times M$ matrix $\mathbf{X}$. As mentioned in Section 13.3.7.1, we also assume that the input data are stationary and that each of the M columns of the stationary data matrix $\mathbf{X}$ has mean $\mu = 0$ and variance $\sigma^2 = 1$, which can be achieved by subtracting the sample mean and dividing by the sample standard deviation for each element x_{ij} of matrix $\mathbf{X}$. Consequently we have created a matrix $\mathbf{X}$ of standardised mean deviations.

PCA is founded on an eigenvalue and eigenvector analysis of:

$$\mathbf{V} = \mathbf{X}' \times \mathbf{X}/N$$

the $M \times M$ symmetric matrix of correlations among the M variables. The principal components are linear combinations of these columns, where the weights are selected according to the following technique:

- The first principal component describes the majority of the total variation in matrix $\mathbf{X}$, the second component describes the majority of the remaining variation, and so on.
- The principal components are uncorrelated with each other.

This can be attained by selecting the weights from the cluster of eigenvectors of the correlation matrix. If $\mathbf{W}$ is the $M \times M$ matrix of eigenvectors of $\mathbf{V}$, we have:

$$\mathbf{V} \times \mathbf{W} = \mathbf{W} \times \mathbf{\Lambda}$$

where $\mathbf{\Lambda}$ is the $M \times M$ diagonal matrix of eigenvalues of $\mathbf{V}$. If matrix $\mathbf{W} = (w_{ij})$ for $i, j = 1, 2, \ldots, M$, then the kth column of $\mathbf{W}$, indicated $\mathbf{w}_k = (w_{1k}, w_{2k}, \ldots, w_{Mk})'$, is the $M \times 1$ eigenvector corresponding to the eigenvalue λ_k. The kth principal component of the system is given by:

$$\mathbf{P}_k = w_{1k} \times \mathbf{X}_1 + w_{2k} \times \mathbf{X}_2 + \cdots + w_{Mk} \times \mathbf{X}_M$$

where $\mathbf{X}_j$ indicates the jth column of matrix $\mathbf{X}$, in other words the standardised historical input data of the jth variable in the initial correlated system. In matrix notation, the kth principal component of the system is given by:

$$\mathbf{P}_k = \mathbf{X} \times \mathbf{w}_k$$

APPENDIX B

The file WD_PCA.xls on the accompanying CD-Rom is an illustration of the PCA method.

In the "Data" sheet of the workbook, and for the sake of simplicity, we retain 122 temperature records in degrees Celsius from 01/09/93 to 31/12/93 for five weather stations. A 10-day period of missing data is artificially created between 01/11/93 and 10/11/93. The common dataset for step 1 of the PCA goes until 31/10/93.

In the "Step 1" sheet of the workbook, to obtain principal components and factor weights, we perform a PCA on St_1, St_2, St_3, St_4 and St_5 using all the data available on St_1 *up to the missing data period* (we have therefore $M = 5$ and $N = 61$). We first standardise the common dataset up to 31/10/93 (cells H3:L63) by subtracting the sample mean and dividing by the sample standard deviation for each temperature record.

To obtain the factor weights, we create two column vectors $\mathbf{a}_1$ and $\mathbf{a}_2$ with five cells, one per weather station (initially for $\mathbf{a}_1$, we set the top cell O5 = 1 and cells O6:O9 = 0). We proceed to compute the first eigenvector using Excel matrix algebra (cells S4:S64 and cell P14) and the Excel Solver: in the Excel Solver window (Figure B13.1), we maximise cell P14 by changing cells O5:O9 subject to cell P15 = 1.

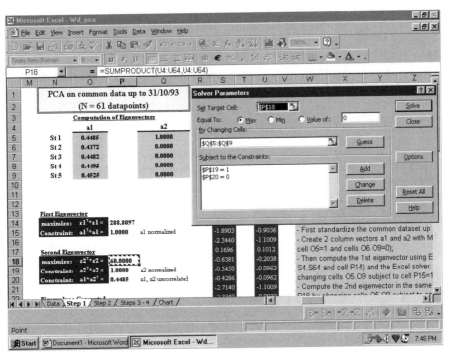

Figure B13.1   Excel Solver window for the second principal component

We compute the second eigenvector exactly in the same way: only this time we maximise cell P18 by changing cells Q5:Q9 subject to cell P19 = 1 *and* cell P20 = 0. The total variance explained by the first two components is computed in cell Q33: at 98.4%, there is obviously no need to look for more principal components. We shall retain the factor weights of St_1 for further use (cells O5:Q5).

In the "Step 2" sheet of the workbook, we perform a second PCA, this time only on St_2, St_3, St_4 and St_5 but using the *entire databank* for these variables and the same two principal components (we have therefore $M = 4$ and $N = 122$). We shall retain the principal components z_1 and z_2 for further use (cells Q4:Q125 and S4:S125).

In the "Steps 3–4" sheet of the workbook, using the factor weights from step 1 (cells B7:B8) and the useful part of the principal components from step 2 (cells A13:A73 and C13:C73), we rebuild a simulated data history of St_1 according to the equation:

$$St_1^* = \mathbf{a}_1\mathbf{z}_1 + \mathbf{a}_2\mathbf{z}_2$$

where $\mathbf{a}_1$ and $\mathbf{a}_2$ are the factor weights for St_1 from step 1 and $\mathbf{z}_1$ and $\mathbf{z}_2$ the principal components from step 2.

In fact, we obtain a standardised series (cells K2:K62) which must be multiplied by the original series standard deviation and added to its mean to get the "reconstructed" temperature data (cells M2:M62).

The choice of the mean and standard deviation is the final and crucial calibration step of the model: here, we take the standard deviation from step 1 (cell E8); for the mean (cell E7), considering both the time dependency of temperature data and the high correlation between weather stations, we decided to take the average of the mean temperature for all stations 15 days before and 15 days after the missing data period with the mean temperature for St_2, St_3, St_4 and St_5 during the missing data period.

Finally, the "Chart" sheet of the workbook plots our results: as can be seen, both actual and PCA-based estimates of the T_{avg} temperature data for St_1 during the 10-day period from 01/11/93 to 10/11/93 are very close, a view confirmed by the average difference of 0.07°C over that period (see cell O63 in the "Steps 3–4" sheet of the workbook).

REFERENCES

Alexander, C. (2001), *Market Models: A Guide to Financial Data Analysis*, John Wiley, Chichester.

Bentz, Y. (2003), "Quantitative Equity Investment Management with Time-Varying Factor Sensitivities", Chapter 7 of this book.

Billio, M. and D. Sartore (2003), "Stochastic Volatility Models: A Survey with Applications to Option Pricing and Value at Risk", Chapter 8 of this book.

Campbell, J. Y., A. W. Lo and A. C. MacKinlay (1997), *The Econometrics of Financial Markets*, Princeton University Press, Princeton, NJ.

Cassola, N. and J. B. Luís (2003), "Modelling the Term Structure of Interest Rates: An Application of Gaussian Affine Models to the German Yield Curve", Chapter 3 of this book.

Corbally, M. and P. Dang (2001), "Risk Products", in E. Banks (ed.), *Weather Risk Management: Market, Products and Applications*, Palgrave, New York, pp. 105–134.

Dempster, A. P., N. M. Laird and D. B. Rubin (1977), "Maximum Likelihood from Incomplete Data via the EM Algorithm", *Journal of the Royal Statistical Society*, B39, **1**, 1–38.

Dunis, C. and X. Huang (2003), "Forecasting and Trading Currency Volatility: An Application of Recurrent Neural Regression and Model Combination", Chapter 4 of this book.

Dunis, C. and J. Jalilov (2002), "Neural Network Regression and Alternative Forecasting Techniques for Predicting Financial Variables", *Neural Network World*, **2**, 113–139.

Dunis, C. and M. Williams (2003), "Applications of Advanced Regression Analysis for Trading and Investment", Chapter 1 of this book.

Greene, W. H. (2000), *Econometric Analysis*, 4th edition, Prentice Hall, Englewood Cliffs, NJ.

Hamilton, J. (1994), *Time Series Analysis*, Princeton University Press, Princeton, NJ.

Harvey, A. C. (1981), *Time Series Models*, Philip Allan, Oxford.

Harvey, A. C. (1989), *Forecasting Structural Time Series Models and the Kalman Filter*, Cambridge University Press, Cambridge.

Henderson, R. (2001), "Pricing Weather Risk", in E. Banks (ed.), *Weather Risk Management: Market, Products and Applications*, Palgrave, New York, pp. 167–199.

Makridakis, S., S. C. Wheelwright and V. E. McGee (1983), *Forecasting: Methods and Applications*, John Wiley & Sons, New York.

Marcus, M. and H. Minc (1988), *Introduction to Linear Algebra*, Dover, New York.

PricewaterhouseCoopers (2002), "The Weather Risk Management Industry: Survey Findings for April 2001 to March 2002", *Weather Risk Management Association*, available at: http://wrma.cyberserv.com/library/public/file346.ppt.

Raspé, A. (2001), "Legal and Regulatory Issues", in E. Banks (ed.), *Weather Risk Management: Market, Products and Applications*, Palgrave, New York, pp. 224–245.

Schafer, J. L. (1997), *Analysis of Incomplete Multivariate Data*, Series Monographs on Statistics and Applied Probability, Vol. 72, Chapman and Hall, London.

Index

Index compiled by Annette Musker

WILEY COPYRIGHT INFORMATION AND TERMS OF USE

CD supplement to *Christian L. Dunis, Jason Laws and Patrick Naïm, Applied Quantitative Methods for Trading and Investment.*

Copyright © 2003 John Wiley & Sons, Ltd.

Published by John Wiley & Sons, Ltd., The Atrium, Southern Gate, Chichester, West Sussex, PO19 8SQ. All rights-reserved.

All material contained herein is protected by copyright, whether or not a copyright notice appears on the particular screen where the material is displayed. No part of the material may be reproduced or transmitted in any form or by any means, or stored in a computer for retrieval purposes or otherwise, without written permission from Wiley, unless this is expressly permitted in a copyright notice or usage statement accompanying the materials. Requests for permission to store or reproduce material for any purpose, or to distribute it on a network, should be addressed to the Permissions Department, John Wiley & Sons, Ltd., The Atrium, Southern Gate, Chichester, West Sussex, PO19 8SQ, UK; fax +44 (0) 1243 770571; Email permreq@wiley.co.uk.

Neither the author nor John Wiley & Sons, Ltd. accept any responsibility or liability for loss or damage occasioned to any person or property through using materials, instructions, methods or ideas contained herein, or acting or refraining from acting as a result of such use. The author and Publisher expressly disclaim all implied warranties, including merchantability or fitness for any particular purpose. There will be no duty on the author or Publisher to correct any errors or defects in the software.

Previa software, copyright Elseware 1994–2003.